TRANSLATION—THEORY AI

TRANSLATION—
THEORY AND PRACTICE:

A HISTORICAL READER

EDITED BY

DANIEL WEISSBORT

AND

ASTRADUR EYSTEINSSON

OXFORD
UNIVERSITY PRESS

OXFORD
UNIVERSITY PRESS

Great Clarendon Street, Oxford OX2 6DP

Oxford University Press is a department of the University of Oxford.
It furthers the University's objective of excellence in research, scholarship,
and education by publishing worldwide in

Oxford New York

Auckland Cape Town Dar es Salaam Hong Kong Karachi
Kuala Lumpur Madrid Melbourne Mexico City Nairobi
New Delhi Shanghai Taipei Toronto

With offices in

Argentina Austria Brazil Chile Czech Republic France Greece
Guatemala Hungary Italy Japan Poland Portugal Singapore
South Korea Switzerland Thailand Turkey Ukraine Vietnam

Oxford is a registered trade mark of Oxford University Press
in the UK and in certain other countries

Published in the United States
by Oxford University Press Inc., New York

© Daniel Weissbort and Astradur Eysteinsson 2006

The moral rights of the authors have been asserted
Database right Oxford University Press (maker)

First published 2006

British Library Cataloguing in Publication Data

Data available

Library of Congress Cataloging in Publication Data

Data available

Typeset by SPI Publisher Services, Pondicherry, India
Printed in Great Britain
on acid-free paper by
Antony Rowe Ltd.,
Chippenham, Wiltshire

ISBN 0–19–871199–9   978–0–19–871199–5
ISBN 0–19–871200–6 (Pbk.)   978–0–19–871200–8 (Pbk.)

PREFACE

The aim of this book is to illuminate the essential activity of translation from a number of perspectives: historical and contemporary, theoretical and practical. At the same time, the contents of the present volume speak in many modes and voices to literary and cultural history, and to cross-cultural relations through the ages. The book draws on several hundred texts, translations, and texts about translation, ranging from classical antiquity to the present. Some are reprinted in their entirety, while others are excerpted, and the editors have supplied notes and introductions. Many of the texts included also themselves contain examples from translations under discussion, so that on the whole, this volume pulls together a sizeable world of translation.

For the sake of coherence and due to obvious limits of magnitude, a large part of the volume focuses on *translation into English*, although it contains several texts that discuss translation in general terms, and others that were orginally written in (and concern translation into) other languages. The volume should be useful for anyone interested in the history and theory of translation, for what is true of the transfer from one specific language and culture into another may obviously be highly relevant—given important and interesting differences—for other parallel situations.

When we first started working on this project together, we had in mind to put together a collection of foundational texts in translation studies, from Cicero to around the mid-twentieth century, including several important prefaces by translators in the English tradition. As work progressed, the concept started changing. We realized that we did not want to limit the volume to a canon of a few statements of translation studies as a theoretical discipline. There were three basic reasons for this.

First, we wanted to bring across to our readers how valuable reflections about translation took form in contexts of actual translation practice. Some of the most important texts in the literary history of the English language, for instance the Bible and the Homeric epics, are translated again and again through the centuries. Hence, it is the need for translation, and the practice of translation, which opens the gateway between the present and history. So the sense of translation practice had to be built into the volume, if only by short examples of the main concern of many of those who have also made important historical comments on translation.

Second, we wanted to end the historical survey with a collection of recent and contemporary material in the field of translation. Ultimately, this material came to constitute the largest chapter of the volume, one that was extremely difficult to select, since we wanted to provide our readers with an insight into both the vibrant and growing field of translation theory, and at the same time to approach translation studies from a broad angle, emphasizing, again, the connection between the critical discussion and the practice of translation (even though we've had to restrain the length of examples from translations).

Third, we felt that limiting our selection to relatively few texts, even though this had the benefit of allowing us to reprint most of them as a whole, did not convey the multifariousness, or indeed the complexity, of translation studies as we understand that term. Yet, the volume must not be allowed to become an oversized collection of short quotations. We wanted to go for both breadth and depth and this is what we struggled with for a long time. The final product contains several texts that appear in their entirety, while we have selected what we felt are the most salient parts of others. Many of the entries focus on a single translator and/or critic, and some of them are presented in more extensive 'collages' (for instance Dryden, Pound, and Nabokov), a mode of selection and introduction we have also used to cover the translation activity in certain periods.

We put some of these collages in charge of specialists in the respective fields, and we should very much like to thank these colleagues for their contributions. They are Jonathan Wilcox, Jane Stevenson, David Hopkins, Ronnie Apter, Jenefer Coates, and Vinay Dharwadker. Most of the entries were prepared jointly by the two editors in what was a long-standing and enjoyable collaboration. In some cases, however, entries were largely selected and introduced by one of us. Thus, Daniel Weissbort prepared 'Classical Latin and Early Christian Latin Translation', 'Late Tudor and Early Jacobean Translation', 'The Authorized (King James) Version of the Bible', 'Anne Dacier', 'Alexander Pope', 'Samuel Johnson', 'Five Nineteenth-Century Translators', 'Martin Buber and Franz Rosenzweig', 'Ethnopoetics: Translation of the Oral and of Oral Performance', 'Translation of Verse Form', and 'Ted Hughes'; while Astradur Eysteinsson prepared 'Renaissance Latin Translation in England', 'Johann Wolfgang von Goethe', 'Friedrich Schleiermacher', 'Victorian Translation and Criticism', 'Walter Benjamin', 'Jiří Levý', 'George Steiner', 'Mary Snell-Hornby', 'Gayatri Spivak', 'Talal Asad', and 'Eva Hoffman'. However, the shaping and presentation of many other entries, as well as the editing of the volume as whole, was our joint effort.

This is not only a book about translators—it is also one in which we had to rely on the help of a number of translators who provided valuable texts: special thanks go to Louis Kelly, but also to Stavros Deligiorgis, Jennifer Tanner, Norma Rinsler, and Gottskalk

Jensson. We thank Gardar Baldvinsson for scanning and other assistance in the preparation of the manuscript, Susan Benner for helping us with the preparation of some texts, Agnes Vogler for her work on the index, and Theo Hermans for his advice concerning the inclusion of material regarding Renaissance Latin translation in England.

We are, last but not least, deeply grateful to our wives, Valentina Polukhina and Anna Johannsdottir, for all their help, advice, and encouragement in the preparation of this book.

D.W. and A.E.

CONTENTS

General Introduction   1

Babel   8

PART I. FROM ANTIQUITY TO MODERN TIMES

1. FROM CICERO TO CAXTON   17

    1.1.   Introduction   17

    1.2.   Classical Latin and Early Christian Latin Translation   20

    1.3.   Old English Translation (Jonathan Wilcox)   34

    1.4.   John of Trevisa   47

    1.5.   William Caxton   51

2. FROM THE REFORMATION AND THE RENAISSANCE
TO THE EIGHTEENTH CENTURY   55

    2.1.   Introduction   55

    2.2.   Martin Luther   57

    2.3.   William Tyndale   68

    2.4.   Estienne Dolet   73

    2.5.   Joachim du Bellay   77

    2.6.   Late Tudor and Early Jacobean Translation   81

    2.7.   Renaissance Latin Translation in England   100

    2.8.   The Catholic Bible in England   110

    2.9.   The Authorized (King James) Version of the Bible   115

    2.10.   Sir John Denham   121

    2.11.   Abraham Cowley   124

    2.12.   Women Translators from the Sixteenth to the Eighteenth Century
(Jane Stevenson)   128

2.13. John Dryden (David Hopkins)   144

2.14. Anne Dacier   160

2.15. Alexander Pope   166

2.16. Samuel Johnson   174

2.17. William Cowper   183

2.18. Alexander Fraser Tytler   188

3. THE NINETEENTH CENTURY   195

3.1. Introduction   195

3.2. Johann Wolfgang von Goethe   198

3.3. Friedrich Schleiermacher   205

3.4. Victorian Translation and Criticism   210

3.5. Six Nineteenth-Century Translators   241

3.6. James Fitzmaurice-Kelly   258

PART II: THE TWENTIETH CENTURY

4. FROM POUND TO NABOKOV   271

4.1. Introduction   271

4.2. Ezra Pound (Ronnie Apter)   274

4.3. Constance Garnett   290

4.4. Walter Benjamin   297

4.5. Martin Buber and Franz Rosenzweig   310

4.6. Jorge Luis Borges   323

4.7. Roman Jakobson   330

4.8. Jiří Levý   337

4.9. Eugene A. Nida   346

4.10. Robert Lowell   352

4.11. Stanley Burnshaw   360

4.12. Laura Bohannan   366

4.13. Vladimir Nabokov (Jenefer Coates)   376

5. Recent and Contemporary Writings 393

    5.1. Introduction 393

    5.2. George Steiner 396

    5.3. James S Holmes 406

    5.4. Itamar Even-Zohar 429

    5.5. André Lefevere 435

    5.6. Mary Snell-Hornby 443

    5.7. Ethnopoetics: Translation of the Oral and of Oral Performance—Dennis Tedlock and Jerome Rothenberg 452

    5.8. Louis and Celia Zukofsky 458

    5.9. Translation of Verse Form 460

    5.10. A. K. Ramanujan (Vinay Dharwadker) 476

    5.11. Gayatri Chakravorty Spivak 486

    5.12. Talal Asad 494

    5.13. Eva Hoffman 502

    5.14. Gregory Rabassa 507

    5.15. Suzanne Jill Levine 512

    5.16. Ted Hughes 521

    5.17. Douglas Robinson 534

    5.18. Lawrence Venuti 546

    5.19. Susan Bassnett 558

    5.20. Everett Fox 562

    5.21. John Felstiner 569

    5.22. W. S. Merwin 582

    5.23. Edwin Morgan 585

    5.24. Seamus Heaney 597

Postface *Daniel Weissbort* 609

Acknowledgements 617

Select Bibliography 625

NOTES ON CONTRIBUTORS

Editors:

Daniel Weissbort (b. 1935) is Emeritus Professor of Comparative Literature at the University of Iowa; Honorary Professor in the Centre for Translation and Comparative Cultural Studies, University of Warwick; Research Fellow, English Department, King's College, London University. He has published poetry of his own and translations of poetry, primarily from Russian. Publications include a number of anthologies, most recently *An Anthology of Contemporary Russian Women's Poetry* (with Valentina Polukhina; University of Iowa Press and Carcanet, 2006) and a translational memoir of Joseph Brodsky, *From Russian with Love* (Anvil, 2004). His *Selected Translations of Ted Hughes* (Faber) is to appear in 2006 and a book on Ted Hughes and translation is forthcoming from OUP. With the late Ted Hughes he founded the magazine, *Modern Poetry in Translation*, which he edited from 1965 to 2003.

Astradur Eysteinsson (b. 1957) is Professor of Comparative Literature at the University of Iceland (Reykjavik). His publications include co-translations of works by Franz Kafka and Max Frisch into Icelandic, several articles in the general area of literary, cultural, and translation studies, various editorial projects, and three books: *The Concept of Modernism* (Cornell UP 1990), *Tvímæli* (on translation and translation studies, University of Iceland Press 1996) and *Umbrot* (on literature and modernity, University of Iceland Press 1999).

Scholars who provided the editors with new translations or who edited some of the individual sections of the volume:

Ronnie Apter is Professor of English at Central Michigan University. Her publications include 20 performable opera translations and the books *Digging for the Treasure: Translation after Pound* (1984; 1987) and a bilingual edition of the Love Songs of Bernart de Ventadorn in Occitan and English: *Sugar and Salt* (1999).

Jenefer Coates teaches literary translation and comparative literature at Middlesex University, London. She has edited various journals including *In Other Words* for the

Translators Association. Besides translating from French and Russian, she also writes on literary subjects, and is completing a book on intertextuality in Vladimir Nabokov, focusing on his use of medieval sources.

Stavros Deligiorgis, a University of Iowa professor emeritus, has published articles on the pre-Socratics, on the Hellenistic and Byzantine romances, and on Chaucer and Boccaccio. Deligiorgis has Englished contemporary Greek fiction (by Thanassis Valtinos; with Jane Assimakopoulos), Romanian poetry by Tristan Tzara, Eugene Ionesco, and Paul Celan, and has regularly participated in performance and inter-media art projects. Currently, he teaches in the Graduate Translation Studies Program of the University of Athens, Greece.

Vinay Dharwadker is Professor of Languages and Cultures of Asia at the University of Wisconsin-Madison, where he teaches Indian literatures, literary studies, and modern theory. A poet, painter, and scholar, he translates poetry from Hindi, Marathi, Sanskrit, Punjabi, and Urdu into English. His publications include *The Oxford Anthology of Modern Indian Poetry* (co-edited, 1994), *The Collected Essays of A. K. Ramanujan* (general editor, 1999), and *Kabir: The Weaver's Songs* (2003; 2005).

David Hopkins is Professor of English Literature at the University of Bristol. His chief research interests are in the English poetry of the seventeenth and eighteenth centuries, and in the reception of Classical literature in England. Among his recent publications are (ed., with Paul Hammond) *The Poems of John Dryden* (5 vols., Longman Annotated English Poets) and (ed. with Stuart Gillespie) *The Oxford History of Literary Translation in English*, Vol. 3: *1660–1790*.

Gottskalk Jensson is a lecturer in Comparative Literature at the University of Iceland. He is a specialist in Classical Literature (Greek and Roman) and his publications include *The Recollections of Encolpius: The Satyrica of Petronius as Milesian Fiction* (2004).

Louis Kelly is Emeritus Professor of Translation History and Theory at the University of Ottawa and Senior Member of Darwin College, Cambridge. His publications include *Twenty-five Centuries of Language Teaching* (1969) and *The True Interpreter* (1979).

Norma Rinsler is Emeritus Professor of French at King's College London, and was Managing Editor of *Modern Poetry in Translation*, 1992–2003. She is currently collaborating on the 5-volume translation of Paul Valéry's *Cahiers/Notebooks* (2000 –).

Jane Stevenson is Professor of Latin at the University of Aberdeen. She has written extensively about early modern women Latinists. Her publications include *Women*

Latin Poets: Language, Gender, and Authority, from Antiquity to the Eighteenth Century (2005).

Jennifer Tanner has a B.A. in German Literature from Oberlin College and a M.F.A. in Literary Translation from the University of Iowa. She is currently working as a freelance translator of German and Russian.

Jonathan Wilcox is Professor of English at the University of Iowa. He is a specialist in Anglo-Saxon Language and Literature and his publications include *Ælfric's Prefaces* (1994; 1996) and *Wulfstan Texts and Other Homiletic Materials* (2000), along with numerous essays on Anglo-Saxon literature and culture.

But clearly there are many more contributors to this book, from Babel to present-day Britain.

GENERAL INTRODUCTION

Astradur Eysteinsson and Daniel Weissbort

How do works of literature and scholarship acquire international status? How have ideas and theories, learning and religion, historical and practical knowledge, traversed the globe? How have various transactions between groups and nations with different customs and conditions been facilitated? How do we learn of what has transpired in distant places?

To a large extent by building linguistic bridges across the channels that divide language spheres and cultural regions, whether by the rewriting of messages and works in another tongue, or through other interventions by individuals who possess knowledge in more than one language and can therefore act as cultural mediators.

In the empires of Antiquity, interpreters were essential intermediaries in trade and the various matters of state. With the onset of printing, some of this work was transferred to translators, who also came to play a key role in disseminating, and passing on to later generations, the documents that were to form the canons of literature, learning, and religion, works such as the Homeric epics, the Bible, and Greek drama, philosophy, and history, to mention obvious examples in the Western tradition.

Translation has been instrumental in the formation of writing and literary culture in every European language ('European' here refers to more than the geographical area of Europe, as defined today). Indeed, the history of international contact and cultural development, within and beyond Europe, can be traced by noting the routes of translation. Translation is still of the utmost importance in the affairs of a world that has gone through the rapid technological development called modernization, which furthermore has enhanced international relations to the point where people feel they can legitimately talk of 'globalization'. While this development is far from having reached all parts of the world in equal measure, it is true that science, media, entertainment, commerce, and the many forms of international relations embrace the globe so extensively now, that translation becomes an almost overwhelming issue, indeed a 'problem' (the notion of the 'problem of translation' has a long and colourful history). Many see a possible solution in the adoption of a single global language, and it seems that English is well on its way to taking on this international role, as Latin did in the very different circumstances of the Late Middle Ages and Renaissance.

But the notion of a global culture in a single language is not a promising prospect; indeed, it is, perhaps fortunately, virtually inconceivable. Vital cultural expressions always involve both the local and the global; the problem of translation is inherent in them, and therefore also in their dispersion and historical delivery. In the world of literature, and in many domains of knowledge and culture, the need for translation is as great as ever. It is a need for trails of understanding between cultures that express themselves in different tongues. The blazing of such trails also facilitates understanding *within* cultures which may be more internally divisive than is apparent. The discovery of the other within ourselves is another by-product of translation.

The aim of this volume is to illuminate translation from a number of perspectives: historical and contemporary, theoretical and practical. The texts are drawn from a long stretch of Western history; from Homeric and biblical texts, via the translation of these and other texts at various times, via numerous commentaries on translation by figures like Cicero, King Alfred, John Dryden, and George Eliot, to translations as well as critical discussions by contemporary authors. The main focus of the anthology is on literary translation, and hence on the art as well as the craft of translation. But this does not imply that we are insisting upon hard and fast lines between literary and other forms of translation, be they scholarly, technical, or pragmatic in any other sense. Literary translation—as much as literature itself—draws on experience from diverse fields of human experience, and its discursive operations overlap with those of other kinds of translation. Literature combines cultural and aesthetic values, and this makes its translation so difficult and challenging, but also so urgent. It is because of this concentrated linguistic expression that poetry has so often been seen as the test case of translation—to the point where it has been defined as that which is not translatable. Yet, a great deal of poetry has been and continues to be translated, and it is important to emphasize that the lessons of literary translation are of course also relevant to other kinds of translation, although there they may often be downplayed by pressing contextual and practical concerns—these, of course, may also operate with regard to literary translation. Literary translation, as much as any other translation activity, takes place in concrete socio-cultural contexts, where a sufficient need has been felt to transport a linguistic product from one language to another. As George Steiner has pointed out, arguments against verse translation are arguments against all translation.[1]

---

[1] 'Attacks on the translation of poetry are simply the barbed edge of the general assertion that no language can be translated without fundamental loss. Formally and substantively the same points can be urged in regard to prose.'

But literary texts of course also demand particular attention to language itself, its resonances and references, its historical depth as well as its personal relevance, and this gives an extra dimension to the 'problem' of the translation. This is obviously not only true of *literature* in the narrow sense, but also in a broader one, not excluding religious, mythological, and oratorical discourse, or various texts of philosophy, history, and other humanistic disciplines. Translation has to attend to the language and cultural heritage of such works, for it also has the function of extending that heritage, of lending it another kind of historical depth, of transforming it into a cross-cultural tradition.

'Translation' is a concept that is missing in Raymond Williams's useful book *Keywords*. It would, quite appropriately, have come right after 'Tradition'. However, it is, to an extent, embodied in Williams's entry on 'tradition', a word that 'came into English in C14 from fw *tradicion*, oF [Old French], *traditionem*, L[atin], from rw *tradere*, L—to hand over or deliver. The Latin noun had the senses of (i) delivery, (ii) handing down knowledge, (iii) passing on a doctrine, (iv) surrender or betrayal'.[2] Translation, too, hands over or delivers, and it is instrumental in passing on and handing down documents deemed worthy of such delivery. Interestingly, the notion of betrayal is also very much a part of the history of the concept of translation, the proverbial truth being that the translator is a traitor ('traduttore traditore'), that he or she is constitutionally incapable of delivering the original. In a recent report, for instance, in the *Guardian* newspaper (Saturday, 12 June 2004, p. 4), on the dropping of Latin and Greek by the largest examination board in the UK, a teacher of Classics, no less, is quoted as saying—quite casually one feels, and not fearing contradiction: 'And it is not enough to trust those who translate, for he who translates, not only explains but corrupts.' Williams says of the 'ceremony, duty and respect' often associated with tradition: 'Considering only how much has been handed down to us, and how various it actually is, this, in its own way, is both a betrayal and a surrender.'[3]

Yet, as Williams points out elsewhere, tradition is always 'selective',[4] this also being true of translation. Moreover, the selection process, in other words canon-formation, that forms the basis of literary traditions, is—unless we are working strictly within national borders—dependent upon translations, which secure the 'survival' of the work and attend to its 'ripening' process, as Walter Benjamin puts it in his well-known article 'Die Aufgabe

---

George Steiner, *After Babel: Aspects of Language and Translation*, (3rd edn.: Oxford and New York: Oxford University Press, 1998), 255.

[2] Raymond Williams, *Keywords: A Vocabulary of Culture and Society* (London: Fontana, 1976), 268–9.

[3] Ibid. 269.

[4] Raymond Williams, *Marxism and Literature* (Oxford: Oxford University Press, 1977), 115.

des Übersetzers' ('The Task of the Translator').[5] Ideas such as 'Western tradition', 'European literature', not to mention 'World Literature', are unthinkable in the absence of translation, and, indeed, of the *tradition of translation*. More practically: one does well to remember that most readers of most if not all the best-known works of Western literature read these works in translation.

The present anthology exemplifies the history and tradition of translation, for instance by highlighting key texts that have been handed down in Western literature through the efforts of translators undeterred by the fact that these texts have been translated many times before. Indeed, many of them are eager to attempt precisely those texts, to remake them, as it were, in the shape and texture of their own age.

Such translation—along with the translation of more recent or even contemporary foreign literature—is obviously a challenge to original writing and is bound to make an impression on its literary culture. Yet this crucial interaction, and the resulting hybrid character of literary history, tends to be left out of documented literary histories or dealt with in a cursory fashion, mostly because they so often work within national borders, identifying national canons and traditions. Still, the situation is changing as a result of a less exclusive concern with one's own culture and of the efforts of many translation activists, such as the late James S Holmes, who titled a talk given to the Translation Programme at the University of Iowa: 'Studying Translations, an underdeveloped Country in the World of Literary Scholarship'. Literary history, as we know it, has been very much a prodigy of Romanticism, cultivating and elevating national legacies.

The historical spectrum of this book, therefore, even though it dwells extensively on a number of canonical texts, challenges canonical literary history in most of its documented forms. The historical focus, as we move out of the Classical period, is on the English language tradition. But when this tradition is viewed from the present perspective, even Shakespeare is no longer as obviously central as he often seems to be—or at least not in the same way. Rather he appears as a writer of transcendent genius who rides a wave of creativity in the English language itself, as it was beginning to benefit from an age of prolific translation. And of course he makes his mark on an English literary culture, which will avidly continue, however, to seek the best way of bringing Homer, Ovid, Virgil, Dante, Beowulf, the Bible, into the living language. The more one familiarizes oneself with this tradition, the clearer it becomes that English possesses a rich history of translation, or what may be called a strong legacy of *translation culture*, one that has buttressed and inspired a great deal of linguistic creativity through the centuries. The poet and

---

[5] Walter Benjamin's essay is included in Sect. 4.4, below.

translator Charles Tomlinson, in his introduction to *The Oxford Book of Verse in English Translation*, draws attention to 'a largely forgotten literature'.[6] Fourteen years before, George Steiner, in his innovative *Penguin Book of Modern Verse Translation*, focuses on the work of translators, without whom, as he puts it, 'we would live in arrogant parishes bordered by silence'.[7]

It is beyond our capacity to do justice to the multiform nature of English, a world language or related world languages or group of related languages. It might even be said that English has become a language pre-eminently of translation, that is, of diffusion and international communication. (Latin was a means of international communication, but did not have the strong basis of a first language that English has.) In a number of countries English exists in a close relationship with another language (Canada, South Africa, India). These are very important sites of translation touched upon in this book only in the case of India. Edwin Morgan's translations into Scots, rather than 'standard' English, has to stand for a range of such possibilities, now that the very notion of a standard English has become problematical, this in its turn allowing for a renewed and non-pedantic, so to speak, interest in foreignizing rather than the more traditional domesticating translation. The book also contains a number of important texts from other languages, from Classical times to the present, which have proved important for the translation debate in English. While a universal textbook might be desirable, this too is simply beyond our means.

A further word about English as the global lingua franca for many purposes, scholarly, scientific, commercial, political. There are, of course, many Englishes today, which, however, are similar enough not yet to require by and large the work of translators to ensure their mutual intelligibility, even if the possibilities of misunderstanding are considerable. It is partly because of its multiform character that English, with its tendency to regard itself as self-sufficient, is also suffering from a paucity of translations into it, whereas, as noted, the language's richness in, say, the Renaissance was largely due to the voluminous importations via translation. As Ezra Pound comments, in his essay on 'Elizabethan Classicists', (1917): 'A great age of literature is perhaps always a great age of translation; or follows it.'[8] The present volume argues, by its very existence, for an inclusive approach to the literary legacies of the world, for greater interaction between them, *especially* in respect to the dominant language, English. Cross-cultural communication involves translation; translation implies cross-

---

[6] Charles Tomlinson, 'Introduction: The Poet as Translator', *The Oxford Book of Verse in English Translation, chosen and edited by C. Tomlinson* (Oxford: Oxford University Press, 1980), p. xvii.

[7] Steiner, 'Introduction', in *The Penguin Book of Modern Verse Translation*, ed. by George Steiner (Harmondsworth: Penguin, 1966), p. 25.

[8] Cf. the Ezra Pound 'collage' in Sect. 4.2, below.

cultural communication; and translation is the principal arena in which differences may be explored, appreciated, and interpreted or understood. The fact that English seems almost self-sufficient at this time disguises the fact that it is also permeated with other language traditions. The present volume, thus, centres on English not in a spirit of chauvinism, but rather the reverse, seeing it as a language of translation.

The link between theory or reflection on translation and the actual practice of it has been emphasized throughout. But valuable insights into the nature and act of translation can also be found in various texts that approach the crossing from one language to another in a more parabolic or allegorical manner, texts that would not be placed under the rubric of translation criticism in any conventional sense. The biblical story of the Tower of Babel is one such text. In attempting to make room for this extra dimension of translation 'studies', we have included a few texts (by Borges, Laura Bohannan, and Eva Hoffman) that illustrate the joys and anxieties of moving across language borders, of striving to represent something from one culture within another.

The primary writers on translation, historically, have been the translators themselves. As noted by Peter France, editor of *The Oxford Guide to Literature in English Translation*: 'until quite recently, with few exceptions, it [i.e. theory] was the work of *practitioners*, some of them eminent ones. Many of the most famous texts are not so much academic treatises as short personal statements.'[9] These statements often take the form of more or less authoritative prefatorial comments. We have also attempted, with the twentieth century, to represent work of writers who might be described as *primarily* theorists or critics. Even in these cases, though, the theoretical comments were in part drawn from or accompanied by actual translation. Thus Walter Benjamin's pivotal essay 'The Task of the Translator' featured first as an introduction to his 1923 translations of Baudelaire's 'Tableaux parisiens' into German. More recently, both Lawrence Venuti, whose comments on the post-colonial developments in translation thought have been influential, and Douglas Robinson, an equally prolific writer on the subject, are also translators of prose and poetry, the one from Italian the other primarily from Finnish. James S Holmes, who was among the pioneers in the emerging discipline of translation studies, was also a major poetry translator (from Dutch). In view of the intimate relationship between theory and practice in so many cases, we have sought to provide excerpts from actual translations (e.g. Benjamin's translation of a Baudelaire poem into German) as well as more general statements on the translation process or the aims of translation.

---

[9] Peter France, 'Theoretical Issues', in France (ed.), *The Oxford Guide to Literature in English Translation* (Oxford: Oxford University Press, 2000), 4.

Since canonical works are constantly retranslated, we have selected significant passages and represented them in several translations: for instance, from Genesis, the story of the Tower of Babel, the informing myth of translation, and the passage from Homer's *Odyssey*, used by Ezra Pound to introduce his *Cantos*; also excerpts from Aeschylus' *Agamemnon*, from Seneca, Juvenal, Ovid, Beowulf, Racine's *Phèdre*, and so forth. Common ground is thus established between individual translators, such as Chapman, Pope, Dryden, Johnson, Browning, Pound, Hughes, and so between different periods of literary history. A history of translation could indeed be written in terms of translations of Homer from Chaucer to, Logue, say—as indeed, George Steiner in effect does in his Penguin *Homer in English* (1996). Considerations of space have obliged us to be highly selective and to abbreviate many documents, but the grouping of related translators in 'collages' will we hope help contextualize their work, drawing attention to the ambience, the cultural-political conditions under which certain developments took place, certain contradictions became apparent. The numerous entries—both the 'collages' and the sections highlighting a single translator and/or translation critic—vary a great deal, both in their content, structure, and introductory material. This variety, so the editors hope, will facilitate the reader's appreciation of the rich mosaic of the tradition of translation which is so much a part of literary and cultural history.

BABEL

The Hebrew Bible and Translation

The Bible is the single most important and most translated text in Western history and culture. Seen as a unifying work and functioning as the basis of organized religion in the West, its translation has often manifested cultural and ideological diversity. The very idea of translating the Bible, 'the Word of God', from the source languages into the vernacular languages has of course led to extensive even deadly controversy. The translation into Latin by St Jerome, known as the Vulgate, was for centuries the official text of the Catholic Church and continued often to be the preferred source for Catholic translators, taking precedence even over the original languages (Hebrew, Aramaic, Greek). The ongoing translation of the Bible, whether directly from the source languages or from the Vulgate— later, Luther's German translation served virtually as an 'original' for some Bible translators—inevitably reflected cultural and linguistic diversity.

The story of this process is, in a sense, contained within the Bible itself, in the Genesis account of the Tower of Babel (Genesis 11: 1–9). This may be regarded as, perhaps, the key myth of translation; clearly, if there were only one human language, there would be no need for translation to facilitate communication between human beings variously located. Of course, since it is God who divides humanity by creating a multiplicity of languages, the attempt to overcome the resulting divisions through translation is evidence of an understandable but sacrilegious desire to return to a condition in which it is practical to consider building a tower! Hence the sense of taboo-breaking that, according to some writers on the subject, is attendant on any act of translation, and hence also the sense of unifying humanity, even in its rich diversity, through the act of translation.

The Babel story is a kind of leitmotif of this volume, and it seems fitting to present it in several translations. The source text, in Hebrew, is given below with an interlinear translation into English (Hebrew, it should be remembered, is read from right to left and the interlinear version, of course, is also to be so read). This is followed by an ancient Greek version, which is part of the first and very important translation, into Greek, of the Jewish Bible, a translation known as the Septuagint. Our readers, thus thrown headlong into the world of translation, are also given two English renderings of the Septuagint Babel story; a mid-nineteenth-century one by Sir Lancelot Brenton, and a new, previously unpublished one by Stavros Deligiorgis, who has also written an introductory note to his translation.

An account of the Septuagint, according to which seventy-two scholars produced identical versions, certain indication of divine intervention, can be found in the entry on Philo Iudaeus (p. 23–4). The Vulgate (Latin) version of the Babel story may be found on p. 113–14, along with the Catholic Douay-Reims translation, which is to a large extent based on the Latin. Other versions may be found on pp. 43–6, 66–7, 72, 119–20, 321–2, 351, and 568.

Genesis 11: 1–9: *The Interlinear Literal Translation of the Hebrew Old Testament*, trans. and ed. George Ricker Berry (Genesis and Exodus) (Hinds and Noble Edition, 1897)

1 וַיְהִי כָל־הָאָרֶץ שָׂפָה אֶחָת
one ¹language [being] earth the all ,pass to came it And

2 וּדְבָרִים אֲחָדִים׃ וַיְהִי בְּנָסְעָם
migrating their in ,pass to came it (and) ; ²same ¹the ³words and

מִקֶּדֶם וַיִּמְצְאוּ בִקְעָה בְּאֶרֶץ
of land the in plain open an found they (and) eastward (from)

3 שִׁנְעָר וַיֵּשְׁבוּ שָׁם׃ וַיֹּאמְרוּ אִישׁ
one each ,said they And .there settled they and ,Shinar

אֶל־רֵעֵהוּ הָבָה נִלְבְּנָה לְבֵנִים וְנִשְׂרְפָה
burn us let and ,bricks make us let ,Come : neighbor his unto

לִשְׂרֵפָה וַתְּהִי לָהֶם הַלְּבֵנָה לְאָבֶן וְהַחֵמָר
bitumen the and stone for brick the them to was and ; burning to

4 הָיָה לָהֶם לַחֹמֶר׃ וַיֹּאמְרוּ הָבָה נִבְנֶה־לָּנוּ
us for build us let ,Come :said they And .mortar for them to was

עִיר וּמִגְדָּל וְרֹאשׁוֹ בַשָּׁמַיִם וְנַעֲשֶׂה־
make us let and ; heavens the in [being] top its (and) ,tower a and city a

לָּנוּ שֵׁם פֶּן־נָפוּץ עַל־פְּנֵי כָל־הָאָרֶץ׃
.earth the all of face the upon scattered be we lest ,name a us for

5 וַיֵּרֶד יְהֹוָה לִרְאֹת אֶת־הָעִיר וְאֶת־הַמִּגְדָּל
,tower the and city the see to Jehovah down came And

6 אֲשֶׁר בָּנוּ בְּנֵי הָאָדָם׃ וַיֹּאמֶר יְהֹוָה הֵן
,Behold ; Jehovah said And .men of sons the built had which

עַם אֶחָד וְשָׂפָה אַחַת לְכֻלָּם וְזֶה
[is] this and ; them of all to ¹one ²language and ,¹one ²people

הַחִלָּם לַעֲשׂוֹת וְעַתָּה לֹא־יִבָּצֵר מֵהֶם
them from off shut be not will now and ; do to beginning their

7 כֹּל אֲשֶׁר יָזְמוּ לַעֲשׂוֹת׃ הָבָה נֵרְדָה
down go us let ,Come .do to plan they which thing any

וְנָבְלָה שָׁם שְׂפָתָם אֲשֶׁר לֹא יִשְׁמְעוּ
hear ²may ¹they ³not that so ,language their there confuse and

8 אִישׁ שְׂפַת רֵעֵהוּ׃ וַיָּפֶץ יְהֹוָה
Jehovah scattered And .neighbor his of language the one each

אֹתָם מִשָּׁם עַל־פְּנֵי כָל־הָאָרֶץ וַיַּחְדְּלוּ
ceased they and ; earth the all of face the upon thence from them

9 לִבְנֹת הָעִיר׃ עַל־כֵּן קָרָא שְׁמָהּ בָּבֶל
,Babel name its called one Therefore .city the build to

כִּי־שָׁם בָּלַל יְהֹוָה שְׂפַת כָּל־הָאָרֶץ
.earth the all of language the Jehovah confused there because

וּמִשָּׁם הֱפִיצָם יְהֹוָה עַל־פְּנֵי
of face the upon Jehovah them scattered thence from and

כָּל־הָאָרֶץ׃
.earth the all

The Greek text: Genesis 11: 1–9, ed. and trans. Sir Lancelot C. L. Brenton, *The Septuagint with Apocrypha: Greek and English* (London: Bagster and Sons, 1851)

Καὶ ἦν πᾶσα ἡ γῆ χεῖλος ἕν, καὶ φωνὴ μία πᾶσι. 11
Καὶ ἐγένετο ἐν τῷ κινῆσαι αὐτοὺς ἀπὸ ἀνατολῶν, εὗρον πεδίον 2
ἐν γῇ Σεναὰρ, καὶ κατῴκησαν ἐκεῖ. Καὶ εἶπεν ἄνθρωπος τῷ 3
πλησίον αὐτοῦ, δεῦτε πλινθεύσωμεν πλίνθους, καὶ ὀπτήσωμεν
αὐτὰς πυρί· καὶ ἐγένετο αὐτοῖς ἡ πλίνθος εἰς λίθον, καὶ ἄσφαλ-
τος ἦν αὐτοῖς ὁ πηλός. Καὶ εἶπαν, δεῦτε οἰκοδομήσωμεν 4
ἑαυτοῖς πόλιν καὶ πύργον, οὗ ἔσται ἡ κεφαλὴ ἕως τοῦ οὐρανοῦ.
καὶ ποιήσωμεν ἑαυτοῖς ὄνομα, πρὸ τοῦ διασπαρῆναι ἡμᾶς ἐπὶ
προσώπου πάσης τῆς γῆς. Καὶ κατέβη Κύριος ἰδεῖν τὴν πόλιν 5
καὶ τὸν πύργον, ὃν ᾠκοδόμησαν οἱ υἱοὶ τῶν ἀνθρώπων. Καὶ 6
εἶπε Κύριος, ἰδοὺ γένος ἕν, καὶ χεῖλος ἓν πάντων, καὶ τοῦτο
ἤρξαντο ποιῆσαι, καὶ νῦν οὐκ ἐκλείψει ἀπ᾽ αὐτῶν πάντα ὅσα ἂν
ἐπιθῶνται ποιεῖν. Δεῦτε, καὶ καταβάντες συγχέωμεν αὐτῶν 7
ἐκεῖ τὴν γλῶσσαν, ἵνα μὴ ἀκούσωσιν ἕκαστος τὴν φωνὴν τοῦ
πλησίον. Καὶ διέσπειρεν αὐτοὺς Κύριος ἐκεῖθεν ἐπὶ πρόσωπον 8
πάσης τῆς γῆς· καὶ ἐπαύσαντο οἰκοδομοῦντες τὴν πόλιν καὶ τὸν
πύργον. Διὰ τοῦτο ἐκλήθη τὸ ὄνομα αὐτῆς, Σύγχυσις, ὅτι ἐκεῖ 9
συνέχεε Κύριος τὰ χείλη πάσης τῆς γῆς, καὶ ἐκεῖθεν διέσπειρεν
αὐτοὺς Κύριος ἐπὶ πρόσωπον πάσης τῆς γῆς.

And all the earth was one lip, and there was one language to all. [2]And it came to pass as they moved from the east, they found a plain in the land of Senaar, and they dwelt there. [3]And a man said to his neighbour, Come, let us make bricks and bake them with fire. And the brick was to them for stone, and their mortar was bitumen. [4]And they said, Come, let us build to ourselves a city and tower, whose top shall be to heaven, and let us make to ourselves a name, before we are scattered abroad upon the face of all the earth.[5] And the Lord came down to see the city and the tower, which the sons of men built. [6]And the Lord said, Behold, *there is* one race, and one lip of all, and they have begun to do this, and now nothing shall fail from them of all that they may have undertaken to do. [7]Come, and having gone down let us there confound their tongue, that they may not understand each the voice of his neighbour. [8]And the Lord scattered them thence over the face of all the earth, and they left off building the city and the tower. [9]On this account its name was called Confusion, because there the Lord confounded the languages of all the earth, and thence the Lord scattered them upon the face of all the earth.

The Septuagint

STAVROS DELIGIORGIS

The greatest human accomplishment in the field of translation may well be the scholarly effort of hundreds of bilingual individuals who, between approximately 250 BCE and 1200 CE, translated almost two thousand Sanscrit Buddhist treatises into Chinese. Neither the vast differences separating the two languages nor the differences between the two cultures stood in the way of the effective, purposeful work (in equal doses of translation and transcendence) that changed the East Asian landscape, on either side of China and India—including Mongolia and Japan—to the philosophical and religious space we recognize today.

By sheer coincidence during approximately the same historical times similar world-changing events were taking place in the Eastern Mediterranean. The languages and the civilizations in question were Hebrew and Greek. They were bracketed, if not quite bridged, by the able, authoritative 'Seventy-two' translators—according to the early *testimonium*, the Epistle of Aristeas (*c.*150 BCE)—who travelled from Jerusalem to Hellenistic Alexandria, possibly on a royal commission, during the reign of Ptolemy Philadelphus (*c.*285 BC). Contrary to widespread opinion, the Jews of Alexandria would not need a translation of the Bible after being dominated by the successors of Alexander of Macedon for only thirty-five years. Jews who had been under foreign domination in other parts of the known world for much longer periods of time were not known to have undertaken translations of their Scriptures. The Epistle of Aristeas records Demetrius Phalereus—like any self-respecting chief librarian—expressed an interest in filling gaps in his 'special collections' and also in the conservation and linguistic accessibility of his acquisitions. A direct quotation from the Epistle makes clear that the reasons for the translation of the Bible were purely intrinsic.

> The Books of the Law of the Jews, with some few others, are wanting. For it happens that these books are written in the Hebrew script and language, but, according to the evidence of the experts, have been somewhat carelessly committed to writing and are not in their original form; for they have never had the benefit of royal attention. It is important that these books, duly corrected, should find a place in your library, because this legislation, in as much as it is divine, is of philosophical importance and of innate integrity.

The legendary 'Seventy' translators had to face, we must assume, texts thick with theological, legal, literary, and political concepts for which the Greek they were translating into had no counterpart. Still, the manner in which the Greek language was mined for words, phrases, and even the retaining of key Hebrew terms in transliteration, is nothing short of an extended tour de force. The end result managed to communicate, if not the precise lexical and syntactic elements of the Hebrew, at least the tone of sublimity and of the sacred associations that the originals as a whole evoked.

The Epistle of Aristeas was the first to mention the enthusiastic approval of the Jewish community of Alexandria when the task was completed. Later Jewish intellectuals of the stature of Josephus and Philo Judaeus held the Septuagint in such high regard they did not hesitate, in their turn, to amplify and elaborate upon Aristeas' original, 'miraculous' report. Early Christian Church Fathers followed suit. They expanded upon Aristeas's themes just as Josephus and Philo had done before them even as they were discovering that the numberless quotations of the Hebrew Bible incorporated in the Gospels and the Epistles of Paul were free as well as literal adaptations of the Septuagint.

Later Jewish communities were eventually to distance themselves from the Septuagint. It was compared to a blasphemy as grievous as the worship of the Golden Calf (*Sepher Torah*, I. 8), the divine displeasure indicated by the plunging of the Earth into three days of unrelieved darkness (*Megillath Taanith*, Book of Fasts, first century CE).

The progressive grounding of the Christian liturgy upon the text of the Septuagint, on the other hand, contributed to its being considered a holy text, and one which other languages would want to approximate through translation. The Arabic, Ethiopic, Armenian, Coptic, and Georgian versions, to mention but a few, were based on the Septuagint. (Augustine of Hippo was so happy with it that he thought Jerome's project of going directly to the Hebrew for his Latin Vulgate to be redundant.)

As a final note we might add that about a thousand years after the Alexandrian drafting of the Septuagint, Greece, and especially the northern city of Thessaloniki, was to become the site of a second map-altering event, comparable in importance to the translation of the Sanskrit scriptures into Chinese. It was the conversion, in the ninth century CE, of the Southern and Eastern Slavic nations to Christianity; the translation of scriptures (by Cyril and Methodius), becoming once again the instrument to that end.

Babel: What Greeks Read Between Some Septuagint Lines

At Babel the post-diluvial God who had promised never to destroy humanity again appears to have noticed a condition that had escaped his earlier wrath: through language humanity could still become one, a creature bigger than its perishable parts. It could overcome its post-lapsarian limitations, in other words, and perhaps even its mortality! The ability of a particular group to communicate with any other group in an unmediated manner is summarily shattered in the same spirit as the removal of the 'exceeding wickedness' of humanity had been dealt with through the flood. Key to the story of the confusion of tongues at Babel is God's perception that human beings would be able to achieve absolutely anything. In paraphrase the Greek of the Septuagint puts it in terrible, litotic language: 'Nothing that they will set out to do will be impossible to them.'

Apart from the occurence of a very familiar universal flood in the opening sections of Plato's *Laws*, the divine judgement against possible hubris in the human undertaking that presumes to reach the seat of the heavenly powers would not have escaped Greek audiences. Plato's dialogue *Protagoras* also dealt with a mythic past in which the primordial human beings began pulling together and joining with one another in order to achieve the mechanisms of self-preservation that the gods had failed to impart to them as they did to all the other animals at the time of the creation.

Genesis 11: 1–9: The Septuagint, translated from the Greek by Stavros Deligiorgis

the entire earth used to be one lip
and one voice to all

it happened
as they moved from the east
they found level ground in the land of Sennaar
and they made their home there

every man urged his neighbour 'come
let us make mud bricks
and let us bake them with fire'

the mudbricks had become to them like stone
asphalt serving for clay

and they said 'come let us build ourselves a city
and a tower
the head of which will reach up to heaven
and let us make ourselves a name
before we are dispersed upon the face
of the whole earth'

and the Lord came down to see the city and the tower
that the sons of men had built

and the Lord said
'here is a single nation and one lip to everybody

and they have begun making this
now nothing that they will set out to do will be impossible to them

let us therefore go down
let us confuse their tongue right there
so no one will be able hear his neighbour's voice'

and the Lord dispersed them from that place
upon the face of the whole earth
and they stopped building the town
and the tower

which is why its name was called Confusion
because that is where the Lord confused the lips
of the whole earth
and it was from there the Lord God dispersed them
upon the face of the whole earth

PART I
FROM ANTIQUITY TO
MODERN TIMES

CHAPTER I

FROM CICERO TO CAXTON

1.1 INTRODUCTION

The English translation tradition, in its earliest manifestations, draws on Classical precedent, mainly on the Classical Latin translation, primarily from the Greek, as well as, of course, on Early Christian Latin Translation from the Scriptures, the Hebrew, Aramaic of the Hebrew Bible and from the Greek of the Gospels.

Clear and forceful as were the Roman writers (Cicero, Horace, Quintilian), their legacy was far from unambiguous and indeed the same oft-quoted remarks or statements of principle were mobilized in support of apparently contradictory positions. The most striking example perhaps is Cicero's famous dictum (in respect to his translation of the two most prominent Ancient Greek orators) promoting sense-for-sense rather than word-for-word translation. This 'free' approach becomes also a defence of *ad verbum* fidelity to the original, since it is taken to be distinct from literary imitation, *à la Romaine*. The 'Classical Latin and Early Christian Latin Translations' collage (Sect. 1.2, below) gives a panoramic view of these developments and controversies.

Nevertheless, while the numerous defensive or aggressive prefaces by translators are indication of strong opposition to Ciceronian freedom, the sense-for-sense approach prevailed, at least as far as non-Scriptural texts were concerned. This is particularly true of a period in which, as in Roman times, a national culture was being constructed, asserting itself, of course, in many ways, but significantly also in the naturalizing (the 'Englishing') of canonical works of Western literature.

With the Scriptures, it was a somewhat different story. The Septuagint or Alexandrian Greek translation of the Hebrew Bible (*c.*285 BC), intended perhaps for the use of the Hellenistic Jews of Alexandria, was by legend held to have been completed in seventy-two days, the number of translators also being seventy-two, producing identical versions, this being proof sufficient of 'divine inspiration'. The intervention of God in the translation of His own Word was necessarily invoked, since without it the translation would be subject to endless questioning, in its turn leading inevitably to religious controversy and conflict.

The Septuagint, then, became a canonical text for later translators, being preferred even to the source, which it would seem to have replaced. Jerome, however, approached this sacrosanct text with Ciceronian caution and returned for verification to the Hebrew and Aramaic. His Vulgate translation, which remained the official Bible of the Catholic Church for centuries, owed its authority not only to the scrupulousness of his scholarship but also to the excellence of his Latin style. His legacy was a dual one of respect for tradition and critical acumen. The Vulgate itself, by virtue of its adoption by the one and only Church, was a text of irreproachable canonicity. It substituted itself for the original until the need began to be widely felt for extension of the readership via translation into the European vernaculars.

The documented fourth-century controversy or debate between the two Church Fathers, Sts Jerome and Augustine, in which no ground was given, expressed irresolvable differences—of temperament, no doubt, as well as of opinion, these differences continuing to operate on into the Renaissance and beyond. One reason for these differences, no doubt, was the fact that Jerome was and Augustine was not a translator. Augustine, intent on establishing an orthodoxy, conscious of the overriding need to provide sure, unambiguous guidance for the faithful, was worried by Jerome's critical examination of hitherto supposedly inspired texts. For Augustine there could be only one true translation of God's word. Deferring to the Septuagint, whose translators had been led by the Holy Spirit, he favoured this translation and regarded it as more reliable and authentic even than the Hebrew and Aramaic originals. He could not approve of Jerome's new version which returned to these sources and which, confusingly and dangerously, he felt, drew attention as well to problematical passages or words therein. Politically more sophisticated than Jerome, Augustine foresaw, for instance, increased disagreement between the Roman and Greek churches, resulting from the existence of different versions of the Scriptures, threatening the unity of the Christian Church. (Of course, he approved of rather than objected to Jerome's translations of the Gospels from the Greek source text.) Two different concepts of scholarship, authenticity, accuracy are at loggerheads here, the prestige of these two great figures ensuring that their difference should continue to reverberate.

Translation into the vernacular (Old and Middle English) paralleled or preceded developments elsewhere in Europe. While early literary activity was mostly in Latin, King Alfred (871–99) initiated a policy of translation. Jonathan Wilcox's collage (Sect. 1.3, below) documents this development and activity, including the translation of important religious works, late Latin works (Boethius), the Bible itself, this being part of a process of education, for the use of those without or with insufficient Latin, in a period of decline in knowledge of the Classical language. Alfred's approach, as befits an educator, was pragmatic, sometimes opting for sense-for-sense, sometimes for the *ad verbum*. In the following century, the Benedictine monk and homilist Aelfric (*c*.990–*c*.1010) translated a part of *Genesis* insisting on the need for interpretation rather than unquestioning literalism.

However, conflict between clerical defenders of Latin and influential laymen persisted, viz the 'Dialogue between a Lord and a Clerk upon Translation', from the translation by John of Trevisa (1326–1412) of Ralph Higden's 1387 world history, *Polychronicon*. The argument advanced by the Clerk is, in effect, an argument against all translation, a defence of the status quo, translation being seen as representing a danger to the fortress of learning, i.e to the exclusivism of those with Latin, mainly the clergy. Trevisa's translation, printed by Caxton, was among the first books to be made widely available. With printing, introduced by William Caxton (*c*.1422–91), texts could of course be far more broadly disseminated. Caxton, a prolific translator himself, also printed many works of translation. The technological revolution initiated by him made possible a great extension of Classical learning and literature, whether for pedagogical, practical purposes, or for entertainment, via vernacular translations, the demand for which of course increased just as the conditions giving rise to that demand also encouraged the expansion of printing. Caxton's last book, itself a translation (of Virgil's *Aeneid*) was based on an intermediary French version. Clearly, although there was a discernible impulse, as noted, to return to source texts, this was not regarded as obligatory. Caxton was undoubtedly the most important early champion of the English language, and translation had a key role in establishing the native language as central to the country's literary life, as a growing percentage of the population gained access to it.

1.2 CLASSICAL LATIN AND EARLY CHRISTIAN LATIN TRANSLATION

Approaches to translation, in the Western tradition, have been seen as oscillating between an attachment to Classical learning, which stresses intellectual flexibility, and the Judaeo-Christian emphasis on the unchanging law of God, embodied in a language which also cannot be changed. The conflict between commitment to stylistic excellence, clarity of expression, and *ad verbum* exactness cannot be resolved, the terms having been established very early on. The principal arena has undoubtedly been the translation of the sacred texts of Judaism and Christianity with the geographic spread of these world religions, as well as the gradual and then incrementally rapid spread of literacy, and self-assertion of the vernacular languages, especially with the disintegration of such supranational entities as the Roman and Holy Roman empires and concomitant rise of nation states.

In Roman times, of course, translation relates to the construction of a supranational culture, based on Rome, and becomes an assertion of Roman cultural independence from or parity with Attic Greece. To achieve this parity, a non-subservient stance was essential.

Late Roman translation from Biblical Greek—St Jerome's handling of the Greek Septuagint, for instance—reflected the high status of the source text. The translations of the Holy Scriptures were necessarily 'inspired' and might enjoy equal and, in the case of the Septuagint, for instance, even superior status to the source text itself. It was in this connection that the myth of the origin of the Septuagint developed, obscuring the reality of the situation (see Philo, below). The Septuagint was held to have been dictated by God, the seventy-two translators functioning as a kind of collective medium for him, the identity of the texts, according to the myth, further testifying to divine intervention.

Jerome, as a 'Ciceronian', even though he agonized over it (*vide* his famous dream) and even though he admitted that in translation of the Scriptures even the order of the words was sacrosanct, was not able to suppress his Classicist leanings, being too committed to the demands of clarity and stylistic excellence, which required a free, or sense-for-sense approach. The Latin legacy, similarly, embodies both pre-Christian and Christian components. It is profoundly ambiguous, and this ambiguity runs through the entire Western tradition of translation, being evident even today, in scarcely less stark a form than at the beginning.

Thanks are due to Professor Louis G. Kelly for his advice, and in particular for the translations of Latin texts which he generously contributed to the present volume.

Marcus Tullius Cicero (106–43 BC)

Cicero, Roman statesman, orator, and philosopher, was regarded as one of the finest Classical stylists. He is credited with the formation of a Latin philosophical vocabulary.

In *De optimo genere oratorum*, his introduction to his translation (not extant) of two speeches by Demosthenes and his arch-rival Aeschines, Demosthenes being the greatest orator of fourth-century Greece, Cicero makes a case for 'free' translation. The essence of successful oratory, he insists, is that it should 'instruct, delight and move the minds of his audience', this being achievable in translation only by conserving the 'force and flavour of the passage', not by translating 'word for word'. While Cicero has been routinely quoted in defence of non-literal translation, it should be remembered that he is instancing the translation of speeches.

The assumption then is that, with sufficient latitude, it is not impossible to convey the persuasiveness of Greek oratory. Cicero's approach is essentially pragmatic. Thus, in the *De finibus bonorum et malorum*, he discusses the translation of Greek philosophical terms into Latin, insisting that Greek neologisms may be rendered by Latin ones, that there is good reason for sometimes translating one Greek word by several Latin ones, and that there should be no injunction against importing Greek words into Latin when there is no adequate Latin term.

'De optimo genere oratorum' (the Best Kind of Orator), iv. 13–v. 14 (46 BC), translated by L. G. Kelly

And this is our conclusion: that, since the most outstanding Greek orators were those from Athens, and that their chief was easily Demosthenes, anybody who imitates him will speak in the Attic style, and excellently to boot. Consequently, since Athenian orators are proposed for our imitation, to speak in the Attic style is to speak well. But, because there are many misconceptions over what constitutes this style of composition, I propose to undertake a task useful for students, but not completely necessary for myself. For I have translated into Latin two of the most eloquent and most noble speeches in Athenian literature, those two speeches in which Aeschines and Demonsthenes oppose each other. And I have not translated like a mere hack, but in the manner of an orator, translating the same themes and their expression and sentence shapes in words consonant with our conventions. In so doing I did not think it necessary to translate word for word, but I have kept the force and flavour of the passage. For I saw my duty not as counting out words for the reader, but as weighing them out. And this is the goal of my project: to give my countrymen an understanding of what they are to seek from those models who aim to be Attic in style, and of the formulas of speech they are to have recourse to.

Quintus Horatius Flaccus (Horace) (65–8 BC)

Horace was an outstanding lyric poet and satirist, friend of the Emperor Augustus and the great epic poet Virgil. His four books of *Carmina* or *Odes* are perhaps his most admired and translated works.

The epistle (*To the Pisones/ Ad Pisones*), known as *Ars Poetica* [Art of Poetry] concentrates on the traditional literary genres of epic and drama, after Aristotle. From the time of Ben Jonson, Horace has been looked upon as a poetic mentor or companion, his passing remarks on translation as influential therefore as Cicero's. Horace appears to disparage the 'faithful' translator, although, somewhat perversely; this criticism has been used to support fidelity to the original, on the grounds that he is alluding not so much to translation, as to literary imitation, in the Roman sense, where fidelity was regarded as somewhat *infra dig*. In calling for a freer treatment of earlier works, Horace echoes Cicero's admonitions to translators of orations, where the aim is not so much a literal transcription of the Greek words as a representation of the persuasiveness of source texts, which are transcriptions of delivered speeches.

From *Ars poetica*, ll. 128–44 (19-17 BC?), translated by Ben Jonson (1573–1637), pub. 1640

'Tis hard, to speake things common properly:
And thou maist better bring a *Rhapsody*
Of *Homers*, forth in acts, then of thine owne,
First publish things unspoken, and unknowne.
Yet common matter thou thine owne maist make,
For, being a Poët, thou maist feigne, create,
Not care, as thou wouldst faithfully translate,
To render word for word: nor with thy sleight
Of imitation, leape into a streight,
From whence thy Modestie, or Poëmes law
Forbids thee forth againe thy foot to draw.
Nor so begin, as did that Circler late,
I sing a noble Warre, and Priam's *Fate.*
What doth this Promiser such gaping worth
Afford? The Mountaines travail'd, and brought forth
A scorned Mouse! O, how much better this,
Who nought assaies unaptly, or amisse?
Speake to me, Muse, the Man, who, after Troy was sack't,

Saw many Townes, and Men, and could their manners tract.
Hee thinkes not, how to give you smoake from light,
But light from smoake; that he may draw his bright
Wonders forth after:

From Horace, *Satires, Epistles and Ars Poetica*, with an English translation by H. Rushton Fairclough (1926; the Loeb Classical Library, Cambridge, Mass. and London: Harvard University Press, 1999)

[A prose version which rather tendentiously translates 'fidus' in 'fidus interpres' as 'slavish' rather than as 'faithful'.]

> It is hard to treat in your own what is common: and you are doing better in spinning into acts a song of Troy than if, for the first time, you were giving the world a theme unknown and unsung. In ground open to all you will win private rights, if you do not linger along the easy and open pathway, if you do not seek to render word for word as a slavish translator.

Philo Iudaeus (Philo of Alexandria) (15/10 BC – 45/50 AD) (fl. 20–40 AD)

Philo was a Greek-speaking Jewish theologian and neo-Platonic philosopher. In the passage below, he describes the origins of the third-century BC translation into Greek by seventy-two translators of the Hebrew Scriptures, the Septuagint. This translation, intended primarily for Jews who had migrated to Egypt and other Greek-speaking lands, became the Old Testament of the Greek-speaking Christians. Philo bases his account on the anonymous letter of Aristeas, under which name a Jewish writer purportedly writes to the Athenian statesman Philocrates before the middle of the third century BC. Philo's addition to the Aristean story emphasizes the divine origin of the translation, claiming that the seventy-two worked independently of one another and yet arrived at an identical text, whereas, according to the earlier account, they collaborated. Divine inspiration alone could validate translation of the Scriptures, the Word of God.

From *The Life of Moses* (*De vita Mosis*, 20 BC) ll. 37–40, by Philo Judaeus, translated by F. H. Colson (London: Heinemann, 1935)

> The translators shut themselves away in seclusion, alone except for the four natural elements of earth, air, fire and water (for the Law begins with the creation of the world).

And then they prophesied as if in ecstasy. They used, not different words, but the same words and sentence structures, as if each was under the guidance of the same invisible Spirit. But is there anybody unaware that every language, and particularly Greek, is rich in words, and that the same thought can be rendered in many ways by ringing the changes on words, using synonyms and, in each case, seeking out the *mot juste*? According to tradition, this did not happen in the translation of our Law, for each Chaldean word was exactly translated by a precise Greek equivalent, which was perfectly adapted to the thing signified. As I see it, this is the same as what happens in geometry or dialectic. There, meanings can not survive ambiguity of expression, as once terminology is established it remains constant. And similarly, our translators found the expressions exactly suitable to the things signified. And these words were the only possible, or at least the words most apt, to render the things signified with perfect clarity. And here is the most striking proof of our claim: whenever a Chaldean who reads Greek, or a Greek who understands Chaldean finds himself before both versions at once, he looks on the Greek and the Chaldean with wonder and respect as two sisters, or rather, as one and the same work in both matter and style [. . .]

but does terminology remain constant

Marcus Fabius Quintillianus (Quintilian) (30? – 96? AD)

Quintilian, like Cicero, was trained as an orator and practised at the bar. Tutor to the family of the Emperor Domitian, he is primarily celebrated as a teacher. Quintilian retired in order to write, his principal work being the *Institutio Oratoria* (Education of an Orator), possibly intended as a primer for the young princes; it is regarded as a basic text in rhetoric, pedagogy and literary criticism. Book X contains a survey of Greek and Latin writers, purporting to show how Latin could match Greek. Translation becomes a way of improving or asserting the value of the vernacular through emulation of Classical models. Quintilian's remarks are in the Ciceronian tradition, whereby translation was seen not only as a tool in the acquisition of a foreign language, but as a means of enriching the target language. He systematizes much of what earlier writers had to say, making clear, for instance, the distinction between *metaphrasis* or word-for-word translation and *paraphrasis* or phrase-by-phrase translation. He is concerned not so much with the painstaking reproduction of earlier texts, as with the preservation of a living tradition. His approach to education was of course highly influential.

In the first passage, below, Quintilian makes it clear that it is permissible and indeed obligatory not only to emulate the Greek models but even to try to excel them.

From *Institute of Oratory; or Education of an Orator* (*Institutio Oratoria*, X. xi. 1–11 (96 CE?), translated by J. S. Watson (London: George Bell, 1876)

From these [Greek] authors, and others worthy to be read, a stock of words, a variety of figures, and the art of composition must be acquired; and our minds must be directed to the imitation of all their excellences; for it cannot be doubted that a great portion of art consists in *imitation*, since, though to invent is first in order of time, and holds the first place in merit, yet it is of advantage to copy what has been invented with success. [. . .] We must, indeed, be either like or unlike those who excel and nature rarely forms one like, though *imitation* does so frequently. But the very circumstance that renders the study of all subjects so much more easy to us, than it was to those who had nothing to imitate, will prove a disadvantage to us, unless it be turned to account with caution and judgement.

Undoubtedly, then, imitation is not sufficient of itself, if for no other reason than that it is the mark of an indolent nature to rest satisfied with what has been invented by others. For what would have been the case, if, in those times which were without any models, mankind had thought that they were not to execute or imagine anything but what they already knew? Assuredly nothing would have been invented. [. . .]

It is dishonourable even to rest satisfied with simply equalling what we imitate. For what would have been the case, again, if no one had accomplished more than he whom he copied? [. . .] But if it is not allowable to add to what has preceded us, how can we ever hope to see a complete orator, when among those, whom we have hitherto recognised as the greatest, no one has been found in whom there is not something defective or censurable? Even those who do not aim at the highest excellence should rather try to excel, than merely follow, their predecessors; for he who makes it his object to get before another, will possibly, if he does not go by him, get abreast of him. But assuredly no one will come up with him in whose steps he thinks that he must tread, for he who follows another must of necessity always be behind him. [. . .]

From *Institutio Oratoria*, X. v. 1–5, translated by L. G. Kelly

Our ancient orators believed that the most efficacious means of acquiring a command of their language was to translate Greek works into Latin. Crassus, quoted in Cicero, *De Oratore* l. 155, says he made a practice of it; and Cicero, speaking in his own name, recommended it very often. And indeed, he published books by Xenophon and Plato he had translated. [. . .] The reason for this exercise is extremely obvious. For Greek authors abound in richness of expression and bring the greatest finesse into their oratory. And therefore those who would translate these authors must use the best of language while relying on their native resources. Because our Roman language is immensely different from Greek, we are bound by a certain need to rethink the many and varied figures with which a work is adorned.

[. . .]

For I do not want translation to be a mere paraphrase, but a struggle and rivalry over the same meanings.

Gaius Plinius Caecilius Secundus (Pliny the Younger) (61?– 112? AD)

A pupil of Quintilian, Pliny was a successful lawyer and orator, serving as praetor and consul. A member of the wealthy classes, raised by his uncle, the literary equestrian Pliny the Elder, he is best known for the nine books of letters on a variety of subjects. These include his official correspondence with the emperor Trajan and amount to a kind of social history of the time. His circle included many of the major figures of the day, such as Tacitus, Suetonius, and Martial.

Epistle VII is influenced by Quintilian's notion of emulation, carrying the argument a stage further into open, almost gloating rivalry.

From Epistle VII. ix. 1–6, *Letter to Fuscus Salinator* (85 AD), translated by L. G. Kelly

You ask my opinion on how you should study during your retirement which you have enjoyed for some time now. As many advise, it is of primary importance to translate from Greek into Latin or from Latin into Greek. By this type of exercise one becomes sensitive to the properties and richness of vocabulary, to the wealth of figures of speech, to effective exposition; and moreover, by the imitation of the best models is learnt the power of writing on the same subject matter. And at the same time, a translator cannot ignore the responsibilities of a reader. For from this comes understanding and critical sense.

When you have read closely enough to retain matter and argument, there is nothing to prevent you from writing like your author's rival and then comparing your work with what you have read. Then you should seek out what is better in your version and better in his. You will have great satisfaction if some of your work is better, and considerable embarrassment if all of his shows more skill. At times one can choose extremely familiar passages, and then seek to excel those you have chosen. Being private this struggle is bold but not out of place: although we do see many who have taken on these contests with much credit to themselves, and who have shown enough self-confidence to surpass those they intended merely to follow.

You can revise what you have written after letting it lie, keep much of it, skim through much of it, add new material, rewrite a lot of it. This is laborious and tedious; but, because of its very difficulty, it bears fruit in bringing you new fire, and giving you new drive when your enthusiasm has flagged. For you will be weaving new members into the complete body without disturbing the balance of the original.

Evagrius (fl. 360?)

Evagrius of Antioch was St Jerome's mentor, his host and patron in Syria. Of noble birth and great wealth, he assisted Damasus in a disputed papal election. He produced a free translation of the *Life of Anthony* (the Egyptian hermit who was reckoned to be the founder of monasticism) by Athanasius of Alexandria (295–373), a Greek Christian writer and opponent of the Arians who denied the divinity of Christ. Athanasius had created a new biographical form that served as a model for later Greek and Latin hagiographers.

In his letter to Pammachius, Jerome cites Evagrius' preface to his translation where, in Ciceronian fashion, he explains how he has attempted to preserve the sense rather than the letter of the text.

From the Prologue to the *Life of St Anthony* (see J. P. Migne, *Patrologia Latina*, 73. 163, Paris [1844–55]), translated by L. G. Kelly

> Word-for-word translation from one language into another clouds the sense, and like uncontrolled weeds, smothers the crop. For, while the original case usages and figures of speech dominate the text, what could have been stated in pithy sentences is hardly made clear by long periphrases. This I have avoided in acceding to your request to translate the life of St Anthony. Even if some words are missing, nothing is missing from the senses. Leave it to others to go chasing after words and syllables; you must look for the sense.

From Epilogue to the *Life of St Anthony* (see *Patrologia Latina*, 73. 167), translated by L. G. Kelly

> Therefore I would ask those prudent people who have been kind enough to read this book to excuse me if, in translating from Greek to Latin, I could not bring over the full power of the Greek. In any case, this was not to my purpose. But we did not take this decision with malice, but knowing full well how Greek loses when translated into Latin. But I preferred to see the Greek suffer this loss, rather than have those who manage to read translations from the Greek suffer loss of divine favour. May almighty God, who inspired St Anthony in his great exploits, also inspire us to imitate him, so that in all things His name may be glorified through Jesus Christ, our Teacher, Counsellor, Redeemer and Saviour, with the Holy Spirit, to whom is glory and everlasting power for ever and ever.

Eusebius Hieronymus, St Jerome (348?–420)

Jerome and Augustine (see below) were the most important of the Church Fathers, as far as translation theory is concerned. Author of the Vulgate Latin translation of the Bible, for centuries the official Bible of the Catholic Church, Jerome also commented in detail on the methods and aims of his translation work, viz. the celebrated letter to his friend Pammachius, which was prompted by the attack on him, in 395, by his former friend and fellow monk Rufinus, himself the author of numerous translations from the Greek.

Born in Dalmatia into a wealthy family, Jerome came to Rome as a boy where he was taught by the foremost grammarian of the age, Aelius Donatus. In a famous dream (375), Jerome was accused by God of being a Ciceronian rather than a Christian, symptom of an internal conflict between his Classical leanings towards free-ranging translation and literalist demands, which stressed the accurate transmission of meaning particularly in the case of Holy Scriptures. After the dream Jerome became a hermit for a while, learning Hebrew; later he was ordained and continued his theological studies in Antioch where he translated or adapted, revised and supplemented the *Chronicle* of the church historian Eusebius of Caesarea, which he discusses in the letter to Pammachius as well as in his Preface to the *Chronicles* (see below). The theoretical basis for Jerome's translation theory is elaborated in his preface to the translation of Eusebius and does not significantly change over the years. On his return to Rome in 382 he became secretary to Pope Damasus and under orders from him began his translation of the Bible, revising the many versions and stylistically improving the old Latin text of the Gospels.

Driven from Rome after Damasus' death in 384, Jerome went to Antioch, Jerusalem and Egypt to study the ascetic life at first hand, and subsequently to Bethlehem, where he founded a monastery and remained for the rest of his life, while continuing to polemicise vigorously. His Vulgate translation of the Bible (391–415), dating from this period, included revisions of earlier New Testament translations and a new translation of the Old Testament, based on Origen's *Hexapla*.

Of all Christian Latin writers Jerome most closely approaches the standards of Classical Rome, having thoroughly assimilated the works of Cicero, Virgil, Horace, and others. On the other hand his letters and controversial writings are extraordinarily irascible. The conflicting demands of Ciceronian aesthetics and Christian asceticism are dramatically exemplified in Jerome's life and work. The apparent contradictions, however, appear less marked if one bears in mind the distinction Jerome himself makes between translation of Holy Scriptures and that of non-sacred texts. He weighs in with devastating effect against the literalists, while at the same time affirming that in the case of the Scriptures the actual words and even their order and significance are to be observed.

From the Preface to *Chronicles* of Eusebius 1–2 (380), translated by L. G. Kelly

There is an old custom among men of letters of translating Greek books into Latin as an intellectual exercise, and also, what is more difficult, of translating fine poetry into Latin verse. The great Cicero translated whole books by Plato with rigorous closeness and, having translated the Roman, Aratus, into hexametres, he turned to Xenophon's *Oeconomicus*. In this, the golden flow of eloquence is sometimes muddied by some scabrous and turbulent shoals so that, those who do not realize that it is a translation, do not credit Cicero with such work. For it is difficult, when following the text of another language, not to overstep the mark in places, and hard to keep in the translation the grace of something well said in the original. Something is signified by the properties of a word: in my language I do not have anything to match, and when I try to render the full sense, I eat up the span of a respectably long life in the resulting sentence. [. . .] If I translate word for word, it sounds absurd; if from necessity, I change something in the word-order or in the language, I am seen to abdicate the responsibility of a translator. [. . .] I pray you that whatever you find disordered in this work, you read with the eye of a friend and not of a critic. And this is doubly important as you know that I dictated this at considerable speed to a secretary; and the difficulty of the task is attested to by the fact that the inspired volumes produced by the Septuagint translators have not kept their flavour in Greek. This consideration drove Aquila, Symmachus and Theodotion [Theodosius] to produce almost a different book from the same work. Aquila tried to translate word for word, Symmachus preferred to follow the sense, and Theodotion did not want to go too far from the ancient versions. [. . .] Thus it came about that Sacred Scripture seemed so rough and uncouth that educated people, not knowing that it had been translated from the Hebrew, looked at the surface instead of the real meat and were put off by the unprepossessing clothing of its style rather than finding the beautiful body underneath. Finally, what is more melodious than the Book of Psalms, which can run in iambics like our Horace or the Greek Pindar, or have the resonance of Alcaeus, or the dignity of Sappho, or the flow of lyric metres. What is more beautiful than the canticle of Deuteronomy and Isaiah, what more dignified than Solomon, or more perfect than Job. Now these, as Josephus and Origen point out, all frame their poetry in hexameters and pentameters. When we read them in Greek, they have a particular sound, and when in Latin, they do not hang together. If there is anybody who does not believe that the power of a language is changed in translation, let him translate Homer literally into Latin—or rather, let him translate Homer into prose. Then he will see a laughable bit of work, and the greatest of poets scarcely able to speak.

From Letter 57, To Pammachius, 'On the Best Method of Translating', translated by L. G. Kelly

[Jerome had been asked by Eusebius of Cremona, an associate who had no Greek, if he would translate into Latin a letter sent by Archbishop Epiphanius to John, Bishop of Jerusalem.]

> [. . .] Not only do I admit, but I proclaim at the top of my voice, that in translating from Greek, except from Sacred Scripture, where even the order of the words is of God's doing, I have not translated word by word, but sense for sense. [. . .]

[Jerome proceeds to cite various Classical authorities, quoting directly from Cicero's preface to his own translation of speeches by Aeschines and Demonsthenes as well as from his own translation of Eusebius' *Chronicles* (see above), after which Jerome moves on to a more contentious area, concerning the translation of Holy Scriptures, even the Septuagint containing passages problematical from the point of view of strict literality.]

> There is nothing extraordinary about this procedure in secular or ecclesiastical writers, when the translators of the Septuagint, the evangelists and the apostles, did the same thing in the sacred books. In St Mark, we read that the Lord said: 'Talitha cumi.' This is commented in the text: 'Which is translated: "My girl, I say to you, get up"' [Mark 5: 41]. Dare you accuse the evangelist of lying because he adds 'I say to you', when all we have in the Hebrew is, 'My girl, get up?' But to make it more emphatic and to translate the nuance of urgent command he added, 'I say to you.' [. . .]

[Jerome gives a number of such examples, stating that 'it is clear that, in their use of the Septuagint translation, the Apostles sought the sense, not words'.]

> The opening words of the Hebrew text of Psalm XXI are the very words Christ spoke on the cross: 'Eli, Eli, lama sabacthani.' This means: 'My God, my God, why have you abandoned me' [Ps. 21: 2; cf. Matthew 27: 46]. Let them state the reason why the Septuagint intercalates 'look at me', for it reads: 'My God, my God, look at me, why have you abandoned me?' They will reply that there is no distortion in the sense if two or three words are added. Let them also realize that the stability of the Church is not threatened if, in the heat of dictation, I leave out a few words.
>
> It is a long job to detail how much the Septuagint adds, how much it leaves out. [. . .] However, it is not for nothing that the Septuagint has become the official church text: it was adopted either because it was the first and was produced before the coming of Christ, or because it was used by the apostles, at least where it did not differ from the Hebrew.

[Jerome then turns, with savage irony, on his critics who accuse him of taking too many liberties. Much later, Martin Luther was to do much the same, when confronting his critics.]

I have gone beyond the length of a letter, but not beyond the measure of my anger. I have been called a fraud, and cackling women tear me to pieces between the shuttle and the loom. But I am content to counter the accusation, rather than to turn it against others. Thus, I leave everything to your judgement. Read the letter itself, in both Greek and Latin, and from it you will quickly judge the sort of cant indulged in by my accusers and the true value of their complaints. For my part, it is enough to have set things right with a very dear friend, and to await the day of judgement hiding in my cell. If possible, despite the raging of my enemies, I would rather comment the Scriptures, than write Philippics in the style of Demosthenes and Cicero.

Aurelius Augustinus, St Augustine (354–430)

Augustine is the most influential of the Church Fathers. Born to a pagan father and Christian mother in Numidia (present-day Algeria), he was sent to Carthage for his education. Originally intending to enter government service he dedicated himself to philosophy, after reading Cicero. He was converted to Christianity in 386. Augustine taught rhetoric in Carthage, Rome and Milan. His masterpiece *Confessions* (397–8) outlines his spiritual development and elaborates a radical doctrine of grace. Augustine was spiritual leader of the Christian Church in Africa, appointed bishop of Hippo in 395. He continued the monastic community life with his clergy and became a dedicated preacher and literary protagonist, struggling doggedly against Manichaeism and other 'heresies'. So forceful was Augustine that he took the Church with him, disposing of rather than attempting to embrace what he saw as schismatic tendencies.

His major works include exegeses of Scriptural texts and, of course, polemics. *On The City of God* (*De Civitate Dei*, 413–26) laid down the basis for the medieval Church.

Augustine regarded translation as a systematic undoing of the linguistic confusion following the destruction of the Tower of Babel. For him there could be only one true translation. In this area (as in others) he strove to establish an orthodoxy, not prevaricating like Jerome who was tormented by the distinction between translation as such and translation of the Word of God. Augustine was committed to establishing the authority of the Church, to this end even condoning persecution. The implications, as far as translation is concerned, are of the utmost significance. His concern for a single, united Church led him to favour the Septuagint translation over the Hebrew and Aramaic source texts, because the Greek translators at Alexandria, it had been held, were guided by the Holy Spirit. He expressed his concern in a respectful but strongly worded letter to Jerome on the latter's plans for a new translation (see below). Of course, Jerome's version of the

Scriptures, the Vulgate, also came to be regarded as inspired and, as such, took precedence over the source or original Scriptural texts. Augustine's literary output, including letters, is vast and shows him to be, like Jerome, a versatile master of Latin style.

Letter 71. 3–4 and 6 (to Jerome on his plans for the Vulgate), translated by L. G. Kelly

I have further comment in this letter: I have just found out that you have translated the Book of Job from the Hebrew, even though we already have a Latin translation of yours from the Greek text. In that translation you marked Hebrew passages missing from the Greek text with asterisks, and with daggers, Greek passages missing in Hebrew. Your diligence was such that we can see in certain passages particular words signifying the stars are in the Hebrew, but not in the Greek. Furthermore, in this last version of yours taken from the Hebrew, we do not find the same fidelity to words. And a careful reader will have some trouble in working out why in your first version asterisks are marked in with such care that we know where even the most minor particles in Hebrew are missing in the Greek texts; and in your second from the Hebrew, this editorial work is so careless, that it seems that the same particles appear in both texts [. . .]

Honestly, I would rather you translate the Scriptures for us from the canonical texts which the seventy translators left us. For it will cause extreme difficulty if your translation is widely adopted: the Latin churches will then differ violently from the Greek churches. Most serious of all, as it is the best known, anybody who disagrees will easily prove you wrong on the strength of the Greek. For anybody who seizes on something he finds strange in a version taken from the Hebrew and accuses you of error, will hardly, if ever, pay regard to the Hebrew by which you defend your reading. And even if your version were to be adopted, who will stand to see the condemnation of so many Greek and Latin traditions? Because even experts in Hebrew can have other answers, it comes to this, that you seem to be the only one competent to prove them wrong. But before what judge, if you can find one perceptive enough?

And so I am immensely grateful to God for your labours in translating the Gospels from the Greek, because in almost no case is there difficulty when we have recourse to the Greek text. If then any controversialist argues for a hoary old false reading, we can bring out the books, compare them, and easily verify or refute. And if certain remarkable cases rightly call forth our assent, is there anybody stubborn enough not to recognize such a useful achievement, or give it its due praise? Would you be good enough to tell me why, in your view, there is so much disagreement between the Hebrew texts and the Greek of the Septuagint? For the Septuagint has so much authority that it has, with reason, been widely disseminated. As I remember, this fact is attested to by the custom of the Apostles, and also by your own testimony. And for this reason, you would have done better if you had given us an accurate translation of the Greek of the Septuagint. The present Latin versions differ so much from manuscript to manuscript that the situation is intolerable; and they are so suspect (it is not unlikely that there is something else in the Greek), that we can hardly expect to prove anything by quoting them.

Anicius Manlius Severinus Boethius (480–524)

Boethius was a late Roman philosopher and statesman, from a family which had held high political office. He was consul in 510 and then political adviser to Theodoric, the Ostrogoth, rising to the rank of *magister officiorum*. He is best known as the author of the Neoplatonic *Consolation of Philosophy* (*De consolatione philosophiae*), a dialogue between himself and Philosophy, mixing prose and verse, written in prison a year before he was put to death for treason. As an outstanding Hellenist, his ambition had been to translate all of Aristotle and Plato. In addition, he wrote textbooks on other subjects, including theology. The *Consolation* was second only to Jerome's Vulgate in popularity during the Middle Ages, and in general Boethius's legacy was immense. His work was translated into Anglo-Saxon by Alfred the Great (see below).

Boethius wrote a Latin commentary on Victorinus' translation of Porphyrius' third century *Eisagoge*, an introduction to Aristotle's logic, which became the standard medieval textbook on the subject; he then retranslated it himself, adding a second volume to his commentary. In his opening to the second volume, he turns Horace on his head, making of him the champion of literalism. Boethius' remarks on translation became commonplaces in the continuing struggle between the word-for-word and sense-for-sense approaches. He extends the theological strictures against free translation to the translation of philosophy.

Introduction to the second edition of the Commentary on Porphyry's *Isagoge*, in *Isagoge Porphyrii Commenta* (510 AD?), translated by L. G. Kelly

This reworking of my commentary is designed to shed light on the matter of our translation. For I am afraid that the translation might earn for me the condemnation due to the 'faithful translator', in that I have manifestly translated each word by one exactly matching it. My reason for this procedure is that, in those texts in which one seeks knowledge of things, it is not the grace of a beautiful style we are to seek, but the uncorrupted truth. Therefore I would seem to have accomplished more if, in philosophical texts written in Latin, the soundness of a close translation should assure that nothing from the Greek text is missing.

1.3 OLD ENGLISH TRANSLATION

JONATHAN WILCOX (UNIVERSITY OF IOWA)

Anglo-Saxon England (*c.*450–*c.*1100) was the home to a vibrant literary culture which developed in the vernacular earlier than in most of medieval Europe. Writing came to Anglo-Saxon England with the conversion to Christianity, a culture of the book, initiated by Augustine's mission of 597. Early literary activity was mostly in Latin until King Alfred initiated a policy of translation, as he explains in the preface to his translation of Gregory's *Pastoral Care* below. Translation blossomed in late Anglo-Saxon England and reached a height in the works of Ælfric, two of whose prefaces are presented here. Within such a culture of translation, there were multiple renditions of the Bible, as seen in the translations of the Babel story presented below. A distinctive tradition of vernacular verse also developed in Anglo-Saxon England. While the most famous vernacular poem, *Beowulf,* is an original story rather than a translation, a similar style of verse was also used to retell incidents from the Bible, including the tower of Babel incident in *Genesis A* presented below.

I have translated these Old English works into fluent Modern English while keeping a foreignizing hint by sometimes staying just slightly closer to the syntax of the original Old English than is comfortable in Modern English. In the case of the biblical translations, I have further emphasized the nature of the original by translating with cognates as indicated in the headnotes. For fuller translations from Old English, see S. A. J. Bradley, *Anglo-Saxon Poetry* (London: Dent, 1981), Michael Swanton, *Anglo-Saxon Prose* (London: Everyman, 1975), and Kevin Crossley-Holland, *The Anglo-Saxon World* (Oxford: Oxford World's Classics, 1984).

King Alfred

In addition to being the most famous king of Wessex (871–99) and, arguably, the first king of a united England (that part, at least, which was not under Viking rule), King Alfred was also a significant translator in his own right and the initiator of a policy of translation. At a military level, Alfred's achievement involved fighting against the Vikings who had overrun most of the country until he finally reigned over a prosperous and expanding nation. At an educational level, his policy is spelled out in the preface to his translation of Gregory's *Pastoral Care,* translated below. Here the king initiates a programme both of translation and of vernacular education, recognizing that Latin learning has declined, aggravated by Viking assaults, to such an extent that it is now necessary to provide learning in the native tongue of his people.

Alfred began his project of translation with Gregory's *Pastoral Care*, presumably to educate and guide his bishops so that they could, in turn, educate the people. Gregory the Great (*c*.540–604) had a special resonance for the English as the pope who initiated Augustine's original mission to convert the country. Alfred's further contributions to those books most needful for all people to know comprise translations of Boethius' *Consolation of Philosophy*, Augustine's *Soliloquies*, and the first fifty Psalms, while his lawcode begins with a translation of Mosaic law. The king undertook such translations with the aid of a seminar of advisers gathered from outside his kingdom, as he outlines in the preface to Gregory's *Pastoral Care*. These advisers also produced other translations associated with Alfred's court, namely of Gregory's *Dialogues*, Orosius' world history, and probably the Old English translations of Bede's *Ecclesiastical History* and of the Martyr-ology. It is within this milieu, too, that the great work of original historical prose, the *Anglo-Saxon Chronicle*, was produced.

The text of the preface to Gregory's *Pastoral Care* below is translated from the edition by Dorothy Whitelock, *Sweet's Anglo-Saxon Reader* (Oxford: Clarendon Press, 1967), based primarily on MS Oxford, Bodleian Library, Hatton 20, the copy sent by the king to the bishopric at Worcester. Other manuscripts of the work survive addressed to other bishops or with the recipient's name left blank. The complete work is edited by Henry Sweet, *King Alfred's West Saxon Version of Gregory's Pastoral Care*, EETS 45, 50 (London, 1871–2). This preface, which is written in prose, is followed by a brief verse preface in which the book is made to describe its origins in the first person. The *æstel* which accompanied copies of the book, mentioned at the end of the passage below, is a unique word of unknown meaning: it is thought to be a book-pointer, which is a likely function for the beautiful (and valuable) Alfred Jewel in the Ashmolean museum. Two other similar objects of somewhat lower status have also been found.

The briefer preface to Boethius' *Consolation of Philosophy* shows more of the king's working method and outlines, in particular, his interesting treatment of the verse elements of the original prosimetrum. These he translated first into prose and subsequently versified from his own prose translation. The text is taken once again from from the edition by Dorothy Whitelock in *Sweet's Anglo-Saxon Reader*, which is drawn primarily from MS Oxford, Bodleian Library, Bodley 180. The complete work is edited by W. J. Sedgefield, *King Alfred's Old English Version of Boethius De Consolatione Philosophiae* (Oxford: Clarendon Press, 1899).

Alfred's life was recorded in a probably contemporary Latin biography by Asser, available in translation by Simon Keynes and Michael Lapidge, *Alfred the Great* (Harmondsworth: Penguin 1983), who also provide a useful introduction and translate many of the king's works. On the king as a literary figure, see also the useful introduction by Allen Frantzen, *King Alfred* (Boston: G. K. Hall, 1986).

King Alfred's Prose Preface to his Translation of Gregory the Great's *Cura pastoralis*, From Dorothy Whitelock (ed.), *Sweet's Anglo-Saxon Reader*

King Alfred commands Bishop Wærferth to be greeted with his words in a loving and friendly manner; and I command it to be made known to you that it has come very often into my mind what wise men there were formerly throughout England, both in religious orders and in secular; and how happy the times then were throughout England; and how the kings who had power over the people were obedient to God and his messengers; and how they kept both their peace and their morals and their authority at home, and also extended their territory abroad; and how they then succeeded both in warfare and in wisdom; and also how eager the religious orders were both about teaching and learning and all those services which they should do for God; and how wisdom and learning were sought from abroad here in this land, and how we now must obtain them from abroad, if we were to have them. It had declined so thoroughly in England that there were very few this side of the Humber who could understand their offices in English or even translate a single letter from Latin into English; and I think that there were not many beyond the Humber! There were so few of them that I cannot think of even a single one south of the Thames when I succeeded to the kingdom. Thanks be to God Almighty that we now have any supply of teachers. Therefore I command you to do as I believe that you want to, that you free yourself of these worldly cares as much as you most often can, so that you may apply that wisdom which God gave you wherever you can apply it. Think what torments came to us in this world then, when we neither loved it ourselves, nor also granted it to other people; we had the name alone that we were Christians, and very few had the practices.

When I recalled all this, then I recalled also how I saw, before it was all plundered and burnt up, how churches throughout all England stood filled with treasures and books, and also a great multitude of God's servants; and then they knew very little benefit of those books, because they could not understand anything of them, because they were not written in their own lanuage. As if they were to have said: 'Our elders, those who kept these places before, they loved wisdom, and through it they obtained riches and left them to us. Here their track may yet be seen, but we cannot follow after it.' And so we have now abandoned both riches and wisdom, because we would not bend down to that trace with our mind.

When I recalled all this, then I wondered very much at the good counsellors who were there before throughout England, and who had studied all those books completely, that they would not turn any portion of them into their own language. But then I immediately answered myself again, and said: 'They did not think that men should ever be so careless and learning so fallen off: they left it undone on purpose, and intended that there would be the more wisdom here in the land, the more we would know languages.'

Then I recalled how the law was first found in the Hebrew language, and afterwards, when the Greeks learned it, then they turned it completely into their own language, and also all other books. And again the Romans did the same, after they learned them, they turned them all through wise translators into their own language. And also all other Christian nations turned some portion of them into their own language. Therefore it seems better to me, if it seems so to you, that we also translate certain books, those which are most needful for all people to know, that we turn those into that language which we can all understand, and bring it about, as we very easily may with God's help, if we have the peace, that all the youth of free men who now are in England, those who have the means that they may apply themselves to it, be set to learning, while they may not be set to any other use, until the time when they can well read English writings. Those may afterwards be taught further in Latin who one wishes to teach further and who are to be placed in higher orders.

When I recalled how the knowledge of Latin had declined before this throughout England, and yet many could read English writings, then I began among various and manifold cares of this kingdom to turn into English that book which is called in Latin *Pastoralis*, and in English 'Shepherd-Book', sometimes word for word, sometimes sense for sense, just as I learned it from Plegmund my archbishop, and from Asser my bishop, and from Grimbold my mass-priest, and from John my mass-priest. After I had learned it, just as I understood it, and as I might most intelligently relate it, I turned it into English; and I intend to send one to each bishopric in my kingdom; and in each is an *æstel*, which is worth fifty mancuses. And I command in God's name that no-one take the *æstel* from the book, nor the book from the cathedral—it being unknown how long there may be such learned bishops as there are now, thanks be to God, almost everywhere. Therefore I intend that it may always be at that place, unless the bishop may have it with him, or it may be on loan anywhere, or anyone may be making a copy from it.

King Alfred's Preface to his Translation of Boethius' *De consolatione philosophiae*, from Dorothy Whitelock (ed.), *Sweet's Anglo-Saxon Reader*

King Alfred was the translator of this book and turned it from Latin into English, as has now been done. Sometimes he set it down word for word, sometimes sense for sense, just as he could relate it most clearly and most meaningfully in light of the various and manifold worldly cares which occupied him both in mind and in body. Those cares are very difficult for us to count which occurred in his days in the kingdom which he had received, and yet, when he had understood this book and turned the substance from Latin into English, then he worked it over again into verse, as has now been done; and now he asks and in God's name beseeches each of those who desires to read this book to pray for him and not to blame him if they can understand it more rightly than he could, because every man must say what he says and do what he does in accordance with the measure of his understanding and in accordance to the time available to him.

Ælfric

In the century following King Alfred, the educational initiative of the king became combined with a revival of monasticism, generally known as the Benedictine reform, to lead to a flowering of intellectual activity in the vernacular. At about the turn of the millennium, this was apparent in the writing down of all four of the major codices of Old English poetry and in the original compositions and translations of English churchmen and intellectuals like Wulfstan, Byrhtferth, and, above all, Ælfric. Ælfric (fl. *c.*990–*c.*1010) was a monk of Cerne Abbas, Dorset, and (from 1005) abbot of Eynsham, a newly founded monastery in Oxfordshire. Ælfric was very concerned with the issue of translation: his most characteristic writings were homilies, which begin with a translation of a gospel pericope and continue with his own conspectus of commentary tradition, translated, combined, and augmented with original moral and topical exhortation. Ælfric shows a strong sensitivity to language, discussing in his homilies, for example, the special processes of signification of the real presence in the Eucharist. Such linguistic sensitivity along with his copious composition in the vernacular make Ælfric particularly qualified to pronounce upon the process of translation.

The preface to his translation of Genesis shows Ælfric's polemical case *against* translation. It introduces his translation of Genesis, a work which he failed to finish for reasons that he explains here. The preface is addressed to Ealdorman Æthelweard, a powerful nobleman, leader of the western counties, and Ælfric's frequent patron. Despite his strong appeal to this patron to be free of translation from henceforth, Ælfric went on writing, producing many further homilies and numerous occasional works. The explanation for this apparent paradox may lie in the kind of works he went on to write. As he outlines here, biblical translation carries special perils both because of the divinely appointed nature of the text and because of the text's significance for its Christian audience. In the polemic of this preface, Ælfric attempts to disallow naively literal readings by providing in miniature homiletic commentary on selected moments in Genesis. The surface narrative may be simple, he suggests, but it requires interpretation in light of the Old Testament's anticipation of the New. Linguistic sense and ultimate meaning are not the same, here seen as the contrasting naked narrative and spiritual significance. By continuing his career as a homilist, Ælfric could satisfy his desire to provide biblical text alongside the interpretation of that text.

Ælfric's translation of Genesis was completed by another writer, as he remarks below. Perhaps the same anonymous translator took over two other substantial translations by Ælfric—of part of the book of Numbers and most of Joshua—and augmented them to make a complete translation of the first six books of the Old Testament. This text was then lavishly illustrated with over 400 coloured drawings (some incomplete) in a high-status and beautiful manuscript, London, British Library, Cotton Claudius B. iv, probably written in the second quarter of the eleventh century at St Augustine's, Canterbury. The illustrated Hexateuch is reproduced in a facsimile edition by C. R. Dodwell and Peter Clemoes, *The Old English Illustrated Hexateuch*, EEMF 18 (Copenhagen: Rosenkilde and Bagger, 1974) and is discussed in *The Old English Hexateuch: Aspects and Approaches*, ed. Rebecca Barnhouse and Benjamin C. Withers (Kalamazoo: Medieval Institute Publications, 2000). The first folio, containing the opening of this preface, has gone missing and so has to be supplied from two other surviving copies (MS Oxford, Bodleian Library, Laud Misc. 509 and Cambridge, University Library, Ii. 1. 33). The text drawn on here is from *Ælfric's Prefaces*, ed. Jonathan Wilcox (Durham Medieval Texts 9, Durham, 1994), where I provide a fuller introduction to Ælfric and his works. For a more general introduction, see James R. Hurt, *Ælfric* (New York: Twayne Publishers, 1972).

While Ælfric's preface to his translation of Genesis contains his most extensive comment on translation practice, the preface to his *Excerptiones de arte grammatica anglice* (conveniently known as Ælfric's Grammar) also shows his self-consciousness about language. He undertook this work after his first two series of *Catholic Homilies*, each of forty homilies, as he states at the opening of the Old English preface below. The Grammar is a translation in that it is primarily drawn from a single Latin work, namely the *Excerptiones de Prisciano*, itself a simplification of Priscian's *Institutiones grammaticae*. Ælfric makes this Latin base text far more useful for classroom practice by writing in English, by omitting abstruse or tangential details, and by providing extensive exemplary paradigms, as is described by Vivien Law, 'Anglo-Saxon England: Aelfric's "Excerptiones de arte grammatica anglice"', *Histoire épistémologie langage*, 9 (1987), 47–71. In the process, he creates the first Latin grammar in a medieval vernacular language. This preface is written in two languages, suggesting the expectation of two distinct audiences: a learned one for the opening Latin part and a broader one for the subsequent discussion. The Latin preface reveals Ælfric's expectation of hostility towards the translation process, which he has to justify as only an exercise to help uneducated children. The English preface reveals through its echoes Ælfric's familiarity with King Alfred's statement on translation, translated above.

Ælfric's Preface to his translation of Genesis, from *Ælfric's Prefaces*, ed. Jonathan Wilcox (Durham, 1994)

Ælfric the monk humbly greets Ealdorman Æthelweard. You bade me, dear sir, that I should turn the book of Genesis for you from Latin into English. Then it seemed difficult to me to grant you that, and you then said that I need not translate more of the book except as far as Isaac, the son of Abraham, because some other person had translated the book for you from Isaac until the end. Now it seems to me, dear sir, that that work is very perilous for me or any man to undertake, because I fear, if some foolish person reads this book or hears it read, that he will think that he may live now in the new law just as the patriarchs lived then in that time before the old law was appointed, or just as men lived under the law of Moses.

Once I knew a certain masspriest, who was my teacher at the time, owned the book of Genesis, and he could understand Latin a little; then he said about the patriarch Jacob, that he had four wives, two sisters and their two handmaidens. What he said was completely true, but he did not know, as did not I at that time, how great a difference there is between the old law and the new. In the beginning of this world, brother took his sister for a wife, and sometimes also a father begot by his own daughter, and many men had multiple wives for the increase of the people, and it was impossible then at the beginning to marry except among relatives. If anyone will live so now after Christ's coming as people lived before the law of Moses or under the law of Moses, such a person is not a Christian at all, nor is he even worthy that any Christian should eat with him.

Unlearned priests, if they understand some small part from Latin books, then it immediately seems to them that they may be glorious teachers; but nevertheless they do not know the spiritual meaning to it and how the old law was symbolic of things to come, or how the new testament after Christ's incarnation was the fulfilment of all those things which the old testament symbolized about the coming of Christ and his chosen ones. They also often talk about Peter—why they may not have a wife, just as Peter the apostle had—and they will not hear or understand that the blessed Peter lived according to the law of Moses until the time of Christ, who first came to humanity at that time and began to preach his holy gospel and chose Peter first to be his companion. Then Peter abandoned his wife rightaway, and all the twelve apostles, those who had wives, abandoned both wives and possessions, and they followed Christ's teaching to the new law and to that chastity, which he himself then raised up. Priests are set up as teachers for lay people. Now it has become fitting for them that they know to understand the old law spiritually, and what Christ himself taught and his apostles in the new testament, so that they could guide the people properly to God's faith and set an example properly in good deeds.

We also say in advance that the book is very profound to understand spiritually, and we are not writing anything more than the naked narrative. Then it may seem to the unlearned that all the sense is enclosed in the simple narrative, but it is very far from that. [. . .] [Ælfric goes on to explain spiritually the opening verse of Genesis and selected episodes as distinct from their naked narrative.]

Now the aforesaid book is very narrowly set in many places, and yet very profoundly in the spiritual sense, and it is ordered just as God himself appointed it to the writer Moses, and we do not dare to write more in English than the Latin has, nor change the order, except for that alone, that Latin and English do not have a single way in the ordering of language. Always whoever translates or teaches from Latin into English must ever order it so that the English has its own way, otherwise it is very misleading for those to read who do not know the ways of Latin.

It should also be known that there were some heretics who would cast away the old law, and some would hold the old and cast away the new, just as the Jews do; but Christ himself and his apostles taught us both to keep the old spiritually and the new literally with deeds. God created for us two eyes and two ears, two nostrils and two lips, two hands and two feet, and he also wanted to have two testaments set in this world, the old and the new, because he does just as is pleasing for himself, and he has no counsellor, nor does he have need for any man to say to him, 'Why do you do so?' We must turn our will to his decrees, and we may not turn his decrees to our desires.

I now say that I do not dare and I will not turn any book after this from Latin into English, and I ask you, dear ealdorman, that you no longer ask me for it, lest I be disobedient to you or lest I be false if I do it. May God be merciful to you forever in eternity.

I now ask in God's name, if anyone wants to copy this book, that he correct it properly against the exemplar, because I do not have control, although someone may bring it to error through false copyists, and then it will be his peril and not mine. The bad copyist does much harm, if he will not correct his error.

Ælfric's Preface to his Grammar, from *Ælfric's Prefaces*, ed. Wilcox

[The following is in Latin:]

I, Ælfric, as one knowing little, have applied myself to translating into your language these excerpts from the lesser and greater Priscian for you tender little boys so that, having read through Donatus's eight parts of speech, you may in this book apply to your tenderness both languages, namely Latin and English, in the time until you reach more perfect studies. Now I know that many will blame me because I have desired to occupy my mind in such studies, namely turning the art of grammar into the English language, but I intend this text to be fitting for ignorant boys, not for their elders.

I know it is possible to translate words in many ways but I follow a simple translation for the sake of avoiding putting off the reader. If, nevertheless, our translation displeases anyone, let him express it however he wants: we are content to express it just as we mastered it in the school of the venerable prelate, Æthelwold, who inspired many to good. It must be known, nevertheless, that the *Ars Grammatica* in many places does not easily receive translation into the English language as, for example, the parts about feet or metres, about which we here keep silent; but we have reckoned, nevertheless, this translation to be useful as a beginning for children, as we have said before. [. . .]

[The following is in Old English:]

I, Ælfric, wanted to turn this little book into the English language from that grammar which is called *Grammatica* after I had translated those two books comprising eighty homilies, because grammar is the key which unlocks the meaning of books, and I thought that this book might help young pupils at the beginning of that craft until they came to greater understanding. [. . .] [Ælfric goes on to stress the responsibility of the wise to teach and of the young to learn.] Whence shall come wise teachers among God's people, unless they learn in youth? And how may the faith be advanced if teaching falls away and teachers fail? It is now essential, therefore, to warn the servants and monks of God, so that holy teaching does not cool or fall away in our days, as it did in England a few years ago from now, such that no English priest knew to write or to explicate a single letter in Latin, until Archbishop Dunstan and Bishop Æthelwold raised up learning again in the monastic life. I do not say therefore that this book may help many to learning, but it is, nonetheless, an introduction to each language, if it pleases anyone.

I now ask in God's name, if anyone wants to copy this book, that he correct it properly according to the exemplar, because I do not have control, although someone may bring it to error through false copyists, and then it will be his peril and not mine. The bad copyist does much harm, if he will not correct his error.

Old English Versions of the Tower of Babel Story

The first of these comes from the translation of Genesis begun by Ælfric and described in the headnote to his prefaces above. At this point different manuscripts give radically different versions, reflecting the work of both Ælfric and the anonymous translator—an appropriate Babel of texts! The last comes from a translation of Genesis into Old English verse. Both accounts are illustrated.

Old English Hexateuch: Genesis 11: 1–9

[MS Cambridge, University Library, Ii. 1. 33 preserves the translation by Ælfric at this point, whereas MS British Library, Cotton Claudius B. iv contains that of an anonymous translator, presumably the one described by Ælfric in his preface to his translation of Genesis. Ælfric's translation is significantly closer than the anonymous translator's to the Vulgate text. It includes, for example, the biblical cadence of repetition in verse 1, ironed out in the brevity of the anonymous rendition, a fuller and more balanced statement of God's intention in verse 6, and a fuller explanation of the name Babel in verse 9. Ælfric himself makes one substantial if characteristic adaptation, notwithstanding the implication of his preface: rather than allow the reader to be distracted by the discussion of building materials in verse 3, he simply omits this matter.

The text is drawn here from *The Old English Version of the Heptateuch*, ed. S. J. Crawford, EETS 160 (London, 1922). To emphasize the minute differences between versions, I have translated particularly closely here, retaining 'speech' for OE *spæc/spræc*, the cognate to which it is etymologically related, and reserving 'language' for *gereord*, even though the sense of these two words is overlapping. Similarly, I have retained the etymological cognate for *stypel*, 'steeple', although the word also means tower, while also retaining a distinction between *ceaster*, 'city', and *burh*, 'town', although the OE distinction is more likely one of etymology than of reference. The anonymous translator's word for the original pre-Babel language in verse 6 suggests that he saw the learned language of the Church as truly a lingua franca!]

Translation by Ælfric (MS CUL Ii. 1. 33)

1. Wæs þa an gereord on eorþan, 7 heora ealre an spræc.
2. Hi ferdon fram eastdele oð þæt hi comon to anum felde on þam lande Sennar, 7 þer wunedon.
3. Þa cwæð gehwa to his nyxtan:
4. Cumað 7 utan wircan us ane burh 7 ænne stypel swa heahne ðæt his rof atille þa heofonan, 7 uton mærsian urne namon, ær þan we beon todælede to eallum landum.
5. God þa nyþer astah, þæt he gesega þa burh 7 þone stypel þe Adames sunus getimbroden.
6. God cwæð þa: Efne þis his an folc 7 gereord him ealum, 7 hi ongunnon þis to wircenne; ne hi ne geswicað heora geþohta, ær þan þe hi mid weorce hi gefyllan.
7. Cumað nu eornostlice 7 uton niþer astigan 7 heora gereord þer towendon, þæt heora nan ne tocnawe his nextan stemne.
8. 7 God þa hi todælde swa of þare stowe to eallum landum, 7 hi geswicon to wrycenne þa buruh.

9. 7 for þi wæs seo burh gehaten Babel, for þan þe ðær wæs todæled þæt gereord ealre eorþan. God þa hi sende þanon ofer bradnesse ealra eorðan.

Literal Translation of Ælfric by J. Wilcox

1. There was then one language on earth and among them all one speech.
2. They went from the east-part until they came to a plain in the land of Sennar, and there they dwelt.
3. Then each one said to his neighbour:
4. Come and let us work a town and a steeple so high that its roof may reach heaven, and let us magnify our name, before we are scattered to all lands.
5. God then came down so that he might see the town and the steeple which Adam's sons built.
6. God then said: Lo this is one people and one language among them all, and they have begun to work this; they will not cease from their intentions before they fulfil them in deed.
7. Come now, therefore, and let us go down and overthrow their language there, so that none of them may understand his neighbour's voice.
8. And so God then scattered them from that place to all lands, and they ceased to build the town.
9. And for that reason the town was called Babel, because there language was scattered over all the earth. God then sent them from there over the breadth of all the earth.

Anonymous translation (MS BL Cotton Claudius B. iv)

1. Truly all people then spoke one speech.
2. When they went from the east-part, they found a plain in Sennarland and they dwelt therein.
3. Then they said among themselves: let us make bricks and bake them in fire. Truly they had bricks for stone and tar for wall-lime.
4. And they said: let us build for ourselves a city and a steeple up to high heaven, and let us honour our name, before we are scattered throughout all the earth.
5. Truly the Lord came down to the point that he might see the town and the steeple which the children of Adam built.
6. And he said: this is one people, and they all speak one Latin and they have begun to work this; they will not cease before it may be complete.
7. Truly let us come and scatter their speech there.
8. So the Lord scattered them from that place throughout all the earth.
9. And for that reason the place was named Babel, because all speech was scattered there.

Old English Verse Translation: *Genesis A*

[A poetic paraphrase of Genesis, composed at an unknown time, survives in MS, Oxford, Bodleian Library, Junius 11, copied at the end of the tenth century. The unknown poet translated most of the biblical book into characteristic Old English verse, written in alliterative four-stress lines using the compressed and distinctive language of poetry. Into this poem, known as *Genesis A*, was subsequently interpolated a distinct account of the fall of the angels and the fall of Adam and Eve conceived in heroic terms and written in a distinctive metre and language adapted from the Old Saxon, known as *Genesis B*. The Tower of Babel episode is included in the original part. The text is here drawn from A. N. Doane (ed.), *Genesis A: A New Edition* (Madison, 1978), whose solutions to some of the many linguistic challenges it presents are readily accepted.

Genesis A suggests a different manner of translation from the super-aware style of Ælfric expounded above. Much of the interest of the poem derives from the poet's readiness to embellish and explain his text as he saw fit, adapting it not just to fit Old English metrics but also to fit the heroic world. This is seen in a willingness to express motivation often left cryptic in the terse Vulgate original. In this episode the building of the town and the tower is *for wlence*, 'out of pride', a motivation familiar to any reader of *Beowulf* as the force that drove Hygelac on his ill-fated raid against the Frisians. When the poet says of the tribes inhabiting Sennar 'the people were of one mind', his adjective, *anmod*, puns on 'proud' (lit.: 'excessively-minded') even as it describes their short-lived unanimity. The very range of vocabulary for a clan, race, or people suggests something of the poet's emphasis. The cost of Babel, the poet stresses, is an acutely perceived social disunity.]

Genesis A, *lines 1635b–1701, From A. N. Doane (ed.),* Genesis A: A New Edition *(Madison: University of Wisconsin Press, 1978)*

There was still then one language in common among the inhabitants of the earth. [. . .]

Then they departed from the east leading goods, cattle and provisions. The people were of one mind. The bold warriors sought a roomier land until they arrived in great bands, a journeying people, where they, children of nobles, firmly took a homeland. In their days the leaders of the people then settled Sennar far and wide with dear men. At that time the green plains of the beautiful earth were a continuous blessing for them, a growing prosperity, for each of their desires.

Then many a one there, a single-minded nobleman, asked one another in the company of his neighbour, about their own honour—before the multitude had to scatter again among the sons of earth, the people of the nation in a search for land—that they might build a town and raise up a tower as a beacon to the stars of heaven. Therefore they visited the field of Sennar as the most mighty leaders of the people, the eldest, often and again were accustomed to in pleasure. They sought men with the knowledge for that work and for that crime, until out of pride and out of recklessness they manifested their skill. Eager for honour, men built a city and raised a ladder up to the heavens, erected a stone wall strongly by hand beyond the measure of men.

Then holy God came to gaze upon that work of the race of men, the warriors' walled city, together with that beacon, which the descendants of Adam began to raise up to the heavens, and the strong-minded king made a restraint for that bad counsel. Then, angry in spirit, he made language dissimilar for the dwellers of earth, so that they did not have success from speech when they met in great numbers, leaders of that project, successful in might, in a group at the tower: none of that tribe of men knew what another said. They could not agree to build that stone wall up from that time onwards, but they wretchedly misbuilt in heaps, separated by langagues. Each lineage had become strange to the other, after the creator through his great power disrupted the speech of men.

The sons of princes scattered then in four directions, disunited, in a search for land. On their track remained a firm stone tower and the soaring town on Sennar both together half-built.

1.4 JOHN OF TREVISA

John of Trevisa (1326–1412) was scholar and translator of the *Polychronicon* of Ralph Higden (1387) and the *De Proprietatibus Rerum* of Bartholomew (1398). The *Polychronicon* is a history of the world, reflecting the historical, geographical, and scientific knowledge of the fourteenth century. Trevisa's translation of Higden contains prologues on translation and was printed by Caxton.

Dialogue between a Lord and a Clerk upon Translation, from Trevisa's Translation of Higden's *Polychronicon*, included in *Fifteenth Century Prose and Verse: An English Garner*, introd. Alfred W. Pollard (Westminster: Archibald Constable, 1903), 203–8.

The LORD.—Sith the time that the great and high tower of Babylon was builded, men have spoken with divers tongues, in such wise that divers men be strange to other and understand not others' speech. Speech is not known but if it be learned; common learning of speech is by hearing, and so alway he that is deaf is alway dumb, for he may not hear speech for to learn. So men of far countries and lands that have divers speeches, if neither of them have learned others' language, neither of them wot what other meaneth. Though they meet and have great need of information and of lore of talking and of speech, be the need never so great, neither of them understandeth other's speech no more than gagling of geese. For jangle that one never so fast, that other is never the wiser, though he shrew him instead of 'good-morrow'! This is a great mischief that followeth now mankind; but God of His mercy and grace hath ordained double remedy. One is that some man learneth and knoweth many divers speeches, and so between strange men, of the which neither understandeth other's speech, such a man may be mean and tell either what other will mean. That other remedy is that one language is learned, used, and known in many nations and lands. And so Latin is learned, known, and used, specially on this half Greece, in all the nations and lands of Europe. Therefore clerks, of their goodness and courtesy, make and write their books in Latin, for their writing and books should be understood in divers nations and lands. And so Ranulphus, monk of Chester (Ralph Higden), wrote in Latin his books of Chronicles, that describeth the world about in length and in breadth, and maketh mention and mind of doings and deeds of marvels and wonders, and reckoneth the years to his last days from the first making of heaven and of earth. And so therein is great and noble information and lore to them that can therein read and understand. Therefore I would have these books of Chronicles translated out of Latin into English, for the more men should them understand and have thereof cunning, information and lore.

THE CLERK.—These books of Chronicles be written in Latin, and Latin is used and understood on this half Greece in all the nations and lands of Europe. And commonly English is not so wide understood, ne known; and the English translation should no man understand but English men alone; then how should the more men understand the Chronicles, though they were translated out of Latin, that is so wide used and known, into English, that is not used and known but of English men alone?

THE LORD.—This question and doubt is easy to assail. For if these Chronicles were translated out of Latin into English, then by that so many the more men should understand them as understand English, and no Latin.

THE CLERK.—Ye can speak, read, and understand Latin; then it needeth not to have such an English translation.

THE LORD.—I deny this argument; for though I can speak, read, and understand Latin, there is much Latin in these books of Chronicles that I can not understand, neither thou, without studying, avisement, and looking of other books. Also, though it were not needful for me, it is needful for other men that understand no Latin.

THE CLERK.—Men that understand no Latin may learn and understand.

THE LORD.—Not all; for some may not for other manner business, some for age, some for default of wit, some for default of chattel, other of friends to find them to school, and some for other divers defaults and lets.

THE CLERK.—It needeth not that all such know the Chronicles.

THE LORD.—Speak not too straitly of thing that needeth; for straitly to speak of thing that needeth, only thing that is, and may not fail, needeth to be. And so it needeth that God be, for God is, and may not fail. And, so for to speak, no man needeth for to know the Chronicles, for it might and may be that no man them knoweth. Otherwise to speak of thing that needeth; somewhat needeth for to sustain or to have other things thereby, and so meat and drink needeth for keeping and sustenance of life. And, so for to speak, no man needeth for to know the Chronicles. But in the third manner to speak of thing that needeth, all that is profitable needeth, and, so for to speak, all men need to know the Chronicles.

THE CLERK.—Then they that understand no Latin may ask and be informed and ytaught of them that understand Latin.

THE LORD.—Thou speakest wonderly, for the lewd man wots not what he should ask, and namely of lore of deeds that come never in his mind; nor wots of whom commonly he should ask. Also, not all men that understand Latin have such books to inform lewd men; also some can not, and some may not, have while, and so it needeth to have an English translation.

THE CLERK.—The Latin is both good and fair, therefore it needeth not to have an English translation.

THE LORD.—The reason is worthy to be plunged in a pludde and laid in powder of lewdness and of shame. It might well be that thou makest only in mirth and in game.

THE CLERK.—The reason must stand but it be assoiled.

THE LORD.—A blear-eyed man, but he were all blind of wit, might see the solution of this reason; and though he were blind he might grope the solution, but if his feeling him failed. For if this reason were aught worth, by such manner arguing men might prove that the three score and ten interpreters, and Aquila, Symachus [Symmachus], Theodocion [Theodosius], and Origines were lewdly occupied when they translated holy writ out of Hebrew into Greek; and also that Saint Jerome was lewdly occupied when he translated holy writ out of Hebrew into Latin, for the Hebrew is both good and fair and y-written by inspiration of the Holy Ghost; and all these for their translations be highly praised of all Holy Church. Then the foresaid lewd reason is worthy to be powdered, laid a-water and y-soused. Also holy writ in Latin is both good and fair, and yet for to make a sermon of holy writ all in Latin to men that can English and no Latin, it were a lewd deed, for they be never the wiser for the Latin, but it be told them in English what it is to mean; and it may not be told in English what the Latin is to mean without translation out of Latin into English. Then it needeth to have an English translation, and for to keep it in mind that it be not forgeten, it is better that such a translation be made and written than said and not written. And so this foresaid lewd reason should move no man that hath any wit to leave the making of English translation.

The CLERK—A great deal of these books standeth much by holy writ, by holy doctors, and by philosophy; then these books should not be translated into English.

The LORD—It is wonder that thou makest so feeble arguments, and hast gone so long to school. Aristotle's books and other books also of logic and of philosophy were translated out of Greek into Latin. Also at praying of King Charles, John Scott translated Deny's books out of Greek into Latin, and then out of Latin into French; then what hath English trespassed that it might not be translated into English? Also King Alfred, that founded the University of Oxford, translated the best laws into English tongue, and a great deal of the Psalter out of Latin into English, and caused Wyrefrith, Bishop of Worcester, to translate Saint Gregory's books, the dialogues, out of Latin into Saxon. Also Caedmon of Whitby was inspired of the Holy Ghost, and made wonder poesies in English nigh of all the stories of holy writ. Also the holy man Beda translated St. John's gospel out of Latin into English. Also thou wotest where the Apocalypse is written in the walls and roof of a chapel, both in Latin and in French. Also the gospel, and prophecy, and the right faith of holy church must be taught and preached to English men that can no Latin. Then the gospel, and prophecy, and the right faith of holy church must be told them in English, and that is not done but by English translation, for such English preaching is very translation, and such English preaching is good and needful; then English translation is good and needful.

The CLERK—If a translation were made that might be amended in any point, some men it would blame.

The LORD—If men blame that is not worthy to be blamed, then they be to blame. Clerks know well enough that no sinful man doth so well that it ne might do better, ne make so good a translation that he ne might be better. Therefore Origines made two translations, and Jerome translated thrice the Psalter. I desire not translation of these the best that might be, for that were an idle desire for any man that is now alive, but I would have a skilful translation, that might be known and understood.

The CLERK—Whether is you liefer have, a translation of these chronicles in rhyme or in prose?

The LORD—In prose, for commonly prose is more clear than rhyme, more easy and more plain to know and understand.

The CLERK—Then God grant us grace grathly to gin, wit and wisdom wisely to work, might and mind of right meaning to make translation trusty and true, pleasing to the Trinity, three persons and one God, in majesty, that ever was and ever shall be, and made heaven and earth, and light for to shine, and departed light and darkness, and called light, day, and darkness, night; and so was made eventide and morrowtide one day, that had no morrowtide. The second day He made the firmament between waters, and departed waters that were under the firmament fro the waters that were above the firmament, and called the firmament heaven. The third day He gathered waters that be under the firmament into one place and made the earth unheled, and named the gathering of waters, seas, and dry earth, land; and made trees and grass. The fourth day he made sun and moon and stars, and set them in the firmament of heaven there for to shine, and to be tokens and signs to depart times and years, night and day. The fifth day He made fowls and birds in the air, and fishes in the water. The sixth day He made beasts of the land, and man of the earth, and put them in Paradise, for he should work and wone therein. But man brake God's hest and fell into sin and was put out of Paradise into woe and sorrow. worthy to be damned to the pain of hell without any end. But the Holy Trinity had mercy of man, and the father sent the Son, and the Holy Ghost alight on a maid, and the Son took flesh and blood of that blissful maid, and died on the Rood to save mankind, and arose the third day, glorious and blissful, and taught his disciples, and ascended into heaven when it was time; and shall come at the day of Doom and deem quick and dead. Then all they that be written in the Book of Life shall wend with Him into the bliss of heaven, and be there in body and soul, and see and know His Godhead and Manhood in joy without any end.

Thus endeth the Dialogue.

1.5 William Caxton

William Caxton (*c*.1422–91), before embarking on his career as the first English printer, was interested in translation. In 1475, he translated Raoul Le Fèvre's *Recueil des histoires de Troye: Recuyell of the Historyes of Troye* (1475), this translation being the first English printed book. He printed some eighty works, himself a translator of twenty-one of them, mostly French romances. Among his most important books was the continuation of John of Trevisa's *Polychronicon*. His last book (1490) was a translation of the *Aeneid* (Eneydos), based on an intermediary French version of the Latin. Major translations published include: *The Golden Legend* (1483), based on an English translation of 1438, a Latin text and a French version; and a modified version of Malory's *Morte d'Arthur* (1485). Caxton's major influence was as a technologist and champion of English rather than Latin as the language for the English printed book. He is a key figure in the history of communication in the broadest sense, translation being an essential component of this activity.

From *The Recuyell of the Histories of Troy*, included in *Fifteenth Century Prose and Verse. An English Garner*, introd. Alfred W. Pollard (Westminster: Archibald Constable, 1903), 213–17

From Title and Prologue to Book I

[…]

When I remember that every man is bounden by the commandment and counsel of the wise man to eschew sloth and idleness, which is mother and nourisher of vices, and ought to put myself unto virtuous occupation and business, then I, having no great charge of occupation, following the said counsel took a French book, and read therein many strange and marvellous histories, wherein I had great pleasure and delight, as well for the novelty of the same as for the fair language of French, which was in prose so well and compendiously set and written, which methought I understood the sentence and substance of every matter. And for so much as this book was new and late made and drawn into French, and never had seen it in our English tongue, I thought in myself it should be a good business to translate it into our English, to the end that it might be had as well in the royaume of England as in other lands, and also for to pass therewith the time, and thus concluded in myself to begin this said work. And forthwith took pen and ink, and began boldly to run forth as blind Bayard in this present work, which is named 'The Recuyell of the Trojan Histories.' And afterward when I remembered myself of my simpleness and unperfectness that I had in both languages, that is to wit in French and in English, for in France was I never, and was born and learned my English in Kent, in the

Weald, where I doubt not is spoken as broad and rude English as in any place of England; and have continued by the space of 30 years for the most part in the countries of Brabant, Flanders, Holland, and Zealand. And thus when all these things came before me, after that I had made and written five or six quires I fell in despair of this work, and purposed no more to have continued therein, and those quires laid apart, and in two years after laboured no more in this work, and was fully in will to have left it, till on a time it fortuned that the right high, excellent, and right virtuous princess, my right redoubted Lady, my Lady Margaret, by the grace of God sister unto the King of England [. . .] sent for me to speak with her good Grace of divers matters, among the which I let her Highness have knowledge of the foresaid beginning of this work, which anon commanded me to show the said five or six quires to her said Grace; and when she had seen them anon she found a default in my English, which she commanded me to amend, and moreover commanded me straitly to continue and make an end of the residue then not translated; whose dreadful commandment I durst in no wise disobey, because I am a servant unto her said Grace and receive of her yearly fee and other many good and great benefits, (and also hope many more to receive of her Highness), but forthwith went and laboured in the said translation after my simple and poor cunning [. . .].

Epilogue to Book II

Thus endeth the second book of the Recule of the Histories of Troy. Which books were late translated into French out of Latin by the labour of the venerable person Raoul le Fèvre, priest, as afore is said; and by me indigne and unworthy, translated into this rude English by the commandment of my said redoubted Lady, Duchess of Burgundy. And for as much as I suppose the said two books be not had before this time in our English language, therefore I had the better will to accomplish this said work; which work was begun in Bruges and continued in Ghent and finished in Cologne, in the time of the troublous world, and of the great divisions being and reigning, as well in the royaumes of England and France as in all other places universally through the world ; that is to wit the year of our Lord a thousand four hundred seventy one. And as for the third book, which treateth of the general and last destruction of Troy, it needeth not to translate it into English, for as much as that worshipful and religious man, Dan John Lidgate, monk of Bury, did translate it but late; after whose work I fear to take upon me, that am not worthy to bear his penner and ink-horn after him, to meddle me in that work. But yet for as much as I am bound to contemplate my said Lady's good grace, and also that his work is in rhyme and as far as I know it is not had in prose in our tongue, and also, peradventure, he translated after some other author than this is; and yet for as much as divers men be of divers desires, some to read in rhyme and metre and some in prose; and also because that I have now good leisure, being in Cologne, and have none other thing to do at this time; in eschewing of idleness, mother of all vices, I have delibered in myself for the contemplation of my said redoubted lady to take this labour in hand, by the sufferance and help of Almighty God; whom I meekly supplye to give me grace to accomplish it to the pleasure of her that is causer thereof, and that she receive it in gree of me, her faithful, true, and most humble servant, etc.

Epilogue to Book III

Thus end I this book, which I have translated after mine Author as nigh as God hath given me cunning, to whom be given the laud and praising. And for as much as in the writing of the same my pen is worn, my hand weary and not steadfast, mine eyne dimmed with overmuch looking on the white paper, and my courage not so prone and ready to labour as it hath been, and that age creepeth on me daily and feebleth all the body, and also because I have promised to divers gentlemen and to my friends to address to them as hastily as I might this said book, therefore I have practised and learned at my great charge and dispense to ordain this said book in print, after the manner and form as ye may here see, and is not written with pen and ink as other books be, to the end that every man may have them at once. [. . .] I beseech Almighty God to reward her [his patron] everlasting bliss after this life, praying her said Grace and all them that shall read this book not to disdain the simple and rude work, neither to reply against the saying of the matters touched in this book, though it accord not unto the translation of others which have written it. For divers men have made divers books which in all points accord not, as Dictes, Dares, and Homer. For Dictes and Homer, as Greeks, say and write favourably for the Greeks, and give to them more worship than to the Trojans; and Dares writeth otherwise than they do. And also as for the proper names, it is no wonder that they accord not, for some one name in these days have divers equivocations after the countries that they dwell in; but all accord in conclusion the general destruction of that noble city of Troy, and the death of so many noble princes, as kings, dukes, earls, barons, knights, and common people, and the ruin irreparable of that city that never since was re-edified; which may be example to all men during the world how dreadful and jeopardous it is to begin a war, and what harms, losses, and death followeth. Therefore the Apostle saith: 'All that is written is written to our doctrine,' which doctrine for the common weal I beseech God may be taken in such place and time as shall be most needful in increasing of peace, love, and charity; which grant us He that suffered for the same to be crucified on the rood tree. And say we all Amen for charity!

CHAPTER 2

FROM THE REFORMATION AND THE RENAISSANCE TO THE EIGHTEENTH CENTURY

2.1 INTRODUCTION

This chapter stretches over a period of two and half centuries, a period of momentous changes in literature and culture, inaugurated by the Reformation and the Renaissance. These movements or paradigms are carried forward in no small part by translation: on the one hand biblical translation, on the other translation of Classical Greek and Roman canons of literary and historical writings, along with an increasing emphasis on more recent European literature.

Martin Luther, the most influential figure of the Reformation and one of its most radical thinkers, is the author of one of the most important Bible translations in European history, and his open letter on translation gives valuable insight into the relationship between the theo-political issues and translation matters. In England, William Tyndale is a key Reformation advocate, and a crucial translator of the Bible into English—and a martyr to that joint venture. One need not be a Bible translator, however, to become a martyr to translation, as witnessed by the case of Estienne Dolet, the French scholar and translator, who wrote an early systematic account of the measures of translation. Dolet's is not the only section in the chapter that testifies to the importance of French translation and translation theory during this period (see also Sects. 2.5 on du Bellay and 2.14 on Anne Dacier), France being of course, ever since the twelfth century, Britain's strong literary neighbour. The sixteenth century, a golden age of translation in England, owes a good deal to France, and some of the translated works came via French into English, notably North's famous version of Plutarch. This and other translations were a shaping influence on English as a literary language and even directly on writers of original works, some of which carry distinct traces of translations, as may be seen in some of Shakespeare's plays.

The strengthening of vernacular tongues and national cultures tends to obscure the view to a cross-cultural linguistic activity which also strongly characterized cultural and scholarly life in Europe in this era. Latin remained an important medium of scholarly and cultural preservation and dissemination, a bridge both across time and space—not least because texts translated into Latin had a potential readership all over Europe. Thus the most glorious period of translation in England was also the scene of much translation into Latin, and readers may catch a glimpse of this below.

Along with the advent of Renaissance humanism, women at last came into sight as makers of written literary culture. Women presumably played a vital role in at least some of the oral traditions that led up to canonical European literary genres and works, but they had been largely excluded from early written literary culture, both religious and secular. For some of them, translation now becomes a means of expression and cultural contribution—a road into the forefront of the literary system.

As we move into the latter part of the period, it becomes clear how translation constitutes a shaping force on English literary and cultural activity. Its two primary flanks are obviously the English versions of the Bible—especially the Authorized (King James) Version, one of the most important texts in English literature—and the translation by Chapman, Dryden, Pope, and many others, of classical works of literature. Methods may vary a great deal, but the line of translators still forms a tradition within the English language, an ever-contested and ever-renewed strand of canonical writing whose significance is thus constantly confirmed even as its previous 'performances' continue to be challenged. There is no better proof of a living tradition.

During the Reformation and Renaissance, and on into the eighteenth century, statements on translation are most frequently made in the context of actual practice, the most prominent platform being the translator's own preface to his or her translation. There are, however, a number of more general and systematic accounts of translation as an act, and of its methods. Such accounts (see Dolet in Sect. 2.4, Laurence Humphrey in Sect. 2.7, and Tytler, who concludes this chapter) need not in themselves provide more of an insight into the act of translation, but they point the way to a more abstract theory, which in turn may help us, as students of translation, to understand this rich field, where translation can never be severed from comments on translation, translation being in itself a form of 'commentary' on another text.

2.2 MARTIN LUTHER

Martin Luther (1483–1546), Augustinian monk and theologian, was the German leader of the Reformation. With his ninety-five theses, nailed to the door of Wittenberg University in 1517, he expressed his dissatisfaction with the penitential system of the Roman Catholic Church. By 1521, the breach with the Church had become irreparable. An effective publicist and great writer of treatises, with a rugged popular style, Luther came to emphasize original writing in the vernacular, but it was through his translation of the Bible (the New Testament, published in 1522, and the Old Testament, in 1534) that he was to establish a norm for written German, and to have a radical and lasting influence on German language and literature. He also wrote hymns, which became very popular and have survived.

As a translator, Luther was distinctly reader-oriented; his aim was to put together a Bible text for the general public. His translation, characterized by a combination of popular speech and poetic dignity, became for many Northern Europeans a new 'original', and served as such as the basis of some Bible translations into the Nordic languages. Luther's *Open Letter on Translation* (1530) is an important text in the history of translation theory, not only because it is intimately connected to a groundbreaking translation, but further because it manifests vividly how the choice of words and expressions in a translation is sometimes intimately linked to a whole ideological and institutional matrix. Luther's choice of the word 'allein', for instance (see below), is a good deal more laden with theological politics than he openly admits.

The letter appears here complete (except for its last part which deals with the question whether deceased saints pray for us), in a new translation, followed by Luther's translation of the Babel story (Genesis 11: 1–9) and a literal rendering into English of Luther's version.

From *Open Letter on Translation* (*Sendbrief vom Dolmetchen*), translated by Jennifer Tanner

> From Wenceslaus Link to all Believers in Christ, God's Grace and Mercy. Solomon the Wise says in Proverbs 11: 26 'He who withholds grain, him the people curse. But blessings will come upon him who sells it.' This passage should be understood to apply to anything that can be of general use or comfort to Christianity. It is for this reason that the master in the Gospel scolds the faithless servant, the lazy rogue, for burying his money in the earth and hiding it. To escape the curse of the Lord and of the community at large I have not suppressed this open letter, which came into my hands from a good friend, but openly published it. For while much idle talk has come about regarding the translation of the

Old and New Testaments, namely, the enemies of the truth purport that the text has in places been changed or even falsified, so that horror and disgust has come over many simple Christians, as well as over the educated who are not familiar with Hebrew and Greek. It is to be hoped that this letter will at least in part hinder the godless in their slander and lift the scruple of the pious; it may even come about that more will be written on this question or matter. I ask therefore that everyone who loves truth take this work on my best recommendation and ask God in good faith for correct understanding of the Holy Writ for the betterment and surfeit of all Christianity. Amen. Nuremberg, 15 September. Anno 1530.

To the Honourable and Circumspect N., my favoured lord and friend

Grace and Peace in Christ. Honourable, circumspect, dear master and friend! I have received your letter with the two questions of which you desire to hear my account: first, why I translated the words of St Paul in 'To the Romans', chapter 3, verse 28: 'Arbitrámur hóminem iustificári ex fíde absque opéribus' into German as: 'We hold that man is justified not by the works of law but by faith alone'—and also regarding the note that the papists have worked themselves into a boundless fury because the word 'sola' (alone) is not found in Paul's text and that such additions to God's Word are not to be tolerated from me, etc.; secondly, if the deceased saints also pray for us, since we read that even the angels pray for us etc. Regarding the first question, if it please you, you may answer your papists on my behalf as such:

First of all. If I, Doctor Luther, had been aware that all the papists together were so skilful that they could translate one chapter of the Holy Writ into German correctly and well, then, truly, I would have been humble and asked them for help and advice in translating the New Testament. But since I knew then and still see now that they have no idea how one should translate or speak German, I spared both them and myself the trouble. But one can clearly see that they learn to speak and write German from my translation and my German and steal my language from me, of which they knew so little before; they do not thank me for it, but rather use it against me. But I will grant them that gladly, because it does me good to know that I have taught my ingrate disciples, also my enemies, to speak.

Further, you can say that I have translated the New Testament into German to the best of my abilities and as conscientiously as possible; I have not forced anyone to read it but simply left it available and only done so as a service to those who cannot do any better. No one has been forbidden to make a better one. Whoever does not want to read it can leave it alone; I am not begging or cajoling anyone to read it. It is my Testament and my translation and shall remain mine. If I have made any mistakes in doing so (which I would not consciously do, nor would I wilfully mistranslate a single letter)—on that

I will not tolerate the papists as my judge, because their ears are too long for that and their 'hee-haw, hee-haw' is too weak for them to judge my translation. I know well, and they know less than the miller's beast, what sort of skill, diligence, judgement, and intelligence are needed for translation, because they have never tried it.

It is said: 'He who works on the road has many masters.' So it has been for me. Those who have never yet been able to speak, let alone translate, they are all my masters and I have to be their disciple. And if I were to ask them how the first two words of Matthew 1: 1: 'Liber Generationis', should be translated into German, not one of them could have said as much as 'cluck'—and now they sit in judgement on the entire work, those fine fellows. So it went for St Hieronymus as well, when he translated the Bible: the whole world was his master and he alone could do nothing right, and the work of this good man was judged by those who were not good enough to shine his shoes for him. This is why one has to have great patience in order to openly do something good; because the world wants to remain Master Cleverly and always has to bridle the horse tail-end first, to be master of everything and itself unable to do anything. That is its nature, which it cannot give up.

I would look with kindness on any papist who would come out and translate any epistle of St Paul or one of the prophets into German. As long as he does not use Luther's German and translation, then one ought to see a fine, lovely, praiseworthy German translation! For we have seen, of course, the Bungler of Dresden, who has shown my New Testament a master (I do not wish to name him in my books any more; besides, he has his judge[1] now and is well known otherwise); he recognizes that my German is sweet and good, and saw rightly that he could not make it better and yet wanted to destroy it, went ahead and took down my New Testament, almost word for word as I did, and removed my preface, commentary, and name, wrote his name, preface, and commentary in their place, and so he sells my New Testament under his own name. Oh, dear children, how it hurt me, when his sovereign, with a dread preface, condemned and forbade that Luther's New Testament should be read, and at the same time commanded that the Bungler's New Testament should be read (which is the very same one that Luther did).

And just so that no one should think that I am lying, take both Testaments in front of you, Luther's and the Bungler's, hold them opposite each other, and you will see who is the translator of both. Because although he has patched and changed things in a few places—although it does not always please me, I can easily bear it and it doesn't hurt me much, as far as the text is concerned; that is why I never bothered to write against it, but had to laugh at the great wisdom, that my New Testament has been so terribly slandered, condemned, and forbidden when it was published under my name, but it must be read, when it is published under another name. But what a virtue that is, to slander and sully another man's book, then steal the very thing and publish it under one's own name, and so by means of someone else's slandered work to seek praise and fame for oneself—I will leave that up to his judge. That is enough for me and I am glad that my work (as St Paul also extols) should also be advanced by my enemies and Luther's book, minus Luther's name, under his enemies' names, should be read. How could I be better avenged?

And to return to the matter at hand: If your papist wants to make a lot of trouble over the word 'sola-alone', then tell him this at once: Doctor Martin Luther wants it that way and says papist and ass are one and the same. Sic vólo, sic iúbeo, sit pro ratióne volúntas. For we do not want to be the pupils or disciples of the papist, but their masters and judges. If they want to strut about and boast with their asses' heads; and as Paul sang his own praises against his holy fools, I will sing my own against these asses. Are they Doctors? So am I! Are they educated? So am I! Are they preachers? So am I! Are they theologians? So am I! Are they debaters? So am I! Are they philosophers? So am I! Are they dialecticians? So am I! Are they lecturers? So am I! They write books? So do I!

And I will keep on praising: I can interpret Psalms and Prophets; they cannot. I can translate; they cannot. I can pray, they cannot. And to speak of lesser things: I understand their entire Dialectic and Philosphy better than any of them. And I know, furthermore, that not one of them understands his Aristotle. And if there is even one of them who correctly understands a preface or chapter of Aristotle, then may I be tossed up in a blanket![2] I won't say too much now, because I was raised and trained in their art from youth onward and I know quite well, how deep and wide it is. And they know just as well that I know and can do everything they can. But still these ruinous people act against me as if I were a guest to their art who only arrived this morning and has never seen or heard the things they learn and can do; and they come on with wondrous displays of their art and teach me things I stamped to pieces twenty years before; so that I find I have to sing along with that harlot to all their blaring and hollering: I knew seven years ago that horseshoe nails are made of iron.

That is in answer to your first question, and I ask that you tell such asses no more in reply to their useless noise about the word 'sola' than this: Luther wants it that way and says he is a Doctor above all Doctors in the entire papacy; it shall remain as it is. I want, from now on, only to disdain them and have them disdained as long as they remain such people, or, should I say, asses. For there are such shameless dunces among them who have never even learned their own art, that of the Sophists, like Doctor Smith and Doctor Snotspoon and his sort; and they set themselves against me in this matter which is not just about sophistry, but also, as St Paul says, about the wisdom and reason of the whole world. It is true: an ass needn't sing very long: we know him soon enough by his ears.

For you and our people, however, I will explain why I decided to use the word 'sola', although in Romans 3: 28 it is not 'sola' but 'solum' or 'tantum' that I have used. See how carefully these asses scrutinize my text! However, I have used 'sola fide' elsewhere and want both of them, 'solum' and 'sola'. I have taken pains in translating in order to render a pure and clear German. And it often happened that we sought and questioned a single word for fourteen days, three, four weeks, and at times still could not find it. In Job we worked this way, Master Philips, Aurogallus, and I, so that in four days sometimes we could hardly finish three lines. Rather—now that it is in German and ready, anyone can read and criticize it. Now a person can fly through three, four pages and never stumble once, but is not aware of the sort of stones and stumps that had been there, where he now walks along as on a smooth-planed board, where we had to sweat and fret before we were able to clear such stones and stumps out of the way so that one could walk along so finely. It is a joy to plough a field that has already been cleared. But rooting out the brush and the stumps and preparing the field—no one wants that part. It is a thankless task. If God Himself can get no thanks for the sun, for heaven and earth, or even for His own son's death: the world is and remains the world in the devil's name, because it won't have it any other way.

Furthermore, I knew very well here, in Romans 3, that the word 'sola' is not found in the Latin and Greek text, and the papists did not need to tell me that. It is true: these four letters 's-o-l-a' are not found there and those asses' heads stare at these letters like cows at a new gate. They do not see that it nevertheless speaks to the sense of the text, and if one wants to translate it into German clearly and powerfully it is needed, because my intention was to speak German, not Latin or Greek, when I undertook to speak German in the translation. That is how German is. When two things are being spoken of, of which one is affirmed and the other negated, then one uses the word 'solum'/*allein* along with the word 'not' or 'no'. As when one says: the farmer brings *allein* grain and no money. No, I really have no money, but *allein* grain. I have *allein* eaten and not yet drunk. Did you *allein* write and not proofread? And countless other such ways in daily use.

Whether Latin or Greek have this as part of their manner of speech or not, German does and that is its nature, that the word *allein* is added to make the word 'not' or 'no' fuller and clearer. For while I could also say: 'The farmer brings grain and no money,' the words 'no money' do not sound as full and clear as when I say 'The farmer brings *allein* grain and no money'; and here the word *allein* helps the word 'no' so that we have a full, clear, German sentence. For one need not ask the letters of the Latin language how one ought to speak German, the way these asses do, rather one should ask the mother in her house, the children in the streets, the common man in the marketplace, about it and see by their mouths how they speak, and translate accordingly: then they understand it well and recognize that one is speaking German to them.

So it is when Christ says: 'Ex abundántia cordis os lóquitur.' If I were to obey the asses, they would lay the letters before me and translate it like this: *Aus dem Überfluß des Herzens redet der Mund.* [Out of the overflow of the heart the mouth speaks.] Tell me: is that German? What German would understand something like that? What is overflow of the heart supposed to be? No German could say that, it would be as if he were trying to say that someone's heart was much too big or that he had too much heart, while that is still not right either. So overflow of the heart is not German, as little as any of these are: overflow of the house, overflow of the tile stove, overflow of the bench, no, but this is how the mother in her house and the common man would say it: *Wes das Herz voll is, des gehet der Mund über* [What the heart is full of will spill over at the mouth]. That is well-spoken German, which I took pains to come up with and unfortunately could not always attain or find. For the Latin letters make it enormously difficult to speak good German.

Likewise, when the traitor Judas says in Matthew 26: 8: 'Ut quid perdítio haec?' and Mark 14: 4: 'Ut quid perdítio ista unguénti facta est?' If I were to obey the asses and literalists, then I would have to translate it as: *Warum ist diese Verlierung der Salben geschehen?* [Why has this loss of ointment occurred?] What kind of German is that? What German would say something like that: Loss of ointment has occurred? And if he actually understands it then he will think that the ointment has been lost and someone should look for it, though even that still sounds vague and dubious. If that is good German, why don't they come forward and make us a fine, lovely new German Testament and leave Luther's Testament alone? I think they ought to show their skill the light of day. But a German man would say it ('Ut quid' etc.) like this: *Was soll doch solcher Unrat?* [Why such a waste?] or: *Was soll doch solcher Schade?* [Why such a loss?] No, it's too bad about the ointment—that is good German, from which one can understand that Magdalene had handled the spilled ointment inexpediently and was wasteful; that was Judas' opinion, since he hoped to find a better use for it.

Likewise, when the angel greets Mary and says: *Gegrüßet seist du, Maria, voll Gnaden, der Herr mit dir* [You are greeted, Mary, full of grace, the Lord is with you]. Now then—there is how is has been translated into German so far, following the Latin letters. Tell me, though, if it is good German as well. Where is the man who speaks that way: you are full of grace? And what German understands what that is supposed to mean: full of grace? He has to think of a keg full of beer or a bag full of money; that is why I have translated it like this: *Du Holdselige* [You blessed woman], by which a German can much better imagine what the angel means by his greeting. But here the papists go mad with fury at me for corrupting the angelic greeting, while I still have not found the best German for it. And if I were to use the best possible German here and translate the greeting into German like this: *Gott grüße dich, du liebe Maria* [Greetings from God, dear Mary] (because this is what the angel is trying to say and this is how he would have said it, if he had wanted to greet her in German), I think they would hang themselves in their colossal fervour over the dear Mary, because I had so destroyed the greeting.

But why should I care if they rage or storm? I do not want to hinder them from translating what they want; but I do want to translate not as they want, but as I want. Whoever does not want it can leave it to me and keep his mastery to himself, for I do not want to see nor hear it; and for my translating they need give neither answer nor account.

" pierced w/ beauty "

Hear me well: I want to say: *du holdselige Maria, du liebe Maria*, and let them say: *du voll Gnaden Maria*. He who knows German knows well what a fine word that is, how it goes straight to the heart: *die liebe Maria, der liebe Gott, der liebe Kaiser, der liebe Fürst, der liebe Mann, das liebe Kind* [the dear Mary, the dear God, the dear emperor, the dear prince, the dear man, the dear child]. And I do not know if one can express the word *liebe* as affectionately and concisely in Latin or other languages, so that it goes straight to the heart and resounds through all the senses, as it does in our language.   *dynamism*

For I hold that St Luke, being a master of Hebrew and Greek, wanted to capture and render the sense of the Hebrew word the angel used by using the Greek word 'kecharitoméni'. And I think the angel Gabriel would have spoken to Mary as he spoke to Daniel, calling him 'hamudóth' and 'isch hamudóth', 'vir desideriórum', that is, *du lieber Daniel*. For that is Gabriel's manner of speaking, as we see in the book of Daniel. If I were to translate the angel's words by following the letters, as is the asses' art, I would have to say: *Daniel, du Mann der Begierungen* [Daniel, you man of desires], or, *Daniel, du Mann der Lüste* [Daniel, you man of of pleasures]. Oh, there's some good German! A German can hear perfectly well that *Mann, Begierungen*, and *Lüste* are German words, although *Begier* and *Lust*, in the singular, would be much better. But when they are joined together in such a way: You man of desires; then no German knows what is being said and thinks perhaps Daniel is full of wicked desires. That would be a fine translation. Therefore, at this point I have to let the letters go their way and seek the way a German man would express what the Hebrew man calls 'Isch hamudóth': and so I find that the German man speaks as such: *Du lieber Daniel, du liebe Maria*, or: *du holdselige Maid, du niedliche Jungfrau, du zartes Weib* [you blessed maid, you sweet virgin, you gentle woman] and so on. For he who wants to translate must have a great hoard of words, so that he can find them right at hand when one refuses to sound right.   *Ideal >*

And why should I have to talk so much and for so long about translation? If I were to note the reasons and thoughts behind all of my words, it would take a year of writing. I have learned well what sort of art and work translation is; therefore I will tolerate no papal ass or mule who has not attempted anything as my judge or critic in this. Whoever does not want my translation can leave it be. The devil thank him who doesn't like it or alters it without my will or knowledge. If it needs to be altered, then I will do it myself. If I do not do it myself, then one should leave me my translation in peace and make himself whatever sort of translation he wants and fare well!

I can testify in good conscience that I have demonstrated my highest faithfulness and diligence in this, and never had any false thoughts—for I have neither taken nor sought a farthing for it, nor won any with it. Neither have I sought honour for myself in this, God knows, my lord; rather I did it as a service to Christianity and in honour of one who sits on high, who does me so much good in all hours that even if I had translated a thousand times as much and as diligently, I still would not have earned an hour to live or have a sound eye: all that I am and have comes from His grace and mercy, indeed, it is from His dear blood and bitter sweat, therefore it should all, God willing, serve to honour Him, with joy and from the heart. Should the bunglers and papal asses slander me, well then, the pious Christians praise me, together with their Lord Christ, and I am all too richly rewarded if just one Christian considers me a faithful worker. I ask the papal asses for nothing, they are not worthy to inspect my work, and I would be sorry to the bottom of my heart if they were to ask that I be pardoned. Their slander is my highest renown and praise. I still want to be a Doctor, an exemplary Doctor, even, and they will not take that name from me until Judgement Day, that I know in truth.

Yet on the other hand, I did not let the letters go too freely, but together with my assistants saw to it with great care that where something depended on it, I kept to the letters and did not deviate from them so freely; as in John 6: 27, where Christ says: *Diesen hat Gott der Vater versiegelt* [God the Father has set His seal on this man]. It would be better German to say: *Diesen hat Gott der Vater gezeichnet* [God the Father has marked this man], or, *diesen meinet Gott der Vater* [God the Father intends this man]. But I would rather do injury to the German language than deviate from the word. Oh, translation is not an art just anyone can do, as the mad holy ones believe; it requires a righteous, pious, faithful, diligent, fearful, Christian, educated, experienced, practised heart. Therefore I hold that no false Christian or factionist can faithfully translate; as is clearly seen in Prophets, translated in Worms, where truly great diligence was applied and closely followed my German. But there were Jews taking part in the work there, who had no great love of Christ—there would have been skill and diligence enough there per se.

That much I have said of translation and the nature of languages. But I was not only trusting and following the nature of languages when I added 'solum' (*allein*) in Romans 3: 28. Rather the text and St Paul's meaning forcefully demand and compel it; for he is dealing here with the main part of Christian teaching itself, namely, that we are justified by faith in Christ, without any works of law; and he so completely cuts off all works that he also says: the works of law (which is of course God's law and word) do not help to justify us; and sets Abraham as an example, as this man was justified so completely without works, since even the highest work, which at that time was newly commanded by God above all other laws and works, namely circumcision, did not help to justify him, but he was justified without circumcision and without any works, through faith, as he says in Chapter 4: 2: 'If Abraham was justified by works, then he can boast, but not before God.' When one so fully excludes all works—and that must indeed be the sense of this, that faith alone can justify, and anyone who wants to speak clearly and concisely about such an exclusion of works must say: Faith alone and not works justifies us. The matter itself compels this, along with the nature of language.

Yes, I know they say: It sounds vexing and the people will understand it to mean that they need do no good works. But what else should one say? Is it not much more vexing

Latn makes it hard
to speak Good Gunen
2.2 MARTIN LUTHER   65

that St Paul himself does not say: 'faith alone', but pours it out much more bluntly, kicks in the bottom of the barrel and says: 'without the works of law', and in Galatians 2: 16: 'Not by the works of law' and so on in other places; for the words 'faith alone' could still be glossed, but the words 'without works of law' are so blunt, vexing, and scandalous that no amount of glossing can help. How much more could the people learn from this to do no good works, where they hear it preached of works in such plain, strong words: 'no work, without works, not by works'. Is that not quite vexing, that one preaches 'without works, no work, not by works'—so why should it be so vexing if one preaches 'faith alone'?

And what is even more vexing: St Paul does not reject simple, ordinary works, but those of the law itself. From that one could grow even more vexed and say, the law be damned and cursed by God and one should do nothing but evil, as they would do in Romans 3: 8: 'Let us do evil, so that good may come', as a factionist began to say in our time as well. Should one, merely on account of such vexation, deny St Paul's words or fail to speak frankly and freely about faith? Rather, precisely St Paul and we want to have and teach such vexation for the sake of no other cause so strongly against works and promote faith alone than that the people should become vexed, kick and fall down, so that they can learn and know that they will not become pious through their good works, but through Christ's death and resurrection alone. If they cannot become pious through good works of law, how much less will they become pious through evil works and without law! One cannot conclude that since good works do not help, therefore evil works help, just as one cannot well conclude that since the sun does not help a blind man to see, therefore the night and darkness must help him to see.

It amazes me, though, that one can struggle and baulk so much within this open matter. Tell me, if Christ's death and resurrection is our work, which we do, or not. It is in no way our work, nor is it the work of any law. Christ's death and resurrection alone make us free from sin and pious, as Paul says in Romans 4: 25: 'He died for our sins and is resurrected for our justification.' Further, tell me: What work is it by which we secure and hold Christ's death and resurrection? It could never be an outward work, but can only be the eternal faith in one's heart; which alone, completely alone and without any works grasps such a death and resurrection, where it is preached through the Gospel. What difference does it make if people rant and rage, cry heresy and burn, although the matter at bottom is clearly printed there and proves that faith alone can secure Christ's death and resurrection without any works and that the same death and resurrection are our life and justification. If it is so obvious that faith alone brings, secures, and gives us this life and justification, why then should one not speak so? It is not heresy that faith alone secures Christ and gives life. But it must be heresy, if one says or speaks of such a thing. Are they not mad, foolish, and senseless? They recognize these matters to be right and yet they punish any speech of the same matter as wrong; there is nothing that may at once be both right and wrong.

Slavonic +
RC
Eastern
mode

Geneva
+
wrest power institutions
from

Furthermore I am not the only one, nor even the first to say that faith alone justifies us. Ambrose, Augustine, and many others have said it before me. And anyone who intends to read and understand St Paul must surely say so and cannot do otherwise. His words are too strong and tolerate no work at all. If it is no work at all, then it must be faith alone. Oh, what a fine, useful, unvexing lesson that would be, if people were to learn that they could become pious through their works along with faith. That would be as much as saying that Christ's death does not take away our sins by itself, but that our works also play a part. What a fine way to honour Christ's death, to say that our works help Him and can also do what He has done, so that we would be just as good and strong as He. That is the talk of the devil, who cannot resist profaning Chist's blood.

Because the matter itself, at bottom, demands that one say: 'Faith *allein* justifies us', as does the nature of our German language, which also teaches us to express it this way. In addition I have the example of the holy fathers and the endangerment of the people forces the matter, in that they keep hanging on works and miss faith and lose Christ, especially in these times, since they have been used to works for so long that they must be torn away from them by force. So it is not only right, but of the highest necessity, that one as clearly and fully as possible state: Faith *allein* without works makes one pious; and I regret that I did not also add *alle* and *aller* [any], as such: *Ohn alle Werk aller Gesetz* [Without any works of any laws], so that it would be fully and roundly said. Therefore it shall remain so in my New Testament, even if all the papal asses go mad and silly they will not make me yield. That is enough about that. I will speak further about this, with God's grace, in my book *De iustificatione*.

As regards the other question, if the deceased saints pray for us [. . .]

TRANSLATOR'S NOTES

1. i.e., has met his maker.
2. A comical punishment; fifty lashes with a wet noodle.

Luther's translation of Genesis 11: 1-9.

Die gantze Heilige Schifft Deudsch (Wittenberg 1545; last edition published in Luther's lifetime), ed. Hanz Volz with Heiz Blanke; text ed. Friedreich Kur (Munich: Rogner & Bernhand, 1972), 41–2

Es hatte aber alle Welt einerley Zungen und sprache. [2]Da sie nu zogen gen Morgen / funden sie ein eben Land / in lande Sinear / vnd woneten daselbs. [3]Vnd sprachen vntereinander / Wolauff / lasst vns Ziegel streichen vnd brennen / Vnd namen ziegel zu stein / vnd thon zu kalck / [4]vnd sprachen / Wolauff / Lasst vns eine Stad vnd Thurn bawen / des spitze bis an den Himel reiche / das wir vns einen namen machen / Denn wir werden vieleicht zerstrewet in alle Lender.

⁵Da fur der HERR ernider / das er sehe die Stad vnd Thurn / die die Menschenkinder baweten. ⁶Vnd der HERR sprach / Sihe / Es ist einerley Volck vnd einerley Sprach vnter jnen allen / vnd haben das angefangen zu thun / sie werden nicht ablassen von allem das sie furgenomen haben zu thun. ⁷Wolauff / lasst vns ernider faren / vnd jre Sprache da selbs verwirren / das keiner des andern sprache verneme. ⁸Also zerstrewet sie der HERR von dannen in alle Lender / das sie musten auffhören die Stad zu bawen / ⁹Da her heisst jr name Babel / das der HERR daselbs verwirret hatte aller Lender sprache / vnd sie zerstrewet von dannen in alle Lender.

Literal translation by Jennifer Tanner

1. Now all the world had but one tongue and language.

2. As they moved towards morning [the east], they found a flat land in the land of Sinar, and they dwelt there.

3. And they spoke among themselves: Well then, let us make[1] and burn bricks. And they took bricks for stone and clay for lime.

4. and said: Well then, let us build a city and a tower whose peak will reach as far as heaven,[2] so that we make a name for ourselves. For we may perhaps be scattered into all lands.

5. Then the LORD came down that he might see the city and the tower that the children of man were building.

6. And the LORD said: See, there is but one people and but one language among all of them, and they have begun to do this; they will not leave off from all that they have undertaken to do.

7. Well then, let us go down and confuse their language there, so that none will discern the language of the other.

8. So the Lord scattered them from there into all lands, so that they had to stop building the city.

9. Therefore its name is called Babel, since in that place the LORD had confused the language of all countries and scattered them from there into all lands.

TRANSLATOR'S NOTES

1. The verb is *streichen*, possibly to spread, i.e., spread the mixture of mud and straw into a mould? Bilingual dictionaries define *streichen* as 'make' with regard to bricks. A closer alternative might be 'cast'. At any rate, it is only the first step, the second being to fire the bricks in a kiln.

2. *Himmel* equally means 'heaven' and 'sky' in German; given the context I chose 'heaven'.

2.3 WILLIAM TYNDALE

William Tyndale (*c.*1494–1536), is by far the most influential Bible translator in the English language. A humanist and theologian, educated at both Oxford and Cambridge, he was determined, in the spirit of the Reformation, to make the Bible widely available in the vernacular to both laymen and clergy. While serving as a tutor, in 1522, he also translated Erasmus's *Enchiridion Militis Christiani* ('The Christian Soldier's Handbook', written in 1502). It was his work on this and subsequent problems with the authorities that persuaded him that ignorance of the Scriptures lay at the root of the theological confusion. In 1524, Tyndale visited Luther in Wittenberg—Luther had published his German translation of the New Testament in 1522—and worked on his translation of the New Testament in Hamburg and Worms, the work being completed in 1525. Much of the commentary is clearly based on Luther's German translation, but Tyndale worked scrupulously from the Greek and Hebrew source texts, using Erasmus's 1522 Greek New Testament. The first English New Testament to be printed, Tyndale's translation was smuggled into England in 1526. Although the bulk of his time went into an extensive revision of his New Testament (1534), he also began work on the Hebrew Bible, producing versions of the Pentateuch and of Jonah. Tyndale, who had spent much of his life in exile, under constant threat of arrest, was eventually captured in Antwerp; he was burned as a heretic at Vilvorde. In 1537, a composite translation of the Bible, containing the work of Tyndale and Coverdale, was issued with the Church's approval.

Tyndale's Bible translation was the dominant stylistic and scholarly influence in the history of English biblical translation. Its mark on the Geneva Bible, the Douay-Reims Bible, and the King James Bible is decisive, although, for doctrinal reasons, not acknowledged. The excellence of his translation, as literature, was increasingly recognized, to the point where its unpedantic directness and idiomatic vigour sometimes served as criteria for more critical evaluation of the elevated style of the revered 1611 Authorized Version, which of course is overwhelmingly indebted to Tyndale's genius.

Tyndale's preface, below, is presented in somewhat modernized spelling. It vividly conveys the passion and conviction that informed Tyndale's activity as a Bible translator, and the physical precariousness of his position, at the very centre of the religious controversies, and the intimidation that he was subject to.

'W.T. To the Reader': Tyndale's Story of His Translation (the preface to Tyndale's translation of Genesis in his Pentateuch, printed in 1530), included in Dewey M. Beegle, *God's Word into English: The Adventure of Bible Translation* (New York: Harper Brothers, 1960)

When I had translated the new testament, I added an epistle unto the latter end, in which I desired them that were learned to amend [it] if aught were found amiss. But our malicious and wily hypocrites which are so stubborn and hard hearted in their wicked abominations that it is not possible for them to amend any thing at all (as we see by daily experience when their both livings and doings are rebuked with the truth) say, some of them that it is impossible to translate the scripture into English, some that it is not lawful for the lay people to have it in their mother tongue, some that it would make them all heretics, as it would no doubt from many things which they of long time have falsely taught, and that it is the whole cause wherefore they forbid it, though they other cloaks pretend. And some or rather every one say that it would make them rise against the king, whom they themselves (unto their damnation) never yet obeyed. And lest the temporal rulers should see their falsehood, if the scripture cam to light, causeth them so to lie.

And as for my translation in which they affirm unto the lay people (as I have heard say) to be I wot not how many thousand heresies, so that it cannot be mended or corrected, they have yet taken so great pain to examyne it, and to compare it unto that they would fain have it and to their own imaginations and juggling terms, and to have somewhat to rail at, and under that cloak to blaspheme the truth, that they might with as little labour (as I suppose) have translated the most part of the bible. For they which in times paste were wont to look on no more scripture then they found in their duns [the commentaries of Duns Scotus] or such like devilish doctrine, have yet now so narrowly looked on my translation, that there is not so much as one I therein if it lack a title over his bed, but they have noted it, and number it unto the ignorant people for an heresy. Finally in this they be all agreed to drive you from the knowledge of the scripture, and that ye shall not have the text thereof in the mother tongue, and to keep the world still in darkness, to the intent they might sit in the conscience of the people, through vain superstition and false doctrine, to satisfy their filthy lusts their proud ambition, and insatiable covetousness, and to exalt their own honour above king & emperour, yea and above god himself.

A thousand books had they lever to be put forth against their abominable doings and doctrine, than that the scripture should come to light. For as long as they may keep that down, they will so darken the right way with the mist of their sophistry, and so tangle them that ether rebuke or despise their abominations with arguments philosophy and with worldly similitude and apparent reasons of natural wisdom. And with wresting the scripture unto their own purpose clean contrary unto the process, order and meaning of the text, and so delude them in descanting upon it with allegories, and amaze them expounding it in many senses before the unlearned lay people (when it hath but one simple literal sense whose light the owls cannot abide) that though thou feel in thine heart and art sure how that all is false that they say, yet couldst thou not solve their subtle riddles.

Which thing only moved me to translate the new testament. Because I had perceived by experience, how that it was impossible to establish the lay people in any truth, except the scripture were plainly laid before their eyes in their mother tongue, that they might see the process, order and meaning of the text: for else whatsoever truth is taught them, these enemies of all truth quench it again, partly with the smoke of their bottomless pit whereof thou readest Apocalypse ix. that is, with apparent reasons of sophistry and traditions of their own making, founded without ground of scripture, and partly in juggling with the text, expounding it in such a sense as is impossible to gather of the text, if thou see the process order and meaning thereof.

And even in the bishop of London's house I intended to have done it. For when I was so turmoiled in the country where I was that I could no longer there dwell (the process whereof were to long here to rehearse) I this wise thought in my self, this I suffer because the priests of the country be unlearned, as god it knoweth there are a full ignorant sort which have seen no more Latin than that they read in their portesses [breviaries or prayers for the canonical hours] and missals which yet many of them can scarcely read (except it be Albertus [i.e. Albertus Magnus] de secretis mulierum in which yet, though they be never so sorely learned, they pour day and night and make notes therein and all to teach the midwives as they say, and Linwood [William Lyndewode's *Provinciale*, a digest of English canon law written in 1433] a book of constitutions to gather tithes, mortuaries [customary gifts claimed from the heirs of dead parishioners], offerings, customs, and other pillage, which they call not theirs, but God's part and the duty of holy church, to discharge their consciences withall: for they are bound that they shall not diminish, but increase all thing unto the utmost of their powers) and therefore (because they are thus unlearned, thought I) when they come together to the alehouse, which is their preaching place, they affirm that my sayings are heresy. And besides that they add to of their own heads which I never spake, as the manner is to prolong the tale to short the time withall, and accuse me secretly to the chancellor [i.e. the Bishop's Chancellor of the diocese] and other bishop's officers. And indeed when I came before the chancellor, he threatened me grievously, and reviled me and rated me as though I had been a dog, and laid to my charge whereof there could be none accuser brought forth (as their manner is not to bring forth the accuser) and yet all the priests of the country were that same day there. As I this thought the bishop of London came to my remembrance whom Erasmus (whose tongue maketh of little gnats great elephants and lifteth up above the stars whosoever giveth him a little exhibition) prayseth exceedingly among other in his annotations on the new testament for his great learning. Then thought I, if I might come to this man's service,

I were happy. And so I got me to London, and through the acquaintance of my master came to Sir Harry Gilford the king's graces controller, and brought him an oration of Isocrates which I had translated out of Greek into English, and desired him to speak unto my lord of London for me, which he also did as he showed me, and willed me to write an epistle to my lord, and to go to him myself which I also did, and delivered my epistle to a servant of his own, one William Hebilthwayte, a man of mine old acquaintance. But god which knoweth what is within hypocrites, saw that I was beguiled, and that the council was not the next way unto my purpose. And therefore he got me no favor in my lord's sight.

Whereupon my lord answered me, his house was full, he had more then he could well find, and advised me to seek in London, where he said I could not lack a service. And so in London I abode almost a year, and marked the course of the world, and heard our praters, I would say our preachers how they boasted themselves and their high authority and beheld the pomp of our prelates and how beside they were as they yet are, to set peace and unite in the world (though it be not possible for them that walk in darkness to country long in peace, for they can not but ether stumble or dash themselves at one thing or another that shall clean unquiet altogether) and saw things whereof I defer to speak at this time, and understood at the last not only that there was no room in my lord of London's palace to translate the new testament, but also that there was no place to do it in all England, as experience doth openly declare.

Under what manner therefore should I now submit this book to be corrected and amended of them, which can suffer nothing to be well? Or what protestation should I make in such a matter unto our prelates those stubborn Nimrods which so mightily fight against god and resist his holy spirit, enforcing with all craft and subtlety to quench the light of the everlasting testament, promises, and appointment made between god and us: and heaping the fierce wrath of god upon all princes and rulers, mocking them with false fained names of hypocrisy, and serving their lusts at all points, and dispensing with them even of the very laws of god, of which Christ himself testifieth, Mathew v. that not so much as one title thereof may perish or be broken. And of which the prophet sayeth Psalm cxviii. Thou hast commanded thy laws to be kept meod, that is in Hebrew exceedingly, with all diligence, might and power, and have made them so mad with their juggling charms and crafty persuasions that they think it full satisfaction for all their wicked living, to torment such as tell them truth, and so born the word of their soul's health and else whosoever believe thereon.

Notwithstanding yet I submit this book and all other that I have other made or translated, or shall in time to come (if it be god's will that I shall further labour in his harvest) unto all them that submit themselves unto the word of god, to be corrected of them, yea and moreover to be disallowed & also burnt, if it seem worthy when they have examined it with the Hebrew, so that they first put forth of their own translating another that is more correct.

Tyndale's Old Testament, **in a modern-spelling edition and with an introduction by David Daniell (New Haven: Yale University Press, 1992), Genesis, 11: 1–9, pp. 25–26**

[See other versions of this passage in the introductory Babel section, and in Sects. 1.3, 2.2, above, and 2.8, 2.9, 4.5, 4.9, 5.20, below.]

And all the world was of one tongue and one language. And as they came from the east, they found a plain in the land of Sinear, and there they dwelled. And they said one to another: come on, let us make brick and burn it with fire. So brick was their stone and slime was their mortar. And they said: Come on, let us build us a city and a tower, that the top may reach unto heaven. And let us make us a name, for peradventure we shall be scattered abroad over all the earth.

And the Lord came down to see the city and the tower which the children of Adam had builded. And the Lord said: See, the people is one and have one tongue among them all. And this have they begun to do, and will not leave off from all that they have purposed to do. Come on, let us descend and mingle their tongue even there, that one understands not what another sayeth. Thus the Lord scattered them from thence upon all the earth. And they left off to build the city. Wherefore the name of it is called Babel, because that the Lord there confounded the tongue of all the world. And because that the Lord from thence, scattered them abroad upon all the earth.

2.4 ESTIENNE DOLET

Estienne Dolet (1509–46) was a French humanist printer, translator, and scholar. He encouraged people to read the Bible in the vernacular and published many Calvinist works. Dolet's fame rests on his commentary on the Latin language (1536–8). As a printer he published his own translations and editions of Classical authors, the New Testament and Psalms, as well as work by François Rabelais.

From Estienne Dolet, *La manière de bien traduire d'vne langve en avltre* [*The Way to Translate Well from One Language to Another*], introd. and trans. by James S. Holmes, *Modern Poetry in Translation*, 41–2 (March 1981), 53–6.

[See Sect. 5.3, below for James S. Holmes]

From Holmes's introduction

> For France, as for England, the sixteenth century was a golden age of translation. Unlike the English, though, the French also carried on a lively theoretical discussion about translating: What is it? How should it, how can it be done? Is it the best way, or a good way, to enrich the vernacular literature? The discussion, begun in translators' prefaces in the 1520s and '30s, was contained in the 1540s and '50s in the major *ars poeticas* of the French Renaissance, those of Sebillet (1548), Du Bellay (1549), and Peletier du Mans (1555). In between, in 1540, a brief essay appeared that was, to my knowledge, the earliest independent treatise to be published in a modern European language on the principles of translation (for the epistle on translation written by Luther ten years earlier, however lively, can hardly be considered that). It also marked the first attempt (later often to be repeated) to reduce the art of translating well to a series of rules.
>
> This essay was *La manière de bien traduire d'vne langve en avltre* by the 'native of Orléans' Estienne Dolet (1509–1546), printed by the author in Lyons in 1540 (and reprinted two years later) in a small booklet also containing two other brief essays, on punctuation and accents in French. The three essays were the first in a series planned by Dolet which, when completed, were to comprise a kind of writer's handbook to bear the title *L'Orateur françoys*. The further studies (on grammar, spelling, pronunciation, the origins of certain terms, the art of oratory, and the art of poetry) were never published, perhaps never written: *L'Orateur* was but one project among many in the life of a busy writer/translator/printer/publisher, and Dolet may have postponed its completion a little too long. For in 1546 he was found guilty of heresy—in his way of translating a passage of good Christian Plato!—and hanged then burnt at the stake, not only translation's theorist but its martyr.

La manière, for all its brevity, must have been a gold-mine of advice for the novice aspiring to the new art of *traduction*. The new art, for in France, more markedly than in England, there was a clear break with the medieval traditions of translating, that of crabbed word-for-wordness in learned glossing and that of uncurbed freedom in literary adapting alike. The break, indeed, was so sharp that it was felt necessary to create a new term for the new art: in the 1530s the verb *traduir* was introduced to contrast with such older activities as *translater* and *truchmanter*, and Dolet went on to form the now-standard nouns *traduction* and *traducteur*.

[…]

The Way to Translate Well from One Language into Another

To translate well from one language into another requires in the main five things.

In the first place, the translator must understand perfectly the sense and matter of the author he is translating, for having this understanding he will never be obscure in his translations, and if the author he is translating is difficult in any way he will be able to render him easy and entirely understandable. And without further ado I shall give you an example of this. In the first book of Cicero's *Questiones Tusculanes* is the following passage: 'Animum autem animam etiam ferè nostri declarant nominari. Nam & agere animam, & efflare dicimus; & animosos, & bene animates: & ex animi sententia. Ipse autem animus ab anima dictus est.'

Translating this work of Cicero's,[1] I remarked as follows. 'One need not dwell at all on the difference,' I said, 'between the terms *animus* and *anima*. For the Latin expressions containing the two terms make clear to us that they mean practically the same thing. It is certain that *animus* is said for *anima*, and that the *animus* expresses itself through the *anima*, as if one would say that the vital principle and its manifestations are the source of the spirit, and that same spirit is an effect of the said vital principle.' Tell me, you who know Latin, whether it would have been possible to translate this passage well without a deep understanding of Cicero's sense. Know then that it is important and necessary for every translator to fathom perfectly the sense of the author he is turning from one language into another. And without that he cannot translate reliably and faithfully.

The second thing that is required in translating is that the translator have perfect knowledge of the language of the author he is translating, and be likewise excellent in the language into which he is going to translate. In this way he will not violate or diminish the majesty of the one language or the other. Do you believe that a man can translate any of Cicero's orations well into French if he be not perfect in the Latin and French tongues? Bethink you that every language has its own properties, turns of phrase, expressions, subtleties, and vehemences that are peculiar to it. If the translator ignores the which, he does injustice to the author he is translating, and also to the language he is turning him into, for he does not represent or express the dignity and richness of the two tongues which he has taken in hand.

The third point is that in translating one must not be servile to the point of rendering word for word. And if someone does that, he is proceeding from poverty and lack of wisdom. For if he has the qualities aforesaid (which he needs in order to be a good translator), he will give thought to meanings without regarding the order of words, and set to work in such a way that the author's intention will be expressed while preserving precisely the property of the one and the other language. And it is too great a precision (or should I say stupidity, or ignorance?) to begin one's translation at the beginning of the sentence: if by changing the order of the words you can express the intention of him you are translating, no one can reprove you for it. Here I do not want to overlook the folly of some translators who submit to servitude in lieu of liberty. That is to say, they are so foolish as to make an effort to render line for line or verse for verse. By which mistake they often corrupt the sense of the author they are translating and do not express the grace and perfection of the one and the other language. You should diligently avoid this vice, which demonstrates nothing but the translator's ignorance.

The fourth rule, which I shall give at this place, is more to be observed in languages not reduced to an art than in others. Not yet reduced to a fixed and accepted art I call such languages as French, Italian, Spanish, that of Germany, of England, and other vulgar tongues. Should it therefore happen that you translate a Latin book into one or another of these (even into French), you should avoid adopting words too close to Latin and little used in the past, but be content with the common tongue without introducing any new terms foolishly or out of reprehensible curiousness. If some do so, do not follow them in this, for their arrogance is of no worth, and is not tolerable among the learned. From this do not understand me to say that the translator should entirely abstain from words that are not in common use, for it is well known that the Greek and Latin languages are much richer in terms than is French. The which often forces us to use rare words. But it should be done only out of sheer necessity. I am further well aware that some might say that most terms in the French language have been derived from the Latin, and that if our predecessors had the authority to introduce them, we moderns and our descendants may do the same. Let all that be debated by babblers, but the best thing is to follow the common tongue. I shall treat this point more amply, with further illustration, in my *Orateur françoys*.

Let us now move on to the fifth rule that should be observed by a good translator. The which is of such great import that lacking it any composition is ponderous and displeasing. But what does it consist of? Nothing other than the observation of rhetorical numbers:[2] that is to say, a joining and arranging of terms with such sweetness that not alone the soul is pleased, but also the ear is delighted and never hurt by such harmony of language. I speak of these rhetorical numbers more copiously in my *Orateur*, hence I shall not discourse of them further here. But here I do advise the translator to have a care for them, for without observing numbers one cannot be admirable in any composition whatsoever, and without them thoughts cannot be serious and have their required and legitimate weight. For do you think that it is enough to have correct and elegant terms without a good joining of them? I say to you that it is just as in a confused heap of various kinds of precious stones, the which cannot display their lustre because they are not properly arranged. Or just as when various musical instruments are badly played by performers who are ignorant of the art of music and know little of its tones and measures. In fine, there is little splendour in words if their order and pattern be not as it should be. And for that in times past the Greek orator Isocrates was esteemed above all, and likewise Demosthenes. Among the Latins Mark Tully Cicero was a great observer of numbers. But do not think that orators should observe them more than historiographers. And that being true you will find that Caesar and Sallust kept their numbers no less than Cicero. The conclusion in this regard is that without closely observing numbers an author is nothing, and if he does observe them he cannot fail to become renowned for eloquence, providing he also is precise in his choice of words, serious in his thoughts, and ingenious in his arguments. These are the points of a perfect orator, one truly arrayed in all glory of eloquence.

NOTES

1. Dolet's translation of the *Tusculan Disputations*, which appeared a few years later, in 1543.
2. Dolet's term is 'oratorical numbers'. Today we would probably talk about 'style'.

2.5 JOACHIM DU BELLAY

Joachim du Bellay (1522–60) was a French poet who, with Pierre de Ronsard led the literary group famously known as La Pléiade. The *Déffense* was, in effect, the group's manifesto. Du Bellay met Jacques Peletier who had translated Horace's *Ars poetica* into French. He studied with Ronsard in Paris. His *Déffense*, an important document in the history of translation studies in France and beyond, was published in 1549, in response to Thomas Sebillet's *Art Poétique* (1548). Du Bellay underwrote Horace's pronouncements, as somewhat simplistically relayed by Sebillet, that one should imitate freely, not translate slavishly. He also wrote a number of major sonnet sequences, some of which were translated by Edmund Spenser under the title of *Visions of Belay*, in 1569.

From *La Déffence et Illustration de la langue françayse* (The Defence and Illustration of the French Language) (1549), trans. James Harry Smith and Edd Winfield, in J. H. Smith and E. Winfield (eds.), *The Great Critics: An Anthology of Literary Criticism* (1932; 3rd edn., New York: W. W. Norton, 1951), 165–77

Book I, Chapter III
Why the French language is not so rich as the Greek and Latin

> And if our language is not as copious and rich as the Greek or Latin, that ought not to be imputed to any fault of the language, as if it of itself could ever be other than poor and sterile: but the fault ought rather to be laid to the ignorance of our ancestors, who (as some one has said in speaking of the ancient Romans), holding in higher respect doing well than talking well, and preferring to leave to their posterity the examples, rather than the rules, of virtuous action, deprived themselves of the glory of their high deeds, and us of the fruit of the imitating of them: and in the same way have left us our language so impoverished and naked that it needs the ornaments and (if I may so speak) the pens of others. But who would say that Greek and Latin had always been of that excellence which we see in the times of Homer, of Demosthenes, of Virgil, of Cicero? And if these authors had considered that, for whatever diligence and cultivation might be expended, their languages would never bear fruit, would they have striven so hard as they have to bring them to the point where we now see them? I can say the same thing of our language, which begins now to flower without bearing fruit, or rather, like a plant stem, has not yet flowered, so far is it from having brought forth all the fruit that it might very well produce. This is certainly not the fault of its nature, which is as fertile as are others, but the fault of those who have had it in charge and have not cultivated it sufficiently: like a wild plant, in the very desert where it had come to life, without watering or pruning,

(or in any way protecting it from the brambles and thorns which overshadowed it), they have left it to grow old and almost die. [...]

Chapter IV
That the French language is not as poor as many think it

I do not, nevertheless, think our vernacular, even as it is now, is so vile and abject as the ambitious admirers of Greek and Latin hold it, who do not think anything good, and who reckon even Pitho, goddess of Persuasion, unable to call anything good, except it be in a foreign tongue and one not understood by the common vulgar. And whoever will look well at it will find that our French language is not so poor that it cannot render faithfully what it borrows from others; so unproductive that it cannot, of itself, bear a fruit of good invention, through the industry and diligence of its cultivators [...]

Chapter V
That translations are not enough to give perfection to the French language

Nevertheless this laudable toil of translating does not seem to me alone a sufficient means of raising our vernacular to be the equal and paragon of other more famous languages. I mean to prove this so clearly that no one, I think, will contradict it, without being manifestly a calumniator of the truth. [...] The office then of the orator is to speak eloquently and at length of each thing proposed. But this faculty of speaking thus of all things can only be acquired by the perfect comprehension of knowledge, which has been the first concern of their Roman imitators. It is necessary that these two languages be understood by those who wish to acquire that abundance and that richness of invention, the first and principal piece of harness for the orator. Once arrived at that point, the faithful translators can grandly serve and assist those who have not the unique accomplishment of devoting themselves to foreign languages. [...] I will never believe that one can learn all that from translations, because it is impossible to translate it with the same grace that the author has put into it: because each language has something indefinably individual only to itself; and if you make an effort to render its innate character into another language, observing the law of translation, so that it is not expanded at all beyond the limits of the author, your diction will be constrained, turgid, and without charm. [...]

Chapter VII
How the Romans have enriched their language

If the Romans (some one will say), did not conquer by the labor of translation, by what means then did they so enrich their language, even almost to equality with the Greek? By imitating the better Greek authors, transforming themselves through them, devouring them; and, after having digested them well, converting them into blood and nurture; each taking to himself according to his nature and the argument which he wishes to choose, the best author, all of whose rarest and most exquisite virtues they observe diligently, appropriating and embodying these, like engraftments, as I have said before, to their language. That caused the Romans to build those sublime writings that we delight in and admire so greatly, counting some equal, others preferable, to the Greek. And what I say Cicero and Virgil well prove, whom gladly I always name among, the Latins, of whom the one, as he was entirely given over to the imitation of the Greeks [...]

Chapter VIII
To enlarge French literature by imitation of the ancient Greek and Latin authors

Write himself, then, must he who wishes to enrich his language, write in imitation of the best Greek and Latin authors; at all their best qualities, as at a fair target, direct the aim of his style; for it cannot be doubted that the great part of the art is contained in imitation: and as it was for the ancients most praiseworthy to invent well, so it is most profitable well to imitate them, even for those whose language is not yet plentiful and rich. But he must understand, who wishes to imitate, that it is no easy thing to follow well the excellent qualities of a good author, as if to transform oneself with him, for nature has so wrought even those things which appeal, most similar, that by some mark or feature they can be distinguished. I say this because there are many in every literature who, without penetrating to the secret, innermost part of an author whom they have approached, adapt themselves solely to first appearances, and spend themselves rather on the beauty of words than on the might of the real content. And certainly, as it is not vicious, but greatly laudable, to borrow from another language sentences and words, and to appropriate them to one's own: so it is greatly reprehensible, and must seem odious to every reader of a liberal, cultivated nature, to see, in the same language, such an imitation, such a one as that of some of the learned, even, who think themselves better in proportion as they resemble an Heroet or a Marot. I charge you (o you who desire the enlargement of your literature and its excellence over the others) not to imitate headlong, as recently some one has said, its most famous authors, as ordinarily do the great part of our French poets, a practice certainly as faulty as it is of no worth to our vernacular: for that is not another thing but to give it (o tremendous liberality) what it already has. I would that our language were so rich in models of its own that we should have no need of recourse to others. But if Virgil and Cicero had been content to imitate the authors of their literature, what should we have had of Latin, beyond Ennius or Lucretius, beyond Crassus or Antonius?

Book II, Chapter IV
What types of poems the French poet should choose

Read then, and re-read, o future poet, handle lovingly, night and day, the exemplary Greek and Latin poets; then leave all those old French poets to the Jenix Floranx of Toulouse and to the Puy of Rouen; such as rondeaux, ballades, virelays, chants royal, chansons, and other such groceries, which corrupt the taste of our language and only serve to bear testimony to our ignorance. Devote yourself to pleasant epigrams, not as made today, by a mob of tellers of new tales, who, in a poem of ten lines, are content to have said nothing which gives value in the first nine lines, provided in the tenth there appear a laughable thing: but to the imitation of a Martial, or of some other excellent poet; if liveliness does not satisfy you, mingle the profitable with the pleasant. Distill with a pen flowing and not scabrous, these plaintive elegies, after the example of an Ovid, a Tibullus, and a Propertius, mingling into it sometimes some of these ancient fables, no small ornaments of poetry. Sing to me those odes, yet unknown to the French muse, on a lute well tuned to the sound of the Greek and Roman lyre, not without a single line in which appears some trace of rare but authentic lore. Material for that the praises of the gods and of great men will furnish you, and the deathward tread of earthly things, and the disquiet of youth: love, the unrestrained rites of wine, and all good cheer. Above all, take care that the type of poetry be far away from the vulgar, enriched and made illustrious with proper words and vigorous epithets, adorned with grave sentences, and varied with all manner of colorful and poetic ornaments [. . .]

2.6. LATE TUDOR AND EARLY JACOBEAN TRANSLATION

'The translators of Elizabeth's age [. . .] sailed the wide ocean of knowledge to plant their colonies of the intellect where they might, or to bring back to our English shores some eloquent stranger, whom their industry had taught to speak with our English tongue.'[1] This 'modern' characterization accords well with Philemon Holland's remark (see his preface to the translation of Pliny's *History of the World*, in which he declares that he 'would wish rather and endeavour, by all means to triumph now over the Romans in subduing their literature under the dent of the English pen, in requitall of the conquest some time over this Island, atchieved by the edge of their sword.'

Translators function as the literary arm, so to speak, of the Merchant Adventurers, their primary aim being the endowment of their country with new benefits or goods. At the same time, however, the aggressive promotion of the English tongue suggests a sense of inferiority vis-à-vis other cultures and languages.

Not surprisingly, then, the emphasis is on 'englishing' in a spirit of defiance rather than humility. English might be prepared to accept any benefits thrust upon it, especially in respect to translation from the Classics, advanced cultures of the European mainland, but this was not to say that it was not also excellently endowed.

Policy and statecraft had much to gain from the imports. The pedagogical purpose of translators is expressed in the dedications and prefaces, dedicatees being selected for their influence, and texts chosen for their educational value.

Providing plots for dramatists, translators also sought to provide entertainment for the 'lettered ease', the focus being on content rather than the elaboration of a theoretical position. The dedications and prefaces have, in fact, comparatively little of substance to communicate about methodology beyond stressing the need to write good English, in general reiterating Cicero's ('Nec verbum verbo curabis reddere fidus / Interpres') counsel, not to be bound by the letter of the source text.

The translators set to work 'in a spirit of sublime unconsciousness. [. . .] The prefaces hardly hint at the complexity of the problem' (Whibley). There were very few scholars with the Classical knowledge of, say, a Philemon Holland. Thus North translated Plutarch's *Lives* via Bishop Amyot's French translation. This 'careless method' seemed to some as wholly positive, resulting in translations 'unsoiled by pedantry [. . .] They call up a vision of space and courage and the open air' (Whibley).

---

[1] Charles Whibley, 'Translators', in Sir A.W. Ward and A.R. Waller (eds.), *The Cambridge History of English Literature*, vol. iv. (1950 edn.), 1–50. Further references to this work appear in the text.

The object was to import valuable works in such a way as to render them widely accessible to a new and expanded reading public. But of course at a price, and later readers, while admiring the conviction of earlier performances, might sometimes feel that they were too distant from their sources, domesticating, to the point of falsification. Translation was not an exclusive craft at this time, and indeed many of those involved were also men of the world (Hoby, for instance, was an ambassador; North, too, was active in politics).

In fact, the Elizabethans seemed not to regard plagiarism as intrinsically dishonest. Indications are that a translator might claim as his own what he had put into English. The most significant examples of the direct influence of translation are of course the use Shakespeare made, in his Roman plays, of North's translation of Amyot's French version of Plutarch's *Lives*. At the time, there was an almost total ignorance of Greek drama, but of the Classical dramatists, Seneca was the most popular, largely on account of his 'ingenious maxims', the focus on which is another indication, surely, of the extent to which content, in particular pedagogical elements, dominated. One might, with regard to Shakespeare and other dramatists of the period, link what was got from Seneca (the five-act form of the drama, the blood-and-guts, the soliloquizing), with what was got from North's translation.

As well as philosophers and moralists, like Cicero (or Seneca in his capacity as a moralist), many Greek and Latin historians were translated, but translations from non-Classical languages were also plentiful.

For a comprehensive listing of the several translations from the Classics, see C. H. Conley, *The First English Translators of the Classics* (1927).

Sir Thomas Elyot (1490–1546)

Elyot was an important prose writer, diplomat, and scholar, who learned Latin and Greek, pupil of Sir Thomas More, a member of the Middle Temple. He published *The Boke Named the Governor* (1531), dedicated to Henry VIII. Often reprinted, it dealt with the complete training, according to classical precedents, of a gentleman of the governing class in leadership. He translated works by Isocrates (436–338 BC); advocate of enlightened monarchy, Plutarch (AD c.46–c.127); and Pico della Mirandola (1463–94) etc. His *Dictionary* (1538) was the first book published in English to bear this title, giving an English vernacular equivalent for each Latin word included. It helped to establish English as the language of learned and practical discourse.

Elyot translated 'The Education or Bringinge up of Children' and 'Howe one may Take Profite of his Enmyes'. *The Image of Governance Compiled of the Actes of Alexander Severus*. The preface shows his aim as being a moral one. Elyot was among the first to translate

Lucian's 'Dialogue of Lucian and Diogenes of the Life Harde and Sharpe, and of the Lyfe Tendre and Delicate'. His translations from Latin ranged from a sermon of St Cyprian to the *Rules of a Christian Life* by the Italian Renaissance writer Giovanni Pico della Mirandola. In the preface to his translation of St Cyprian's fourth-century CE *A sweet and Devout Sermon* (1534) (to which is appended a work by Pico della Mirandola), he wrote:

> I have translated this little book: not superstitiously following the letter, which is verily elegant, and therefore the harder to translate into our language, but keeping the sentence and intent of the Author I have attempted (not with little study) to reduce into English the right phrase or form of speaking, used in this treatise, which I have dedicated and sent unto you for a token: that ye shall perceive, that I do not forget you: and that I do unfaynedly love you, not only for our alliance, but also much more for your perseverance in virtue & marks of true faith, praying you to communicate it with our two sisters religious Dorothy & Eleanor, and to join in your prayers to god for me [. . .]

From 'The Letter to Nicocles', (1531), published in *The Doctrinal of Princes* (London: Thomas Bershelet, 1534), translated from Isocrates

> This little book (which in mine opinion) is to be compared in counsel and short sentence with any book, holy scripture excepted, I have translated out of Greek, not presuming to contend with them, which have done the same in Latin: but to the intent only that I would assay, if our English tongue might receive the quick and proper sentences pronounced by the Greeks. And in this experience I have found (if I be not much deceived) that in the form or speaking, used of the Greeks, called in Greek, and also in Latin, *Phrasis* [i.e. style, here applied particularly to conscious art in the construction of sentences] much near approcheth to that, which at this day we use: than the order of the Latin tongue I mean in the sentences, and not in the words: which I doubt not shall be affirmed by them, who sufficiently instructed in all the said three tongues, shall with a good judgement read this work. Wherefore good sister, for as much as I do consider, with what fertility almighty god hath endowed you, to my great comfort, if your children do prosper in virtue and learning, I therefore in times vacant from business & other more serious study, as it were for my solace & recreation have translated for you this little treatise entitled the Education of children, and made by Plutarch the excellent philosopher and master to Trajan, most virtuous & noble of all Emperors: whereby ye shall be marvellously instructed... [. . .] Also of purpose I have omitted to translate some part of this matter, contained as well in the Greek as in the Latin, partly for that it is strange from the experience or usage of this present time, partly that some vices be in those tongues reproved, which ought rather to be unknown, than in a vulgar tongue to be expressed.

Sir Thomas Hoby (1530–1566)

Famous as a linguist and a traveller in Italy and France, Hoby was knighted in 1566. At the time of his death in Paris, he was English ambassador. He made available in English the great Renaissance handbook on the fashioning of a courtier, *Il cortegiano*, by Baldassare Castiglione: *The Courtier* (1561).

From 'The Epistle of the Translator', in Baldasar Castiglione, *the Book of the Courtier . . . done into English by Sir Thomas Hoby* (1561) (The Tudor Translations; London: David Nutt, 1900)

And where it shall not perhaps thoroughly please, by reason my final understanding in the tongue, and less practise in the matters herein contained, is not of force to give it the brightness and full perfection in this our tongue that it hath in the Italian, it shall suffice yet that I have shed my self obedient in the respect a man ought to have towards his betters: and no more can they avoid the blame to charge me withal, than I to undertake it. Beside that, I have declared my good will and well meaning, no less then if my cunning were great, and could extend much farther. [. . .] But in case, judgements now feint, or mine interpretation seem not pithy, but rude, not proper, but cold, there is no more imperfection in this Courtier, then in Cirus himself, in the translation of Xenophon into the Italian or any other tongue, the one as necessary and proper for a Gentleman of the court, as the other for a king. And I shall desire my labour may so be taken well in worth, as I have endeavoured my self to follow the very meaning and words of the Author, without being misled by fantasy, or leaving out any parcel one or other, whereof I know not how some interpreters of this book into other languages can excuse themselves, and the more they be conferred, the more it will perchance appear.

Thomas Newton and Alexander Neville

Senecca, His Tenne Tragedies, edited by Thomas Newton, published in 1581, is the most important Elizabethan translation of Classical drama. Most of the translations date from the 1560s and were first published then. Alexander Neville (1544–1614) is responsible for the *Oedipus*. Other translators are Jasper Heywood, John Studley, Thomas Nuce, and Newton himself. The translations are written primarily in the 'fourteener', take liberties with content, elaborating and explaining Seneca's rhetoric, and adding and adapting episodes and choric interludes.

Alexander Neville (1544–1614) was secretary successively to Archbishops Parker, Grindal, and Whitgift. His brother, Thomas, actively defended Puritanism at Cambridge in 1595. Neville himself was a member of Gray's Inn. The translator, only 16 at the time, states that he translated *Oedipus* to be acted at Cambridge. Opposition to liberal influences was aggressive, as many translators testify. Hence the value of the protection of powerful patrons, in this case Dr Wotton, a member of the Privy Council. Opponents were characterized as Zoilists (i.e. obscurantists, anti-humanists).

Oedipus, the Fifth Tragedy of Seneca (1560), translation by Alexander Neville

From Neville's 'Preface to the Reader'
[This ranges from an apology for liberties taken to an assertion of puritanical moral uplift.]

> Behold here before thy Face (good Reader) the most lamentable Tragedy of that most Unfortunate Prince Oedipus, for thy profit rudely translated. Wonder not at the grossness of the Style: neither yet account the Inventors Diligence disgraced by the Translators Negligence: Who though that he hath sometimes boldly presumed to err from his Author, roving at random where he list: adding and subtracting at pleasure: yet let not that engender disdainful suspicion within thy learned breast. [. . .] Only wish I all men by this Tragical history (for to that intent was it written) to beware of sin: the end whereof is shameful and miserable. [. . .] But whereas no man lives so uprightly, whom slandering tongues leave undiffamed, I refer myself to the Judgement of the wisest, little esteeming the prejudicial mouths of such carping Merchants, which suffer no men's doings almost to escape undefiled. In fine, I beseech all together (if so it might be) to bear with my rudeness, and consider the grossness of our own Country language, which can by no means aspire to the high lofty Latinists style. Mine only intent was to exhort men to embrace Virtue and shun Vice, according to that of the right famous and excellent Poet Virgil
>
> Discite justiciam moniti, et non temnere divos
>
> This obtained: I hold myself thoroughly contented: In the mean season I end: wishing all men to shun Sin, the plain (but most perilous) pathway to perfect infelicity.

From Act 2

[See also Sect. 5.16, below, for Ted Hughes's version of the same passage, as well as literal versions by F. J. Miller and that of David Turner. Oedipus, in dialogue with Creon, Queen Jocasta's brother, unwittingly calls for expiation for the murder of his predecessor King Laius (a murder committed, of course, by himself, after which he married Jocasta, his mother), which may bring about deliverance from the scourge that is afflicting Thebes.]

Let us (sith God commaunds) forthwith some good atonement make
If any way, or means there be their wrathful rage to slake.
Thou God that sits on seate on high, and all the world dost guide,
And thou by whose commaundment the Starres in Skies do glide:
Thou, thou that onely ruler art of Seas, of Floods, and all,
On thee and on thy Godhead great, for these requestes I call.
Who so hath slayne king Laius, oh Jove I do thee pray,
Let thousand ills upon him fall, before his dying day.
Let him no health ne comfort have, but al to crusht with cares,
Consume his wretched yeares in griefe, and though that Death him spares
Awhyle. Yet mischiefes all, at length uppon him light.
With all the evile under Sun, that ugly monster smight.
In exile let him live a Slave, the rated course of life.
In shame, in care, in penury, in daunger and in strife.
Let no man on him pity take, let all men him revile.
Let him his Mothers sacred Bed incestuously defile.
Let him his father kill. And yet let him do mischiefes more.

Arthur Golding (1536–1606)

Educated at Jesus College, Cambridge, Golding entered the service of the Protector Somerset. His most important work was his translation of Ovid's *Metamorphoses* (1565 and 1567). The translation, like Chapman's version of Homer's *Iliad*, is in fourteeners. This was the Ovid Shakespeare read, although, despite his (relatively) 'little Latin', the latter had access to the source text. Golding also produced the first complete translation of Caesar's *Commentaries* (1565), the rest of his translations being of Calvinistic works of religious commentary, including Calvin's own commentaries on the Psalms and Theodore Beza's *Tragedie of Abraham's Sacrifice* (1577). In addition, Golding translated a dialogue of Seneca, *De Beneficiis* (1578), and completed Sir Philip Sidney's translation of Philippe de Mornay's *A Worke concerning the Trewnesse of the Christian Religion* (1604).

The verse introduction to *The Metamorphoses* describes Ovid's work as one of edification, teaching the mutability of all things. Ezra Pound, who called Golding's version the most beautiful book in the English language, wrote: 'He is intent on conveying a meaning, and not on bemusing them with a rumble' ('Notes on Elizabethan Classicists', 1917). In Pound's view: 'The quality of translations declined in measure as the translators ceased to be absorbed in the subject matter of their original.'

Golding's was the first major English translation of *The Metamorphoses*. Its importance can hardly be exaggerated; Shakespeare's allusions to Classical mythology, particularly, of course, in his two narrative poems, are drawn largely from Ovid, both source text and Golding's translation. The Ovidian echoes are more persistent than any others.

From the 'Preface to the Reader', in *Ovid's Metamorphoses: The Arthur Golding Translation 1567*, ed. John Frederick Nimms (Philadelphia: Paul Dry Books, 2000), 427–8

Through Ovids woorke of turned shapes I have with peinfull pace
Past on untill I have him made so well acquainted with our toong
As that he may in English verse as in his owne bee soong.
Wherein although for pleasant style, I cannot make account,
To match myne author, who in that all other dooth surmount:
Yit (gentle Reader) doo I rrust my travail in this cace
May purchase favour in thy sight my dooings to embrace:
Considring what a sea of goodes and Jewelles thou shalt fynd,
Not more delyghtfull to the eare than frutefull to the mynd.
For this doo lerned persons deeme, of Ovids present woorke:
That in no one of all his bookes the which he wrate, doo lurke
Mo darke and secret misteries, mo counselles wyse and sage,
Mo good ensamples, mo reprooves of vyce in youth and age,
Mo fyne inventions to delight, mo matters clerkly knit,
No, nor more straunge varietie to shew a lerned wit.
The high, the lowe: the riche, the poore: the mayster, and the slave:
The mayd, the wife: the man, the chyld: the simple and the brave:
The yoong, the old: the good, the bad: the warriour strong and stout:
The wyse, the foole: the countrie cloyne: the lerned and the lout:
And every other living wight shall in this mirrour see
His whole estate, thoughtes, woordes and deeedes expresly shewd to bee.
[. . .]

Ovid, *The Metamorphoses*, Book IV, lines 440–55, the tale of Salmacis and Hermaphrodite

[The Nymph Salmacis has thrown herself upon the double-sexed, reluctant Hermaphroditus (offspring of Hermes [Mercury] and Aphrodite [Venus]), who is bathing in her pool and for whom she has developed an overwhelming passion. See Sect. 5. 16, below for translation of the same passage by Ted Hughes.]

Arthur Golding's translation

The prize is won (cride Salmacis aloud) he is mine owne.
And therewithall in all post hast she having lightly throwne
Hir garments off, flew to the Poole and cast hir thereinto
And caught him fast between hir armes, for ought that he could doe:
Yea maugre all his wrestling and his struggling to and fro,
She held him still, and kissed him a hundred times and mo.
and willde he nillde he with hir handes she toucht his naked brest:
And now on this side now on that (for all he did resist
And strive to wrest him from hir gripes) she clung unto him fast:
And wound about him like a Snake which snatched up in hast
And being by the Prince of Birdes borne lightly up aloft,
Doth writhe hir selfe about his necke and griping talants oft:
And cast hir taile about his wings displayed in the winde:
Or like as Ivie runnes on trees about the utter rinde:
Or as the Crabfish having caught his enmy in the Seas,
Doth claspe him in on every side with all his crooked cleas.

Prose version by Frank Justus Miller (rev. G. P. Goold), *Ovid Metamorphoses books I–VIII* (1916; Cambridge, Mass: Harvard University Press, 1999), 203–4

'I win, and he is mine!' cries the naiad, and casting off all her garments dives also into the waters: she holds him fast though he strives against her, steals reluctant kisses, fondles him, touches his unwilling breast, clings to him on this side and on that. At length, as he tries his best to break away from her, she wraps him round with her embrace, as a serpent, when the king of birds has caught her and is bearing her on high: which, hanging from his claws, wraps her folds about his head and feet and entangles his flapping wings with her tail: or as the ivy oft-times embraces great trunks of trees, or as the sea-polyp holds its enemy caught beneath the sea, its tentacles embracing him on every side.

Thomas Wilson (1525?–1581)

Thomas Wilson was a scholar at King's College, Cambridge. Member of Parliament, he served as Secretary of State (1577–81). From 1553 Wilson was also a staunch adherent of the Dudley family (John Dudley, Duke of Nothumberland was a patron of the new learning). He was a close friend of the noted Greek scholar and leading Cambridge humanist Sir John Cheeke and was one of the Protestant exiles during the time of Queen Mary, when

Protestantism and the new learning were banned. Wilson recalls Cheeke's concern for English exiles and his reading to and interpreting for them 'certaine orations of Demosthenes in Greeke …'. He translated Quintilian, Aristotle, and Cicero, *Arte of Rhetorique* (1553), and Demosthenes *Orations* (1570), published just after the Catholic uprising in 1569.

Wilson's patron was none other than Queen Elizabeth's 'principall Secretarie', Sir William Cecil. Whether it be true that Wilson had translated Demosthenes' orations at the instance of the government to strengthen the country's morale during a time of threatened interference from Spain, the political purpose of the translation is clearly proclaimed on the title page, Philip of Macedon being code for Philip of Spain. The dedication and other prefatory matter pointedly refer to love of country and the need for loyalty, especially at so critical a moment in the national history.

While stressing the difficulty of rendering Demosthenes in English (or in Latin) Wilson insists that English is as good an instrument as any, seeing himself as steering a course between the apparently too literal translation and the too free. He castigates those who criticize translations without themselves attempting to translate.

Thomas Wilson from Dedication, *Three Orations of Demosthenes* (London: imprinted by Henrie Denhan, 1570)

Yea, the more that I look upon this Orator to bring his sentences and words known to our common speech and language: the more doe I find him hard and unable to be translated, according to the excellence of his tongue. And many times I have been ashamed of my self, when I compared his Greek and my English together. And no marvel neither. For the Latin translators being otherwise most excellent men, have not always satisfied themselves, much less answered to their charge and enterprise in the opinion of others that compared their doings and the Greek together. […] For this must I needs confess, that I am altogether unable to doe so in English, as the excellence of this orator deserveth in Greek. And yet the cunning is no less, and the praise as great in my judgement to translate any thing excellently into English, as into any other language. […] And in deed my labour can be no hurt to any body, except it be to my self. For the Greek is as it was […]. And such as have no Greek, may go to the Latin for all my doings, or any other translation else in any other strange tongue or language. For as I do hear say, certain pieces of Demosthenes are translated also into divers other tongues. But such as are grieved with translated books, are like to them that eating fine Manchet, are angry with others that feed on Cheate bread. And yet God knoweth men would as gladly eat Manchet as they, if they had it. But all can not wear Velvet, or feed with the best, and therefore such are contented for necesity's sake to wear our Country cloth, and to take themselves to hard fare, that can have no better. But what reason have they I pray you that will not suffer men to write reason as well as to speak reason? for this I dare say, that even those men, if they have any reason with them at all, will use in their proofs upon weighty matters, the arguments of Demosthenes or reasons of like value. And may not I or any other set down those reasons by pen, in our English language, the which are uttered daily in our common speech, by men of understanding? [...] And thus having done my voluntary task, I desire none other thanks for all my labour and travail herein, but your favourable defence against certain, that will doe nothing themselves, and yet will find fault with all things, being in nature Drones, and no Bees: Lubbers and no learners: as void of sound judgement and understanding, as they are out of reason curious judges, over the travail and pains taking of others. But who can stop these open mouthed talkers? empty vessels make the greatest sound, and ring out a hollow noise to small purpose, and so do these that have the least skill and smallest knowledge, make the mightiest brag, and are the boldest of all others without cause or reason god he knoweth. Of which croking paddocks, and manifest overweeners of themselves: I do make very little account, or no reckoning at all. [...]

Sir Thomas North (1539–1602/3)

Son of the first Baron North, lawyer and politician, Thomas North was educated at Peterhouse, Cambridge and Lincoln's Inn. He was knighted for his part in preparations to withstand possible invasion at the time of the Armada. It is possible or even likely that North met Bishop Amyot, the celebrated French translator of Plutarch, who had been appointed Grand Almoner of France, when he visited the country in the retinue of his brother, on an embassy to the French court.

In addition to his translation of Plutarch, North also translated *The Morall Philosophie of Doni*, and *The Diall of Princes*, a translation of Antonio de Guevara's *Libro dureo de Marco aurelio* (1528), a spurious autobiography, expanded in the political treatise the *Relox de principes* (1529). Plutarch was translated via the French version of the Greek original by Amyot (1569). It is arguable that, since he was working from an almost contemporary French intermediary, North might have been somewhat less inclined to adhere closely to the 'source' text. His style was intensely dramatic, which above all is what commended it to Shakespeare, who drew freely on it in his three Roman tragedies (*Julius Caesar, Anthony and Cleopatra*, and *Coriolanus*). The perceived importance of the source is of course implicit in the dedication of the translation to Queen Elizabeth herself. F. O. Matthiessen (*Translation: An Elizabethan Art*, 1931) regarded North's translation of Plutarch as the earliest great masterpiece of English prose, after Malory's *Morte D'Arthur* and the *Book of Common Prayer*.

From the Dedication 'To the Most High and Mighty Princess Elizabeth, By the Grace of God, of England, France and Ireland Queen, Defender of the Faith: etc.', in *Plutarch's Lives of the Noble Grecians and Romans, Englished by Sir Thomas North* **(1579; London: David Nutt, 1896)**

How many examples shall your subjects read here, of several persons, and whole armies, of noble and base, of young and olde, that both by sea and land, at home and abroad, have strained their wits, not regarded their states, ventured their persons, cast away their lives, not only for the honour and safety, but also for the pleasure of their Princes?

Then well may the Readers think, if they have done this for heathen Kings, what should we do for Christian Princes? If they have done this for glory, what should we do for religion? if they have done this without hope of heaven, what should we do that look for immortality? And so adding the encouragement of these examples, to the forwardness of their Owen dispositions: what service is there in war, what honour in peace, which they will not be ready to doe, for their worthy Queen?

A comparison between Amyot, North, and a more recent literal translation (Bernadotte Perrin, The Loeb Classical Library) of Plutarch's *Parallel Lives,* **'Life of Brutus'**

Perrin's translation

And it is said that Caesar, when he first heard Brutus speak in public, said to his friends: 'I know not what this young man wants, but all that he wants he wants very much.' For the weight of his character, and the fact that no one found it easy to make him listen to appeals for favour, but that he accomplished his ends by reasoning and the adoption of noble principles, made his efforts, withersoever directed, powerful and efficacious.

North's translation

They say also that Caesar said, when he heard Brutus plead; 'I know not,' said he, 'what this young man would; but, what he would, he willeth it vehemently.' For, as Brutus' gravity and constant mind would not grant all men their requests that sued unto him, but being moved with reason and discretion did always incline to that which was good and honest, even so, when it was moved to follow any matter, he used a kind of forcible and vehement persuasion that calmed not till he had obtained his desire.

[North's translation is highly colloquial, for example, his use of doublets for single words, not so much to enhance the meaning as for sound. In general, his changes were in the interest of precise detailing and dramatic effect. Where Amyot is dignified and restrained, North is often picturesquely vigorous, using the language of direct instead of indirect speech, drawing on proverbial phrases etc. His dramatization of the text, of course, made it particularly attractive for the playwright. North gave Shakespeare not only material for plots but living characters and very often the very words they were likely to use:]

Amyot: Mais ilz ne disent pas la verite
Perrin: But it is not so
North: But this holdeth no water

Amyot: luy donna une couple de soufflets
Perrin: sprang up and gave him a thrashing
North: rose up on his feet and gave him two good whirts on the ear.

[handwritten: adding much detail]

Comparison between North and Shakespeare in *Coriolanus*

[Shakespeare drew both plot and a good deal of the actual wording from North's translation. In *Coriolanus*, for instance, his indebtedness to North is transparent, although, as in the passage below, it is also clear that Shakespeare does not simply plagiarize but adds some significant touches, heightening the text (e.g. 'Whoop'd out of Rome') at moments crucial to the plot. He was able to use North's text as a basis, at certain points almost as if they were joint-authors. No doubt the pressure under which he was working rendered him less likely to have qualms about such borrowings. In *Coriolanus*, a late play, the principal character resembles Othello in his nobility and naivety. He is brought low by the baseness and treachery of others. Shakespeare takes the substance of the plot from North. It is also noticeable that much of North's text falls naturally into heroic metre.]

Shakespeare, Coriolanus*, Act IV, Scene v*

CORIOLANUS (unmuffling). If, Tullus,
Not yet thou know'st me, and seeing me, dost not
Think me for the man I am, necessity
Commands me name myself . . .
My name is Caius Marcius, who hath done
to thee particularly, and to all the Volsces,
Great hurt and mischief; thereto witness may
My surname, Coriolanus: the painful service,
The extreme dangers, and the drops of blood
Shed for my thankless country, are requited
But with that surname; a good memory,
And witness of the malice and displeasure
Which thou shouldst bear me: only that name remains;
The cruelty and envy of the people,

Permitted by our dastard nobles, who
Have all forsook me, hath devour'd the rest;
And suffer'd me by the voice of slaves to be
Whoop'd out of Rome. Now this extremity
Hath brought me to thy hearth; not out of hope,
Mistake me not, to save my life; for if
I had fear'd death, of all the men i' the world
I would have 'voided thee; but in mere spite
To be full quit of those my banishers,
Stand I before thee here ...

North

Then Martius unmuffled himself, and after he had paused a while, making no answer, he said unto him: If thou knowest me not yet, Tullus, and seeing me, dost not perhaps believe me to be the man I am in deed, I must of necessity bewraye my self to be that I am. I am Caius Martius, who hath done to thy self particularly, and to all the Volsces generally, great hurt and mischief, which I cannot deny for my surname of Coriolanus that I bear. For I never had other benefit nor recompense, of all the true and painful service I have done, and the extreme dangers I have been in, but this only surname: a good memory and witness, of the malice and displeasure thou showldest bear me. In deed the name only remaineth with me: for the rest, the envy and cruelty of the people of Rome have taken from me, by the sufferance of the dastardly nobility and magistrates, who have forsaken me, and let me be banished by the people. This extremity hath now driven me to come as a poor suitor, to take thy chimney hearth, not out of any hope I have to save my life thereby. For if I had feared death, I would not have come hither to put my life in hazard: but prickt forward with spite and desire I have to be revenged of them that thus have banished me.

John Florio (1553–1625)

Giovanni or John Florio, translator and lexicographer, was the son of an Italian Protestant refugee. His *A World of Words*, a vast folio Italian–English dictionary, published in 1598, was a landmark and standard throughout the seventeenth century. This was followed by *The Essays, or Moral, Politic, and Military Discourse of Lo. Michael de Montaigne* (1595; 1603). Under James I, Florio became tutor to Prince Henry. A passionate enthusiast about words, he wrote in euphuistic style (with a multitude of compound words, doublings, etc). Shakespeare was greatly influenced by the Montaigne translation. Whibley's comment that it has 'neither the sentiment of North, nor the scholarship of Holland', seems too negative (See also F. O. Matthiessen, *Translation, An Elizabethan Art* (Harvard, 1931), 'Florio's Montaigne' (1603) for additional comments.)

From Florio's 'Dedication to the second book' *Essays of Montaigne* **(London: V. Sims, 1603)**

Montaigne was worth translating, because of his 'so pleasing passages, so judicious discourses, so delightsome varieties, so persuasive conclusions, such learning of all sortes, and above all, so elegant a French style'

From *Firste Fruites* (London: Thomas Dawson, for Thomas Woodcocke, 1578)

[Florio expresses his dissatisfaction with English.]

It doth not like me at all, because it is a language confused, bepeesed with many tongues: it taketh many words of the latin, & more from the French, & more from the Italian, and many more from the Dutch, some also from the Greek & from the Britai, so that if every language had his own words again, there would but a few remain for Englishmen, and yet every day they add. Take a book and read, but mark well, and you shall not read four words together of true English.

[The translation demonstrates his passionate delight in words. Added words are italicized in the following example:]

M. J'en ay veu engloutir du sable, de la cendre, & se travailler à point nommé de ruiner leur estomac, pour acquerir les pasles couleurs."

F. I have seen some swallow gravell, ashes, *coales*, *dust*, *tallow*, *candles*, and for the-nonce, labour and *toyle* themselves to spoile their stomacke, only to get a pale-*bleake* colour.

"These boistrous billows" for "ces flots"

M. Je ne voy rien autour de moy que couvert & masqué

F. I see nothing about me, but *inscrutable hearts*, *hollow mindes*, fained *looks*, dissembled *speeches*, and *counterfeit actions*.

George Chapman (1559/60–1634)

Chapman wrote much poetry and drama, but is best known for his translations of Homer. He published the first seven books of the *Iliad* in 1598, followed by the whole work (1611), the *Odyssey* (1614–15) and Homeric 'Hymns' (1616), as well as translations from Petrarch

(1612), Musaeus (1616), Hesiod (1618), and Juvenal (1629). To some extent superseded by Pope's Homer, Chapman's was the subject of a celebrated poem by John Keats ('On First Looking Into Chapman's Homer', 1816) and remained in print.

Keats's resonant sonnet is of interest, taking Chapman at his word, and testifying to the translation's enduring freshness and originality:

> Oft of one wide expanse had I been told
>   That deep-brow'd Homer ruled as his demesne;
>   Yet did I never breathe its pure serene
> Till I heard Chapman speak out loud and bold:
> Then felt I like some watcher of the skies
>   When a new planet swims into his ken [...]

Chapman + Keats' [handwritten annotation]

Chapman's observations on translation in the verse preface to the 1611 *Iliad*, 'To The Reader', hardly describe his method, but embody a passionate defence of Homer and a defiant attack on the translator's detractors. Chapman's insistence on non-literalism makes it clear that accusations of inaccuracy were a staple of criticism. As regards his tendency to elaborate, Chapman points to his predecessors. Only poetic licence or inspiration can help in the translation of poetry. He does not argue but simply affirms the appropriateness of the fourteener (fourteen-syllable line). Regarding the use of fourteeners in the *Iliad* as against pentametric couplets in the *Odyssey*, the longer line works well enough if the enjambments, varying the otherwise jog-trot alternation of 4-stress 3-stress hemistiches, are carefully observed.

The same indulgence may be granted Chapman which he would claim for Homer, that he 'not bee read for a few lynes with leaves turned over capriciously in dismembred fractions, but throughout, the whole drift, weight and height of his workes set before the apprensive eye of his judge.'

Chapman translated directly from the original, with errors due to ignorance or haste. He vindicates his 'varietie of new wordes'. If 'my countrey language were an usurer, he would thank me for enriching him'. He dismisses Scaliger, the greatest Classical scholar of the time, as 'soul-blind Scaliger', and compares Virgil and Homer to the disadvantage of the former, Homer's poem being 'writ from a free fury', whereas Virgil's comes out of a 'courtly, laborious, and altogether imitatory spirit'.

> I must confesse I hardly dare referre
>   To reading judgements, since so generally
> Custome hath made even th'ablest Agents erre
>   In these translations: all so much apply
> Their paines and cunning word for word to render

Their patient authors, when they may as well
Make fish with fowle, Camels with Whales engender,
   Or their tongues' speech in other mouths compell.
For even as different a production
   Aske Greeke and English, since, as they in sounds
And letters shunne one forme and unison,
   So have their sense and elegancie bounds
In their distinguisht natures, and require
   Onely a judgement to make both consent
In sense and elocution, and aspire
   As well to reach the spirit that was spent
In his example, as with arte to pierce
   His Grammar and etymologie of words.
But as great Clerkes can write no English verse
   Because (alas! great Clerks) English affords,
Say they, no height nor copie—a rude toung
   (Since 'tis their Native)—but in Greeke or Latin
Their writs are rare, for thence true Poesie sprong—
   Though them (Truth knowes) they have but skil to chat-in
Compar'd with that they might say in their owne,
   Since thither th'other's full soule cannot make
The ample transmigration to be showne
   In Nature-loving Poesie, so the brake
That those Translatours sticke in that affect
   Their word-for-word tradujctions (where they lose
The free grace of their naturall Dialect
   And shame their authors with a forced Glose)
I laugh to see—and yet as much abhorre
   More licence from the words than may expresse
Their full compression and make cleare the Author.
From whose truth if you thinke my feet digresse
[. . .]
   (In some maine parts) that were his Commentars.
But (as the illustration of the Sunne
   Should be attempted by the erring starres)

> They fail'd to search his deepe and treasurous hart.
>   The cause was since they wanted the fit key
> Of Nature, in their down-right strength of Art,
>   With Poesie to open Poesie—
> Which in my Poeme of the mysteries
>   Reveal'd in Homer I will clearly prove,
> Till whose neere birth suspend your Calumnies
>   And farre-wide imputations of selfe love.

From Homer, *Odyssey*, Book XI

[See other versions of the same passage elsewhere in the volume.]

From *The Odysseys of Homer Together With The Shorter Poems Translated According To The Greek By George Chapman* (1614–15)

> Arriv'd now at our ship, we launch'd, and set
> Our mast up, put forth sail, and in did get
> Our late-got cattle. Up our sails, we went
> My wayward fellows mourning now th'event.
> A good companion yet, a foreright wind,
> Circe (the excellent utt'rer of her mind)
> Supplied our murmuring consorts with, that was
> Both speed and guide to our adventurous pass.
> All day our sails stood to the winds, and made
> Our voyage prosp'rous. Sun then set, and shade
> All ways obscuring, on the bounds we fell
> Of deep Oceanus, where people dwell
> Whom a perpetual cloud obscures outright,
> To whom the cheerful sun lends never light,
> Nor when he mounts the star-sustaining heaven,
> Nor when he stoops earth, and sets up the even,
> But night holds fix'd wings, feather'd all with banes,
> Above those most unblest Cimmerians.
> Here drew we up our ship, our sheep withdrew,
> And walk'd the shore till we attain'd the view
> Of that sad region Circe had foreshow'd [...]

Greek source text and *ad verbum* translation by Gottskalk Jensson

Homer, *Odyssey*, II. 1–22

Αὐτὰρ ἐπεί ῥ' ἐπὶ νῆα κατήλθομεν ἠδὲ θάλασσαν,
νῆα μὲν ἂρ πάμπρωτον ἐρύσσαμεν εἰς ἅλα δῖαν,
ἐν δ' ἱστὸν τιθέμεσθα καὶ ἱστία νηΐ μελαίνῃ,
ἐν δὲ τὰ μῆλα λαβόντες ἐβήσαμεν, ἂν δὲ καὶ αὐτοὶ
βαίνομεν ἀχνύμενοι, θαλερὸν κατὰ δάκρυ χέοντες.
ἡμῖν δ' αὖ κατόπισθε νεὸς κυανοπρῴροιο
ἴκμενον οὖρον ἵει πλησίστιον, ἐσθλὸν ἑταῖρον,
Κίρκη ἐϋπλόκαμος, δεινὴ θεὸς αὐδήεσσα.
ἡμεῖς δ' ὅπλα ἕκαστα πονησάμενοι κατὰ νῆα
ἥμεθα· τὴν δ' ἄνεμός τε κυβερνήτης τ' ἴθυνε.
τῆς δὲ πανημερίης τέταθ' ἱστία ποντοπορούσης.
δύσετό τ' ἠέλιος σκιόωντό τε πᾶσαι ἀγυιαί·
ἡ δ' ἐς πείραθ' ἵκανε βαθυρρόου Ὠκεανοῖο.
ἔνθα δὲ Κιμμερίων ἀνδρῶν δῆμός τε πόλις τε,
ἠέρι καὶ νεφέλῃ κεκαλυμμένοι· οὐδέ ποτ' αὐτοὺς
Ἠέλιος φαέθων καταδέρκεται ἀκτίνεσσιν,
οὔθ' ὁπότ' ἂν στείχῃσι πρὸς οὐρανὸν ἀστερόεντα,
οὔθ' ὅτ' ἂν ἂψ ἐπὶ γαῖαν ἀπ' οὐρανόθεν προτράπηται,
ἀλλ' ἐπὶ νὺξ ὀλοὴ τέταται δειλοῖσι βροτοῖσι.
νῆα μὲν ἔνθ' ἐλθόντες ἐκέλσαμεν, ἐκ δὲ τὰ μῆλα
εἱλόμεθ'· αὐτοὶ δ' αὖτε παρὰ ῥόον Ὠκεανοῖο
ᾔομεν, ὄφρ' ἐς χῶρον ἀφικόμεθ', ὃν φράσε Κίρκη.

English crib

'But when we had come down to the ship and the sea, we first of all drew the ship into the divine sea, and set the mast and the sail in the black ship, and took the sheep and put them aboard, and ourselves embarked sorrowing, shedding big tears. And for us fair-haired Kirke, dread goddess of human speech, sent behind the dark-prowed ship a favourable wind to fill the sail, a good companion. Having taken care of every bit of tackle throughout the ship, we sat down; the wind and the helmsman steered her. All day long the sail was stretched as she cruised over the sea. And the sun set and all roads were darkened; and she came to the edges of deep-flowing Okeanos. There is the people and city of Kimmerian men, wrapped in mist and cloud; and never does the shining sun look down upon them with rays, either when climbing the starry heaven or when going on to earth from heaven, but destructive night is stretched over poor mortals. Coming to this place we beached the ship, and took out the sheep; and ourselves went along the stream of Okeanos, until we came to the place, which Kirke had pointed out.'

Philemon Holland (1552–1637)

Even more prolific than North, Holland went directly to the Classical source, rather than using intermediaries, but loved ornament. He was no pedant, unashamedly clothing his Classical authors in Elizabethan garb: 'if I have called again into use some old words, let it be attributed to the love of my country language: if the sentence be not so concise, couched and knit together as the originall, loth I was to be obscure and darke: have I not Englished every word aptly? Each nation hath several manners, yea, and tearmes appropriate by themselves.' Still, Holland, did also go in for much ornament, as for instance with regard to Pliny's 'Historie of the World' (1634), where famously he expressed the ambition 'by all means to triumph now over the Romans in subduing their literature under the dent of the English pen, in requital of the conquest some time over this Island, achieved by the edge of their sword.' There have been understandably few attempts to translate Pliny the Elder's enormous *Naturalis Historia* (Natural History).[1] Nearly three centuries were to pass before there was another version.

[1] See Peter France (ed.), The Oxford Guide to Literature in English Translation (Oxford: OUP, (2000), 539.)

Holland, like other translators of the period makes the source text accessible to his contemporaries. Thus, the opening of his translation of Plutarch's *Moralia*, the section on 'The Education of Children', in the fairly literal Loeb edition runs: 'Let us consider what may be said of the education of freeborn children, and what advantages they should enjoy to give them a sound character when they grow up. It is perhaps better to begin with their parentage first'; Holland has: 'Ereasmuch as we are to consider what may be said as touching the education of children, free born and descended from gentle blood, how and by what discipline they may become honest and virtuous, we shall perhaps treat hereof the better, if we begin at their generation and nativity.'

Livy *Ab urbe condita* (From the Foundation of the City), 142 books covering seven-and-a-half centuries of Roman history; first complete translation of the thirty-five surviving books by Philemon Holland

Dedication to Queen Elizabeth

From Preface to the Reader

I framed my pen, not to any affected phrase, but to a mean and popular style [...] if the sentence be not so concise, couched and knit together, as the original, loth I was to be obscure and dark.

2.7. RENAISSANCE LATIN TRANSLATION IN ENGLAND

Latin was the lingua franca of European intellectual life for centuries. It moved north across Europe along with institutional Christianity, which reached the shores of Iceland in the year 1000. From around that time and into the seventeenth century—and to a degree even into the nineteenth—Latin was a language in which intellectuals pursued a dialogue across borders, from the Mediterranean to the Arctic Ocean, and across time, for certain areas of Latin discourse established themselves as traditions which were very much kept alive from one era to another.

This is a part of European cultural legacy which is often downplayed in national histories—including literary histories—and sometimes passed over in relative silence, just like the vital role of Arab scholars in preserving and mediating Classical European learning after the demise of Ancient Greece and Rome, in many cases passing it back into Europe through the cross-cultural efforts of translators in Spain, under Muslim leadership.

Translation was also a central activity in European Latinity. The most powerful text of this period was a translation: the Vulgate version of the Bible. And while that translation was often considered a kind of holy 'original'—the very core of the Catholic Church—and the translation of holy scripture into other languages could involve severe complications and penalties, the Church encouraged and relied on the translation of various other texts.

With the onset of the Renaissance, translation also comes to figure prominently in other areas of scholarship, literature, politics, and social life. Translation from and into Latin becomes a central undertaking. Latin is the source language of countless translations into the various vernacular tongues that now take on new cultural roles. But since Latin is an international medium, shared by intellectuals in different countries, it was an obvious language to translate into, not only the great library of Greek texts from an extensive period, but also salient documents written in other languages. Of course, many documents of all kinds were also composed in Latin by individuals in various parts of Europe. One of the key works of English literature, Thomas More's *Utopia* (1516), was written in Latin. In fact, the same individual might on different occasions write in the respective vernacular, in Latin, or translate texts from one to the other. This bilingual aspect of the intellectual pursuit is one of the most striking characteristics of this period in European cultural history.

Compiled on the basis of J. W. Binns's *Intellectual Culture in Elizabethan and Jacobean England: The Latin Writings of the Age* (ARCA Classical and Medieval Texts, Papers and Monographs, 24; Leeds: Francis Cairns Publications Ltd., 1990).

The following quotations and excerpts are taken from the book *Intellectual Culture in Elizabethan and Jacobean England: The Latin Writings of the Age* (ARCA Classical and Medieval Texts, Papers and Monographs 24; Leeds: Francis Cairns (Publications) Ltd. 1990), by Dr J. W. Binns, formerly of the Centre for Medieval Studies, at the University of York, England. In this impressive work, Professor Binns gives a detailed account of Latin writings in Renaissance England. He points out that alongside the literary activity in the English language at this time, there was a vast but now 'virtually unremarked' quantity of writing in Latin 'that stands at the centre of the revival of English intellectual life in the years of Elizabeth and James. About one in ten of the items printed in England between *c.*1550–1640 is in Latin. This may not seem a large percentage, but the importance of this forgotten tenth is greater than the proportion might suggest, because far more vernacular than Latin items were ephemeral and of slight intellectual interest [. . .] whereas Latin writings were usually serious in purpose and often intended for posterity' (pp. 1–2).

In our time, when English seems to be headed for a global linguistic dominance in a number of ways, it puts things into a striking historical perspective to be reminded that Latin, this 'dead language', used to have such a status in Europe, while English, in the age of Shakespeare, to the 'scholarly continental public', was 'a minor and unknown tongue' (p. 241). 'So it made sense for any serious English writer to write in Latin, a language of unquestioned prestige, which could be read by intellectuals all over Europe, which had endured pre-eminent for a millennium and a half, and which there was no reason to doubt would last for ever' (p. 3). In some cases the act of writing in or translating into Latin, as Binns points out, was spurred by burning contemporary, ideological and theological issues, especially when spokesmen of the Church of England sought to justify the Reformation and defend their church against Catholics on the Continent (p. 242).

Binns gives a scholarly account of poetry and drama, as well as the various non-fictional and scholarly works, composed by English writers in Latin. But he also covers the 'English' translations into Latin of texts originally written in Greek or in English and other European vernaculars. Parts of this discussion are included below, along with Binns's translation of comments made by these translators on their work.[1] Judging by these comments, no single method appears to reign supreme, but they offer valuable insights into textual and contextual matters of translation. The collage concludes with Binns's summary of a treatise written in Latin by one of the leading translators, Laurence Humphrey, a significant work in the history of translation theory, but one that has gone largely unnoticed. Humphrey's tripartite notion of translation methods pre-dates by more than a century Dryden's similar and much-quoted description of the different kinds of translation, although what Humphrey understood by 'imitation' is somewhat different, relating to the Classical pedagogical notion, rather than extravagant self-expression.

From J. W. Binns, *Intellectual Culture in Elizabethan and Jacobean England: The Latin Writings of the Age* (ARCA Classical and Medieval Texts, Papers and Monographs 24; Leeds: Francis Cairns (Publications) Ltd., 1990)

John Christopherson and Laurence Humphrey

The most prominent class of Greek writers to engage the attention of English translators were the Greek Fathers, together with some early Christian and Byzantine religious writings. Here the motive for translation is clearly theological: to make available to the wider Latinate audience important religious and theological texts. In this area the work of John Christopherson is prominent.

The Latin translations by John Christopherson of Eusebius' *Historia ecclesiastica* and *De vita Constantini*, of Socrates' *Historia ecclesiastica* and of the writings on Church history of Theodoretus, Theodore, Sozomen, and Evagrius Scholasticus were first printed in Louvain in 1569 under the title *Historia ecclesiastica scriptores graeci* [. . .]. Christopherson, a Catholic, had been made Master of Trinity College, Cambridge, in the reign of Queen Mary, to whom he had been appointed chaplain and confessor. He died in 1558 [. . .].

In an introductory 'Prooemium Interpretis', Christopherson himself writes that he is translating the works of the Greek Fathers to make more widely known their spiritual discipline and moral precepts, and so that the excellent examples of their lives might become better known. [. . .]

Christopherson goes on to say that those who publish fine editions of the Greek and Latin Fathers have conferred a great blessing on the Church. Therefore he had decided to embark upon his present work:

> I consider that it would be not inconvenient for me to interpret this work, and that it would be not unpleasant for others to read: so long as I turned it into Latin in such a way as both to express truly the sense and meaning of the author, and to adumbrate its form of speech and harmony by imitating them, so that the whole work might be articulated by features either identical to, or else not greatly dissimilar from, the original.

Christopherson continues to give further revealing glimpses of his thought in this 'Prooemium', which is in effect a miniature treatise on the Art of Translation. In translating from Greek into Latin, Christopherson says that four things are desirable:

> In translating Greek, it seems to me, contemplating the matter with keen attention, that four things in particular are required: a true explanation of sense and meaning, good latinity, harmony, and that perspicuity of speech which I have mentioned. The first is usually held to be relevant for fidelity, the second for delight, the third for the judgement of the ears, the fourth for the understanding. For who will believe if

the meaning is suspect? Who will take pleasure in reading, if the speech is rude and unpolished? Whose ears will not be disgusted, if the speech is disconnected and confused? Whom will it not deter, if it seems obscure and shrouded by darkness? And although those ideals are in the highest degree both useful and necessary in translating the books of philosophers, orators and poets, who have written about the humane disciplines and polite literature, yet in rendering the writings of saints and apostles, the things which are handed down by them about our religion ought rightly to be considered no less necessary and much more useful. For although in translating the Scriptures the order of the words should be retained, as St Jerome says, because it is a mystery: yet in the translation of other Greek writings, on the same authority of Jerome (when he cites and imitates Cicero), we should translate not word for word, but meaning for meaning.

In other words, says Christopherson, the meaning of the text ought not to be subordin-ated to a good style, desirable though the latter may be. On the other hand, inflexible adherence to the letter rather than the spirit is to be avoided. True eloquence, he continues, is not empty verbalising, but the articulation of wisdom:

> For eloquence is not that empty and almost puerile verbal volubility which often insolently advances itself among the common people, but wisdom which speaking eloquently and copiously glides into the minds of the prudent with sweetness. For if you take away wisdom, the death of eloquence will follow.

(pp. 218–21)

Laurence Humphrey, (1527?-1590), President of Magdalen College, Oxford, was one of the most learned of the Latin writers of Elizabethan England. [. . .]

Laurence Humphrey's translation of St Cyril of Alexandria's *Commentariorum in Hesaiam prophetam libri quinque* was printed at Basle, 1563, and was dedicated to Queen Elizabeth, whilst his translation of the *Disputatio contra Marcionistas*, attributed to Origen, appeared in the complete Latin translation of Origen by a variety of hands published at Basle in 1571 and reprinted at Paris in 1572–4 and 1604. The title page of the second volume claims Humphrey's Latin version as the first available anywhere (*nunc primum latine redditi per Laurentium Humfridum Anglum*). Humphrey's translation is dedicated on 6 August 1557 to an otherwise obscure Sir Anthony Cave, and Humphrey writes in the dedication that he had translated the work from a Greek codex belonging to Froben:

> I translated the work from the Greek from a manuscript codex of Froben, rendering the meaning not the words, having regard not to the number of words but to their weight, everywhere taking precautions to the best of my ability that the meaning of the Greek should not be overthrown, as usually happens, and perish in translation.

In this dedication Humphrey proclaims the ethical and educational virtue of the Greek Fathers, both in inculcating good morality and in their rhetorical style. It was, we may be sure, the passionate interest of these translators in morals and in schooling that drew them to such works:

> I wish that the *Homilies* of Chrysostom and the speeches of Gregory and of Basil the Great could occupy some place (in schools) since not only are they bestrewn and crammed with metaphors, similes, and proverbs, but they excel in all kinds of doctrine and learning.
>
> (pp. 224–5)

Patrick Young and Richard Brett

The translation by Patrick Young, the biblical scholar and librarian to James I and Charles I, of Pope Clement I's (fl. A.D. 96) *Clementis ad Corinthios epistola prior*, appeared at Oxford in 1633, and was dedicated to King Charles. [. . .]. Young says that his translation is a plain one, and maintains that it is strictly faithful and literal:

> Subtracting nothing, and adding nothing of my own, not a syllable, not a letter, . . . I have as far as was possible translated most faithfully.

His version was not distinguished for elegance of style:

> If you seek for the charm of eloquence, or the splendour of rhetorical speech in my version you will do so in vain. I aimed in this matter at fidelity, not ornament, or verbal elegance.
>
> (p. 226)

In 1597, Richard Brett, Fellow of Lincoln College, Oxford, published a Latin translation of a work by Simeon Metaphrastes, a Byzantine writer from Constantinople who flourished at the beginning of the tenth century, the *Vitae sanctorum evangilistarum Iohannis et Lucae, a Simeone Metaphraste olim concinnatae, iam recens traductae*. This work appeared from the press of Joseph Barnes, the university printer, and it contains an edition of the Greek text parallel to the Latin. Brett, who was later one of the translators of King James' Bible, dedicates the work to the judge, Thomas Owen, and in his dedication he makes it clear that he has allowed himself a good deal of freedom. The translation had occupied him for a month:

> Where my author is sportive with repetition, there I have wielded my axe, and cut out his tautologies. Where he progresses with too much compression and obscurely, there I have introduced some light and charm. Where he progresses in too expansive a manner, uniting in a single sentence matters ill-digested or very numerous and conflicting, there indeed I have given the most correct shape to single items as

I thought best, and broken it up into sometimes two, sometimes three, periods without any harm to the meaning... For what a task it was for a man in intervals of leisure from higher cares to have transcribed, translated, copied out again and submitted to the press this work in the space of one month? I do not say 'polished the work', since I had neither the time nor the inclination to do so.

(pp. 226–7)

Lord Bacon

The most important English author to gain a continental audience in Latin guise at this time was [...] undoubtedly Lord [Francis] Bacon. Those of his works that were not written in Latin from the start were soon made available to a European audience in Latin versions. William Rawley, chaplain and amanuensis to Lord Bacon and editor of the London, 1623 edition of *De augmentis scientiarum*, the first book of which incorporates a Latin translation of Bacon's *The Advancement of Learning*, writes in his dedicatory letter to the reader:

> Not long ago he formed the intention that it should be translated into Latin, since he had heard that the work was being sought after by foreigners. Nay, he was wont frequently to say that books written in modern languages would not very long after go bankrupt. And so he now publishes his translation of the work, which has been worked on by certain men who are fairly well known for their eloquence, and then purified by his own revision too.

The words of Bacon himself which Rawley cites provide the clearest proof possible of the relative status of English and Latin in this period. This Latin version of Bacon was widely reprinted all over Europe—at Paris in 1624, Strasbourg in 1635 and 1654, Leyden in 1645 and 1652, Amsterdam in 1662; and indeed it was never really out of circulation, since it was re-issued in the eighteenth century at Lugano, 1763 and Würzburg, 1779 and in the nineteenth century at Nuremburg, 1829.

Some explanation of 'men ... well known for their eloquence' may be worthwhile. Bacon had written earlier to Dr Playfere, the Lady Margaret Professor of Divinity at Cambridge, asking him to translate the *Advancement of Learning* into Latin on the grounds that English was still very much a 'private' language:

> And therefore the privateness of the language considered wherein it is written, excluding so many readers, (as, on the one side, the obscurity of the argument in many parts of it excludeth many others), I must account it a second birth of that work, if it might be translated into Latin, without manifest sense of loss of the sense and matter.

It appears, however, that Dr Playfere produced an over-elaborate specimen of a translation, which did not please Bacon, who may have thought that such a translation would distract from the meaning. Rawley's friend Thomas Tenison reports:

he sent a specimen of such superfine Latinity, that the Lord Bacon did not encourage him to labour further in that work, in the penning of which, he desired not so much neat and polite, as clear, masculine, and apt expression.

So it appears that Playfere was not one of the translators, who according to Tenison included the poet George Herbert. Nevertheless it is clear that Bacon himself exercised final supervision over the version.

(pp. 252–3)

Sir Francis Kynaston

[The following is from Binns's account of the Latin translation of Chaucer's *Troilus and Criseyde*, Books I and II, by Sir Francis Kynaston, a courtier and poet:]

Amorum Troili et Creseidae [. . .] printed in parallel with the English text of Thynne, and dedicated to Patrick Young, the Royal Librarian, throws important light on the literary and cultural aspirations of the English at this time. The impulse behind it, as is clear from the dedication and the many prefatory poems, was to preserve a great literary work from neglect, and to make it available both to a European audience, and to Kynaston's own English contemporaries, for whom the archeisms of Chaucerian English were an obstacle to understanding. Thus it has nationalistic and literary aims in a number of dimensions. [. . .]

In a subsequent 'address to the reader', Kynaston explains the spirit in which he had undertaken the work, and the difficulties he had encountered. He again explains that he had seen Chaucer becoming obsolete and despised for the archaism of his English, so that to preserve the poem, it seemed advisable to put it into Latin:

> It seemed most advisable to me to endow the poem with a new tongue, and to adorn it with a new kind of rhythm and song; and to support it on the eternal column of Roman eloquence and to render it stable and unmoving (as much as is in my power) throughout all time.

He could, he says, have provided an English modernization of the poem, just as the *Roman de la Rose* had been seven times modernized in France since it was first written. But he thought that to change even an iota of Chaucer's writings would be a sin, for they were worthy of remaining sacred and untouched for ever.

Kynaston adopts an unusual verse form in attempting to convey the Chaucerian metre as closely as possible in Latin. He explains that it would have been easier to put the poem into Latin hexameters and pentameters. But when he remembered that the seven-line stanza (of pentameters) had been used by both Tasso and Ariosto, and that it was popular with the English and French, then he thought that he would attempt to write Latin in the same metre. Kynaston discusses his metrical scheme in some detail, writing that he will try to preserve the rhythms and rhymes of the original to the best of his ability.

He outlines a number of difficulties—discussing the meaning of obsolete words and the fact that English words are often monosyllabic, while Latin words are polysyllabic, various problems in rhyme and quantity, the necessity of reproducing Chaucer's puns etc. He stresses his faithful rendering. This thoroughly renaissance perception of his original and of his duties toward it is reinforced by his distinction between the rhymes used in his own lines and the barbarous stressed metres of (rhyming) monkish verse. At first sight the result is somewhat disconcerting. The lines appear to have no shape in quantitative terms, nor do they seem to have any apparent rhythmic structure. The number of syllables (11, i.e., an attempt to reproduce the Chaucerian pentameter in a Latin guise) is however fairly constant; and if the lines are read with the strong iambic rhythm of the original in mind, they work fairly well. A singly stanza of the Latin with Chaucer's original at its side will exemplify these features. The opening stanza is:

Dolorem *Troili* duplicem narrare,	The double sorwe of Troilus to tellen,
Qui Priami Regis Troiae fuit gnatus,	That was the king Priamus sone of Troye,
Ut primum illi contigit amare,	In lovynge, how his aventures fellen
Ut miser, felix, et infortunatus	Fro wo to wele, and after out of joie,
Erat, decessum ante sum conatus.	My purpos is, er that I parte fro ye.
Tisiphone fer opem recensere	Thesiphone, thow help me for t'endite
Hos versus, qui, dum scribo, visi flere.	Thise woful vers, that wepen as I write.

(pp. 253–6)

Humphrey's Treatise on Translation

[In his book, Binns discusses Laurence Humphrey's views on Ciceronianism, as expressed in his *Interpretatio linguarum, seu de ratione convertendi et explicandi autores tam sacros quam prophanos, libri tres* (Basle, 1559), i.e. 'The translation of languages, or On the logic of converting/translating and explaining authors, sacred as well as profane, three books'. He points out, however, that this treatise is 'worthy of attention on its own account as a study of the theory of translation' whereupon he gives the following summary of Humphrey's work:]

It is over 600 pages long, and is dedicated to Sir Thomas Wroth. In the dedication Humphrey states that literature and religion are the two things which bring the most happiness to men. Literature however depended on languages, and languages could not be made known without the aid of translation. Humphrey praises the inherent value and dignity of translation and also women who have translated works into the vernacular— the daughters of Sir Thomas More, learned in Latin and Greek, Lady Jane Grey, the daughters of Sir Anthony Cooke, and the newly succeeded Queen Elizabeth herself, whose accomplishments in Greek, Latin, Italian and French he praises. Humphrey says that he approves of the translation of the Bible into the vernacular, especially since such texts as Ovid's *Metamorphoses* and *Amores* were available in vernacular translation. Indeed he calls for the Bible to be translated into every tongue, so that even Saracens, Sarmatians, Indians and others could be guided by the knowledge of Christ. Humphrey concludes the dedication by noting that he is dedicating the work to Wroth at the suggestion of Edwin Sandys and Sir Francis Walsingham.

Book I of the *Interpretatio linguarum* starts with arguments in favour of knowing other languages. Then Humphrey discusses the three types of translation; the purely literal, word for word kind, which is the lowest type; the excessively free type, which is too self-indulgent, and third, the middle way between the two extremes, which is both faithful and elegant. After a section discussing Ciceronianism in Biblical translation, Humphrey urges his readers to pay equal attention to words and subject matter, and to maintain the stylistic differences (whether high, middle, or low) of the original. Joachim Perionius' translation of Aristotle is, he says, an admirable example of success in these respects. All languages are similar to each other, but they differ too. Greek and Latin differ very greatly. There was a danger, so far as the English were concerned, that the English idiom might creep into Latin. For 'someone is knocking at the door', the English were liable to say *Aliquem pulsare ad ostium* rather than the Terentian *pulsare fores*. In this first book, Humphrey praises Latin in particular as a language generally known, which belongs to the Christian world, and into which works in other languages are often translated. People ought not only to be not ignorant of the language but also to know it well. Greek too was important, and so was Hebrew. Churchmen ought to learn these languages, and universities too ought to promote them. The first book ends with a schematic guide to the work, with a list of authors cited, and a short index.

Book II of the *Interpretatio linguarum* is devoted principally to a discussion of imitation. Humphrey approves of it, because, as he says, one needs a guide. Whom one should choose to imitate is important. It is in this context that a further discussion of Ciceronianism is introduced. Humphrey gives detailed precepts on such topics as the correct and true formulation of sentences, the removal of ambiguities, whether or not to change metaphors, and so forth. The importance of constant practice is stressed. Book II also includes a section on poetical imitation. The third book is concerned to put into practice the theoretical precepts taught in Book I on the virtues and responsibilities of translation, and in Book II on imitation. One should first read quickly the work to be translated, and observe the drift of the argument. Book III is full of direct practical advice and discusses such subjects as the choice of words. Humphrey maintains that when one is translating from the Bible, one should translate not word for word, but meaning for meaning. Humphrey also stresses the importance of correct and versatile style.

He discusses rhetorical ornament, the use of synonyms, metaphors, and periphrasis etc. He praises in particular Sir John Cheke's Latin translation of the Emperor Leo's *De bellico apparatu*. This section of the work concludes with an encomium of Englishmen who had translated various works, and whose memories had been forgotten in England, so Humphrey says. In particular he praises Henry Howard, Earl of Surrey, the translator of Virgil; and Thomas Wyatt, whose translation of the Psalter he had heard of by repute. Humphrey also quotes Leland's praise of Wyatt and Surrey, and mentions poems and sonnets after the Italian fashion written by Edmund Sheffield, who died in the Norfolk rebellion. Sir Thomas Chaloner's translation of Erasmus into English is also lauded by Humphrey, as is Richard Cavendish's translation of Euclid, and works translated by Richard Eden. The translation out of French of Calvin's *An Epistle both of Godly Consolacion and also of Aduertisement* (London, 1550), by Edward Seymour, Duke of Somerset, is mentioned, along with the work of Sir Thomas Elyot, Katherine Parr, John Caius, and Nicholas Udall. Humphrey calls for Livy, Cicero, Plato and Aristotle to be translated into English: and also for translations of the Bible, Church histories, and works of Christian antiquity. Oxford and Cambridge Universities could produce many men capable of doing the job, if they would only be diligent. Humphrey praises the endeavours of Thomas Cooper, later to be the author of the *Thesaurus linguae romanae et britannicae* (London, 1565), the standard Elizabethan Latin dictionary. This section demonstrates very well Humphrey's awareness of, and interest in, the vernacular culture of his day.

Then Humphrey recommends the practice of turning prose into verse and of metaphrase. In an interesting passage, he remarks that the English language has been corrupted by the influx of French and Latin words. The book closes with some practical illustrations of translation from various languages, and with a Latin translation of a short treatise by Philo Judaeus, all designed for practice in the art of translation. The *Interpretatio linguarum* is a formidably erudite work, the product of a well-read, learned intellectual, and, considering the part that translation from and into English and Latin played in Elizabethan intellectual life, its significance should be stressed. (pp. 209–12)

1. [Binns places these translations in parentheses following the Latin texts, which for lack of space are not included here. Binns's numerous references to exact paginations in his sources are not included in the excerpts from his book.]

2.8. THE CATHOLIC BIBLE IN ENGLAND

The Douay version or Catholic Bible originated in the need for a translation of the Bible for use of Roman Catholics during a time of religious controversy (the Reformation), the many Protestant versions, preceding the Authorized Version of 1611, having been used by reformers for polemical purposes. The work of preparation was undertaken by the members of the English College at Douai, in Flanders, founded by William Allen (afterwards Cardinal Allen) in 1568, the translation being chiefly the work of Gregory Martin, formerly of St John's College, Oxford, revised by Thomas Worthington, Richard Bristowe, John Reynolds, and Allen himself.

In view of the intended purpose of the translation, the scholars worked directly, not from the original Hebrew or Greek, but from the Latin Vulgate of St Jerome, this being the official text authorized by the Catholic Church. This text, it should be noted, was in any case held to be more reliable than others, in view of the authenticity of the source texts to which Jerome had access at the time. Many ecclesiastical terms, derived from Latin, were retained; in some cases, the Latin word itself being kept, in an Anglicized form. The Douay-Reims Bible, not surprisingly in view of its intended polemical use, included a comprehensive array of annotations interpreting the text in conformity with Catholic orthodoxy, to combat the equally assertive biblical commentaries of Reformers. The result, admittedly, was somewhat cumbersome, but the standard of scholarship was relatively high.

In 1578, the college was temporarily transferred, on account of political troubles, from Douai to Reims, and the translation of the New Testament was published there in 1582. The Old Testament was delayed until the whole Bible was published in 1609 and 1610, by which time the college had returned to Douai. The New Testament, thus, appeared nearly thirty years before the Authorized Version and, although not acknowledged, influenced the latter to a considerable extent.

Although the Bibles used by the Catholics of England and Ireland subsequently are popularly styled the Douay Version, from the eighteenth century into the twentieth century they were, in fact, the result of a series of revisions by Bishop Richard Challoner (published 1749-52), in most cases his changes bringing the Catholic Bible closer to the Authorized Version. Challoner's revision considerably reduced the annotations. A revision of the Reims-Challoner New Testament was published by the Catholic Bible Society of America in 1941, sponsored by the Confraternity of Christian Doctrine. The Old Testament was, in fact, a new translation, based now on the source texts (1948–69). In 1970 a new version of the New Testament, based now on the Greek rather than the Latin

Vulgate, was published. Other versions, initiated by or intended for the Roman Catholic Church, included *The Westminster Version of the Sacred Scriptures*, and the version by one man, Mgr. Ronald Knox (1945-9), the limitations of this work clearly indicated, since it is described as '[a] translation of the Latin Vulgate in the light of the Hebrew and Greek originals'. Movement towards an ecumenical Bible translation takes a step forward with *The Jerusalem Bible*, inspired by and largely based on the French Dominican translation *La Bible de Jérusalem* (1956). The English version, inspired by and referring to the French, returns to the Hebrew, Aramaic, and Greek originals. Since use of the original sources, as it were following the example of St Jerome himself, is now accepted, many of the obstacles in the way of an ecumenical translation have been removed.

Gregory Martin (1540-82), principle translator of the Douay Version, was assisted by several of the other scholars then residing in the English College at Douay, but it was Martin who made the whole translation in the first instance. He was a brilliant scholar and linguist, ordained priest in 1573, three years later going to Rome to assist Allen in the foundation of the English College there. He remained in Rome two years, then being recalled by Allen to Reims.

It was after his return from Rome that he embarked on his Bible translation. In accuracy and scholarship, as noted, if not in rhythmic harmony, it was superior to any of the English versions which had preceded it. Beside his Bible translation, Martin published a *Treatise of Schisme* (Douai, 1578); *Discovery of the Manifold Corruptions of the Holy Scriptures by the Heretikes of our Daies* (Reims, 1582; this attacked various Protestant translations and occasioned a fierce paragraph by paragraph refutation by William Fulke, in 1583); *Treatise of Christian Peregrination* (Reims, 1583); *Of the Love of the Soul* (St Omer, 1603); and *Gregorius Martinus ad Adolphum Mekerchum pro veteri et vera Græcarum Literarum Pronunciatione* (Oxford, 1712).

From Gregory Martin, 'The Preface to the Reader', *The New Testament of Jesus Christ* (1582)

2. Which translation we do not for all that publish upon erroneous opinion of necessity that the Holy Scriptures should always be in our mother tongue, or that they ought, or were ordained by God, to be read indifferently of all, or could be easily understood of everyone that reads or hears them in a known language, or that they were not often through man's malice or infirmity pernicious and much hurtful to many; or that we generally and absolutely deemed it more convenient in itself, and more agreeable to God's word and honour or edification of the faithful, to have them turned into vulgar tongues, than to be kept and studied only in the ecclesiastical learned languages. Not for

these nor any such like causes do we translate this sacred book, but upon special consideration of the present time, state, and condition of our country, unto which diverse things are either necessary or profitable and medicinable now that otherwise in the peace of the Church were neither much requisite nor perchance wholly tolerable.

3. In this matter, to mark only the wisdom and moderation of holy Church and the governors thereof on the one side, and the indiscreet zeal of the popular, and their factious leaders, on the other, is a high point of prudence. These latter, partly of simplicity, partly of curiosity, and specially of pride and disobedience, have made claim in this case for the common people, with plausible pretences many, but good reasons none at all. The other, to whom Christ has given charge of our souls, the dispensing of God's mysteries and treasures (among which Holy Scripture is no small store) and the feeding of his family in season with food fit for every sort, have neither of old nor of late ever wholly condemned all vulgar versions of Scripture, nor have at any time generally forbidden the faithful to read the same; yet they have not by public authority prescribed, commanded, or authentically ever recommended any such inter-pretation to be indifferently used of all men.

[. . .]

4. [. . .] In our own country, notwithstanding the Latin tongue was ever (to use Venerable Bede's words) common to all the provinces of the same for meditation or study of Scriptures, and no vulgar translation commonly used or occupied of the multitude, yet there were extant in English even before the troubles that Wycliffe and his followers raised in our Church, as appears as well by some pieces yet remaining as by a provincial Constitution of Thomas Arundel Archbishop of Canterbury, in a Council held at Oxford, where strait provision was made that no heretical version set forth by Wycliffe or his adherents should be suffered, nor any other in or after his time be published or permitted to be read, being not approved and allowed by the Diocesan before, alleaging St. Hierom for the difficulty and danger of interpreting the holy Scripture out of one tongue into another, though by learned and Catholic men. So also it is there insinuated that neither the translations set forth before the heretic's time nor other afterward being approved by the lawful ordinaries, were ever in our country wholly forbidden, though they were not (to say the truth) in quiet and better times (much less when the people were prone to alteration heresy, or novelty), either hastily admitted ordinarily read of the vulgar, but used only, or specially, of some devout religious and contemplative persons, in reverence, secrecy, and silence, for their spiritual comfort.

5. Now since Luther's revolt also, diverse learned Catholics, for the more speedy abolishing of a number of false and impious translations put forth by sundry sects, and for the better preservation or reclaim of many good souls endangered thereby, have published the Bible in the several languages of almost all the principal provinces of the Latin Church; no other books in the world being so pernicious as heretical translations of

the Scriptures, poisoning the people under colour of divine authority, and not many other remedies being more sovereign against the same (if it be used in order discretion and humility) than the truth, faithful, and sincere interpretation opposed thereunto.

6. Which causes the holy Church not to forbid utterly any Catholic translation, though she allow not the publishing or reading of any absolutely and without exception, or limitation: knowing by her divine and most sincere wisdom, how, where, when, and to whom these her Master's and Spouse's gifts are to be bestowed to the most good of the faithful; and therefore neither generally permits that which must needs do hurt to the unworthy nor absolutely condemns that which may do much good to the worthy. [...]

Genesis 11, 'The Tower of Babel'

From the Douay-Reims translation of the Bible (1609–10)

1 And the earth was of one tongue, and of the same speech. 2 And when they removed from the east, they found a plain in the land of Sennaar, and dwelt in it. 3 And each one said to his neighbour: Come, let us make brick, and bake them with fire. And they had brick instead of stones, and slime instead of mortar. 4 And they said: Come, let us make a city and a tower, the top whereof may reach to heaven: and let us make our name famous before we be scattered abroad into all lands. 5 And the Lord came down to see the city and the tower, which the children of Adam were building.

6 And he said: Behold, it is one people, and all have one tongue: and they have begun to do this, neither will they leave off from their designs, till they accomplish them in deed. 7 Come ye, therefore, let us go down, and there confound their tongue, that they may not understand one another's speech. 8 And so the Lord scattered them from that place into all lands, and they ceased to build the city. 9 And therefore the name thereof was called *Babel*, because there the language of the whole earth was confounded: and from thence the Lord scattered them abroad upon the face of all countries.

Latin Vulgate Translation

1. erat autem terra labii unius et sermonum eorundem
2. cumque proficiscerentur de oriente invenerunt campum in terra Sennaar et habitaverunt in eo
3. dixitque alter ad proximum suum venite faciamus lateres et coquamus eos igni habueruntque lateres pro saxis et bitumen pro cemento
4. et dixerunt venite faciamus nobis civitatem et turrem cuius culmen pertingat ad caelum et celebremus nomen nostrum antequam dividamur in universas terras
5. descendit autem Dominus ut videret civitatem et turrem quam aedificabant filii Adam

6. et dixit ecce unus est populus et unum labium omnibus coeperuntque hoc facere nec desistent a cogitationibus suis donec eas opere conpleant

7. venite igitur descendamus et confundamus ibi linguam eorum ut non audiat unusquisque vocem proximi sui

8. atque ita divisit eos Dominus ex illo loco in universas terras et cessaverunt aedificare civitatem

9. et idcirco vocatum est nomen eius Babel quia ibi confusum est labium universae terrae et inde dispersit eos Dominus super faciem cunctarum regionum

2.9. THE AUTHORIZED (KING JAMES) VERSION OF THE BIBLE

Miles Smith (d. 1624), Classical scholar and orientalist, was one of the translators appointed by James I to make a new version of the Bible, and was also assigned the task of writing the preface. Educated at Oxford, he served in a variety of ecclesiastical positions, being rewarded for his work on the Bible with the bishopric of Gloucester. His lengthy preface, excerpts from which are included below, is frequently omitted from editions of the King James Bible.

It was in the first year of his reign that King James held a conference at Hampton Court (1604), which authorized fifty-four scholars to undertake a revision of the existing English translations of the Bible. A list of fifteen rules was drawn up, the first being that the translators should follow the Bishops Bible (1568) as closely as possible, this being largely based on Tyndale's translation (1525, 1531; see Sect. 2.3, above). The committee's work was undertaken in a non-competitive, scholarly, and, for the time, remarkably unprejudiced fashion. The King's objective was similar to that of Pope Damasus when charging Jerome with the revision of the texts of the Latin Bible, namely, in the interest of unity, to arrive at a single authoritative text. He was also concerned to heal divisions, working towards a religious consensus in what was clearly a dangerous situation, with the divisions in Christianity abroad and at home.

The influence of this text on English literature has been enormous, indeed overwhelming at times, even negatively, as Ezra Pound was to note with regard to translations of Homer, which he characterized as 'King James fustian'. So seductive are its cadences that the Authorized Version is seen as one of the most important literary works in the English language, for which reason we include two other striking excerpts, in addition to the Babel story.

Smith reiterates, with numerous examples, the populist case for making the Scriptures accessible in the vernacular, 'for the behoof and edifying of the unlearned which [. . .] had souls to be saved as well . . .' He contrasts this inclusiveness with the attitude of the Catholic Church, which had just produced its own translation into English of the Bible (Reims/Douay, 1582, 1609, see Sect. 2.8, above). This, he claimed, was reluctantly under-taken: 'Yea, so unwilling they are to communicate the Scriptures to the people's under-standing in any sort, that they are not ashamed to confess that we forced them to translate it into English against their wills.' Later he notes that, for instance, with regard to ecclesiastical terms, he and his colleagues have avoided the obscure terms employed by the 'Papists', which might seem to defeat the object of the operation.

The introduction includes a short history of Bible translation and reiterates that the translators are building on the work of their predecessors, notably of St Jerome. The polemic with the Catholic translators still continued, but in general the tone is conciliatory.

From 'The Translators to the Reader', Preface to the King James Version of the Bible, 1611

Happy is the man that delighted in the Scripture, and thrice happy that meditateth in it day and night.

But how shall men meditate in that, which they cannot understand? How shall they understand that which is kept close in an unknown tongue? as it is written, 'Except I know the power of the voice, I shall be to him that speaketh, a Barbarian, and he that speaketh, shall be a Barbarian to me.' [1 Cor. 14]

[. . .]

Therefore as one complaineth, that always in the Senate of Rome, there was one or other that called for an interpreter: [Cicero 5 :: de finibus.] so lest the Church be driven to the like exigent, it is necessary to have translations in a readiness. Translation it is that openeth the window, to let in the light; that breaketh the shell, that we may eat the kernel; that putteth aside the curtain, that we may look into the most Holy place; that removeth the cover of the well, that we may come by the water, even as Jacob rolled away the stone from the mouth of the well, by which means the flocks of Laban were watered [Gen. 29: 10]. Indeed without translation into the vulgar tongue, the unlearned are but like children at Jacob's well (which is deep) [John 4: 11] without a bucket or something to draw with; or as that person mentioned by Isaiah, to whom when a sealed book was delivered, with this motion, 'Read this, I pray thee,' he was fain to make this answer, 'I cannot, for it is sealed.' [Isa. 29: 11]

[. . .]

Many men's mouths have been open a good while (and yet are not stopped) with speeches about the Translation so long in hand, or rather perusale of Translations made before: and ask what may be the reason, what the necessity of the employment: Hath the Church been deceived, say they, all this while? Hath her sweet bread been mingled with leaven, here silver with dross, her wine with water, her milk with lime? (Lacte gypsum male miscetur, saith S. Ireney,) [S. Iren. 3. lib. cap. 19.] We hoped that we had been in the right way, that we had the Oracles of God delivered unto us, and that though all the world had cause to be offended and to complain, yet that we had none. Hath the nurse holden out the breast, and nothing but wind in it? Hath the bread been delivered by the fathers of the Church, and the same proved to be lapidosus, as Seneca speaketh? What is it to handle the word of God deceitfully, if this be not? Thus certain brethren. Also the adversaries of Judah and Jerusalem, like Sanballat in Nehemiah, mock, as we hear, both the work and the workmen, saying; 'What do these weak Jews, etc. will they make the stones whole again out of the heaps of dust which are burnt? although they build, yet if a fox go up, he shall even break down their stony wall." [Neh. 4: 3] Was their Translation good before? Why do they now mend it? Was it not good? Why then was it obtruded to the people? Yea, why did the Catholics (meaning Popish Romanlets) always go in jeopardy, for refusing to go to hear it? Nay, if it must be translated into English, Catholics are fittest to do it. They have learning, and they know when a thing is well, they can manure de tabula. We will answer them both briefly: and the former, being brethren, thus, with S. Jerome, 'Damnamus veteres? Mineme, sed post priorum studia in domo Domini quod possums laboramus.' [S. Jerome. Apolog. advers. Ruffin.] That is, 'Do we condemn the ancient? In no case: but after the endeavors of them that were before us, we take the best pains we can in the house of God.' As if he said, Being provoked by the example of the learned men that lived before my time, I have thought it my duty, to assay whether my talent in the knowledge of the tongues, may be profitable in any measure to God's Church, lest I should seem to labour in them in vain, and lest I should be thought to glory in men, (although ancient,) above that which was in them. Thus S. Jerome may be thought to speak.

And to the same effect say we, that we are so far oft from condemning any of their labours that travailed before us in this kind [. . .] that we acknowledge them to have been raised up of God, for the building and furnishing of his Church, and that they deserve to be had of us and of posterity in everlasting remembrance. [. . .] Yet for all that, as nothing is begun and perfected at the same time, and the later thoughts are thought to be the Wiser: so, if We building upon their foundation that went before us, and being holpen by their labours, do endeavor to make that better which they left so good; no man, we are sure, hath cause to mislike us; they, we persuade ourselves, it they were alive, would thank us. [. . .]

But it is high time to leave them [earlier translators], and to show in brief what we proposed to ourselves, and what course we held in this our perusal and survey of the Bible. Truly (good Christian Reader) we never thought from the beginning, that we should need to make a new Translation, nor yet to make of a bad one a good one, (for then the imputation of Sixtus had been true in some sort, that our people had been fed with gall of Dragons instead of wine, with whey instead of milk:) but to make a good one better, or out of many good ones, one principal good one, not justly to be excepted against; that hath been our endeavor, that our mark. [. . .] S. Jerome maketh no mention of the Greek tongue, wherein yet he did excel, because he translated not the old Testament out of Greek, but out of Hebrew. And in what sort did these assemble? In the trust of their own knowledge, or of their sharpness of wit, or deepness of judgment, as it were in an arm of flesh? At no hand. They trusted in him that hath the key of David, opening and no man shutting; they prayed to the Lord the Father of our Lord, to the effect that S. Augustine did; 'O let thy Scriptures be my pure delight, let me not be deceived in them, neither let me deceive by them.' [S. Aug. lib. II. Confess. cap. 2.] In this confidence, and with this devotion did they assemble together; not too many, lest one should trouble another; and yet many, lest many things haply might escape them. If you ask what they had before them, truly it was the Hebrew text of the Old Testament, the Greek of the New. These are the two golden pipes, or rather conduits, where-through the olive branches empty themselves into the gold. Saint Augustine calleth them precedent, or original tongues; [S. August. 3. de doctr. c. 3. etc.] Saint Jerome, fountains. [S. Jerome. ad Sunjam et Fretel.] The same Saint Jerome affirmeth, [S. Jerome. ad Lucinium, Diet. 9 ut veterum.] and Gratian hath not spared to put it into his Decree, That 'as the credit of the old Books' (he meaneth of the Old Testament) 'is to be tried by the Hebrew Volumes, so of the New by the Greek tongue,' he meaneth by the original Greek. If truth be tried by these tongues, then whence should a Translation be made, but out of them? These tongues therefore, the Scriptures we say in those tongues, we set before us to translate, being the tongues wherein God was pleased to speak to his Church by the Prophets and Apostles. Neither did we run over the work with that posting haste that the Septuagint did, if that be true which is reported of them, that they finished it in 72 days; [Joseph. Antiq. fib. 12.] neither were we barred or hindered from going over it again, having once done it, like S. Jerome, if that be true which himself reporteth, that he could no sooner write anything, but presently it was caught from him, and published, and he could not have leave to mend it: [S. Jerome. ad Pammac. pro libr. advers. Iovinian.] neither, to be short, were we the first that tell in hand with translating the Scripture into English, and consequently destitute of former helps, as it is written of Origen, that he was the first in a manner, that put his hand to write Commentaries upon the Scriptures, [Sophoc. in Elect.] and therefore no marvel, if he overshot himself many times. None of these things: the work hath not been huddled up in 72 days, but hath cost the workmen, as light as it seemeth, the pains of twice seven times seventy two days and more: matters of such weight and consequence are to be speeded with maturity: for in a business of movement a man feareth not the blame of convenient slackness. [S. Chrysost, in II. Thess. cap. 2.] Neither did we think much to consult the Translators or Commentators, Chaldee, Hebrew, Syrian, Greek or Latin, no nor the Spanish, French, Italian, or Dutch; neither did we disdain to revise that which we had done, and to bring back to the anvil that which we had hammered: but having and using as great helps as were needful, and fearing no reproach for slowness, nor coveting praise for expedition, we have at length, through the good hand of the Lord upon us, brought the work to that pass that you see.

[. . .]

Another thing we think good to admonish thee of (gentle Reader) that we have not tied ourselves to an uniformity of phrasing, or to an identity of words, as some peradventure would wish that we had done, because they observe, that some learned men somewhere, have been as exact as they could that way. Truly, that we might not vary from the sense of that which we had translated before, if the word signified that same in both places (for there be some words that be not the same sense everywhere) we were especially careful, and made a conscience, according to our duty. But, that we should express the same notion in the same particular word; as for example, if we translate the Hebrew or Greek word once by PURPOSE, never to call it INTENT; if one where JOURNEYING, never TRAVELING; if one where THINK, never SUPPOSE; if one where PAIN, never ACHE; if one where JOY, never GLADNESS, etc. Thus to mince the matter, we thought to savour more of curiosity than wisdom, and that rather it would breed scorn in the Atheist, than bring profit to the godly Reader. For is the kingdom of God to become words or syllables? Why should we be in bondage to them if we may be free, use one precisely when we may use another no less fit, as commodiously?[1]

[...]

Add hereunto, that niceness in words was always counted the next step to trifling, and so was to be curious about names too: also that we cannot follow a better pattern for elocution than God himself; therefore he using divers words, in his holy writ, and indifferently for one thing in nature: [see Euseb. li. 12. ex Platon.] we, if we will not be superstitious, may use the same liberty in our English versions out of Hebrew and Greek, for that copy or store that he hath given us. Lastly, we have on the one side avoided the scrupulosity of the Puritans, who leave the old Ecclesiastical words, and betake them to other, as when they put WASHING for BAPTISM, and CONGREGATION instead of CHURCH: as also on the other side we have shunned the obscurity of the Papists, in their AZIMES, TUNIKE, RATIONAL, HOLOCAUSTS, PRAEPUCE, PASCHE, and a number of such like, whereof their late Translation is full, and that of purpose to darken the sense, that since they must needs translate the Bible, yet by the language thereof, it may be kept from being understood. But we desire that the Scripture may speak like itself, as in the language of Canaan, that it may be understood even of the very vulgar.

[...]

EDITORS' NOTE

1. [This contrasts with the concern of a modern translator, Everett Fox (see Sect. 5.20, below), and before him, Buber and Rosenzweig (see Sect. 4.5, below), for verbal patterns (parallelisms, etc.).]

From the Authorized Version

Genesis 11: 1–9

1 And the whole earth was of one language, and of one speech.

2 And it came to pass, as they journeyed from the east, that they found a plain in the land of Shinar; and they dwelt there.

3 And they said one to another, Go to, let us make brick, and burn them throughly. And they had brick for stone, and slime had they for mortar.

4 And they said, Go to, let us build us a city and a tower, whose top *may reach* unto heaven; and let us make us a name, lest we be scattered abroad upon the face of the whole earth.

5 And the LORD came down to see the city and the tower, which the children of men builded.

6 And the LORD said, Behold, the people *is* one, and they have all one language; and this they begin to do: and now nothing will be restrained from them, which they have imagined to do.

7 Go to, let us go down, and there confound their language, that they may not understand one another's speech.

8 So the LORD scattered them abroad from thence upon the face of all the earth: and they left off to build the city.

9 Therefore is the name of it called Babel; because the LORD did there confound the language of all the earth: and from thence did the LORD scatter them abroad upon the face of all the earth.

Psalm 23

A Psalm of David

1 The LORD *is* my shepherd; I shall not want.

2 He maketh me to lie down in green pastures: he leadeth me beside the still waters.

3 He restoreth my soul: he leadeth me in the paths of righteousness for his name's sake.

4 Yea, though I walk through the valley of the shadow of death, I will fear no evil: for thou *art* with me; thy rod and thy staff they comfort me.

5 Thou preparest a table before me in the presence of mine enemies: thou anointest my head with oil; my cup runneth over.

6 Surely goodness and mercy shall follow me all the days of my life: and I will dwell in the house of the LORD for ever.

St. John 1: 1-5

1 In the beginning was the Word, and the Word was with God, and the Word was God.

2 The same was in the beginning with God.

3 All things were made by him; and without him was not any thing made that was made.

4 In him was life; and the life was the light of men.

5 And the light shineth in darkness; and the darkness comprehended it not.

2.10 SIR JOHN DENHAM

Sir John Denham (1615–69), courtier, wit, and poet, is best known in literary history for his national panegyric *Cooper's Hill*, which influenced georgic and descriptive poetry for over a hundred years. More than half of his poetical works were translations, some of which were later praised by Pope and Dryden, and incorporated into their works. At about the same time that translators in his Royalist circle were eschewing literalism in translation, Denham proposed his 'new way', a method both poetic and accurate. Dryden was to commend Denham and Abraham Cowley for freeing translation from servility, but also to disparage their excessive liberties.

'To Sir Richard Fanshaw upon his Translation of Pastor Fido' (1648)

> Such is our Pride, our Folly, or our Fate,
> That few but such as cannot write, Translate.
> But what in them is want of Art, or voice,
> In thee is either Modesty or Choice.
> Whiles this great piece, restor'd by thee doth stand
> Free from the blemish of an Artless hand.
> Secure of Fame, thou justly dost esteem
> Less honour to create, than to redeem.
> Nor ought a Genius less than his that writ,
> Attempt Translation; for transplanted wit,
> All the defects of air and soil doth share,
> And colder brains like colder Climates are:
> In vain they toil, since nothing can beget
> A vital spirit, but a vital heat.
> That servile path thou nobly dost decline
> Of tracing word by word, and line by line.
> Those are the labour'd births of slavish brains,
> Not the effects of Poetry, but pains;
> Cheap vulgar arts, whose narrowness affords
> No flight for thoughts, but poorly sticks at words.
> A new and nobler way thou dost pursue
> To make Translations and Translators too.
> They but preserve the Ashes, thou the Flame,
> True to his sense, but truer to his fame.

Foording his current, where thou find'st it low
Let'st in thine own to make it rise and flow;
Wisely restoring whatsoever grace
It lost by change of Times, or Tongues, or Place.
Nor fetter'd to his Numbers, and his Times,
Betray'st his Musick to unhappy Rimes,
Nor are the nerves of his compacted strength
Stretch'd and dissolv'd into unsinnewed length:
Yet after all, (lest we should think it thine)
Thy spirit to his circle dost confine.
New names, new dressings, and the modern cast,
Some Scenes some persons alter'd, had out-fac'd
The world, it were thy work; for we have known
Some thank't and prais'd for what was less their own.
That Masters hand which to the life can trace
The airs, the lines, and features of a face,
May with a free and bolder stroke express
A varyed posture, or a flatt'ring Dress;
He could have made those like, who made the rest,
But that he knew his own design was best.

'The Preface' to *The Destruction of Troy* (1656), from T. R. Steiner (ed.), *English Translation Theory, 1650–1800* (Assen and Amsterdam: Van Gorum, 1975), 63–5

There are so few Translations which deserve praise, that I scarce ever saw any which deserv'd pardon; those who travel in that kind, being for the most part so unhappy, as to rob others, without enriching themselves, pulling down the fame of good Authors, without raising their own: Neither hath any Author been more hardly dealt withal than this our Master; and the reason is evident, for, what is most excellent, is most inimitable; and if even the worst Authors are yet made worse by their Translators, how impossible is it not to do great injury to the best? And therefore I have not the vanity to think my Copy equal to the Original, nor (consequently) my self altogether guiltless of what I accuse others; but if I can do *Virgil* less injury than others have done, it will be, in some degree to do him right; and indeed, the hope of doing him more right, is the only scope of this Essay, by opening this new way of translating this Author, to those whom youth, leisure, and better fortune makes fitter for such undertakings.

I conceive it a vulgar error in translating Poets, to affect being *Fidus Interpres*; let that care be with them who deal in matters of Fact, or matters, of Faith: but whosoever aims at it in Poetry, as he attempts what is not required, so he shall never perform what he attempts; for it is not his busines alone to translate Language into Language, but Poesie into Poesie; & Poesie is of so subtile a spirit, that in pouring out of one Language into another, it will all evaporate; and if a new spirit be not added in the transfusion, there will remain nothing but a *Caput mortuum*, there being certain Graces and Happinesses peculiar to every Language, which gives life and energy to the words; and whosoever offers at Verbal Translation, shall have the misfortune of that young Traveller, who lost his own language abroad, and brought home no other instead of it: for the grace of the Latine will be lost by being turned into English words; and the grace of the English, by being turned into the Latine Phrase. And as speech is the apparel of our thoughts, so are there certain Garbs and Modes of speaking, which vary with the times; the fashion of our clothes being not more subject to alteration, than that of our speech: and this I think *Tacitus* means, by that which he calls *Sermonem temporis istius auribus accommodatum*; the delight of change being as due to the curiosity of the ear, as of the eye; and therefore if *Virgil* must needs speak English, it were fit he should speak not only as a man of this Nation, but as a man of this age; and if this disguise I have put upon him (I wish I could give it a better name) fit not naturally and easily on so grave a person, yet it may become him better than that Fools-Coat wherein the French and Italian have of late presented him; at least, I hope, it will not make him appear deformed, by making any part enormously bigger or less than the life, (I having made it my principal care to follow him, as he made it his to follow Nature in all his proportions). Neither have I any where offered such violence to his sense, as to make it seem mine, and not his. Where my expressions are not so full as his, either our Language, or my Art were defective (but I rather suspect my self;) but where mine are fuller than his, they are but the impressions which the often reading of him, hath left upon my thoughts; so that if they are not his own Conceptions, they are at least the results of them; and if (being conscious of making him speak worse than he did almost in every line) I erre in endeavouring sometimes to make him speak better; I hope it will be judged an error on the right hand, and such an one as may deserve pardon, if not imitation.

2.11 ABRAHAM COWLEY

Abraham Cowley (1618–67) was a committed Royalist, poet (usually thought of as a Metaphysical poet), and wit, educated at Cambridge. He was regarded as the greatest poet of his age, ranging very widely, writing English and Latin poetry, plays, essays, and prose work. Cowley is now perhaps best remembered for his approach to translation of the Pindaric ode, which established this form in English. In his preface to the *Pindariques*, he advanced the notion of 'Imitation', an ultra-free type of translation. Dryden, who greatly admired Cowley and was indebted to him, particularly in respect to his mastery of the heroic couplet, criticized his notion of imitation insofar as it aspired to normativeness, although he approved it in the case of Cowley himself and of so problematical a source text as the Greek poet Pindar's Odes.

Preface to the *Pindariques*, included in Abraham Cowley, *The Complete Works in Verse and Prose*, ed. Alexander B. Grosart (Facs. edn., New York, 1967)

If a man should undertake to translate Pindar Word for Word, it would be thought that one Madman had translated another; as may appear, when he that understands not the Original, reads the verbal Traduction of him into Latin Prose, than which nothing seems more Raving. And sure, Rhyme without the Addition of Wit, and the Spirit of Poetry (quod nequeo monstrare & sentio tantum) would but make it ten times more distracted than it is in Prose. We must consider in Pindar the great Difference of Time betwixt his Age and ours, which changes, as in Pictures, at least the Colours of Poetry; the no less Difference betwixt the Religions and Customs of our Countries, and a thousand Particularities of Places, Persons, and Manners, which do but confusedly appear to our Eyes at so great a Distance. And lastly (which were enough alone for my purpose) we must consider that our Ears are Strangers to the Music of his Numbers, which sometimes (especially in Songs and Odes) almost without any thing else, makes an excellent Poet. For though the Grammarians and Critics have laboured to reduce his Verses into regular Feet and Measures (as they have also those of the Greek and Latin Comedies) yet in effect they are little better than Prose to our Ears. And I would gladly know what Applause our best Pieces of English Poesies could expect from a Frenchman or Italian, if converted faithfully, and Word for Word into French or Italian Prose. And when we have considered all this, we must needs confess that after all these Losses sustained by Pindar, all we can add to him by our Wit or Invention (not deserting still his Subject) is not like to make him a Richer Man than he was in his own Country. This is in some measure to be applied to all Translations; and the not observing of it, is the Cause that all which ever I yet saw are so much inferior to their Originals. The like happens too in Pictures, from the same Root of exact Imitation; which being a vile and unworthy kind of Servitude, is incapable of producing any thing good or noble. I have seen Originals both in Painting and Poesy, much more beautiful than their natural Objects; but I never saw a Copy better than the Original, which indeed cannot be otherwise; for Men resolving in no case to shoot beyond the Mark, it is a thousand to one if they shoot not short of it. It does not at all trouble me that the Grammarians perhaps will not suffer this libertine way of rendering foreign Authors, to be called Translation; for I am not so much enamoured of the Name Translator as not to wish rather to be Something Better, though it want yet a Name. I speak not so much all this, in Defence of my manner of Translating, or Imitating (or what other Title they please) the two ensuing Odes of Pindar; for that would not deserve half these Words, as by this Occasion to rectify the Opinion of divers Men upon this matter. The Psalms of David, (which I believe to have been in their Original, to the Hebrews of his Time, though not to our Hebrews of Buxtorfius's making, the most exalted Pieces of Poesy) are a great Example of what I have said; all the translators of which (even Mr. Sands himself; for in despite of popular Error, I will be bold not to except him) for this very Reason, that they have not sought to supply the lost Excellencies of another Language with new ones in their own; are so far from doing Honour, or at least Justice to that Divine Poet, that methinks they revile him worse than Shimei. And Buchanan himself (though much the best of them all, and indeed a great Person) comes in my Opinion no less short of David, than his Country does of Judæa. Upon this ground, I have in these two Odes of Pindar, taken, left out, and added what I please; nor make it so much my Aim to let the Reader know precisely what he spoke, as what was his Way and Manner of speaking; which has not been yet (that I know of) introduced into English, though it be the noblest and highest kind of writing in Verse; and which might, perhaps, be put into the List of Pancirollus, among the lost Inventions of Antiquity. This Essay is but to try how it will look in an English Habit: For which Experiment, I have chosen one of his Olympique, and another of his Nemaean Odes; which are as followeth.

Comparison of translations of one of Pindar's Odes

[A comparison of the two excerpts below provides ample evidence of what 'Imitation' meant in practice, the extent to which Cowley diverges from the source text.]

From 'The Second Olympique Ode' of Pindar (written in praise of Theron, Prince of Agrigentum, Sicily), stanzas 1 and 2, trans. Abraham Cowley, included in Abraham Cowley, *The Complete Works in Verse and Prose,* ed. Alexander B. Grosart (Facs. edn., New York, 1976).

> Queen of all Harmonious things,
>   Dancing Words, and Speaking Strings,
>   What God, what hero wilt thou sing?
>   What happy Man to equal Glories bring?

Begin, begin thy noble choice,
And let the Hills around reflect the Image of thy Voice.
    Pisa does to Jove belong.
    Jove and Pisa claim thy Song,
The fair First-Fruits of War, the' Olympique Games
    Alcides offer'd up to Jove;
    Alcides too thy strings may move;
But, oh, what Man to joyn with these can worthy prove,
Joyn Theron boldly to their sacred Names;
    Theron the next honour claimes;
    Theron to no man gives place,
Is first in Pisa's, and in Virtue's Race;
    Theron there, and he alone,
Even his own swift Fore-fathers has out-gone.

They through rough ways, o'er many stops they past,
    'Till on the fatal bank at last
They Agrigentum built, the beauteous Eye
    Of fair-faces Sicilie,
    Which does it self i' th' River by
    With Pride and Joy espy.
Then cheerful Notes their Painted Years did sing,
And Wealth was one, and Honor th' other Wing.
Their genuine Virtues did more sweet and clear,
    In Fortune's graceful dress appear.
    To which great son of Rhea, say
The Firm Word which forbids things to Decay.
    If in Olympus Top, where thou
    Sit'st to behold thy Sacred Show,
    If in Alpheus silver flight,
    If in my Verse thou dost delight,
    My Verse, O Rhea's Son, which is
    Lofty as that, and smooth as this. [. . .]

Literal translation from Pindar I, ed. *and trans. William H. Race (Loeb Classical Library;*
Cambridge, Mass. and London: Harvard University Press, 1997), 63–4

Hymns that rule the lye,
What god, what hero, and what man shall we celebrate?
Indeed, Pisa belongs to Zeus, while Herakles

    established the Olympic festival
as the firstfruit of war;
but Theron, because of his victorious four-horse chariot
must be proclaimed—a man just in his regard for guests,
    bulwark of Akragas,
and foremost upholder of his city from a line of famous
    ancestors,

who suffered much in their hearts
to win a holy dwelling place on the river and they were
the eye of Sicily, while their allotted time drew on, adding
    wealth and glory
to their native virtues.
O son of Kronos and Rhea, ruling over your abode on Olympos,
over the pinnacle of contests, and over Alpheos' course,
    cheered by my songs
graciously preserve their ancestral land [...]

2.12 WOMEN TRANSLATORS FROM THE SIXTEENTH TO THE EIGHTEENTH CENTURY

Jane Stevenson
(University of Aberdeen)

Translation was important to early modern women. In these centuries, to be educated implied familiarity with Latin, and to some extent Greek, but very few women were taught these languages. However, as J. W. Saunders has pointed out, as early as the mid-sixteenth century, when few Latin texts were easily available in translation, 'John Croke's wife and Edmund Becke's cousin who knew no Latin secured the poems they wanted'—that is, they were able to find some Latinate individual in their circle to translate them. As the sixteenth century progressed, it was increasingly possible just to go out and buy a copy of a particular work. Great numbers of translations were published, and widely circulated— for example Shakespeare, though he had been to a grammar school, was more comfortable with English translations of Classical texts, and also read Italian literature in translation. Thus, classical *learning* could easily be acquired by reading English or French translations, as we can see from a woman such as the seventeenth-century Dame Sarah Cowper, daughter of one of the Lord Mayors of London, who left a memorandum of the books she owned: these include all kinds of texts originally written in Latin, Greek, and French. Aphra Behn hailed Creech's translation of the Latin philosopher Lucretius with delight:

> Till now, I curst my Birth, my Education
> And more the scanted Customes of the Nation.
> Permitting not the Female Sex to tread
> The Mighty Paths of Learned Heroes dead . . .
> So thou by this Translation dost advance
> Our Knowledg from the State of Ignorance,
> And equals us to Man: Ah how can we
> Enough Adore, or Sacrifice enough to thee!

The sense that Classical learning *was* available to them, because ever more works were translated, is reiterated by women writers in the later seventeenth century. For example, Elizabeth Rowe's *Poems on Several Occasions* includes a preface by her friend Elizabeth Johnson, signed as from Hardings-rents on 10 May of that year, explaining one of her references with the words, 'for you must know we Read Plutarch now 'tis Translated'. Even in a scholarly family such as that of the Newdigates, the fact that her husband's Classical studies were mostly pursued via translations meant that Dame Alice Newdigate was in a position to imbibe a great deal of Classical lore, and did so. One of several women's responses to John Sprint's attempt to circumscribe women's role entirely to the service of men, *The Ladies Defence, or, The Bride-Woman's Counsellor Answer'd, a Poem in a Dialogue between Sir John Brute, Sir William Loveall, Melissa, and a Parson*, includes an 'Epistle Dedicatory' by the poet Mary, Lady Chudleigh, advising women to read Classics in translation (Seneca, Plutarch, Epictetus, then the poets). A French critic, H.-J. Martin, has described the seventeenth century as 'the time of translations', reflecting the astonishing amount of translation from Latin into French in the seventeenth century (some of it by women, notably Anne Dacier (1651–1720)) so much so, that by the mid-century, access to all Classical texts of importance could be achieved without the trouble of learning Latin or Greek. The cultural dominance of French, not merely in France but in Europe more generally, is witnessed by a letter sent from John Norris, a philosopher sympathetic to women's learning, to the bluestocking poet Elizabeth Thomas (1675–1731) with a sort of curriculum, in which he says: 'for some of them [the authors mentioned] there will be a Necessity of a Language or two, Latin is more difficult, and French will now answer all, which therefore I would have you learn out of Hand. It is the most commanding, and therefore most useful Language at present.'

In the eighteenth century, women continued to be concerned with translation. Mrs Chapone, a very influential voice in the education of girls in the eighteenth century, was ambivalent about their actually studying the classical languages: 'I respect the abilities and application of those ladies who have attained them [. . .] yet I would by no means advise [. . .] [any] woman who is not strongly impelled by a particular genius to engage in such studies,' but her grounds are that 'the real knowledge that they supply is not essential, since the English, French, or Italian tongues afford tolerable translations of all the most valuable productions of antiquity'. She assumes as a matter of course that a properly educated woman will read seriously in Classical literature, and says of Homer and Virgil in translation, 'every body reads [them] that reads at all'—she strongly recommended that Virgil be read in Annibale Caro's Italian version, because she considered that the closest to the original.

The Sixteenth Century

It is not surprising, given the immense cultural importance of translation in this period, to find early modern women engaging in translations themselves. It is possible to find English women translators as early as the fifteenth century: Henry VII's mother, Lady Margaret Beaufort, translated from French, and so did a London woman, Dame Eleanor Hull. It seems probable that for early modern women, translation offered a means of self-expression which was seen as relatively legitimate because the writer was not herself claiming the dignity of an author, but merely representing the work of someone else— though a number of writers indicate some anxiety about whether it is appropriate for a woman to write. In the sixteenth century, very few Englishwomen published anything at all. Of the nineteen known to me, just over half were translators. They include Mary Bassett and Anne Cooke, two of the best-educated women in English, who were both serious students of Greek and Latin, Queen Elizabeth herself, Mary Sidney the Countess of Pembroke (the sister of Sir Philip Sidney), and a middle-class woman, Margaret Tyler.

There are also many interesting translations by sixteenth-century women which were not published. New Year's gifts are an important part of sixteenth-century English culture, as Christmas gifts are today, and it was considered appropriate to give something which you had made. The English princesses, both Mary and Elizabeth, made translations as New Year's gifts, which showed off their accomplishments. Mary Tudor's translation of the Prayer of St Thomas Aquinas, made from Latin when she was twelve, still survives, and so do translations by Elizabeth, including a French translation of a work by Marguerite d'Angou-lême which was made as a present for her father Henry VIII. Other women did the same: both Lady Jane and Lady Mary Fitzalan (1536–76, 1540–57), the two daughters of the scholarly Earl of Arundel, made a series of translations from Latin and Greek as presents for their father which survive in the British Library. Lady Jane has left a translation of Isocrates from Greek to Latin, and a translation of Euripides' *Iphigeneia* into English, which she loved doing ('I have taken an incredible pleasure from this reading', she noted), and her sister Lady Mary similarly left four small quarto volumes of exercises, presented to her father as successive New Year's gifts from her thirteenth to seventeenth year, a book of moral sayings attributed to Classical authors such as Plato, Aristotle, and Seneca translated from Latin to English, a volume of translations from Alexander Severus, more moral sayings translated from Greek to English, and a fourth set translated from Greek to Latin: it is possible to see that each was more challenging than the last.

Mary Clark, later Mary Bassett, née Roper

Mary Clark, daughter of Margaret Roper, and granddaughter of Sir Thomas More, was classically educated, as her mother had been, and like her mother, put her languages to use. She translated her grandfather Sir Thomas More's *History of The Passion* from Latin to English and was considered one of the learned lights of Queen Mary Tudor's court. John Harpsfield asserts that Mary Roper was 'well experted in the latine and greeke tonges; she hath very hansomely and learnedly translated out of the greeke into the englishe all the ecclesiasticall storye of Eusebius, with Socrates, Theodoretus, Sozomenus and Euagrius, albeit of modestie she suppresseth it, and keepeth it from the print'. A manuscript now in the British Library, Harley 1860, contains the Eusebius translation, a Latin version of the first book of Eusebius's *Ecclesiastical History* with an English version of the first five books, dedicated to the future Queen Mary Tudor, *c.* 1550. It seems to be the actual manuscript copy presented to Mary, though it has lost the binding of purple velvet we know it originally had. Mary Clark's attitude to her work is apologetic:

> When I for myne owne onely exercyse had of late, most noble pryncesse, translated some part of thecclesyastycall storye [history] of Eusebius out of Greke into englysshe, not myndyng to have bestowed my fardour labour, as taken more payne therein, veryly [truly] accomptyng all my whole busyness brought to a fynall ende and conclusyion[. . .]

She is apparently dismissing her work as casually produced, nothing more than a private exercise; which she was somehow persuaded to extend into this huge, formal manuscript. It is common for early modern women translators to downplay their work in this way, assuring the reader that they are not trying to show off in an inappropriate, unfeminine fashion: we will see that similar points are made by Lucy Hutchinson in the seventeenth century.

Margaret Tyler

Another Elizabethan woman, Margaret Tyler, who translated a Spanish chivalric romance, is also conscious that people may find this strange. Interestingly, in excusing herself for translating a book on a manly subject (warfare), she shifts the ground by pointing out that according to legend, some women used to be warriors: thus, she implies, there is nothing very odd in a woman merely writing about war. The following passages give a sense of the flavour of her work.

Apology

> Such deliverie as I have made I hope thou wilt friendly acept, the rather for that it is a womans worke, though in a storye prophane, and a matter more manlike than becometh my sexe. But as for the manlinesse of the matter, thou knowest that it is not necessarie for every trumpetter or drumstare [drummer] in the warre to be a good fighter [. . .] it is no sinne to talke of *Robinhood*, though you never shot in his bowe: or be it that the attempt were bolde to intermeddle in armes, so as the auncient *Amazons* did and in this storie *Claridiana* doth, and in other stories not a few, yet to report of armes is not so odious but

that it may be borne withall, not only in you men which your selves are fighters, but in us women, to whome the benefit in equall part apperteineth of your victories.

Diego Ortúnez de Calaharra: *The Mirrour of Princely Deedes and Knyghthood*, **London, T. East, 1578, ch. 32.**

In the fresh and pleasant moneth of May, when the greene boughes and sweete smelling flowers renewe joye and gladnesse in the heartes of young folke, the great Citte of *London* and wide fieldes there-about, seemed not lesse covered with armed knights, then if the mightie hoasts of *Darius and Alexander* had thether assembled. For the great Feasts and Justes [jousts] were so diligently publyshed in everie Region and Countrey, and the prizes which the king had set, were of such valour, that there came thether from divers farre and straunge landes, so manye knights and ladies, as that the number of them was infinit.

Mildred Cecil, Lady Burghley, née Cooke (1526–1589)

One of the few women in the sixteenth century to say anything much about her practice as a translator is Mildred Cecil, wife of Elizabeth's chancellor, Lord Burghley. Like her sister Anne Bacon, who has already been mentioned, she was extremely well educated. At an early point in her life, before Elizabeth came to the throne, when she and her husband were very much the clients and protégés of the Duke of Somerset, Lord Protector of England during the minority of Edward VI, Mildred Cecil made a translation for Lady Somerset of a sermon by an early Christian Greek writer, St Basil the Great. This is prefaced by a letter 'to the veray noble and vertuose Duchesse of Summarsid hir ryght good lady and Mystres'. She describes her translation as follows, focusing on a perennial difficulty:

I have somwhat superstitiosely observid the nature of the greke phrase not omittyng the congruety of english speche but rather the use, that the treatye of so goode an Author shold not in to[o] moch serving the english tongue lese his owne efficacie and value. Thynkyng it lesse faute [fault] that thautor [the author] sholde speake grekish English and save his own sence, than english greke and confound it with a doutful, in this sheweng the propertie of the tonge, in the other the Veritie [truth] of the matter.

The Seventeenth Century

If we turn now to translation in the seventeenth century, there is a number of important women translators, most of whom were educated gentlewomen. As Isaac Watts observes, there were many Stuart gentlewomen 'rich in Learning, yet averse to Show'. Among numerous other examples, we may consider Martha, Lady Giffard, who read Latin with ease, made an accomplished English version of Horace's poem 'O fons Bandusiae', and advised her niece, Lady Berkeley in 1698, 'I would faine advise about your reading what I practice myself not to read anything very serious before you goe to bed; that would be a good time to read Virgil in, and let your Turkish history only goe a dayes.' Similarly, Anna Hume, daughter of the Scots historian, poet, and essayist David Hume of Godscroft, is usually given credit for the English translation of the Latin verses in her father's *History of the Houses of Douglas and Angus*. Elizabeth Cary, Lady Falkland (1585–1639), author of the closet drama *Mariamne*, translated all her life. Her daughter testifies in her biography of her mother, 'Afterwards, by herself, without a teacher, and while still a child, she learned French, Spanish and Italian (which she always understood quite perfectly). She learned Latin in the same manner (without being taught) and understood it perfectly when she was young, translating the Epistles of Seneca from Latin to English. After having long discontinued it, she was much more imperfect in it, so when a little time before her death she translated some of Blosius out of Latin, she was fain to help herself somewhat with the Spanish translation.' These translations seem to have been private, but later in her life, she attempted to aid the cause of Catholicism in England by translating Cardinal Perron's *Replique à la response du serenissime roy de la Grand Bretagne* (Perron was an internationally important figure, with a considerable influence on the religious life of England), which was printed with a dedication to her patroness, Queen Henrietta Maria: most of the copies were seized and burnt.

Katherine Phillips (1631–1664)

Katherine Phillips is the first successful woman playwright, though unlike Aphra Behn, she did not write for the commercial stage. Nonetheless, her translation of Corneille's *La Mort de Pompée* made her famous. She was a Royalist married to a Parliamentarian, and due to the political difficulties this posed, she and her husband lived quietly in Wales throughout the Civil War. However, she became known as a poet in her late teens, and at the Restoration in 1661, she became more publicly visible. In 1662, her close friend Anne Owen married the distinguished Anglo-Irish Royalist Marcus Trevor, of County Down, and Katherine was invited to accompany her on the nuptial journey to her husband's house at Rostrevor. Katherine's reputation as a poet preceded her and she was enthusiastically received by Dublin society. The Earl of Orrery, having seen her translation of a single scene, 'earnestly importuned' her to execute a complete translation of Corneille's play. This was ready by November and produced at the Theatre Royal, Smock Alley,

Dublin, in February 1663. Phillips's attitude towards her own work is extremely modest; but however, her own views of translation come out in a letter she sent to her friend and adviser, Sir Charles Cottrell, in her criticism of a rival translation of *Pompée* by 'Certain Persons of Honour':

'Pharsalian Kites' for 'les Vautours de Pharsale', I cannot relish; his englishing 'le dernier preuve de leur Amitie', 'their new friendship' & many additions & omissions of the authors sence. then in the second, & fourth Acts, (which are all I have) unless the parts acted, were much reform'd from this coppy, there are as many faults as ever I saw in a good Poem; which were I neare you, I could much better ask your opinion of, onely let me now inquire what you think of these words

> Ne me parlez donc plus de Tage & de Gange
> je connoy ma portée, & ne prends point de change

which they have english'd thus:

> Talk not to me of Tagus, nor of Ganges
> I know my right & care not for yr changes.

And calling Juba Scipio the Pompey's Sons, (for a Rime too), Daring Sprights, making Cleopatra say she courts Caesar, & add 10: or 12 lines of Romes becoming a Monarchy, for which as there is no ground in Corneille, so I see not how it would have been proper for her to say at that time, when Caesar had just refus'd a Crown being piqué d'honneur, not to be thought Rome's Soveraign, though he was her Master. I think a translation ought not to be used as Musicians doe a Ground, with all the liberty of descant, but as Painters when they coppy, & the rule that I understood of translations till these Gentlemen inform'd me better, was to write to Corneille's sence, as it is to be supposed Corneille would have done, if he had been an Englishman, not confind to his lines, nor his numbers (unless we can doe it happily) but always to his meaning, or to say all, to translate as the temple of death is translated, where the Originall appears in its own true undisfigured proportion, & yet beautify'd with all the riches of another tongue.

(*The Temple of Death* was a translation by Cottrell himself, of Habert's *Le Temple de Mort*, so the allusion is a compliment to him.) The texture of Phillips's own translation, notably smoother than that of the 'Certain Persons of Honour', is illustrated below.

Cornelia's speech to Caesar

> CORNELIA. Caesar, that envious Fate which I can brave,
> Makes me thy Prisoner, but not thy Slave:
> Expect not then my Heart should e're afford
> To pay thee Homage, or to call thee Lord:

How rude soever Fortune makes her Blow;
I Crassus Widow once, and Pompey's now;
Great Scipio's Daughter, (and what's higher yet)
A Roman, have a Courage still more great;
And of all Stroaks her Cruelty can give,
Nothing can make me blush, but that I live,
And have not follow'd Pompey, when he dy'd;
For though the Means to do it were deny'd,
And Cruel Pity would not let me have
The quick assistance of a Steel or Wave,
Yet I'm asham'd, that after such a Woe,
Grief had not done as much as they could do:
Death had been glorious, and had set me free
As from my Sorrow then, so now from Thee.
Yet I must thank the Gods, though so severe,
That since I must come hither, Thou art here:
That Caesar reigns here, and not Ptolomy;
And yet, O Heaven! what Stars do govern me?
That some faint kind of satisfaction 'tis,
To meet here with my greatest Enemies;
And into their Hands that I rather fall,
Then into His that ow'd my Husband all.
But of thy Conquest, Caesar, make no boast,
Which to my single Destiny thou ow'st;
I both my Husbands Fortunes have defac'd,
And twice have caus'd th'whole World to be disgrac'd;
My Nuptial Knot twice ominously ty'd,
Banish'd the Gods from the Uprighter Side;
Happy in misery I had been, if it,
For Romes advantage, had with Thee been Knit;
And on thy House that I could so dispense
All my own Stars malignant influence:
For never think my Hatred can grow less,
Since I the Roman Constancy profess;
And though thy Captive, yet a Heart like mine,
Can never stoop to hope for ought from Thine:
Command, but think not to subject my Will,
Remember this, I am Cornelia still.

Lucy Hutchinson, née Apsley (1620 – after 1662)

The highly educated Lucy Hutchinson produced two significant translations, neither of which was published; one of the classical Latin poet Lucretius, the other of a Latin theological work by John Owen. She was a precocious child: according to her own account of her life, she could read by the age of four, and by the time she was seven, she had eight tutors in languages, music, dancing, writing, and needlework. She also learned Latin, at the express wish of her father. She shows another side of the difficulties women faced as writers in the following letter which she wrote as an introduction of her translation of Lucretius, a manuscript presented to the Earl of Anglesey, in which she is anxious to demonstrate the amateur character of her work:

> When I present this unworthy translation to your Lordship, I sacrifice my shame to my obedience, for (though a masculine witt hath thought it work printing his head in a laurell crowne for the version of one of these bookes) I am so farre from gloriing [glorying] in my six, that had they not by misfortune bene gone out of my hands in one lost copie, even your Lordships command, which hath more authority with me, then any humane thing I pay reverence to, should not have redeemd it from the fire [...] And therefore, since I did attempt things out of my own Sphaere, I am sorry I had not the capacity of making a worke, nor the good fortune of chusing a subject, worthy of being presented to your Lordship [...] Afterward being convincd of the sin of amusing my selfe with such vaine Philosophy (which even at the first I did not employ any serious studie in, for I turnd it into English in a roome where my children practizd the severall quallities they were taught with their Tutors, and I numbred the sillables of my translation by the threds of the canvas I wrought in, and sett them downe with a pen and inke that stood by me; (how superficially it must needs be done in this manner, the thing itselfe will shew,) but I say afterwards as my judgement grew riper, and my mind was fixt in more profitable contemplations, I thought this booke not worthy either of review or correction, the whole worke being one fault.

Lucy Hutchinson is sincere in what she says here: she was deeply devout, and she clearly had misgivings about spending time on Lucretius, known as 'the atheist philosopher'. But there are also issues here about writing as a woman, 'whose more becoming vertue is silence', as she says elsewhere in this introduction. Like the much earlier Mary Clark, she claims a degree of amateurism which is belied by the translation itself, a very large, ambitious production translated from a classical language. Both women, however, created a single, handsomely written presentation manuscript, which was an end in itself rather than intended as the fair copy for a subsequent edition. Both also claim, implausibly, that the work was achieved casually, almost accidentally, without any desire to profit from it. They thus get their apology in first, disarming criticism of both the woman for writing, and of the work itself, establishing that their work should not be measured against the serious work of university-educated men. However, the impression is inevitably given by the translation itself that it is possible for a woman to produce high-quality translation while supervising a roomful of children and embroidering with the other hand, suggesting an almost superhuman ease and confidence. Hutchinson's translation of the third book of Lucretius can usefully be contrasted with that of John Dryden, 'Translation of the Last Part of the Third Book of Lucretius: Against the Fear of Death' (1685), which is printed in Sect. 2.13, below.

> Now though the nature of the soule, dismist
> From humane bodies, could with sence subsist,
> Yett that concerns not us, who have alone
> Our life and being in their conjuctions.
> Neither though time should after death restore
> Our matter to the state it had before,
> And us in regions of the light revive
> Coud we a benifitt from thence derive,
> After the chaine of life were broke, and we
> Once interrupted in our memorie.
> We now in life are not sollicitous
> For what was done before nor anxious
> For what our matter shall hereafter doe
> When time shall our dissolved frames renew.
> For when we look back on vast ages gone,
> And on the matters various motion,
> Tis easie to believe the seeds have bene
> In the same positures oft, that now they'are in.
> But tis not to our memories disclosd
> Because lifes pawses oft are interpos'd
> In which with diverse wandring motions they
> Long time devested of all sences stray.
> To future woes ordeind, men must survive
> In that time when those evills may arrive.
> Now, since death doth our former beings cease,
> And this which the like troubles may distresse
> Prohibitts to have bene before, wee see
> Theres nothing to be feard in death, and he

Who hath no being, feeles no calamitie.
In men, whom never-failing death deprives
Of mortall being, whither unborne their lives
Never begin, or spun out vanish thus
The difference is not aniething to us.

Aphra Behn, née Johnson (?1640–1689)

Aphra Behn is very well known as the first successful woman playwright in English. She made a reasonable living as a dramatist from 1670 until 1682, when London's two theatre companies amalgamated into the United Company, halving the demand for new plays. Thereafter she augmented her income with translations, from French and Latin (the latter from intermediate English versions), as well as poetry. As a dramatist, she declared her pride in her work, her desire for fame and literary recognition as well as money. It is therefore not surprising to find that her translation work was ambitious. One of the most famous and often-quoted works on translation theory in her time was the *Essay on Translated Verse* by Wentworth Dillon, fourth Earl of Roscommon (?1633–85). Aphra Behn's translation of Bernard de Fontenelle's *A Discovery of New Worlds* is prefaced by an essay on the translation of prose which explicitly measures itself against Roscommon's work, and offers an analysis of the particular difficulties offered by various European languages, based on their linguistic history. She is therefore claiming a space for herself not as a mere hack, but as a public intellectual, an approach completely different from that of contemporaries such as Lucy Hutchinson and Katherine Phillips, who present their work as private and amateur.

The Translator's PREFACE

> The General Applause this little Book of the Plurality of Worlds has met with, both in France and England in the Original, made me attempt to translate it into English. The Reputation of the Author, (who is the same, who writ the *Dialogues of the Dead*) the Novelty of the Subject in vulgar Languages, and the Authors introducing a Woman as one of the speakers in these five Discourses, were further Motives for me to undertake this little work; for I thought an English Woman might adventure to translate any thing, a French Woman may be supposed to have spoken: But when I had made a Tryal, I found the Task not so easie as I believed at first. Therefore, before I say any thing, either of the Design of the Author, or of the Book it self, give me leave to say something of Translation of Prose in general: As for Translation of Verse, nothing can be added to that Incomparable Essay of the late Earl of Roscommon, the nearer the Idioms or turn of the Phrase

of two Languages agree, 'tis the easier to translate one into the other. The Italian, Spanish and French, are all three at best Corruptions of the Latin, with the mixture of Gothic, Arabick and Gaulish Words. The Italian, as it is nearest the Latin, is also nearest the English: For its mixture being composed of Latin, and the Language of the Goths, Vandals, and other Northern Nations, who over-ran the Roman Empire, and conquer'd its Language with its Provinces, most of these Northern Nations spoke the Teutonick or Dialects of it, of which the English is one also; and that's the Reason, that the English and Italian learn the Language of one another sooner than any other; because not only the Phrase, but the Accent of both do very much agree, the Spanish is next of kin to the English, for almost the same Reason: Because the Goths and Vandals having over-run Africk, and kept Possession of it for some hundred of Years, where mixing with the Moors, no doubt, gave them a great Tincture of their Tongue. These Moors afterwards invaded and conquered Spain; besides Spain was before that also invaded and conquered by the Goths, who possessed it long after the time of the two Sons of Theodosius the Great, Arcadus and Honorius. The French, as it is most remote from the Latin, so the Phrase and Accent differ most from the English: It may be, it is more agreeable with the Welsh, which is near a-kin to the Basbritton and Biscagne Languages [Breton and Basque], which is derived from the old Celtick Tongue, the first that was spoken amongst the Ancient Gauls, who descended from the Celts.

The French therefore is of all the hardest to translate into English. For proof of this, there are other Reasons also. And first, the nearer the Genious and Humour of two Nations agree, the Idioms of their Speech are the nearer; and every Body knows there is more Affinity between the English and Italian People, than the English and the French, as to their Humours; and for that Reason, and for what I have said before, it is very difficult to translate Spanish into French; and I believe hardly possible to translate French into Dutch. The Second Reason is, the Italian Language is the same now as it was some hundred of Years ago, so is the Spanish, not only as to the Phrase, but even as to the Words and Orthography; whereas the French Language has suffered more Changes this hundred Years past, since Francis the first, than the Fashion of their Cloths, and Ribbons, in Phrase, Words and Orthography. So that I am confident a French Man a hundred Years hence will no more understand an old Edition of Froisard's *History* [Jean Froissard's *Chronicles*, written in the late fourteenth century], than he will understand Arabick. I confess the French Arms, Money and Intrigues have made their Language very universal of late, for this they to be commended. It is an Accident, which they owe to the greatness of their King and their own Industry; and it may fall out hereafter to be otherwise. A third Reason is as I said before, that the French being a Corruption of the Latin, French Authors take a liberty to borrow a Word they want from the Latin, without farther Ceremony, especially when they treat of Sciences. This the English do not do, but at second hand from the French. It is Modish to Ape the French in every thing: Therefore, we not only naturalize their words, but words they steal from other Languages. I wish in this and several other things, we had a little more of the Italian and Spanish Humour, and did not chop and change our language, as we do our Cloths, at the Pleasure of every French Tailor.

In translating French into English, most People are very cautious and unwilling to print a French Word at first out of a new Book, till Use has rendered it more familiar to us; and therefore it runs a little rough in English, to express one French Word, by two or three of ours; and thus much, as to the Ease and Difficulty of translating these Languages in general: But, as to the French in particular, it has as many Advantages of the English, as to the Sound, as ours has of the French, as to the Signification: which is another Argument of the different Genius of the two Nations. Almost all the Relatives, Articles, and Pronouns in the French Language, end in Vowels, and are written with two or three Letters. Many of their words begin with Vowels, so that when a word after a Relative, Pronoun or Article, ends with a Vowel, and begins with another, they admit of their beloved Figure Apostrophe, and cut off the first Vowel. This they do to shun an ill sound; and they are so musical as to that, that they will go against all the Rules of Sense and Grammar, rather than fail; as for Speaking of a Man's Wife they say, son Epouse; whereas in Grammar, it ought to be sa Epouse; but this would throw a French-Man into a Fit of a Fever, to hear one say, by way of Apostrophe S'Epouse, as this makes their Language to run smoother, so by this they express several Words very shortly, as qu'entend je, in English, what do I hear? In this Example, three words have the Sound but of one, for Sound prevails with them in the beginning, middle and end. Secondly, their words generally end in Vowels, or if they do not, they do not pronounce the Consonant, for the most part unless there be two together, or that the next word begins with a Vowel. Thirdly, by the help of their Relatives, they can shortly, and with ease resume a long Preceeding Sentence, in two or three short words; these are the Advantages of the French Tongue, all which they borrow from the Latin. But as the French do not value a plain Suit without a Garniture, they are not satisfied with the Advantages they have, but confound their own Language with needless Repetitions and Tautologies; and by a certain Rhetorical Figure, peculiar to themselves, imply twenty Lines, to express what an English Man would say, with more Ease and Sense in five; and this is the great Misfortune of translating French into English: If one endeavours to make it English Standard, it is no Translation. If one follows their Flourishes and Embroideries, it is worse than French Tinsel. But these defects are only comparatively, in respect of English: And I do not say this so much, to condemn the French, as to praise our own Mother-Tongue, for what we think a Deformity, they may think a Perfection; as the Negroes of Guinney think us as ugly, as we think them.

[Behn translates Fontenelle's own preface in the following manner, showing also why she found this work on popular science interesting: it was an attempt to make contemporary ideas about physics and the nature of the universe accessible to people without a university education, and was particularly aimed at women.]

The Author's PREFACE

I find my self reduced almost to the same Condition in which Cicero was, when he undertook to put Matters of Philosophy in Latin; which, till that time, had never been treated of, but in Greek. He tells us, it would be said, his Works would be unprofitable, since those who loved Philosophy, having already taken the pains to find it in the Greek, would neglect, after that, to read it again in Latin (that not being the Original;) and that who did not care for Philosophy, would not seek it, either in the Latin, or the Greek. But to this *Cicero* himself answer, and says, That those who were not Philosophers would be tempted to the Reading of it, by the Facility they Would find in its being in the Latin Tongue; and that those who were Philosophers would be curious enough to see how well it had been turned from the Greek to the Latin.

Cicero had reason to answer in this manner; the Excellency of his Genius, and the great Reputation he had already acquired sufficiently defend this new Undertaking of his, which he had dedicated to the benefit of the Publick. For my part, I am far from offering at any Defence for this of mine, though the Enterprize be the same; for I would treat of Philosophy in a manner altogether unphilosophical, and have endeavoured to bring it to a Point not too rough and harsh for the Capacity of the Numbers, nor too light and trivial for the *Learned* [...]

In this Discourse I have introduced a fair Lady to be instructed in Philosophy, which, till now, never heard any speak of it; imagining, by this Fiction, I shall render my Work more agreeable, and to encourage the fair Sex (who lose so much time at their Toylet in a less charming Study) by the Example of a Lady who had no supernatural Character, and who never goes beyond the Bounds of a Person who has no Tincture of Learning, and yet understands all that is told her.

The Eighteenth Century

The most famous learned woman of eighteenth-century England was Elizabeth Carter, because she translated from Greek, but while the depth of her knowledge of Greek is something very out of the ordinary, as a student of Latin, she is a less isolated figure than she appears: to name only other obvious bluestockings (as learned ladies of the eighteenth century were called), Hannah Thrale read Latin and translated Latin poetry (for example, she translates a little poem by the Emperor Hadrian in her *Retrospection* (1801), i. 44).

Another famous bluestocking, Hannah More, novelist, poet, and moralist, also knew Latin. Lady Mary Wortley Montagu taught herself Latin, so effectively that her juvenilia at sixteen or so includes an imitation of Ovid's *Heroides*, the death of Adonis from his *Metamorphoses*, and an imitation of Virgil's tenth eclogue. All this activity suggests, rightly, that Englishwomen continued to take a lively interest in translation, even from classical languages.

Elizabeth Carter (1717–1806)

Montagu Pennington, in his *Memoirs of Mrs Elizabeth Carter* (London, 1807), states, 'It was her most eager desire to be a scholar [. . .] the slowness with which she conquered the impediments, that always oppose the beginning of the study of the dead languages, was such as wearied even the patience of her father [. . .] but she was determined to overcome the difficulty.' If this is the case, then she triumphed over her slowness, and became the most famous woman scholar of her generation. She was also known as a poet and writer, and translated Crousaz's *Examination of Mr Pope's Essay on Man* (1738) from French, and Algarotti's *Sir Isaac Newton's Philosophy Explain'd, for the Use of the Ladies* (1739) from Italian, but her chief claim to fame was her translation of Epictetus from ancient Greek. Curiously, she is the second woman to translate this Stoic philosopher, though she was not aware of the fact (the learned Dane Birgitte Thott published a Danish translation in Copenhagen in 1661). She comments briefly on her method of translation in the preface below.

From *All the Works of Epictetus which are now Extant* (1758)

It was judged proper, that a Translation of him should be undertaken; there being none, I believe, but of the Enchiridion, in any modern Language, excepting a pretty good French one, published about a hundred and fifty years ago, and so extremely scarce, that I was unable to procure it, till Mr Harris obligingly lent it me, after I had published the Proposals for printing this: which notwithstanding the Assistance given me in the Prosecution of it, hath still, I am sensible, great Faults. But they, who will see them the most clearly, will be the readiest to excuse, as they will know best the Difficulty of avoiding them. There is one Circumstance, which, I am apprehensive, must be particularly striking, and possibly shocking to many, the frequent Use of some Words in an unpopular Sense: an Inconvenience, which, however, I flatter myself, the Introduction and Notes will, in some Degree, remove. In the Translation of technical terms, if the same *Greek* word had not always been rendered in the same manner, at least when the Propriety of our Language will at all permit it, every new Expression would have been apt to raise a new Idea. The Reader, I hope, will pardon, if not approve, the Uncouthness, in many Places, of a Translation pretty strictly literal: as it seemed necessary, upon the whole, to preserve the original Spirit, the peculiar Turn, and characteristic Roughness of the Author.

[This is a sample of the actual translation (bk II, ch. xi, pp. 147–8).]

The Beginning of Philosophy is this: The being sensible of the Disagreement of Men with each other: an Inquiry into the Cause of this Disagreement; and a Disapprobation, and Distrust of what merely *seems*: a certain Examination into what seems, whether it seem rightly: and an Invention of some Rule, like a Balance, for the Determination of Weights; like a Square for strait and crooked.

2.13 JOHN DRYDEN

David Hopkins
(University of Bristol)

Dryden's writings on translation are best considered not as a fixed body of theory or doctrine, but as the working notes of a practitioner, based on broad principles established early in his translating career, but continually modified, enriched, and transformed by subsequent discoveries and challenges in the field. Dryden's translations, from the Classical poets Homer, Horace, Juvenal, Lucretius, Ovid, Persius, Virgil, and Theocritus, and from the medieval writers Chaucer and Boccaccio, constitute about two-thirds of his non-dramatic verse. They were the poet's main source of income in the last decade of his life, and were widely regarded, for well over a hundred years after his death, as the crown of his creative achievement. Dryden was, by inclination, an 'occasional' translator, who preferred to select poems and passages which had 'affected' him with a particular vividness and urgency 'in the reading', or to whose authors he felt he had a 'soul congenial'. (His version of the works of Virgil—his only attempt at rendering another author's oeuvre in its entirety, and the only one of his translations about which he expresses any weariness or misgivings—is the exception which proves the rule). Dryden's translations reveal him constantly (in T. S. Eliot's words) 'giving the original through himself and finding himself through the original'. A study of Dryden's translating practice is thus, necessarily and simultaneously, a study of the poet's imaginative communings with a number of his favourite fellow-writers.

Dryden's main reflections on translation are to be found in the prefaces and dedicatory epistles prefixed to the various miscellanies and collections in which his versions appeared between 1680 and 1700. These discussions focus on a number of recurring questions and preoccupations: the kinds of knowledge that any successful translator needs to possess; the kind of fidelity to his original which he should seek; the ways in which he might best preserve the distinctive 'character' of each of their originals; the degree to which he might properly add to, subtract from, or 'update' material in his original; the larger contribution which translation might make to the culture and language of the nation. In the Preface to *Ovid's Epistles* (1680), Dryden proposed his celebrated tripartite division of translation into 'metaphrase', 'paraphrase', and 'imitation'. 'Metaphrase' is rejected on the grounds that it produces versions of such crabbed awkwardness that they can give little idea of the artistic quality of their originals. 'Imitation' is criticized because of an excessive freedom which makes it more properly regarded as original poetry than as translation.

'Paraphrase'—translation in which the contours of the original are attentively observed, but with a freedom which allows the translator to convey the 'spirit' and 'sense' rather than merely the 'letter' of the original—is offered as the ideal *via media* between the two extremes.

Dryden broadly adhered to 'paraphrase' throughout his translating career, but his later prefaces and practice reveal him constantly modifying his theory both in details (elements of 'metaphrase' and 'imitation' are frequently incorporated piecemeal at the local level) and in larger responses to specific challenges posed by particular writers. In the Preface to *Sylvae* (1685), Dryden, buoyed up with confidence by the 'hot fit' of activity which had recently produced his masterly renderings of Lucretius, Horace, and Virgil, claims the right to exercise a greater degree of freedom than he had exercised hitherto, in order to produce translations which, if his original 'were living, and Englishman, . . . are such as he would probably have written'. And when preparing his versions of the highly allusive and topical Roman satirists Juvenal and Persius (1692; dated 1693), Dryden clearly became convinced that further liberties were necessary if his versions were to convey to cultivated English readers a comprehensible and vivid impression of the pointed and acerbic wit which characterized his originals.

By the Preface to his last volume, *Fables Ancient and Modern*, Dryden's discussions of translation had moved beyond the specifics of method and technique, to present the translator's art in quasi-mystical terms, as a kind of spiritual 'transfusion' or metempsychosis, in which the souls of particular poets, like the constituent elements of individual human beings described by Ovid's Pythagoras, are imagined as achieving posthumous life, in a perpetual cycle of flux and renewal, through the renderings and reimaginings of their successors.

Dryden on Translation

From Preface to *Ovid's Epistles* (London: J. Tonson, 1680)

Three Types of Translation

All translation, I suppose, may be reduced to these three heads.

First, that of metaphrase, or turning an author word by word and line by line, from one language into another. Thus, or near this manner, was Horace his *Art of Poetry* translated by Ben Jonson. The second way is that of paraphrase, or translation with latitude, where the author is kept in view by the translator so as never to be lost, but his words are not so strictly followed as his sense, and that too is admitted to be amplified, but not altered. Such is Mr Waller's translation of Virgil's Fourth *Aeneid*. The third way is that of imitation, where the translator (if now he has not lost that name) assumes the liberty not only to vary from the words and sense, but to forsake them both as he sees occasion, and taking only some general hints from the original, to run division on the groundwork as he pleases. Such is Mr Cowley's practice in turning two Odes of Pindar, and one of Horace, into English.

The Hazards of 'Metaphrase'

'Tis almost impossible to translate verbally and well at the same time; for the Latin (a most severe and compendious language) often expresses that in one word which either the barbarity or the narrowness of modern tongues cannot supply in more. [...] the verbal copier is encumbered with so many difficulties at once that he can never disentangle himself from all. He is to consider at the same time the thought of his author and his words, and to find out the counterpart to each in another language; and besides this, he is to confine himself to the compass of numbers, and the slavery of rhyme. 'Tis much like dancing on ropes with fettered legs: a man may shun a fall by using caution; but the gracefulness of motion is not to be expected: and when we have said the best of it, 'tis but a foolish task; for no sober man would put himself into a danger for the applause of 'scaping without breaking his neck.

The Translator's Language

No man is capable of translating poetry who, besides a genius to that art, is not a master both of his author's language and of his own. Nor must we understand the language only of the poet, but his particular turn of thoughts and of expression, which are the characters that distinguish, and, as it were, individuate him from all other writers. When we are come thus far, 'tis time to look into ourselves, to conform our genius to his, to give his thought either the same turn, if our tongue will bear it, or, if not, to vary but the dress, not to alter or destroy the substance. The like care must be taken of the more outward ornaments, the words. When they appear (which is but seldom) literally graceful, it were an injury to the author that they should be changed. But since every language is so full of its own proprieties, that what is beautiful in one is often barbarous, nay sometimes nonsense, in another, it would be unreasonable to limit a translator to the narrow compass of his author's words: 'tis enough if he choose out some expression which does not vitiate the sense. I suppose he may stretch his chain to such a latitude; but by innovation of thoughts, methinks he breaks it. By this means the spirit of an author may be transfused, and yet not lost: and thus 'tis plain that the reason alleged by Sir John Denham has no farther force than to expression; for thought, if it be translated truly, cannot be lost in another language; but the words that convey it to our apprehension (which are the image and ornament of that thought) may be so ill chosen as to make it appear in an unhandsome dress, and rob it of its native lustre. There is therefore a liberty to be allowed for the expression, neither is it necessary that words and lines should be confined to the measure of their original. The sense of an author, generally speaking, is to be sacred and inviolable.

From Preface to *Sylvae* (London: printed for Jacob Tonson, 1685)

Freedom and Pedantry in Translation

I have both added and omitted, and even sometimes very boldly made such expositions of my authors, as no Dutch commentator will forgive me. Perhaps, in such particular passages, I have thought that I discovered some beauty yet undiscovered by those pedants, which none but a poet could have found. Where I have taken away some of their expressions, and cut them shorter, it may possibly be on this consideration, that what was beautiful in the Greek or Latin would not appear so shining in the English: and where I have enlarged them, I desire the false critics would not always think that those thoughts are wholly mine, but that either they are secretly in the poet, or may be fairly deduced from him: or at least, if both those considerations should fail, that my own is of a piece with his, and that if he were living, and an Englishman, they are such as he would probably have written.

For, after all, a translator is to make his author appear as charming as possibly he can, provided he maintains his character, and makes him not unlike himself. Translation is a kind of drawing after the life; where every one will acknowledge there is a double sort of likeness, a good one and a bad. 'Tis one thing to draw the outlines true, the features like, the proportions exact, the colouring itself perhaps tolerable; and another thing to make all these graceful by the posture, the shadowings, and chiefly by the spirit which animates the whole. I cannot without some indignation look on an ill copy of an excellent original; much less can I behold with patience Virgil, Homer, and some others, whose beauties I have been endeavouring all my life to imitate, so abused, as I may say to their faces, by a botching interpreter. What English readers, unacquainted with Greek or Latin, will believe me, or any other man, when we commend those authors, and confess we derive all that is pardonable in us from their fountains, if they take those to be the same poets whom our Ogilbys have translated? But I dare assure them that a good poet is no more like himself in a dull translation, than his carcass would be to his living body. There are many who understand Greek and Latin, and yet are ignorant of their mother tongue. The proprieties and delicacies of the English are known to few; 'tis impossible even for a good wit to understand and practise them, without the help of a liberal education, long reading, and digesting of those few good authors we have amongst us, the knowledge of men and manners, the freedom of habitudes and conversation with the best company of both sexes; and, in short, without wearing off the rust which he contracted while he was laying in a stock of learning.

Maintaining the Character of an Original

Thus it appears necessary that a man should be a nice critic in his mother tongue before he attempts to translate a foreign language. Neither is it sufficient that he be able to judge of words and style; but he must be a master of them too. He must perfectly understand his author's tongue, and absolutely command his own; so that to be a thorough translator, he must be a thorough poet. Neither is it enough to give his author's sense in good English, in poetical expressions, and in musical numbers. For, although all these are exceeding difficult to perform, there yet remains an harder task; and 'tis a secret of which few translators have sufficiently thought. I have already hinted a word or two concerning it; that is, the maintaining the character of an author, which distinguishes him from all others, and makes him appear that individual poet whom you would interpret. For example, not only the thoughts, but the style and versification of Virgil and Ovid are very different. Yet I see, even in our best poets who have translated some parts of them, that they have confounded their several talents; and by endeavouring only at the sweetness and harmony of numbers, have made them both so much alike that, if I did not know the originals, I should never be able to judge by the copies which was Virgil and which was Ovid. It was objected against a late noble painter, that he drew many graceful pictures, but few of them were like. And this happened to him because he always studied himself more than those who sat to him. In such translators I can easily distinguish the hand which performed the work, but I cannot distinguish their poet from another.

The Challenge of Translating Lucretius

If I am not mistaken, the distinguishing character of Lucretius (I mean of his soul and genius) is a certain kind of noble pride, and positive assertion of his opinions. He is everywhere confident of his own reason, and assuming an absolute command, not only over his vulgar reader, but even his patron Memmius. For he is always bidding him attend, as if he had the rod over him; and using a magisterial authority while he instructs him. [. . .] He seems to disdain all manner of replies, and is so confident of his cause that he is beforehand with his antagonists, urging for them whatever he imagined they could say, and leaving them, as he supposes, without an objection for the future. All this, too, with so much scorn and indignation, as if he were assured of the triumph before he entered into the lists. From this sublime and daring genius of his, it must of necessity come to pass that his thoughts must be masculine, full of argumentation, and that sufficiently warm. From the same fiery temper proceeds the loftiness of his expressions, and the perpetual torrent of his verse, where the barrenness of his subject does not too much restrain the quickness of his fancy. [. . .] These are the considerations which I had of that author, before I attempted to translate some parts of him. And accordingly I laid by my natural diffidence and scepticism for a while, to take up that dogmatical way of his, which, as I said, is so much his character as to make him that individual poet.

Capturing the Character of Horace

That which will distinguish his style from all other poets is the elegance of his words, and the numerousness of this verse; there is nothing so delicately turned in all the Roman language. There appears in every part of his diction, or (to speak English) in all his expressions, a kind of noble and bold purity. His words are chosen with as much exactness as Virgil's; but there seems to be a greater spirit in them. [...] But the most distinguishing part of all his character seems to me to be his briskness, his jollity, and his good humour; and those I have chiefly endeavoured to copy; his other excellencies, I confess, are above my imitation. One ode which infinitely pleased me in the reading, I have attempted to translate in Pindaric verse; 'tis that which is inscribed to the present Earl of Rochester, to whom I have particular obligations, which this small testimony of my gratitude can never pay. 'Tis his darling in the Latin, and I have taken some pains to make it my masterpiece in English: for which reason I took this kind of verse, which allows more latitude than any other.

From Dedication to the *Aeneis* (1697), in *The Works of Virgil*, translated into English verse by Mr Dryden (London: printed for Jacob Tonson, 1697)

Imitating Virgil's Numbers

His words are not only chosen, but the places in which he ranks them for the sound. He who removes them from the station wherein their master sets them spoils the harmony. What he says of the Sibyl's prophecies may be as properly applied to every word of his: they must be read in order as they lie; the least breath discomposes them; and somewhat of their divinity is lost. I cannot boast that I have been thus exact in my verses; but I have endeavoured to follow the example of my master, and am the first Englishman, perhaps, who made it his design to copy him in his numbers, his choice of words, and his placing them for the sweetness of the sound. On this last consideration, I have shunned the caesura [elision] as much as possibly I could; for, wherever that is used it gives a roughness to the verse, of which we have little need in a language which is overstocked with consonants. Such is not the Latin, where the vowels and consonants are mixed in proportion to each other: yet Virgil judged the vowels to have somewhat of an overbalance, and therefore tempers their sweetness with caesuras. Such difference there is in tongues, that the same figure which roughens one gives majesty to another; and that was it which Virgil studied in his verses.

Dryden's Freedoms in Translating Virgil

The way I have taken is not so strait as metaphrase, nor so loose as paraphrase; some things too I have omitted, and sometimes have added of my own. Yet the omissions, I hope, are but of circumstances, and such as would have no grace in English; and the additions, I also hope, are easily deduced from Virgil's sense. They will seem (at least I have the vanity to think so) not stuck into him, but growing out of him. He studies brevity more than any other poet: but he had the advantage of a language wherein much may be comprehended in a little space. We, and all the modern tongues, have more articles and pronouns, besides signs of tenses and cases, and other barbarities on which our speech is built by the faults of our forefathers. [. . .] I thought fit to steer betwixt the two extremes of paraphrase and literal translation; to keep as near my author as I could, without losing all his graces, the most eminent of which are in the beauty of his words; and those words, I must add, are always figurative. Such of these as would retain their elegance in our tongue, I have endeavoured to graff on it; but most of them are of necessity to be lost, because they will not shine in any but their own. Virgil has sometimes two of them in a line; but the scantiness of our heroic verse is not capable of receiving more than one; and that too must expiate for many others, which have none. Such is the difference of the languages, or such my want of skill in choosing words. Yet I may presume to say [. . .] that, taking all the materials of this divine author, I have endeavoured to make Virgil speak such English as he would himself had spoken, if he had been born in England, and in this present age.

The Translator's Burden

But slaves we are, and labour on another man's plantation; we dress the vineyard, but the wine is the owner's; if the soil be sometime barren, then we are sure of being scourged: if it be fruitful, and our care succeeds, we are not thanked; for the proud reader will only say, the poor drudge has done his duty. But this is nothing to what follows; for being obliged to make his sense intelligible, we are forced to untune our own verses, that we may give his meaning to the reader. He who invents is master of his thoughts and words; he can turn and vary them as he pleases, till he renders them harmonious; but the wretched translator has no such privilege; for being tied to the thoughts, he must make what music he can in the expression; and, for this reason, it cannot always be so sweet as the original.

From Preface to *Fables Ancient and Modern* (London: Jacob Tonson, 1700)

Dryden's Affinity with Chaucer

Chaucer, I confess, is a rough diamond, and must first be polished ere he shines. I deny not likewise that, living in the early days of our poetry, he writes not always of a piece; but sometimes mingles trivial things with those of greater moment. Sometimes also, though not often, he runs riot, like Ovid, and knows not when he has said enough. [. . .] Having observed this redundancy in Chaucer [. . .] I have not tied myself to a literal translation; but have often omitted what I judged unnecessary, or not of dignity enough to appear in the company of better thoughts. I have presumed farther in some places, and added somewhat of my own where I thought my author was deficient, and had not given his thoughts their true lustre, for want of words in the beginning of our language. And to this I was the more emboldened, because (if I may be permitted to say it of myself) I found I had a soul congenial to his, and that I had been conversant in the same studies. Another poet, in another age, may take the same liberty with my writings, if at least they live long enough to deserve correction.

From 'Of the Pythagorean Philosophy, from Ovid's *Metamorphoses*, Book XV' (1700)

Translation and Immortality

> Then to be born is to begin to be
> Some other thing we were not formerly,
> And what we call to die is not t' appear
> Or be the thing that formerly we were.
> Those very elements which we partake
> Alive, when dead some other bodies make;
> Translated grow, have sense or can discourse;
> But death on deathless substance has no force.

Dryden the Translator

From 'Translation of the Last Part of the Third Book of Lucretius: Against the Fear of Death' (1685)

The finality of death

> Nay, ev'n suppose when we have suffered fate,
> The soul could feel in her divided state,
> What's that to us? for we are only we
> While souls and bodies in one frame agree.
> Nay, though our atoms should revolve by chance,
> And matter leap into the former dance;
> Though time our life and motion could restore,
> And make our bodies what they were before,
> What gain to us would all this bustle bring?

The new-made man would be another thing;
When once an interrupting pause is made,
That individual being is decayed.
We, who are dead and gone, shall bear no part
In all the pleasures, nor shall feel the smart,
Which to that other mortal shall accrue,
Whom of our matter time shall mould anew.
      For backward if you look on that long space
Of ages past, and view the changing face
Of matter, tossed and variously combined
In sundry shapes, 'tis easy for the mind
From thence t' infer that seeds of things have been
In the same order as they now are seen;
Which yet our dark remembrance cannot trace,
Because a pause of life, a gaping space
Has come betwixt, where memory lies dead,
And all the wandering motions from the sense are fled.
For whosoe'er shall in misfortunes live,
Must *be* when those misfortunes shall arrive;
And since the man who *is* not, feels not woe
(For death exempts him, and wards off the blow,
Which we the living only feel and bear),
What is there left for us in death to fear?
When once that pause of life has come between,
'Tis just the same as we had never been.

From 'Horace, Ode 29, Book 3, Paraphrased in Pindaric Verse, and Inscribed to the Right Honourable Lawrence, Earl of Rochester' (1685)

Living in the Present

Enjoy the present smiling hour,
   And put it out of Fortune's power;
The tide of business, like the running stream,
   Is sometimes high and sometimes low,
A quiet ebb or a tempestuous flow,
         And always in extreme.
   Now with a noiseless gentle course
   It keeps within the middle bed;
   Anon it lifts aloft the head,
And bears down all before it with impetuous force:

And trunks of trees come rolling down,
   Sheep and their folds together drown;
Both house and homestead into seas are borne,
And rocks are from their old foundations torn,
And woods made thin with winds their scattered honours mourn.

   Happy the man, and happy he alone,
     He who can call today his own:
     He who secure within can say,
'Tomorrow do thy worst, for I have lived today:
     Be fair, or foul, or rain, or shine,
The joys I have possessed, in spite of Fate, are mine;
     Not heaven itself upon the past has power,
But what has been has been, and I have had my hour.'

From 'The Tenth Satire of Juvenal' (1692; dated 1693)

The Fall of Sejanus

Some ask for envied power, which public hate
Pursues, and hurries headlong to their fate:
Down go the titles, and the statue crowned
Is by base hands in the next river drowned.
The guiltless horses and the chariot wheel
The same effects of vulgar fury feel:
The smith prepares his hammer for the stroke,
While the lunged bellows hissing fire provoke.
Sejanus, almost first of Roman names,
The great Sejanus crackles in the flames:
Formed in the forge, the pliant brass is laid
On anvils; and of head and limbs are made
Pans, cans and piss-pots, a whole kitchen trade.

Hannibal

Ask what a face belonged to this high fame;
His picture scarcely would deserve a frame:
A sign-post dauber would disdain to paint
The one-eyed hero on his elephant.
Now what's his end, O charming Glory, say:
What rare fifth act to crown this huffing play?
In one deciding battle overcome,

He flies, is banished from his native home;
Begs refuge in a foreign court, and there
Attends, his mean petition to prefer;
Repulsed by surly grooms, who wait before
The sleeping tyrant's interdicted door.
What wondrous sort of death has heaven designed,
Distinguished from the herd of human kind,
For so untamed, so turbulent a mind?
Nor swords at hand, nor hissing darts afar,
Are doomed t' avenge the tedious, bloody war;
But poison, drawn through a ring's hollow plate,
Must finish him: a sucking infant's fate.
Go, climb the rugged Alps, ambitious fool,
To please the boys, and be a theme at school!

The miseries of old age

'Jove, grant me length of life, and years' good store
Heap on my bending back: I ask no more.'
Both sick and healthful, old and young, conspire
In this one silly, mischievous desire.
Mistaken blessing which old age they call:
'Tis a long, nasty, darksome hospital;
A ropy chain of rheums, a visage rough,
Deformed, unfeatured, and a skin of buff;
A stitch-fall'n cheek that hangs below the jaw;
Such wrinkles as a skilful hand would draw
For an old grandam ape, when, with a grace,
She sits at squat and scrubs her leathern face.
   In youth, distinctions infinite abound;
No shape or feature just alike are found:
The fair, the black, the feeble, and the strong.
But the same foulness does to age belong,
The self-same palsy both in limbs and tongue;
The skull and forehead one bald barren plain,
And gums unarmed to mumble meat in vain;
Besides th' eternal drivel that supplies
The dropping beard from nostrils, mouth, and eyes.
His wife and children loathe him, and, what's worse,
Himself does his offensive carrion curse!

Flatt'rers forsake him too; for who would kill
Himself to be remembered in a will?
His taste not only palled to wine and meat,
But to the relish of a nobler treat.
The limber nerve, in vain provoked to rise,
Inglorious from the field of battle flies;
Poor feeble dotard, how could he advance
With his blue headpiece and his broken lance?
Add that, endeavouring still without effect,
A lust more sordid justly we suspect.

From 'The Second Book of Virgil's *Aeneis*' (1697)

The Death of Priam

'Perhaps you may of Priam's fate enquire.
He, when he saw his regal town on fire,
His ruined palace and his entering foes,
On every side inevitable woes,
In arms disused invests his limbs, decayed
Like them with age, a late and useless aid.
His feeble shoulders scarce the weight sustain:
Loaded, not armed, he creeps along with pain,
Despairing of success, ambitious to be slain.
    Uncovered but by heaven, there stood in
An altar: near the hearth a laurel grew,
Doddered with age, whose boughs encompass round
The household gods, and shade the holy ground.
Here Hecuba with all her helpless train
Of dames for shelter sought, but sought in vain.
Driv'n like a flock of doves along the sky,
Their images they hug, and to their altars fly.
The queen, when she beheld her trembling lord,
And hanging by his side a heavy sword,
'What rage,' she cried, 'has seized my husband's mind?
What arms are these, and to what use designed?
These times want other aids: were Hector here,
Ev'n Hector now in vain, like Priam, would appear.
With us one common shelter thou shalt find,
Or in one common fate with us be joined.'
She said, and with a last salute embraced

The poor old man, and by the laurel placed.
   Behold Polites, one of Priam's sons,
Pursued by Pyrrhus there for safety runs.
Through swords and foes amazed and hurt, he flies
Through empty courts and open galleries.
Him Pyrrhus, urging with his lance, pursues,
And often reaches, and his thrusts renews.
The youth transfixed, with lamentable cries
Expires before his wretched parent's eyes:
Whom gasping at his feet when Priam saw,
The fear of death gave place to nature's law,
And shaking more with anger than with age,
'The gods,' said he, 'requite thy brutal rage—
As sure they will, barbarian, sure they must,
If there be gods in heaven, and gods be just—
Who tak'st in wrongs an insolent delight;
With a son's death t' infect a father's sight.
Not he, whom thou and lying Fame conspire
To call thee his; not he, thy vaunted sire,
Thus used my wretched age: the gods he feared;
The laws of nature and of nations heard.
He cheered my sorrows, and for sums of gold
The bloodless carcass of my Hector sold;
Pitied the woes a parent underwent,
And sent me back in safety from his tent.'
   This said, his feeble hand a javelin threw,
Which, fluttering, seemed to loiter as it flew:
Just, and but barely, to the mark it held,
And faintly tinkled on the brazen shield.
   Then Pyrrhus thus: 'Go thou from me to Fate,
And to my father my foul deeds relate:
Now die!' With that, he dragged the trembling sire,
Sliddering through clottered blood and holy mire
(The mingled paste his murdered son had made),
Hauled from beneath the violated shade,
And on the sacred pile the royal victim laid.
His right hand held his bloody falchion bare,
His left he twisted in his hoary hair;

Then with a speeding thrust his heart he found;
The lukewarm blood came rushing through the wound,
And sanguine streams distained the sacred ground.
   Thus Priam fell, and shared one common fate
With Troy in ashes, and his ruined state:
He who the sceptre of all Asia swayed,
Whom monarchs like domestic slaves obeyed.
On the bleak shore now lies th' abandoned king,
A headless carcass and a nameless thing.

From 'Sigismonda and Guiscardo, from Boccace' [Boccaccio] (1700)

Sigismonda defends her clandestine marriage to her father's squire, Guiscardo

'Tancred, I neither am disposed to make
Request for life, nor offered life to take:
Much less deny the deed; but least of all
Beneath pretended justice weakly fall.
My words to sacred truth shall be confined;
My deeds shall show the greatness of my mind.
That I have loved, I own; that still I love,
I call to witness all the powers above.
Yet more I own: to Guiscard's love I give
The small remaining time I have to live;
And if beyond this life desire can be
Not Fate itself shall set my passion free.
   This first avowed, nor folly warped my mind,
Nor the frail texture of the female kind
Betrayed my virtue; for too well I knew
What honour was, and honour had his due:
Before the holy priest my vows were tied,
So came I not a strumpet, but a bride.
This for my fame, and for the public voice;
Yet more, his merits justified my choice:
Which had they not, the first election thine
That bond dissolved, the next is freely mine:
Or grant I erred—which yet I must deny—
Had parents power ev'n second vows to tie,
Thy little care to mend my widowed nights
Has forced me to recourse of marriage rites,
To fill an empty side, and follow known delights.
What have I done in this deserving blame?

State laws may alter: nature's are the same;
Those are usurped on helpless womankind,
Made without our consent, and wanting power to bind.'

From 'The First Book of Homer's *Ilias*'

Achilles vents his wrath on Agamemnon

'Dastard and drunkard, mean and insolent,
Tongue-valiant hero, vaunter of thy might,
In threats the foremost, but the lag in fight;
When didst thou thrust amid the mingled press,
Content to bid the war aloof in peace?
Arms are the trade of each plebeian soul;
'Tis death to fight, but kingly to control.
Lordlike at ease, with arbitrary power,
To peel the chiefs, the people to devour;
These, traitor, are thy talents; safer far
Than to contend in fields and toils of war.
Nor couldst thou thus have dared the common hate,
Were not their souls as abject as their state.
But by this sceptre solemnly I swear—
Which never more green leaf or growing branch shall bear,
Torn from the tree and giv'n by Jove to those
Who laws dispense and mighty wrongs oppose—
That when the Grecians want my wonted aid,
No gift shall bribe it, and no prayer persuade.
When Hector comes, the homicide, to wield
His conquering arms, with corpse to strew the field;
Then shalt thou mourn thy pride, and late confess
My wrong repented when 'tis past redress.'
    He said, and with disdain in open view,
Against the ground his golden sceptre threw.

From 'The Flower and the Leaf' (1700)

Spring

Now turning from the wintry signs, the sun
His course exalted through the Ram had run,
And whirling up the skies, his chariot drove
Through Taurus, and the lightsome realms of love,

Where Venus from her orb descends in showers
To glad the ground, and paint the fields with flowers;
When first the tender blades of grass appear,
And buds that yet the blast of Eurus fear,
Stand at the door of life, and doubt to clothe the year;
Till gentle heat, and soft repeated rains
Make the green blood to dance within their veins;
Then, at their call, emboldened out they come,
And swell the gems, and burst the narrow room;
Broader and broader yet, their blooms display,
Salute the welcome sun, and entertain the day.
Then from their breathing souls the sweets repair
To scent the skies, and purge th' unwholesome air;
Joy spreads the heart, and with a general song,
Spring issues out, and leads the jolly months along.

2.14 ANNE DACIER

Anne Dacier (1654–1720), daughter of the classical scholar Tanneguy Lefebvre, published fragments from the Alexandrian poet Callimachus as early as 1674. This was so well received that she was chosen by Pierre-Daniel Huet, as one of the editors of the collection of classics *Ad usum Delphini*, for the use of the Dauphin. She married a student of her father's, the philologist André Dacier. Her many translations include Anacreon and Sappho (1681); several plays by Plautus and Aristophanes (1683–84); Terence (1688); and the *Iliad* (1699) and *Odyssey* (1708).

Dacier's translation of the *Iliad* into prose included a long preface in response to Homer's critics. This document figures prominently in the ongoing quarrel between the Ancients (to which group she belonged) and the Moderns, the latter being critical of Classical literature, including the Homeric poems, and insisting on the right and duty of contemporary authors to modify them according to their own supposedly superior aesthetic standards. By the time Boileau, a defender of the Ancients, died in 1711, the concern for accurate translations of the classics had been swept away by the Moderns' tireless promotion of contemporary literature. In a letter to Dacier (1720), Voltaire, who had lauded her as 'one of the prodigies of the century of Louis XIV', made his own position clear: 'I am convinced that we have two or three poets in France who would be able to translate Homer very well; but I am equally convinced that nobody will read them unless they soften and embellish almost everything because, Madame, you have to write for your own time, not for the past.'[1]

Scholarly writings by Anne Dacier and others are convincing evidence of the significant part played by women writers who appreciated the opportunity offered by translation as a way of contributing to and shaping the culture of the Enlightenment. Dacier's renown spread beyond France, Alexander Pope, for instance, valuing her work, as is clear, if with some reservations, from his introductory comments to his 'Observations on the First Book' of the *Iliad* (i.e. his notes). He claims that previous commentators on Homer have very little on the 'poetical beauties of the author', their remarks being 'rather philosophical, historical, geographical, allegorical, or in short rather any thing than critical and poetical', and he quotes at length from Eustathius, a Constantinople cleric and classical scholar, whose many works included vast commentaries on the *Iliad* and the *Odyssey*. But he also makes great use of Dacier's notes, pointing out that she too is indebted to Eustathius, adding: 'She has made a farther attempt than her predecessors to discover

---

[1] See A. Lefevere, *Translation/History/Culture*, (London: Routledge, 1992), 30.

the beauties of the Poet; tho' we have often only her general praises and exclamations instead of reasons. But her remarks all together are the most judicious collection extant of the scatter'd observations of the ancients and moderns, as her preface is excellent, and her translation equally careful and elegant.'[2]

From *The Iliad of Homer*, translated from the Greek into blank verse by Mr Ozell, Mr Broom, and Mr Oldisworth (London: G. James, for Bernard Lintott, 1712), including an English translation of Dacier's Preface

[John Ozell in his Preface to the English Translation reiterates much of what Dacier has to say, but national prejudice also receives an airing. French is 'the most unfitted language for such subjects, whereas English is the "fittest" '; 'In Matters of Cookery, indeed, the French Language abounds beyond any other; for which Reason as a great Critic observes, the Italians call it the Kitchen-language'; French 'wants Sinews and Strength to alay the excessive softness of it', this putting it at a great disadvantage when trying to convey 'Manly Passions', the description of which is of the essence in Homer. And as if that is not enough, French 'versification' is 'intolerably tedious', there being no 'Variety of Numbers [...] but the same eternal cadence upon the last syllable of each Word'.

This is good enough reason for translation of the Greek poets into French prose rather than poetry, although the same argument does not apply to English, where the preferred medium is blank verse. Had Homer lived today and written in English, he 'would most certainly have chosen the same sort of Verse, which our English Homer, Milton did.' Ozell is even critical of the revered Dryden, who, unlike Mme Dacier, was led by rhyme into making errors.]

Ozell's Notes and Preface

Dacier's notes, which were of primary importance to her, comment, albeit acutely, on the message, rather than on the medium, the translation being treated, in effect, as a source text. She insists on the need for them, since 'It is quite impossible to render all those several Beauties discernible by Translation alone; it is absolutely necessary to accompany this with Remarks'. The English translators included Dacier's notes, many of them quite copious, implicitly of course taking her side in the *Querelle*. She observes: 'I have very rarely thought fit to descend to criticise upon Words; nothing can be more dry, more barren, or more disagreeable.' We might beg to differ, but she continues: 'I am of the Opinion, that what is most advantageous, and of the highest Importance, is to make the Reader thoroughly apprehend the Delicacy and Energy of Homer's Turns and Thoughts.' Thus, the *Iliad*,

---

[2] See Pope's Preface to *The Iliad of Homer* (1715–20; London: Penguin 1996, (1743 edn.)).

Book 1, line 1, Sing, Goddess the Resentment of Achilles ... is fleshed out by this note: 'The Invention is an essential part of an Epic Poem, and indispensably necessary upon many Accounts. The Poet, being to relate an infinite Number of Things, which he is not willing to be reckon'd the Inventor of, but delivers for true [...]; and being often oblig'd to display the most hidden causes, and most Secret springs of Actions; he must necessarily have recourse to some Deity, to inspire him with them; for he neither ought nor can know them any other way [...]'.

Dacier examines 'the opinion of those, who have believ'd, that Homer's principle aim, in his poem, was to please; that Instruction is but incidental; that Morality is there in subordinate to Pleasure, and only made use of as a surer way to please'. She concludes: 'To affirm that to please is the ultimate End of Epic Poetry is like maintaining that Pleasure is the only end of Architecture, and that a Palace is built only to entertain the Eye without any Regard had to the Lodging, and Conveniency of the Owner.' That is, the moral reasons for translating Homer are so overwhelming that the task must be undertaken, in spite of its near impossibility, French verse being so inadequate.

Dacier states unequivocally that 'Poets translated into verse, cease to be Poets', maintaining that this can be demonstrated. Accordingly, she recommends prose, in support of which she alludes to 'the Hebrews who [...] have made a sort of Poetry of their Prose'. She insists that she does not mean by this [i.e. prose translation] servile translation. At the very least, translation obliges one to read more deeply and to discover new beauties and meanings.

On the one hand, Dacier can say of her notes that these remarks 'may be serviceable to the Reader for unravelling of the Poet's Art [...]', by which evidently she had in mind something other than prosody or aesthetics, while on the other characterizing Homer's poetry as being 'like Musick, which can bring under its Command, and reduce to Harmony, the most disagreeable and unharmonious Sounds; all things submit to it, and concur to work the Effects it enjoins'. Since 'the Beauties are not, however, the most valuable part', the attempt to reproduce these, if self-evidently impossible, must and indeed can be made.

From Anne Dacier's 'Preface', translated by Ozell

> But this mixed composition, the source of these beauties, is unknown to our tongue; it does not, at all, allow of these different turns; it knows not what to do with a mean, hard, or disagreeable word; it has no treasure in reserve, to conceal what is defective; it neither has those numerous particles to support its words, nor that different harmony, proceeding from the various ranging of terms; and consequently, it is incapable of expressing most of the beauties which shines in that poem. This is my condemnation, and a very just one too, if I am tried with rigor; for, I own, in every verse in Homer I find a beauty, a force, a harmony, a grace, which it has been impossible for me to preserve.

χοζρανικα

To what purpose was it, then, to attempt a thing I could not succeed in? I will here give my reasons; perhaps they may make a tolerable excuse.

The wonders of Homer's style, and the beauties he has drawn from his tongue, are not the most valuable part of his poetry; there are beauties above those of the language, and such as cannot fail moving those who are not altogether insensible. The most barbarous nations, who have no notion of fine poetry, or the energy and harmony of language, could not forbear being sensible of the loftiness of his ideas, the majesty of his subject, that beautiful nature which reigns throughout every part of him, and the surprising variety of his character, which differ very much, even in the same kind of virtues. For instance, Ulysses and Nestor, both of them men of profound prudence, are not the same. Achilles, Diomedes, and Ajax, all of them brave, are yet so in a different manner. The Indians and the Persians have Homer translated into their languages; and it is positively said, there is a Chaldaic or Syriac translation of him. I am of opinion, a French translation may be as good as those, and better preserve most of the beauties of the style, or give a better sense of them.

Besides, I do not write for the learned, who read Homer in his own tongue; they know him better than I pretend to; I write for those who do not know him, that is, for the greater number, in respect of whom this poet is as it were dead; I write also for those who learn to read him, and are to take pains to understand him before they can be sensible of his beauties.

As for the first of them, that is, those who are deprived of the pleasure of reading him in Greek, let them give me leave here to make a comparison which, by letting them see the judgment I make myself of my work, will put my translation out of the reach of their censure, and secure the original from their contempt. Can images be more properly made use of than when we speak of the father of poetry? [...]

This is the most impartial idea I can give of my translation; I own, it is not Homer alive and animated, but still it is Homer; there will not be found in him that energy, that grace, that life, those ravishing charms, and that fire, which warms all that comes near it; but every feature, and the admirable symmetry of all his parts will be picked out; nay, I dare be so bold as to hope, he will still retain lively colours enough to make it doubtful for a moment whether there are not yet some remains of life in him. In a word, it is Homer, and Homer much less altered than in the translations that have been hitherto made, which have so strangely disfigured him, that he is no longer to be known.

Some will say, there is a surer way of approaching to the original, which is to translate it into verse; for, as they allege, poets are to be translated into verse, to retain their fire. This would certainly be best, were it practicable; but to believe it possible is a mistake, capable, in my opinion, of demonstration. [...]

A translator, in prose, may say all that Homer has said; this he can never do in verse, especially in our tongue, where he must of necessity be always altering, retrenching,

what makes
him poet in
the first place?

adding. Now, what Homer has thought and said, though rendered in a plainer and less poetical manner than he has done, is certainly much better than what those who translate him in verse are forced to lend him.

This is my first reason. There is another, which is the same I have already explained. Our poetry is not capable of expressing all the beauties of Homer, and soaring to his height; it may follow him in some select places; it may successfully hit off two, four, or six of his verses [...]; but at length, the connection will be so weak that nothing will be more languid. And what can be imagined meaner than a cold and flat piece of poetry, wherein nothing is tolerable that is not excellent? I could make this very obvious by examples, but that they are common, and every man may convince himself of this truth. Nay, I am not afraid to say, and could be able to prove it, that poets translated into verse cease to be poets. [...]

It is not so in prose, which can follow all the poet's notions, retain the beauty of his images, say all he has said; and if at any time it is obliged to lend something to him, which must be done but very rarely, as being dangerous, it only borrows from him whatsoever it lends him; and, even under its plainness and mediocrity, fails not to support itself. I do not say I have performed all this, I only say it may be done in prose. [...]

We must then be content with prose for translating of the poets, and endeavour to imitate the Hebrews, who having no poetry (that is, a sort of speech confined to a certain number of feet, and long or short syllables) have made a sort of poetry of their prose, by means of a more beautified, more sprightly, and a more figurative language; and it has succeeded so well, that nothing represents more lively ideas to the mind than the canticles, the psalms, and some passages in the prophets.

It is certain that prose, supported by and composed with art, will come nearer to poetry than a translation into verse [...] But I do not think it enough to say that prose may come near to poetry; I will go yet farther and affirm that in case of translation, which is the matter in hand, there is sometimes such a niceness, a beauty, and an energy in prose as poetry cannot come near. The books of the prophets and the psalms, even in the Vulgate, are full of such passages, as the greatest poet in the world could not put into verse without losing much of their majesty and pathos.

When I speak of a translation of prose, I do not mean a servile translation, I mean a noble and generous translation which, adhering strictly to the way of thinking in the original, searches out the beauties of its language and represents the images without retailing the words. The first sort of translation becomes unfaithful through too scrupulous a faithfulness; for it loses the spirit to preserve the letter, which is the work of a cold and barren genius; whereas the other, though chiefly aiming to retain the spirit, yet fails not, in its greatest liberties, to retain the letter; and by means of its bold but true strokes becomes not only a faithful copy of its original, but even a second original; which cannot be executed but by a solid, noble and fruitful genius.

What I have here said is to undeceive some persons who, being unacquainted with the nature and beauty of writings, have more particularly a very disadvantageous and false notion of translations. They fancy it is a servile imitation, wherein the flower of wit and fancy have no share; in a word; that there is no creation. This is certainly a gross mistake; translation is not like the copy of a picture, wherein the copier is tied down to the features, the colours, the proportions, the contours, and the attitudes of the original he follows; all this is quite otherwise, a good translator is not so confined; he is, at most, like a statuary [sculptor] who works after a picture, or like a painter who copies after a piece of statuary; he is like Virgil, who describes the Laocoon from the marble original, that wonderful piece, which he had before him. In this imitation, as in all others, the soul, full of those beauties it intends to represent, and inebriated with the pleasing vapours arising from these abundance springs, is to suffer itself to be ravished and transported by that foreign enthusiasm; and to make it its own, and so to produce very different representations and expressions, though resembling the others. [. . .] This, if I mistake not, is the difference between good and bad translations; the one, by a low and servile imitation, gives the letter, without the spirit; the other by a free and noble imitation, retains the spirit, without departing from the letter; and makes quite a new thing of that which was already known. [. . .]

If I understood him [Homer] tolerably, it was only by labouring to make him understood by others. When we read only for ourselves, we are often satisfied with a slight and superficial perusal; but when we read for others, the obligation we lie under of giving clear and distinct ideas makes us stop to drive deeper into the subject, and necessity then serving as a spur to the mind, causes it to discover those beauties and meanings which cursory reading had not permitted it to take notice of. [. . .]

2.15   ALEXANDER POPE

Alexander Pope (1688–1744), born in London into a Catholic family, was a major translator of poetry as well as poet. In 1712, he published his mock-heroic masterpiece *The Rape of the Lock*, preceded by his precociously brilliant *An Essay on Criticism* (1711). *The Iliad* was published in six volumes (1715–20), Pope having taken ten years over it. In 1728, *The Dunciad* inaugurated his later career as the principal satirist of his age. Associated with this are the *Imitations of Horace*. *The Odyssey*, with the assistance of William Broome and Elijah Fenton, took a further three years (5 vols., 1725–6). The unprecedented commercial success of Pope's Homer made its author independently wealthy. Later he published translations from Chaucer. Also notable among his translations are *Imitations of Horace* (1734–7), with the Latin original *en face*, encouraging comparison between his transformation of the original and the source text, since an informed readership could be expected by and large to have access to the Latin. His prefaces to the *Iliad* and *Odyssey* are among his best pieces of sustained critical writing.[1]

Pope's interest in Homer, as noted by Steiner,[2] dates from childhood, and he drew 'richly if critically' on the work of predecessors, like Chapman and Dryden, aiming not at bland accuracy, of course, but at some sort of poetic equivalency of effect. He benefited also from the scholarship of his French contemporary Anne Dacier (see Sect. 2.14, above). whose own Homeric translation, however, was into prose. Pope's translation of the Homeric epic is perhaps the greatest example of elevated style in English literature; he took what he saw as essential liberties, varying the repetitive epithets, suppressing what was considered offensive to contemporary taste. The so-called Augustan period was arguably the last period in which a convincing recreation of epic poetry in English could be attempted, and Pope, with his incomparable mastery of the heroic couplet, the energy and vigour of his writing, his prosodic inventiveness, allied to a remarkable scholarliness, was the man for the job. The resulting poem, inevitably, was thoroughly domesticated, making Homer supremely readable in terms of the neo-classical aesthetic and notions of propriety. Pope, as Steiner notes, 'elaborates on the pictorial elements and the morally sententious'. Even some contemporaries, however, found Pope's text lacking in precision and too dependent on the requirements of the time ('A very pretty poem, Mr Pope, but you must not call it Homer,' famously commented Richard Bentley, Master of Trinity).

[1] See also H. A. Mason, *To Homer through Pope: An Introduction to Homer's 'Iliad' and Pope's Translation* (London: Chatto and Windus, 1972) for a detailed discussion of the Homeric poems.
[2] See *Homer in English*, ed. George Steiner (London: Penguin, 1996).

The reaction was swift and inevitable, as evinced, for example, by William Cowper (see Sect. 2.17, below), with his blank-verse translation. But one cannot argue with Steiner's contention that Pope's Homers 'constitute the principal "epic act" after Milton in the language'. The translation can be characterized as visionary, in that Pope has dynamically grasped its scope, while remaining brilliantly attentive to detail. The aphoristic tendency, implicit in the heroic couplet, is expertly controlled, the poem being organized, as it were, into verse paragraphs and these into chapters, without sacrifice of the couplet's incisiveness.

The prefaces, especially that to *The Iliad*, are striking examples of polemical and at the same time scholarly critical writing and attest to Pope's commitment to and appreciation of Homer's rapturous, fiery genius, so attractive to Chapman as well, and his conviction that a balance had to be maintained between fidelity and freedom: 'It is certain no literal translation can be just to an excellent original in a superior language; but it is a great mistake to imagine [...] that a rash paraphrase can make amends for its general defect'. Pope's footnotes are, indeed, among the finest examples of close textual criticism in the eighteenth century. Steiner concludes, somewhat caustically: 'Pope's main detractors have been those who have not read him.' And it is indeed a formidable undertaking to read Pope's Homer today, since the translation is a masterpiece in its own right, whereas the modern reader generally seeks out texts which draw somewhat less attention to themselves (Christopher's Logue's ongoing Homer is an exception to this). Ezra Pound remarked, with somewhat grudging approval, that 'he [Pope] has at least the merit of translating Homer into *something*'.[3] But this is in the context of his own agenda and it is possible now to enjoy and admire Pope, without any sense of having abandoned one's search for the 'real' Homer.

From Alexander Pope's Preface to *The Iliad* of Homer (1715–20; London: Penguin, 1996 (using 1743 edn.)), 3–22, contained also in *The Twickenham Edition of the Poems of Alexander Pope*, ed. Maynard Mack (London and New Haven: Methuen and Yale University Press, 1938–68), vols. vii–x

> Homer is universally allowed to have had the greatest invention of any writer whatever. The praise of judgment Virgil has justly contested with him, and others may have their pretensions as to particular excellences; but his invention remains yet unrivalled. Nor is it a wonder if he has ever been acknowledged the greatest of poets, who most excelled in that which is the very foundation of poetry. [...]

[3] 'Translators of Greek: Early Translators of Homer' (1920), repr. in *Literary Essays of Ezra Pound* (New York: New Directions, 1968), 250.

Our author's work is a wild paradise, where, if we cannot see all the beauties so distinctly as in an ordered garden, it is only because the number of them is infinitely greater. It is like a copious nursery, which contains the seeds and first productions of every kind, out of which those who followed him have but selected some particular plants, each according to his fancy, to cultivate and beautify. If some things are too luxuriant it is owing to the richness of the soil; and if others are not arrived to perfection or maturity, it is only because they are overrun and oppressed by those of a stronger nature. It is to the strength of this amazing invention we are to attribute that unequalled fire and rapture which is so forcible in Homer, that no man of a true poetical spirit is master of himself while he reads him. [. . .]

I shall here endeavour to show how this vast invention exerts itself in a manner superior to that of any poet through all the main constituents parts of his work; as it is the great and peculiar characteristic, which distinguishes him from all other authors. [. . .]

Fable may be divided into the probable, the allegorical, and the marvellous.

The probable fable is the recital of such actions as, though they did not matter, yet might in the common course of nature; or of such as, though they did, became fables by the additional episodes and manner of telling them. [. . .] The action is hurried on with the most vehement spirit, and its whole duration employs not so much as fifty days. Virgil, for want of so warm a genius, aided himself by taking in a more extensive subject, as well as a greater length of time, and contracting the design of both Homer's poems into one, which is yet but a fourth part as large as his. The other epic poets have used the same practice, but generally carried it so far as to superinduce a multiplicity of fables, destroy the unity of action, and lose their readers in an unreasonable length of time. [. . .]

To proceed to the allegorical fable, if we reflect upon those innumerable knowledges, those secrets of nature and physical philosophy which Homer is generally supposed to have wrapped up in his allegories, what a new and ample scene of wonder may this consideration afford us! How fertile will that imagination appear, which was able to clothe all the properties of elements, the qualifications of the mind, the virtues and vices, in forms and persons, and to introduce them into actions agreeable to the nature of the things they shadowed! This is the field in which no succeeding poet could dispute with Homer [. . .]

The marvellous fable includes whatever is supernatural and especially the machines of the gods. If Homer was not the first who introduced the deities (as Herodotus imagines) into the religion of Greece, he seems the first who brought them into a system of machinery for poetry, [. . .] [N]one has been able to enlarge the sphere of poetry beyond the limits he has set; every attempt of this nature has proved unsuccessful; and after all the various changes of times and religions, his gods continue to this day the gods of poetry.

We now come to the character of his persons; and here we shall find no author has ever drawn so many, with so visible and surprising a variety, or given us such lively and affecting impressions of them. Every one has something so singularly his own, that no painter could have distinguished them more by their features, than the poet has by their manners. Nothing can be more exact than the distinctions he has observed in the different degrees of virtues and vices. The single quality of courage is wonderfully diversified in the several characters of the Iliad. [. . .] The characters of Virgil are far from striking us in this open manner. [. . .]

The speeches are to be considered as they flow from the characters, being perfect or defective as they agree or disagree with the manners of those who utter them. As there is more variety of characters in the Iliad, so there is of speeches, than in any other poem. [. . .] In Virgil, the dramatic part is less in proportion to the narrative, and the speeches often consist of general reflections or thoughts, which might be equally just in any person's mouth upon the same occasion. [. . .] We oftener think of the author himself when we read Virgil than when we are engaged in Homer. [. . .] Homer makes us hearers, and Virgil leaves us readers.

If, in the next place, we take a view of the sentiments, the same presiding faculty is eminent in the sublimity and spirit of the thoughts. Longinus has given his opinion that it was in this part Homer principally excelled. What were alone sufficient to prove the grandeur and excellence of his sentiments in general is that they have so remarkable a parity with those of the Scripture. [. . .] And it is with justice an excellent modern writer allows, that if Virgil has not so many thoughts that are low and vulgar, he has not so many that are sublime and noble, and that the Roman author seldom rises into very astonishing sentiments where he is not fired by the Iliad.

If we observe his descriptions, images, and similes, we shall find the invention still predominant. To what else can we ascribe that vast comprehension of images of every sort, where we see each circumstance of art and individual of nature summoned together by the extent and fecundity of his imagination [. . .] [I]t is evident of Virgil especially, that he has scarce any comparisons which are not drawn from his master.

If we descend from hence to the expression, we see the bright imagination of Homer shining out in the most enlivened forms of it. We acknowledge him the father of poetical diction, the first who taught that 'language of the gods' to men. [. . .] To throw his language more out of prose, Homer seems to have affected the compound epithets. This was a sort of composition peculiarly proper to poetry, not only as it heightened the diction, but as it assisted and filled the numbers with greater sound and pomp, and likewise conduced in some measure to thicken the images. On this last consideration I cannot but attribute these also to the fruitfulness of his invention, since (as he has managed them) they are a sort of supernumerary pictures of the persons or things to which they were joined. [. . .] As a metaphor is a short simile, one of these epithets is a short description.

Lastly, if we consider his versification, we shall be sensible what a share of praise is due to his invention in that also. He was not satisfied with his language as he found it settled in any one part of Greece, but searched through its different dialects with this particular view, to beautify and perfect his numbers. [. . .]

It is often hard to distinguish exactly where the virtue ends or the fault begins. As prudence may sometimes sink to suspicion, so may a great judgment decline to coldness; and as magnanimity may run to profusion or extravagance, so may a great invention to redundancy or wildness. [. . .] It is owing to the same vast invention, that his similes have been thought too exuberant and full of circumstances. The force of this faculty is seen in nothing more than in its inability to confine itself to that single circumstance upon which the comparison is grounded. [. . .] If there are others which seem rather to charge him with a defect or narrowness of genius, than an excess of it, those seeming defects will be found upon examination to proceed wholly from the nature of the times he lived in. Such are his grosser representation of the gods, and the vicious and imperfect manner of his heroes. [. . .] It must be a strange partiality to antiquity, to think with Madame Dacier, 'that those times and manners are so much the more excellent, as they are more contrary to ours.' [. . .]

Having now spoken of the beauties and defects of the original, it remains to treat of the translation, with the same view to the chief characteristics. As far as that is seen in the main parts of the poem, such as the fable, manners, and sentiments, no translator can prejudice it but by wilful omissions or contractions. As it also breaks out in every particular image, description, and simile, whoever lessens or too much softens those takes off from this chief character. It is the first grand duty of an interpreter to give his author entire and unmaimed; and for the rest, the diction and versification only are his proper province, since these must be his own, but the others he should take as he finds them.

It should then be considered what methods may afford some equivalent in our language for the graces of these in the Greek. It is certain no literal translation can be just to an excellent original in a superior language: but it is a great mistake to imagine (as many have done) that a rash paraphrase can make amends for this general defect. [. . .] It is not to be doubted that the fire of the poem is what a translator should principally regard, as it is most likely to expire in his managing [. . .] Where his diction is bold and lofty, let us raise ours as high as we can, but where his is plain and humble, we ought not to be deterred from imitating him by the fear of incurring the censure of a mere English critic.

Nothing that belongs to Homer seems to have been more commonly mistaken than the just pitch of his style [. . .] There is a graceful and dignified simplicity, as well as a bold and sordid one, which differ as much from each other as the air of a plain man from that of a sloven [. . .] This pure and noble simplicity is nowhere in such perfection as in the Scripture and our author. One may affirm with all respect to the inspired writings, that the Divine Spirit made use of no other words but what were intelligible and common to men at that time, and in that part of the world; and, as Homer is the author nearest to those, his style must of course bear a greater resemblance to the sacred books than that of any other writer. [. . .]

Perhaps the mixture of some Graecisms and old words after the manner of Milton, if done without too much affectation, might not have an ill effect in a version of this particular work, which most of any other seems to require a venerable, antique cast. But certainly the use of modern terms [...] cannot be allowable, those only excepted without which it is impossible to treat the subjects in any living language.

There are two peculiarities in Homer's diction which are a sort of marks or moles by which every common eye distinguishes him at first sight [...] I speak of his compound epithets, and of his repetitions. Many of the former cannot be done literally into English without destroying the purity of our language. I believe such should be retained as slide easily of themselves into an English compound, without violence to the ear or to the received rules of composition [...] Some that cannot be so turned, as to preserve their full image by one or two words, may have justice done them by circumlocution. [...] Upon the whole, it will be necessary to avoid that perpetual repetition of the same epithets which we find in Homer, and which, though it might be accommodated (as has been already shown) to the ear of those times, is by no means so to ours [...]

As for Homer's repetitions, we may divide them into three sorts: of whole narrations and speeches, of single sentences, and of one verse or hemistitch. I hope it is not impossible to have such a regard to these, as neither to lose so known a mark of the author on the one hand, nor to offend the reader too much on the other. [...] I believe the best rule is to be guided by the nearness, or distance at which the repetitions are placed in the original. When they follow too close, one may vary the expression; but it is a question, whether a professed translator be authorized to omit any. If they be tedious, the author is to answer for it.

It only remains to speak of the versification. Homer (as has been said) is perpetually applying the sound to the sense, and varying it on every new subject. [...] Few readers have the ear to be judges of it: but those who have will see I have endeavoured at this beauty.

Upon the whole, I must confess myself utterly incapable of doing justice to Homer. I attempt him in no other hope but that which one may entertain without much vanity, of giving a more tolerable copy of him than any entire translation in verse has yet done. [...] Chapman has taken the advantage of an immeasurable length of verse, notwithstanding which, there is scarce any paraphrase more loose and rambling than his. [...] He appears to have had a strong affectation of extracting new meanings out of his author; insomuch as to promise in his rhyming preface, a poem of the mysteries he had revealed in Homer [...] But that which is to be allowed him, and which very much contributed to cover his defects, is a daring fiery spirit that animates his translation, which is something like what one might imagine Homer himself would have writ before he arrived at years of discretion. [...] It is a great loss to the poetical world that Mr Dryden did not live to translate the Iliad. He has left us only the first book, and a small part of the sixth [...] He seems to have had too much regard to Chapman, whose words he sometimes copies, and has unhappily followed him in passages where he wanders from the original. However, had he translated the whole work, I would not more have attempted Homer after him than Virgil, his version of whom (notwithstanding some human errors) is the most noble and spirited translation I know in any language. [...]

That which, in my opinion, ought to be the endeavour of any one who translates Homer, is above all things to keep alive that spirit and fire which makes his chief character. [...]

From *The Iliad* of Homer, Book 1, ll. 297–324

[Achilles confronts Agamemnon who has offended him by seizing Briseïs, a beautiful captive who had been allotted to Achilles. See the same passage in Dryden's translation, Sect. 2.13, above.]

> O monster, mix'd of insolence and fear,
> Thou dog in forehead, but in heart a deer!
> When wert thou known in ambush'd fights to dare,
> Or nobly face the horrid front of war?
> 'Tis ours, the chance of fighting fields to try,
> Thine to look on, and bid the Valiant die.
> So much 'tis safer thro' the camp to go,
> And rob a subject, than despoil a foe.
> Scourge of thy people, violent and base!
> Sent in Jove's anger on a slavish race,
> Who lost to sense of gen'rous freedom past,
> Are tam'd to wrongs, or this had been thy last.
> Now by this sacred sceptre, hear me swear,
> Which never more shall leaves or blossoms bear,
> Which sever'd from the trunk (as I from thee)
> On the bare mountains left its parent tree;
> This sceptre, form'd by temper'd steel to prove
> An ensign of the delegates of Jove,
> From whom the pow'r of laws and justice springs:
> (Tremendous oath! Inviolate to Kings)
> By this I swear, when bleeding Greece again
> Shall call Achilles, she shall call in vain.
> When flush'd with slaughter, Hector comes, to spread
> The purpled shore with mountains of the dead,
> Then shalt thou mourn th'affront thy madness gave,
> Forc'd to deplore, when impotent to save:

> Then rage in bitterness of soul, to know
> This act has made the bravest Greek thy foe.

From *The Odyssey* of Homer (London: Lintot, 1725–6), opening lines of Book XI

[See also translations by Chapman, Sect. 2.6; Cowper, Sect. 2.17; Morris, Sect. 3.5; Pound, Sect. 4.2.]

> Now to the shores we bend, a mournful train,
> Climb the tall bark, and launch into the main:
> At once the mast we rear, at once unbind
> The spacious sheet, and stretch it to the wind;
> Then pale and pensive stand, with cares opprest,
> And solemn horrour saddens every breast.
> A freshening breeze the Magic Pow'r supply'd,
> While the wing'd vessel flew along the tyde:
> Our oars we shipp'd: all day the swelling sails
> Full from the guiding pilot catch'd the gales.
>   Now sunk the Sun from his aerial height,
> And o'er the shaded billows rush'd the night:
> When lo! We reach'd old ocean's utmost bounds,
> Where rocks controul his waves with ever-during mounds.
>   There is a lonely land, and gloomy cells,
> The dusky nation of Cimmeria dwells;
> The sun ne'er views th' uncomfortable seats,
> When radiant he advances, or retreats:
> Unhappy race! whom endless night invades,
> Clouds the dull air, and wraps them round in shades.
>   The ship we moor on these obscure abodes;
> Dis-bark the sheep, an offering to the Gods;
> And hellward bending, o'er the beach descry
> The dolesome passage to th' infernal sky.

2.16 SAMUEL JOHNSON

Samuel Johnson (1709–84), poet, playwright, educator, journalist, literary critic and biographer, lexicographer, moralist, as early as 1731 completed a Latin translation of Pope's *Messiah*. Another early translation, from a French version, was of *A Voyage to Abyssinia* (1735) by Father Jeronimo Lobo, a Portuguese Jesuit. Johnson moved from Lichfield to London where, as a journalist, he was always on the verge of abject poverty.

A Poem in Imitation of the Third Satire of Juvenal was published in 1738. And in 1749, *The Vanity of Human Wishes: The Tenth Satire of Juvenal* appeared. Johnson was a master of the noble and sententious style, his couplets not as flexible as Pope's, but filled with gravitas. As his biography of his master Dryden indicates, Johnson saw an opportunity for himself in the translation of Juvenal, even if some passages translated by Dryden could not be bettered.

He worked on his celebrated *Dictionary* from 1746 to 1754, *The Plan of an English Dictionary* appearing in 1747. The *Dictionary* was first published in two volumes in 1755, the first major English dictionary to include historical citations. Some of the definitions offered were far from neutral but reflected Johnson's prejudices, such as his anti-Scottish ones.

In 1750–2 appeared his essays for the *Rambler*, a semi-weekly publication. Other short essays, known as the *Idler* essays, were also published from 1757. Johnson met Boswell in 1763. His Idler essays (especially nos. 68 and 69 [1759], see below), as T. R. Steiner puts it (*English Translation Theory: 1650–1800*, 1975), form a 'capsule history' of translation. In general Johnson adheres to the middle way, promoted by Dryden, advocating freedom rather than slavishness, but not in a spirit of 'licentiousness' or at the expense of accuracy. In 1765, Johnson's eight-volume edition of *The Plays of William Shakespeare* was published, several times reissued with additional notes. These were sensitive reading, stressing the utilitarian value of literature and treating Shakespeare as a 'moralist'. As a member of 'The Club' of literary men, Johnson was a master of the conversational art, brilliantly captured by Boswell in his *Life of Johnson*.

Johnson also wrote introductions for a collection of English poetry, revised and corrected as *The Lives of the Most Eminent English Poets with Critical Observations on Their Work*, in three volumes (1779–81), including the lives of such as Pope, Dryden, and Cowley, with commentary on their translations. With regard to Pope's Homer, Johnson insisted that it was written to be read and that 'criticism which would destroy the power of pleasing must be blown aside'. Pope's debt to Dryden is noted and carefully delineated; at the same time the English language's debt to Pope for his translation is insisted upon. It can hardly be denied that if a translation is not accessible, it cannot do its work, this being essentially linked to the age in which it is produced, since no one can legislate for succeeding ages or predict what will be required then. This is an argument used with some legitimacy by publishers when rejecting certain approaches to translation, such as that for instance of radical foreignization, although of course the same arguments can be used in a philistine fashion which does not necessarily reflect the capacity of a readership to absorb what is challenging.

Johnson once asserted unequivocally to Boswell (Boswell's *Life of Johnson* contains many of his comments on translation) that since 'poetry cannot be translated', the criterion must be the success of the translation as an English poem. This commonsensical point of view, up till quite recently, might have been taken as standard, although in its time of course it was radical enough. In his biographical-critical sketches of Cowley, Dryden, Pope, and others who contributed to the development of translation, Johnson keeps to the middle path, defined by Dryden, while being not unsympathetic to the even greater liberties claimed by later poets-translators, himself included (see below, for his version of Juvenal, as compared to Dryden's).

Johnson on Translation

From *A Dictionary of the English Language* (1755): definitions

TO TRANSLATE. To transport; to remove. It is particularly used of the removal of a bishop from one see to another. To transfer from one to another; to convey; to change; to interpret to another language; to change into another language retaining the sense.

TRANSLATION. Removal, act of removing; the removal of a bishop to another see; the act of turning into another language; interpretation; something made by translation; version.

TRANSLATOR. One that turns anything into another language.

From *The Idler*, 68/69 (1759): 'both faithful and pleasing'

He that reviews the progress of English literature, will find that translation was very early cultivated among us, but that some principles, either wholly erroneous or too far extended, hindered our success from being always equal to our diligence. [. . .]

[. . .] It may be supposed that Chaucer would apply more than common attention to an author of so much celebrity [Boethius], yet he has attempted nothing higher than a version strictly literal, and has degraded the poetical parts to prose, that the constraints of versification might not obstruct his zeal for fidelity. [. . .]

Caxton proceeded as he began, and, except the poems of Gower and Chaucer, printed nothing but translations from the French, in which the original is so scrupulously followed, that they afford us little knowledge or our own language: though the words are English, the phrase is foreign.

As learning advanced, new works were adopted into our language, but I think with little improvement of the art of translation, though foreign nations and other languages offered us models of a better method; till in the age of Elizabeth we began to find that greater liberty was necessary to elegance, and that elegance was necessary to general reception; some essays were then made upon the Italian poets, which deserve the praise and gratitude of posterity.

But the old practice was not suddenly forsaken: Holland [Philemon Holland, see Sect. 2.6, above] filled the nation with literal translation; and, what is yet more strange, the same exactness was obstinately practised in the versions of the poets. This absurd labour of construing into rhyme was countenanced by Jonson in his version of Horace [*The Art of Poetry*, 1640]; and whether it be that more men have learning than genius, or that the endeavours of that time were more directed towards knowledge than delight, the accuracy of Jonson found more imitators than the elegance of Fairfax; and May, Sandys and Holiday, confined themselves to the toil of rendering line for line, not indeed with equal felicity, for May and Sandys were poets, and Holiday only a scholar and a critick.

Feltham appears to consider it as the established law of poetical translation that the lines should be neither more nor fewer than those of the original; and so long had this prejudice prevailed, that Denham praises Fanshaw's version of Guarini [see Sect. 2.10, above] as the example of a *new and noble way*, as the first attempt to break the boundaries of custom and assert the natural freedom of the Muse.

In the general emulation of wit and genius which the festivity of the Restoration produced, the poets shook off their constraint, and considered translation as no longer confined to servile closeness. [. . .] The wits of Charles's time had seldom more than slight and superficial views; and their care was to hide their want of learning behind the colours of a gay imagination; they, therefore, translated always with freedom, sometimes with licentiousness, and, perhaps, expected that their readers should accept sprightliness for knowledge, and considered ignorance and mistake as the impatience and negligence of a mind too rapid to stop at difficulties, and too elevated to descend to minuteness. [. . .]

There is undoubtedly a mean to be observed. Dryden saw very early that closeness best preserved an author's sense, and that freedom best exhibited his spirit; he, therefore, will deserve the highest praise, who can give a representation at once faithful and pleasing, who can convey the same thoughts with the same graces, and who, when he translates, changes nothing but the language.

From *The Lives of the Poets*, 'Cowley': The Pindarique Odes

[Johnson, the liberal and far from pompous critic, nevertheless draws attention to the limitations in Cowley's appreciation of Pindar, which has encouraged him in a mistaken freedom, failing, if understandably, to perceive the regularities in the Greek poet's verse. Nevertheless, later translators are in Cowley's debt for helping to free translation from 'servility'.]

His endeavour was, not to shew *precisely what Pindar spoke, but his manner of speaking.* He was therefore not at all restrained to his expressions, nor much to his sentiments; nothing was required for him, but not to write as Pindar would not have written. [. . .] Though the English ode cannot be called a translation, it may be very properly consulted as a commentary. [. . .]

To the disproportion and incongruity of Cowley's sentiments must be added the uncertainty and looseness of his measures. He takes the liberty of using in any place a verse of any length, from two syllables to twelve. The verses of Pindar have, as he observes, very little harmony to a modern ear; yet by examining the syllables we perceive them to be regular, and have reason enough for supposing that the ancient audiences were delighted with the sound. The imitator ought therefore to have adopted what he found, and to have added what was wanting: to have preserved a constant return of the same numbers, and to have supplied smoothness of transition and continuity of thought.

Our debt to Cowley

[. . .] that he was among those who freed translation from servility, and, instead of following his author at a distance, walked by his side.

From *The Lives of the Poets*, 'Roscommon'

'It was my Lord Roscommon's Essay on Translated Verse', [Wentworth Dillon, Earl of Roscommon, *An Essay on Translated Verse* (1684)] says Dryden, 'which made me uneasy, till I tried whether or no I was capable of following his rules, and of reducing the speculation into practice. For many a fair precept in poetry is like a seeming demonstration in mathematicks, very specious in the diagram, but failing in the mechanick operation. [. . .]'

He that can abstract his mind from the elegance of the poetry, and confine it to the sense of the precepts, will find no other direction than that the author should be suitable to the translator's genius; that he should be such as may deserve a translation; that he who intends to translate him should endeavour to understand him; that perspicuity should be studied, and unusual and uncouth names sparingly inserted; and that the style of the original should be copied in its elevation and depression. These are the rules that are celebrated as so definite and important; and for the delivery of which to mankind so much honour has been paid. Roscommon has indeed deserved his praises, had they been given with descernment, and bestowed not on the rules themselves, but the art with which they are introduced, and the decorations with which they are adored.

From *The Lives of the Poets*, 'Dryden'

[Against servility, but guided by Dryden, Johnson, as in the *Idler* essays, again encapsulates the history of English translation.]

Cowley says that such *copyers* [Ben Jonson, Feltham, Sandys, etc.] were a *servile race*; he asserted his liberty, and spread his wings so boldly that he left his authors. It was reserved for Dryden to fix the limits of poetical liberty, and give us just rules and examples of translation. [...]

In the proper choice of style consists the resemblance which Dryden principally exacts from the translator. He is to exhibit his author's thoughts in such a dress of diction as the author would have given them, had his language been English [...] A translator is to be like his author; it is not his business to excel him.

[The 'declamatory grandeur' of Juvenal] The general character of this translation will be given, when it is said to preserve the wit, but to want the dignity of the original. The peculiarity of Juvenal is a mixture of gaiety and stateliness, of pointed sentences and declamatory grandeur. [...] It is therefore perhaps possible to give a better representation of that great satirist, even in those parts which Dryden himself has translated, some passages excepted, which will never be excelled.

[Homer and Virgil] In the comparison of Homer and Virgil, the discriminative excellence of Homer is elevation and comprehension of thought, and that of Virgil is grace and splendour of diction. The beauties of Homer are therefore difficult to be lost, and those of Virgil difficult to be retained. [...]

All these obstacles Dryden saw, and all these he determined to encounter. [...]

From *The Lives of the Poets*, 'Pope': 'that poetical wonder, the translation of the *Iliad*'

The chief help of Pope in this arduous undertaking was drawn from the versions of Dryden. Virgil had borrowed much of his imagery from Homer, and part of the debt was now paid by his translator. Pope searched the pages of Dryden for happy combinations of heroick diction; but it will not be denied that he added much to what he found. He cultivated our language with so much diligence and art, that he has left in his *Homer* a treasure of poetical elegances to posterity. His version may be said to have tuned the English tongue; for since its appearance no writer, however deficient in other powers, has wanted melody. Such a series of lines so elaborately corrected, and so sweetly modulated, took possession of the public ear; the vulgar was enamoured of the poem, and the learned wondered at the translation.

But in the most general applause discordant voices will always be heard. It has been objected by some, who wish to be numbered among the sons of learning, that Pope's version of Homer is not Homerical; that it exhibits no resemblance of the original characteristick manner of the Father of Poetry, as it wants his awful simplicity, his artless grandeur, his unaffected majesty. This cannot be totally denied; but it must be remembered that *necessitas quod cogit defendit*; that may be lawfully done which cannot be forborn. Time and place will always enforce regard. In estimating this translation, consideration must be had of the nature of our language, the form of our metre, and, above all, of the change which two thousand year have made in the modes of life and habits of thought. [...]

Thus it will be found, in the progress of learning, that in all nations the first writers are simple, and that every age improves in elegance. One refinement always makes way for another, and what was expedient to Virgil was necessary to Pope. [...]

To a thousand cavils one answer is sufficient; the purpose of a writer is to be read, and the criticism which would destroy the power of pleasing must be blown aside. Pope wrote for his own age and his own nation: he knew that it was necessary to colour the images and point the sentiments of his author; he therefore made him graceful, but lost him some of his sublimity. [...]

Johnson the Translator

Juvenal, Satire X

[See Sect. 2.13, above, for Dryden's Version of Satire X and Sect. 4.10, below, for Robert Lowell's version.]

From The Vanity of Human Wishes, the Tenth Satire of Juvenal Imitated
by Samuel Johnson (London, 1749), *lines 73–90*

Unnumber'd suppliants crowd Preferment's gate,
Athirst for wealth, and burning to be great;
Delusive Fortune hears the'incessant call,
They mount, they shine, evaporate, and fall.
On ev'ry stage the foes of peace attend,
Hate dogs their flight, and insult mocks their end.
Love ends with hope, the sinking statesman's door

Pours in the morning worshipers no more;
For growing names the weekly scribbler lies,
To growing wealth the dedicator flies,
From every room descends the painted face,
That hung the bright Palladium of the place,
And smoak'd in kitchens, or in auctions sold,
To better features yields the frame of gold;
For now no more we trace in ev'ry line
Heroic worth, benevolence divine:
The form distorted justifies the fall,
And detestation rids the'indignant wall. [...]

Niall Rudd, Johnson's Juvenal, London and The Vanity of Human Wishes *(Bristol: Bristol Classical Press, 1981),* literal version of the above passage

So these requests for which it is right to cover the knees of the gods with wax [tablets containing prayers], are either superfluous or harmful. Some men are sent hurtling down by the virulent resentment to which their power exposes them; they are destroyed by their long and impressive list of honours. Down come their statues drawn by the rope; then axe-blows smash their chariot wheels, and the legs of their innocent horses are broken. Now the flames are roaring; now bellows and furnace bring a glow to the head that was worshipped by the people; the mighty Sejanus is crackling; then from the face which was number two in the whole world are made pitchers, basins, saucepans, and dishes. [...]

Johnson, lines 211–22

[The subject here is the heroic warrior, in this case, the historical Charles XII of Sweden, instead of Hannibal as in Juvenal]

The vanquish'd hero leaves his broken bands,
and shews his miseries in distant lands;
Condemn'd a needy supplicant to wait,
While ladies interpose, and slaves debate.
But did not Chance at length her error mend?
Did no subverted empire mark his end?
Did rival monarchs give the fatal wound?
Or hostile millions press him to the ground?
His fall was destin'd to a barren strand,
A petty fortress, and a dubious hand;
He left the name, at which the world grew pale,
To point a moral, or adorn a tale.

Niall Rudd

Lord, what a sight! What a picture he would have made! A one-eyed general riding on a huge Gaetulian beast [elephant]. So how did he finish up? Alas for his dreams of glory! The great man, if you please, is beaten; he escapes with frantic haste into exile; and there he sits in the hall of the king's palace, an important and impressive client, waiting until it should please his Bithynian lord [King Prusias] to wake up. That soul which once turned the world upside down will meet its end, not from a sword or from stones or spears, but from something which will avenge Cannae and take reprisal for all that blood – a little ring. [i.e poison] [...]

Johnson, lines 255–74

[The subject here, of course, is old age.]

> Enlarge my life with multitude of days,
> In health, in sickness, thus the suppliant prays;
> Hides from himself his state, and shuns to know
> That life protracted is protracted woe.
> Time hovers o'er, impatient to destroy,
> And shuts up all the passages of joy:
> In vain their gifts the bounteous seasons pour,
> The fruit autumnal, and the vernal flow'r,
> With listless eyes the dotard views the store,
> He views, and wonders that they please no more;
> Now pall the tasteless meats and joyless wines,
> And Luxury with sighs her slave resigns.
> Approach, ye minstrels, try the soothing strain,
> And yield the tuneful lenitives of pain:
> No sounds alas would touch the'impervious ear,
> Though dancing mountains witness'd Orpheus near;
> Nor lute nor lyre his feeble pow'rs attend,
> Nor sweeter musick of a virtuous friend,
> But everlasting dictates crowd his tongue,
> Perversely grave, or positively wrong. [...]

Niall Rudd

'Grant me a long life, Jupiter; grant me many years!' This is the one thing you pray for, whether your complexion is healthy or pale. But think of the endless and bitter afflictions that go with longevity. First, look at the face—so misshapen and hideous as to be unrecognizable; a misshapen hide instead of human flesh; baggy cheeks, and wrinkles such as an old mother ape has long had etched on her muzzle, where Thabraca [on the North African coast] spreads its leafy glades. Young men have many individual features: A is more handsome than B and B than C; D is far more powerfully built than E; but old men all look alike—a trembling body and voice, a now hairless pate, and an infant's running nose. The poor old fellow has to chew his bread with gums which have lost their cutting edge. He is repellent to his wife, his children, and himself; he even provokes the disgust of Cossus the legacy-hunter. As his palate loses its sensitivity, he no longer takes the same pleasure in food and wine; he has long since forgotten what sex was like; if you try to stimulate him, his thin tool with its enlarged vein lies limp and will remain so although it be caressed all night. What have they to look forward to, these white-haired, incapacitated lions? Moreover, one rightly regards with suspicion the kind of lust that hankers after sex without the power to achieve it. Consider now the loss of another faculty. What pleasure can he get from a musician, even if he be an eminent harpist, or Seleucus or one of the other pipers who wear those fashionable mantles of gleaming gold? [. . .]

2.17 WILLIAM COWPER

William Cowper (1731–1800), English poet, letter-writer, essayist, was trained as a lawyer. Cowper wrote many hymns, as well as *The Task, a Poem in Six Books* (1785): 'God made the Country and Man made the Town.' The success of *The Task* encouraged Cowper to produce his blank verse version of Homer (1785–91), a translation which remained popular well into the nineteenth century. Cowper's comments on Pope are an indication of Pope's prominence as a translator of epic poetry. He objected to Pope's rhyming-couplet approach, dismissing the notion that the translator should try to imagine how the original author would have written in contemporary English. He himself wrote in the Miltonic tradition, meditatively and didactically, in fact also translating some of Milton's Latin and Italian poems (1808) into English. Cowper also translated two poems of Horace early on and towards the end of his life he produced poems from the French of Mme de la Motte Guyon (1801). His observations and caveats regarding the translation of such ancient texts as the Homeric epics remain pertinent.

From Cowper's 'Preface' to *The Iliad of Homer*, ed. R. Southey (1791; London, 1854)

Whether a translation of Homer may be best executed in blank verse or in rhyme, is a question in the decision of which no man can find difficulty, who has ever duly considered what translation ought to be, or who is in any degree practically acquainted with those very different kinds of versification. I will venture to assert that a just translation of any ancient poet in rhyme, is impossible. No human ingenuity can be equal to the task of closing every couplet with sounds homotonous, expressing at the same time the full sense, and only the full sense, of his original. The translator's ingenuity, indeed, in this case, becomes itself a snare, and the readier he is at invention and expedient, the more likely he is to be betrayed into the widest departures from the guide whom he professes to follow. Hence it has happened, that although the public have long been in possession of an English Homer by a poet whose writings have done immortal honour to his country, the demand of a new one, and especially in blank verse, has been repeatedly and loudly made by some of the best judges and ablest writers of the present day.

I have no contest with my predecessor. None is supposeable between performers on different instruments. Mr Pope has surmounted all difficulties in his version of Homer that it was possible to surmount in rhyme. [. . .]

I number myself among the warmest admirers of Mr Pope as an original writer, and I allow him all the merit he can justly claim as the translator of this chief of poets. He has given us the *Tale of Troy* divine in smooth verse, generally in correct and elegant language, and in diction often highly poetical. Bur his deviations are so many, occasioned chiefly by the cause already mentioned, that, much as he has done, and valuable as his work is on some accounts, it was yet in the humble province of a translator that I thought it possible even for me to follow him with some advantage.

That he has sometimes altogether suppressed the sense of his author, and has not seldom intermingled his own ideas with it, is a remark which, on this occasion, nothing but necessity should have extorted from me. But we differ sometimes so widely in our matter, that unless this remark, invidious as it seems, be premised, I know not how to obviate a suspicion, on the one hand, of careless oversight, or of factitious embellishment on the other. On this head, therefore, the English reader is to be admonished, that the matter found in me, whether he like it or not, is found also in Homer, and that the matter not found in me, how much soever he may admire it, is found only in Mr Pope. I have omitted nothing; I have invented nothing.

Are we allowed to invent in poetry?

[. . .]

It will however be necessary to speak a little more largely to this subject, on which discordant opinions prevail even among good judges.

The free and the close translation have, each, their advocates. But inconveniences belong to both. The former can hardly be true to the original author's style and manner, and the latter is apt to be servile. The one loses his peculiarities, and the other his spirit. Were it possible, therefore, to find an exact medium, a manner so close that it should let slip nothing of the text, nor mingle any thing extraneous with it, and at the same time so free as to have an air of originality, this seems precisely the mode in which an author might be best rendered. I can assure my readers from my own experience, that to discover this very delicate line is difficult, and to proceed by it when found, through the whole length of a poet voluminous as Homer, nearly impossible. I can only pretend to have endeavoured it.

It is an opinion commonly received, but, like many others indebted for its prevalence to mere want of examination, that a translator should imagine to himself the style which his author would probably have used, had the language into which he is rendered been his own; a direction which wants nothing but practicability to recommend it. For suppose six persons equally qualified for the task, employed to translate the same Ancient into their own language, with this rule to guide them. In the event it would be found that each had fallen on a manner different from that of all the rest, and by probable inference it would follow that none had fallen on the right. [. . .]

I have no fear of judges familiar with Homer in the original. They need not be told that a translation of him is an arduous enterprize, and as such, entitled to some favour. From these, therefore, I shall expect, and shall not be disappointed, considerable candour and allowance. Especially *they* will be candid, and I believe that there are many such, who have occasionally tried their own strength in this *bow of Ulysses*, They have not found it supple and pliable, and with me are perhaps ready to acknowledge that they could not always even approach with it the mark of their ambition. But I would willingly, were it possible, obviate uncandid criticism, because to answer it is lost labour, and to receive it in silence has the appearance of stately reserve, and self-importance.

To those, therefore, who shall be inclined to tell me hereafter that my diction is often plain and unelevated, I reply beforehand that I know it,—that it would be absurd were it otherwise, and that Homer himself stands in the same predicament. In fact, it is one of his numberless excellencies, and a point in which his judgement never fails him, that he is grand and lofty always in the right place, and knows infallibly how to rise and fall with his subject. *Big words on small matters* may serve as a pretty exact definition of the burlesque, an instance of which they will find in the Battle of the Frogs and Mice, but none in the Iliad.

By others I expect to be told that my numbers, though here and there tolerably smooth, are not always such, but have, now and then, an ugly hitch in their gait, ungraceful in itself, and inconvenient to the reader. To this charge also I plead guilty, but beg leave in alleviation of judgement to add, that my limping lines are not numerous, compared with those that limp not. The truth is, that not one of them all escaped me, but, such as they are, they were all made such with a wilful intention. In poems of great length there is no blemish more to be feared than sameness of numbers, and every art is useful by which it may be avoided. A line, rough in itself, has yet its recommendations; it saves the ear the pain of an irksome monotony, and seems even to add greater smoothness to others. Milton, whose ear and taste were exquisite, has exemplified in his Paradise Lost the effect of this practice frequently.

Having mentioned Milton, I cannot but add an observation on the similitude of his manner to that of Homer. It is such that no person familiar with both, can read either without being reminded of the other; and it is in those breaks and pauses, to which the numbers of the English poet are so much indebted both for their dignity and variety, that he chiefly copies the Grecian. But these are graces to which rhyme is not competent; so broken, it loses all its music; of which any person may convince himself by reading a page only of any of our poets anterior to Denham, Waller, and Dryden. A translator of Homer, therefore, seems directed by Homer himself to the use of blank verse, as to that alone in which he can be rendered with any tolerable representation of his manner in this particular. [. . .]

A word or two on the subject of the following translation, and I have done.

My chief boast is that I have adhered closely to my original, convinced that every departure from him would be punished with the forfeiture of some grace or beauty for which I could substitute no equivalent. The epithets that would consent to an English form I have preserved as epithets; others that would not, I have melted into the context. There are none, I believe, which I have not translated in one way or other, though the reader will not find them repeated so often as most of them are in HOMER, for a reason that need not be mentioned.

Few persons of any consideration are introduced either in the Iliad or Odyssey by their own name only, but their patronymic is given also. To this ceremonial I have generally attended, because it is a circumstance of my author's manner.

Homer never allots less than a whole line to the introduction of a speaker. No, not even when the speech itself is no longer than the line that leads it. A practice to which, since he never departs from it, he must have been determined by some cogent reason. He probably deemed it a formality necessary to the majesty of his narration. In this article, therefore, I have scrupulously adhered to my pattern, considering these introductory lines as heralds in a procession; important persons, because employed to usher in persons more important than themselves.

It has been my point everywhere to be as little verbose as possible, though at the same time, my constant determination not to sacrifice my author's full meaning to an affected brevity.

In the affair of style, I have endeavoured neither to creep nor to bluster, for no author is so likely to betray his translator into both these faults, as Homer, though himself never guilty of either. I have cautiously avoided all terms of new invention, with an abundance of which, persons of more ingenuity than judgement have not enriched our language, but incumbered it. I have also everywhere used an unabbreviated fullness of phrase as most suited to the nature of the work, and above all, have studied perspicuity, not only because verse is good for little that wants it, but because Homer is the most perspicuous of all poets.

In all difficult places I have consulted the best commentators, and where they have differed, or have given, as is often the case, a variety of solutions, I have ever exercised my best judgement, and selected that which appears, at least to myself, the most probable interpretation. On this ground, and on account of the fidelity which I have already boasted, I may venture, I believe, to recommend my work as promising some usefulness to young students of the original.

The passages which will be least noticed, and possibly not at all, except by those who shall wish to find me at a fault, are those which have cost me abundantly the most labour. It is difficult to kill a sheep with dignity in a modern language, to flay and to prepare it for the table, detailing every circumstance of the process. Difficult also, without sinking below the level of poetry, to harness mules to a waggon, particularizing every article of their furniture, straps, rings, staples, and even the tying of the knots that kept all together. Homer, who writes always to the eye, with all his sublimity and grandeur, has the minuteness of a Flemish painter.

But in what degree I have succeeded in my version either of these passages, and such as these, or of others more buoyant and above-ground, and especially of the most sublime, is now submitted to the decision of the reader, to whom I am ready enough to confess that I have not at all consulted their approbation, who account nothing grand that is not turgid, or elegant that is not bedizened with metaphor.

[…]

From *The Odyssey of Homer*, Book XI, trans. William Cowper, (London: printed for J. Johnson, 1791)

Arriving on the shore, and launching, first,
Our bark into the sacred Deep, we set
Our mast and sails, and stow'd secure on board
The ram and ewe, then, weeping, and with hearts
Sad and disconsolate, embark'd ourselves.
And now, melodious Circe, nymph divine,
Sent after us a canvas-stretching breeze,
Pleasant companion of our course, and we
(The decks and benches clear'd) untoiling sat,
While managed gales sped swift the bark along.
All day, with sails distended, e'er the Deep
She flew, and when the sun, at length, declined,
And twilight dim had shadow'd all the ways,
Approach'd the bourn of Ocean's vast profound.
The city, there, of the Cimmerians stands
With clouds and darkness veil'd, on whom the sun
Deigns not to look with his beam-darting eye,
Or when he climbs the starry arch, or when
Earthward he slopes again his west'ring wheels,
But sad night canopies the woeful race.
We haled the bark aground, and, landing there
The ram and sable ewe, journey'd beside
The Deep, till we arrived where Circe bade.

2.18 ALEXANDER FRASER TYTLER

Alexander Fraser Tytler (1747–1813) was a Scottish lawyer and historian, whose *Essay on the Principles of Translation* (1791) is often seen as the first extended thesis on translation written in English. Tytler's common-sense approach still appeals, even if it must now be questioned by translation scholars.

Today's reader of Tytler, aware of the preoccupations of contemporary translators, will boggle at the certainties or convictions that evidently informed Tytler's thinking. To take only the three principles that he formulates. (1) How can a 'complete transcription of the ideas of the original work' be given, seeing that style or form and content are indissoluble? (2) How can 'the style and manner of writing [. . .] be of the same character with that of the original', when the languages are different? (The problem seems to lie in Tytler's use of the uncompromising term 'same' rather than, for instance, 'similar'). (3) As for the requirement that 'the Translation should have all the ease of original composition', translators today often go so far as deliberately to eschew fluency. In any case, in itself it is no longer a priority—although the popular taste, and most publishers, still demand it. This problem is already anticipated, as Holmes notes in his Introduction (see below), at the time when Tytler was writing his *Essay.*

In general, the reader today might feel that Tytler's perception of the translator's duties is presumptuous to a degree, transcending the bounds even of his own common-sense thinking, as for instance when, even with a caution, he allows the translator to 'add to the idea of the original what may appear to give greater force or illustration etc'. When it comes to poetry, he goes even further: 'I conceive it to be the duty of a poetical translator, never to suffer his original to fall.' Such confidence would give the translator a partnership role with the original authority, intervening at a later stage in order, as it were, to finalize or perfect the text. By this account, the translation might seem to be superior to the original, since the blemishes will have been removed.

What picture of the translator, then, emerges from Tytler's account? He appears as a latter-day judge, combining the qualities of critic and peerless writer, whose task it is to present the original author, as he himself would have wished to be presented, free of blemishes and faults. The translator, in effect, functions as a kind of censor, who always has the true interest of author and reader in view. Nevertheless, Tytler's strictures, even today, cannot be easily dismissed, however much we may question his concept of good writing. Many contemporary translation critics will salute his prioritizing of 'sense', for instance.

For Tytler, then, the status of a translator could hardly be higher ('[H]e only is perfectly accomplished for the duty of a translator who possesses genius akin to that of the original author'). The translator appears as the partner of the original author, fully equal and in some ways even superior!

From James S Holmes's introduction to his shortened version of Tytler's *Essay on the Principles of Translation, Modern Poetry in Translation*, 43 (Autumn, 1981), 27–46

Throughout the nineteenth century, and far into the twentieth, the best known and most read of books in English on the nature of translation was surely Alexander Fraser Tytler's *Essay on the Principles of Translation*. One of the problems facing anyone reading the *Essay* is however that one constantly loses the main thread of the argument, led astray by the abundance of illustrative material jampacked into the book. What I have attempted to do here is to strip away all this illustrative flesh to reveal the skeleton of theory giving the *Essay* its shape: Tytler's bare bones. One result is no doubt a decrease in exciting reading, for many of those lopped-off examples were brilliant finds. [We have, with regrets, lopped off even the little that Holmes left, so that what we have here are the bare bones of the bare bones.]

[. . .]

One of the things that becomes clearer as a result of this drastic operation is that Tytler's thinking about translating takes on the shape of a system, a normative model that the translator can actually make use of, to a greater extent than any earlier text that I know on the subject. Not only does he develop his three translation rules (possibly borrowed—or plagiarized—from his contemporary and fellow townsman George Campbell); he also establishes an hierarchical order to guide the choices of the translator attempting to observe those rules.

Today [Holmes was writing in 1979 or 1980] we would formulate the rules differently and question the universal applicability of the hierarchy. Even so, the structure of this skeleton remains as an impressive monument epitomizing eighteenth-century common-sense thinking on translation. Even as Tytler was writing the *Essay*, of course, the floodtide of Romanticism and *Sturm und Drang* that would sweep away that edifice was swelling in England and Germany. The last edition of the *Essay* to be prepared by Tytler himself appeared in the year of his death, 1813; it was that same year that Schleiermacher delivered to the Prussian Academy his address on the two methods of translating, but the two men seem to be separated by a revolution in thinking of Andean proportions. [. . .]

From Alexander Fraser Tytler (Lord Woodhouselee), *Essay on the Principles of Translation* (1791, 1797, 1813); based on 'The Essential Tytler' by James S Holmes, *Modern Poetry in Translation*, 43 (Autumn 1981), 27–46

If it were possible accurately to define, or, perhaps more properly, to describe what is meant by a *good Translation*, it is evident that a considerable progress would be made towards establishing the Rules of the *Art*; for these Rules would flow naturally from that definition or description. But there is no subject or criticism where there has been so much difference of opinion. If the genius and character of all languages were the same, it would be an easy task to translate from one into another; nor would any thing more be requisite on the part of the translator, than fidelity and attention. But as the genius and character of languages is confessedly very different, it has hence become a common opinion, that it is the duty of a translator to attend only to the sense and spirit of his original, to make himself perfectly master of his author's ideas, and to communicate them in those expressions which he judges to be best suited to convey them. It has, on the other hand, been maintained, that, in order to constitute a perfect translation, it is not only requisite that the ideas and sentiments of the original author should be conveyed, but likewise his style and manner of writing, which, it is supposed, cannot be done without a strict attention to the arrangement of his sentences, and even to their order and construction. According to the former idea of translation, it is allowable to improve and to embellish; according to the latter, it is necessary to preserve even blemishes and defects and to these must likewise be superadded the harshness that must attend every copy in which the artist scrupulously studies to imitate the minutest lines or traces of his original.

As these two opinions form opposite extremes, it is not improbable that the point of perfection should be found between the two. I would therefore describe a good translation to be, *That, in which the merit of the original work is so completely transfused into another language, as to be as distinctly apprehended, and as strongly felt, by a native of the country to which that language belongs, as it is by those who speak the language of the original work.* [...]

It will follow,

  I. That the Translation should give a complete transcript of the ideas of the original work.

  II. That the style and manner of writing should be of the same character with that of the original.

  III. That the Translation should have all the ease of original composition.

[...]

First General Rule [...]

In order that a translator may be enabled to give a complete transcript of the ideas of the original work, it is indispensably necessary, that he should have a perfect knowledge of the language of the original, and a competent acquaintance with the subject of which it treats. [...]

The extreme difficulty of translating from the works of the ancients, is most discernible to those who are best acquainted with the ancient languages. It is but a small part of the genius and powers of a language which is to be learnt from dictionaries and grammars. There are innumerable niceties, not only of construction and idiom, but even in the signification of words, which are discovered only by much reading, and critical attention.

A very learned author, and acute critic [George Campbell, 'Preliminary Dissertations of a New Translation of the Gospels', 1789] has, in treating 'of the causes of the differences in languages', remarked that a principal difficulty in the art of translating arises from this circumstance, 'that there are certain words in every language which but imperfectly correspond to any of the words of other languages'. Of this kind, he observes, are most of the terms relating to morals, to the passions, to matters of sentiment, or to the objects of the reflex and internal senses. [. . .]

Where the sense of an author is doubtful, and where more than one meaning can be given to the same passage or expression, (which, by the way, is always a defect in composition), the translator is called upon to exercise his judgement, and to select that meaning which is most consonant to the train of thought in the whole passage, or to the author's usual mode of thinking, and of expressing himself. To imitate the obscurity or ambiguity of the original, is a fault; and it is still a greater, to give more than one meaning. [. . .]

If it is necessary that a translator should give a complete transcript of the ideas of the original work, it becomes a question, whether it is allowable in any case to add to the ideas of the original what may appear to give greater force or illustration; or to take from them what may seem to weaken them from redundancy. To give a general answer to this question, I would say, that this liberty may be used, but with the greatest caution. [. . .] Under these limitations, a translator may exercise his judgement, and assume to himself, in so far, the character of an original writer. An improvement is sometimes very happily made, by substituting figure and metaphor to simple sentiment. [. . .]

Analogous to this liberty of adding to or retrenching from the ideas of the original, is the liberty which a translator may take of correcting what appear to him a careless or inaccurate expression of the original, where that inaccuracy seems materially to affect the sense. [. . .]

[. . .] I conceive it to be the duty of a poetical translator, never to suffer his original to fall. He must maintain with him a perpetual contest of genius; he must attend him in his highest flights, and soar, if he can, beyond him; and when he perceives, at any time, a diminution of his powers, when he sees a drooping wing, he must raise him on his own pinions. Homer has been judged by the best critics to fall at times beneath himself, and to offend, by introducing low images and puerile allusions. Yet how admirably is this defect veiled over, or altogether removed, by his translator Pope. [. . .]

It is always a fault when the translator adds to the sentiment of the original author, what does not strictly accord with his characteristic mode of thinking, or expressing himself. But if authors, even of taste and genius, are found at times to have made an injudicious use of that liberty which is allowed in the translation of poetry, we must expect to see it miserably abused indeed, where those talents are evidently wanting.

Second General Rule [. . .]

[. . .] A good translator must be able to discover at once the true character of his author's style [. . .] [T]hese characteristic qualities he must have the capacity of rendering equally conspicuous in the translation as in the original. If a translator fails in this discernment, and wants this capacity, let him be ever so thoroughly master of the sense of his author, he will present him through a distorting medium, or exhibit him often in a garb that is unsuitable to his character. [. . .]

But a translator may discern the general character of his author's style, and yet fail remarkably in the imitation of it. Unless he is possessed of the most correct taste, he will be in continual danger of presenting an exaggerated picture or a caricatura of his original. The distinction between good and bad writing is often of so very slender a nature, and the shadowing of difference so extremely delicate, that a very nice perception alone can at all times define the limits. Thus, in the hands of some translators, who have discernment to perceive the general character of their author's style, but want this correctness of taste, the grave style of the original becomes heavy and formal in the translation; the elevated swells into bombast, the lively froths up into the petulant, and the simple and *naif* degenerates into the childish and insipid.

[. . .]

The rule which enjoins to a translator the imitation of the style of the original author, demands several limitations.

1. This imitation must always be regulated by the nature or genius of the language of the original and of the translation.

The Latin language admits of a brevity, which cannot be successfully imitated in the English. [. . .]

2. The Latin and Greek languages admit of inversions which are inconsistent with the genius of the English.

3. The English language is not incapable of an elliptical mode of expression; but it does not admit of it to the same degree as the Latin.

[. . .]

Third General Rule [. . .]

When we consider those restraints within which a translator finds himself necessarily confined, with regard to the sentiments and manner of his original, it will soon appear that this last requisite includes the most difficult part of his walk. To one who walks in trammels, it is not easy to exhibit an air of grace and freedom. [. . .] The more he studies a scrupulous imitation, the less his copy will reflect the ease and spirit of the original. How then shall a translator accomplish this difficult union of ease with fidelity? To use a bold expression, he must adopt the very soul of his author, which must speak through his own organs. [...]

But while a translator thus endeavours to transfuse into his work all the ease of the original, the most correct taste is requisite to prevent that ease from degenerating into licentiousness. [...]

If the order in which I have classed the three general laws of translation is their just and natural arrangement, which I think will hardly be denied, it will follow, that in all cases where a sacrifice is necessary to be made of one of those laws to another, a due regard ought to be paid to their rank and comparative importance, the different genius of the languages of the original and translation, will often make it necessary to depart from the manner of the original, in order to convey a faithful picture of the sense; but it would be highly preposterous to depart, in any case, from the sense, for the sake of imitating the manner. Equally improper would it be, to sacrifice either the sense or manner of the original, if these can be preserved consistently with purity of expression, to a fancied ease or superior gracefulness of composition. [...]

[...]

It may perhaps appear paradoxical to assert, that it is less difficult to give to a poetical translation all the ease of original composition, than to give the same degree of ease to a prose translation. Yet the truth of this assertion will be readily admitted, if assent is given to that observation [... t]hat a superior degree of liberty is allowed to a poetical translator in amplifying, retrenching from, and embellishing his original, than to a prose translator. For without some portion of this liberty, there can be no ease of composition; and where the greatest liberty is allowable, there that ease will be most apparent, as it is less difficult to attain to it. [...]

[...]

While a translator endeavours to give to his work all the ease of original composition, the chief difficulty he has to encounter will be found in the translation of idioms, or those turns of expression which do not belong to universal grammar, but of which every language has its own, that are exclusively proper to it. [...]

The translation is perfect, when the translator finds in his own language an idiomatic phrase corresponding to that of the original.

As there is nothing which so much conduces both to the ease and spirit of composition, as a happy use of idiomatic phrases, there is nothing which a translator, who has a moderate command of his own language, is so apt to carry to a licentious extreme.

In the use of idiomatic phrases, a translator frequently forgets both the country of his original author, and the age in which he wrote; and while he makes a Greek or a Roman speak French or English, he unwittingly puts into his mouth allusions to the manners of modern France or England. [. . .]

A translator will often meet with idiomatic phrases in the original author, to which no corresponding idiom can be found in the language of the translation. As a literal translation of such phrases cannot be tolerated, the only resource is, to express the sense in plain and easy language.

But this resource, of translating the idiomatic phrase into easy language must fail, where the merit of the passage to be translated actually lies in that expression which is idiomatical. This will often occur in epigrams, many of which are therefore incapable of translation [. . .]

[. . .]

In a preceding chapter, while treating of the translation of idiomatic phrases, we censured the use of such idioms in the translation as do not correspond with the age or country of the original. There is, however, one species of translation, in which that violation of the *costume* is not only blameless, but seems essential to the nature of the composition: I mean burlesque translation, or Travesty. This species of writing partakes in a great degree, of original composition and is therefore not to be measured by the laws of serious translation. [. . .]

But this species of composition pleases only in a short specimen. We can not bear a lengthened work in Travesty. The incongruous association of dignity and meanness excites risibility chiefly from its being unexpected. [. . .]

[. . .]

From the consideration of those general rules of translation which in the foregoing essay I have endeavoured to illustrate, it will appear no unnatural conclusion to assert, that he only is perfectly accomplished for the duty of a translator who possesses genius akin to that of the original author. [. . .] Thus we shall observe invariably, that the best translators have been those writers who have composed original works of the same species with those which they have translated. [. . .]

We have observed, in the preceding part of this essay, that poetical translation is less subjected to restraint than prose translation, and allows more of the freedom of original composition. It will hence follow, that to exercise this freedom with propriety, a translator must have the talent of original composition in poetry; and therefore, that in this species of translation, the possession of a genius akin to that of his author, is more essentially necessary than in any other. [. . .] The best translators of poetry, therefore, have been those who have approved their talents in original poetical composition. [. . .]

CHAPTER 3

THE NINETEENTH CENTURY

3.1 INTRODUCTION

Several of the key statements of the nineteenth-century philosophy and policy of translation were made by German scholars and writers who were, in one way or another, active in the period generally characterized as 'Romantic'. Herder, Goethe, Humboldt, the Schlegel brothers, and Schleiermacher all wrote important documents about translation. These texts were clearly linked to recent and contemporary practice of translation into German (especially translations of the Homeric epics, the Greek tragedies, and Shakespeare's plays), but they also made their mark as theoretical pronouncements both in and beyond the German sphere, especially some of Goethe's statements (see Sect. 3.2, below) and Schleiermacher's 'On the Different Methods of Translating' (excerpts from which are included in Sect. 3.3, below).

According to André Lefevere, these writers are part of a 'German tradition' that he sees originating in Martin Luther (see Sect. 2.2, above), moving through Gottsched and Lessing into the Romantic period, and then on to Nietzsche, Benjamin, and Rosenzweig (see Sects. 4.4 and 4.5, below).[1] Luther is obviously important for most German translation critics, and Goethe sees Luther's translation method as a valuable first step or 'epoch' in bringing foreign works into German. It is equally true, however, that Goethe and some of the other key people mentioned above felt that they had moved beyond this mode of translation and were eager to witness closer encounters with foreign languages and texts. In this respect, rather than thinking of themselves as participating in a German tradition, they often defined themselves *against* what they saw as a French tradition of translation, characterized by appropriation and domestication. It it important to remember that French had for a long time been the most respected literary vernacular in Europe, one that often served as an intermediary language for translators. There had in fact been cases

---

[1] André Lefevere: *Translating Literature: The German Tradition from Luther to Rosenzweig* (Assen/Amsterdam: Van Gorcum, 1977).

when a work would be translated into German from a French translation even when the German translator did in fact know the original language of the work.[2]

Hence, translation and the translation debate in the early nineteenth century served to enhance the striving for an independent literary language in Germany. French, as we have seen, had also often served as the intermediary language for English translators, and while the cultural and national context in Britain was completely different from that of Germany, many English translators and scholars welcomed the new German 'movement', while others sought to point out a way in between the German 'close' method and the French 'loose' one, often associated with 'les belles infidèles' (the beautiful but unfaithful).[3] No single theoretical texts were written in English that can be compared with those of the leading German thinkers, but a lively translation debate was conducted in books and journals in Britain, and *translation criticism* becomes comparatively more prominent than ever before or indeed after. Reviews, sometimes long and detailed, that centred around recent translations, would often contain a good deal of general discussion about translation methods and the cultural cross-over that characterizes the translated text. The best-known interchange about Victorian translation is the debate between Matthew Arnold and Francis Newman, but this is in fact very much an integral part of a wider critical discourse, samples of which can be found in 'Victorian Translation and Criticism' (Sect. 3.4, below, see also the introduction to that section).

By the beginning of the period covered in this section, the Western canon was largely in place, and its key works are at the centre of the translation debate in Britain: Homer especially, but also the Greek tragedies, Virgil's *Aeneid*, and other significant works written in Classical Greek and Latin, still the two towering original languages against which the qualities of the English language are measured. But translation from the other European vernaculars was on the rise; Dante is close to the heart of the canon, and as recent a writer as Goethe rapidly becomes a writer of paradigmatic significance, one whose works appear in a succession of (re)translations. But while many scholars and translators largely agreed about what texts possessed the value which the target language and culture needed most, or would thrive on, there was fierce disagreement about the method of bringing these texts across the language barrier.

It is interesting to note that while respect for Homer is generally crystallized in the discussion about the appropriate metre to use for the Greek epics in English, there are also those who suggest that *prose* is the most appropriate form for Homer and for several other

---

[2] Cf. Jürgen Stackelberg: *Übersetzungen aus zweiter Hand: Rezeptionsvorgänge in der europäischen Literatur vom 14. bis zum 18. Jahrhundert* (Berlin and New York: Walter de Gruyter, 1984) 126.

[3] This well-known feminized (sexist?) metaphor for translation was first used by Nicolas Perrot d'Ablancourt (1606–64), French translator of many Classical authors.

Classical writings. We are, after all, in the age of the novel by now. But what kind of prose? Some suggest that the prose style of the Bible is the key to the Classical poetic and dramatic epics. This is a wonderful manifestation of the interplay, so often ignored or not recognized, between translation, literary language, and literary history. The Bible in a 'Classical' translation—having become a kind of tradition in the language and the literary culture—is drawn on in translating Classical works into a *modern* form.

It should come as no surprise, therefore, that nineteenth-century translation into English evinces a pluralistic spectrum of methods, more in fact than one could conjecture from the scholarly discussion, which tended to be limited to translation of works from the Western tradition. Not only is there a good deal of translation of 'popular' literature, notably novels, from other European languages, which do not get much critical attention, but some of the most popular (and some of the most notorious) literary works in Victorian Britain were translated texts that originated outside Europe. The British response to the literature of the 'Orient' was sometimes deeply coloured by imperial confidence, sometimes arrogance, most ignobly expressed, perhaps, in Thomas Babington Macaulay's statement in 1835 that a single shelf in 'a good European library' was more valuable than the combined literature of India and the Arab world.[4] Some may hear an echo of this attitude in the words of Edward FitzGerald about the original *Rubáiyát* text that he turned into tremendously popular English poetry (see Sect. 3.5, below). A very different kind of response to the 'exotic' can be seen in William Morris's response to classical Icelandic literature, which he brought into an archaicized English, challenging popular taste for the exotic by a different sort of 'nostalgic' approach.

The reader will find examples from numerous translations in the two large 'collages' that make up the bulk of the following chapter, which concludes, however, with James Fitzmaurice-Kelly's swift historical overview from 1911 of the whole period covered by the volume up to that point.

---

[4] Cf. Tejaswini Niranjana: *Siting Translation: History, Post-Structuralism, and the Colonial Context* (Berkeley and Los Angeles: University of California Press, 1992), 31.

3.2 JOHANN WOLFGANG VON GOETHE

Johann Wolfgang von Goethe (1749–1832), pre-eminent German poet and writer, was also a lawyer, politician, civil servant, botanist, zoologist, physicist, painter, theatre manager, and literary critic. Author of *Faust, Die Leiden des jungen Werthers* (The Sufferings of Young Werther), *Iphigenie auf Tauris, Wilhelm Meisters Lehrjahre* (Wilhelm Meister's Apprenticeship), and several celebrated poems, Goethe is one of the most important European writers of his time, both as a master of many genres, and as someone who was instrumental in the whole crucible of movements and counter-movements: from *Sturm und Drang* (storm and stress) and early Romantic revolt against the rationalism of the Enlightenment, toward a re-evaluation of Classicism and Humanism, along with the development of Romanticism. Notions of both nationhood and universality, and their linguistic and symbolic modes of expression, are crucial to Goethe's world view, suspended as it is between organic growth and metamorphosis. For Goethe, as for many of his German contemporaries, such as J. G. Herder, A. W. Schlegel, Wilhelm von Humboldt, and Friedrich Schleiermacher, translation—both as linguistic fact and as metaphor—was a gateway between on the one hand the strengthening notions of nationality and the Western tradition, and on the other, in some cases, the broader world (especially the 'Orient').

In the case of Goethe, this gateway is closely linked to 'world literature', a concept that he, more than anyone else, brought into prominence, a concept that clearly is heavily dependent upon translation. Eckermann's record of Goethe's most famous comment on world literature is included below, and when we look beyond the few lines usually cited, we see that Goethe's reflections are started by his observations about a Chinese novel he is reading (almost certainly in translation, but ironically the text is never fully identified). His conclusion, in this case, may seem to reinstate the Western canon as the cornerstone ('we must always return to the ancient Greeks'), but in one of his best-known comments about translation—his notes to the cycle of poems *West-Östlicher Divan* (1819), which signalled his discovery of the Orient in the poetry of the Persian poet Hafiz—the opposite seems to be true. There he moves from German translations of Homer, Ariosto, etc., to the important task of translating Persian and Indian literature into German (see excerpt below), although the final comment does, significantly, relate this whole translation endeavour to interlinear versions of the Bible.

It should be stressed that this selection of statements by Goethe does not constitute a single systematic theory, or even view, of translation (for this see Schleiermacher in Sect. 3.3, below). Goethe made these statements in different contexts at different times, but he gradually came to place more and more emphasis on the movement toward the foreign, as we see in his notion of the 'third epoch' of translation, in which the translation is not received 'instead of' the other text (the original), but rather 'in the other's stead'; its stage is that of the foreign text; the foreign text itself may in fact be that 'stead [*Stelle*]'. Or as Goethe said late in his life: 'When translating, one should go as far as the untranslatable; only then does one become aware of the foreign nation and the foreign language.'[1] This view of the foreign (along with the metaphoric reference to the interlinear version) is clearly a major source of inspiration for Walter Benjamin in his seminal article 'The Task of the Translator' (see Sect. 4.4, below).

On Translation

The following three comments of Goethe on translation, translated by André Lefevere, are taken from Lefevere's *Translating Literature: The German Tradition from Luther to Rosenzweig* (Assen/Amsterdam: Van Gorcum, 1977), 35–9 (printed here in a chronological sequence).

From *Dichtung und Wahrheit* (1811–1814)

Wieland's translation [of Shakespeare] appeared. It was devoured, shared with and recommended to friends and acquaintances. We Germans had the advantage that many important works of foreign nations were first translated in a light and bantering vein. The translations of Shakespeare in prose, first Wieland's, then [Johann Joachim] Eschenburg's, could quickly spread as reading matter. They were generally intelligible and suited to the common reader. I honour both rhythm and rhyme, through which poetry become poetry indeed, but what is really deeply and thought operative, what really shapes and improves, is what is left of a poet when he has been translated into prose. What remains then is the pure, perfect essence which a blinding exterior often succeeds in deluding us with when it is not there, and in hiding when it is. That is why I think translations into prose are more advantageous than translations into verse in the first stages of education; one can see that boys, who turn everything into a joke, make fun of the sound of words, the fall of syllables, and destroy the deep essence of the noblest work out of a certain sense of parodistic devilry. I should therefore like you to consider whether we are not in need of a prose translation of Homer; it should, of course, be

---

[1] 'Beim Übersetzen muß man bis ans Unübersetzliche herangehen; alsdann wird man aber erst die fremde Nation und die fremde Sprache gewahr', quoted in Hans Joachim Störig, 'Einleitung', in Störig (ed.), *Das Problem des Übersetzens* (Stuttgart: Henry Goverts Verlag 1963), p. viii.

worthy of the level that German literature has reached by now. I leave this and what I said before to the consideration of our worthy pedagogues who can rely on extensive experience in this matter. I simply want to remind you of Luther's Bible translation as an argument in favour of my proposal. That this excellent man offered us in our mother tongue, and as it were in one piece, a work written in the most different styles, as well as its poetic, historical, imperative, didactic tone, has helped religion more than if he had aspired to recreate the idiosyncracies of that original down to the smallest detail. Later translators have tried in vain to make us enjoy the book of Job, the Psalms, and other canticles in their poetic form. If you want to influence the masses, a simple translation is always best. Critical translations vying with the original are really of use only for conversations conducted by the learned among themselves.

From 'Zum brüderlichen Andenken Wielands' (1813)

There are two maxims in translation: one requires that the author of a foreign nation be brought across to us in such a way that we can look on him as ours; the other requires that we should go across to what is foreign and adapt ourselves to its conditions, its use of language, its peculiarities. The advantages of both are sufficiently known to educated people through perfect examples. Our friend [Wieland], who looked for the middle way in this, too, tried to reconcile both, but as a man of feeling and taste he preferred the first maxim when in doubt.

From *West-Östlicher Divan* (1819)

There are three kinds of translation. The first acquaints us with foreign countries on our own terms; a simple prosaic translation is best in this respect. For since prose totally cancels all peculiarities of any kind of poetic art, and since prose itself pulls poetic enthusiasm down to a common water-level, it does the greatest service in the beginning, by surprising us with foreign excellence in the midst of our national homeliness, our everyday existence; it offers us a higher mood and real edification while we do not realize what is happening to us. Luther's Bible translation will produce this kind of effect at any time.

If the *Nibelungen* had been put into decent prose at the outset, and if it had been stamped a popular romance, much would have been gained and the singular, dark, noble, awesome sense of chivalry would have addressed itself to us with its full strength. Whether this is still advisable or feasible now will best be judged by those who have applied themselves more thoroughly to these matters of great antiquity.

A second epoch follows in which [the translator] really only tries to appropriate foreign content and to reproduce it in his own sense, even though he tries to transport himself into foreign situations. I would like to call this kind of epoch the parodistic one, in the fullest sense of that word. In most cases men of wit feel called to this kind of trade. The French use this method in their translations of all poetic works; hundreds of examples can be found in the translations produced by [Abbé Jacques] Delille [a well-known and prolific translator of the day]. Just as the French adapt foreign words to their pronunciations, just so do they treat feelings, thoughts, even objects; for every foreign fruit they demand a counterfeit grown in their own soil.

Wieland's translations are of this kind; he too had a singular sense of understanding and taste which brought him close to antiquity and to foreign countries only to the extent to which he could still feel comfortable. This excellent man may be considered the representative of his time; he has had an extraordinary impact, precisely because what he found pleasing, how he appropriated it, and how he communicated it in his turn seemed pleasing and enjoyable also to his contemporaries.

Since it is impossible to linger too long either in the perfect or in the imperfect and one change must of necessity follow another, we experienced the third epoch, which is to be called the highest and the final one, namely the one in which the aim is to make the translation identical with the original, so that one would not be valued instead of the other, but in the other's stead.[1]

This kind had to overcome the greatest resistance originally; for the translator who attaches himself closely to his original more or less abandons the originality of his nation, and so a third comes into existence, and the taste of the multitude must first be shaped towards it.

Voss [Johann Heinrich Voss, the translator of Homer into hexameters], who will never be praised enough, could not satisfy the public initially; yet slowly, bit by bit, it listened itself into his new manner and made itself comfortable in it. But whoever can now see what has happened, what versatility has come to the Germans, what rhetorical, rhythmical, metrical advantages are at the disposal of the talented and knowledgeable youngster, how Ariosto and Tasso, Shakespeare and Calderón are now presented to us twice and three times over as germanized foreigners, may hope that literary history will plainly state who was the first to take this road in spite of so many obstacles.

The works of von Hammer [the Viennese Orientalist Joseph von Hammer-Purgstall] point for the most part to a similar treatment of Oriental masterpieces, in which approximation to the external form is to be most recommended. The passage of a translation by Firdausi which our friend has given us reveal themselves as endlessly more profitable when compared to those of an adaptor whom we can read excerpts of in the *Fundgruben* [*des Orients*, a review of Oriental studies edited by von Hammer]. Adapting a poet in this way is, in my opinion, the saddest mistake a diligent translator, who is moreover well suited to his task, could make. But since these three epochs are repeated and inverted in every literature; since, indeed, these three methods can be applied simultaneously, a translation into prose of the *Sháh-náma* [Book of Kings, the Persian poet's Firdausi's long poem] and the works of Nizāmī is still in order. It could be used for rapid reading which would open up the main sense; we would be pleased with the historical, the legendary, and the generally ethical and we would move closer and closer to moods and ways of thought, until we could totally fraternize with them at last.

Remember the most resolute recognition we Germans have given such a translation of the *Sakuntalá* [by the Indian dramatist Kâlidâsa]; we can ascribe its great impact to the general prose in which the poem has been diluted. But it is about time now for someone to offer it to us in a translation of the third type, which would correspond to the different dialects as well as to the rhythmical, metrical, and prosaic ways of speech in the original, and which would allow us to enjoy that poem anew in all its idiosyncrasy and to naturalize it for us. Since a manuscript of this eternal work may be found in Paris, a German who lives there could gain undying merit among us if he were to undertake such a work.

The English translator of [Kâlidâsa's] *Messenger of the Clouds*, or *Meghadúta* [Horace H. Wilson] is also worthy of all praise, because the first acquaintance with such a work is always momentous in one's life. But his translation really belongs in the second period, in that it is supplementary and paraphrastic; it flatters the Northeasterly ear and sense through the iambic pentameter. I am indebted to our Kosegarten [Luwig Gotthard Kosegarten, a scholar-author of the time] for a few lines translated directly from the original language, and they give a totally different impression indeed. The Englishman has, moreover, allowed himself transpositions of motifs which the trained esthetic eye immediately discovers and disapproves of. It remains to explain in a few words why we called the third epoch the final one. A translation which attempts to identify itself with the original in the end comes close to an interlinear version and greatly enhances our understanding of the original; this in turn leads us, compels us as it were, towards the source text, and so the circle is closed at last. Inside it the coming together of the foreign and the native, the unknown approximation and the known, keep moving towards each other.

EDITORS' NOTE

1. [Here is this important statement in Goethe's original: 'wo man die Übersetzung dem Original identisch machen möchte, so daß eins nicht anstatt des andern, sondern an der Stelle des andern gelten soll'. J. W. von Goethe: 'Drei Stücke zum Thema Übersetzen', in Hans Joachim Störig (ed.): *Das Problem des Übersetzens* (Stuttgart: Henry Goverts Verlag, 1963), 36. In his translation Lefevere has made 'the original identical with the translation', almost certainly an accident in typing, which we decided to correct.]

On World Literature

From J. W. Goethe, *Conversations with Eckermann* (1823–32), trans. John Oxenford (San Francisco: North Point Press, 1984), 132–3

Wednesday, January 31 [1827]

Dined with Goethe. 'Within the last few days, since I saw you,' said he, 'I'll have read many things; especially a Chinese novel, which occupies me still and seems to me very remarkable.'

'Chinese novel!' said I; 'that must look strange enough.'

'Not so much as you might think,' said Goethe; 'the Chinese think, act, and feel almost exactly like us; and we soon find that we are perfectly like them, except that all they do is more clear, pure, and decorous, than with us.

'With them all is orderly, citizen-like, without great passion or poetic flight; and there is a strong resemblance to my *Hermann and Dorothea*, as well as to the English novels of Richardson. They likewise differ from us in that with them external nature is always associated with the human figures. You always hear the goldfish splashing in the pond, the birds are always singing on the bough; the day is always serene and sunny, the night is always clear. There is much talk about the moon; but it does not alter the landscape, its light is conceived to be as bright as day itself; and the interior of the houses is as neat and elegant as their pictures. For instance, "I heard the lovely girls laughing, and when I got sight of them they were sitting on cane chairs." There you have, at once, the prettiest situation; for cane chairs are necessarily associated with the greatest lightness and elegance. Then there is an infinite number of legends which are constantly introduced into the narrative and are applied almost like proverbs: as, for instance, one of a girl who was so light and graceful in the feet that she could balance herself on a flower without breaking it; and then another, of a young man so virtuous and brave that in his thirtieth year he had the honour to talk with the Emperor; then there is another of two lovers who showed such great purity during a long acquaintance that, when they were on one occasion obliged to pass the night in the same chamber, they occupied the time with conversation and did not approach one another.'

'There are innumerable other legends, all turning upon what is moral and proper. It is by this severe moderation in everything that the Chinese Empire has sustained itself for thousands of years, and will endure hereafter.'

'I find a highly remarkable contrast to this Chinese novel in the *Chansons de Béranger*, which have, almost every one, some immoral licentious subject for their foundation, and which would be extremely odious to me if managed by a genius inferior to Béranger; he, however, has made them not only tolerable, but pleasing. Tell me yourself, is it not remarkable that the subjects of the Chinese poet should be so thoroughly moral, and those of the first French poet of the present day be exactly the contrary?'

'Such a talent as Béranger's,' said I, 'would find no field in moral subjects.'

'You are right,' said Goethe; 'the very perversions of his time have revealed and developed his better nature.'

'But,' said I, 'is this Chinese romance one of their best?'

'By no means,' said Goethe; 'the Chinese have thousands of them, and had when our forefathers were still living in the woods.'

'I am more and more convinced,' he continued, 'that poetry is the universal possession of mankind, revealing itself everywhere and at all times in hundreds and hundreds of men. One makes it a little better than another, and swims on the surface a little longer than another—that is all. Herr von Matthisson must not think he is the man, nor must I think that I am the man; but each must say to himself that the gift of poetry is by no means so very rare, and that nobody need think very much of himself because he has written a good poem.'

'But, really, we Germans are very likely to fall too easily into this pedantic conceit, when we do not look beyond the narrow circle that surrounds us. I therefore like to look about me in foreign nations, and advise everyone to do the same. National literature is now rather an unmeaning term; the epoch of world literature is at hand, and everyone must strive to hasten its approach. But, while we thus value what is foreign, we must not bind ourselves to some particular thing, and regard it as a model. We must not give this value to the Chinese, or the Serbian, or Calderón, or the *Nibelungen*; but if we really want a pattern, we must always return to the ancient Greeks, in whose works the beauty of mankind is constantly represented. All the rest we must look at only historically; appropriating to ourselves what is good, so far as it goes.'

3.3   FRIEDRICH SCHLEIERMACHER

Friedrich Schleiermacher (1768–1834) was an influential German theologian and one of the key scholarly figures of German Romanticism; professor of theology, first at Halle, later in Berlin; often regarded as the founder of secular hermeneutics, since his theories of interpretation form a bridge from religion to the humanities in general. His important lecture 'On the Different Methods of Translating', delivered to the Royal Academy of Sciences in Berlin in 1813, contains a systematic analysis of the Romantic concept of translation, urging that the reader be brought to the author, that the reader learn to accept 'alienation', or what would now be called foreignization of translations.

Schleiermacher opens his lecture (excerpts of which appear below) by discussing translation as a general feature of understanding and language, then narrows the focus to two kinds of transference: interpreting ('Dolmetchen'), whereby he refers not only to oral interpreting, but to this linguistic act in the general 'field of commerce', whereas the 'translator proper operates mainly in the fields of art and scholarship', especially as he tackles creative texts that constitute 'a new element in the life of a language' (see below). It is the latter which is Schleiermacher's concern, but he goes on to exclude also looser versions of translation, namely 'paraphrase' and 'imitation'. What we are left with then are the two basic methods of translation proper: moving the author to the reader or the reader to the author. Translators pursuing the first method often claim that they want to make their author speak the way he would have spoken had he written the work in the translator's language. This has long been a popular expression (Dryden is often quoted to this effect) among translators who wish to argue that the liberties they have taken are based on some more integral aspects of the work, aspects which are thus being rendered in spite of the changes made. In his lecture, Schleiermacher goes after this formula with a vengeance, and argues in detail (which space does not allow us to include) why the method behind it does not hold water. In fact, he more than once implies that this method often turns out to be imitation in disguise. Hence, there seems to be only one option left for the translator who wants to transmit 'the living power' which 'creates new forms by means of the plastic material of language'; the reader has to be brought to the author, and Schleiermacher comes up with his own metaphoric formula to describe this translation: it will be 'perfect in its kind when one can say that if the author had learnt German as well as the translator has learnt Latin he would not have translated the work he originally wrote in Latin any differently than the translator has done.' This clever move of casting the author as a potential translator of his work (rather than a writer of it in another language) dramatizes the relationship between the author, translator and reader in a thought-provoking way.

And while at one point he talks about moving the reader to the author, Schleiermacher also describes them as meeting 'at a certain point in the middle', i.e. they meet through and 'in' a translator who opens up the gateway of the foreign.

However, this foreignizing method clearly challenges the reader and it places a strain on the language of the translation. Schleiermacher notes that not every language is ready for this, but he clearly has great faith in the German language and its ability not only to incorporate the foreign, but to house the extensive number of translated works which he finds necessary for the method to make sense in the long run. Schleiermacher not only sees translation as a crucial national enterprise, but he also dreams of the German language as a linguistic empire where the various works of world literary history are all gathered together.

From 'On the Different Methods of Translating', trans. André Lefevere, in Lefevere's *Translating Literature: The German Tradition from Luther to Rosenzweig* **(Assen and Amsterdam: Van Gorcum 1977), 67–89**

On the one hand every man is in the power of the language he speaks, and all his thinking is a product thereof. He cannot think anything with great precision which would lie outside the limits of language; the shape of his concepts, the nature and the limits of the way in which they can be connected, is prescribed for him by the language in which he is born and educated—intellect and imagination are bound by it. Yet on the other hand every freely thinking, mentally self-employed human being shapes his own language. For in what other way—except precisely by means of these influences—would it have developed and grown from its first raw state to its more perfect elaboration in scholarship and art? In this sense, therefore, it is the living power of the individual which creates new forms by means of the plastic material of language, at first only for the immediate purpose of communicating a passing consciousness; yet now more, now less of it remains behind in the language, is taken up by others, and reaches out, a shaping force. It might even be said that a person deserves to be heard beyond his immediate environment only to the extent to which he influences language. Any verbal text soon dies away of necessity if it can be reproduced by a thousand organs in a form which is always the same; only that text can and may endure longer which constitutes a new element in the life of a language itself. Therefore, each free and higher speech needs to be understood twice, once out of the spirit of the language of whose elements it is composed, as a living representation bound and defined by that spirit and conceived out of it in the speaker, and once out of the speaker's emotions, as his action, as produced and explicable only out of his own being. (p. 71)

If his readers are to understand, they must perceive the spirit of the language which was the author's own and be able to see his peculiar way of thinking and feeling, and to realize these two aims the translator can offer them nothing but his own language, which at no point fully corresponds to the other, and his own person, whose understanding of his author is now more, now less clear, and whose admiration and approval of him is now greater, now less. Does not translation, considered in this way, seem a foolish enterprise? That is why people, in despair at not reaching this goal, or, if you prefer, before they had reached the stage at which all this could be clearly thought out, discovered two other methods of becoming acquainted with works in foreign languages, not with a view to gathering their real artistic or linguistic sense, but rather to fill a need and to contemplate spiritual art; in the methods some of these difficulties are forcibly removed, others slyly circumvented, but the concept of translation adduced here is completely abandoned. These two methods are paraphrase and imitation. Paraphrase strives to conquer the irrationality of languages, but only in a mechanical way. It says; even if I do not find a word in my language which corresponds to a work in the original language, I still want to try to penetrate its value by adding both restrictive expansive definitions. [. . .] Imitation, on the other hand, submits to the irrationality of languages, it grants that one cannot render a copy—which would correspond precisely to the original in all its parts—of a verbal artefact in another language, and that, given the difference between languages, with which so many other differences are connected, there is no option but to produce an imitation, a whole which is composed of parts obviously different from the parts of the original, but which would yet in its effects come as close to that whole as the difference in material allows. [. . .] The imitator, therefore, does not attempt to bring the two parties—the writer and the reader of the imitation—together, because he does not think a direct relationship between them is possible; he merely wants to produce on the reader an impression similar to that received from the original by its contemporaries who spoke the same language. (pp. 72–3)

But what of the genuine translator, who wants to bring those two completely separated persons, his author and his reader, truly together, and who would like to bring the latter to an understanding and enjoyment of the former as correct and complete as possible without inviting him to leave the sphere of his mother tongue—what roads are open to him? In my opinion there are only two. Either the translator leaves the author in peace, as much as possible, and moves the reader towards him; or he leaves the reader in peace, as much as possible, and moves the author towards him. The two roads are so completely separate from each other that one or the other must be followed as closely as possible, and that a highly unreliable result would proceed from any mixture, so that it is to be feared that author and reader would not meet at all. The difference between the two methods, and the fact that they stand in this relationship, must be immediately obvious. For in the first case the translator tries, by means of his work, to replace for the reader the understanding of the original language that the reader does not have. He tries to communicate to the readers the same image, the same impression he himself has gained—through his knowledge of the original language—of the work as it stands, and in doing so he tries to move the readers towards his point of view, which is essentially foreign to them. But if the translation wants to let its Roman author, for instance, speak the way he would have spoken to Germans, but Latin; rather it drags him directly into the world of the German readers and transforms him into their equal—and that, precisely, is the other case. The first translation will be perfect in its kind when one can say that if the author had learnt German as well as the translator has learnt Latin he would not have translated the work he originally wrote in Latin any differently than the translator has done. But the second, which does not show the author as he himself would have translated but as he, as a German, would have originally written German, can have no other measure of perfection than if it could be certified that, could all German readers be changed into experts and contemporaries of the author, the original would have meant exactly the same to them as what the translation means to them now—that the author has changed himself into a German. This method is obviously meant by all those who use the formula that one should translate an author in such a way as he himself would have written German. From this opposition it is immediately obvious how different the procedure must be in every detail, and how, if one tried to switch methods in the course of one and the same project, everything would become unintelligible as well as unpalatable. I merely would like to add that there cannot be a third method, with a precisely delimited goal over and above these two. The two separated parties must either meet at a certain point in the middle, and that will always be the translator, or one must completely join up with the other, and of these two possibilities only the first belongs to the field of translation; the other would be realized if, in our case, the German readers totally mastered Latin, or rather if that language totally mastered them. (pp. 74–5)

If we except those miraculous masters to whom many languages are as one [...]—all others retain a sense of the strange, no matter how fluently they read a foreign language. How should the translator transfer this feeling—that they have something foreign before them—to the readers whom he offers a translation in their mother tongue? Of course you will say that the answer to this riddle has been given long ago, and that the problem has often been solved more than well enough in our case, for the more closely the translation follows the turns taken by the original, the more foreign it will seem to the reader. That may well be true, and it is easy enough to ridicule this position in general. But if this joy is not to be purchased too cheaply, if the most magisterial is not to be thrown out in one bath with the worst and the most schoolboyish, it will have to be admitted that an indispensable requirement of this method of translation is a feeling for language which is not only not colloquial, but also causes us to suspect that it has now grown in total freedom but rather has been bent towards a foreign likeness; and it must be admitted that to do this artfully and with measure, without disadvantage to one's own language or oneself, is probably the greatest difficulty our translator has to overcome.

[. . .] Who would willingly force himself to appear in movements less light and elegant than those he is capable of, to seem brutal and stiff, at least at times, and to shock the reader as much as is necessary to keep him aware of what he is doing? (pp. 78–9)

[Schleiermacher goes on to argue that this kind of translation may not work in languages that are 'captives of too strict a bond of classical expression' (p. 79), but that it should work in languages 'which are freer, in which innovations and deviations are tolerated to a greater extent, in such a way that their accumulation may, under certain circumstances, generate a certain characteristic mode of expression' (p. 80). Thus, the characteristics of, and differences between, the different foreign languages and literatures will emerge in a broad-based literature in translation, in which the reader has a comparative perspective:]

These comparisons are not available if only isolated works of masters of isolated genres are sporadically translated into a language. In this way even the most educated readers can achieve only a very deficient knowledge of what is foreign by means of translation, and it is inconceivable that they would be able to reach any judgment of either the translation or the original. This method of translation must therefore be applied extensively, a transplantation of whole literatures into a language, and it makes sense and is of value only to a nation that has the definite inclination to appropriate what is foreign. (p. 80)

Just as our soil itself has no doubt become richer and more fertile and our climate milder and more pleasant only after much transplantation of foreign flora, just so we sense that our language, because we exercise it less owing to our Nordic sluggishness, can thrive in all its freshness and completely develop its own power only through the most many-sided contacts with what is foreign. And coincidentally our nation may be destined, because of its respect for what is foreign and its nature which is one of mediation, to carry all the treasures of foreign art and scholarship, together with its own, in its language, to unite them into a great historical whole, so to speak, which would be preserved in the centre and heart of Europe, so that, with the help of our language, whatever beauty the most different times have brought forth can be enjoyed by all people, as purely and perfectly as is possible for a foreigner. This appears indeed to be the real historical aim of translation in general, as we are used to it now. (p. 88)

3.4 Victorian Translation and Criticism

Britain was the scene of much translation activity during the nineteenth century and translation was taken very seriously in the critical forum. Publications such as *The Athenaeum, Classical Museum*, and *Edinburgh Review* regularly featured articles on translation as well as reviews of newly published translations. Some of these reviews are lengthy and include a good deal of general discussion about translation methods, most frequently in relation to the translation of poetry (lyrical, epic, dramatic). Many of these critical pieces are veritable storehouses of strong opinions, as can be gauged from the excerpts in the following selection.

The debate is clearly fuelled by a strong conviction that translation is crucial for literary life in Britain. The Homeric epics seem to become even more important than before; how Homer is rendered in English is for many one of the key issues of contemporary literary activity. This is the source of the well-known controversy between Matthew Arnold (1822–88), poet and professor of poetry at Oxford, and Francis W. Newman (1805–97), professor of Latin at University College London (brother of the famous cardinal John Henry Newman). It started with Arnold's critique (in his lectures 'On Translating Homer', 1861) of Newman's translation of the *Iliad*. Newman wrote a detailed reply and Arnold responded in his 'Last Words on Translating Homer'. It has often been assumed that Arnold had the last word in more than one sense; most readers have in fact approached the debate through editions of Arnold's criticism, where Newman's reply is printed in between Arnold's pieces, and it often feels as if Newman has been simply absorbed in, and 'contained' by, the most powerful critical voice of Victorian England.

In the following 'collage', we have included parts of Newman's preface to his translation, together with an example from the translation, as well as sections of the ensuing debate, concluding with a passage from the *Iliad* as translated by Newman and Arnold respectively. The issues at hand, when observed closely, turn out to be quite complex, and not only as regards the choice of metre, where they were at loggerheads. Newman's aim is an ambitious one, since he wanted to allude to a broad readership while at the same time staying true to the various 'peculiarities' of Homer's epic, and the broad spectrum of expressions he found in it. He felt that Arnold was attacking the scholarly mainstay of his translation and answered accordingly; Arnold then turned the tables on him by claiming that it was not so much in the realm of scholarship as in poetic delivery that Newman has failed. From a contemporary point of view, the relationship between theory and practice becomes very complicated here. Several modern translation scholars seem to work on premises that are quite close to those of Newman; that does not mean they necessarily approve of his actual translation.

Translation scholars frequently refer to the Newman–Arnold controversy, but rarely discuss it in the context of Victorian translation criticism, but this is the context in which it appears here. Homer was of primary significance throughout the nineteenth century, but other works from the Western canon also remain important sources of new English texts, notably works of epic and dramatic poetry: the Greek tragedies, Virgil's *Aeneid*, Dante's *Divina Commedia*. As for more recent literature, however, the canonical paradigm begins to shift as we move into the nineteenth century. France, a powerful literary neighbour for centuries, is now seriously challenged by Germany. Some of the excerpts below bear witness to the awareness of and respect not only for recent German literature and philosophy (Goethe, Schiller, Kant), but also for German achievements in translation, which was seen as striving for formal and semantic accuracy in the incorporation of Classical literature— Shakespeare, as well as Homer, Aeschylus, Sophocles—into the world of modern German writing (see also Sects. 3.2 and 3.3, above, on Goethe and Schleiermacher respectively).

But amidst the widespread interest in translation, there was an anxiety about the receptiveness of the literary public to older and more recent canonical works in English translation. This anxiety is echoed in an anonymous review of John Stewart Blackie's translation of Aeschylus' lyrical dramas. 'There are few literary callings which have been more affected by the changes of public taste than that of the translator. From the time of the Restoration, if not earlier, to the beginning of the present century, the achievement of a decently successful version of a classic author conferred on a man a species of immortality. Those who stood highest as original poets felt that their assurance of posthumous fame was doubly sure when they had associated their names with Homer or Virgil.' But why has this changed? The reviewer goes on: 'After the public had once become accustomed to Byron and Scott, they began to care little for translations; and the more recent influences of Shelley and Wordsworth have not been more favourable to these unfortunate attempts to entwine the old with the new'[1].

It is probably true that in Britain, in some contrast to what happened in Germany, contemporary Romantic literature did not develop at close quarters with the translation of the canonical literature, and that many readers leaned more to the former than the latter. But the diminished status of the translator—which for instance Richard E. Young finds manifested in his study of Victorian translation criticism[2]—is also a result of the very criteria of some of the prominent views of translation. When the novelist George Eliot, herself a translator and an active spokeswoman of German culture in Britain, notes that

[1] *Edinburgh Review*, 92 (July 1850), 173.
[2] Richard Emerson Young: *Theories of Translating Poetry in Victorian England*, unpublished Ph.D dissertation (University of Michican, 1964), 137.

'a good translator is infinitely below the man who produces *good* original works',[3] she is not holding up any objective measuring stick, but rather following a dominant notion of the translator's task.

This notion—marked by what one might call an anxiety of creativity—crops up in some of the texts below. To some extent it is summed up in a review (see below) of the translations of James Clarence Mangan, an important literary figure in nineteenth-century Ireland. The reviewer is full of praise: 'Mr Mangan's mind is precisely of that plastic character which is indispensable for spirited and truthful translations. He possesses, in a high degree, the art of thoroughly divesting himself, in his capacity of translator, of every individuality, of thought and of manner, and becoming, so to speak, the mere instrument of the author whom he translates.' This is of course a well-known trope, the invisible translator, who does not remind readers that they are reading a translation.[4]

Many critics (and translators) are sceptical of the overly visible or creative translator, and of what they perceive of as highly liberal translation methods in the past, even in the celebrated translations of Dryden and Pope, and they attempt to set up new parameters of accuracy. This debate, which can get quite heated, also sometimes becomes rather confusing, especially when it gets entangled with the question whether to translate classical epic or dramatic poetry into the same or somehow equivalent English metres, or whether to opt for prose. Some critics see prose translation as a means of guaranteeing a close rendering of the meaning of the original or even a 'literal' transposition; yet at the same time prose clearly allows the translator more room to move in and such freedom also risks distancing the text from the original, the verse form of which has already been discarded. In some essays and reviews of the period, for instance in the review, excerpted below, of Buckley's and Blackie's Aeschylus translations, the *values* that the critic seems to be after in translation end up in conflict against one another.

John Stuart Blackie (1809–95)—who has been foregrounded in the collage with excerpts from four of his critical pieces and one of his translations—was one of the most prominent figures in the field of translation during this period. First a professor at the University of Aberdeen, and later Chair of Greek at the University of Edinburgh, he was not only a Classics scholar, but also a specialist in German and Scottish literature and culture, and one of Scotland's leading cultural figures. While many of his colleagues seemed to be actively redrawing a map of classic polarized dichotomy of translation methods, Blackie

---

[3] See George Eliot's review, printed in its entirety below, in which she discusses works of translation from the German, but also critiques the celebrated German translations of Shakespeare, showing that they are not as infallible as one might have assumed.

[4] See Lawrence Venuti: *The Translator's Invisibility: A History of Translation* (London and New York: Routledge, 1995), for a historical and general study of this view of the translator and his or her work.

sought to define an equally classic idea of 'the golden mean'; in this case 'between the painful minuteness of the German, and the loose diffusion of the vulgar English school'.

But ideas were in a flux during this period and the excerpts will show that Blackie changed his mind about certain key issues, for instance that of metre and rhyme. As noted, there was an avid debate not only about whether epic and dramatic poetry should be translated into poetry, but also about what English form was most suited as a substitute for the original hexameter, especially that of the Homeric epics. What was the status of that form in its source language and culture? Could one translate the works into English hexameter, or was blank verse perhaps the 'national' British equivalent? Matthew Arnold famously entered precisely this debate as he criticized Francis W. Newman's translation of the *Iliad*.

The Victorian translation debate as a whole, while parts of it may have contributed to the diminished status of the translator, actually points in the other direction. For as Blackie states: 'Translation is really one of the most difficult kinds of literary work; and requires, for a decided success, such a combination of learning, judgment, perseverance, enthusiasm and taste, as is seldom found in the same person.'

Words and Verse Form

From R. H. Horne's 'Remarks on Translation', *Classical Museum*, 1/4 (1843), 398–403

Words, and symbols—which latter include sculpture and painting—are the only medium of communication between the generations of mankind. We shall speak chiefly of the first, and most enduring; referring to the latter occasionally in illustration.

The medium of an author's thoughts must be his words; words are the sole material by which he permanently expresses what has passed in his mind; they are the only form and image his ideas assume in developing a particular train of thought or condition of emotion. The only merit therefore in a translation is that of giving the words of an author in another language, as nearly by equivalents as possible. [. . .] No professions of admiration and thorough comprehension on the part of the translator are any excuse for abandoning the words of his author. The instant a man says, 'I will give the *spirit* of the author in the words that author would have used had he lived now, and written in this other language,' it is all over with the original. Translation, in such a case, becomes a mere cover for individual egotism and vanity,—often for presumption—always for something other than it pretends to be. Sometimes it will be necessary to render one idiom by another, as one proverb may often be rendered by another; but the literal words of the original should be given in a note. [. . .] (p. 398)

The English language is lamentably deficient in faithful translations of the ancients; indeed, it may be said, that for the literature of this country the whole business of translating the ancients has yet to be done. Those which we most read are, unfortunately, the least like the originals. Of Herodotus, simple, naive, and truthful, I believe the translation that is read most, is one that was made from a French translation. [...] How turgid and mawkish are our versions of Pindar and Theocritus! How, also, has 'dear Don Quixote' suffered in his time! We have no faithful translation of Juvenal; still less of Ovid; and Dryden's Virgil might have been written by him without Virgil. [...] Perhaps it may be said, that with regard to translating poetry, our tendency to do so in *rhyme*, is at the root of the evil. There may be much in that, but the evil itself is the false principle; it is the substitution of the translator's mind for the mind of the man translated. Therefore the blank verse (rarely used) is, for the most part, as unfaithful as the rhyme, whenever any difficult passage occurs, or one of more than ordinary energy and ornament. In the latter case, the translator is hampered by his notion of the laws of metre, and his fears of being thought rugged, or of giving 'a school-boy version.' O, that we could once see a good, innocent, truthful, schoolboy-like translation of a great author!—for that would be a right beginning, and constitute a new 'school of translation' in this country, where it is so much needed. But nearly all these versifications are rhymed, and polished up on the model of Pope's dulcet monotony, the metrical system of ten-syllable finger-counting, instead of allowing any guidance of the ear in the 'beats of time,' which lead to the energetic freedom of rhythmic harmonies. To that narrow scholastic metre-law, and to the rhymes, anything that appeared obscure or obstinate on the part of the original, has been sacrificed without the slightest hesitation.

Perhaps there is no instance of the licentious spirit of English translations more complete than in those purporting to be from Homer. The name of George Chapman, I mention with reverence and admiration; but his truly-grand version of Homer must nevertheless be declared *no* translation. Chapman's version of Homer is a paraphrase by a kindred spirit; that of Pope is a paraphrase in his own spirit. The works might be appropriately contra-distinguished as 'Homer's Chapman,' and 'Pope's Homer.' [...] (pp. 399–400)

Germans in English

From William Empson, 'Hayward's Translation of Faust', *Edinburgh Review*, 57 (Apr. 1833), 107–43.

[A review of *Faust: A Dramatic Poem by Goethe. Translated* [by Abraham Hayward] *into English Prose, with remarks on former Translations and Notes* (London, 1833).]

The translator of a poem has his choice whether he will employ verse or prose. Adopting the form of prose, he tells you plainly what you are to expect, nothing more than the substance honestly 'done into English.' Assuming the outward and visible signs of poetry, he too frequently hangs out false colours. [. . .] A prose translation, designed for a higher purpose than for the use or abuse of schoolboys, is a novelty in English literature deserving of attention on its first appearance. (p. 107)

If the difficulty of the particular metre, or of metre generally, can be mastered without sacrificing more on their account then they are worth, they ought undoubtedly to be preserved. What, however, in any given case, is a nation to do, until a genius shall arise who can reconcile contradictions which are too strong for ordinary hands? In the meanwhile, is it not the wisest course, to make the most favourable bargain that the nature of the dilemma offers. [. . .] What is the best? Surely that in which the least of the original is lost—least lost of those qualities which are the most important. The native air and real meaning of a work are more essential qualities, than the charm of its numbers, or the embellishments and the passion of its poetic style. [. . .] Goethe has borne personal testimony to the specific and powerful influence which translations in prose may exercise upon the poetical character of a nation.[1] (pp. 112–13)

Mr Hayward says that one of the highest triumphs of a translator, in a passage capable of various meanings, is to shadow out them all. In reply to this, our first remark is that his own practice, according to his account of it, is inconsistent with his rule. In the course of his enquiries, he says, that 'he has not unfrequently had three or four different interpret-ations suggested to him by as many accomplished German scholars, each ready to do battle for his own against the world.' What then? Does he say that he has attempted to shadow out them all? So far from it, he insists—we dare say with justice—that readers who may miss their favourite interpretation in his version of any passage, are bound to give him the credit of having wilfully 'rejected it.' [. . .] Whenever a word or a sentence is capable of several meanings, the ambiguity must operate either as a beauty or as a defect. There can be no difficulty in telling which. Nor does it make any difference for this purpose, whether the ambiguity arises from the general nature of the language, or is attributable solely to the author. In the few instances where an uncertainty of this kind is a beauty, it is of course a translator's business as much to give the double, as in other instances to give the single meaning. In the great majority of cases where the uncertainty is a defect, an obligation on the tailor to preserve the patches and the spots of the pattern coat, (especially spots of this nature,) strikes us as very Chinese proceeding.[2] To avoid these blemishes is not to falsify; it is simple justice toward an original of any merit. (p. 133)

EDITORS' NOTES

1. [Cf. the Goethe entry in Sect. 3.2, above.]
2. [Presumably a reference to 'Chinese copy', i.e. an exact copy of an original.]

From an anonymous review in *The Athenaeum*, 5 July 1834, of three English translations of Goethe's *Faust*

[A review of Hayward's prose translation (2nd edn.) and verse translations by John S. Blackie and David Syme.]

If the number of labourers in the rich harvest field of German letters affords any proof of the increasing thirst after this noble literature amongst our countrymen, it is assuredly a matter of no mean import to all well-wishers of a nearer and kindlier intercourse between the master minds of both nations, that the first quarter of this year brought forward three separate translations of the same matchless original.
[...]
   Mr Hayward's translation, we admit, is a most useful companion for the learner, as a sort of grammatical key. But, when for this he has used it—and it will but seldom lead him astray—poorly indeed must he feel the power of the master poet, if he again opens it.
[...]
   We have said that justice cannot be done Faust in English prose; and the translations of Mr Blackie and Mr Syme have each failed, in our judgment, in attempting to catch Goethe's mantle in poetry. Comparing the original, for one instant and in one point of view, to a Titian of inestimable price, we are ill content to see this copied by a statue, which can give us none of the painter's splendid colouring. But it is true, that we may find there the grace and soul of beauty of the picture: and this better than a copy in oils, where the tone and tint or Titian's glories are lost—the masterly handling of his subject travestied and degraded. Both of these translators in verse confess, in their prefaces, to minor changes of words, and omissions, here and there, to give increased poetical power to the whole! We reprobate all such irreverent tampering. It would never have been dreamed of by any one who *could* feel and translate Goethe. It has been remarked before, that much of the charm of Goethe's numbers lies in their exquisite unity with the thoughts they breathe. This beauty our translators could not imitate, and have not preserved.

From an anonymous review of James Clarence Mangan's *Anthologia Germanica— German Anthology; a Series of Translations from the most Popular of the German Poets*, 2 vols., *Dublin Review*, 19 (Dec. 1845), 312–31

Poetical translations from the foreign languages, especially the German, have multiplied so rapidly of late years, that the English reader is often bewildered in attempting to make a selection. [...]
   The volumes now before us will introduce the reader to many poets who are comparatively unknown, but whose acquaintance notwithstanding, will, we make no doubt, prove little less agreeable than that of the old and traditionary representatives of

German literature. [... We] have no hesitation in saying, that the *German Anthology* is destined to take its place in the very highest rank of poetical translations. Mr Mangan's mind is precisely of that plastic character which is indispensable for spirited and truthful translations. He possesses, in a high degree, the art of thoroughly divesting himself, in his capacity of translator, of every individuality, of thought and of manner, and becoming, so to speak, the mere instrument of the author whom he translates. The moment he takes up the pen, he forgets himself altogether; or rather he, as it were, converts himself into his original thinking and writing in a new language; so that not alone the thought, but the words, the form, the style, the manner, the very metre, arc faithfully rendered back. With him translation is a mere process of fusion; but the metal is recast in precisely the same mould, and preserves not alone the substance, but the most minute and delicate peculiarities of form which characterised its original structure.

And this faculty is still more extraordinary when exercised, as here, upon an almost endless variety of subjects. [. . .] Mr Mangan has tried his hand on more than forty different models, and appears equally at home with all. With that strange faculty of which naturalists tell, his pen seems to take its colour from the food it feeds upon—it is pious and didactic with Hölty or Klopstock—humorous and burlesque with Dunkel—it plunges into the depths of mysticism with De la Motte Fouqué—and laughs at the world with Kotzebue or Bürger. The writer is a complete literary Proteus. He appears to be equally in his element among the fairy tales of Schnezler, and the philosophic reveries of Schiller or Goethe; and after throwing his whole soul into one of the fiery philippics of Freiligrath or Kerner, can return to dream over the melancholy sentimentalism of Tieck, or Simrock, or Rückert, as though he had lived his whole life long in those dreamy halls,

'Where melancholy music ceaseless swells.'

George Eliot, 'Translations and Translators', *The Leader*, 20 Oct 1855

[A review of *Critique of Pure Reason*, translated 'from the German of Emanuel Kant' by J. M. D. Meiklejohn (Bohn's Philosophical Library); and *Specimens of the Choicest Lyrical Productions of the most Celebrated German Poets*, with Biographical and Literary Notes, translated in English Verse by Mary Anne Burt (2nd edn. London: Hall, Virtue, and Co.)]

A clergyman (of the Charles Honeyman species) once told us that he never set about preparing his sermons till Saturday evening, for he 'trusted to Providence'. A similar kind of trust, we suppose, must be prevalent among translators, for many of them are evidently relying on some power which

> Can teach all people to translate,
> Though out of languages in which
> They understand no part of speech—

a *Nachklang,* or resonance, perhaps, of the famous legend about those early translators, the Seventy who turned the Old Testament into Greek, which legend tells how Ptolemy shut them up in separate cells to do their work, and how, when they came to compare their renderings, there was perfect agreement! We are convinced, however, that the translators of the Septuagint had some understanding of their business to begin with, or this supernatural aid would not have been given, for in the matter of translation, at least, we have observed, that 'God helps them who help themselves.' A view of the case, which we commend to all young ladies and some middle-aged gentlemen, who consider a very imperfect acquaintance with their own language, and an anticipatory acquaintance with the foreign language, quite a sufficient equipment for the office of translator.

It is perfectly true that, though geniuses have often undertaken translation, translation does not often demand genius. The power required in the translation varies with the power exhibited in the original work: very modest qualifications will suffice to enable a person to translate a book of ordinary travels, or a slight novel, while a work of reasoning or science can be adequately rendered only by means of what is at present exceptional faculty and exceptional knowledge. Among books of this latter kind, Kant's *Critique of Pure Reason* is perhaps the very hardest nut—the peach-stone—for a translator to crack so as to lay open the entire uninjured kernel of meaning, and we are glad at last to believe that a translator of adequate power has been employed upon it. For so far as we have examined the version placed at the head of our article, it appears to us very different indeed from the many renderings of German metaphysical works, in which the transla-tor, having ventured into deep waters without learning to swim, clings to the dictionary, and commends himself to Providence. Mr Meiklejohn's translation—so far, we must again observe, as we have examined it—indicates a real mastery of his author, and, for the first time, makes Kant's *Critik der reinen Vernunft* accessible to English readers.

It may seem odd that we should associate with this mighty book—this terrible ninety-gun ship—such a little painted pleasure-boat as Miss (or Mrs) Burt's miscellaneous collection of translations from German lyric poets. But we are concerning ourselves here simply with translation—not at all with Kant's philosophy or with German lyrics considered in themselves, and these two volumes happen to be the specimens of translation most recently presented to our notice. With regard to prose, we may very generally use Goldsmith's critical recipe, and say that the translation would have been better if the translator had taken more pains; but of poetical attempts we are often sure that no amount of pains would produce a satisfactory result. And so it is with Miss Burt's *Specimens of the German Poets.* She appears to have the knowledge and the industry which many translators want, but she has not the poetic power which makes poetical transla-tions endurable to those acquainted with the originals. Amongst others, however, who have no such acquaintance, Miss Burt's translations seem to have been in some demand, since they have reached a second edition. She has been bold enough to attempt a version of Goethe's exquisite *Zueignung* (*Dedication*), and here is a specimen of her rendering. Goethe sings with divine feeling and music—

> Für andre wächst in mir das edle Gut,
> Ich kann und will das Pfund nicht mehr vergraben,
> Warum sucht' ich den Weg so sehnsuchtsvoll,
> Wenn ich ihn nicht den Brüdern zeigen soll?

Miss Burt follows him much as a Jew's harp would follow a piano—

> Entombed no longer shall my *talent* be,
> That treasure I amass, shall others share?
> To find the road—oh, why such zeal display,
> If I guide not my brethren on their way?

A version like this bears about the same relation to the original as the portraits in an illustrated newspaper bear to the living face of the distinguished gentlemen they misrepresent; and considering how often we hear opinions delivered on foreign poets by people who only know those poets at second hand, it becomes the reviewer's duty to insist again and again on the inadequacy of poetic translations.

The Germans render our poetry better than we render theirs, for their language, as slow and unwieldy as their own post-horses in prose, becomes in poetry graceful and strong and flexible as an Arabian war-horse. Besides, translation among them is more often undertaken by men of genius. We remember, for example, some translations of Burns, by Freiligrath, which would have arrested us by their beauty if we had seen the poems for the first time, in this language. It is true the Germans think a little too highly of their translations, and especially are under the illusion, encouraged by some silly English people, that Shakespeare according to Schlegel is better than Shakespeare himself—not simply better to a German as being easier for him to understand, but absolutely better as poetry. A very close and admirable rendering Schlegel's assuredly is, and it is a high pleasure to track it in its faithful adherence to the original, just as it is to examine a fine engraving of a favourite picture. Sometimes the German is as good as the English—the same music played on another but as good an instrument. But more frequently the German is a feeble echo, and here and there it breaks down in a supremely fine passage. An instance of this kind occurs in the famous speech of Lorenzo to Jessica. Shakespeare says—

> Soft stillness and the night
> Become the touches of sweet harmony.

This Schlegel renders—

> Sanfte Still und Nacht
> Sie werden *Tasten* süsser Harmonie.

That is to say, 'Soft stillness and the night *are* the *finger-board* of sweet harmony.' A still worse blunder is made by Tieck (whose translation is the rival of Schlegel's) in the monologue of Macbeth. In the lines—

> That but this blow
> Might be the be-all and the end-all here—
> But here upon this bank and shoal of time,
> I'd jump the life to come—

Tieck renders, 'Upon this bank and shoal of time,' 'Auf dieser *Schülerbank* der Gegenwart', that is, 'On this *school-bench* of the present!' These are cases of gross inaccuracy arising from an imperfect understanding of the original. Here is an instance of feebleness. Coriolanus says—

> And like an eagle in the dovecote, I
> Flutter'd the Volscians in Corioli.

For the admirably descriptive word 'fluttered,' Schlegel gives '*schlug*' which simply means 'slew'. Weak renderings of this kind are abundant.

Such examples of translators' fallibility in men like Schlegel and Tieck might well make less accomplished persons more backward in undertaking the translation of great poems, and by showing the difficulty of the translator's task, might make it an object of ambition to real ability. Though a good translator is infinitely below the man who produces *good* original works, he is infinitely above the man who produces *feeble* original works. We had meant to say something of the moral qualities especially demanded in the translator—the patience, the rigid fidelity, and the sense of responsibility in interpreting another man's mind. But we have gossiped on this subject long enough.

John Stuart Blackie

From J. S. Blackie, 'Recent translations of the Agamemnon', *Classical Museum*, 6 (1848), 432–63

[A review of two translations of Aeschylus' *Agamemnon*, by W. Sewell (1846) and John Conington (1848).]

The English and the Germans, so diversely constituted in most particulars, and forming, in fact, opposite poles of the intellectual and moral world, stand peculiarly contrasted in that department of literature which seeks to appropriate the products of foreign and far distant minds by the engine of translation. Scarcely does the theology or the metaphysics of our trans-Rhenane brethren present a stronger contrast to ours, than Pope's Homer forms to that of Voss. In the transfusion of ancient Greek and Roman poetry into our tongue, the main object of the English translator has always been to be free and graceful, spirited and energetic; while, with an instinct no less distinctly national, the German, religiously laborious, strives after accuracy of erudition, and profundity of philosophical appreciation. (p. 432)

[. . .] though Mr Conington may not have succeeded in dethroning Mr Symmons from the position which he holds, as the most poetical of all the English translators of the Agamemnon, he has produced a work of high merit, satisfying at once the demands of the man of taste and the minute student of Aeschylus, in a fashion of which the English school of translation has hitherto presented very few examples. Such a beginning certainly affords the best reason to hope that this country may yet give birth to a series of translations, realizing the true golden mean between the painful minuteness of the German, and the loose diffusion of the vulgar English school. (p. 463)

From Blackie's preface to his translation of *The Lyrical Dramas of Aeschylus* (1850; London J. M. Dent & Sons, 1906)

The proper problem of an English translator is not *how to say a thing as the author would have said it, had he been an Englishman;* but *how, through the medium of the English language, to make the English reader feel both what he said and how he said it, being a Greek.* Now, any one who is familiar with the general run of English rhythmical translations, of which Pope's Iliad is the pattern, must be aware that they have too often been executed under the influence of the former of these principles rather than the latter. In Pope's Homer, and in Sotheby's also, I must add, we find many, perhaps all the finest passages very finely done; but so as Pope or Sotheby might have done themselves in an original poem written at the present day, while that which is most peculiarly Homeric, a certain blunt naturalness and a talkative simplicity, we do not find in these translators at all. [. . .]

Now, I at once admit that a good prose translation—that is to say, a prose translation done by a poet or a man of poetical culture—of such an author as Homer, is preferable, for many purposes, to a poetical translation so elegantly defaced as that of Pope. A prose translation, also, of any poet, done accurately in a prosaic style by a proser, however much of a parody or a caricature in point of taste, may not be without its use, if in no other way, as a ready check on the free licence of omission or inoculation which rhythmical translators are so fond to usurp. But it is a mistake to suppose, because Pope, under the influence of Louis XIV and Queen Anne, could not write a good poetical translation of Homer, that therefore such a work is beyond the compass of the English language.[1] I believe that, if Alfred Tennyson were to give the world a translation of the Iliad in the measure of *Locksley Hall*, he would cut Pope out of the market of the million, even at this eleventh hour. We are, in the present epoch of our literary history, arrived at a very favourable moment for producing good translations. A band of highly-original and richly-furnished minds has just left the stage, leaving us the legacy of a poetical language which, under their hand, received a degree of rhythmical culture, of which it had been before considered incapable. The example of the Germans, also, now no longer confined to the knowledge of a few, stands forth to show us how excellent poetical translations may be made, free, at least, from those faults from which we have suffered. There is no reason why we should despair of producing poetical versions of the Classics which shall be at once graceful as English compositions, and characteristic as productions of the Greek or Roman mind. I, for one, have already passed this judgment on my own attempt, that if I have failed in these pages to bring out what is Greek and what is Aeschylean prominently, in combination with force, grace, and clearness of English expression, it is for lack of skill in the workman, not for want of edge in the tool. (pp. 3–4)

NOTE

1. Southey requested a Frenchman ambitious of translating his Roderick, to do so in prose, not because he preferred that method in general, but because he believed that '*poetry of the higher order is as impossible in French, as it is in Chinese.*'—*Life*, Vol. IV, p. 100. [*italics in original*]

From Blackie's translation of Aeschylus' *Agamemnon*, included in *The Lyrical Dramas of Aeschylus*, pp. 45–6

[Cf. the passage as translated below by Browning (Sect. 3.5) Lowell (Sect. 4.10) and Hughes (Sect. 5.16)]

> I'll voice the strain. What though the arm be weak
>> That once was strong,
> The suasive breath of Heaven-sent memories stirs
>> The old man's breast with song.
>> My age hath virtue left
> To sing what fateful omens strangely beckoned
>>> The twin kings to the fray,
>>> What time to Troy contentuous marched
>>> The embattled Greek array.
> Jove's swooping bird, king of all birds, led on
> The kings of the fleet with spear and vengeful hand:
> By the way-side from shining seats serene,
> Close by the palace, on the spear-hand seen,
>> Two eagles flapped the air,
> One black, the other silver-tipt behind,
> And with keen talons seized a timorous hare,
>> Whose strength could run no more,

Itself, and the live burden which it bore.
Sing woe and well-a-day! But still
May the good omens shame the ill.

From Blackie's 'A Few Remarks on English Hexameters', *Classical Museum*, 4/3 (1856), p. 319–30

The general principle, then, on which a metrical translation must proceed is plain enough. The reader of a translated work is entitled to demand a fac-simile of the original; but this *only in so far as is consistent with the grammatical and rhythmical genius of the language in which the translation is made.* Now what is included in that wide word the GENIUS of a language? It includes two things essentially different [...] in the first place, and principally, whatever belongs organically to the grammatical and metrical *structure* of the language; and in the second place, whatever belongs by use and habit and association to the characteristic *style* and peculiar living expression of the language. Thus, the English language, by its structure, most naturally falls into the iambic movement [...] but it is also capable, without any painful effort, of the trochaic movement; and when stirred with high lyric emotion, it does not refuse the tribrachic measure [...]. (p. 321)

The matter then comes to a very short issue. The man who shall sit down to write a translation of the *Iliad* in English hexameters, must do so with the full consciousness that he is making a very deliberate and doubtful experiment against the literary use and wont of a highly cultivated language [...]. (p. 327)

If, on account of epic associations, our ten-syllabled verse is to be used in rendering Homer, there can be no question that, in this particular matter, Cowper was nearer the mark than Pope, and that, in this case, blank verse is preferable to rhyme. But it admits, we think, of the clearest proof on the strictest aesthetic principles—principles which it might go hard even with our hardy German friends to disprove—that the proper English correlative of the Greek hexameter of Homer, (Virgil may be different,) is Chapman's old iambic verse of fourteen syllables; or better still—because, like dactylic verse, it commences with the accent—the trochaic measure of fifteen syllables, so felicitously used by Mr Tennyson in his luxuriant poem, 'Locksley Hall.' [...] The only doubt that can be stated is, whether this measure, iambic or trochaic, should be used with or without rhyme. The English ear unquestionably would prefer rhyme; but for the sake both of accuracy in the version, and variety in the pause, we should like to see the experiment made without rhyme. (pp. 329–30)

From Blackie's 'Homer and his Translators', *Macmillan Magazine*, 4 (Aug. 1861), 268–80

Why have we so few first-rate poetical translations? For several reasons. *First*, because there is no great demand for them. [...] *Second*, because the work of translation, like that of criticism, is more exposed to be undertaken by unqualified persons than almost any other work. [. . .] But a *third* reason is stronger than these. Translation is really one of the most difficult kinds of literary work; and requires, for a decided success, such a combination of learning, judgment, perseverance, enthusiasm and taste, as is seldom found in the same person. (268)

Homer is an ἀοιδός or popular minstrel, who addressed his narrative songs to the ear of the masses for their amusement—not a ποιητής, or modern poetic man of genius, who addresses his epos to the cultivated understanding and the polished taste of the reading public, or, it may be, only a small fraction of that public. This truth must be admitted, and its significance known and felt, before a single step can be taken towards a translation of Homer in the spirit of which Homer was written. (p. 272)

The great excellence of Cowper lies in his avoidance of the two grand faults of his two great predecessors [Chapman and Pope]: when they are turgid, bombastical, and be-spangled with artificial conceits, he is always chaste, simple, natural, and at the same time dignified. But he wants fire and rapidity—a very great defect in the popular epos, and very un-Homeric—nor can he pretend to equal Pope in sound, or Chapman in vigour. In the 'Odyssey' this quiet manner is more at home, and his translation of that work is perhaps the best version of any Homeric poem existing in the English language. (p. 274)

[Blackie goes on to discuss why different varieties of blank verse will not do.]

[. . .] Pope will beat them all, you may depend upon it. And why will Pope beat them all? Perhaps for several reasons; but certainly for this one—because he rhymes. And in favour of rhyme, that good old English luxury—that happy modern invention—I must here, before proceeding further, put in a strong plea,—partly because it is the fashion, in certain quarters, to talk cheaply of it; partly because Professor Arnold most unhand-somely disowns it; and partly because I am certain that no translation of Homer, however well executed, will have any chance of popularity without it. (p. 274)

One thing remains. Professor Arnold, in the ingenious, graceful, and thoughtful little book, which has given occasion to these critical remarks, showed a good example to all critics by giving a specimen of the sort of hexameters into which he was of opinion that Homer should be translated. I should consider myself somewhat of a sneak if after having commented so freely on his opinions, I should not follow his practice. Here, therefore, I fling down for his critical dissection and disapproval—for I cannot expect him to approve of my ballad measure any more than I do of his hexameters—the well known smart interlude between Ulysses and Thersites, in the second book of the Iliad.

[. . .]
Soothly Achilles lacketh gall, and droops his princely wing,
Or this were the last of insults, cast from the lips of this faithless king!

Such reckless works Thersites dared from venomed heart to fling
Against the monarch; but Ulysses darkly-scowling came,
And swift pursued the railer rude with words of bitter blame.
Thersites, sense-confounding fool, thy mouth of fluent prate
Learn now to gag; against the kings this ribald talk abate!
I tell thee true, of all the crew from Greece to Troy that came,
Vilest art thou: there breathes not one, who owns a fouler name!

[...] (p. 279)

Newman, Arnold, Homer

From F. W. Newman, 'Preface' to *The Iliad of Homer: Faithfully Translated into Unrhymed English Metre* **by F. W. Newman (London: Walton and Maberly, 1856), pp. iii–xx**

In discerning the mind of Homer—as to its intellectual and moral tone—we get discernment not into one Greek only, but into all the Greeks, of whom he is emphatically a noble type. In this respect, the substance of what he tells is often of less importance to us than the manner in which he tells it, and it becomes a first-rate duty of a translator to adhere closely to his manner and habit of thought, as also to his moral sentiments. (p. iii)

[Homer] is alternately Poet, Orator, Historian, Theologian, Geographer, Traveller, jocose as well as serious, dramatic as well as descriptive. [...] it suffices to warn the reader not to expect, *or to wish*, Homer to be always at the same high pitch of poetry. He rises and sinks with his subject, is prosaic when it is tame, is low when it is mean. To express this suitably, we need a diction sufficiently antiquated to obtain pardon of the reader for its frequent homeliness.

The style of Homer himself is direct, popular, forcible, quaint, flowing, garrulous, abounding with formulas, redundant in particles and affirmatory interjections, as also in grammatical connectives of time, place, and argument. In all those respects it is similar to the old English ballad, and is in sharp contrast to the polished style of Pope, Sotheby, and Cowper, the best known English translators of Homer. (p. iv)

[...] the first matter of all is to select the metre, with which the style is intimately connected. The moral qualities of Homer's style being like those of the English ballad, we need a metre of the same genius. It must be fundamentally musical and popular. (p. v)

These considerations convinced me *à priori* that the English metre fitted to translate Homer's hexameter must be a long line composed of two short ones, having each either *three* beats or four *beats*. [...] But beside this I held it as an axiom that rhyme must be abandoned. [...] Yet on abandoning rhyme, to which our ears are accustomed in the popular ballad, I found an unpleasant void, until I gave a double ending to the verse, *i.e.*, one (unaccented) syllable more than our Common Metre allows. (pp. vi–vii)

A few remarks here on the problem presented to a translator seem to me the more needful, because some reviewers of my translation of Horace's Odes laid down as axioms (to which they assumed my agreement), principles which I regard to be utterly false and ruinous to translation. One of these is, that the reader ought, if possible, to forget that it is a translation at all, and be lulled into the illusion that he is reading an original work. Of course, a necessary inference from such a dogma is that whatever has a foreign colour is undesirable and is even a grave defect. The translator, it seems, must carefully obliterate all that is characteristic of the original, unless it happen to be identical in spirit to something already familiar in English. From such a notion I cannot too strongly express my intense dissent. I aim at precisely the opposite—to retain every peculiarity of the original, so far as I am able, *with the greater care the more foreign it may be*—whether it be a matter of taste, of intellect, or of morals. (pp. xv–xvi)

[handwritten margin note: tinge of the foreign]

From Newman's translation of *The Iliad of Homer*, Book 1, pp. 7–8 (ll. 225–44)

[Achilles confronts Agamemnon. For the same passage, translated by Dryden and Pope respectively, see Sects. 2.13 and 2.15, above.]

'O gorg'd with wine! the eyes of dog, but heart of deer, who bearest,
Never didst thou with all the folk   put corslet on for battle,
Nor hardihood of soul hast thou   among Achaia's chieftains
On ambuscade to go; but this   to thee destruction seemeth.
Truly more gainful is it, mid   Achaia's ample army
To plunder of his gifts, whoe'er   a word against thee sayeth;—
A king who doth his folk devour,   for-that they all are worthless;
Else, verily, Atrides! this   were now thy final outrage.
But roundly will I say,—and swear   a mighty oath upon it:
That by the sceptre in my hand,   whence leaf or twig shall never
Sprout forth, sithence the parent trunk it left upon the mountains;
Nor bud will it; for by the brass   both leaf and bark around it
Are peel'd away; but now in turn   Achaia's children bear it,—
Servants of Justice,—in their palms; by Jupiter deputed
To enforce observance of the Right: (a mighty oath I tender):
There shall upon Achaia's sons   a longing for Achilles
Come, soon or late, on one and all;   but them though pierc'd with anguish,
Unable wilt thou be to help,   when hero-slaying Hector
Shall hew them down in crowds: but thou thy soul within shalt mangle
Enrag'd, that thou didst vilely treat   the noblest of the Achaians.'

From Matthew Arnold's *On Translating Homer* (1861), repr. in *Matthew Arnold's Essays, Literary and Critical* (London: Dent, 1906), 210–75

[...] The translator's 'first duty', says Mr Newman, is a historical one: to be faithful. Probably both sides would agree that the translator's 'first duty is to be faithful'; but the question at issue between them is, in what faithfulness consists.

My one object is to give practical advice to a translator; and I shall not the least concern myself with theories of translation as such. But I advise the translator not to try 'to rear on the basis of the Iliad, a poem that shall affect our countrymen as the original may be conceived to have affected its natural hearers'; and for this simple reason, that we cannot possibly tell *how* the *Iliad* 'affected its natural hearers.' [...] Evidently the translator needs some more practical directions than these. No one can tell him how Homer affected the Greeks; but there are those who can tell him how Homer affects *them*. These are scholars; who possess, at the same time with knowledge of Greek, adequate poetical taste and feeling. No translation will seem to them of much worth compared with the original; but they alone can say whether the translation produces more or less the same effect upon them as the original. They are the only competent tribunal in this matter: the Greeks are dead; the unlearned Englishman has not the data for judging; and no man can safely confide in his own single judgment of his own work. (pp. 211–12)

Mr Newman says that 'the entire dialect of Homer being essentially archaic, that of a translator ought to be as much Saxo-Norman as possible, and owe as little as possible to the elements thrown into our language by classical learning.' Mr Newman is unfortunate in the observance of his own theory, for I continually find in his translation words of Latin origin, which seem to me quite alien to the simplicity of Homer—'responsive' for instance, which is a favourite word of Mr Newman, to represent the Homeric ἀμειβόμενος:

> Great Hector of the motley helm thus spake to her *responsive*.

> But thus *responsively* to him spake godlike Alexander.

And the word 'celestial', again, in the grand address of Zeus to the horses of Achilles,

> You, who are born celestial, from Eld and Death exempted!

seems to me in that place exactly to jar upon the feeling as too bookish. But, apart from the question of Mr Newman's fidelity to his own theory, such a theory seems to me both dangerous for a translator and false in itself. Dangerous for a translator; because, wherever one finds such a theory announced (and one finds it pretty often), it is generally followed by an explosion of pedantry; and pedantry is of all things in the world the most un-Homeric. False in itself; because, in fact, we owe to the Latin element in our language most of that very rapidity and clear decisiveness by which it is contradistinguished from the German, and in sympathy with the languages of Greece and Rome: so that to limit an English translator of Homer to words of Saxon origin is to deprive him of one of his special advantages for translating Homer. In Voss's well-known translation of Homer, it is precisely the qualities of his German language itself, something heavy and trailing both in the structure of its sentence and in the words of which it is composed, which prevent his translation, in spite of the hexameters, in spite of his fidelity, from creating in us the impression created by the Greek. Mr Newman's prescription, if followed, would just strip the English translator of the advantage which he has over Voss. (pp. 213–14)

Homer is rapid in his movement, Homer is plain in his words and style, Homer is simple in his ideas, Homer is noble in his manner. Cowper renders him ill because he is slow in his movement, and elaborate in his style; Pope renders him ill because he is artificial both in his style and his words; Chapman renders him ill because he is fantastic in his ideas; Mr Newman renders him ill because he is odd in his words and ignoble in his manner. [...] Mr Newman's movement, grammatical style, and ideas, are a thousand times in strong contrast with Homer's; still it is by the oddness of his diction and the ignobleness of his manner that he contrasts with Homer the most violently. (p. 250)

So the translator really has no good model before him for any part of his work, and has to invent everything for himself. [...] Pope certainly had a quick and darting spirit, as he had, also, real nobleness; yet Pope does not render the movement of Homer. To render this the translator must have, besides, his natural qualifications, an appropriate metre.

I have sufficiently shown why I think all forms of our ballad-metre unsuited to Homer. It seems to me to be beyond question that, for epic poetry, only three metres can seriously claim to be accounted capable of the grand style. Two of these will at once occur to everyone,—the ten-syllable, or so-called *heroic*, couplet, and blank verse. (p. 251)

[Arnold then explains why he finds that neither of these two metres, nor in fact the Spenserian stanza, work for Homer.]

When I say this, I point to the metre which seems to me to give the translator the best chance of preserving the general effect of Homer,—that third metre which I have not yet expressly named, the hexameter. I know all that is said against the use of hexameters in English poetry; but it comes only to this, that, among us, they have not yet been used on any considerable scale with success. *Solvitur ambulando:* this is an objection which can best be met by *producing* good English hexameters. And there is no reason in the nature of the English language why it should not adapt itself to hexameters as well as the German language does; nay, the English language, from its greater rapidity, is itself better suited than the German for them. [...] Applied to Homer, this metre affords to the translator the immense support of keeping him more nearly than any other metre to Homer's movement [...] (257)

[The translator] will find one English book and one book only, where, as in the *Iliad* itself, perfect plainness of speech is allied with perfect nobleness; and that book is the Bible. No one could see this more clearly than Pope saw it: 'This pure and noble simplicity,' he says, 'is nowhere in such perfection as in the Scripture and Homer': yet even with Pope a woman is a 'fair,' a father is a 'sire' and an old man a 'reverend sage,' and so on through all the phrases of that pseudo-Augustan, and most unbiblical, vocabulary. The Bible, however, is undoubtedly the grand mine of diction for the translator of Homer; and, if he knows how to discriminate truly between what will suit him and what will not, the Bible may afford him also invaluable lessons of style. (p. 264)

So essentially characteristic of Homer is his plainness and naturalness of thought, that to the preservation of this in his own version the translator must without scruple sacrifice, where it is necessary, verbal fidelity to his original, rather than run any risk of producing, by literalness, an odd and unnatural effect. The double epithets so constantly occurring in Homer must be dealt with according to this rule; these epithets come quite naturally in Homer's poetry; in English poetry they, in nine cases out of ten, come, when literally rendered, quite unnaturally. I will not now discuss why this is so, I assume it as an indisputable fact that it is so; that Homer's μερόπων ἀνθρώπων comes to the reader as something perfectly natural, while Mr Newman's 'voice-dividing mortals' comes to him as something perfectly unnatural. (pp. 265–6)

So I proceed at once to give, in conclusion, one or two passages in which I have tried to follow those principle of Homeric translation which I have laid down. [. . .] I take first a passage of which I have already spoken, the comparison of the Trojan fires to the stars. [. . .] I want to show you that it is possible, in a plain passage of this sort, to keep Homer's simplicity without being heavy and dull; and to keep his dignity without bringing in pomp and ornament. 'As numerous as are the stars on a clear night,' says Homer,

> So shone forth, in front of Troy, by the bed of Xanthus,
> Between that and the ships, the Trojan's numerous fires.
> In the plain there were kindled a thousand fires: by each one
> There sat fifty men, in the ruddy light of the fire:
> By their chariots stood the steeds, and champed the white barley
> While their masters sat by the fire, and waited for Morning.

Here, in order to keep Homer's effect of perfect plainness and directness, I repeat the word 'fires' as he repeats πυρά, without scruple; although in a more elaborate and literary style of poetry this recurrence of the same word would be a fault to be avoided. I omit the epithet of Morning, and whereas Homer says that the steeds 'waited for Morning,' I prefer to attribute this expectation of Morning to the master and not the horse. Very likely in this particular, as in any other single particular, I may be wrong: what I wish you to remark is my endeavour after absolute plainness of speech, my care to avoid anything which may the least check or surprise the reader, whom Homer does not check or surprise. (pp. 267–8)

From *Homeric Translation in Theory and Practice*, a Reply to Matthew Arnold, Esq., Professor of Poetry, Oxford, by Francis W. Newman, a Translator of the Iliad (London and Edinburgh: Williams and Norgate, 1861) (also in *Matthew Arnold's Essays*, pp. 276–336)

Scholars are the tribunal of Erudition, but of Taste the educated but unlearned public is the only rightful judge; and to it I wish to appeal. [. . .] Where I differ in Taste from Mr Arnold, it is very difficult to find 'the scholars' tribunal,' [. . .] but as regards Erudition, this difficulty does not occur, and I shall fully reply to the numerous dogmatisms by which he settles the case against me. (p. 2)

[Regarding hexameters:] The method could not be profitably used for translating Homer or Virgil, plainly because it is impossible to say for whose service such a translation would be executed. Those who can read the original will never care to read *through* any translation; and the unlearned look on all, even the best hexameters, whether from Southey, Lockhart or Longfellow, as odd and disagreeable prose. [. . .] 'Homer is popular,' is one of the very few matters of fact in this controversy on which Mr Arnold and I are agreed. 'English hexameters are not popular,' is a truth so obvious, that I do not yet believe he will deny it. Therefore, 'Hexameters are not the metre for translating Homer.' Q.E.D. (pp. 12–13)

At length I come to the topic of Diction, where Mr Arnold and I are at variance not only as to taste, but to the main facts of Greek literature. I had called Homer's style quaint and garrulous; and said that he rises and falls with his subject, being prosaic when it is tame, and low when it is mean. I added no proof; for I did not dream that it was needed. Mr Arnold not only absolutely denies all this, and denies it without proof; but adds, that these assertions prove my incompetence, and account for my total and conspicuous failure. (p. 31)

I regard it as quaint in Homer to call Juno *white-arm'd goddess* and *large-ey'd*. (I have not rendered βοῶπις *ox-ey'd*, because in a case of doubt I shrank to obtrude anything so grotesque to us.) It is quaint to say 'the lord of bright-haired Juno lightens' for 'it lightens'; or 'my heart in my *shaggy* bosom is divided,' for 'I doubt' [. . .]. If the whole Greek nation by long familiarity had become inobservant of Homer's 'oddities' (conceding this for the moment), that also would be no fault of mine. That Homer *is* extremely peculiar, even if the Greeks had become deadened to the sense of it, the proof on all sides is overpowering.

It is very quaint to say, 'the outwork (or rampart) of the teeth' instead of 'the lips.' If Mr Arnold will call it portentous in my English, let him produce some shadow of reason for denying it to be portentous in Greek. [. . .] (pp. 50–51)

It is not to be expected, that one who is blind to superficial facts so very prominent as those which I have recounted, should retain any delicate perception of that highly coloured, intense, and very eccentric diction of Homer, even if he has ever understood it, which he forces me to doubt. [. . .]

I have not adduced, in proof of Homer's quaintness, the monstrous simile given to us in Iliad 13, 754; viz. Hector 'darted forward screaming like a snowy mountain, and flew through the Trojans and allies:' for I cannot believe that the poet wrote anything so absurd. Rather than admit this, I have suggested that the text is corrupt, and that for ὄρεϊ νιφόεντι we should read ὀρνέῳ θύοντι,—'darted forth screaming *like a raging bird*.' Yet, as far as I know, I am the first man that has here impugned the text. [. . .] (p. 54)

From 'Last Words on Translating Homer. A reply to Francis W. Newman by Matthew Arnold' (1862), in *Matthew Arnold's Essays*, pp. 337–80

I think that in England, partly from the want of an Academy, partly from a national habit of intellect to which that want of an Academy is itself due, there exists too little of what I may call a public force of correct literary opinion, possessing within certain limits a clear sense of what is right and wrong, sound and unsound, and sharply recalling men of ability and learning from any flagrant misdirection of these their advantages. (p. 340)

Mr Newman errs by not perceiving that the question is not one of scholarship, but of a poetical translation of Homer. This, I say, should be perfectly simple and intelligible. He replies by telling me that ἀδινός, εἰλίποδες and σιγαλόεις are hard words. Well, but what does he infer from that? That the poetical translation, in his rendering of them, is to give us a sense of the difficulties of the scholar, and so is to make his translation obscure? [. . .] It may even be affirmed that everyone who reads Homer perpetually for the sake of enjoying his poetry (and no one who does not so read him will ever translate him well), comes at last to form a perfectly clear sense in his own mind for every important word in Homer, such as ἀδινός, or ἠλίβατος, whatever the scholar's doubts about the word may be. And this sense is present to his mind with perfect clearness and fullness, whenever the word recurs, although as a scholar he may know that he cannot be sure whether this sense is the right one or not. But poetically he feels clearly about the word, although philologically he may not. [. . .]

Perplexed by his knowledge of the philological aspect of Homer's language, encumbered by his own learning, Mr Newman, I say, misses the poetical aspect, misses that with which alone we are here concerned. [...] He talks of my 'monomaniac fancy that there is nothing quaint or antique in Homer.' Terrible learning, I cannot help in my turn exclaiming, terrible learning, which discovers so much! (pp. 350–2)

Translations of the *Iliad*

[It seems appropriate to conclude this interchange between Newman and Arnold with a few lines from the *Iliad* as translated by these two eminent men. Arnold criticizes the way in which both Chapman and Newman translated the dialogue between Achilles and his horse and proceeds to give his own translation (p. 273). In his reply, Newman complains that Arnold does not in fact quote relevant lines of his translation, which he in turn includes (p. 30). Here are the first eleven lines:]

Arnold's version

'Xanthus and Balius both, ye far-famed seed of Podarga!
See that ye bring your master home to the host of the Argives
In some other sort than your last, when the battle is ended;
And not leave him behind, a corpse on the plain, like Patrocles.'
    Then from beneath the yoke, the fleet horse Xanthus addressed him;
Sudden he bowed his head, and all his mane, as he bowed it,
Streamed to the ground by the yoke, escaping from under the collar;
And he was given a voice by the white-armed Goddess Hera.
    'Truly, yet this time will we save thee, mighty Achilles!
But thy day of death is at hand; nor shall *we* be the reason—
No, but the will of heaven, and Fate's invincible power.'

Newman's version

'*Chestnut* and *Spotted*! noble pair!   farfamous brood of *Spry-foot*!
In other guise now ponder ye   your charioteer to rescue
Back to the troop of Danaï,   when we have done with battle:
Nor leave him dead upon the field,   as late ye left Patroclus.'
But him the dapplefooted steed   under the yoke accosted;
(And droop'd his auburn head aside   straightway; and thro' the collar,
His full mane, streaming to the ground,   over the yoke was scatter'd:
Him Juno, whitearm'd goddess, then   with voice of man endowèd:)
'Now and again we verily   will save and more than save thee,
Dreadful Achilles! yet for thee   the deadly day approacheth.
Not ours the guilt; but mighty God   and stubborn Fate are guilty.'

Translating the European Tradition

From an anonymous review of translations of Aeschylus, *The North British Review,* 16 (Nov. 1851), 259–78

[A review of *The Tragedies of Aeschylus*, 'Literally translated by Theodore Alois Buckley', (London, 1849), and *The Lyrical Dramas of Aeschylus*, from the Greek 'Translated into English Verse by John Stuart Blackie', 2 vols. (London 1850).]

That every civilized modern nation ought to possess a complete series of translations of all the Greek and Latin Classics, is an assertion that will be universally admitted. (p. 259)

[The reviewer claims that a large proportion of the translation of the Classics has been vitiated by a 'false method' of 'loose and elegant paraphrase'.] The country has a right to look to Oxford and Cambridge for the filling up of that blank in our literature to which we have alluded—a complete and trustworthy translation, suitable for the popular English reader, of all the works that the genius and learning of antiquity have bequeathed to us. [. . .]

And with what kind of translations is it that, under such an arrangement, the ordinary scholarship of Oxford and Cambridge, or the similarly educated talent throughout the country, might be fairly expected to provide us? With this, surely, at the least—good literal prose translations of all the Greek and Latin Classics, accompanied with such illustrative notes as would make the text thoroughly intelligible to the careful English reader. The prime and essential characteristic of such translations ought to be rigid and punctilious literality. [. . .] All attempts to escape this, all pretensions about giving the 'spirit' of the original, but not the exact words, we would treat as dishonest subterfuges. There is no security that we see for giving the spirit of the original, unless by giving an exact version of the words. (pp. 260–2)

It remains true, nevertheless, that no mere intellectual rendering of a poetical passage, however faithful, can equal the force and intention of the original; and hence we are prepared to say, in the second place, with Professor Blackie, that, in every case where it is possible consistently with entire faithfulness to the meaning, the translation of a poetical passage ought to be in verse. Here, however, a rule suggests itself, so obvious that, were it not more frequently transgressed than kept, it might seem unnecessary to mention it. It is this, that every poetical translation of a poetical passage should, wherever it is possible, be in the same metre as the original. [. . .] But how are we to act in the more difficult business of translating the ancient poets, whose metres are, for the most part, obsolete? Here, at best, our procedure must be in a spirit of compromise. [. . .] A metrical *fac-simile* in English, of the Odes of Horace, would be about as pleasant a spectacle as a box of corkscrews; and even Homer would be intolerable in English, whatever he is in German, Hexameters. [...] In short, if still we resolve that our translations shall be metrical [...] we have clearly but one resource—namely, to exercise our own taste and ear in finding metres which shall satisfy, as nearly as possible, all the demands of the original, at the same time that they fulfil all native conditions. And this is what Professor Blackie professes to have done with Aeschylus. (pp. 267–9)

In the two works before us—the one a literal prose translation of the plays of Aeschylus by an Oxford scholar; the other a poetical translation of the same plays by one who is both a scholar and a man of genius—the question as between prose translations and poetical translations of poetry of such a kind and so ancient a date, is brought to a practical issue. (p. 271)

Mr Buckley's prose translation of Aeschylus [...] is certainly done on the principle of literal exactness. We cannot say much, however, in favour of Mr Buckley's power of reconciling literal exactness with other qualities. The literality of his translation is frequently of that helpless kind which ends in unintelligibility; not a few of the passages in his version looking like the efforts of a faithful but somewhat dull schoolboy, who, after annexing to every word in a sentence its dictionary-meaning, remains without the slightest glimpse of the sense which the words convey as a whole. [...]

Professor Blackie's translation of Aeschylus belongs, of course, by its very nature, to a far higher order of performance than Mr Buckley's. And, in that order, it is infinitely better done. The translation of the great tragic poet has evidently been to Professor Blackie a labour of love. Every line of the original has been conscientiously gone through by the translator, and the meaning rendered in a manner thoroughly intelligible to the English reader. Here, also, we have spirit, strength, large command of language, and abundant proof of a mind not only of original literary faculty, and native poetical tendency, but also richly cultured in classic lore. (p. 273)

And yet, if, passing from the consideration of the merit of Professor Blackie's translation, as a general literary feat, we view it specially with relation to the question, how far this large amount of the labour of one of our really able men has contributed to bring Aeschylus, in all his force and all his peculiarity, more closely and vividly before the minds of modern British readers than could have been possible without such help, we shall be forced to confess that, judging according to such a mode, we should have preferred being left with but a bald literal version, enjoying, at the same time, the pleasure of seeing so large a surplus of talent judiciously laid out on some independent performance. [...]

[The reviewer stresses and gives an example of Blackie's excellent rendering of various passages.] But on the whole, such is the value of literal adherence to the very words of a poet like Aeschylus, and so inevitable are the deviations from this absolute literality in even the most painstaking poetical translator, that we are not sure whether, if we desired to give an intelligent English reader a clear and exact idea of the old Greek bard, we should not put Mr Buckley's prose translation, with all its faults, into his hands, rather than Professor Blackie's poetical translation, with all its merits—only advising him to read Professor Blackie's translation afterwards, or to keep it by him at the time, in order to read his fine renderings of some of the grander and more difficult passages. (pp. 274–5)

From an anonymous review in *Athenaeum*, 23 March 1844, pp. 267–9, of two Dante translations

[A review of *The Inferno of Dante Alighieri*, trans. in the *terza rima* of the original by John Dayman, and *The First Ten Cantos of the Inferno of Dante Alighieri*, trans. T. W. Parsons.]

These translators are bold men to venture on Dante, after Mr Cary and Mr Wright. Mr Dayman's version is veritable *terza rima*. Mr Parsons substitutes a stanza that looks, by the printer's aid, like the same measure, but is after all only the common quatrain licentiously used. One great difficulty in Dante (perhaps the greatest), is the conciseness of his style; nothing tries a translator more than this. Only great authors write concisely, and they can do it with both energy and grace; in inferior hands, the concise style becomes hard and stiff. The American translator [Parsons] before us quarrels sadly with his tools. He writes irreverently of Dante's 'curt parsimony of phrase,' and even calls him an 'imperfect speaker.' Implicit faith is needed in the translator, to render the poet *con amore*; what is here described as a puzzle, should be felt as a charm. It is suspicious when a translator impeaches his poet of faults, by way of excuse for the defects of his own version. We would permit the facts to be stated, but not as blemishes. Is it a fault in the Ulyssean bow, that inferior strengths fail in bending it? Let us then cease to doubt whether Dante's 'brevity of description' is 'uniformly a merit.'

[. . .]

Mr Dayman, unlike his American competitor, has declined to burthen himself with the yoke of making Dante popular. On the contrary, perhaps, he has somewhat too much restricted himself from some liberties that might have been allowed to him. Not only has he undertaken in English the difficult measure of the original, but, *maugre* the acknowledged paucity of rhymes in our language, has endeavoured to follow the example of his author, in using as seldom as possible, the same rhyme twice in the same canto. This shows, at any rate, a determination to conquer rather than to avoid difficulties. We have, therefore, two modes of performing the same task before us.

[. . .]

One of these versions is evidently constructed on the principle of popularizing the original, and the other on that of faithfully reflecting it. Without referring now to the comparative correctness of the two translations, but confining ourselves to the mere results—or the actual effects produced on the mind by their perusal—let us ask which has best attained the end of impressing the feeling of poetic excellence and power? We answer that the award must be given in favour of Mr Dayman. The versification of his rival is smooth and intelligible; but it has not the force and harmony, the variety and combination of musical elements that distinguish his own. We have a shrewd suspicion, then, that the best translation, even for popular purposes, would, not only in the long run, but in the immediate effect, be that which proceeded on the strictest pinciples of conformity to the style and measure of the original poem.

From an anonymous review of *The Roman Poets of the Republic* by W. Y. Sellar, and *The Aeneid of Virgil in English Blank Verse*, trans. by John Miller, *Athenaeum*, 10 Oct 1863, pp. 459–61

Mr Miller's translation of Virgil's Aeneid adds one to the many metrical translations of Virgil, of which there exist nearly 200. In English alone the bibliographical authorities give upwards of thirty poetical versions of part or the whole of Virgil's works. Admitting that Dryden is not faultless, and we are not *tam fautores inepte* as to maintain that he is, the man must, nevertheless, be very bold who enters the lists with a view to supersede him. Dryden is, upon the whole, undoubtedly too diffuse; but any one who will take the trouble to look through the Earl of Surry's version (1557), or Phaer and Twine's (1607), will easily understand the reactionary feeling which made him err in this direction. The present generation is striving to correct the loose disposition to paraphrase which characterized our greatest translators; but in doing so it runs great risk of falling into the bald and inartistic prose-poetry of a more primitive age. At the head of the loose translators of the Aeneid stands Delille, whose only aim seems to be to travel as far from the original as his utmost ingenuity will enable him to do. Mr Miller—we regret that we must say, the *late* Mr Miller—possessed very great poetical powers, as the prophetic lines, foreshadows of his death, sad preface to his book, sufficiently testify. As a translator, he is less successful, but his work is creditably accomplished. Apart from occasional liberties with the metre (such as the uncalled-for introduction of anapaests and tribrachs), we have no special fault to indicate. Dr Kennedy gave to the world a very fair translation of Virgil some years ago. Mr Miller's is rather superior, in point of fire, to that of the learned head-master of Shrewsbury.

As a matter of curiosity, it may not be uninteresting to see the different phraseology in which some half-dozen translators have clothed the same passage; we, therefore, append a few lines from the Second Book of the Aeneid as rendered by the Earl of Surrey, Phaer and Twine, &c. and Mr Miller, respectively.

The Earl of Surrey, 1557:

> They whisted all with fixed face attent
> When Prince Aeneas from the royal seat
> Thus gan to speak. O Quene, it is thy wil
> I should renew a woe cannot be told:
> How that the Grekes did spoile and overthrow
> The Phrygian wealth and wailful realm of Troy,
> Those ruthful things that I myself beheld,
> And whereof, no small part fel to my share.

Phaer and Twine, 1607:

> They whistled (whisted?) all, and fixt with eyes ententive did behold,
> When Lord Aeneas where he sat from hie bench thus he told.
> A dolefull worke me to renew O Queen thou dost constraine
> To tell how Greek the Troian wealth and lamentable reigne
> Did overthrow, which I myself have seene and bene a part
> No small thereof.

Dryden:

> All were attentive to the godlike man
> When from his lofty couch he thus began:
> Great Queen, what you command me to relate,
> Renews the sad remembrance of our fate;
> An empire from its old foundations rent,
> And every woe the Trojans underwent;
> A peopled city made a desert place,
> All that I saw, and part of which I was.

Pitt, 1740:

> All gazed in silence with an eager look,
> Then from the golden couch the hero spoke:
> 'Ah mighty Queen! You urge me to disclose,
> And feel, once more, unutterable woes;
> How vengeful Greece with victory was crown'd,
> And Troy's fair empire humbled to the ground;
> Those direful scenes I saw on Phrygia's shore,
> Those wars in which so large a part I bore,' &c.

Delille:

> On se tait, on attend dans un profond silence,
> Alors, environné d'une assemblée immense,

> De la conche élevée où siége le héros
> Il s'adresse à Didon, et commence dans ces mots:
> 'Reine! de ce beau jour faut-il troubler les charmes,
> Et rouvrir à vos yeux la source de nos larmes;
> Vous raconter la nuit, l'épouvantable nuit
> Qui vit Pergame en cendre et son règne détruit;
> Ces derniers coups du sort, ce triomphe du crime,
> Dont je fus le témoin, hélas! et la victime?'

Dr Kennedy:

> Silent were all, in deep attention fix'd,
> When from high couch the sire Aeneas spake:
> At thy command, O Queen, woes I renew
> Unspeakable, showing Troy's power and realm
> By Greeks o'erthrown, most mournful scenes, which I
> Viewed, and wherein so large a part I bore.

Mr Miller:

> Silent were all and turned their eyes intent,
> When sire Aeneas from his high couch began:
> Oh mighty Queen, thou orderest to renew
> Unutterable sorrow; how the Greeks
> The Trojan splendours and that hapless realm
> O'erthrew; those dark calamities which I
> Both saw and largely shared.

Mr Miller's interpretation will be found to be careful and conscientious; and the description of the death of Cacus, and other similar passages, though a long way behind the grand original, are by no means destitute of spirit.

From S. H. Butcher and A. Lang's 'Preface' to their translation of *The Odyssey of Homer* (1878; 4th rev. edn. London: Macmillan 1883), pp. v–x

There would have been less controversy about the proper method of Homeric translation, if critics had recognised that the question is a purely relative one, that of Homer there can be no final translation. The taste and the literary habits of each age demand different qualities in poetry, and therefore a different sort of rendering of Homer. To the men of the time of Elizabeth, Homer would have appeared bald, it seems, and lacking in ingenuity, if he had been presented in his antique simplicity. For the Elizabethan age, Chapman supplied what was then necessary, and the mannerisms that were then deemed of the essence of poetry, namely, daring and luxurious conceits. Thus in Chapman's verse

Troy must 'shed her towers for tears of overthrow,' and when the winds toss Odysseus about, their sport must be called 'the horrid tennis.'

In the age of Anne, 'dignity' and 'correctness' had to be given to Homer, and Pope gave them by aid of his dazzling rhetoric, his antithesis, his *netteté*, his command of his every conventional and favourite artifice. [. . .]

The epics are stories about the adventures of men living in most respects like the men of our own race who dwelt in Iceland, Norway, Denmark, and Sweden. The epics are, in a way, and as far as manners and institutions are concerned, historical documents. Whoever regards them in this way, must wish to read them exactly as they have reached us, without modern ornament, with nothing added or omitted. He must recognise, with Mr Matthew Arnold, that what he now wants, namely, the simple truth about the matter of the poem, can only be given in prose, 'for in a verse translation no original work is any longer recognisable.' It is for this reason that we have attempted to tell once more, in simple prose, the story of Odysseus. We have tried to transfer, not all the truth about the poem, but the historical truth, into English. In this process Homer must lose at least half his charm, his bright and equable speed, the musical current of that narrative, which, like the river of Egypt, flows from an indiscoverable source, and mirrors the temples and the palaces of unforgotten gods and kings. Without this music of verse, only a half truth about Homer can be told, but then it is that half of the truth which, at this moment, it seems most necessary to tell. This is the half of the truth that the translators who use verse cannot easily tell. [. . .]

We do not know whether it is necessary to defend our choice of a somewhat antiquated prose. Homer has no ideas which cannot be expressed in words that are 'old and plain,' and to words that are old and plain, and, as a rule, to such terms as, being used by the Translators of the Bible, are still not unfamiliar, we have tried to restrict ourselves. It may be objected, that the employment of language which does not come spontaneously to the lips, is an affectation out of place in a version of the Odyssey. To this we may answer that the Greek Epic dialect, like the English of our Bible, was a thing of slow growth and composite nature, that it was never a spoken language, nor, except for certain poetical purposes, a written language. Thus the Biblical English seems as nearly analogous to the Epic Greek, as anything that our tongue has to offer.

The Odyssey, Book XI (opening lines), trans. Butcher and Lang, p. 172

[Cf. the same passage as translated by others, pp. 97–8, 173, 187, 255–6, and 286–7.]

Now when we had gone down to the ship and to the sea, first of all we drew the ship unto the fair salt water, and placed the mast and sails in the black ship, and took those sheep and put them therein, and ourselves too climbed on board, sorrowing and shedding big tears. And in the wake of our dark-prowed ship she sent a favouring wind that filled the sails, a kindly escort,—even Circe of the braided tresses, a dread goddess of human speech. And we set in order all the gear throughout the ship and sat us down; and the wind and the helmsman guided our barque. And all day long her sails were stretched in her seafaring; and the suns sank and all the ways were darkened.

She came to the limits of the world, to the deep flowing Oceanus. There is the land and the city of the Cimmerians, shrouded in mist and cloud, and never does the shining sun look down on them with his rays, neither when he climbs up the starry heavens, nor when again he turns earthward from the firmament, but deadly night is outspread over miserable mortals. Thither we came and ran the ship ashore and took out the sheep; but for our part we held on our way along the stream of Oceanus, till we came to the place which Circe had declared to us.

3.5 SIX NINETEETH-CENTURY TRANSLATORS

The nineteenth century, unlike the Tudor and Jacobean period, is not generally thought of as a great age of translation. It saw a burgeoning of Romantic poetry and the development of the novel into a major art form. As is apparent from the Newman–Arnold debate and more specifically from the excerpts of Victorian criticism (see Sect. 3.4, above) there was a lively debate, spurred in part by developments in German letters. The German example of close (i.e. 'literal' and often 'foreignizing') renderings helped to expand the understanding of varieties of translation, associated with Dryden (see Sect. 2.13, above).

In the practice of translation, no approach could be said to dominate. Robert Browning's version of the *Agamemnon*, in its literalism, may be contrasted with Edward FitzGerald's radically 'free' ('domesticating') version of the *Rubáiyát* of Omar Khayyam, not to mention Longfellow's epic imitation, in *The Song of Hiawatha*, of the Finnish *Kalevala*, a prime example of the intercultural effect, at this time, of translation. Of course, in the case of FitzGerald, the 'free' approach may have had more than a little to do with the fact that he was translating a non-Western text, whereas Browning's 'fidelity' can be partly attributed to the fact that he was translating one of the canonical works of Western literature. At another extreme is William Morris, who combines close translation with an archaizing tendency, attempting thereby to connect with a pre-Latinate, pre-Norman stratum of English. FitzGerald's (on the surface) almost dismissive attitude may be gauged by his remark, in a letter to his (far more respectful) mentor, E. B. Cowell: 'It is an amusement to me to take what Liberties I like with these Persians, who (as I think) are not Poets enough to frighten one from such excursions, and who really do want a little Art to shape them'.[1]

Henry Wadsworth Longfellow

Henry Wadsworth Longfellow (1807–82), author of *The Song of Hiawatha* (1855), is the most popular of all American poets. A European trip brought him into contact with Scandinavian and German Romantic poetry. During his stay in Stockholm in 1852, he read the *Kalevala*, a collection of Finnish folk poems, edited into a coherent national epic cycle (1835) by Elias Lönnrot (1802–84), comparable with the Icelandic Edda. Attempting to

---

[1] *Letters of Edward FitzGerald*, i (London, Macmillan and Co., 1894), 319.

learn Finnish, Longfellow in fact read the poem in translation from that language, this inspiring him to write *Hiawatha*, on the *Kalevala* model, as an American epic poem. It was, thus, far from a direct translation, but the stanza form was acknowledged as deriving from the Finnish collection as well as from a translation into English of Chippewa legends. Shortly after its publication, Longfellow wrote, in somewhat more respectful terms perhaps than FitzGerald: 'I have tried to do for our old Indian legends what the unknown Finnish poets had done for theirs, and in doing this I have employed the same meter, but of course have not adopted any of their legends' ('In "Hiawatha" ', November 1855). All of this, of course, is to be understood in the context of the national sentiment inspired by the German Romantics, such as Johann Gottfried Herder, theoretician of the *Sturm und Drang*, preoccupied with folk poetry. Longfellow spent the summer of 1835 in Sweden, this resulting, two years later, in an essay in the *North American Review* (1837) on Esaias Tegnér's enormously popular and much translated heroic poem *Frithiof's Saga* (1825), a Romantic cycle on an old Norse theme. Longfellow translated selected passages in the original metres and included these in his essay.

In the early nineteenth century, comprehensive translation of the German Romantics helped to promote interest in medieval epic as well. Thus, both Longfellow (*The Golden Legend*, 1851) and Rossetti (*Henry the Leper*, 1846) offered versions of *Der arme Heinrich* (Poor Henry), a story by Hartmann von Aue, a dominant figure of the high Middle Ages. A more modern example (see below) is Longfellow's translation of Goethe's poem 'Wanderers Nachtlied II' ('Über allen Gipfeln'). By this time Professor of Modern Languages at Harvard (1834), Longfellow was also captivated by some Spanish poems, recreating the Spanish ballad in *The Secret of the Sea* (1849), this not being his first venture into medieval Spanish, since, in 1833, he had published a version of Jorge Manrique's *Coplas por la muerte de su padre* (1479): 'Verses for his father's Death', the most famous elegy in Spanish, Longfellow's version being a recreation rather than a strict translation. He also translated Dante's *Divine Comedy* into blank terzines (1865–7), a compromise between *terza rima* and the blank verse employed, for instance by Henry Francis Cary (1814), the best-known nineteenth-century Dante translator (see below).

Comparison of translations of Dante Alighieri, *Divine Comedy*

Opening lines of Inferno, canto 1, in Italian original

Nel mezzo del cammin di nostra vita
mi ritrovi per una selva oscura
che la diritta via era smarrita.

Ah quanto a dir qual era è cosa dura
  esta selva selvaggia e aspra e forte
  che nel pensier rinova la paura!
Tant' è amara che poco è più morte;
  ma per trattar del ben ch'io vi trovai,
diro dell'altre cose ch'i' v'ho scorte.

Longfellow's translation (London: Routledge, 1867)

Midway upon the journey of our life
  I found myself within a forest dark,
  For the straightforward pathway had been lost.

Ah me! how hard a thing it is to say
  What was this forest savage, rough, and stern,
  Which in the very thought renews the fear.
So bitter is it, death is little more;
  But of the good to treat, which there I found,
  Speak will I of the other things I saw there.

Henry Francis Cary's version (1818)

In the midway of this our mortal life,
I found me in a gloomy wood, astray
Gone from the path direct: and e'en to tell,
It were no easy task, how savage wild
That forest, how robust and rough its growth,
Which to remember only, my dismay
Renews, in bitterness not far from death.
Yet, to discourse of what there good befell,
All else will I relate discovered there.

Mark Musa's version (1971)

Midway along the journey of our life
  I woke to find myself in some dark woods,
  for I had wandered off from the straight path.

How hard it is to tell what it was like,
  this wood of wilderness, savage and stubborn
  (the thought of it brings back all my old fears),

a bitter place! Death could scarce be bitterer.
But if I would show the good that came of it
I must talk about things other than the good.

Comparison of translations of Goethe's 'Wanderers Nachtlied II'

Longfellow's translation, from The Poetical Works of Henry Wadsworth Longfellow
(London: Frederick Warne and Co., 1882), 595

Wanderer's Night-Song II

O'er all the hill-tops
Is quiet now,
In all the tree-tops
Hearest thou
Hardly a breath;
The birds are asleep in the trees.
Wait; soon like these
Thou too shalt rest.

German source text

Über allen Gipfeln
Ist Ruh,
In allen Wipfeln
Spürest du
Kaum einen Hauch;
Die Vögelein schweigen im Walde,
Warte nur, balde
Ruhest du auch.

Plain prose translation by David Luke from Goethe Selected Verse
(London: Penguin, 1986), 50

The Wayfarer's Nightsong ll

Over all the hill-tops
it is still,
In all the tree-tops
you can hardly
Feel a breath stirring.
The little birds are silent in the forest.
Wait! Soon
You too will be still.

Edward FitzGerald

Edward FitzGerald (1809–83) was a poet, a prolific letter-writer, and the renowned translator of the *Rubáiyát* of Omar Khayyam, probably the most popular English poem of the nineteenth century. He was a typical, amiable, upper-class Victorian man-of-letters, able to indulge his interests and curiosities, much loved—by Thackeray, Tennyson, and Carlyle, among others. In 1837 FitzGerald settled down to a peaceful, uneventful life in Suffolk. However, in 1845, he met E. B. Cowell, an established Oriental scholar and linguist. Cowell introduced FitzGerald to Persian and to Spanish literature, guaranteeing to teach him the grammar in one day! In 1856, Cowell went to India, becoming Professor of English at Calcutta. Just before his departure, he and FitzGerald read 'Some curious infidel and epicurean Tetrastichs by a Persian of the Eleventh Century' (from a letter to Tennyson, July 1856) which Cowell had found in a fifteenth-century Persian manuscript in the Bodleian Library and had copied for his friend.

In 1857, amid marital troubles, FitzGerald found that Omar Khayyam 'breathes a sort of consolation!' He jokingly signed his name, in letters to Cowell, 'Edward FitzOmar'. A stanza crystallized in his mind fairly early, and, in a letter to Cowell in 1857, he wrote: 'I see how a very pretty Eclogue might be tessellated [mosaiced] out of his scattered Quatrains.' He became obsessed with the translation, but was of course aware of its outrageous nature, publishing the work in 1859, anonymously, in a limited edition. He had turned these spontaneous occasional short poems into a continuous, dramatically unified sequence, sometimes compressing more than one poem into one of his own quatrains. It was only after some time, once it had been discovered by Rossetti, Swinburne, and Ruskin, that the poem became widely known, achieving its heights, in fact, only after the translator's death, and it was not until 1869 that the American scholar Charles Eliot Norton reviewed it in the most flattering terms: 'He is to be called "translator" only in default of a better word, one which should express the poetic transfusion of a poetic spirit from one language to another, and the representation of the ideas and images of the original in a form not altogether diverse from their own but perfectly adapted to the new conditions of time, place, custom, and habit of mind in which they reappear.' Norton, with whom FitzGerald corresponded, added, in a manner which the seventeenth-century exponents of what Dryden called Imitation might have echoed: 'It is the work of a poet inspired by the work of a poet; not a copy, but a reproduction, not a translation, but the redelivery of a poetic inspiration.' FitzGerald himself, however, writing to Cowell in 1858, expressed perhaps a certain unease: 'My Translation will interest you from its Form, and also in many respects in its Detail: very un-literal as it is. Many Quatrains are mashed together and something lost, I doubt, of Omar's Simplicity, which is so much a Virtue in him.'

The success of the poem may be explained in terms of Khayyam's evident rebellion against bigotry and religious dogmatism. The translation addressed several prevalent concerns: divine justice versus hedonism; science versus religion; as well as catering to the taste for eastern art and bric-a-brac. The only consolation, in a puzzling life, was physical pleasure. The 'sceptical' *Rubáiyát* seemed appropriately published in the same year as *Origin of Species*, although FitzGerald himself was no atheist or agnostic. He felt a kinship with Omar, tinged with guilt, whereas Cowell himself openly disapproved of Omar's pessimism about life and especially about the certainty of a Hereafter.

Like Ruskin, FitzGerald found himself out of step with the 'march of progress', lamenting the spoliation of nature and, in fact, turning for relief to the less vulnerable sea. He produced translations of plays by Calderón (1853), Aeschylus (*The Agamemnon*, 1876), and Sophocles. His other translations from Persian included Attar-ut-Tair's thirteenth-century text *The Bird Parliament* (1859), a kind of ornithological *Pilgrim's Progress*, affirming in this case the benevolence of God, and Jami's *Salaman and Absal* (1856). A critic, while regretting FitzGerald's somewhat deficient Persian, seemed to approve his work in general, writing that 'As a first attempt, however, to make Jami accessible to the English reader, this little volume is deserving of commendation.'

FitzGerald's approach to translation in general was typified by the freedom he felt appropriate in his treatment of Omar. In a letter to Cowell (1859) he famously wrote: 'I suppose very few People have ever taken such Pains in Translation as I have: though certainly not to be literal. But at all costs a thing must live: with a transfusion for one's own life if one can't retain the Original's better. Better a live Sparrow than a stuffed Eagle.' In a letter to James Russell Lowell, the American poet, essayist, and editor, he underlined this sentiment, writing explicitly of his approach to translation:

> I am persuaded that, to keep Life in the Work (as Drama must) the Translator (however inferior to his Original) must re-cast that original into his own Likeness, more or less: the less like his original, so much the worse: but still, the live Dog better than the dead Lion; in Drama, I say. [. . .] Another shot have I made at Faust in Bayard Taylor's Version: but I do not even get on with him as with Hayward, hampered as he (Taylor) is with his allegiance to original metres, etc. His Notes I was interested in: but I shall die ungoethed [. . .]

Already in his work on the Quaker poet Bernard Barton in 1849, FitzGerald had commented: 'Some of the poems I take entire, some half—some only a few stanzas, and these dovetailed together—with a change of word or even of a line here and there, to give them logic and fluency ... I am sure I have distilled many pretty little poems out of long dull ones which the world has discarded.' If this was how he could describe his editorial duties with respect to an English-language poet, it is not surprising that he gave himself maximum latitude in his translations. His candidly unapologetic description of his own approach affords insight into the priorities of at least some prominent nineteenth-century translators and exemplifies the polarization that had taken place in an era of translation characterized also by scholarly literalism.

From Edward FitzGerald's Introduction to the *Rubáiyát* of Omar Khayyam (1st edn. London: B. Quaritch, 1859)

With regard to the present Translation. The original Rubáiyát (as, missing an Arabic Guttural, these *Tetrastichs* are more musically called), are independent Stanzas, consisting each of four lines of equal, though varied, Prosody, sometimes *all* rhyming, but oftener (as here attempted) the third line suspending the Cadence by which the last atones with the former Two. Something as in the Greek Alcaic, where the third line seems to lift and suspend the Wave that falls over in the last. As usual with such kind of Oriental Verse, the Rubáiyát follow one another according to Alphabetic Rhyme—a strange Farrago of Grave and Gay. Those here selected are strung into something of an Eclogue, with perhaps a less than equal proportion of the 'Drink and make-merry', which (genuine or not) recurs over-frequently in the Original. For Lucretian as Omar's Genius might be, he cross'd that darker Mood with much of Oliver de Basselin Humour. Any way, the Result is sad enough: saddest perhaps when most ostentatiously merry: any way, fitter to move Sorrow than Anger towards the old Tentmaker, who after vainly endeavouring to unshackle his Steps from Destiny, and to catch some authentic Glimpse of TOMORROW, fell back upon TODAY (which has out-lasted so many Tomorrows!) as the only Ground he got to stand upon, however momentarily slipping from under his Feet.

From *The Rubáiyát* of Omar Khayyám (first version, 1859), stanzas 1–3

> Wake! For Morning in the Bowl of Night
> Has flung the Stone that puts the Stars to Flight:
>   And Lo! The Hunter of the East has caught
> The Sultán's Turret in a Noose of Light.
>
> Dreaming when Dawn's Left Hand was in the Sky
> I heard a Voice within the Tavern cry,
>   'Awake, my Little ones, and fill the Cup

'Before Life's Liquor in its Cup be dry.'

And, as the Cock crew, those who stood before
The Tavern shouted—'Open then the Door!
  'You know how little while we have to stay,
'And, once departed, may return no more.'

Comparison between FitzGerald's fifth version (1879) and that of Robert Graves and Omar Ali-Shah (*The Original Rubaíyyat of Omar Khayaam,* in new translation with critical commentaries, 1968)

[Note, these stanzas by FitzGerald are, in fact, rendered fairly literally (see L. P. Elwell-Sutton, 'the Rubaiyat Revisited', *Delos*, 3 (1969), 170–91).]

FitzGerald, stanza 44

Why, if the Soul can fling the Dust aside,
And naked on the Air of Heaven ride,
  Were't not a shame—were't not a Shame for him
In this clay carcase crippled to abide?

Robert Graves, stanza 47

Dear love, when you are free to slough your skin
And become naked spirit, soaring far
Across God's Empyrean, you will blush
That you lay cramped so long in body's gaol.

FitzGerald, stanza 95

And much as Wine has played the Infidel,
And robb'd me of my Robe of Honour—Well,
I wonder often what the Vintners buy
One half so precious as the stuff they sell.

Robert Graves, stanza 102

Though drink has rotted my high reputation,
Reject it I will not, while yet I breathe,
Wondering often what the vintners buy
Equal in value with the wine they sell.

Robert Browning

Robert Browning (1812–89) was a major English poet of the nineteenth century. His father taught him Greek and Latin but he had little formal education. He published prolifically before his marriage to Elizabeth Barrett, at the time better known than him. The couple lived in Italy until Elizabeth's death in 1861. Browning experimented with form and content, turning away from direct self-expression to dramatic monologues, implanting his own ideas in a context of historical personalities and period atmosphere; his work has greatly influenced twentieth-century poets who use dramatic monologue, especially Eliot and Pound. He ignored the extravagant imagery and vagueness of the Romantics, his chief source of inspiration being the Italian late Renaissance. In later life, he published an ultra-literal translation of Aeschylus' *Agamemnon* (1877), which he defended convincingly in his preface, proclaiming his belief in the need for translation to be 'literal at every cost save that of absolute violence to our language' (see below). Pound castigated this version as an example of Victorian fustian, although much of his own translation work, of course, could also be described as literalistic, if in an updated way. Browning's translation of *Agamemnon* reflected also his continuing interest in dramatic writing. If at one time it seemed unreadable, it is once again, perhaps, becoming accessible since 'standard' English is no longer as dominant as it was.

From the Preface (1877) to the *Agamemnon,* **included in** *The Poetical Works of Robert Browning,* **vol. xi (London: Smith, Elder, 1903), 511–12**

If, because of the immense fame of the following Tragedy, I wished to acquaint myself with it, and could only do so by the help of a translator, I should require him to be literal at every cost save that of absolute violence to our language. The use of certain allowable constructions which, happening to be out of daily favour, are all the more appropriate to archaic workmanship, is no violence: but I would be tolerant for once,—in the case of so immensely famous an original,—of even a clumsy attempt to furnish me with the very turn of each phrase in as Greek a fashion as English will bear: while, with respect to amplifications and embellishments,—anything rather than, with the good farmer, experience that most signal of mortifications, 'to gape for Aeschylus and get Theognis.' I should especially decline—what may appear to brighten up a passage—the employment of a new word for some old one [. . .]—if I obtained a mere strict bald version of thing by thing, or at least word pregnant with thing, I should hardly look for an impossible transmission of the reputed magniloquence and sonority of the Greek; and this with the less regret, inasmuch as there is abundant musicality elsewhere, but nowhere else than in his poem the ideas of the poet. [...] Fortunately, the poorest translation, provided only it be faithful,—though it reproduce all the artistic confusion of tenses, moods, and persons, with which the original teems,—will not only suffice to display what an eloquent friend maintains to be the all-in-all of poetry—'the action of the piece'—but may help to illustrate his assurance that 'the Greeks are the highest models of expression, the unapproached masters of the grand style: their expression is so excellent because it is so admirably kept in its right degree of prominence, because it is so simple and so well subordinated, because it draws its force directly from the pregnancy of the matter which it conveys ... not a word wasted, not a sentiment capriciously thrown in, stroke on stroke!'[1]

NOTE

1.　*Poems*, by Matthew Arnold, Preface.

From Browning's translation of Aeschylus' *Agamemnon*

[See J. S. Blackie's, Robert Lowell's, and Ted Hughes's versions of these lines, in Sect. 3.4, 4.10, and 5.16, below. Hughes's notion of literalism seems more concerned with 'playability' than Browning's.]

[This excerpt, spoken by the Chorus, constituting, in fact, the first choral ode or Parodos, describes the embarkation for Troy of the Argive fleet under the monarchs Agamemnon and Menelaus, brothers, after Menelaus' wife Helen has fled to Troy with Paris. The ominous killing of a pregnant hare by two birds of prey, is recounted.]

> How the fierce bird against the Teukris land
> Despatched, with spear and executing hand,
> The Achaian's two-throned empery—o'er Hellas' youth
> Two rulers with one mind:
> The birds' king to these kings of ships, on high,
> —The black sort, and the sort that's white behind,—
> Appearing by the palace, on the spear-throw side,
> In right sky-regions, visible far and wide,—
> Devouring a hare-creature, great with young,
> Baulked of more racings they, as she from whom they sprung!

Literal translation of this passage, from *Aeschylus: Oresteia*, trans. with notes by Hugh Lloyd-Jones (London: Duckworth, 1979)

[This is a modern scholarly literal version. Lloyd-Jones's note on this section begins: 'The Chorus now sings the Parodos proper, "the longest [only the first part is given here] and richest chorus extant in Greek tragedy" (Franekel). It falls into 3 sections, differentiated by sense as well as metre [. . .]'.]

> I have power to tell of the auspicious command of the
>   expedition, the command of men
> in authority; for still from the gods am I inspired
> with persuasive power, my strength in song, by the life that
>   has grown up with me:
> to tell how the two-throned command of the Achaeans, of the
>   youth of Hellas
> the concordant leadership,
> as sped with avenging spear and arm
> by the warlike bird of omen to the Teucrian land,
> the king of birds appearing to the kings of the ships,
> the black eagle and behind it the white one,
> appearing near the palace on the hand in which the spear is
>   brandished,
> in seats conspicuous,
> feeding upon the hare, her womb teeming with young,
> checked from running her final course.
> Sing sorrow, sorrow, but may the good prevail.

Richard Burton

Explorer, Orientalist, scholar, linguist, sexologist, mystic, and spy or diplomat, Richard Burton (1821–90) was raised in France and Italy and studied at Oxford. He saw active service in the Indian Army and served in the Crimean War. During the course of an adventurous life, Burton learned over thirty languages. He wrote voluminously, achieving fame or notoriety for a literary style that combined an Elizabethan richness with a vocabulary replete with local colour. He was one of the first Englishmen, in disguise, to make the pilgrimage to Mecca (1853), writing A *Personal Narrative of a Pilgrimage to Mecca and Al-Madina*, and he also travelled widely for the British government, serving as British Consul off the coast of Equatorial Guinea, in Brazil, Damascus, and Trieste, where he died. Burton was one of the first Europeans to explore East Africa. His other expeditions included one across the United States to Salt Lake City, and a voyage up the Congo river. Knighted in 1885, Burton produced the first unexpurgated translation of *The Arabian Nights' Entertainments or the Book of a Thousand Nights and a Night* (1885–8). In addition, in 1883, he produced a translation of the erotic classic *The Kama Sutras of Vatsayayana*, *The Ananda Ranga*, and *The Scented Garden of*

Sheikh Nefzawi. His frankness about sexuality was the most likely reason that his widow, in an effort to 'preserve his reputation', burned his memoirs after his death. He was also the author of an archaizing translation of the Portuguese epic *The Lusiads* (1880).

From *The Arabian Nights*, 'The Tale Of The Bull And The Ass'

Know, O my daughter, that there was once a merchant who owned much money and many men, and who was rich in cattle and camels. He had also a wife and family, and he dwelt in the country, being experienced in husbandry and devoted to agriculture. Now Allah Most High had endowed him with understanding the tongues of beasts and birds of every kind, but under pain of death if he divulged the gift to any. So he kept it secret for very fear. He had in his cow house a bull and an ass, each tethered in his own stall, one hard by the other. As the merchant was sitting near-hand one day with his servants and his children were playing about him, he heard the bull say to the ass:

'Hail and health to thee O Father of Waking! for that thou enjoyest rest and good ministering. All under thee is clean-swept and fresh-sprinkled. Men wait upon thee and feed thee, and thy provaunt is sifted barley and thy drink pure spring water, while I (unhappy creature!) am led forth in the middle of the night, when they set on my neck the plow and a something called yoke, and I tire at cleaving the earth from dawn of day till set of sun. I am forced to do more than I can and to bear all manner of ill-treatment from night to night. After which they take me back with my sides torn, my neck flayed, my legs aching, and mine eyelids sored with tears. Then they shut me up in the byre and throw me beans and crushed straw mixed with dirt and chaff, and I lie in dung and filth and foul stinks through the livelong night. But thou art ever in a place swept and sprinkled and cleansed, and thou art always lying at ease, save when it happens (and seldom enough!) that the master hath some business, when he mounts thee and rides thee to town and returns with thee forthright. So it happens that I am toiling and distrest while thou takest thine ease and thy rest. Thou sleepest while I am sleepless, I hunger still while thou eatest thy fill, and I win contempt while thou winnest goodwill.'

When the bull ceased speaking, the ass turned toward him and said: 'O Broad-o'-Brow, O thou lost one! He lied not who dubbed thee bullhead, for thou, O father of a bull, hast neither forethought nor contrivance. Thou art the simplest of simpletons, and thou knowest naught of good advisers. Hast thou not heard the saying of the wise?

> 'For others these hardships and labours I bear,
> And theirs is the pleasure and mine is the care,
> As the bleacher who blacketh his brow in the sun
> To whiten the raiment which other men wear.'

Dante Gabriel Rossetti

Dante Gabriel Rossetti (1828–82), painter and poet, like his sister Christina, was bilingual in Italian and English. He took after his father, who became Professor of Italian at King's College London, in the dissemination of Italian culture in England. With William Holman Hunt and John Everett Millais, fellow students at the Antique School of the Royal Academy, Rossetti helped found the Pre-Raphaelite Brotherhood in 1848 (the name coming partly from Keats's claim that earlier Italian painters were greater than Raphael). Love of Dante and the earlier Italian poets influenced Rossetti's own work, and through him, the Pre-Raphaelite movement influenced literature as well. Thus, English readers came to the lost art of the Troubadours (eleventh to thirteenth centuries) through Dante's commendation of them in the *Divine Comedy*, interest in Dante and his circle having been stimulated by the Pre-Raphaelites. The Romantics and Pre-Raphaelites established a style in translation which prevailed for the next half-century, as exemplified in Ezra Pound's early work, which may be regarded as both the last flowering of it and as the beginning of a new way.

In 1861, Rossetti published his influential *The Early Italian Poets from Ciullo d'Alcamo to Dante* (revised as *Dante and His Circle*, 1874). Rossetti's brother William translated Dante's *Inferno* in 1865. Rossetti himself also translated medieval and Romantic German and French poetry, including François Villon, the interest in medieval culture extending also to medieval epic and Minnesang. As noted above (see Longfellow), Rosetti's paraphrase of Hartmann's *Der arme Heinrich*, *Henry the Lepper*, was imitated by Longfellow in *The Golden Legend* (1851). As his Preface indicates, Rossetti, while insisting on the need for inspiration ('a good poem shall not be turned into a bad one'), as it were, also fully acknowledged the constraints that a desire for fidelity imposes ('The task of the translator [. . .] is one of some self-denial'). One might speculate that his non-native ancestry made him somewhat less cavalier in this latter respect than, say, Burton or FitzGerald.

From the Preface to the First Edition (1861) of *The Early Italian Poets together with Dante's Vita Nuova*, included in *Collected Works of Dante Gabriel Rossetti*, vol. li (Boston: Roberts Bros. 1887), pp. xii–xvi

Much has been said, and in many respects justly, against the value of metrical translation. But I think it would be admitted that the tributary art might find a not illegitimate use in the case of poems which come down to us in such a form as do these early Italian ones. Struggling originally with corrupt dialect and imperfect expression, and hardly kept alive through centuries of neglect, they have reached that last and worst state in which the *coup-de-grâce* has almost been dealt them by clumsy transcription and pedantic super-structure. At this stage the task of talking much more about them in any language is hardly to be entered upon; and a translation (involving as it does the necessity of settling many points without discussion,) remains perhaps the most direct form of commentary.

The life-blood of rhythmical translation is this commandment,—that a good poem shall not be turned into a bad one. The only true motive for putting poetry into a fresh language must be to endow a fresh nation, as far as possible with one more possession of beauty. Poetry not being an exact science, literality of rendering is altogether secondary to this chief law. I say *literality,*—not fidelity, which is by no means the same thing. When literality can be combined with what is thus the primary condition of success, the translator is fortunate, and must strive his utmost to unite them; when such object can only be attained by paraphrase, that is his only path.

[. . .]

[. . .] The task of the translator (and with all humility be it spoken) is one of some self-denial. Often would he avail himself of any special grace of his own idiom and epoch, if only his will belonged to him; often would some cadence serve him but for his author's structure—some structure but for his author's cadence; often the beautiful turn of a stanza must be weakened to adopt some rhyme which will tally, and he sees the poet revelling in abundance of language where himself is scantily supplied. Now he would slight the matter for the music, and now the music for the matter; but no,—he must deal to each alike. Sometimes too a flaw in the work galls him, and he would fain remove it, doing for the poet that which his age is denied him; but no,—it is not in the bond. His path is like that of Aladdin through the enchanted vaults: many are the precious fruits and flowers which he must pass by unheeded in search for the lamp alone; happy if at last, when brought to light, it does not prove that his old lamp has been exchanged for a new one,—glittering indeed to the eye, but scarcely of the same virtue nor with the same genius at its summons.

'Ballata', from Dante Gabriel Rossetti, *Poems and Translations*
(London: J.-M. Dent & Sons), 313

He will gaze upon Beatrice

> Because mine eyes can never have their fill
>   Of looking at my lady's lovely face
>   I will so fix my gaze
> That I may become bless'd, beholding her.
> Even as an angel up at his great height
> Standing amid the light,
>   Becometh bless'd by only seeing God:—
> So, though I be a simple earthly wight,
> Yet none the less I might,
>   Beholding her who is my heart's dear load,
>   Be bless'd, and in the spirit soar abroad.

Such power abideth in that gracious one;
    Albeit felt of none
      Save of him who, desiring, honours her.

William Morris

William Morris (1834–96), poet and designer, was also an important political writer. Influenced by Burne-Jones and Ruskin, he turned to architecture; Rossetti it was who encouraged him to take up painting. Later Morris took up design, furniture, and decoration, attempting to combine the aesthetic and the useful, with an emphasis on craftsmanship. His brand of utopian socialism was based on hatred of capitalism and the effects of the industrial revolution. In 1890, Morris founded the Kelmscott Press, experimenting with printing and book design, inspired by medieval design and the tradition of illumination. The immensely long *The Earthly Paradise* (1868) incorporated Greek and Norse legend. Morris visited Iceland twice (1871 and 1873). He got to know an Icelandic scholar, Eiríkur Magnússon, with whom he translated a number of sagas, six volumes of an intended comprehensive collection being completed. Morris tries to retain the syntax and employed archaisms, often making these texts a challenge to read, although accuracy, one of his prime concerns, suffered less. His translations from Icelandic profoundly influenced his own poetry.

    Morris's version of *Beowulf* from Old English, based on a prose rendering by the Anglo-Saxon scholar A. J. Wyatt, echoed Old English metre, again retaining the syntax and exploiting archaic diction. Morris's version was so closely mimetic that it was felt by some to be more obscure than the original. It was as though there had been no Norman conquest or traffic with the Latin world. His translation of Homer is also characterized by his desire to preserve and cultivate the Northern roots of the English language. In his archaizing rendering of Virgil (1875), Morris turned to the fourteener, as used by Chapman in his seventeenth-century translation of Homer's *Iliad* (see Sect. 2.6, above). Below, his translation of the first part of Book XI of the *Odyssey* (see other translations of the same passage in this volume), is followed by a passage from *Beowulf* (see also translations by Morgan and Heaney respectively, in Sects. 5.23 and 5.24, below), and a passage from the Icelandic saga of Grettir the Strong. It is in fact one of the scenes which has led many to believe that the *Saga of Grettir* is either influenced by *Beowulf* or that the two works share literary roots.

From the *Odyssey* of Homer (1887), Book XI, translated by William Morris
(London: Reeves & Turner, 1887)

So when adown we were gotten to the ship's side and the shore,
Then into the holy salt-sea we thrust her down once more,

And in the black ship hoisted the sail upon the mast.
And the sheep we gat aboard her, and aboard we also passed
Sore sorrowing, pouring the tear-drops swift-following each on each.
But the fair-haired Circe beworshipped, the Goddess of the speech,
For us had thought behind us and our black-prowed ship to send
The following breeze sail-filling, a goodly faring-friend.

So we, when all the tackling about the ship we had dight,
Sat still, while wind and rudder bore on the keel aright,
And the sails of our seafarer were filled with the wind all day:
But now the sun sank under and dusk on all roads lay,
And at last unto the utmost of deep Ocean-stream we came,
Where is the folk Cimmerian and the city of their name,
By the mist and the cloud-rack covered, and never on a day
On them doth the sun bright-shining look down with his many a ray;
Nay, not when the starry heaven he climbeth aloft, nor when
From the heavens again he turneth to the Earth and the lands of men,
But over those men unhappy hangs night for ever dead.

There then our ship did we beach, and the sheep therefrom we led,
And along the shores of Ocean ourselves the way did we hold,
Till we came to the land and the country whereof had Circe told,
[. . .]

From *Beowulf*, translated by William Morris and A. J. Wyatt (1895),
repr. in *The Collected Works of William Morris*, x
(London: Longmans Green and Company 1911), 203

[Beowulf fights Grendel.]

Naught would the earls' help for anything thenceforth
That murder-comer yet quick let loose of,
Nor his life-days forsooth to any of folk
Told he for useful. Out then drew full many
Of Beowulf's earls the heir-loom of old days,
For their lord and their master's fair life would they ward,
That mighty of Princes, if so might they do it.
For this did they know not when they the strife dreed,
Those hardy-minded men of the battle,
And on every half there thought to be hewing,
And search out his soul, that the ceaseless scather
Not any on earth of the choice of all irons,
Not one of the war-bills, would greet home for ever,
For he had forsworn him from victory-weapons,

And each one of edges. But his sundering of soul
In the days that we tell of, the day of this life,
Should be weary and woeful, the ghost wending elsewhere
To the wielding of fiends to wend him afar.
Then found he out this, he who mickle erst made
Out of mirth of his mood unto children of men
And had fram'd many crimes, he the foeman of God,
That the body of him would not bide to avail him,
But the hardy of mood, even Hygelac's kinsman,
Had him fast by the hand: now was each to the other
All loathly while living: his body-sore bided
The monster: was manifest now on his shoulder
The unceasing wound, sprang the sinews asunder,
The bone-lockers bursted. To Beowulf now
Was the battle-fame given [. . .]

From *Grettis Saga*: *The Story of Grettir the Strong*, translated by Eiríkur Magnússon and William Morris (1869), repr. in *The Collected Works of William Morris*, vii (London: Longmans Green and Company, 1911), 162–3

[Grettir (as 'Guest') fights a troll-woman]

Now it is to be told of Guest, that when it drew towards midnight, he heard great din without, and thereafter into the hall came a huge troll-wife, with a trough in one hand and a chopper wondrous great in the other; she peered about when she came in, and saw where Guest lay, and ran at him; but he sprang up to meet her, and they fell a-wrestling terribly, and struggled together for long in the hall. She was the stronger, but he gave back with craft, and all that was before them was broken, yea, the cross-panelling withal of the chamber. She dragged him out through the door, and so into the outer doorway, and then he betook himself to struggling hard against her. She was fain to drag him from the house, but might not until they had broken away all the fittings of the outer door, and borne them out on their shoulders: then she laboured away with him down towards the river, and right down to the deep gulfs.

By then was Guest exceeding weary, yet must he either gather his might together, or be cast by her into the gulf. All night did they contend in such wise; never, he deemed, had he fought with such a horror for her strength's sake; she held him to her so hard that he might turn his arms to no account save to keep fast hold on the middle of the witch.

But now when they came on to the gulf of the river, he gives the hag a swing round, and therewith got his right hand free, and swiftly seized the short-sword that he was girt withal, and smote the troll therewith on the shoulder, and struck off her arm; and therewithal was he free, but she fell into the gulf and was carried down the force.

3.6 JAMES FITZMAURICE-KELLY

James Fitzmaurice-Kelly (1857–1923) was Gilmour Professor of Spanish Language and Literature at the University of Liverpool (1909–16) and later Cervantes Professor of Spanish Language and Literature, King's College London (1916–20). He was a major British authority on Spanish and Spanish literature in his time. Among his publications are *Life of Miguel de Cervantes Saavedra* (1892); *History of Spanish Literature* (1898: new editions 1913, 1926); an edition, with John Ormsby, of *Don Quixote* (1898–9); *The Oxford Book of Spanish Verse* (1913); *Cervantes and Shakespeare* (1916); and *Cambridge Readings in Spanish Literature* (1920). All his principal works were translated into Spanish. He contributed several articles on Spanish literature and authors to the eleventh edition of *Encyclopaedia Britannica* in 1911, but also wrote a general entry on translation. This article, included below, is very much a solid product of nineteenth-century historical scholarship, and the author's emphasis on the historical significance of translation—while it runs counter to most histories of national literature—grows out of a considerable critical tradition in Victorian Britain (cf. the collage of Victorian translation criticism in Sect. 3.4, above). Fitzmaurice-Kelly has a keen sense of the multicultural twists and turns in the history of translation, but at the same time he is thoroughly traditional in his unhesitant fusion of critical and historical judgement on the one hand and personal taste on the other. Many will disagree with his harsh treatment of Cowper and especially Pope, or with his lenient appraisal of Morris's *Beowulf.* Mabbe's version of *Celestina*, notes Fitzmaurice-Kelly, 'deserved a success which it failed to obtain.' But while much recent scholarship in both literary and translation studies has moved away from this kind of evaluative discourse, it has in fact remained a strong current in the critical, if not academic, debate right up to the present.

Translation, *Encyclopædia Britannica* (11th edn., Cambridge, 1911), vol. xxvii, pp. 183–6

TRANSLATION (Lat. *trans*, across, and *latus*, the participle of *ferre*, to carry), literally a carrying over or transference from one to another, and so from one medium to another. Among the more literal usages is the translation of Enoch in the Bible (Heb. xi. 5), or the ecclesiastical removal of a bishop to another see. But the commonest sense of the word is in connexion with the rendering of one language into another.

The characteristics of a good translation in the literary sense, and the history of the influence, through translations, of one literature on another, are worth more detailed notice. Dryden has prescribed the course to be followed in the execution of the ideal translation: 'A translator that would write with any force or spirit of an original must never dwell on the words of his author. He ought to possess himself entirely, and perfectly comprehend the genius and sense of his author, the nature of the subject, and the terms of the art or subject treated of; and then he will express himself as justly, and with as much life, as if he wrote an original; whereas, he who copies word for word loses all the spirit in the tedious transfusion.' Comparatively few translators have satisfied this canon. A writer capable of attaining the standard set up by Dryden is naturally more disposed to use his powers to express his own views than those of his foreign predecessors. No doubt at all times, and in all countries, translations have usually been produced for utilitarian purposes, and not from artistic motives. In the first instance we may assume that translations were undertaken in a spirit of educational propaganda as a means of communicating new ideas and new facts to a somewhat uninstructed and uncritical public, indifferent as to matters of form. But, though the translator's primary motive is didactic, he is insensibly led to reproduce the manner as well as the matter of his original as closely as possible. Montaigne warns aspirants of the difficulty in dealing with authors remarkable for the finish of their execution. 'Il faict bon,' he writes in the *Apologie de Raimond Sebonde*, 'traduire les aucteurs comme celuy-là ou il n'y a guères que la matière à représenter: mais ceux qui ont donné beaucoup à la grace et à l'élégance de langage ils sont dangereux à entreprendre nommément pour les rapporter à un idiome plus foible.' As it happens, however, the task of translating foreign masterpieces has frequently been undertaken by writers of undisputed literary accomplishment whose renderings have had a permanent effect on the literature of their native country.

It was certainly the case when Rome, having conquered Greece, was captured by her captive. There is much point and little exaggeration in the statement that 'when the Greek nation became a province of Rome, the Latin literature became a province of the Greek'; and this peaceful victory was initiated by a series of translations made by writers of exceptional ability and, in some cases, of real genius. The first translator whose name is recorded in the history of European literature is L. Livius Andronicus, a manumitted Greek slave who about 240 B.C., rendered the *Odyssey* into Saturnian verse. This translation, of which some fragments are preserved, was long in use as a school text, for Horace studied it under the formidable Orbilius; but Andronicus appears to have recognized his mistake in using the native Latin measure as a vehicle of literary expression, and is said to have rendered Greek tragedies and comedies into metres corresponding to those of his Greek originals. The decision was momentous, for it influenced the whole metrical development of Latin poetry. The example set by Andronicus was followed by Naevius and Ennius, both of whom laid the foundations of the Latin theatre by translating Greek plays—especially those of Euripides—and naturalized in Rome the hexameter, which, as practised later by Lucretius and Virgil, was destined to become 'the stateliest measure ever moulded by the lips of man.' The tradition of translating more or less freely was continued by Pacuvius, the nephew of Ennius, as well as by Plautus and Terence, whose comedies are skilful renderings or adaptations from the New Attic Comedy of Philemon, Diphilus and Menander. A persistent translator from the Greek was Cicero, who interpolates in his prose writings versified renderings of passages from Homer, Aeschylus, Sophocles and Euripides which prove the injustice of the popular verdict on his merits as a poet. Cicero not only translated the oration of Demosthenes *On the Crown*, but also made Latin versions of Plato's *Timaeus* (part of which survives), of Xenophon's *Oeconomicus*, and of the *Phaenomena*, an astronomical poem by Aratus of Soli, an Alexandrian imitator of Hesiod. This last performance was a tribute to the prevailing fashion of the moment, for the Alexandrian poets had supplanted the early Greek school in favour among the literary circles of Rome. To the foregoing list may be added the great name of Catullus, whose *Coma Berenices* is translated from Callimachus, and Cornelius Gallus is mentioned as a translator of Euphorion. Complete translations became less and less necessary as a knowledge of Greek spread among the educated class. But the practice of translating fragments of Greek verse continued throughout the classic period of Latin literature, and the translations of Greek originals incorporated by Virgil were duly pointed out by Octavius Avitus.

The knowledge of Greek declined with the empire, and translations were accordingly produced for the benefit of students who were curious concerning the philosophic doctrines of the Athenians and the Neoplatonists. Porphyry's introduction to Aristotle's *Categories* was translated by Victorinus about the reign of Julian the Apostate; at the end of the 5th century this introduction was once more translated by Boetius, whose translations of Aristotle's *Categories* and other logical treatises began the movement which ended in establishing the Greek philosopher as the most profound and authoritative exponent of intellectual problems during the middle ages. Plato was less fortunate, for he was known to students chiefly by the Latin version of the *Timaeus* made by Chalcidius (it is said) for Hosius, the bishop of Cordova. Cassiodorus, the contemporary of Boetius, went farther afield when he ordered a Latin translation of Josephus to be prepared; but the interest in Aristotle extended to the East, and in the 6th century he was translated into Syriac by Sergius of Resaina. The Syrians acted as interpreters of Greek learning to the Arabs, and during the 8th and 9th centuries—chiefly through the staff of translators organized at Bagdad by Honein ibn Ishak—the works of Plato and Aristotle, as well as those of Hippocrates and Galen, were translated into Arabic. These translations are of capital importance in the history of European thought. Many of them were introduced into Spain by the Arabs, and were rendered—in some cases through the intermediary of a Castilian-speaking Jew—into Latin at the college of translators founded in 1130 (or shortly afterwards) at Toledo by Raymund, archbishop of that city. Circulating widely throughout western Europe, these Latin translations supplied the learned with a third- or fourth-hand knowledge of Greek philosophy. When Albertus Magnus, St Thomas Aquinas, or any other early light of the schools refers to Aristotle, it must be borne in mind that he often had no more exact acquaintance with the text which he expounds or confutes than could be gathered from an indirect Latin version of an Arabic rendering of a Syriac translation of a Greek original. This accounts for many misunderstandings and errors which would otherwise be incomprehensible. Among the earliest European translators who made their way to Toledo were Adelard of Bath, who rendered an Arabic version of Euclid into Latin; the Englishman known as Robert de Retines, afterwards archdeacon of Pamplona, the first translator of the Koran, which he did into Latin in 1141–1143 by order of Peter the Venerable; and Gerard of Cremona, who, towards the end of the 12th century, was responsible for over seventy translations from the Arabic, including Ptolemy's *Almagest* and many of Aristotle's treatises, as well as works by Galen, Hippocrates and Avicenna. Early in the 13th century Michael Scot, who had begun his Arabic studies at Palermo, visited Toledo and (perhaps with the help of the Jew Andreas, if we are to believe the statement of Hermann the German, repeated by Roger Bacon) translated into Latin various works of Aristotle, Avicenna, and—more especially—Averroes. These Latin translations by Michael Scot introduced Averroes to the notice of Western scholars, and the fact that they were used at the universities of Paris and Bologna gave the first impetus to the vogue of Averroistic doctrine which lasted from the time of St Thomas Aquinas to the rise of Martin Luther. At Toledo, between 1240 and 1256, Hermann the German translated into Latin the commentaries of Averroes on Aristotle's *Ethics*, together with abridgments of the *Poetic* and the *Rhetoric* made respectively by Averroes and Alfarabi. But, at the very period of Hermann the German's residence at Toledo, a more satisfactory method of translation was begun. Within half a century of the conquest of Constantinople in 1204 a visit to Spain was no longer indispensable for a would-be translator of Greek philosophical treatises. The original texts slowly became more available, and a Latin translation of Aristotle's *Ethics* seems to have been made from the Greek by order of Robert Grosseteste, bishop of Lincoln, between 1240–1244. Towards the end of the century the indefatigable William of Moerbeke (near Ghent)—mentioned as 'William the Fleming' by Roger Bacon—produced, amongst numerous other Latin renderings from the Greek, versions of Aristotle's *Rhetoric* and *Politics* which have commended themselves to more exact scholars of the modern German type. The Latin renderings from the Arabic were current till a much later date; but it was henceforth accepted, at least in principle, that translations of the Greek classics should be made direct from the original text.

Meanwhile the work of translating foreign productions into the local vernacular had been begun in the north and west of Europe. Towards the end of the 9th century an illustrious English translator appeared in the person of King Alfred, who rendered St Gregory the Great's *Cura pastoralis* into West Saxon 'sometimes word for word, sometimes sense for sense.' Alfred is also regarded, though with less certainty, as the translator of Bede's *Historia ecclesiastica* and the *Historia adversus paganos* of Orosius. The version of St Gregory's treatise is the most literal of the three; omissions are frequent in the renderings of Bede and Orosius, and in all the diction is disfigured by latinisms. A larger conception of a translator's function is noticeable in Alfred's version of Boetius's *De consolatione philosophiae*, a famous Neoplatonic treatise which was the delight of the middle ages, and was translated later into German by Notker Labeo, into French by Jean de Meung, and twice again into English by Chaucer and by Queen Elizabeth respectively. In translating Boetius, Alfred deals more freely with his author, interpolates passages not to be found in the extant texts of the original, and yet succeeds in giving an adequate interpretation which is also an excellent specimen of English prose. If the alliterative verses found in one manuscript of Alfred's translation are accepted as his work, it is clear that he had no poetic faculty; but he has the credit of opening up a new path, of bringing England into contact with European thought, and of stimulating such writers as Werferth, bishop of Worcester—the translator of St Gregory's *Dialogues*—to proceed on the same line. Some forty years earlier John Scotus (Erigena) had won celebrity as a translator by his Latin renderings of works ascribed to the mysterious 5th century Neoplatonist who passes under the name of Dionysius the Areopagite. Towards the close of Alfred's reign some countrymen of Erigena bettered his example by producing Irish versions of Hippocrates and Galen at St Gallen. St Gallen became a centre of translation, and there, at the beginning of the 11th century, Notker Labeo presided over a committee of interpreters who issued German renderings of certain treatises by Aristotle, Terence's *Andria* and Virgil's *Eclogues*. Far greater literary importance attaches to *Syntipas*, the title given by Michael Andreopulos to a collection of ancient Oriental tales which he translated from an intermediate Syriac version into Greek at the request of the Armenian duke of Melitene about the end of the 11th century. These stories were retranslated into French verse and (by Jean de Haute-Seille) into Latin during the course of the 12th century under the respective titles of the *Sept sages de Rome* and *Dolopathos*; they were utilized in the *Cento novelle antiche*, in the *Libro dei sette savj*, and in the *Decamerone*, and were finally absorbed by every literature in Europe. Immense popularity was won by the *Liber gestorum Barlaam et Josaphat*, a Latin translation made in the 11th or 12th century from the Greek, and recast in many European languages during the 13th century. The book is in fact a legendary life of Buddha adapted to the purposes of Christianity by a monk; but it was accepted as an historical record, the undiscerning credulity of the faithful informally canonized Barlaam and Josaphat, and ultimately compelled the Latin Church to include these two fictitious beings as saints in the *Martyrologium romanum*. This is perhaps the most curious result attained by any translation. The interest in Eastern apologues and moralizing stories, which was early shown in Marie de France's translation of Aesopic fables, was further demonstrated by the Castilian translations of *Kalilah and*

Dimnah and *Sindibad* made about the middle of the 13th century, by (or at the command of) Alphonso the Learned and his brother the Infante Fadrique respectively.

The enthusiasm for these Oriental stories was communicated to the rest of Europe by John of Capua's *Directorium humanae vitae* (1270), a Latin translation of *Kalilah and Dimnah*; but, in the meanwhile, as the younger European literatures grew in power and variety, the field of translation necessarily widened to such an extent that detailed description becomes impossible. Geoffrey of Monmouth's *Historia regum Britanniae*, which purports to be a free version of an unnamed Breton book, is the source of the Arthurian legends which reappeared transformed in elaborate French versions, and were transmitted to the rest of Europe during the 12th and 13th centuries. During this period of French literary supremacy instances of bilingual faculty are not wanting in the form of translations: shortly after the middle of the 13th century Brunetto Latini translated passages of Cicero into Italian, and selections from Sallust into French. A hundred years later there are unmistakable indications that the middle ages are departing, that the French suzerainty over literature is at an end, and that the advent of the New Humanism is an accomplished fact. The early Renaissance had already dawned in Italy: a renewed interest in the Latin classics (Greek was not yet generally cultivated by scholars) proved that there was a revival of learning in France. Livy was done into French by Bersuire, Seneca by Bauchant, Boccaccio by Laureat de Premier Fait, and a celebrated translator appeared in the person of Nicolas Oresme, who, however, rendered Aristotle from a Latin version. In England Chaucer executed translations of Boetius and part of the *Roman de la rose*, and succeeded equally in interpreting the philosophic treatise and the allegorical poem. A still further advance is discernible in the book of travels ascribed to Sir John Mandeville: this work, which seems to have been originally written in French, is rendered into English with an exceptional felicity which has won for the translator the loose-fitting but not altogether inappropriate title of 'the father of English prose.' The English version of Mandeville is assigned to the beginning of the 15th century. About 1470 Sir Thomas Malory produced from French originals his *Morte d'Arthur*, a pastiche of different texts translated with a consummate art which amounts to originality. Malory's inspired version, together with the numerous renderings from the French issued (and often made personally) by Caxton, stimulated the public taste for romantic narrative, raised the standard of execution, and invested the translator with a new air of dignity and importance.

Yet the 15th century has a fair claim to be regarded as the golden age of translation. The Gothic version of the Bible, made by Ulfilas during the 4th century almost simultaneously with St Jerome's Vulgate, is invaluable as the sole literary monument of a vanished language; the 14th century English version by Wycliffe and the 15th century English versions which bear the names of Tyndale and Coverdale are interesting in themselves, and are also interesting as having contributed to the actual Authorized

Version of 1611. But they are incomparably less important than Luther's German translation of the Bible (1522–1534) which, apart from its significance as indicating the complete victory of the liberal middle class and the irremediable downfall of the feudal and ecclesiastical autocracy, supplanted minor dialects and fixed the norm of literary expression in German-speaking countries. Luther, it has been truly said, endowed Germany with a uniform literary language, a possession which she had lost for nearly three hundred years. The effect of profane literature was speedily visible in Fischart's translations of Rabelais's *Pantagruéline* (1572) and the first book of *Gargantua* (1575). But before this date France had produced a prince of translators in Jacques Amyot, bishop of Auxerre. In 1548 Nicolas de Herberay had published a French translation of *Amadis de Gaule* which enchanted the polite world at the court of Henry II., had its day, and is forgotten. But Amyot's translation of Plutarch (1559) remains an acknowledged master-piece, surviving all changes of taste and all variations of the canon of translation. Montaigne writes: 'Je donne la palme avecque raison, ce me semble, à Jacques Amyot, sur tous nos escripvains François.' If 'escripvain' be understood to mean 'translator,' this judgment is beyond appeal.

Lord Berners will not bear comparison with Amyot in achievement or influence; but, though less completely equipped and less uniformly happy in his choice of texts (for Amyot translated the *Aethiopian History* and *Daphnis and Chloe* as well as Plutarch), Lord Berners holds a distinguished place in the ranks of English translators. His renderings of Fernández de San Pedro's *Cárcel de amor* and of Guevara's *Libro aureo* are now read solely by specialists engaged in tracing English euphuism to its remoter sources, and some of his other translations—the *Boke of Duke Huon of Burdeux* and *Arthur of Little Britain*—are too poor in substance to be interesting nowadays. But Lord Berners is justly remembered by his notable translation of Froissart (1523–1525). Froissart offers fewer opportunities than Guevara for the display of that 'fecundious art of rhetoric' in which the English translator thought himself deficient, and, with this temptation removed, Lord Berners is seen at his best. In his version of Froissart, apart from endless confusion of proper names, he makes few mistakes of any real importance, and, if he scarcely equals his original in *brio*, he is almost invariably adequate in reproducing the French blend of simplicity with stateliness. Such translations as Phaer's *Virgil* (1557) and Golding's *Ovid* (1561) have not the historical importance of William Painter's *Palace of Pleasure*, a miscellaneous collection of stories rendered from the Italian, nor of Jasper Heywood's version of Seneca (1581) whose plays had exercised immense influence upon the methods of Garnier and Montchrétien in France. Though Kyd translated Garnier's *Cornélie*, the Senecan system was destined to defeat in England, and Heywood's translation did not even postpone the catastrophe. On the other hand Marlowe found the subject of his *Tamburlaine* in Painter's collection, and thus began the systematic exploitation of the *Palace of Pleasure* which was continued by his successors on the stage. A translator of the rarest excellence was forthcoming in Sir Thomas North, who rendered Guevara (1557) from the French (revising his second edition from the Spanish), and *The Morall Philosophie of Doni*—'a worke first compiled in the Indian tongue'—from the Italian (1570). But, good as they are, both these versions are overshadowed by the famous translation of Plutarch which North published in 1579. He may have referred occasionally to the Greek, or perhaps to some intermediate Latin rendering; but the basis of his work is Amyot, and his English is not inferior to the French in sonority and cadence of phrase. This retranslation of a translation is a masterpiece of which fragments are incorporated with scarcely any change in *Coriolanus*, *Julius Caesar* and *Antony and Cleopatra*; and touches from North have been noted also in the *Midsummer Night's Dream* and in *Timon of Athens*. Amyot greatly influenced the development of French prose, and his translation was the source of Racine's *Mithridate*; but, if we reflect that Shakespeare not only took some of his subjects from the English Plutarch and found nothing to amend in the diction of many passages, North's triumph may be reckoned as even more signal than Amyot's. Very little below North's translation of Plutarch comes John Florio's translation of Montaigne (1603), a fantastically ingenious performance which contributed a celebrated passage to *The Tempest* and introduced the practice of the essay into England. It is impossible to cope with the activity of English translators during the last half of the 16th century and the first half of the 17th. To this period belongs Chapman's impressive and resounding translation (1598–1616) of Homer, which was to enrapture Keats two hundred years later. Adlington's version of Apuleius, Underdown's renderings of Heliodorus and Ovid, the translations of Livy, Pliny, Suetonius and Xenophon issued in quick succession by Philemon Holland are vivid and often extravagantly picturesque in their conveyance of classic authors into Elizabethan prose. With them must be named the translator of Tacitus (1591), Sir Henry Savile, who served later on the committee which prepared the Authorized Version of the Bible, and must therefore be counted amongst those who have exercised a permanent influence on English prose style. Thomas Shelton produced the earliest translation (1612) of *Don Quixote*, a version which, in spite of its inaccuracies and freakishness, preserves much of the tone and atmosphere of the original. Mabbe's translation (1622) of *Guzmán de Alfarache* was lauded by Ben Jonson, and widely read during the 17th century, and his version of the *Celestina* deserved a success which it failed to obtain. It compares most favourably with a version of Tasso (1600) by Edward Fairfax, who has been persistently overpraised. But the Puritanical instinct of the English people, powerful even when not in the ascendant, was an insuperable obstacle to the acclimatization of Spanish literature in England. The *Leviathan* has obscured Hobbes's fame as a translator, but he is known to scholars by his sound but crabbed rendering of Thucydides (1629) and by a wholly unnecessary version of Homer which he published at the very end of his career (1674). Sir Roger L'Estrange is responsible for translations of Seneca, Cicero and Josephus, which are usually lively enough to be readable and unfaithful enough to be misleading; the most popular of his renderings is a translation of Quevedo's *Sueños* (made through the French) which owes most of its vogue during the Restoration rather to its reckless indecency than to its intrinsic merit. Dryden's free translations of Juvenal (1693) and Virgil (1697) treat the original authors with a cavalier freedom, but at least they preserve the meaning, if not the conciseness and point, of the Latin.

Among the multitudinous English translations of the 18th century it is only necessary to mention Pope's versions of the *Iliad* (1715–1720) and the *Odyssey* (1725–1726) and Cowper's rendering of Homer, issued in 1791. These neat translations necessarily fail to convey any impression of Homer's epical grandeur, and they set a mischievous fashion of artificial 'elegance' which has been too often adopted by their successors; but both Pope and Cowper conform faithfully to the mistaken canon of their age, and both have fugitive moments of felicity. A posthumous translation of *Don Quixote* bearing the name of Charles Jarvis appeared in 1742, has been reprinted times innumerable ever since, and has helped to make Cervantes's masterpiece known to generations of English-speaking people. Defective in point of exact scholarship, it has the merit of agreeable perspicuity, and there seems no reason to believe the remark, ascribed by Warburton to Pope, that Jarvis 'translated *Don Quixote* without knowing Spanish': the available evidence is strongly against this malicious theory. The most remarkable translations of the 18th century, however, appeared in Germany: these are the versions of the *Odyssey* (1781) and *Iliad* (1793) by Voss, and A. W. von Schlegel's rendering of Shakespeare (1797–1810), which gave a powerful impulse to the romantic movement on the Continent.

Byron's version of a Spanish ballad and Shelley's renderings of Calderón are interesting exhibitions of original genius voluntarily accepting a subordinate role. More importance attaches to Carlyle's translation of *Wilhelm Meister* (1824), a faithful rendering free from the intolerable mannerisms and tricks which the translator developed subsequently in his original writings. William Taylor had long before translated Bürger's *Lenore*, Lessing's *Nathan* and Goethe's *Iphigenia*; but such interest as the English nation has been induced to take in German literature dates from the appearance of Carlyle's translation. If he did nothing more, he compelled recognition of the fact that Germany had at last produced an original genius of the highest class. Calderón found accomplished translators in Denis Florence MacCarthy (1848–1873) and in Edward FitzGerald (1853), who also attempted to render Sophocles into English; but these are on a much lower plane than the translation of the *Rubaiyát* (1859) of Omar Khayyam, in which, by a miracle of intrepid dexterity, a half-forgotten Persian poet is transfigured into a pessimistic English genius of the 19th century. Versions of Dante by Longfellow (whose translations of poems by minor authors are often admirable), of Latin or Greek classics by Conington, Munro, Jowett and Jebb, maintain the best traditions of the best translators. William Morris was less happy in his poetical versions of *Virgil* (1875) and the *Odyssey* (1887) than in his prose translations of *The Story of Grettir the Strong* (1869) and *The Volsunga Saga* (1870)—both made in collaboration with Magnússon—and in his rendering of *Beowulf* (1895). In his *Lays of France* (1872) Arthur O'Shaughnessy skirts the borders of translation without quite entering into the field; he elaborates, paraphrases and embroiders rather than translates the *lais* of Marie de France.

Most versions of modern foreign writers are mere hackwork carelessly executed by incompetent hands, and this is even more true of England than of France and Germany. But, with the development of literature in countries whose languages are unfamiliar, the function of the translator increases in importance, and in some few cases he has risen to his opportunity. Through translations the works of the great Russian novelists have become known to the rest of Europe, and through translations of Ibsen the dramatic methods of the modern stage have undergone a revolution.

PART II
THE TWENTIETH CENTURY

CHAPTER 4

FROM POUND TO NABOKOV

4.1 INTRODUCTION

Ezra Pound is one of the most important figures in the history of translation into English and a key figure for the development of translation in the twentieth-century (see Ronnie Apter's collage in Sect. 4.2, below). Associated with his friend and fellow-deracinated American T. S. Eliot as a founding figure of Modernism, Pound was obsessed with the tradition he was trying, in a sense, to liberate himself from or at least make work for him. His translations (ranging from Chinese to Provençal) constitute a significant body of work, informing much of his other writing (for instance, his own poems and his influential essays, including his important anthology (with Marcella Spann) *Confucius to Cummings*, 1958). While the amount of material translated by Pound is not so vast, it has been extraordinarily influential, accompanied by his polemicizing essays and promoted by the forceful and charismatic poet himself. It has even been suggested that one may speak of poetry translation in the modern period as either pre- or post-Poundian, although some chronologically post-Poundians, e.g. Michael Hamburger, have objected to this.

Pound the Modernist was, of course, also a Victorian and many of his translations carry the imprint of that period with, for instance, their recourse to archaicizing (not unreminiscent of Browning or even Morris). At the same time, with his incomparably well-tuned ear, Pound was able frequently to approximate the very sound structure of his source texts (see in particular his version from the Anglo-Saxon of 'The Seafarer'). An apparent paradox is perhaps explicable in terms of Pound's (American?) pragmatism. He attempted to resolve some of the problems (not to say imponderabilities) of poetic translation by, in a sense, constructing from elements, borrowed or plundered from world literature, a language which he used in his translation work and also in his original poetry (somewhat as Brodsky (see Sect. 5.9 below), in a more limited way created his own English to accommodate the structures and the very sound of Russian verse).

Nevertheless, while Pound had followers, they could hardly be regarded as mainstream; the English tradition, as defined by Dryden, was disturbed but not disrupted by this 'foreignizing' reinforcement of what had preceded it and had reached England via German Romanticism, in particular Schleiermacher (see above, Sect. 3.3, and Sect. 3.1: Introduction). Pound's was one among a number of competing influences, all of which however examined their provenance critically or perhaps with less confidence than earlier translators, like Pope. That was unless the job in hand was so pressing and so extensive that there was little time for theorizing! Such was the case of Constance Garnett (see Sect. 4.3, below), her mission being to bring into readable English and in sufficient bulk the extraordinary achievements of nineteenth- and early twentieth-century Russian prose.

This period is marked by the work of a number of influential writers and thinkers, who not only translated but wrote about translation in the most challenging manner, their work forming the basis for much of the discussion that follows. Walter Benjamin (see Sect. 4.4, below for a discussion of his landmark essay 'The Task of the Translator') laid the foundations for subsequent discourse on the place, the actual objectives of translation, from both personal and socio-historical points of view. Foreignizing has now been problematized to the point where it can still inform translation; George Steiner, for instance, builds on Benjamin's mystical notion of translation as an *Ursprache*.

One consequence, of course, is the notion of translation as embodying a distinct language, a composite or synthesis of source and target languages. (That may be somewhat misleading, since the language of the translation is, for practical purposes, closer to the target—even if the latter has been rendered more permeable—than to the source.) Similarly universalizing intellectual currents are discernible not only in the writings of George Steiner, but also in the writings and practice of Martin Buber and Franz Rosenzweig in their German Bible translation and more recently Everett Fox's in his translation of the Hebrew Pentateuch into English. The prevalence of these preoccupations is reflected in this chapter which draws on writings more internationally than earlier ones, especially on work being done by American-based scholars and writers. Agendas are somewhat more clearly definable, perhaps because we are approaching the present day and so are more familiar with the context. Thus the pragmatic Eugene Nida, a major force in the translation of the Christian Scriptures, is clearly guided by proselytizing aims. Clear objectives, however, need not be religious ones. Robert Lowell is similarly concerned with the readerly reader, rather than the scholar or even scholarly reader! Vladimir Nabokov (see Sect. 4.13, below), a major novelist in Russian and English as well as translator from Russian into English, was in effect a radical foreignizer, although himself rooted in a source language, Russian. His notion of the capabilities of translation is limited—even so, he goes too far evidently for many English readers. His great test case, of course, is Pushkin's novel-in-verse, *Eugene Onegin*.

By restricting the scope of direct translation, Nabokov renders it, as he thought, more possible if, in a sense, less ambitious, although it must be added that his own work (as suggested by Jenefer Coates in Sect. 4.13) is permeated by his vast readings in other literary traditions, this too constituting a kind of translation. Nabokov's translations, his version of disciplined literalism also create a new language. He combines scholarship and literalism, his comprehensive, sometimes fulsome, notes being integral to the text, the translation. Stanley Burnshaw, the American poet and critic, in his important anthology *The Poem Itself*, similarly supplies 'literal' translations, accompanied by basic syntactical and contextual notes, providing the committed reader with materials, as it were, towards the construction of a simulacrum of the original.

While the end result appears to be the elaboration of a specialized language of translation, only the more devoted or committed reader can be expected to follow a Nabokov, for whom however there was no alternative. Ezra Pound, on the other hand, strives to create a language of poetry that convincingly establishes its own terms, allowing translations to convey something like the totality of the poetic experience in the source language. Both a Pound and a Nabokov, however, are crucially aware of the need to go beyond plain naturalizing ('domesticating'), if the 'other' is to be introduced into the lifestream of the native literary culture.

4.2 Ezra Pound

Ronnie Apter
(Central Michigan University)

Ezra Pound (1885–1972) declared, 'A great age of literature is perhaps always a great age of translations; or follows it' ('Notes on Elizabethan Classicists' p. 232). He was right. And, aided by his own gifts as a poet, he helped make the latter half of the twentieth century a period of great translation. When he began translating and writing about translation in the 1910s, the translation of older poetry into English was dominated by the use of Wardour Street, a pseudo-archaic *mélange* of modern English and archaisms from any of five centuries, which Rossetti, Swinburne, and lesser lights had made popular. Words like 'hath' and 'methinks' were meant to indicate the age of the source text. In the hands of good poets like Dante Gabriel Rossetti and Charles Algernon Swinburne, the method produced glamorously romantic translations. Those less adept produced translations which made the great poets of the past sound all alike and equally irrelevant to the present. Pound is remembered as the translator and theorist who put paid to that tradition. His letters and essays usually urged translation into fully modern English and advocated free verse as an English equivalent to quantitative or syllabic verse (see 'Cavalcanti'). His enormously influential translations from Chinese in *Cathay*, such as 'South Folk in Cold Country' (see below) taught translators how to use a neutral modern, semi-formal diction to convey a simultaneous sense of antiquity and timelessness. His correspondence with W. H. D. Rouse (see below), a prose translator of the *Odyssey*, again and again urges Rouse to find the modern phrase, the living idiom.

Yet, strangely enough, Pound himself rarely translated older poetry without incorporating some form of archaizing. One of his great translations, 'The Seafarer' (see below), uses Wardour Street with the best of them. At the same time, it uses a highly original form of free verse to express the movement of the Anglo-Saxon: a roughly four-stress line, low in unstressed syllables, with much alliteration. The power and flexibility of this form has influenced most subsequent translation of Old English. In still other translations, Pound experimented with using a specific earlier period of English (see the translations at the end of 'Cavalcanti'), or with mixing different periods on purpose, each locution being intended to call to mind the *Weltanschauung* of its particular time, in an attempt to convey ideas not available to modern English (see 'How to Read,' section on Logopoeia).

Against the anti-translation attitude still all too prevalent ('Poetry is what is lost in translation'), Pound advocated respect for the English tradition of translation, calling attention particularly to the beauties of Elizabethan translation: Golding's *Metamorphoses*, Gavin Douglas's *Aeneid*, and Marlowe's *Eclogues* from Ovid (see 'Translators of Greek'). He pointed out that Elizabethans saw earlier literature, not as a set of words to be faithfully reproduced, but as a set of ideas to be absorbed and refashioned. He set about following their lead himself to outraged howls about his lack of literality. Canto 1, for instance, translates not the *Odyssey*, but a 1538 translation of it into Latin by Andreas Divus Justinopolitanus (see below). Moreover, Pound's verse form for the translation is the roughly four-stress, alliterative free verse he had earlier invented for his translation of 'The Seafarer'. That translation chain shades into his own poem. Few translators or critics accept Pound's Elizabethan approach, yet many cannot but admire the verve of his translations, and accept that somehow, for all his errors and 'errors', he has come closer to the spirit of the originals than many a careful classicist.

For Pound, translation is a form of criticism (see 'Date Line'), its purpose for readers to point out and make accessible works of importance; its purpose for writers to help them, in their struggle to match the voice of another, to find their own.

From 'Notes on Elizabethan Classicists', in *Literary Essays*, ed. and introd. T. S. Eliot (New York: New Directions, 1968), 227–48 (First published as 'Elizabethan Classicists', *The Egoist*, 4. 8–10 (1917) and 5. 1 (1918))

A great age of literature is perhaps always a great age of translations; or follows it. The Victorians in lesser degree had FitzGerald, and Swinburne's Villon, and Rossetti. One is at first a little surprised at the importance which historians of Spanish poetry give to Boscan, but our histories give our own translators too little. And worse, we have long since fallen under the blight of the Miltonic or noise tradition, to a stilted dialect in translating the classics, a dialect which imitates the idiom of the ancients rather than seeking their meaning, a state of mind which aims at teaching the boy his Latin or Greek or whatever it may be, but has long since ceased to care for the beauty of the original; or which perhaps thinks 'appreciation' obligatory, and the meaning and content mere accessories. (232)

Or is a fine poet ever translated until another his equal invents a new style in a later language? Can we, for our part, know our Ovid until we find him in Golding? Is there one of us so good at his Latin, and so ready in imagination that Golding will not throw upon his mind shades and glamours inherent in the original text which had for all that escaped him? Is any foreign speech ever our own, ever so full of beauty as our *lingua materna* (whatever *lingua materna* that may be)? Or is not a new beauty created, an old beauty doubled when the overchange is well done? (235)

From 'Cavalcanti', in *Literary Essays*, 149–200 (first published in *Make It New* (1934))

As to the use of canzoni in English, whether for composition or in translation: it is not that there aren't rhymes in English; or enough rhymes or even enough two-syllable rhymes, but that the English two-syllable rhymes are of the wrong timbre and weight. They have extra consonants at the end, as in *flowing* and *going*; or they go squashy; or they fluff up as in *snowy* and *goeth*. They are not *rime agute*; they do not offer readily the qualities and contrasts that Dante has discussed so ably in *De Eloquio*.

Even so, it is not that one 'cannot' use them but that they demand at times, sacrifice of values that had not come into being and were therefore not missed in Limoges, A.D. 1200. Against which we have our concealed rhymes and our semi-submerged alliteration. (*En passant*, the alliteration in Guido's canzone is almost as marked as the rhyming though it enters as free component.)

It is not that one language cannot be made to do what another has done, but that it is not always expeditious to approach the same goal by the same alley. I do not think rhyme-aesthetic, *any* rhyme-aesthetic, can ever do as much damage to English verse as that done by latinization, in Milton's time and before. The rhyme pattern is, after all, a matter of chiselling, and a question of the *lima amorosa*, whereas latinization is a matter or compost, and in the very substance of the speech. By latinization I mean here the attempt to use an uninflected language as if it were an inflected one, i.e. as if each word had a little label or postscript telling the reader at once what part it takes in the sentence, and specifying its several relations. Not only does such usage—with remnants of Latin order—ruin the word order in English, but it shows a fundamental mis-comprehension of the organism of the language, and fundamental stupidity of this kind is bound to spread its effects through the whole fibre of a man's writing.

Hendecasyllables

Another prevalent error is that of dealing with Italian hendecasyllables as if they were English 'iambic pentameter'. One is told in college that Italian verse is not accentual but syllabic but I can't remember anyone's having ever presented the Anglo-American reader with a lucid discrimination between the two systems of measurement. (168–9)

As to the atrocities of my translation [of Guido's canzone 'Donna mi prega'], all that can be said in excuse is that they are, I hope, for the most part intentional, and committed with the aim of driving the reader's perception further into the original than it would without them have penetrated. The melodic structure is properly indicated—and for the first time—by my disposition of the Italian text, but even that firm indication of the rhyme and the articulation of the strophe does not stress *all* the properties of Guido's triumph in sheer musicality. [. . .]

I have not given an English 'equivalent' for the *Donna mi Prega*; at the utmost I have provided the reader, unfamiliar with old Italian, an instrument that may assist him in gauging *some* of the qualities of the original.

All this is not so unconnected with our own time as it might seem. Those writers to whom *vers libre* was a mere 'runnin' dahn th' road', videlicet escape, and who were impelled thereto by no inner need of, or curiosity concerning, the quantitative element in metric, having come to the end of that lurch, lurch back not into experiment with the canzone or any other unexplored form, but into the stock and trade sonnet. (pp. 172–3)

When I 'translated' Guido eighteen years ago [1912] I did *not* see Guido at all [. . .].

My perception was not obfuscated by Guido's Italian, difficult as it then was for me to read. I was obfuscated by the Victorian language.

[. . .] I began by meaning merely to give prose translation so that the reader ignorant of Italian could see what the melodic original meant. It is, however, an illusion to suppose that more than one person in every 300,000 has the patience or the intelligence to read a foreign tongue for its sound, or even to read what are known to be the masterworks of foreign melody, in order to learn the qualities of that melody, or to see where one's own falls short.

What obfuscated me was not the Italian but the crust of dead English, the sediment present in my own available vocabulary—which I, let us hope, got rid of a few years later. You can't go round this sort of thing. It takes six or eight years to get educated in one's art, and another ten to get rid of that education.

Neither can anyone learn English, one can only learn a series of Englishes. Rossetti made his own language. I hadn't in 1910 made a language, I don't mean a language to use, but even a language to think in. [. . .]

Where both Rossetti and I went off the rails was in taking an English sonnet as the equivalent for a sonnet in Italian. (pp. 193–4)

[Having noted the cultural influence of Italy on Elizabethan England, Pound asks:] What happens when you idly attempt to translate early Italian into English, unclogged by the Victorian era, freed from sonnet obsession, but trying merely to sing and to leave out the dull bits in the Italian, or the bits you don't understand?

I offer you a poem that 'don't matter' ['Madonna la vostra belta enfolio']. [. . .] It is not very attractive: until one starts playing with the simplest English equivalent.

> 'Lady thy beauty doth so mad mine eyes,
> Driving my heart to strife wherein he dies.'

[. . .]

The next line is rather a cliché; the line after more or less lacking in interest. We pull up on:

'Whereby thou seest how fair thy beauty is
To compass doom'.

That would be very nice, but it is hardly translation. [. . .]

My two lines take the opening and two and a half of the Italian, English more concise; and the octave gets too light for the sestet. Lighten the sestet.

'So unto Pity must I cry
Not for safety, but to die.
Cruel Death is now mine ease
If that he thine envoy is.'

We are preserving one value of early Italian work, the cantabile; and we are losing another, that is, the specific weight. (pp. 195–6)

But by taking these Italian sonnets, which are not metrically the equivalent of the English sonnet, by sacrificing, or losing, or simply not feeling and understanding their cogency, their sobriety, and by seeking simply that far from quickly or so-easily-as-it-looks attainable thing, the perfect melody, careless of exactitude of idea, or careless as to which profound and fundamental idea you, at that moment, utter, perhaps in precise enough phrases, by cutting away the apparently non-functioning phrases (whose appearance deceives) you find yourself in the English *seicento* song-books.

Death has become melodious; sorrow is as serious as the nightingale's, tombstones are shelves for the reception of rose-leaves. And there is, quite often, a Mozartian perfection of melody, a wisdom, almost perhaps an ultimate wisdom, deplorably lacking in guts. (p. 197) As second exercise, we may try the sonnet by Guido Orlando ['Onde si move e donde nasce Amore'] which is supposed to have invited Cavalcanti's *Donna mi Prega*.

'Say what is Love, whence doth he start
Through what be his courses bent
Memory, substance, accident
A chance of eye or will of heart

Whence he state or madness leadeth
Burns he with consuming pain
Tell me, friend, on what he feedeth
How, where, and o'er whom doth he reign

Say what is Love, hath he a face
True form or vain similitude
Is the Love life, or is he death

Thou shouldst know for rumour saith:
Servant should know his master's mood —
Oft art thou ta'en in his dwelling-place.'

[...] there is no deception, I have invented nothing, I have given a *verbal* weight about equal to that of the original, and arrived at this equality by dropping a couple of syllables per line. [...]

→ growth by reduction

There is no question of giving Guido in an English contemporary to himself, the ultimate Britons were at that date unbreeched, painted in woad, and grunting in an idiom far more difficult for us to master than the Langue d'Oc of the Plantagenets or the Lingua di Si.

If, however, we reach back to pre-Elizabethan English, of a period when the writers were still intent on clarity and explicitness, still preferring them to magniloquence and the thundering phrase, our trial [translation of 'Chi è questa che vien, ch' ogni uom la mira', by Guido Cavalcanti], or mine at least, results in:

> 'Who is she that comes, makyng turn every man's eye
> And makyng the air to tremble with a bright clearenesse
> That leadeth with her Love, in such nearness
> No man may proffer of speech more than a sigh?
>
> Ah God, what she is like when her owne eye turneth, is
> Fit for Amor to speake, for I cannot at all;
> Such is her modesty, I would call
> Every woman else but an useless uneasiness.
>
> No one could ever tell all of her pleasauntness
> In that every high noble vertu leaneth to herward,
> So Beauty sheweth her forth as her Godhede;
>
> Never before so high was our mind led,
> Nor have we so much of heal as will afford
> That our mind may take her immediate in its embrace.'

The objections to such a method are: the doubt as to whether one has the right to take a serious poem and turn it into a mere exercise in quaintness; the 'misrepresentation' not of the poem's antiquity, but of the proportionate feel of that antiquity, by which I mean that Guido's thirteenth-century language is to twentieth-century Italian sense much less archaic than any fourteenth-, fifteenth-, or early sixteenth-century English is for us. [...] And as [the fervour of the original] simply does not occur in English poetry in those centuries there is no ready-made verbal pigment for its objectification.

In the long run the translator is in all probability impotent to do *all* of the work for the linguistically lazy reader. He can show where the treasure lies, he can guide the reader in choice of what tongue is to be studied. [...]

This refers to 'interpretative translation'. The 'other sort', I mean in cases where the 'translator' is definitely making a new poem, falls simply in the domain of original writing, or if it does not it must be censured according to equal standards, and praised with some sort of just deduction, assessable only in the particular case. (198–200)

'South-Folk in Cold Country,' from *Cathay* (1915), included in *Personae: The Collected Shorter Poems of Ezra Pound*, introd. Hugh Kenner (London and Boston: Faber and Faber, 1971), 139; also in *Translations* (1970), 200, and *Poems and Translations* (2003), 259

> The Dai horse neighs against the bleak wind of Etsu,
> The birds of Etsu have no love for En, in the north,
> Emotion is born out of habit.
> Yesterday we went out of the Wild-Goose gate,
> To-day from the Dragon-Pen.[1]
> Surprised. Desert turmoil. Sea sun.
> Flying snow bewilders the barbarian heaven.
>
> Lice swarm like ants over our accoutrements.
> Mind and spirit drive on the feathery banners.
> Hard fight gets no reward.
> Loyalty is hard to explain.
> Who will be sorry for General Rishogu,
>   the swift moving,
> Whose white head is lost for this province?
>
>   (*Li T'ai Po*)

NOTE

1. *i.e.*, we have been warring from one end of the empire to the other, now east, now west, on each border.

Letters to W. H. D. Rouse, from *The Letters of Ezra Pound 1907–1941*, pref. Mark Van Doren, ed. D. D. Paige (New York: Harcourt, Brace, and World, 1950)

Letter 290, Rapallo, February 1935

I don't see that one translates by leaving in unnecessary words; that is, words not necessary to the meaning of the whole passage, any whole passage. An author uses a certain number of blank words for the timing, the movement, etc., to make his work sound like natural speech. I believe one shd. check up all that verbiage as say 4% blanks, to be used where and when wanted in the translation, but perhaps never, or at any rate not usually where the original author has used them. [. . .]

When I suggest your doing a translation with all the meaning, I didn't mean merely to put back words, or translations for words. (269)

Letter 292, Rapallo, 18 March 1935

NO NO! Doc: Here you are backslidin' on all your highly respectable principles and slinging in licherary langwidg and puttin' yer sentences all out of whack.

'Odysseus' boy jumped out of bed as rednailed etc. appeared thru the dawn mist,' or whatever; and if he reached for his six-shooter before puttin' on his boots, that is a point to be made, as highly illustrative of the era. A guards officer wdn't. But I reckon in Idaho in the 80's Blue Dick or Curly might have. And for his feet, they ought to be well-kept, or elegant or patrician otherwise they slide into book-talk.

Tain't what a man sez, but wot he means that the traducer has got to bring over. The implication of the word.

As fer them feet, the blighter had been usin cold cream, the bloomin' Bloomsbury knut!! [. . .]

I think the openings of the books need especial care. This first page of book two is *bad*. I mean it is just translation of words, without your imagining the scene and event enough, and without attending to the English idiom. [. . .]

People have been trying to translate this [book] for 400 years. Can't be done easy. Very definite sense: Telemachus growing up and asserting himself. It is the vividness and rapidity of narration, three little scenes, all alive. That is writing. I just don't think you've yet got it. At any rate I'd like to see a 'rewrite' as if you didn't know the words of the original and were telling what happened.

Excuse this firmness, but hang it, anything else wd. be waste of both our time. (pp. 271–2)

Letter 294, Rapallo, 17 April 1935

I don't know that I have been clear enough re recurrable epithets—either to be simple and natural so that repeat don't worry one, or else strange and part of definite intended stylization.

Glaux, owl, totem or symbolic bird (gods connected with the divine animals, as stupid bitch Hera has her bull eyes), glare-eyed, owl-eyed Athena.

The Apollo at Villa Giulia gives tip to Mediterranean gods; startling, sudden, none of that washy late stuff done by sculpting slave models, nor afternoon-tea Xtian piety. Gods tricky as nature.

'Wine dark' I shd. accept. It is outside northern belief, but tells something about Mediterranean water that has to be seen.

Blond Menelaus: small dark Pelasgians or Mediterraneans still believe in cuckolding large Nordic fatheads. Cucufier un anglais, etc. At any rate, he has blond temperament, not redhead but note that as language you can repeat carrot-top, sorrel-top, reddy, whereas hair colours sound literary. As black-headed, etc.

The Nordic Menelaus. As to character of Odysseus. Anything but the bright little Rollo of Chambers' Journal brought up on Sam Smiles. Born on po' misero, don't want to go to war, little runt who finally has to do all the hard work, gets all Don Juan's chances with the ladies and can't really enjoy 'em. Circe, Calypso, Nausicaa. Always some fly in the ointment, last to volunteer on stiff jobs. (p. 273)

Letter 295, Rapallo, April 1935

Dear Dr Rouse: Sorry, but I am afraid I think the start of V. just plain damn bad. Careless, frivolous. Missed opportunities <u>all</u> over it.
Let's list the aims:
    1. Real speech <u>in</u> the English version.
    2. Fidelity to the original
        a. meaning
        b. atmosphere
No need of keeping verbal literality for phrases which sing and run naturally in the original. But, the THEOIO is strong magic.

The Argicide, Hermes, carried past, the movement with the wind takes the god into nature. It is raw cut of concrete reality combined with the tremendous energy, the contact with the natural force. The reality that becomes mere pompous rhetoric in Milton. The miracle of Homer is that great poesy is everywhere latent and that the literary finish is up to Henry James. (273–4)

Letter 296, Rapallo, 23 May 1995

The *first* essential is the narrative movement, forward, not blocking the road as Chapman does. Everything that stops the reader must <u>go</u>, be cut out. And then everything that holds the mind, long after the reading, i.e., as much as is humanly possible, must be clamped back on the moving prose. It is enough to break six men's backs, and if you hadn't <u>been there</u> in a sailing boat, I shd. lie down and surrender [. . .]. (275)

Letter 297, Rapallo, 6 June 1935

Dear Dr Rouse: I thought I <u>had</u> given plenary approval to Nanny and all yr. country idiom, any real speech [. . .]

[Same letter as above] 13 June 1935

The chief impression in reading Homer is freshness. Whether illusion or not, this is the classic quality. 3000 years old and still <u>fresh</u>. A trans. that misses that is bad. Must get <u>new</u> combinations of words. I can't recall 'patient protagonist' as occurring in English. I use this as example. A trans of meaning. I repeat Dazzi's scandal re using 'paroles en liberté' and also wonder about Aeschylus and syntax, whether editors haven't tried to put back too much. (275)

Letter 332, Rapallo, 4 November 1937

Benedictions: No, I am not cursing you fer not makin your kings talk like gangsters. [...]

Where the translation can be improved is in dimension of inflection of the voice. Possibly <u>no</u> change of vocabulary required, but the greater variety of intonation and of sentence movement. The indication of tone of voice and varying speeds of utterance. In that, Homer is never excelled by Flaubert or James or any of 'em. <u>But</u> it needs the technique of one or more life times.

I dare say (in private) that the use of slang is merely a sign of imperfect technique. The slanger <u>wants</u> to get the real sound of speech as spoken, and can only get near it by using the expression of the moment. <u>Limited</u>, this view, by fact that the god damn iggurunt often think they are using vulgah and slangy eggspreshuns when they are using words right out er Bill Shxpr, such as 'boosing' or 'bowsing,' etc. Look at <u>Pericles</u>:

<u>Faith</u>, she would serve, (pause)
        after a long voyage at sea.

The cadence is so well-taken that even the archaism in the first word doesn't dim the naturalness of the <u>sentence.</u>

    1. words
    2. sentences and movements of same—
two parts of writin'.

I come back to Ulysses the <u>toff</u>, liftin his imaginary highhat as he comes out of the underbrush. (pp. 298–9)

From 'The Seafarer' [1912], included in *The Translations of Ezra Pound*, introd. Hugh Kenner (London and Boston: Faber & Faber, 1970), 207–9; also in *Poems and Translations*, pp. 236–8)

[From the Anglo-Saxon.]

> May I for my own self song's truth reckon,
> Journey's jargon, how I in harsh days
> Hardship endured oft.
> Bitter breast-cares have I abided,
> Known on my keel many a care's hold,
> And dire sea-surge, and there I oft spent
> Narrow nightwatch nigh the ship's head
> While she tossed close to cliffs. Coldly afflicted,
> My feet were by frost benumbed.

Chill its chains are; chafing sighs
Hew my heart round and hunger begot
Mere-weary mood. Lest man know not
That he on dry land loveliest liveth,
List how I, care-wretched, on ice-cold sea,
Weathered the winter, wretched outcast
Deprived of my kinsmen;
Hung with hard ice-flakes, where hail-scur flew,
There I heard naught save the harsh sea
And ice-cold wave, at whiles the swan cries,
Did for my games the gannet's clamour,
Sea-fowls' loudness was for me laughter,
The mews' singing all my mead-drink.
Storms, on the stone-cliffs beaten, fell on the stern
In icy feathers; full oft the eagle screamed
With spray on his pinion.
                    Not any protector
May make merry man faring needy.
This he little believes, who aye in winsome life
Abides 'mid burghers some heavy business,
Wealthy and wine-flushed, how I weary oft
Must bide above brine.
Neareth nightshade, snoweth from north,
Frost froze the land, hail fell on earth then,
Corn of the coldest. Nathless there knocketh now
The heart's thought that I on high streams
The salt-wavy tumult traverse alone.
Moaneth alway my mind's lust
That I fare forth, that I afar hence
Seek out a foreign fastness.
For this there's no mood-lofty man over earth's midst,
Not though he be given his good, but will have in his youth greed;
Nor his deed to the daring, nor his king to the faithful
But shall have his sorrow for sea-fare
Whatever his lord will.
He hath not heart for harping, nor in ring-having
Nor winsomeness to wife, nor world's delight
Nor any whit else save the wave's slash,
Yet longing comes upon him to fare forth on the water.
[. . .]

From 'How to Read' (first appeared in the *New York Herald Tribune*, 'Books', 1929), included in *Literary Essays*, 15–40

If we chuck out the classifications which apply to the outer shape of the work, or to its occasion, and if we look at what actually happens, in, let us say, poetry, we will find that the language is charged or energized in various manners.

That is to say, there are three 'kinds of poetry':

MELOPOEIA, wherein the words are charged, over and above their plain meaning, with some musical property, which directs the bearing or trend of that meaning.

PHANOPOEIA, which is a casting of images upon the visual imagination.

LOGOPOEIA, 'the dance of the intellect among words', that is to say, it employs words not only for their direct meaning, but it takes count in a special way of habits of usage, of the context we *expect* to find with the word, its usual concomitants, of its known acceptances, and of ironical play. It holds the aesthetic content which is peculiarly the domain of verbal manifestation, and cannot possibly be contained in plastic or in music. It is the latest come, and perhaps most tricky and undependable mode.

The *melopoeia* can be appreciated by a foreigner with a sensitive ear, even though he be ignorant of the language in which the poem is written. It is practically impossible to transfer or translate it from one language to another, save perhaps by divine accident, and for half a line at a time.

Phanopoeia can, on the other hand, be translated almost, or wholly, intact. When it is good enough, it is practically impossible for the translator to destroy it save by very crass bungling, and the neglect of perfectly well-known and formulative rules.

Logopoeia does not translate; though the attitude of mind it expresses may pass through a paraphrase. Or one might say, you can *not* translate it 'locally', but having determined the original author's state of mind, you may or may not be able to find a derivative or an equivalent. (25)

From 'Translators of Greek: Early Translators of Homer' (1920), included in *Literary Essays*, 249–79

We have drifted out of touch with the Latin authors [. . .] and we have mislaid the fine English versions: Golding's *Metamorphoses*; Gavin Douglas's *Aeneids*; Marlowe's *Eclogues* from Ovid, in each of which books a great poet has compensated, by his own skill, any loss in transition; a new beauty has in each case been created. (249)

Pope [. . .] has at least the merit of translating Homer into *something*. The nadir of Homeric translation is reached by the Leaf-Lang prose; Victorian faddism having persuaded these gentlemen to a belief in King James fustian; their alleged prose has neither the concision of verse nor the virtues of direct motion. [...] their version is full of 'Now behold I' and 'yea even as' and 'even as when' tushery [...] (250)

Obscurities *not inherent in* the matter, obscurities due not to the thing but to the wording, are a botch, and are *not* worth preserving in a translation. The work lives not by them but despite them.

Rossetti is in this matter sounder than Browning, when be says that the only thing worth bringing over is the beauty of the original; and despite Rossetti's purple plush and molasses trimmings he meant by 'beauty' something fairly near what we mean by the 'emotional intensity' of his original. (268)

One might almost say that Aeschylus' Greek is agglutinative, that his general drive, especially in choruses, is merely to remind the audience of the events of the Trojan war; that syntax is subordinate, and duly subordinated, left out, that he is not austere, but often even verbose after a fashion (not Euripides' fashion).

A reading version might omit various things which would be of true service only if the English were actually to be sung on a stage, or chanted to the movements of the choric dance or procession. (273)

Comparison of translations of Homer, *The Odyssey*, beginning of canto 1

Beginning of 'Canto 1' (1917; final rev. 1925), in The Cantos of Ezra Pound *(1993) 3–5.*

[The Andreas Divus mentioned is Andreas Divus Justinopolitanus, translator of the *Odyssey* into Latin (Parisiis: In officina Christiani Wecheli, 1538), a book bought second-hand by Pound sometime between 1906 and 1910. Pound relates this provenance in 'Translators of Greek: Early Translators of Homer', *Literary Essays*, p. 259. Divus's version appears below.]

> And then went down to the ship,
> Set keel to breakers, forth on the godly sea, and
> We set up mast and sail on that swart ship,
> Bore sheep aboard her, and our bodies also
> Heavy with weeping, and winds from sternward
> Bore us out onward with bellying canvas,
> Circe's this craft, the trim-coifed goddess.
> Then sat we amidships, wind jamming the tiller,
> Thus with stretched sail, we went over sea till day's end.
> Sun to his slumber, shadows o'er all the ocean,
> Came we then to the bounds of deepest water,
> To the Kimmerian lands, and peopled cities
> Covered with close-webbed mist, unpierced ever

With glitter of sun-rays
Nor with stars stretched, nor looking back from heaven
Swartest night stretched over wretched men there.
The ocean flowing backward, came we then to the place
Aforesaid by Circe.
[. . .]
Lie quiet Divus. I mean, that is Andreas Divus,
In officina Wecheli, 1538, out of Homer.
And he sailed, by Sirens and thence outward and away
And unto Circe.
          Venerandam,
[. . .]

Andreas Divus's Latin translation, used by Pound, with ad verbum *translation of the Latin by Gottskalk Jensson.*

[Divus's version stays very close to the Greek source text (see the Greek with literal translation after Chapman's version in Sect. 2.6, above).]

Andreas Divus (1538)

'At postquam ad navem descendimus, et mare,
Nauem quidem primum deduximus in mare diuum.
Et malum posuimus et vela in navi nigra:
Intrò autem oues accipientes ire fecimus, intrò et ipsi
Iuimus dolentes, huberes lachrymas fundentes:
Nobis autem a tergo navis nigrae prorae
Prosperum ventum imisit pandentem velum bonum amicum
Circe benecomata gravis Dea altiloqua.
Nos autem arma singula expendientes in navi
Sedebamus: hanc autem ventusque gubernatorque dirigebat:
Huius at per totum diem extensa sunt vela pontum transientis:
Occidit tunc Sol, obumbratae sunt omnes viae:
Haec autem in fines pervenit profundi Oceani:
Illic autem Cimmeriorum virorum populusque civitasque,
Caligine et nebula cooperti, neque unquam ipsos
Sol lucidus aspicit radiis,
Neque quando tendit ad coelum stellatum,
Neque quando retro in terram a coelo vertitur:
Sed nox perniciosa extenditur miseris hominibus:
Navem quidem illuc venientes traximus, extra autem oves
Accepimus: ipsi autem rursus apud fluxum Oceani
Iuimus, ut in locum perveniremus quem dixit Circe:'

English crib

'And when we had descended to the ship, and the sea, we indeed first drew the ship down into the divine sea. And we put the mast and sails in the black ship; and taking the sheep we made them go aboard the ship, ourselves also going aboard lamenting, shedding abundant tears. But for us fair-haired Circe, weighty goddess of lofty speech, sent behind the dark-prowed ship a favourable wind filling the sail, a good friend. And having arranged every bit of tackle in the ship we remained seated; but her the wind and the steersman directed; and throughout the entire day her sails were stretched as she cruised over the sea. The sun then set, all roads were overshadowed; and she came to the ends of deep Ocean; and there is the people and city of Cimmerian men, covered in mist and cloud, and never does the shining sun look upon them with rays, not when tending to the starry sky, nor when turning back to earth from heaven. But pernicious night is extended over miserable humans. Indeed coming to this place we pulled the ship, and took the sheep out; and we ourselves went back beside the stream of Ocean, until we came to the place which Circe pointed out.'

From 'Date Line' (originally in *Make It New*, 1934), included in *Literary Essays*, 74–87

Criticism has at least the following categories [...]

   1. Criticism by discussion [...]

   2. Criticism by translation.

   3. Criticism by exercise in the style of a given period. [...]until a man can actually control a given set of procedures there must be many elements in them of which he has but an imperfect knowledge.

This introduces almost a personal note, or at least a long-delayed reply to carpers who objected to my spending three days in translating Fontenelle on the ground that I should have been 'doing original work and not wasting my energies in translation'. [...]

   4. Criticism via music, meaning definitely the setting of a poet's words; e.g. in [my opera] *Le Testament*, Villon's words, and in [my melopoetic translations in] *Cavalcanti*, I have set Guido's and Sordello's. [...]

This is the most intense form of criticism save:

   5. Criticism in new composition. [...]

Criticism so far as I have discovered has two functions:

   1. Theoretically it tries to forerun composition, to serve as gunsight, though there is, I believe, no recorded instance of the foresight having EVER been of the slightest use save to actual composers. I mean the man who formulates any forward reach of co-ordinating principle is the man who produces the demonstration. [...]

   2. Excernment. The general ordering and weeding out of what has actually been performed. [...]

The ordering of knowledge so that the next man (or generation) can most readily find the live part of it, and waste the least possible time among obsolete issues. (74–5)

Further Reading

Works by Pound or translated by Pound

The Cantos of Ezra Pound (New York: New Directions, 1993).

The Letters of Ezra Pound, 1907–1941, preface by Mark Van Doren, ed. D. D. Paige (New York: Harcourt, Brace, and World, 1950).

Literary Essays of Ezra Pound, introd. and ed. T. S. Eliot (New York: New Directions, 1968).

Poems and Translations, ed. Richard Sieburth (The Library of America, 2003).

Personae: The Collected Shorter Poems of Ezra Pound (New York: New Directions, 1971).

The Translations of Ezra Pound introd. Hugh Kenner (London and Boston: Faber and Faber, 1970).

Works on Pound

Apter, Ronnie, *Digging for the Treasure: Translation after Pound* (New York: Paragon, 1987).

Kenner, Hugh, *The Pound Era* (Berkeley and Los Angeles: University of California Press, 1971).

Sullivan, J. P., *Ezra Pound and Sextus Propertius: A Study in Creative Translation* (Austin: University of Texas Press, 1964).

Yip, Wai-lim, *Ezra Pound's 'Cathay'*, (Princeton: Princeton UP, 1969).

4.3 CONSTANCE GARNETT

Constance Garnett (1861–1946) translated a substantial portion of the classical (nineteenth-century) corpus of Russian literature, with the exception of its poetry, some sixty volumes, including the major works of Turgenev, Goncharov, Dostoevsky, Tolstoy, Gogol, Herzen, and Chekhov.

Constance was married to Edward Garnett, son of Richard Garnett, Keeper of Printed Books at the British Museum (now the British Library). He was a minor writer but an influential publisher's reader, encouraging many important writers, including Joseph Conrad and D. H. Lawrence. David Garnett, their novelist son, who has written a biography of Constance, comments on the liberality of what in many respects was a respectable Victorian household. Constance worked for an educational and recreational charitable organization in London and also joined the socialist Fabian Society, for a while serving on the executive committee, although she later withdrew when it became increasingly dominated by advocates of state socialism.

In 1891 the Garnetts moved out of London to the country. Edward, however, who had met a number of political exiles, especially populist (*narodnik*) Russian thinkers and writers in London, invited one of them, Feliks Volkhovsky, to visit them, and it is from this visit that Constance's involvement with Russia and Russian literature dates, Volkhovsky persuading her to learn Russian, which she did with remarkable speed by the long-standing method of translating literary texts. She was introduced to other Russian exiles, most importantly the political activist Sergei Stepniak-Kravchinsky, who encouraged Constance to continue as a translator, which he saw as an effective means of propagating the ideology of liberation.

Part of Constance Garnett's success obviously lay in the appeal of a newly discovered major literature, but the sheer extent of her work also helps explain its impact, and should be borne in mind when assessing individual works. Her first translation, 1894, was of Ivan Goncharov's *A Common Story* which had been published in Russia in 1847. Goncharov, of course, is best known as the author of *Oblomov* (1859, first English translation not until 1915), it being Garnett evidently who introduced his work. The same year she published a translation of Tolstoy's *The Kingdom of God is Within You*, and scarcely a year passed without her publishing one or more major translation, notably the complete works of Ivan Turgenev, who died in 1883, in fifteen volumes (1894–9), hers not being the first translation of Turgenev, but by far the most substantial. In 1898, on the first of her two trips to Russia, she visited Tolstoyan schools for peasants and Tolstoy himself. She went on to translate *Anna Karenina, War and Peace*, as well as a number of his short stories (1901–4).

Garnett's translation of Dostoevsky's *Brothers Karamazov* in 1912 began the vogue for Russian writing and in particular for that of Fyodor Dostoevsky himself, whose entire oeuvre she translated, in thirteen volumes (1912–1920), still managing to complete a translation of all Chekhov's stories (1916–22). Her translations of Chekhov's plays have perhaps occasioned the most criticism (see Crankshaw's memoir below), but they were also influential in their time; Bernard Shaw's *Heartbreak House* owed much to Garnett's translation of *The Cherry Orchard*. Other important translations are *My Life and Works*, memoirs of the philosopher and radical political thinker Alexander Herzen (1924–7), and the works of Nikolay Gogol, in six volumes.

The impact of Russian prose on English literature can hardly be exaggerated, and no more can Constance Garnett's role, this being acknowledged, for instance, by Katherine Mansfield who clearly was greatly in debt to Garnett for her translations of Chekhov's short stories.

Garnett had, of course, had the advantage in some cases (Turgenev, Tolstoy, Dostoevsky, Chekhov) of translating work by writers who were almost contemporaries. The scale of her work was astonishing even if she was not in every case the first in the field, with the notable exceptions of Anton Chekhov and Fyodor Dostoevsky. As the most prolific of translators, she, above all, was responsible for the vogue for Russian writing, this being fuelled to some extent by the modernist spirit and progressive political views of the Bloomsbury group, at the centre of which she and Edward found themselves. As George Hyde puts it,[1] this modern spirit 'called out across the decades to Russia, finding in the writing of a dispossessed and oppressed "intelligentsia" an analogy for their sense of stylistic and emotional crisis, of a comprehensive loss of identity (Joyce compared his own writing to Lermontov's in 1905)'. Constance's sympathy for the exploited is evident, but she was out of step with the new generation of socialists, holding that the economic interpretation of history was too narrow.

Constance Garnett's translations made Russian literature accessible to an English-language public, already disposed to appreciate it. Whatever their shortcomings, they unquestionably inaugurated the Russian fever of the early twentieth century. Her importance for many major writers is a matter of record: Joseph Conrad, for instance, in a letter to Edward Garnett (see Crankshaw's, memoir, below); Constance herself received a letter from the then unknown Katherine Mansfield, testifying to an attitude almost of veneration: 'My generation (I am 32) and the younger generation owe you more than we ourselves are able to realize. These books have changed our lives, no less. What could it be like to be without them!' Edward Crankshaw, while not uncritical, draws

---

[1] In Peter France (ed.), *The Oxford Guide to Literative in English Translation* (Oxford: OUP, 2000), 586.

attention to her essential merits as an interpreter of Russian literature. In particular, her versions of Chekhov revolutionized the art of the short story, crucially influencing the likes of the aforementioned Mansfield and of D. H. Lawrence, who was among her most ardent admirers.

A few weeks before her death, Constance Garnett was invited to broadcast. She was already 84 years old, crippled and ill, but the invitation led her to talk about the subject of translation, on which she had not expressed herself in print before. Her remarks are informal and anecdotal but even so afford insights into both her methodology and her general approach. In any case, this is virtually all we have, since her translations never included prefatory comments by herself, although some (a few Turgenev novels) were introduced, in fairly general terms, by her husband Edward. Her son, David Garnett, made rapid notes of the conversation, which was published, as far as possible in her own words, in *The Listener*, 30 January 1947. The same issue contained a useful memoir by the journalist and political commentator Edward Crankshaw, which is excerpted below.

Constance Garnett, The Art of Translation, conversation recorded in *The Listener*, 30 January 1947

I should like to be judged by my translation of Tolstoy's *War and Peace*. But Tolstoy's simple style goes straight into English without any trouble. There's no difficulty. Dostoevsky is so obscure and so careless a writer that one can scarcely help clarifying him—sometimes it needs some penetration to see what he is trying to say. Turgenev is much the most difficult of the Russians to translate because his style is the most beautiful.

Once when I was translating *The Sportman's Sketches* [Turgenev], I gave the first draft of six of the stories to the Russian revolutionary leader, Stepniak, to read over. I had put, as I always did, alternative words above the line, whenever I was in some doubt of the right word. Well, when I had finished all the stories in the volume, I asked Stepniak for my manuscript, but he declared he had given it back to me. However, I could not remember his doing so, and it was nowhere to be found. So I translated the six stories again. When I had done this Stepniak found my first translation among his papers and returned it, so I compared the two translations to choose the best passages from each. To my surprise I found they were identical; I had hesitated in the same places, over the same words, and had written the same possible alternatives above the line in the same places. I concluded that though someone else might do a better version, it was clear that I could not myself. I had done the only version I was capable of. I took far more trouble over my translations of Turgenev and of Chekhov than over any of my other translations because their Russian is so beautiful. I was very much pleased because the Russian critic, Zhdanov, said it was impossible to translate Turgenev, and afterwards took the trouble to go through some of my translations carefully, and said he was amazed that it was possible for them to have been so well done.

Sometimes a word eludes me. One of the best translations I made was of the title of Dostoevsky's story 'An Unpleasant Predicament'. The word 'predicament' eluded me and I tried 'experience' and other words. Suddenly the word 'predicament' came and it was the exact equivalent of the Russian.

There have been such infamously bad translations. For example, someone did a translation of Chekhov's story which I called 'The Nightmare'—the Russian is *Koshmar*—from the French word *Cauchemar*. He called it 'The Incubus'. The story is about someone who makes a complaint to the bishop against a poor village priest and discovers later that he is starving, and the whole village is dying of starvation under nightmarish conditions. The title 'The Incubus', has no meaning in relation to the story, or quite the wrong associations. Again, I made a mistake in judgment in translating one of Turgenev's stories as *A House of Gentlefolk*. The Russian means 'A Nest of Gentlefolk', but I was afraid the public would think it too queer. Afterwards someone published a version called *A Nest of Hereditary Legislators*, and my title has now been changed to *A Nest of Gentlefolk*, quite rightly.

The qualifications for a translator are to be in sympathy with the author he is translating, and most important of all to be in love with words and interested in all their meanings. The language of a country is the soul of its people, and if you debase the language you debase the people and rob them of their heritage. The BBC has done such splendid work by awakening the musical taste of the people: I should like to say that it ought to do the same for the English language, the richest and the most beautiful in the world, by awakening the people to the beauty of the language and avoiding the debased jargon that is spreading everywhere.

The desire to modernise an author arises from ignorance of the past and from bad taste. I have always tried to translate the Russians into the language of the period in which they wrote, which is of course possible with Russian literature, since it is all relatively modern. It would show grotesque insensibility to produce a translation of Gogol's *Dead Souls*, written at the same time as *Pickwick*, in the language of today's newspapers. I am particularly proud of having translated *Dead Souls* into English of the period in which it was written. I agree there are obvious limits to this: there would be no advantage in trying to translate 'The Odyssey' into the language of Chaucer—on the other hand no one would want to translate it into modern slang. Thus with *Dead Souls*, one cannot translate the language of Russian serfs before their emancipation into that of the proletariat of today. One's aim should always be to translate into the language of the corresponding way of life.

Edward Crankshaw, 'Work of Constance Garnett', printed in *The Listener*, 30 January 1947

[. . .] [S]he was the first, and she was an artist in her own right. The English language is poor in its translations from other tongues: there have been only a handful of really inspired translators since the authorised version of the Bible set the standard. The chances of any of these knowing Russian must have been, statistically, very slender. But Constance Garnett turned out to be one of them. [. . .] It is not necessary to know a language well by examination standards to become a good translator. It is only necessary to have the translator's gift, which is a rare thing. If you have that it means that your feeling for words and shades of expression is so highly developed that you know instinctively what your author is trying to say, his tone of voice, his mood, his intentions, and his ambiguities—even if you cannot tell, without looking up a word or two in a dictionary, the technical equivalent in English of all the words he has used. Constance Garnett had that gift, though with certain blind spots, which we shall come to later. [. . .] [T]ranslation at this level of experience is something entirely different in kind as well as in degree from turning passages of Russian prose into respectable English prose: it is the recreation of original thought and perceptions into a new medium. This Mrs Garnett did. She re-created the great Russian classics in another medium: the medium of English experience. It was summed up very nicely by Joseph Conrad in a letter to his friend and adviser, Edward Garnett: 'For the rest, Turgenev for me is Constance Garnett and Constance Garnett *is* Turgenev. She has done the marvellous thing of placing the man's work inside English literature, and it is there that I see it—or rather that I feel it'. It was particularly necessary for Conrad to be able to feel Turgenev in this way because, for personal as well as general reasons, he abhorred Russia like the plague. But he could not do without Turgenev.

It is the same for all of us today—those of us who were not brought up to speak Russian. And we should add to Turgenev, Chekhov. Chekhov, for us, is Mrs Garnett, and Mrs Garnett is Chekhov—for better or for worse. These were the two great writers whom Mrs Garnett made supremely her own. She translated others, too. She threw herself into Tolstoy and Dostoevsky. But for these she was not necessary, as she was for Turgenev and Chekhov. The flat, didactic cadences of Tolstoy relentlessly batter their way into the paralysed consciousness of the most inept translator and reproduce themselves in English with sufficient resemblance to their original state to achieve, by their inspired accumulation, what Henry James would have called, had he been Tolstoy's admirer, 'the sought total effect'—though in fact, not at all admiring, he called both Tolstoy and Dostoevsky 'fluid puddings'. Dostoevsky, too, with the overpowering vehemence of his subject-matter and his manner, takes the thing out of the translator's hands and sweeps the reader along in an indiscriminate, headlong rush. It is not until you read and re-read one of the familiar poor translations that you realise how much more sharply you are aware of the depth and detail of that overpowering landscape when Mrs Garnett takes you over it. It is simply that you can do without her. In Turgenev, however, and in the tales of Chekhov, you cannot. For here we enter the realm of the significant word. If Tolstoy thought in terms of chapters and Dostoevsky in terms of paragraphs, Chekhov thought in terms of sentences, while Turgenev thought in terms of words and syllables— and silences. A bad translator could have killed them both stone-dead by reducing them to nonsense. But by an amazing piece of good luck they found Mrs Garnett, and, through her, entered in their full stature into English literature. And, having entered it, they changed it. This means, in effect, that Mrs Garnett gave us a new literature.

I am not trying to suggest that without Constance Garnett the voices of the great Russians would never have reached this country. What she did was to give them authenticity and bring them into the common consciousness. Her own original contribution, which we owe to her and to no one else at all, was the work of Chekhov, which completely revolutionised the English short story, so that English short story writers— and novelists—writing today, even if they have never read a word of Chekhov for themselves, are writing as they do largely because of Chekhov—and Mrs Garnett. [. . .] And until a year or two before the late war almost all the best and much of the worst in English fiction was permeated with Chekhov—not, alas, by the best and truest in that genius, whose immense and terrible stature is still not realised in this country, but by certain aspects of his technique and his approach. But that is not the fault of Constance Garnett. It is the fault of the writers themselves. And the same goes for the theatre, though here, too, the influence of Chekhov's plays, through Mrs Garnett's translations, immense though it is, and often beneficial, is by no means everything that it should be. And this time the translator is not entirely blameless. I spoke earlier of certain blind spots in her so highly developed instinct for words and meaning. And the greatest of these appears when it comes to dramatic writing involving dialogue. She did, it seems to me, lack the sense of dialogue. [. . .]

You may wonder whether I know what I am saying when I use the word 'genius' in connection with a translation—well, I think I do. If you will listen a moment to a certain passage from Turgenev as re-created by Mrs Garnett I think you will understand why. It comes from 'The Tryst' in *A Sportsman's Sketches*:

> I sat looking about and listening. The leaves faintly rustled over my head; from the sound of them alone one could tell what time of year it was. It was not the gay laughing tremor of the spring, nor the subdued whispering, the prolonged gossip of the summer, nor the chill and timid faltering of late autumn, but a scarcely audible, drowsy chatter. A slight breeze was faintly humming in the tree-tops. Wet with the rain the copse in its inmost recesses was for ever changing as the sun shone or hid behind a cloud; at one moment it was all radiance, as though suddenly everything

were smiling in it; the slender stems of the thinly-growing birch trees took all at once the soft lustre of white silk, the tiny leaves lying on the earth were on a sudden flecked and flaring with purplish gold, and the graceful stalks of the high, curly bracken, decked already in their autumn colour, the hue of an over-ripe grape, seemed interlacing in endlessly tangling criss-cross before one's eyes. . . .

That is the kind of thing before which, whether in the Russian of Turgenev or the English of Constance Garnett, you have to throw up your hands in acknowledgment of magic. There is no knowing how it is done, the translation no less than the original. And if that is not genius, then I don't know what is.

Fyodor Dostoevsky, *Crime and Punishment* (Heinemann, 1914) (opening paragraphs), translated by Constance Garnett

On an exceptionally hot evening early in July a young man came out of the garret in which he lodged in S. Place and walked slowly, as though in hesitation, towards K. Bridge.

He had successfully avoided meeting his landlady on the staircase. His garret was under the roof of a high, five-storeyed house, and was more like a cupboard than a room. The landlady, who provided him with garret, dinners and attendance, lived on the floor below and every time he went out he was obliged to pass her kitchen, the door of which invariably stood open. And each time he passed, the young man had a sick, frightened feeling, which made him scowl and feel ashamed. He was hopelessly in debt to his landlady and was afraid of meeting her.

This was not because he was cowardly and abject, quite the contrary: but for some time past he had been in an over-strained, irritable condition, verging on hypochondria. He had become so completely absorbed in himself and isolated from his fellows that he dreaded meeting not only his landlady but anyone at all. He was crushed by poverty, but the anxieties of his position had of late ceased to weigh upon him. He had given up attending to matters of practical importance; he had lost all desire to do so. Nothing that any landlady could do had a real terror for him. But to be stopped on the stairs to be forced to listen to her trivial, irrelevant gossip, to pestering demands for payment, threats and complaints, and to rack his brains for excuses, to prevaricate, to lie—no, rather than that, he would creep down the stairs like a cat and slip out unseen.

This evening, however, on coming out into the street, he became acutely aware of his fears.

4.4 WALTER BENJAMIN

Walter Benjamin (1892–1940), German-Jewish essayist, outstanding cultural and literary critic, has been a shaping force in modern literary studies and more broadly in what has come to be called cultural studies. His independent way of blending Marxist and materialist approaches with Jewish Messianic and Kabbalistic ideas took form in a variety of books and essays on literature, theatre, art, and technology, on the modern city, on history, and on language. Benjamin's favourite critical genre was the essay, which allowed him to combine scholarly analysis with free-flowing reflections, granting him room for metaphoric speculation, where political and poetical elements sometimes meet in an unexpected fashion.

When Benjamin brought out his translation of Baudelaire's *Tableaux parisiens* (Heidelberg, 1923), he wrote an introduction in the form of an essay, which is arguably the single most important piece of modern translation studies. It is somehow typical of Benjamin that he never mentions Baudelaire (whom he wrote about elsewhere) by name in the introduction, nor so much as touches on the fact that the book in hand contains his own translations of several poems by Baudelaire. It seems that he wants to leave it wholly up to the reader to make the connection; this may in fact be an illustration, in practice, of what he says in the opening words of the introduction; in experiencing and getting to know a work or form of art, it is of little use to take heed of the audience.

The introduction as a whole is in fact expressive of this 'lack' of consideration. This is a complex piece of writing, packed with valuable observations, which the reader may have a hard time fitting together into a coherent argument of a conventional kind. The meeting of languages, which takes place in the act of translation—and the third space that thus comes into being—is for Benjamin a manifestation of certain basic elements of language as a human faculty, indeed of a unifying 'pure' language, which may remain hidden in any language, and which translation has a unique capacity to bring out, if not to capture. Benjamin's approach is clearly indebted to German Romantic scholars and translators (Schleiermacher, Goethe, Humboldt, Hölderlin), but he has given this line of thought a strong modern twist, in some sense his own brand of what has been called the 'linguistic turn', including his understanding of history as containing 'messianic' moments, which can suddenly let in historical experiences from the past and open up the future.

The introduction, entitled 'Die Aufgabe des Übersetzers' ('The Task of the Translator'), has been reprinted several times, in German and in several other languages, but generally as a separate essay. In fact it is often discussed and referred to without any mention of the fact that it originally served as an 'introduction' to a collection of translated poems. It was brought into English in 1968, in two different translations: by Harry Zohn, as a part of the well-known collection *Illuminations* (ed. Hanna Arendt), and by James Hynd and E. M. Valk, with a facing German text, in the journal *Delos* (ed. D. S. Carne-Ross), the organ of the short-lived National Translation Center, Austin, Texas. The first of these has been reprinted many times, but the present editors decided to reprint, in full, the Hynd and Valk translation. It is followed by one of Benjamin's translations of Baudelaire from the 1923 edition. We are indebted to Professor Norma Rinsler for the literal English version of Benjamin's German translation and for the accompanying notes, as well as for her help with and comments on the literal version of Baudelaire's French original.

The Task of the Translator, translated by James Hynd and E. M. Valk, *Delos*, 2 (1968), 76–96

To know a work of art or a genre well, it is of little use to take heed of the audience, of the respondent. One does not merely go wrong when relating a work of art to a specific public or to the representative of such a public; the very notion of an ideal 'receiver' vitiates any theory of art. By definition such a theory presupposes man's being and nature. Art does exactly the same: it merely presupposes a physical and spiritual human presence. But never a specific act of response. For no poem is intended for its reader, no painting for its viewer, no symphony for its listener.

Is a translation intended for readers who do not understand the language of the original? That would seem to be an adequate explanation of the different status of original and translation in the realm of art. Moreover, this appears to be the only reason for saying 'the same thing' twice. What *does* a work of literature 'say'? What does it communicate? Very little to someone who understands it. It does not, by its essential nature, inform or assert. Nevertheless, the translation that was concerned merely to communicate could transmit simply that—communication: in other words, the non-essential. And this is a characteristic of bad translations. But what there is besides communication in a literary work—and even the bad translator admits that this is the essential: is it not the illimitable, the inapprehensible, the 'poetic'? Which the translator can only render if he too is a poet? To this in fact is due a second characteristic of the bad translation, which can therefore be defined as an inaccurate rendering of non-essential content. Translation can be nothing more than that so long as it persists in serving the reader. Yet if it were intended for the reader, so would the original be. If the original does not exist for the reader, how should a translation?

Translation is a form. To understand it as such means going back to the original. Because the original contains, in its translatability, the law that governs the translation. This question of a work's 'translatability' is two-fold. It can mean: will the work ever find its proper translator among all its possible readers; or—and more to the point—does it, by its nature, permit translation and therefore, given the significance of the form, demand it? Basically, the first question must be decided contingently, the second is a matter of demonstration. Only a superficial approach that denied the independent meaning of the second possibility would take them to be the same. In this connection, it might be pointed out that certain concepts are best grasped if they are not associated, a priori, exclusively with man. Thus one might speak of a life or a moment as 'unforgettable' even if all men had forgotten it. If its essence required that it not be forgotten, then that assertion would not be false: it would only point to a requirement not satisfied by man and, simultaneously, to a realm in which it could be satisfied: the memory of God. By the same token, the question of the translatability of certain works would remain open even if they were untranslatable for man. And indeed, given an exacting concept of translation, should this not be the case to some extent? It is in the light of such an analysis that one can ask whether a given work of literature *requires* translation. The relevant proposition is this: if translation is a form, then the condition of translatability must be ontologically necessary to certain works.

Translatability is an essential property of certain works—which is not to say that their translation is essential to them in themselves, but merely that a particular significance inherent in the original takes expression in its translatability. One gains the insight that a translation, however good, cannot be of any significance to the original. Nevertheless it has the closest tie with the original: because the original is translatable. Indeed, this tie is the more intimate since it no longer signifies anything to the original. It may be called a natural or, more precisely, a vital tie. Just as the expressions of life are most intimately tied to the living thing, but without significance to it, so translation issues from the original. Though less from its life than from its 'surviving life.' Coming after the original, translation marks for significant works, which never find their proper translator in the era of their creation, the stage of their continuing life. And the life and continuing life of works of art must be understood not metaphorically but as simple matters of fact. Even when thought was at its narrowest, life, it seemed, could not be limited to organic matter alone. But one cannot bring this expanded dominion under the incompetent sway of soul, as Fechner attempted; and the occasions of animal experience, those of sensation, of which life is only intermittently conscious, are even less adequate to define it. In fact, the concept only has its due when life is recognized in whatever is subject to the continuing perspective of history, but not limited to it. For it is history alone, not nature, and certainly not the fitfulness of sensation or soul, that can finally determine the scope of life. And here the philosopher finds his task: to understand all natural life from the encompassing life of history. And surely the continuing life of works is easier to grasp than that of creatures. Great works of art can trace their descent from their sources, their production in the time of their creators, and the subsequent periods of a continuing

reincarnation

life that is fundamentally eternal. This, when it occurs, is called fame. Translations which do more than transmit communication occur when a work has reached the era of its fame in its continuing life. Far, then, from promoting that fame, as bad translators are apt to claim for their work, the translation owes its existence to it. The life of the original reaches its ever-recurring, latest and most complete unfolding in translation.

This unfolding, as that of a special and higher life, is determined by a special and higher purpose. Life and rational purpose—the interdependence of the two notions looks patent; yet it eludes our understanding. Or rather, we can grasp it when we think of 'purpose' in a higher, generalized sphere, *not* in any particular, self-contained 'goal.' All purposeful phenomena of life, like their rational purpose in general, are finally purposeful not for life itself but for the expression of its essence, for the representation of its total significance. Thus translation's ultimate purpose is to express the innermost relation between languages. It cannot possibly, in itself, reveal or create this hidden relation; but it can represent it by realizing it in germ or intention. And in fact this representation of a total significance through the attempt, the germ, of its creation is a quite special mode of representation, virtually confined to the linguistic province of life. Elsewhere, other types of signification—signs and analogies—are used, not intension, which realizes by anticipation and allusion. But the inner relation presumed between languages is that of a special convergence. It consists in this: that languages are not alien to each other but, a priori and apart from all historical connection, are related in that which they wish to say.

"generative" translation

what about translation of translation

This search for clarification may seem to have led the inquiry, after futile detours, back to the traditional theory of translation. How can the kinship of the languages be validated in translations, if not by conveying as precisely as possible the form and sense of the original? The traditional theory could of course gain no exact concept of that precision and thus could not, finally, give any account of what is the essence of translation. In truth, the kinship of languages proves itself, in translation, to be something much more profound and specific than the superficial and indefinable similarity of two literary works. To grasp the true relation between original and translation requires a method and an aim quite analogous to the procedure by which epistemology must prove the impossibility of a picture theory of languages. If it is shown there that knowledge could not be objective, could not even lay claim to objectivity if knowledge consisted of pictures of reality, then it can be demonstrated here that no translation would be possible if similarity with the original were the ultimate object of its being. In its continuing life— how could one speak of 'continuing life' if the process did not involve the metamorphosis and renewal of a life force—the original work changes. Words also, and be they firmly writ, have their slow ripening. What in the author's time may have been an extension of his literary language may later be worked through; some new extension immanent in the created work can become actual. What once was new can later sound trite; what once was viable can sound archaic. To seek the essence of such changes, and of the no less incessant transformations of sense, in the subjectivity of succeeding generations rather than in the life of language itself and its works would be to confuse—even allowing for the crudest kind of psychologism—the basis and the substance of a fact; or, to put it more strongly, to deny, from intellectual inadequacy, one of the most extraordinary and productive of historical processes. And even if one were to make the final stroke of the author's pen the work's *coup de grâce*, that moribund theory of translation could not be saved. For just as in the course of the centuries the tone and meaning of the great literary works are completely transformed, so too is the translator's native language. Indeed, while the writer's words survive in his own language, even the greatest translation is destined to diminish through the growth of the translator's language and to be lost in its renewed life. Translation is far removed from being the deaf, inert equation of two dead tongues. Translation is, among all communicative modes, the one most concerned to mark the ripening process in a foreign language and the pulse of changing life in its own.[1]

translation as a measure of one's own language

    If the kinship of the languages is revealed in translation, this is due to something other than the vague similarity between reproduction and original. Resemblance, obviously, need not involve kinship. The concept of kinship is consistent, in this context, with its narrower use; for identity of origin does not provide a sufficient definition in either case, although, of course, the concept of origin will remain necessary for the definition of the narrower sense. How are the two languages related, apart from their historical connection? Certainly as little by the resemblance of two literary works as by the resemblance of words. Rather, all kinship of languages that goes beyond historical derivation is based on this: that in each of them individually one thing, in fact the same thing, is meant—something, however, that cannot be attained by any one language alone, but only by the totality of their mutually supplementary intentions: pure, universal language. While, in fact, all the individual elements—words, sentences, contexts—in foreign languages exclude each other, in their intentions the languages supplement each other. The desire to comprehend this principle exactly—one of the fundamental principles of the philosophy of language—is implicit in the intention to distinguish between *what* is meant and the *manner* of meaning. In 'Brot' and 'pain,' the same object is designated but not signified. Due to the manner of meaning, the two words always signify something different for the German and the Frenchman, they are not interchangeable and in fact tend ultimately to be mutually exclusive; but due to what is meant, taken absolutely, they signify one and the same thing. Although the manner of meaning is thus quite at variance in the two words, in the languages to which these words belong their manners of meaning supplement each other. In these languages, in fact, the manner of meaning is integrated into what is meant. That is, in the individual languages lacking this supplementary relation, what is meant is never found in relative independence, as in individual words and sentences; but it is subject to constant transformations until, out of the harmony of

a Platonic form of the sign for bread?

all these manners of meaning, that which is meant emerges as universal language. Until then, it remains hidden in the individual languages. But if these continue to grow in this way till the messianic end of their history, then it is translation which takes fire in the eternal continuing life of the works and in their ceaseless renewal, again and again testing the holy growth of language—how far distant the hidden may be from revelation, how conscious the awareness of this distance may be.

This is of course to admit that every translation is a somehow provisional manner of coming to terms with the otherness of languages. A solution to this 'otherness,' one that is not provisional and subject to time but both instant and final, is denied to man or at least cannot be pursued immediately. But mediately, it is the growth of religion which ripens in languages the concealed seed of a higher language. Translation, therefore, although it can raise no claim for the permanence of its creations, and in this is unlike art, does not disown its movement towards an ultimate, final and decisive stage of all linguistic ordonnance. In it the original grows upwards as if in a higher and purer climate of language. Translation, admittedly, cannot live there permanently any more than it can reach there in every part of its form. Yet with marvellous insistence it at least points to that as the realm, predestined and denied, where language is reconciled and fulfilled. The original does not reach there root and branch, but whatever in a translation is more than communication stands in this realm. This essential element can be more exactly defined as whatever in a translation is not retranslatable. That is, one may take from it all the information one can, and translate it; yet there remains the intangible at which the true translator aims. Unlike the language of the original author, this intangible cannot be translated, since the relation of content to language is utterly different in original and translation. In the original, they form an assured unity, the unity of fruit and rind, while the language of the translation invests its content in the ample folds of a royal mantle. For it signifies a higher language than it is, and thus, in its alien dimensions, must always be unsuited to its content. This incongruity hampers any further transposition even as it renders it superfluous. For every translation of a work from one set point in the history of language represents, with regard to one set aspect of its content, those in all other languages. At least to that extent, then, translation transplants the original—ironically enough—to a more final realm of language, because the original cannot be transferred from this realm by any further rendering. All that can happen is that its other and different aspects can in their turn be raised to this higher realm. The word 'ironical' may bring to mind the thinking of the Romantics, and with reason. They possessed particularly keen insight into the life of works of art, the life to which translation is one of the highest testimonies. Of course, they scarcely recognized it as such but rather turned their whole attention to criticism, which constitutes another, if less important, moment in the continuing life of a work of art. But even if their theory was scarcely concerned with translation, their great achievement as translators showed their feeling for the essence and

language is an imperfect signifier, always lexical gap in the extreme

the dignity of the medium. Everything suggests that this feeling need not necessarily be uppermost in a writer's mind; indeed it may play a very minor role there. History does nothing to confirm the conventional preconception according to which the important translators should be true writers and the unimportant translators inferior writers. Take some of the major figures like Luther, Voss, Schlegel: they are incomparably more important as translators than as writers; while others among the greatest, like Hölderlin and George, given the complete range of their work, cannot be classified simply as poets. Nor, above all, as translators. Just as translation is a unique form, so too the task of the translator may be taken as unique and clearly differentiated from that of the writer.

The task is this: to find in the translator's language that latent structure which can awake an echo of the original. It is this characteristic of translation that distinguishes it in every way from an original work, since the design of the original is never directed to language as such, its totality, but only, and immediately, to certain specific linguistic clusters. But translation, unlike an original work, does not see itself as within the forest depths of language but rather outside it, facing it; without itself entering those depths, it calls the original inside, at that one point where, at a given moment, the echo in the translator's language can resound to the work in the foreign language. Not only does the design aim at something different for translation and original, since translation proceeds from a single foreign work to language in its totality; the design itself is different. That of the writer is naïve, primary, concrete; that of the translator derivative, final, conceptual. For the great impulse that charges the translator's work is the integration of the many languages into one true language. In that integration, admittedly, individual sentences, creations, value judgments do not concur—which is why it remains dependent on translation. But the languages themselves, completed and reconciled in the manner of their meaning, do come to agreement. If there is a language of truth, in which the final secrets that draw the effort of all thinking are held in silent repose, then this language of truth is—true language. And it is precisely this language—to glimpse or describe it is the only perfection the philosopher can hope for—that is concealed, intensively, in translations. There is no muse of philosophy, there is no muse of translation either. Yet these are no philistine pursuits, as sentimental artists like to suppose. For philosophy has a genius whose typical longing is for that language which is revealed in translation. 'Les langues imparfaites en cela que plusieurs, manque la suprême: penser étant ecrire sans accessoires, ni chuchotement mais tacite encore l'immortelle parole, la diversité sur terre des idiomes empêche personne de proférer les mots qui sinon se trouveraient, par une frappe unique, elle-même matériellement la vérité.' If what Mallarmé is thinking in these words can be strictly determined by the philosopher, then translation, bearing the seeds of such a language, stands midway between creative writing and teaching. Its work does not rank with theirs in expressiveness, yet it makes as deep a mark on history.

If the task of the translator becomes clear in such a light, the path to its solution threatens to become more impassably obscure. The task, in fact—to bring the seeds of universal language to ripeness in translation—seems to defy solution, to be impervious to all solution. For isn't the basis of any such solution removed if the rendering of sense ceases to matter? And, if you look at it negatively, it is to this point that everything said so far leads. Fidelity and freedom—freedom to render the sense and, in its service, fidelity to the word—are the hoary concepts that occur in every discussion of translation. They seem of no further service to a theory that seeks in translation something other than rendering of sense. Even though the traditional use of these concepts always sees them in incessant conflict. What exactly can fidelity bring, in a specific way, to the rendering of sense? Fidelity in the rendering of individual words can almost never carry over fully the sense they have in the original. For this sense is not exhausted, in its creative significance for the original, in what is meant; rather, it acquires this significance precisely as *what* is meant is bound, in the specific word, to the *manner* of meaning. This is commonly expressed in the formula that the word carries its emotional tone. In particular, literalness in regard to syntax destroys any rendering of sense whatever and is in danger of becoming unintelligible. To the nineteenth century, Hölderlin's translations of Sophocles were monstrous and glaring examples of such literalness. How much harder, finally, the rendering of sense is made by fidelity in the rendering of form requires no explanation. Hence the demand for literalness cannot be ascribed to the concern for preserving the significance. The sense is much better served—though the work and the language, of course, much less—by the undisciplined freedom of the bad translator. Necessarily, then, the demand for literalness—the reason for which is obvious, though the underlying motive may be deeply concealed—must be more convincingly grounded. Just as the broken pieces of a vase, to be joined again, must fit at every point, though none may be exactly like the other; so translation, rather than following the sense of the original, must fit itself in its own language, with loving particularity, to the original's manner of meaning: so that both languages (like fragments of one vase) may be recognized as fragments of a greater language. Precisely for this reason, translation must largely disregard the aim of communication, the aim of rendering the sense; and the original is essential to it only in so far as it relieves the translator (and his work) from the task of defining and ordering the communicable. In this realm of translation it is also true that ἐν ἀρχῇ ἦν ὁ λόγος. In the beginning was the Word. Yet the language of the translation can—indeed must—let itself go with respect to the sense of the original, in order that the *intentio* of that sense may resonate with its own kind of *intentio*—not as reproduction, but as harmony and as completion of the language in which it appears. It is therefore not the highest tribute to a translation, especially in the period when it is produced, to say that it reads like an original. The real meaning of fidelity, which is vouched for by literalness, is rather that the great longing for completion of the languages speaks from the work. Genuine translation is translucid; it does not veil the original text nor shadow it. Rather, it allows the radiance of universal language, a radiance intensified by the particular idiom, to fall the more brightly on the original. Such focusing, such richening of light, is achieved mainly by fidelity to syntax—a fidelity which proves that words, not propositions, are the translator's true raw material. The proposition, the sentence-unit is a wall around the idiom of the original; fidelity to the word, literalness of felt verbal meaning, is the colonnade through which the original can be seen.

If fidelity and freedom in translation have in the past been regarded as conflicting tendencies, then seemingly this deeper interpretation of one of these concepts, far from reconciling the two, denies the other any legitimacy at all. To what does freedom refer if not to the rendering of sense, which is no longer to be the ruling principle? Only if the sense of a linguistic creation can be taken as identical with the sense it communicates, it retains over and above all communication—so close, yet so utterly remote; hidden under it, or rendered the more distinct; broken by it, or rendered the more powerful— something final, decisive. In all languages and their creations there remains, beyond the communicable, something incommunicable, something symbolizing or symbolized, according to context. Symbolizing only, in the ultimate creations of the languages; symbolized, in the evolutions of the languages themselves. And what seeks to come forward, indeed to come to birth, in the evolution of the languages is the germ of universal language. But if this germ, though hidden and fragmentary, is nonetheless present in actual life as that which is symbolized, it exists in works of art only in the form of its symbolic representation. If that final essence, which is universal language itself, is in individual languages confined to the linguistic and its transformations, then in works of art it suffers from the burden of an alien sense. To free it, to transform the symbolizing into the symbolized, to restore universal language, fully formed, to linguistic growth and movement, this is the prodigious, the unique power of translation. Within this universal language, which no longer signifies anything and no longer expresses anything, but which as inexpressive and creative Word is what is signified in every language, all communication, all sense and all design finally converge at a level where their extinction is ordained. And there, precisely, freedom of language is confirmed in a new and higher right. Not freedom to transmit communicable sense, since the task of fidelity is just to emancipate translation from this necessity. Rather, freedom validates itself in its own language for the sake of universal language. The task of the translator is this: in his own language to redeem universal language from exile in the alien, to free it by translation from the work that enthralls it. For its sake he breaks down the rotting barriers of his own language: Luther, Voss, Hölderlin, George extended the boundaries of German. What importance the sense retains afterwards, for the relation of original and translation, can be caught in a simile. Just as a tangent glancingly, at a single point only, touches the circle, and as the contact and not the point prescribes the law by which it draws its straight line out to infinity, in the same way, glancingly, and only at the infinitely small point of the sense does the translation touch the original, to follow its personal course, set by the law of fidelity, in the freedom of linguistic growth and movement. It was Rudolph Pannwitz, in his *krisis der europäischen kultur*, who recognized the true significance of this freedom—though he did not call it that nor expound it. Here is the passage; with Goethe's notes to his *Divan*, it is easily the best thing published in Germany on the theory of translation:

> our translations, even the best, proceed from a false premise, they want to german-ize hindi, greek, english, instead of hindi-izing, grecizing, anglicizing german. they have a much greater respect for the little ways of their own language than for the spirit of the foreign work. the fundamental error of the translator is that he maintains the accidental state of his own language, instead of letting it suffer the shock of the foreign language. he must, particularly if he translates a language very remote from his own, penetrate to the ultimate elements of language itself, where word, image, tone become one; he must widen and deepen his language through the foreign one. no one realizes just how possible this is, to what degree every language is capable of transformation, and language differs from language almost as little as dialect from dialect; but this is so only when one takes it not as something merely superficial, but as a matter of the deepest gravity.

How far a translation can accord with the essence of this form is objectively determined by the translatability of the original. The less the quality and dignity of its language, the greater the element of communication, the less it offers to translation. A text that offered nothing but communicable sense, far from providing the occasion for a model translation, would defeat translation altogether. The higher the nature of the work, the more translatable it is even at the most glancing contact with the sense. This of course applies only to original works. Translations are untranslatable not because of the difficulty of the undertaking but from the all too limited way the sense adheres to them. Here, as in every other essential respect; the affirmative case is made by Hölderlin's translations, especially those of the two Sophoclean tragedies. In them the harmony of the two languages is so profound that sense is hardly touched by language, touched like an Aeolian harp by the wind. Hölderlin's translations are archetypes of their form; they bear, to even the most consummate versions of their text, the relation of archetype to prototype—compare Hölderlin's and Borchardt's versions of Pindar's Third Pythian Ode. For this very reason, in them more than in any others, resides the uncanny, primordial danger of all translation: that the gates of language so wrenched from their hinges, so forced and traversed, should slam and enclose the translator in silence. The Sophocles translations were Hölderlin's last work. In them sense plunges from abyss to abyss until it threatens to vanish in unsound-able depths of language. But there is a stay. Of all texts it is granted only to the Scriptures, in which sense has stopped to be the watershed for the flow of language and the flow of revelation. Where the text belongs immediately, without mediation of sense, in its literalness, to true universal language, to truth and teaching, it is translatable absolutely. No longer for its own sake, but exclusively for the sake of the languages. In that encounter, so limitless a confidence is demanded of translation that, like language and revelation in the text, literalness and freedom must without strain unite in the translation in the form of the interlinear version. For in some degree, all great writings, but the Scriptures in the highest degree, contain between the lines their virtual translation. The interlinear version of the Scriptures is the archetype or ideal of all translation.

EDITORS' NOTE

1. [The last two sentences are a translation of the following German sentence: 'So weit ist sie entfernt, von zwei erstorbenen Sprachen die taube Gleichung zu sein, daß gerade unter allen Formen ihr als Eigenstes es zufällt, auf jene Nachreife des fremden Wortes, auf die Wehen des eigenen zu merken', i.e. 'It [translation] is so far removed from being the deaf equation of two dead languages, that of all forms it is in fact the one that is most inherently concerned with watching over the ripening process of the foreign word, the labour pains of its own [word]'. Given Benjamin's dense expressive mode, it may seem important not to split the sentence in two. 'Nachreife' is a pregnant word here, referring as it does to the process of ripening *after* harvesting; this may have significant resonances when used for the 'farming' and historical cultivation of language. Similarly, in view of Benjamin's use of imagery in the article, it may be questionable not to keep the metaphor of 'Wehen', language 'in labour'. But translating this particular text is no easy or painless task and it goes to show that translating a critical or theoretical text can in certain cases be as arduous a struggle with dense and slippery language as is frequently the case with poetry or other literary texts (see also the introduction to Sect. 5.11, below on Gayatri Spivak).]

Baudelaire and Benjamin

Charles Baudelaire, 'La lune offensée'

French original

O Lune qu'adoraient discrètement nos pères,
Du haut des pay bleus où, radieux sérail,
Les astres vont te suivre en pimpant attirail,
Ma vieille Cynthia, lampe de nos repaires,

Vois-tu les amoureux, sur leurs grabats prospères,
De leur bouche en dormant montrer le frais émail?
Le poëte buter du front sur son travail?
Ou sous les gazons secs s'accoupler les vipères?

Sous ton domino jaune, et d'un pied clandestin,
Vas-tu, comme jadis, du soir jusqu'au matin,
Baiser d'Endymion les grâces surannées?

- 'Je vois ta mère, enfant de siècle appauvri,
Qui vers son miroir penche un lourd amas d'années,
Et plâtre artistement le sein qui t'a nourri!'

Literal version of Baudelaire's French, trans. Norma Rinsler

[See also Sect. 4.10, below. for Robert Lowell's version.]

The Insulted/Injured Moon

O Moon that our fathers circumspectly adored
From the height of the blue countries where the stars,
A brilliant seraglio, will follow you in trim gear,[1]
Old Cynthia mine, lamp of our retreats/hideouts,

Do you see the lovers, on their prosperous beds/pallets,[2]
As they sleep, displaying their mouths' fresh/bright enamel.
The poet beating his brow against his work/the page?
Or under the dry sod the viper couple?

Beneath your yellow cape/domino, and with stealthy foot,
Will, as of old, from dusk till dawn,
Kiss Endymion's antiquated charms?

'I see your mother, child of this indigent age,
Leaning towards the mirror her burden of years
And artfully powdering the breast that nourished you!"

TRANSLATOR'S NOTES

1. 'pimpant attirail' seems faintly derisive in this context, more colloquially translated, perhaps, as 'dressed to kill' or 'dressed up to the nines'.
2. This phrase suggests a luxury hotel. 'Lucky/fortunate beds'—for the lovers, that is—is a possibility.

German translation by Walter Benjamin

Die Kränkung der Luna

O Luna deren Dienst nun Tote wahren
Kannst du von droben wo bei steifen Feiern
Die Sterne mit dir ziehn in Strahlenschleiern
Betagte du mit der wir munter waren

Auf ihrer Streu die Liebenden gewahren
Wenn schlummernd sie den reinen Mund entschleiern
Und wie des Dichters Haupt von Mühen bleiern
Und wie im trocknen Gras sich Vipern paaren?

Bliebst du in deinem gelben Domino
Endymions verbuhlter Anmut froh
Bei der du dich bis in den Tag verpaßt?

-'Jüngst wies also deine Mutter ich bestrahlte
Ihr Spiegel wie sie die bejahrte Last
Des Busens der dich nährte sorgsam malte.'

Literal version of Benjamin's German translation, trans. Norma Rinsler

O Moon whose worship dead men now preserve
Can you from up above where in formal solemnities
The stars move with you in veils of radiance[1]
You ancient one with whom we used to be merry

Perceive[2] the lovers on their bed of straw
When sleeping they reveal their pure mouths
And how the poet's head is leaden with his toil
And how in the dry grass the vipers couple?[3]

Did you remain in your yellow domino
Happy in Endymion's wanton grace
With which you let yourself go[4] until dawn?

—Just now therefore I revealed your mother I lit up[5]
Her mirror where she the aged burden
Of the breast that nourished you was painting.

TRANSLATOR'S NOTES

An absence of punctuation does not make German clearer! Line 9, *Bliebst,* is past tense, and one would have expected *Bleibst,* which if not future as in French, is at least present tense. But the first tercet is in the past tense too.

1. 'Strahlenschleiern' in German: 'radiance-veils', a lovely coinage.
2. The sense is 'Can you... Perceive...' but the distance is more normal in German than in English.
3. Another poem written about the same time ('La Voix') has, to describe the poet's inner darkness, 'Je traîne des serpent qui mordent mes souliers'. So, maybe the poet finds these vipers underfoot too.
4. It is 'forget yourself', in the sense not of finding Nirvana but of losing one's dignity. *Bei der* can only refer to *Anmut*, not to Endymion, so it's not 'with whom'.
5. I am reading this as *wies ich [und] bestrahlte*, i.e. two verbs dependent on one subject.

4.5 MARTIN BUBER AND FRANZ ROSENZWEIG

Martin Buber (1878–1965) was one of the most influential figures in the study of philosophy and religion in the twentieth century. Among his books are *I and Thou, Good and Evil, On Judaism, Tales of the Hasidim*, and *On the Bible*. Franz Rosenzweig (1886–1929) was a theologian and translator (with Buber) of the Hebrew Bible, his principal work being *The Star of Redemption* (1921). A collection of their writings on the Bible and its translation appeared in 1936 under the title *Die Schrift und ihre Verdeutschung*; an English version, *Scripture and Translation*, from which the excerpts below were taken, was published in 1994.

The translation of the Bible into German by Buber and Rosenzweig represents a landmark in Bible translation, with its close philological reading of the Hebrew and Aramaic source texts (cf. the example from Genesis 11 below). The translators focused, notably, on the technical use of the 'leading-word' ('Leitwort') technique, parallelisms, treating the text as oral in origin, the Hebrew Bible regarded as a whole, in effect an anthology extensively cross-referencing itself. It was therefore essential to render the cross-referencing accurately and clearly, not to blur it, as in the King James translation, where the focus had been also on the potential of the English language, with its richness of synonyms. It is on principles defined by Buber and Rosenzweig that Everett Fox (see Sect. 5.20, below) based his own translation of *The Five Books of Moses* (1995). The basic choice in biblical translation has been between literal and dynamic (as propounded by Eugene Nida, for instance, see Sect. 4.9, below) approaches, both of which may of course be guided by religious impulses, although the dynamic approach usually indicates a concern with proselytism, whereas the literal indicates greater attention to the wording of the original text and is sometimes directed at scholars rather than the general reader.

Fox's English translation reproduces features, in Buberian/Rosenzweigian fashion, of the Hebrew biblical language. It is worth noting that this coincides with a renewed interest in foreignization. While foreignization is not in the first place tied to literalistic rendering of the Scriptures, the climate created by its renewed acceptability is more hospitable to the kind of translation practised by Fox, which thus seems more linked to radical or progressive developments, than to the *ad verbum* medieval tradition. Ted Hughes is quoted on the back cover of *The Five Books of Moses*: 'Everett Fox's new translation of the Old Testament must be one of the most important books. For once since the King James, a translation that comes right out of the heart of the living culture of the thing. I read with read excitement, like a wholly new real text.' The fact that for Hughes it read like a 'real text' (meaning presumably an original rather than a translation text) is a significant contemporary testimony to the success of Fox's procedure.

Tyndale, it is true, translated the Bible so it should be accessible to every ploughboy, whereas those who want still to hear his cadences are governed by a spirit of esotericism rather, its remoteness from contemporary speech giving it the hallmark of the sacred. It was the mellifluousness of the King James translators' language that ensured the longevity of the so-called Authorized Version. It seems unlikely that a version today, designed to be read in churches, could possess such lasting qualities. But it would be invidious to argue that changes in the English language itself might account for this. It is clear to many translation commentators today (see various contributions to Peter France's *The Oxford Guide to Literature in English Translation*, 2000) that intelligibility must take precedence over preserving traditional language, which no longer communicates effectively. This does not, of course, address the question of the validity of the Fox translation, to which Hughes responded so positively, sensing that a primary connection with the ancient source had been restored.

Buber and Rosenzweig were, of course, active at a time of dire crisis for European Jewish culture. Buber wanted passionately to renew, as he put it, 'the dialogue between heaven and earth'. In 1938, in an essay written in Palestine, 'The How and Why of our Bible Translation' (see *Scripture and Translation*, pp. 205–19), Buber alludes to the German assault on the Hebrew Bible, seeking to separate Old and New Testaments in a Nazi-inspired attempt to purge 'Jewish influence' from German culture. The bulk of Buber's and Rosenzweig's collaborative translation work, of course, was done some years before (1925–9), but these disturbing political-cultural developments were apparent already. The aim of the two translator-philosophers was, idealistically, to bring to life a spoken sacred text, in a time of crisis, to recover the Word embedded in that text and make it resonate in the living language of their contemporaries, as Luther had done during the Reformation, but by returning in the first place to the text itself rather than projecting it immediately onto the German language. Their motivation was essentially religious, but their practice was text-based.

From Franz Rosenzweig, 'Scripture and Word: On the New Bible Translation' (late 1925), in Martin Buber and Franz Rosenzweig, *Scripture and Translation*, trans. by Lawrence Rosenwald with Everett Fox (Bloomington, Ind.: Indiana University Press, 1994), 40–2

[The radical agenda of restoring orality to what has been written down is here spelled out. Rosenzweig's fervour is clearly discernible in his desire that God's word should sound again, be conveyed somehow in writing. A reform of the written scriptures amounts to a kind of religious revival. Rosenzweig announces a revitalization of the language of religion, through translation, as Luther had done almost exactly four centuries before.]

Every word is a spoken word. The book originally served the word, whether declaimed, sung, or spoken; it sometimes still serves it today, as in theatrically living drama or opera. Opera people talk of the script as something technical, instrumental, provisional; once, that was how people characterized the rank and condition of books generally, vis-à-vis the spoken word. But technique has a dangerous power over those who wield it; all unintentionally the means become an end, the provisional becomes the permanent, the technical becomes a magic spell. The book no longer serves the word. It becomes the word's ruler and hindrance; it becomes Holy Scripture. [. . .]

But one book—and precisely the book from which in our Judeo-Christian culture this fateful scripturalization and literarization of the word had its beginning, and in connection with which the antidotes of oral teaching and of tradition were first tried out—one book alone among all the books of our cultural horizon cannot content itself with this antidote of an oral tradition to complement it. This book alone must not, even *qua* book, enter entirely into *Schrifttum* into literature.[1] Its unique content forbids it to become wholly *Schrift*. It must remain word. It cannot attain the autonomous, aesthetic value of *Schrift* because it cannot attain the distance that is the precondition of this value. Its content, the essential part of its content, refuses displacement into the objectivity, the separatedness, the *madeness* that characterize all that becomes literature. Only its accessories are capable of becoming literature, and it is these accessories that a literary consideration must content itself with. But the essential content is precisely what escapes the specifying and distancing power of *Schrift*: the word of God to man, the word of man to God, the word of men before God. We have only to consider the letter—the most legitimate form of writing, the form always addressed to an immediate need and necessity,[2] the form from which all other forms borrow whatever legitimacy they have—to see that this legitimation of writing can never pertain to the word of and to and before God; God is *present*, and if he acts through messengers, they are not postmen bringing yesterday's news, which perhaps in the meantime has already been overtaken by the intervening events; rather in this moment of theirs God is what acts immediately in them and speaks immediately through them.

It is, accordingly, a vital question for Scripture, for this one *Schrift*, whether the word is to be merely adjacent to it or within it. The word of God cannot dispense with the word of man—the true, spoken, sounding word of man. The Bible alone, among all books of the literary epoch, whether literary or pre-literary, demands a pre-literary mode of reading—demands, that is, what the Hebrew expression for reading means, which is familiar in the west from the Koran and which has also yielded what words pertaining to writing have not yielded, namely the most familiar term denoting the Old Testament: the *qeri'ah*, the 'calling out'. It is in response to this command that in all worship Scripture is customarily read aloud; it is in the service of this command that Luther in his translation has recourse to the spoken language of the people. The crucial question to ask of any new translation is whether this command has been fulfilled at a given time and for a given people.

The fetters that today hold all written German mute are constituted by the semantic system in which the words are embedded: punctuation. [...] When, therefore, these fetters must be loosed at any cost [...] we need [...] drastic measures. Martin Buber has found these measures. The bond of the tongue must be loosed by the eye. We must free from beneath the logical punctuation that is sometimes its ally and sometimes its foe the fundamental principle of natural, oral punctuation: the act of breathing.

Breath is the stuff of speech; the drawing of breath is accordingly the natural segmenting of speech. [...]

TRANSLATORS' NOTES

1. The German *Schrifttum* is often translated 'literature'; but it is, as Rosenzweig goes on to suggest, simply an extension of *Schrift*; if *Schrift* is 'writing', *Schrifttum* is 'writingness.' 'Writingness', however, transgresses what Rosenzweig calls the 'boundaries of linguistic possibility'; so the translation retains the German term.

   Readers should be reminded of the multiple meanings of *Schrift*: 'Scripture', 'writing', 'literature'. When those various terms appear in the translation they most often render the one German term; when the precise term is crucial to the argument the translation retains the German.

2. There's a crucial pun here: because, Rosenzweig writes, the letter comes in aid of an immediate need (*Not*, 'need'), it is truly necessary (*not-wendig*, 'necessary'). Now *wendig* means 'averting' or 'turning'; so by separating the two components of the word Rosenzweig suggests that that is necessary which averts our need, or which we turn to in our need.

From Franz Rosenzweig, 'Scripture and Luther' (July 1926), in Buber and Rosenzweig, *Scripture and Translation*, 47–8

[See also Sect. 2.2, above on Luther.]

[Much of this essay has to do with the uniqueness of Luther's translation, with the fact, as Rosenzweig sees it, that 'every great work of one language can in a certain sense be translated into another language only once'. There is one particular moment in which 'the genii of the two languages are wedded'. At such a moment, the translator 'will be led by the honourable belief that the more faithfully the original enters his language, the more abundantly the needs of this great national hour will be fulfilled'. This is a unique historical moment that 'does not return, because it does not need to return'. 'No new translation, therefore, can attain a comparable national significance. Luther may have allowed for and indeed demanded revision, but this is now impossible, because his translation has become the fundamental book not only of a particular church but of the national language itself.' Attempts to improve on Luther, from a Bible criticism point of view (*Wissenschaft*) have not succeeded.

The translator however can and must leap over the obstacles, 'if only that we may be free then to stand still, and not be in danger.']

> Of Luther's comments on his translation, the most widely known are those articulating his desire to make his translation German, generally comprehensible German: 'to produce clear language, comprehensible to everyone, with an undistorted sense and meaning.' Such comments are in fact predominant in his work; and the great advance he made over previous Bible translations was most striking for his contemporaries in precisely this respect.
>
> But he was also altogether conscious of the other side of his work, of the movement of the German reader in the direction of the alien original, the genius of the alien language. The separate preface to the German Psalter is the most instructive of all Luther's writings on translation. [. . .]
>
> The reasons, or reason rather, for which Luther sometimes asks his reader to 'give the Hebrew some room' and to 'put up with such words' are stated by him [. . .]

>> But we have also sometimes translated word for word though we could have done it otherwise and more clearly, and for this reason: the words have something import-ant in them. Psalm 68:18, for example: 'Thou art gone up on high, and hast led captivity captive.' An idiomatic translation would be: 'hast freed the prisoners.' But that is too weak and does not yield the rich, subtle sense of the Hebrew: 'thou hast led captivity captive'—that is, not only has Christ released the prisoners, but he has in the process taken away the prison, taken it captive, so that it can never again take us prisoner, and our redemption is eternal. [. . .] To honor such teaching, and for the comfort of our souls, we must retain such words, must put up with them, and so give the Hebrew some room where it does better than German can.

It is perfectly clear here how the realms of the two principles, that of moving the text and that of moving the reader, are bounded [Rosenzweig has previously referred to Schleiermacher's distinction between translations that leave the writer in peace and move the reader in his direction, and those that leave the reader in peace and move the writer]. The former principle is ordinarily the dominant one, for Luther as for every other translator [. . .] and that Luther speaks at such length of this self-evident side of his work becomes intelligible only when we understand that he may well have felt himself the first competent practitioner of the translator's art. The translations of his predecessors swarmed with Latinisms—not, however, in adherence to the latter principle, but simply from bungling.

[. . .] But where, according to Luther, does the necessity arise 'to give the Hebrew some room'? Where the statement is very important, directed to us, 'to our souls'—that is, where for Luther, for the living Christian, the Scriptures are the immediate compelling word of God, living truth and living consolation [. . .] where for him, the Christian, it was the living word of God—there and only there, but there necessarily, it had to be taken word for word, and translated in 'rigid' literalness. Elsewhere—and for Luther in the Old Testament 'elsewhere' was the chief part of the text—[. . .] the translator 'sends the Hebrew words packing, and speaks the meaning of them in the best German he can'.

Luther's belief, then, determines at every level how the work of mediation is to proceed—that is, where to leave the word in peace and where the hearer. But Luther's belief implies Luther's concept of a delimitable (because limited) religious content. Our time has lost his notion of revelation [. . .] Our time, then, must in translating be permitted to ask the book the essential religious question all over again, as firmly and assuredly as it can [. . .]

[. . .] Writing does of course everywhere shape turns of oral expression in accord with its own formality; but outside the sphere of experience where writing reigns, the language remains free and productively powerful. [. . .] So also in the life of a people: a moment comes when writing ceases to be a handmaiden of language and becomes its mistress. This moment comes when a matter encompassing the whole life of the people has been cast into writing, i.e., when there is for the first time a book that everyone simply 'must have read.' [. . .]

For the voice of the Bible is not to be enclosed in any space—not in the inner sanctum of a church, not in the linguistic sanctum of a people, not in the circle of the heavenly images moving above a nation's sky. Rather this voice seeks again and again to resound from outside—from outside this church, this people, this heaven. It does not keep its sound from echoing in this or that restricted space, but it wants itself to remain free. If somewhere it has become a familiar, customary possession, it must again and anew, as a foreign and unfamiliar sound, stir up the complacent satedness of its alleged possessor from outside. This book and this book alone among all the books of humankind must not find its end in the treasure-house of human culture—because, precisely, it must not find an end in the first place. [. . .]

The Luther Bible was when first written what the Bible should be, was the thing through which, as often as the Bible becomes it, it establishes itself as unique among all human, i.e., merely human books: a sensation. [. . .] The Luther Bible was, then, a trumpet-call in the ear of those who had fallen asleep happy in their possession of the 'received and certified text.' But it did not remain that; it became itself a possession, a national possession. [. . .] [O]nly once was it a storm churning up the waters of the national life before these were gathered and channelled into their individual channels; and having been that once it could not be that again, since it was now a possession and thus safely chained up again. [. . .]

[. . .] Scripture must be read differently and transmitted differently than Luther read and transmitted it? Luther had his reasons for sometimes giving the Hebrew some room, for expanding German till it accustomed itself to the Hebrew, namely that on occasion the text spoke of 'teaching' and the 'comfort of our souls.' We do not know from what words teaching and comfort may come; we believe that the hidden springs of teaching and comfort may someday break through to us from every word of this book. Ought not Luther's reasons incline us to a new reverence toward the word, to a reverence that necessarily must renew our reading, our understanding, and our translation.

[Rosenzweig then pronounces on the limitations of *Wissenschaft* translation (i.e. translation based on biblical criticism), which has dispersed the aura of sanctity once surrounding the Bible, humanizing it and 'offering readers of every sort the content of the Old Testament, with the means of current biblical research, in clear contemporary German' (Foreword to Kautzsch-Bertholet *Textbibel*).]

> For—it is almost embarrassing to state such truisms, but also necessary—it is impossible to transmit the content without at the same time transmitting the form. How something is said is not peripheral to what is said. The melody makes the music. [. . .]
>
> Again: this argument is not at all aimed at the disparagement of individual translators, who surely gave this translation their best efforts. Rather it is aimed at *Wissenschaft* itself, which in translating is simply not *wissenschaftlich* enough. It has shaken many persons' trust in the Luther translation; but it has not put in place of that translation the translation of contemporary belief and its expressive forms—which is, after all, consciously or unconsciously, what all its work is meant to serve. [. . .]
>
> Aside, then, from its correction of particular errors, the modern translation offers even in a scholarly sense very little that is better, and much that is worse, than Luther.

Luther himself saw the scholarly significance of his work as lying in his return to the original text. [. . .] Luther the revolutionary, however, was still inwardly linked to what he was overthrowing. The vulgate was indeed [. . .] a soothing pillow for the conscience and a padding for the door of the cultivated man's study against disruptive noises from outside. [. . .] In other words: when Luther investigated the meaning of the Hebrew text, he was not thinking hebraically; nor was he, as he later did in rendering the investigated meaning into German, thinking Germanically; he was thinking Latinately.

NOTE

1. Preface to the Book of Job, editions of 1524 and 1525.

From Martin Buber, '*Leitwort* Style in Pentateuch Narrative' (from a lecture, January 1927), in Buber and Rosenzweig, *Scripture and Translation*, 114–28

[In this lecture, Buber identifies a salient feature of biblical prosody, ignored in Ciceronian fashion by the King James translators, who on the contrary exploited the multiplicity of

English synonyms (see Sect. 2.9, above, on the Authorized (King James) Version). With their emphasis on structure and on the poetics of the text, Buber and Rosenzweig strove to represent more fully the parallelism in the Bible. Buber stresses, however, that the recommended procedure should be adhered to only where appropriate; it is emphatically not to be regarded as a general rule or as an insistence on a metaphrastic approach. The translator's task, in Rosenzweig's words, is 'to weigh the claims of local context against the claims of global context'. Buber gives no useful advice on how this is to be accomplished, but the example set by him and Rosenzweig in identifying 'thematic resonances' is illuminating.]

> By *Leitwort* I understand a word or word root that is meaningfully repeated within a text or sequence of texts or complex of texts; those who attend to these repetitions will find a meaning of the text revealed or clarified, or at any rate made more emphatic. [...] Such measured repetition, corresponding to the inner rhythm of the text—or rather issuing from it—is probably the strongest of all techniques for making a meaning available without articulating it explicitly [...] [S]uch repetition can achieve not only aesthetic value, as manifested notably in the verse-forms of the Elder Edda, but also a special and irreplaceable value of *statement*. This value consists in the fact that the meaning to be stated is portrayed without any tacked-on moral, i.e., without any disruption or distortion of the pure form of the narrative. [...]
>
> But nowhere, probably, does this happen with such singular power as in the narratives of the Pentateuch. The strictness of the form here arises from the profound intention to report, and *only* to report; and precisely for this reason the message may not impose itself on the form. [...] [T]hose who listen will hear the higher meaning in the similarity of sound. A connection is established between one passage and another, and thus between one stage of the story and another—a connection that articulates the deep motive of the narrated event more immediately than could a pinned-on moral. Epic diction never overflows, never becomes rhetoric or lyric; the *Leitwort* rhythm is a genuinely epic rhythm, the appropriate artistic *signum* of a mystery stretching around and into the world of aesthetic form.

[Buber then gives examples, mostly from Genesis and Numbers of 'verbal atmosphere' generated by multiple recurrences, which communicates to the reader what is at issue in any particular instance.]

From Martin Buber, 'On Word Choice in Translating the Bible: In Memoriam Franz Rosenzweig', (Summer 1930), in Buber and Rosenzweig, *Scripture and Translation*, 73–89

[Intense concentration on the text as such is passionately urged. The verbal texture as a whole is considered, as a living or organic whole, rather than the focus being exclusively on the particular *Leitwort*, with its thematic significance.]

The special obligation to create a new version of the Bible, which came alive in our time and led to our undertaking, resulted from the discovery that the passage of time had largely turned the Bible into a palimpsest [...] The Bible asks us for a reverent intimacy with its meaning and its sensory concreteness; but that has been replaced by a mix of uncomprehending respect and unthinking familiarity [...] and its relation to the real Bible resembles the relation of the murdered God of our time [...] to the living God of reality. [...]

[...] Even the most significant translations of the Bible that we possess [...] do not aim principally at maintaining the original character of the book as manifested in word choice, in syntax, and in rhythmical articulation. They aim rather at transmitting to the translators' actual community... a reliable foundational document [...] [T]hey do not *a priori* ignore the peculiarities of its constituent elements, of its structure, of its dynamic; but they easily enough sacrifice those peculiarities when stubborn 'form' seems to hinder the rendering of 'content' [...] Revelation is accomplished in the human body and the human voice, i.e. in *this* body and *this* voice, in the mystery of their uniqueness. The prophet's proclamation consists not only of its symbols and parables, but also of the fundamental sensory concreteness of even the subtlest Hebrew concepts, of the taut stretching in the architecture of the ancient Hebrew sentence, of the Hebrew manner of relating adjacent or even widely separated words through similarity of verbal root or similarity of sound, of the powerful movement of Hebrew rhythm that goes beyond all meter [...] *Theoretically* speaking, the biblical messages cannot be rendered in their fusion of meaning and sound; but practically speaking they can. Can, that is, approximately—as approximately as one is allowed by the boundaries of the language one translates into. But the translator must press towards these boundaries again and again—to the real boundaries, that is—and must accept instruction as to what is permitted him and what is not only from the mouths of the supreme watchmen of language.

[However, Buber is careful not to overemphasize the potential of this method. As a translator himself, he is conscious of the practical limitations, but insists on the need to listen with great concentration to the source text, its resonances, its echoes, to always bear in mind that its origin is in the spoken not the written word. At the same time, this practical intelligence leads him to recommend freedom in expanding the word store, creating neologisms, resuscitating obsolete terms. As Buber says, 'It has been one of the strongest confirmations of our method that we have been able to reproduce such verbal patterns' (he has discussed the translation of *ohel mo'ed*, referring to the movable sanctuary of the desert). 'In both their breadth of manifestation and in their unity', he sees it as the translator's function to return to terms, which have become technical, their living associations (e.g. *Shabbat* must be delivered 'from the rigidity of "Sabbath"'. He discusses also the awesome task of rendering of the name of God, the tetragrammaton YHWH.]

[...] The auditory patterns of German can never *reproduce* the auditory forms of Hebrew; but they can, in growing from an analogous impulse and in exercising an analogous effect, *correspond* to them Germanically, can *Germanize* them.

To meet the demands of such a task, the translator must elicit from the letter of the Hebrew text its actual auditory form; he must understand the writtenness of Scripture as for the most part the record of its spokenness [...]

The auditory form of the German translation should then correspond to spokenness [...] [I]ts unfamiliarity is itself necessary, is indeed the one necessity, if [...] a translation is to produce an encounter between the Bible and the people today [...], to create a western equivalent of this, a German equivalent, we have to reach past the present verbal repertory towards the defamiliarized—indeed toward the obsolete and forgotten [...] Sometimes the translator must venture new formations, if he can find in the established German vocabulary no exact equivalent for a biblical institution or concept. No doubt the biblical world will seem [...] in many ways linguistically sharper and more vivid [...]; concepts will in the translation be distanced from the familiar, and will accordingly present their concrete fundamental significance more emphatically than they do in the original [...]

From Martin Buber, 'A Translation of the Bible' (1927), in Buber and Rosenzweig, *Scripture and Translation*, 166–71

[Martin Buber sums up what Rosenzweig's and his aims were. So radical and audacious are they even now, pushing language to its limits that some repetition seems in order. Buber, below, reiterates the same message even more emphatically than before, in terms that are echoed later by the likes of Rothenberg and Tedlock (see Sect. 5.7, below, Ethnopoetics)].

The 'Old Testament' has never before been translated by writers seeking to return to the concrete, fundamental meaning of each individual word: previous translators have been contented to put down something 'appropriate', something 'corresponding'. [...] [I]n Leviticus the 'man who takes the wife of his brother' is assigned a punishment corresponding to the sin: 'he has revealed the nakedness of his brother, and they will remain naked of children.' That is why Abraham calls himself not 'childless' but 'childbare', 'childstripped.' To undertake a genuine translation of the Bible entails now and then venturing such words; whether posterity will receive them or reject them is not for the living to know.

We have attempted also [. . .] to distinguish synonyms wherever German permits, i.e., not to render two distinct Hebrew words by one German one, nor—at least within a single sequence—to render a single Hebrew word by two German ones. We have further attempted, in cases where a common root linked various words, to retain that link in German. [. . .]

The individual word, then, in its original concrete meaning is crucial to us. But that is not to say that the Hebrew verbal sequence is something secondary, something not to be maintained against the conventions of the language into which we are translating. We know of no 'content' separable from this form in which it has been transmitted to us, and transferable into a form of a different sort. What matters is to naturalize this form in a quantitatively different language in such a way as the limits of the language allow—the time, and not merely the conventions. [. . .]

We take seriously not only the text's semantic characteristics but also its acoustic ones. It became clear to us, accordingly, that the text's abundant alliterations and assonances could not be understood in aesthetic terms alone; often if not always it is passages of religious importance in which assonance and alliteration occur, and both assonance and alliteration thus help make this importance emerge more vividly. [. . .]

We have, as I said, had in mind the Bible 'aloud'. We proceed from the notion that the Bible is a product of living recitation, and is intended for living recitation; that speech is its nature, and the written text only a form for preserving it. Hence our method of rendering its rhythm. Our translation is the first *colometric* translation [. . .] i.e. the first that gives the text its natural division into lines of meaning as these are determined by the laws of human breathing and human speech, with each line constituting a rhythmic unit. [. . .]

[The final passage actually precedes the last of the above passages, but is placed here as an introduction to the translation of the Buber Rosenzweig German translation of the Babel story (which it would be appropriate, of course, to compare with the Everett Fox translation of the same biblical passage, quoted below. See also other versions of this famous biblical passage).]

[. . .] the remarkable account of how the architects of Babel built of *lebenah*, brick, rather than *eben*, stone, and used as mortar not *homer*, loam or clay, but *hemar*, pitch or asphalt [. . .] This is no pun; rather the acoustic similarity emphasizes the nature of the situation, in which the builders must discard natural materials for artificial ones, or at any rate for materials that can be brought out of the earth only with considerable effort. The first half of the verse, 'so for them brick-stone [*Backstein*] was like building-stone [*Baustein*]', worked well enough; but the second half needs improvement.

Genesis 11: 1–9 in Buber and Rosenzweig's translation.

From Die Schrift (Die fünf Bücher der Weisung), *Verdeutscht von Martin Buber gemeinsam mit Franz Rosenzweig (12., verbesserte Auflage der neubearbeiteten Ausgabe von 1954) (Darmstadt: Wissenschaftliche Buchgesellschaft, 1997), 33–4.*

11, 1 Über die Erde allhin war eine Mundart und einerlei Rede.

2 Da wars wie sie nach Osten wanderten: sie fanded ein Gesenk im Lande Schinar und setzten sich dort fest.

3 Sie sprachen ein Mann zum Genossen:

Heran! backen wir Backsteine und brennen wir sie zu Brande!

So war ihnen der Backstein statt Bausteins und das Roherdpech war ihnen statt Roterd-mörtels.

4 Nun sprachen sie:

Heran! bauen wir uns eine Stadt und einen Turm, sein Haupt bis an den Himmel,

und machen wir uns einen Namen,

sonst werden wir zerstreut übers Antlitz aller Erde!

5 ER fuhr nieder,

die Stadt und den Turm to besehen, die die Söhne des Menschen bauten.

6 ER sprach:

Da, einerlei Volk ist es und eine Mundart in allen, und nur der Beginn dies ihres Tuns—

nichts wäre nunmehr ihnen zu steil, was alles sie zu tun sich ersännen.

Heran! fahren wir nieder und vermengen wir dort ihre Mundart,

daß sie nich mehr vernehmen ein Mann den Mund des Genossen.

8 ER zerstreute sie von dort übers Antlitz aller Erde,

daß sie es lassen mußen, die Stadt zu bauen.

9 Darum ruft man ihren Namen Babel, Gemenge,

den vermengt hat ER dort die Mundart aller Erde,

und zerstreut von dort hat ER sie übers Antlitz aller Erde.

Literal translation by A. Eysteinsson

11, 1 Over all the Earth there was one way of mouth and one kind of speech.

2 Then it was that they wandered to the East: they found a valley/lower land in the land of Shinar and they settled there.

3 They spoke, each man to his fellow man:

Go to it! let us bake stones of brick and let us burn them in the fire! [repetitive and alliterative: backen/Backsteine; brennen/Brande]

So for them the brickstone was instead of building stone, and the raw pitch was for them instead of red mortar.

4 Now they spoke:

Go to it! Let us build ourselves a city and a tower, its head as far as the sky,

and let us make ourselves a name,

or else we shall be dispersed over the face of the whole Earth!

5 HE went down,

to look at the city and the tower, which the sons of man were building.

6 HE spoke:

There, this is one kind of people and one way of mouth in all, and now the beginning of this deed of theirs—

nothing would hereafter be too steep for them, whatever they would think to do.

7 Go to it! let us go down there we shall mix/confuse their way of mouth,

so that each man no longer perceives the mouth of his fellow man.

8 HE dispersed them from there over the face of the whole Earth,

so they had to cease building the city.

9 There one calls their name Babel, mixture/confusion,

for there HE confused the way of mouth of the whole Earth,

and HE dispersed them from there over the face of the whole Earth.

4.6 JORGE LUIS BORGES

Jorge Luis Borges (1899–1986) was the most prominent Argentinian writer of his time. He was educated in Europe and was himself very influenced by English and American literature. His reputation as a major writer is principally based on two collections of short fictions, masquerading as essays, detective stories, literary criticism, or biography, *Ficciones* (1944) and *El Aleph* (1949). Borges was also a distinguished Anglo-Saxon scholar. He was the first writer to come to world prominence during the course of the so-called Latin American Boom in the 1960s. The blurring of linguistic and cultural frontiers implicit in the boom provides some sort of context for Borges's perennially intriguing fable 'Pierre Menard, Author of *Don Quixote*', in which French writer Menard learns Spanish and immerses himself in Cervantes's work, so as to translate or rewrite *Don Quixote*. This playful story is concerned with an obsessive interest in a 'foreign' work, and at a metaliterary level it addresses some crucial aspects of the personal and historical relationships implicated in the making of a translation.

From *Ficciones*, ed. and introd. Anthony Kerrigan (New York: Grove Press, Inc, 1962)

'*Pierre Menard, Author of* Don Quixote', *trans. Anthony Bonner*

To Silvina Ocampo

The *visible* works left by this novelist are easily and briefly enumerated. It is therefore impossible to forgive the omissions and additions perpetrated by Madame Henri Bachelier in a fallacious catalogue that a certain newspaper, whose Protestant tendencies are no secret, was inconsiderate enough to inflict on its wretched readers— even though they are few and Calvinist, if not Masonic and circumcized. Menard's true friends regarded this catalogue with alarm, and even with a certain sadness. It is as if yesterday we were gathered together before the final marble and the fateful cypresses, and already Error is trying to tarnish his Memory. ... Decidedly, a brief rectification is inevitable.

I am certain that it would be very easy to challenge my meager authority. I hope, nevertheless, that I will not be prevented from mentioning two important testimonials. The Baroness de Bacourt (at whose unforgettable *vendredis* I had the honor of becoming acquainted with the late lamented poet) has seen fit to approve these lines. The Countess de Bagnoregio, one of the most refined minds in the Principality of Monaco (and now of Pittsburgh, Pennsylvania, since her recent marriage to the international philanthropist Simon Kautsch who, alas, has been so slandered by the victims of his disinterested handiwork) has sacrificed to 'truth and death' (those are her words) that majestic reserve which distinguishes her, and in an open letter published in the magazine *Luxe* also grants me her consent. These authorizations, I believe, are not insufficient.

I have said that Menard's *visible* lifework is easily enumerated. Having carefully examined his private archives, I have been able to verify that it consists of the following:

a)   A symbolist sonnet which appeared twice (with variations) in the magazine *La Conque* (the March and October issues of 1899).

b)   A monograph on the possibility of constructing a poetic vocabulary of concepts that would not be synonyms or periphrases of those which make up ordinary language, 'but ideal objects created by means of common agreement and destined essentially to fill poetic needs' (Nîmes, 1901).

c)   A monograph on 'certain connections or affinities' among the ideas of Descartes, Leibnitz and John Wilkins (Nîmes, 1903).

d)   A monograph on the *Characteristica Universalis* of Leibnitz (Nîmes, 1904).

e)   A technical article on the possibility of enriching the game of chess by means of eliminating one of the rooks' pawns. Menard proposes, recommends, disputes, and ends by rejecting this innovation.

f)   A monograph on the *Ars Magna Generalis* of Ramón Lull (Nîmes, 1906).

g)   A translation with prologue and notes of the *Libro de la invención y arte del juego del axedrez* by Ruy López de Segura (Paris, 1907).

h)   The rough draft of a monograph on the symbolic logic of George Boole.

i)   An examination of the metric laws essential to French prose, illustrated with examples from Saint-Simon (*Revue des langues romanes*, Montpellier, October, 1909).

j)   An answer to Luc Durtain (who had denied the existence of such laws) illustrated with examples from Luc Durtain (*Revue des langues romanes*, Montpellier, December, 1909).

k)   A manuscript translation of the *Aguja de navegar cultos* of Quevedo, entitled *La boussole des précieux*.

l)   A preface to the catalogue of the exposition of lithographs by Carolus Hourcade (Nîmes, 1914).

m)   His work, *Les problèmes d'un problème* (Paris, 1917), which takes up in chronological order the various solutions of the famous problem of Achilles and the tortoise. Two editions of this book have appeared so far; the second has as an epigraph Leibnitz' advice 'Ne craignez point, monsieur, la tortue,' and contains revisions of the chapters dedicated to Russell and Descartes.

n)   An obstinate analysis of the 'syntactic habits' of Toulet (*N.R.F.*, March, 1921). I remember that Menard used to declare that censuring and praising were sentimental operations which had nothing to do with criticism.

o) A transposition into Alexandrines of *Le Cimetière marin* of Paul Valéry (*N.R.F.*, January, 1928).

p) An invective against Paul Valéry in the *Journal for the Suppression of Reality* of Jacques Reboul. (This invective, it should be stated parenthetically, is the exact reverse of his true opinion of Valéry. The latter understood it as such, and the old friendship between the two was never endangered.)

q) A 'definition' of the Countess of Bagnoregio in the 'victorious volume'—the phrase is that of another collaborator, Gabriele d'Annunzio—which this lady publishes yearly to rectify the inevitable falsifications of journalism and to present 'to the world and to Italy' an authentic effigy of her person, which is so exposed (by reason of her beauty and her activities) to erroneous or hasty interpretations.

r) A cycle of admirable sonnets for the Baroness de Bacourt (1934).

s) A manuscript list of verses which owe their effectiveness to punctuation.[1]

Up to this point (with no other omission than that of some vague, circumstantial sonnets for the hospitable, or greedy, album of Madame Henri Bachelier) we have the *visible* part of Menard's works in chronological order. Now I will pass over to that other part, which is subterranean, interminably heroic, and unequalled, and which is also—oh, the possibilities inherent in the man!—inconclusive. This work, possibly the most significant of our time, consists of the ninth and thirty-eighth chapters of Part One of *Don Quixote* and a fragment of the twenty-second chapter. I realize that such an affirmation seems absurd; but the justification of this 'absurdity' is the primary object of this note.[2]

Two texts of unequal value inspired the undertaking. One was that philological fragment of Novalis—No. 2005 of the Dresden edition—which outlines the theme of *total* identification with a specific author. The other was one of those parasitic books which places Christ on a boulevard, Hamlet on the Cannebière and Don Quixote on Wall Street. Like any man of good taste, Menard detested these useless carnivals, only suitable—he used to say—for evoking plebeian delight in anachronism, or (what is worse) charming us with the primary idea that all epochs are the same, or that they are different. He considered more interesting, even though it had been carried out in a contradictory and superficial way, Daudet's famous plan: to unite in *one* figure, Tartarin, the Ingenious Gentleman and his squire.... Any insinuation that Menard dedicated his life to the writing of a contemporary *Don Quixote* is a calumny of his illustrious memory.

---

[1] Madame Henri Bachelier also lists a literal translation of a literal translation done by Quevedo of the *Introduction à la vie dévote* of Saint Francis of Sales. In Pierre Menard's library there are no traces of such a work. She must have misunderstood a remark of his which he had intended as a joke.

[2] I also had another, secondary intent—that of sketching a portrait of Pierre Menard. But how would I dare to compete with the golden pages the Baroness de Bacourt tells me she is preparing, or with the delicate and precise pencil of Carolus Hourcade?

He did not want to compose another *Don Quixote* which would be easy—but *the Don Quixote.* It is unnecessary to add that his aim was never to produce a mechanical transcription of the original; he did not propose to copy it. His admirable ambition was to produce pages which would coincide—word for word and line for line—with those of Miguel de Cervantes.

'My intent is merely astonishing,' he wrote me from Bayonne on December 30th, 1934. 'The ultimate goal of a theological or metaphysical demonstration—the external world, God, chance, universal forms—are no less anterior or common than this novel which I am now developing. The only difference is that philosophers publish in pleasant volumes the intermediary stages of their work and that I have decided to lose them.' And, in fact, not one page of a rough draft remain to bear witness to this work of years.

The initial method he conceived was relatively simple: to know Spanish well, to re-embrace the Catholic faith, to fight against Moors and Turks, to forget European history between 1602 and 1918, and to *be* Miguel de Cervantes. Pierre Menard studied this procedure (I know that he arrived at a rather faithful handling of seventeenth-century Spanish) but rejected it as too easy. Rather because it was impossible, the reader will say! I agree, but the undertaking was impossible from the start, and of all the possible means of carrying it out, this one was the least interesting. To be, in the twentieth century, a popular novelist of the seventeenth seemed to him a diminution. To be, in some way, Cervantes and to arrive at *Don Quixote* seemed to him less arduous—and consequently less interesting—than to continue being Pierre Menard and to arrive at *Don Quixote* through the experiences of Pierre Menard. (This conviction, let it be said in passing, forced him to exclude the autobiographical prologue of the second part of *Don Quixote.* To include this prologue would have meant creating another personage—Cervantes— but it would also have meant presenting *Don Quixote* as the work of this personage and not of Menard. He naturally denied himself such an easy solution.) 'My undertaking is not essentially difficult,' I read in another part of the same letter. 'I would only have to be immortal in order to carry it out.' Shall I confess that I often imagine that he finished it and that I am reading *Don Quixote*—the entire work—as if Menard had conceived it? Several nights ago, while leafing through Chapter XXVI—which he had never attempted—I recognized our friend's style and, as it were, his voice in this exceptional phrase: *the nymphs of the rivers, mournful and humid Echo.* This effective combination of two adjectives, one moral and the other physical, reminded me of a line from Shakespeare which we discussed one afternoon:

Where a malignant and turbaned Turk ...

Why precisely *Don Quixote,* our reader will ask. Such a preference would not have been inexplicable in a Spaniard; but it undoubtedly was in a symbolist from Nîmes, essentially devoted to Poe, who engendered Baudelaire, who engendered Mallarmé, who engendered Valéry, who engendered Edmond Teste. The letter quoted above clarifies this point. '*Don Quixote*,' Menard explains, 'interests me profoundly, but it does not seem to me to have been—how shall I say it—inevitable. I cannot imagine the universe without the interjection of Edgar Allan Poe

Ah, bear in mind this garden was enchanted!

or without the *Bateau ivre* or the *Ancient Mariner*, but I know that I am capable of imagining it without *Don Quixote*. (I speak, naturally, of my personal capacity, not of the historical repercussions of these works.) *Don Quixote* is an accidental book, *Don Quixote* is unnecessary. I can premeditate writing, I can write it, without incurring a tautology. When I was twelve or thirteen years old I read it, perhaps in its entirety. Since then I have reread several chapters attentively, but not the ones I am going to undertake. I have likewise studied the *entremeses,* the comedies, the *Galatea*, the exemplary novels, and the undoubtedly laborious efforts of *Pérsiles y Sigismunda* and the *Viaje al Parnaso*. . . . My general memory of *Don Quixote*, simplified by forgetfulness and indifference, is much the same as the imprecise, anterior image of a book not yet written. Once this image (which no one can deny me in good faith) has been postulated, my problems are undeniably considerably more difficult than those which Cervantes faced. My affable precursor did not refuse the collaboration of fate; he went along composing his immortal work a little *à la diable*, swept along by inertias of language and invention. I have contracted the mysterious duty of reconstructing literally his spontaneous work. My solitary game is governed by two polar laws. The first permits me to attempt variants of a formal and psychological nature; the second obliges me to sacrifice them to the "original" text and irrefutably to rationalize this annihilation. . . . To these artificial obstacles one must add another congenital one. To compose *Don Quixote* at the beginning of the seventeenth century was a reasonable, necessary and perhaps inevitable undertaking; at the beginning of the twentieth century it is almost impossible. It is not in vain that three hundred years have passed, charged with the most complex happenings—among them, to mention only one, that same *Don Quixote*.'

  In spite of these three obstacles, the fragmentary *Don Quixote* of Menard is more subtle than that of Cervantes. The latter indulges in a rather coarse opposition between tales of knighthood and the meager, provincial reality of his country; Menard chooses as 'reality' the land of Carmen during the century of Lepanto and Lope. What Hispanophile would not have advised Maurice Barrès or Dr Rodríguez Larreta to make such a choice! Menard, as if it were the most natural thing in the world, eludes them. In his work there are neither bands of gypsies, conquistadors, mystics, Philip the Seconds, nor autos-da-fé. He disregards or proscribes local color. This disdain indicates a new approach to the historical novel. This disdain condemns *Salammbô* without appeal.

It is no less astonishing to consider isolated chapters. Let us examine, for instance, Chapter XXXVIII of Part One 'which treats of the curious discourse that Don Quixote delivered on the subject of arms and letters.' As is known, Don Quixote (like Quevedo in a later, analogous passage of *La hora de todos*) passes judgment against letters, and in favor of arms. Cervantes was an old soldier, which explains such a judgment. But that the *Don Quixote* of Pierre Menard—a contemporary of *La trahison des clercs* and Bertrand Russell—should relapse into these nebulous sophistries! Madame Bachelier has seen in them an admirable and typical subordination of the author to the psychology of the hero; others (by no means perspicaciously) a *transcription of Don Quixote*; the Baroness de Bacourt, the influence of Nietzsche. To this third interpretation (which seems to me irrefutable) I do not know if I would dare to add a fourth, which coincides very well with the divine modesty of Pierre Menard: his resigned or ironic habit of propounding ideas which were the strict reverse of those he preferred. (One will remember his diatribe against Paul Valéry in the ephemeral journal of the superrealist Jacques Reboul.) The text of Cervantes and that of Menard are verbally identical, but the second is almost infinitely richer. (More ambiguous, his detractors will say; but ambiguity is a richness.) It is a revelation to compare the *Don Quixote* of Menard with that of Cervantes. The latter, for instance, wrote (*Don Quixote*, Part One, Chapter Nine):

> *. . . la verdad, cuya madre es la historia, émula del tiempo, depósito de las acciones, testigo de lo pasado, ejemplo y aviso de lo presente, advertencia de lo por venir.*

> [. . . truth, whose mother is history, who is the rival of time, depository of deeds, witness of the past, example and lesson to the present, and warning to the future.]

Written in the seventeenth century, written by the 'ingenious layman' Cervantes, this enumeration is a mere rhetorical eulogy of history. Menard, on the other hand, writes:

> *. . . la verdad, cuya madre es la historia, émula del tiempo, depósito de las acciones, testigo de lo pasado, ejemplo y aviso de lo presente, advertencia de lo por venir.*

> [. . . truth, whose mother is history, who is the rival of time, depository of deeds, witness of the past, example and lesson to the present, and warning to the future.]

History, *mother* of truth; the idea is astounding. Menard, a contemporary of William James, does not define history as an investigation of reality, but as its origin. Historical truth, for him, is not what took place; it is what we think took place. The final clauses—*example and lesson to the present, and warning to the future*—are shamelessly pragmatic.

Equally vivid is the contrast in styles. The archaic style of Menard—in the last analysis, a foreigner—suffers from a certain affectation. Not so that of his precursor, who handles easily the ordinary Spanish of his time.

There is no intellectual exercise which is not ultimately useless. A philosophical doctrine is in the beginning a seemingly true description of the universe; as the years pass it becomes a mere chapter—if not a paragraph or a noun in the history of philosophy. In literature, this ultimate decay is even more notorious. '*Don Quixote,*' Menard once told me, 'was above all an agreeable book; now it is an occasion for patriotic toasts, grammatical arrogance and obscene deluxe editions. Glory is an incomprehension, and perhaps the worst.'

These nihilist arguments contain nothing new; what is unusual is the decision Pierre Menard derived from them. He resolved to outstrip that vanity which awaits all the woes of mankind; he undertook a task that was complex in the extreme and futile from the outset. He dedicated his conscience and nightly studies to the repetition of a pre-existing book in a foreign tongue. The number of rough drafts kept on increasing; he tenaciously made corrections and tore up thousands of manuscript pages.[3] He did not permit them to be examined, and he took great care that they would not survive him. It is in vain that I have tried to reconstruct them.

I have thought that it is legitimate to consider the 'final' *Don Quixote* as a kind of palimpsest, in which should appear traces—tenuous but not undecipherable—of the 'previous' handwriting of our friend. Unfortunately, only a second Pierre Menard, inverting the work of the former, could exhume and rescuscitate these Troys. . . .

'To think, analyze and invent,' he also wrote me, 'are not anomalous acts, but the normal respiration of the intelligence. To glorify the occasional fulfillment of this function, to treasure ancient thoughts of others, to remember with incredulous amazement that the *doctor universalis* thought, is to confess our languor or barbarism. Every man should be capable of all ideas, and I believe that in the future he will be.'

Menard (perhaps without wishing to) has enriched, by means of a new technique, the hesitant and rudimentary art of reading: the technique is one of deliberate anachronism and erroneous attributions. This technique, with its infinite applications, urges us to run through the *Odyssey* as if it were written after the *Aeneid*, and to read *Le jardin du Centaure* by Madame Henri Bachelier as if it were by Madame Henri Bachelier. This technique would fill the dullest books with adventure. Would not the attributing of *The Imitation of Christ* to Louis Ferdinand Céline or James Joyce be a sufficient renovation of its tenuous spiritual counsels?

Nîmes

1939

---

[3] I remember his square-ruled notebooks, the black streaks where he had crossed out words, his peculiar typographical symbols and his insect-like handwriting. In the late afternoon he liked to go for walks on the outskirts of Nîmes; he would take a notebook with him and make a gay bonfire.

4.7 ROMAN JAKOBSON

Roman Jakobson (1896–1982), literary theorist and linguist, was born and educated in Moscow. He was associated with a number of Futurist painters and poets, and himself experimented with 'supraconscious' poems. Jakobson was particularly friendly with and influenced by the radically experimental poet Khlebnikov, about whose work he wrote extensively. He was friendly with Mayakovsky from 1916 until the poet's suicide in 1930, writing extensively about his work. Jakobson was co-founder of both the Moscow Linguistic Circle, in 1915, and the Prague Linguistic Circle, in 1926, and was thus a key figure both in the development of Russian Formalism and Czech Structuralism. In 1916, he had collaborated with Petersburg literary scholars in establishing a formalist group, called the Society for the Study of Poetic Language (OPOJAZ). Jakobson came to the USA in 1941, teaching at Harvard and MIT. His essay, 'On Linguistic Aspects of Translation' extends the significance of translation to include intralingual and intersemiotic translation. It first appeared in Reuben Brower's landmark volume, *On Translation* (Cambridge, Mass. Harvard University Press, 1959). Jakobson's emphasis on the functional role of linguistic elements in the translated text had a positive effect on the work of poetry translators. Regarding poetry by definition as untranslatable, Jakobson believed in the inevitability of 'creative transposition'.

'On Linguistic Aspects of Translation', in R. Jakobson, *Language in Literature*, ed. Krystyna Pomorska and Stephen Rudy (Cambridge, Mass.: Harvard University Press, 1987), 428–35

According to Bertrand Russell, 'no one can understand the word "cheese" unless he has a nonlinguistic acquaintance with cheese.'[1] If, however, we follow Russell's fundamental precept and place our 'emphasis upon the linguistic aspects of traditional philosophical problems,' then we are obliged to state that no one can understand the word *cheese* unless he has an acquaintance with the meaning assigned to this word in the lexical code of English. Any representative of a cheese-less culinary culture will understand the English word *cheese* if he is aware that in this language it means 'food made of pressed curds' and if he has at least a linguistic acquaintance with *curds*. We never consumed ambrosia or nectar and have only a linguistic acquaintance with the words *ambrosia, nectar*, and *gods*—the name of their mythical users; nonetheless, we understand these words and know in what contexts each of them may be used.

The meaning of the words *cheese, apple, nectar, acquaintance, but, mere*, and of any word or phrase whatsoever is definitely a linguistic—or to be more precise and less narrow—a semiotic fact. Against those who assign meaning (*signatum*) not to the sign, but to the thing itself, the simplest and truest argument would be that nobody has ever smelled or tasted the meaning of *cheese* or of *apple*. There is no *signatum* without *signum*. The meaning of the word 'cheese' cannot be inferred from a nonlinguistic acquaintance with cheddar or with camembert without the assistance of the verbal code. An array of linguistic signs is needed to introduce an unfamiliar word. Mere pointing will not teach us whether *cheese* is the name of the given specimen, or of any box of camembert, or of camembert in general or of any cheese, any milk product, any food, any refreshment, or perhaps any box irrespective of contents. Finally, does a word simply name the thing in question, or does it imply a meaning such as offering, sale, prohibition, or malediction? (Pointing actually may mean malediction; in some cultures, particularly in Africa, it is an ominous gesture.)

For us, both as linguists and as ordinary word-users, the meaning of any linguistic sign is its translation into some further, alternative sign, especially a sign 'in which it is more fully developed,' as Peirce, the deepest inquirer into the essence of signs, insistently stated.[2] The term 'bachelor' may be converted into a more explicit designation, 'unmarried man,' whenever higher explicitness is required. We distinguish three ways of interpreting a verbal sign: it may be translated into other signs of the same language, into another language, or into another, nonverbal system of symbols. These three kinds of translation are to be differently labeled:

(1) Intralingual translation or *rewording* is an interpretation of verbal signs by means of other signs of the same language.

(2) Interlingual translation or *translation proper* is an interpretation of verbal signs by means of some other language.

(3) Intersemiotic translation or *transmutation* is an interpretation of verbal signs by means of signs of nonverbal sign systems.

The intralingual translation of a word uses either another, more or less synonymous, word or resorts to a circumlocution. Yet synonymy, as a rule, is not complete equivalence: for example, 'every celibate is a bachelor, but not every bachelor is a celibate.' A word or an idiomatic phraseword, briefly a code-unit of the highest level, may be fully interpreted only by means of an equivalent combination of code-units, i.e., a message referring to this code-unit: 'every bachelor is an unmarried man, and every unmarried man is a bachelor,' or 'every celibate is bound not to marry, and everyone who is bound not to marry is a celibate.'

Likewise, on the level of interlingual translation, there is ordinarily no full equivalence between code-units, while messages may serve as adequate interpretations of alien code-units or messages. The English word cheese cannot be completely identified with its standard Russian heteronym *syr* because cottage cheese is a cheese but not a *syr*. Russians say: *prinesi syru i tvorogu*, (bring cheese and [sic] cottage cheese). In standard Russian, the food made of pressed curds is called *syr* only if ferment is used.

Most frequently, however, translation from one language into another substitutes messages in one language not for separate code-units but for entire messages in some other language. Such a translation is a reported speech; the translator recodes and transmits a message received from another source. Thus translation involves two equivalent messages in two different codes.

Equivalence in difference is the cardinal problem of language and the pivotal concern of linguistics. Like any receiver of verbal messages, the linguist acts as their interpreter. No linguistic specimen may be interpreted by the science of language without a translation of its signs into other signs of the same system or into signs of another system. Any comparison of two languages implies an examination of their mutual translatability; widespread practice of interlingual communication, particularly translating activities, must be kept under constant scrutiny by linguistic science. It is difficult to overestimate the urgent need for and the theoretical and practical significance of differential bilingual dictionaries with careful comparative definition of all the corresponding units in their intension and extension. Likewise differential bilingual grammars should define what unifies and what differentiates the two languages in their selection and delimitation of grammatical concepts.

Both the practice and the theory of translation abound with intricacies, and from time to time attempts are made to sever the Gordian knot by proclaiming the dogma of untranslatability. 'Mr Everyman, the natural logician,' vividly imagined by Benjamin Whorf, is supposed to have arrived at the following bit of reasoning: 'Facts are unlike to speakers whose language background provides for unlike formulation of them.'[3] In the first years of the Russian revolution there were fanatic visionaries who argued in Soviet periodicals for a radical revision of traditional language and particularly for the weeding out of such misleading expressions as 'sunrise' or 'sunset.' Yet we still use this Ptolemaic imagery without implying a rejection of Copernican doctrine, and we can easily transform our customary talk about the rising and setting sun into a picture of the earth's rotation simply because any sign is translatable into a sign in which it appears to us more fully developed and precise.

An ability to speak a given language implies a faculty of talking about this language. Such a metalinguistic operation permits revision and redefinition of the vocabulary used. The complementarity of both levels—object-language and metalanguage—was brought out by Niels Bohr: all well-defined experimental evidence must be expressed in ordinary language, 'in which the practical use of every word stands in complementary relation to attempts of its strict definition.'[4]

All cognitive experience and its classification is conveyable in any existing language. Whenever there is deficiency, terminology may be qualified and amplified by loanwords or loan-translations, neologisms or semantic shifts, and finally, by circumlocutions. Thus in the newborn literary language of the Northeast Siberian Chukchees, 'screw' is rendered as 'rotating nail,' 'steel' as 'hard iron,' 'tin' as 'thin iron,' 'chalk' as 'writing soap,' 'watch' as 'hammering heart.' Even seemingly contradictory circumlocutions, like 'electrical horsecar' (èlektričeskaja konka), the first Russian name of the horseless street car, or 'flying steamship' (jeha paraqot), the Koryak term for the airplane, simply designate the electrical analogue of the horsecar and the flying analogue of the steamer and do not impede communication, just as there is no semantic 'noise' and disturbance in the double oxymoron—'cold beef-and-pork hot dog.'

No lack of grammatical device in the language translated into makes impossible a literal translation of the entire conceptual information contained in the original. The traditional conjunctions 'and,' 'or' are now supplemented by a new connective—'and/ or'—which was discussed a few years ago in the witty book *Federal Prose – How to Write in and/or for Washington*.[5] Of these three conjunctions, only the latter occurs in one of the Samoyed languages.[6] Despite these differences in the inventory of conjunctions, all three varieties of messages observed in 'federal prose' may be distinctly translated both into traditional English and into this Samoyed language. Federal prose: 1) John and Peter, 2) John or Peter, 3) John and/or Peter will come. Traditional English: 3) John and Peter or one of them will come. Samoyed: John and/or Peter both will come, 2) John and/or Peter, one of them will come.

If some grammatical category is absent in a given language, its meaning may be translated into this language by lexical means. Dual forms like Old Russian *brata* are translated with the help of the numeral: 'two brothers.' It is more difficult to remain faithful to the original when we translate into a language provided with a certain grammatical category from a language devoid of such a category. When translating the English sentence *She has brothers* into a language which discriminates dual and plural, we are compelled either to make our own choice between two statements 'She has two brothers'—'She has more than two' or to leave the decision to the listener and say: 'She has either two or more than two brothers.' Again in translating from a language without grammatical number into English one is obliged to select one of the two possibilities— *brother* or *brothers* or to confront the receiver of this message with a two-choice situation: *She has either one or more than one brother.*

As Franz Boas neatly observed, the grammatical pattern of a language (as opposed to its lexical stock) determines those aspects of each experience that must be expressed in the given language: 'We have to choose between these aspects, and one or the other must be chosen.'[7] In order to translate accurately the English sentence *I hired a worker*, a Russian needs supplementary information, whether this action was completed or not and whether the worker was a man or a woman, because he must make his choice between a verb of completive or noncompletive aspect—*nanjal* or *nanimal*—and between a masculine and feminine noun—*rabotnika* or *rabotnicu*. If I ask the utterer of the English sentence whether the worker was male or female, my question may be judged irrelevant or indiscreet, whereas in the Russian version of this sentence an answer to this question is obligatory. On the other hand, whatever the choice of Russian grammatical forms to translate the quoted English message, the translation will give no answer to the question of whether I *hired* or *have hired* the worker, or whether he/she was an indefinite or definite worker (*a* or *the*). Because the information required by the English and Russian grammatical pattern is unlike, we face quite different sets of two-choice situations; therefore a chain of translations of one and the same isolated sentence from English into Russian and vice versa could entirely deprive such a message of its initial content. The Geneva linguist S. Karcevskij used to compare such a gradual loss with a circular series of unfavorable currency transactions. But evidently the richer the context of a message, the smaller the loss of information.

Languages differ essentially in what they *must* convey and not in what they *can* convey. Each verb of a given language imperatively raises a set of specific yes-or-no questions, as for instance: is the narrated event conceived with or without reference to its completion? Is the narrated event presented as prior to the speech event or not? Naturally the attention of native speakers and listeners will be constantly focused on such items as are compulsory in their verbal code.

In its cognitive function, language is minimally dependent on the grammatical pattern because the definition of our experience stands in complementary relation to metalinguistic operations—the cognitive level of language not only admits but directly requires recoding interpretation, that is, translation. Any assumption of ineffable or untranslatable cognitive data would be a contradiction in terms. But in jest, in dreams, in magic, briefly, in what one would call everyday verbal mythology and in poetry above all, the grammatical categories carry a high semantic import. In these conditions, the question of translation becomes much more entangled and controversial.

Even such a category as grammatical gender, often cited as merely formal, plays a great role in the mythological attitudes of a speech community. In Russian the feminine cannot designate a male person, nor the masculine specify a female. Ways of personifying or metaphorically interpreting inanimate nouns are prompted by their gender. A test in the Moscow Psychological Institute (1915) showed that Russians, prone to personify the weekdays, consistently represented Monday, Tuesday, and Thursday as males and Wednesday, Friday, and Saturday as females, without realizing that this distribution was due to the masculine gender of the first three names (*ponedel'nik*, *vtornik*, *četverg*) as against the feminine gender of the others (*sreda*, *pjatnica*, *subbota*). The fact that the word for Friday is masculine in some Slavic languages and feminine in others is reflected in the folk traditions of the corresponding peoples, which differ in their Friday ritual. The widespread Russian superstition that a dropped knife presages a male guest and a dropped fork a female one is determined by the masculine gender of *nož* (knife) and the feminine of *vilka* (fork) in Russian. In Slavic and other languages where 'day' is masculine and 'night' feminine, day is represented by poets as the lover of night. The Russian painter Repin was baffled as to why Sin had been depicted as a woman by German artists: he did not realize that 'sin' is feminine in German (*die Sünde*), but masculine in Russian (*grex*). Likewise a Russian child, while reading a translation of German tales, was astounded to find that Death, obviously a woman (Russian *smert'*, fem.), was pictured as an old man (German *der Tod,* masc.). *My Sister Life,* the title of a book of poems by Boris Pasternak, is quite natural in Russian, where 'life' is feminine (*žizn'*), but was enough to reduce to despair the Czech poet Josef Hora in his attempt to translate these poems, since in Czech this noun is masculine (*život*).

What was the first problem which arose in Slavic literature at its very beginning? Curiously enough, the translator's difficulty in preserving the symbolism of genders, and the cognitive irrelevance of this difficulty, appears to be the main topic of the earliest Slavic original work, the preface to the first translation of the *Evangeliarium,* made in the early 860's by the founder of Slavic letters and liturgy, Constantine the Philosopher, and recently restored and interpreted by André Vaillant.[8] 'Greek, when translated into another language, cannot always be reproduced identically, and that happens to each language being translated,' the Slavic apostle states. 'Masculine nouns like *potamos* (river) and *aster* (star) in Greek, are feminine in another language like *rěka* and *zvězda* in Slavic.' According to Vaillant's commentary, this divergence effaces the symbolic identification of the rivers with demons and of the stars with angels in the Slavic translation of two of Matthew's verses (7: 25 and 2: 9). But to this poetic obstacle, Saint Constantine resolutely opposes the precept of Dionysius the Areopagite, who called for chief attention to the cognitive values (*silě razumu*) and not to the words themselves.

In poetry, verbal equations become a constructive principle of the text. Syntactic and morphological categories, roots, and affixes, phonemes and their components (distinctive features)—in short, any constituents of the verbal code—are confronted, juxtaposed, brought into contiguous relation according to the principle of similarity and contrast and carry their own autonomous signification. Phonemic similarity is sensed as semantic relationship. The pun, or to use a more erudite, and perhaps more precise term—paronomasia, reigns over poetic art, and whether its rule is absolute or limited, poetry by definition is untranslatable. Only creative transposition is possible: either intralingual transposition—from one poetic shape into another, or interlingual transposition—from one language into another, or finally intersemiotic transposition—from one system of signs into another (from verbal art into music, dance, cinema, or painting).

If we were to translate into English the traditional formula *Traduttore, traditore* as 'the translator is a betrayer,' we would deprive the Italian rhyming epigram of all its paronomastic value. Hence a cognitive attitude would compel us to change this aphorism into a more explicit statement and to answer the questions: translator of what messages? betrayer of what values?

NOTES

1. Bertrand Russell, 'Logical Positivism,' *Revue Internationale de philosophie,* 4 (1950), 18; cf. p. 3.
2. Cf. John Dewey, 'Peirce's Theory of Linguistic Signs, Thought, and Meaning,' *Journal of Philosophy,* 43 (1946), 91.
3. Benjamin Lee Whorf, *Language, Thought, and Reality* (Cambridge, Mass., 1956), p. 235.
4. Niels Bohr, 'On the Notions of Causality and Complementarity,' *Dialectica,* 1 (1948), 317 ff.
5. James R. Masterson and Wendell Brooks Phillips, *Federal Prose* (Chapel Hill, 1948), 40–41.
6. Cf. Knut Bergsland, 'Finsk-ugrisk og almen sprakvitenskap,' *Norsk Tidsskrift for Sprogvidenskap,* 15 (1949), 374–375.
7. Franz Boas, 'Language,' *General Anthropology* (Boston, 1938), 132–133.
8. Andre Vaillant, 'Le Préface de l'Evangeliaire vieux-slave,' *Revue des études slaves,* 24 (1948), 5–6.

4.8 JIŘÍ LEVÝ

Jiří Levý (1926–67) was a Czech theorist and historian of literature, who became at an early age a leading scholar of translation in what used to be called 'Eastern Europe'. His work built and extended upon the research of Russian formalism and the Czech structuralism of the Prague school, aimed as it was at combining structural analysis of literary works with a semantic one, emphasizing, for instance, the information value of the formal components of poetry. In 1957 he brought out an anthology of Czech theories of translation, and in 1963 the book *Umění překladu* ('The Art of Translation'), which he later reworked in preparation for Russian and German translations. The German translation, by Walter Schamschula, was published in 1969 under the title *Die literarische Übersetzung. Theorie einer Kunstgattung*. The German version was later translated into English by Susanne Flatauer (the manuscript is entitled *Literary Translation as an Art Form*), but it was not published at the time, and as far as we can establish, no part of it has appeared until now— see excerpts below. Hence, many students of translation know Levý only through a few articles, especially the often-quoted 1967 article 'Translation as a Decision-Making Process' (*To Honor Roman Jakobson*, vol. ii, (The Hague)).

The parts of Levý's book included below manifest several of his key conceptions of translation. He situates literary translation within a general communicative theory of translation (cf. also Mary Snell-Hornby in Sect. 5.6, below) and he seeks to locate the aesthetic qualities of literary works through a structural analysis in which he establishes the interplay and hierarchy of textual aspects. Since the translator cannot bring everything across, it is important to decide firmly what elements of the work must be preserved in order for it to function as a whole in its new language. Levý is fully aware that translation is a hybrid phenomenon, one that is often riddled with contradiction between the foreign and the native, but he sees it as the translator's task to minimize the wrinkles caused by this state of affairs, and to put together a textual whole which will function in its new context without calling too much attention to the fact that it is a translation. His book is a theory of what he himself calls the 'illusionist' method of translation; in his book he also talks about the 'principle of realist translation'—this approach runs counter to theories of foreignization represented by several critcs in this volume (see e.g. Sect. 3.2, 3.3, 4.4, and 5.2 on Goethe, Schleiermacher, Benjamin, Steiner respectively). 'A good translator must above all be an efficient reader', Levý says, a reader who refashions the work for another reader who is not to be made conscious of the kind of performance the translator is involved in. In fact, Levý repeatedly compares translation to the performing arts, especially dramatic performance. He sees the Stanislawskian theatre training (i.e. in method acting) as the closest analogy to the education of a good translator.

From *Literary Translation as an Art Form*, translated by Susanne Flatauer

A good starting-point from which detailed and specialized theories of translation may be developed is the precedence according to which individual aspects of the translated text are preserved—and this precedence depends on the structure of the written or spoken text, and not on the purpose which the translation is to serve. In the process of translation, the message may be divided into (a) elements which remain, or ought to remain, constant = i; and (b) variable elements which are being replaced by an equivalent in the target language = v. This may be illustrated for some of the most important types of texts and for some basic linguistic factors, as follows:

	technical text	journalistic and rhetorical prose	literary prose and drama	free verse	rhymed verse	musical text (libretto)	dubbing
denotative meaning	i	i	i	i	i	i–v	i–v
connotative meaning	v	i–v	i	i	i	i	i
stylistic classification of the word	i–v	i	i	i	i	i	i
syntax	v	i–v	i	i	i	i	i
repetition of qualities of sound (rhythm, rhyme)	v	v	v	i–v	i	i	i–v
length and pitch of vowels	v	v	v	i–v	i–v	i	i
characteristics of enunciation	v	v	v	i–v	i–v	i–v	i

The difficulty of translation increases during the course of transition from technical text to dubbing, for here factors are added which must be constant. The emphasis shifts toward invariability of the respective lower linguistic elements, and at the same time, the demand for invariability of the higher components is often relaxed: in poetry it is sometimes more important to retain the connotative rather than the denotative meaning. This becomes even more obvious in the translation of opera libretti. Our diagram is, admittedly, only a very rough sketch. Thus the statement that in dubbing the form of enunciation should be preserved needs to be defined exactly to the effect that what is important is 'the visual form of movement of enunciation'. Of course, whether the individual linguistic elements are obligatory or not (i–v), e.g. in poetry, depends, and this will be readily understood, on genre, etc.

[. . .]

Thus it remains for us to define the conception of translation on which this book is based. The 'conciseness' of a translation as well as the truthfulness of figuration, the probability of motivation, etc., are special instances of one single general category which we may call neotic compatibility. And attitudes to this category lie essentially between two extremes: illusionism and anti-illusionism.

Illusionist methods demand that the work should 'look like the original, like reality'. This may be seen clearly in the illusionist theatre which dresses up its actors and builds its scenery with scrupulous historical correctness. The novel is based on the illusion of the author's omniscience and presents its narrative as an objective record of reality, in which the author does not interfere. The illusionist translator hides behind the original which he presents to the reader, as it were, without a mediator, in order to evoke in him an illusion by translation: that is to say, the illusion of reading the original text. In every case, this is an illusion which relies on a tacit agreement with the reader or spectator: the playgoer knows that what he sees on the stage is not reality, but he demands that it should look like reality; the novel-reader knows that he is reading an invented story, but he demands that the novel should keep to the rules of probability. Thus the reader of a translation, too, knows that he is not reading the original, but he demands that the translation should retain the quality of the original. Then he will be ready to believe that he is reading *Faust, Buddenbrooks*, or *Dead Souls*.

Anti-illusionist methods trifle boldly with the fact that it is only an imitation of reality which they are offering to the public. The figure on the stage proclaims himself to be an actor, and, taking off his mask, he points at a tree and announces that this tree represents a forest. The novelist digresses from epic illusion; addressing his reader, he discusses with him what he ought to do with the figure of his hero. The translator, too, may digress from his illusion by translation. He does this by revealing his standpoint as observer, by not simulating an original work, but by annotating it, or by 'nudging' the reader with the help of personal and topical allusions. Anti-illusionist translation is rare (basically it includes parody and caricature), for the aim of translation is primarily representative; it is to 'grasp' the text. An abstract athematic translation would really be an anti-translation.

Thus our book makes the attempt of establishing an 'illusionist' theory of translation. In so doing, we do not deny the possibility of experiments, though these will always have to be understood with the 'normal' translation forming a background for them. Whether we shall characterize this standpoint as functional, using the linguistic conception, or as realistic, using the aesthetic conception, will depend on the content which we attribute to these conceptions. The important thing is not going to be the preservation of 'the work as such', but to maintain its value for the recipient (that is to say, the distinctive or sociological functions of its elements). We shall not insist upon the experience of the reader of the original having to be identical with that of the reader of the translation. Instead we shall insist upon an identity from the point of view of the function in the overall structure of the socio-historical contexts of both readers. What is important is to subordinate the details to the whole, be it in regard to their function in the system or in regard to a schematized validity.

[. . .]

To translate is to communicate. Strictly speaking, the translator decodes the information contained in the original author's text and reformulates, or encodes, it in his own language. The reader, in turn, decodes the information contained in the text of the translation. Thus a chain of communication is formed which can be diagrammatically illustrated:

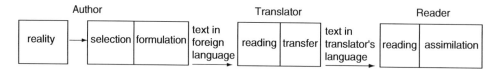

This chain is further complicated in the course of the production of a translated play: the cast decodes the text of the translation and performs the new information which is then taken in by the audience.

An analysis of the meaning of a work of art may be considered from two possible angles: (a) the communicative aspect which establishes the processes taking place during the transfer of the statement from author to recipient; and (b) the representative aspect, with the essential criterion of what the work embodies, as well as the relationship of its contents to its creator and to the interplay of the surrounding factors. Our knowledge of the former aspect has been defined mainly by the theory of information and its conception of language as a code (i.e. as as system of units, and of rules for linking them), in addition to the conception of a work as encoded information. The theory of information enables us to determine which elements of a translation must remain unchanged (i.e. information) and which will have to be replaced (i.e. the linguistic code).

Up to now, our knowledge of the latter aspect (discussed by as early a philosopher as Aristotle in his theory of mimesis) has been extensively defined by Marxist philosophy of art and its interpretation of a work of art as a representation of reality, for the analysis of which it has, above all, applied the dialectics of the object and subject.

[. . .]

Having outlined the process of creating a translation, we shall attempt to formulate some of the demands which are made of the translator's work. Starting from the thesis that his original represents the material with which he must deal artistically, we can summarize the demands made upon the translator in three ways. He must

(1) fully comprehend the original,

(2) interpret the original,

(3) translate the original.

Comprehension of the original:

We expect that the artist who has created the original work should have comprehended the reality he represents, and that the translator, in turn, should comprehend the work he translates. A good translator must above all be an efficient reader.

[...]

Not until the translator has grasped the reality in the form in which it has been executed in the work, will he be able to create an artistically true translation.

Educational means which might lead to such a comprehension of the reality, will first have to be established. Certainly, to gain experience in the dramaturgic interpretation of plays will have to be one of these means, as well as the concentrated thinking through of literary works. A part of this education would consist of detailed analysis of the heroes' mental and physical characteristics, in descriptions of the place of action and of situations; in subtle analysis of interrelationships between the characters, or between action and scenery, author and work, work and time; in an analysis of the reflection of an alien milieu in the work; in an analysis of its meaning, etc. It will surely be possible to find methods similar to those used by Stanislavski for the training of actors, in order to reveal hidden textual meanings and develop the translator's imagination.

[...]

A translated work is a hybrid form. A translation is not a homogenous work, but a conglomerate, a blending of two structures: on the one hand, there is its content, its meaning, as well as its formal outline; on the other hand, the whole system of language-related traits which the translator has added to the work. Between these two layers—or rather qualities which intermingle throughout the work as a whole—there exists a state of tension, which may result in conflict.

The content of the work is dependent on an alien milieu; its language is the mother tongue. The reader is conscious of this dichotomy only when there is a clear conflict between the milieu of the action and the specifically native expression. There are cases where even the best possible solution is a compromise which cannot quite conceal the contradictions in the translation.

[...]

The more perfect the translation, the better able it is to overcome its unavoidable quality of being contradictory. That is why translating requires—in addition to all that translation and original work presuppose equally—one particular ability: the translator must know how to compensate for contradictions which will arise of necessity in the translated work owing to its ambivalent character. For it requires only one small detail to draw the reader's attention to the fact that he is reading a book which has been transplanted into an alien soil, just as the spectator will be reminded by some minor clumsiness that the figures on the stage are only pretending, which will instantly disrupt his immediate enjoyment of the play. It is this which misleads critics into clinging to details and to emphasizing, above all, the negative facets of a translation.

In translation more than anywhere else a consistency of conception is needed, i.e. a definite grasp of the work and a consistent basic attitude to it. Then again, we may very often observe a degree of uncertainty in the use of techniques, and this depends entirely on the translator's resourcefulness. Translators using dialects frequently allow one person to use the same word in different guise. The translation often shows how, step by step, the translator managed to find better solutions for constantly recurring situations. In the methods used we can also sometimes trace vacillation between the intention of either bringing the work to the reader or taking him to it. First and foremost, though, a translator must have a consistent aim in his own mind, and this must be given precedence over partial solutions.

[. . .]

A literary work is an historically conditioned fact which cannot be repeated. There can be no identity between original and translation, and that is why the exclusive element cannot be wholly retained. To demand this would result in literal translation, in a naturalistic copying of dialects which are conditioned socially as well as by time and place, in formalist adherence to metre and, theoretically, to the thesis of the untranslatability of any work. Strictly speaking, however, there is, between an original and its translation, not the same relationship as between an object and its reflection (i.e. reality and art, or literary model and independent variations on it), and that is why the important aspects of a translation are neither artistic transformation nor taking to an intellectual conclusion of the exclusive traits of the original. In practice this would lead to actualization and adaptation to local realities, and in theory to the thesis that a translation must be better than its original. The relationship between a translation and its original is that of a work and its actualization in another material; therefore, on no account should it be the realization of the form : content unity in the linguistic material which is regarded as the constant factor, but the realization of that unity in the mind of the receptor, or, in more simple terms, the impression the work makes on the reader. For the reader, then, the important feature of translation is not mechanical retention of form, but of its semantic and aesthetic values; not the retention of all those details which emphasize the historical milieu of the time of a work's creation, is the important feature of the specifically national and temporal aspect, but to awaken in the reader the impression, the illusion of a definite historical national milieu. Several working principles may be established from this.

A literary work takes its material from the social consciousness of its surroundings and realizes it through the communication medium, i.e. language. Thus, only when the social consciousness and the communication media of both author and reader are the same, will the realization of a work not be distorted. Due to the continuous development of the social consciousness of the nation in which the work was created, some elements in its content will, in the course of this development, cease to be wholly comprehensible even within the context of its native literature, or perhaps their sense will be distorted; among these elements are time-related facts, human relationships, etc. In the same way, language develops in the main stylistically: an expression regarded by the author as a colloquial phrase and understood as such by the contemporary reader, can lose its popular character in generations to come and finally turn into an archaism. That is why today a foreign reader will catch the distorted meaning of the work. And that is why the translation should start out from the undistorted original realization.

Only those specific elements should be retained in a translation which the reader will be able to perceive as characteristic of the foreign milieu, i.e. only those capable of being vehicles for the meaning of national and temporal characteristics. All the rest which the reader no longer perceives as a reflection of the milieu, will lose substance and deteriorate into becoming form without content, since they can no longer be realized.

In consideration of these facts the translator from the Russian will preserve the patronymic form (Vasilij Ivanovitch) because we already regard it as typically Russian. Conversely, a translator from the English will not retain the custom for a married woman to be known not only by her husband's surname, but also by his Christian name, because the reader will not recognize the typically English mode of appellation. Amelia Sedley, Thackeray's heroine in *Vanity Fair*, is called Mrs George Osborne after her marriage; as a rule, this is not translated [into German] as *Frau Georg Osborne*, but as *Frau Osborne* or *Frau Amelie Osborne*.

[...]

In contrast to an original work, a translation is not an independent literary entity. It is meant to be the reproduction of another work, and this very relationship to the original is its fundamental characteristic. In this genre it is precisely because we evaluate a translation according to its relation to the original that we find the course between beginning and end of the creative process of such absorbing interest. For this reason, an analysis of how a translation is created is extremely important. At the same time, the process of creation is harder to evaluate in connection with translators than with the original author, because evidence of this process may be detected only in the linguistic expression, usually in delicate semantic nuances, and it is this very wording which is so often interfered with by editors, publishers and other adaptors.

If conclusions about the relationship of the translated version and its original are to be reliable, it will in the first place be necessary to establish reliably which text the translator used as his original. Work on the history of a translation, particularly an earlier one, is made more difficult by the fact that many writers, including eminent authors, translate, as it were, second-hand, and this takes place not only from oriental but also from most of the minor European literatures. When translating from oriental works, it is very frequently the English text which serves as a link; and the German when translating from minor European literatures, but there are others as well. Thus at about 1800 Czech translators would translate via German and Polish texts. Conversely Czech texts have been the starting point for Polish translators from the time of Humanism. The scholar investigating a translator's conception of his original text might end up by describing in fact an extraneous translation on which the translator's version had been based.

Mostly it is misunderstandings and deviations hard to attribute to a direct translation which draw our attention to a dependence on an extraneous translation.

In 1889, the *Bibliothèque populaire* published a French translation of short stories by Jan Neruda under the title *Contes tchèques*. Several misunderstandings clearly point to the fact that this is not a direct translation from the Czech, but a translation via the German. *Selský trh* : *Bauernmarkt* : *Marché aux Maçons* (instead of *Marché aux Paysans*), *Petřín* : *Laurenziberg* : *le Mont Saint-Laurent* (instead of *le Mont Saint-Pierre*). It is not difficult to find the German link text: Jurenka's translation of *Kleinsaitner Geschichten* (Tales from Kleinseiten) and Smital's translation of *Genrebilder* (Genre Pieces) which appeared in *Reclam's Universal Library* during the years 1883–6. [. . .].

Admittedly, second-hand translating has not always been as simple as that. We must take into account that often the translator worked with several texts, and that he either used an extraneous translation to help him find a solution for semantically or stylistically difficult details or that, conversely, he later compared and checked with the original a translation which had been prepared from an extraneous translation. Moreover, in such cases it is usually possible to establish the method of working.

[. . .]

As soon as the historian has ascertained the points of reference from which the translator started out, he will be able to tackle his main task, namely the analysis of the principles of the translator's conception and working methods. Technically speaking, there exists in every translation a certain percentage—which varies according to its accuracy—of different values which the translator has added to the text. It is precisely these deviations from his original which will reveal most clearly the translator's methods and his attitude to the translated work. That is why the analysis of a translation must begin with a careful comparison of the translated version and the original text and, in addition, with, so-to-speak, statistical recordings of deviations in details as far they can be ascertained. Here we may say again that while a number of deviations will be accidental, a proportion will be characteristic for the relationship between the translator's personal style and the style of the period in which the original was written, for the relationship between his conception of the work and its objective idea. Among accidental deviations—which, at the most, may serve as evidence of the translator's linguistic knowledge or conscientiousness—are obvious semantic mistakes. Most reviews of translations concentrate precisely on these mistakes, and for that reason this material will not provide a very rich source for work on the history of translation. We shall find other inaccuracies which, at least partly, can be classified in several groups all of which are invariably characterized by some kind of semantic or aesthetic shifting vis-à-vis the original. These groups of deviations will indicate clearly the translator's main principles of interpretation.

4.9 EUGENE A. NIDA

Eugene A. Nida (b. 1914), American pioneer in development of theory and practice of Bible translation, took a degree in Greek, encountering the works of such linguists as Edward Sapir and Leonard Bloomfield. From 1946 until his retirement in the 1980s, he was executive secretary for Translations of the American Bible Society.

Nida undertook a series of field trips in Africa and Latin America, during which he worked with missionary translators on linguistic problems, and searched for potential indigenous translators. He emphasized the need to provide translators with better models, resources, and training, building a translations network and organizational structure that became the global United Bible Societies Translations Program (UBS). Nida has published widely, including *Toward a Science of Translating* (Brill, 1964), and later *The Theory and Practice of Translation* (Brill, 1969, with C. R. Taber), expounding a theory of dynamic (functional) equivalence, an approach designed to enable the translator to capture the meaning and spirit of the original language text without being bound to its linguistic structure.

The excerpt below deals with Nida's key notion of dynamic equivalence. This is followed by the *Good News Bible* version of Genesis 11, The Tower of Babel. *The Good News Bible* is the best-known example of a biblical translation based on a model of dynamic equivalence. See also other versions of this passage, e.g. Septuagint, Tyndale (Sect. 2.3), Authorized Version (Sect. 2.9), and Fox (Sect. 5.20) (this last based on diametrically different Bible translation principles).

From *Toward a Science of Translating: With Special Reference to Principles and Procedures Involved in Bible Translating* **(Leiden: E. J. Brill, 1964), 156–60**

> Since no two languages are identical, either in the meanings given to corresponding symbols or in the ways in which such symbols are arranged in phrases and sentences, it stands to reason that there can be no absolute correspondence between languages. Hence there can be no fully exact translations. The total impact of a translation may be reasonably close to the original, but there can be no identity in detail. Constance B. West (1932, p. 344) clearly states the problem: 'Whoever takes upon himself to translate contracts a debt; to discharge it, he must pay not with the same money, but the same sum.' One must not imagine that the process of translation can avoid a certain degree of interpretation by the translator. In fact, as D. G. Rossetti stated in 1874 (Fang, 1953), 'A translation remains perhaps the most direct form of commentary.'

Different Types of Translations

No statement of the principles of correspondence in translating can be complete without recognizing the many different types of translations (Herbert P. Phillips, 1959). Traditionally, we have tended to think in terms of free or paraphrastic translations as contrasted with close or literal ones. Actually, there are many more grades of translating than these extremes imply. There are, for example, such ultraliteral translations as interlinears; while others involve highly concordant relationships, e.g. the same source-language word is always translated by one—and only one—receptor-language word. Still others may be quite devoid of artificial restrictions in form, but nevertheless may be overtraditional and even archaizing. Some translations aim at very close formal and semantic correspondence, but are generously supplied with notes and commentary. Many are not so much concerned with giving information as with creating in the reader something of the same mood as was conveyed by the original.

Differences in translations can generally be accounted for by three basic factors in translating: (1) the nature of the message, (2) the purpose or purposes of the author and, by proxy, of the translator, and (3) the type of audience.

Messages differ primarily in the degree to which content or form is the dominant consideration. Of course, the content of a message can never be completely abstracted from the form, and form is nothing apart from content; but in some messages the content is of primary consideration, and in others the form must be given a higher priority. For example, in the Sermon on the Mount, despite certain important stylistic qualities, the importance of the message far exceeds considerations of form. On the other hand, some of the acrostic poems of the Old Testament are obviously designed to fit a very strict formal 'strait jacket.' But even the contents of a message may differ widely in applicability to the receptor-language audience. For example, the folk tale of the Bauré Indians of Bolivia, about a giant who led the animals in a symbolic dance, is interesting to an English-speaking audience, but to them it has not the same relevance as the Sermon on the Mount. And even the Bauré Indians themselves recognize the Sermon on the Mount as more significant than their favorite 'how-it-happened' story. At the same time of course, the Sermon on the Mount has greater relevance to these Indians than have some passages in Leviticus.

In poetry there is obviously a greater focus of attention upon formal elements than one normally finds in prose. Not that content is necessarily sacrificed in translation of a poem, but the content is necessarily constricted into certain formal molds. Only rarely can one reproduce both content and form in a translation, and hence in general the form is usually sacrificed for the sake of the content. On the other hand, a lyric poem translated as prose is not an adequate equivalent of the original. Though it may reproduce the conceptual content, it falls far short of reproducing the emotional intensity and flavor. However, the translating of some types of poetry by prose may be dictated by important cultural considerations. For example, Homer's epic poetry reproduced in English poetic form usually seems to us antique and queer—with nothing of the liveliness and spontaneity characteristic of Homer's style. One reason is that we are not accustomed to having stories told to us in poetic form. In our Western European tradition such epics are related in prose. For this reason E. V. Rieu chose prose rather than poetry as the more appropriate medium by which to render the *Iliad* and the *Odyssey*.

The particular purposes of the translator are also important factors in dictating the type of translation. Of course, it is assumed that the translator has purposes generally similar to, or at least compatible with, those of the original author, but this is not necessarily so. For example, a San Bias story-teller is interested only in amusing his audience but an ethnographer who sets about translating such stories may be much more concerned in giving his audience an insight into San Bias personality structure. Since, however, the purposes of the translator are the primary ones to be considered in studying the types of translation which result, the principal purposes that underlie the choice of one or another way to render a particular message are important.

The primary purpose of the translator may be information as to both content and form. One intended type of response to such an informative type of translation is largely cognitive, e.g. an ethnographer's translation of texts from informants, or a philosopher's translation of Heidegger. A largely informative translation may, on the other hand, be designed to elicit an emotional response of pleasure from the reader or listener.

A translator's purposes may involve much more than information. He may, for example, want to suggest a particular type of behavior by means of a translation. Under such circumstances he is likely to aim at full intelligibility, and to make certain minor adjustments in detail so that the reader may understand the full implications of the message for his own circumstances. In such a situation a translator is not content to have receptors say, 'This is intelligible to us.' Rather, he is looking for some such response as, 'This is meaningful for us.' In terms of Bible translating, the people might understand a phrase such as 'to change one's mind about sin' as meaning 'repentance.' But if the indigenous way of talking about repentance is 'spit on the ground in front of,' as in Shilluk,[1] spoken in the Sudan, the translator will obviously aim at the more meaningful idiom. On a similar basis, 'white as snow' may be rendered as 'white as egret feathers', if the people of the receptor language are not acquainted with snow but speak of anything very white by this phrase.

A still greater degree of adaptation is likely to occur in a translation which has an imperative purpose. Here the translator feels constrained not merely to suggest a possible line of behavior, but to make such an action explicit and compelling. He is not content to translate in such a way that the people are likely to understand; rather, he insists that the translation must be so clear that no one can possibly misunderstand.

In addition to the different types of messages and the diverse purposes of translators, one must also consider the extent to which prospective audiences differ both in decoding ability and in potential interest.

Decoding ability in any language involves at least four principal levels: (1) the capacity of children, whose vocabulary and cultural experience are limited; (2) the double-standard capacity of new literates, who can decode oral messages with facility but whose ability to decode written messages is limited; (3) the capacity of the average literate adult, who can handle both oral and written messages with relative ease; and (4) the unusually high capacity of specialists (doctors, theologians, philosophers, scientists, etc.), when they are decoding messages within their own area of specialization. Obviously a translation designed for children cannot be the same as one prepared for specialists, nor can a translation for children be the same as one for a newly literate adult.

Prospective audiences differ not only in decoding ability, but perhaps even more in their interests. For example, a translation designed to stimulate reading for pleasure will be quite different from one intended for a person anxious to learn how to assemble a complicated machine. Moreover, a translator of African myths for persons who simply want to satisfy their curiosity about strange peoples and places will produce a different piece of work from one who renders these same myths in a form acceptable to linguists, who are more interested in the linguistic structure underlying the translation than in cultural novelty.

Two Basic Orientations in Translating

Since 'there are, properly speaking, no such things as identical equivalents' (Belloc 1931a and b, p. 37), one must in translating seek to find the closest possible equivalent. However, there are fundamentally two different types of equivalence: one which may be called formal and another which is primarily dynamic.

Formal equivalence focuses attention on the message itself, in both form and content. In such a translation one is concerned with such correspondences as poetry to poetry, sentence to sentence, and concept to concept. Viewed from this formal orientation, one is concerned that the message in the receptor language should match as closely as possible the different elements in the source language. This means, for example, that the message in the receptor culture is constantly compared with the message in the source culture to determine standards of accuracy and correctness.

The type of translation which most completely typifies this structural equivalence might be called a 'gloss translation,' in which the translator attempts to reproduce as literally and meaningfully as possible the form and content of the original. Such a translation might be a rendering of some Medieval French text into English, intended for students of certain aspects of early French literature not requiring a knowledge of the original language of the text. Their needs call for a relatively close approximation to the structure of the early French text, both as to form (e.g. syntax and idioms) and content (e.g. themes and concepts). Such a translation would require numerous footnotes in order to make the text fully comprehensible.

A gloss translation of this type is designed to permit the reader to identify himself as fully as possible with a person in the source-language context, and to understand as much as he can of the customs, manner of thought, and means of expression. For example, a phrase such as 'holy kiss' (Romans 16: 16) in a gloss translation would be rendered literally, and would probably be supplemented with a footnote explaining that this was a customary method of greeting in New Testament times.

In contrast, a translation which attempts to produce a dynamic rather than a formal equivalence is based upon 'the principle of equivalent effect' (Rieu and Phillips, 1954). In such a translation one is not so concerned with matching the receptor-language message with the source-language message, but with the dynamic relationship [. . .], that the relationship between receptor and message should be substantially the same as that which existed between the original receptors and the message.

A translation of dynamic equivalence aims at complete naturalness of expression, and tries to relate the receptor to modes of behavior relevant within the context of his own culture; it does not insist that he understand the cultural patterns of the source-language context in order to comprehend the message. Of course, there are varying degrees of such dynamic-equivalence translations. One of the modern English translations which, perhaps more than any other, seeks for equivalent effect is J. B. Phillips' rendering of the New Testament. In Romans 16: 16 he quite naturally translates 'greet one another with a holy kiss' as 'give one another a hearty handshake all around.'

Between the two poles of translating (i.e. between strict formal equivalence and complete dynamic equivalence) there are a number of intervening grades, representing various acceptable standards of literary translating. During the past fifty years, however, there has been a marked shift of emphasis from the formal to the dynamic dimension. A recent summary of opinion on translating by literary artists, publishers, educators, and professional translators indicates clearly that the present direction is toward increasing emphasis on dynamic equivalences (Cary, 1959b).

[handwritten margin note: against Schleiermacher + Humboldt]

NOTE

1. This idiom is based upon the requirement that plaintiffs and defendants spit on the ground in front of each other when a case has been finally tried and punishment meted out. The spitting indicates that all is forgiven and that the accusations can never be brought into court again.

BIBLIOGRAPHY

Hilaire Belloc (1931a) *On Translation*. Oxford University Press.
Hilaire Belloc (1931b) 'On translation.' *Bookman* 74. 32–39, 179–185 (reprinted *BT* 10. 83–100. 1959).
Edmond Cary, ed. (1959b) 'Notre enquête.' *Babel* 5. 61–106.

Achilles Fang (1953) 'Some reflections on the difficulty of translation.' In Arthur F. Wright, ed., *Studies in Chinese Thought*. (Am. Anthropol. Assoc., Vol. 55, Memoir 75.) Chicago: Univ. Chicago Press, pp. 263–285. (Reprinted in Reuben A. Brower, ed. *On Translation*. Cambridge, Mass.: Harvard Univ. Press, pp. 111–133.

Herbert P. Phillips (1959) 'Problems of translation and meaning in field work.' *Human Organization* 18. 184–192.

E. V. Rieu and J.B. Phillips (1954) 'Translating the Gospels.' *Concordia Theol. Monthly* 25. 754–765.

Constance B. West (1932) 'La théorie de la traduction au XVIIIe siècle.' *Revue Littérature Comparée* 12. 330–355.

The Babel story, Genesis 11: 1–9, included in *The Good News Bible: Today's English Version* (The Bible Societies, Collins/Fontana, 1976), 15

1 At first, the people of the whole world had only one language and used the same words. 2 As they wandered about in the East, they came to a plain in Babylonia and settled there. 3 They said to one another, 'Come on! Let's make bricks and bake them hard.' So they had bricks to build with and tar to hold them together. 4 They said, 'Now let's build a city with a tower that reaches the sky, so that we can make a name for ourselves and not be scattered all over the earth.'

5 Then the LORD came down to see the city and the tower which those men had built, 6 and he said, 'Now then, these are all one people and they speak one language; this is just the beginning of what they are going to do. Soon they will be able to do anything they want! 7 Let us go down and mix up their language so that they will not understand one another.' 8 So the LORD scattered them all over the earth, and they stopped building the city. 9 The city was called Babylon,[1] because there the LORD mixed up the language of all the people, and from there he scattered them all over the earth.

NOTE

1. BABYLON: This name sounds like Hebrew for 'mixed up.'

4.10 ROBERT LOWELL

Robert Lowell (1917–77), American poet, was also a playwright and translator. From a distinguished New England family, Lowell was the dominant poetic voice of his era. Trained in the Classics, Lowell turned to translation in a major way with *Phaedra* (1960), a version from the French of Racine. *Imitations* (1961), a collection of free versions of European poets, from Homer to Pasternak, for which he revived Dryden's term for the least source-text based form of poetry translation, marked a significant moment in the history of post-war poetry translation, with its radically domesticating approach. Lowell's career itself seems to reflect a turn from academic verse to the freer approach of Whitman or the spoken-voice rhythms of W. C. Williams, as well as to more self-exposure. His verse play treatment of Aeschylus' *Prometheus Bound* (1967) creates a new play. *Near the Ocean* (1967) includes rather closer versions of Horace, Dante, Quevedo, Góngora, and of Juvenal's Tenth Satire, titled like Samuel Johnson's imitation, 'The Vanity of Human Wishes'. As Lowell says in a note: 'The theme that connects my translations is Rome, the greatness and horror of her Empire.' The political implications, as regards his own country, are clear. Lowell's version of Aeschylus's *Oresteia* was published posthumously, in 1978. Like Ted Hughes's, it was based on other translations, especially Richmond Lattimore's, even though Lowell had had a classical education.

Though his own translations tended to be highly personal, Lowell was also committed to translation in a general sense, serving on the board of the relatively short-lived National Translation Centre, Austin, Texas, founded in 1965. In an interview with D. S. Carne-Ross, and published in the first issue of the NTC's journal *Delos*, edited by Carne-Ross, Lowell said: '[T]he whole point of translating [. . .] is to bring into English something that didn't exist in English before. I don't think I've ever done a translation of a poem I could have written myself.' Nevertheless, as Carne-Ross suggests, Lowell's method is to 'take possession of the original and dominate it'.

The introduction to *Imitations* as a statement became something of a benchmark for later discussions of poetry translation. Lowell is quite frank about his intentions, taking as a precedent the tradition of 'imitation', as characterized, for instance, by Dryden (see Sect. 2.13, above). Nevertheless, his work was frequently attacked for not being what it in fact explicitly rejects. Ted Hughes's interest in translation (see Sect. 5.16, below) was awakened to some extent by Lowell, and even if his approach was different, it is relatable to Lowell's endeavours.

Imitations, being the work of a major poet, helped draw attention to the art of translation, and to its importance in the context of literature in general. The terms of the debate generated by this work were perhaps somewhat stark, but maybe this helped get it a hearing. Lowell, of course, must have been well aware of many of the issues raised by his statement. *Imitations* itself, although of intrinsic interest as work by a major talent, cannot be read even as a reduced anthology of European poetry, but is certainly of moment as an ambitious attempt to re-create in English works of genius in other languages; by definition, as Lowell is obliged by his credo to claim, this requires similar inspiration. One might suppose that the likelihood of this occurring, also by definition, is minimal, and that it is therefore the near impossible that Lowell is attempting, particularly since, as he puts it, he was writing these translations 'from time to time when I was unable to do anything of my own'. He does not apologize but rather makes a virtue of the highly personal nature of his motivation, although the combativeness of his tone also suggests that he is aware of the risks involved.

At the same time, he insists on the value of 'modest photographic prose translations', as against would-be poetic versions by inferior poets or by good poets working below par. Ted Hughes, coming to translation a little later, bases his own work, to a far greater extent, on these 'modest' versions which he evidently believes capable of conveying the force of works of genius. However, even if the results are quite different, less divides Lowell and a Hughes than is immediately apparent, both being fully aware of the problems and of the risks.

From *Imitations* (New York: Farrar, Straus and Giroux, 1961)

'Introduction', pp. xi–xiii

This book is partly self-sufficient and separate from its sources, and should be first read as a sequence, one voice running through many personalities, contrasts and repetitions. I have hoped somehow for a whole, to make a single volume, a small anthology of European poetry. The dark and against the grain stand out, but there are other modifying strands. I have tried to keep something equivalent to the fire and finish of my originals. This has forced me to do considerable re-writing.

Boris Pasternak has said that the usual reliable translator gets the literal meaning but misses the tone, and that in poetry tone is of course everything. I have been reckless with literal meaning, and laboured hard to get the tone. Most often this has been *a* tone, for *the* tone is something that will always more or less escape transference to another language and cultural moment. I have tried to write alive English and to do what my authors might have done if they were writing their poems now and in America.

Most poetic translations come to grief and are less enjoyable than modest photographic prose translations, such as George Kay has offered in his *Penguin Book of Italian*

Verse. Strict metrical translators still exist. They seem to live in a pure world untouched by contemporary poetry. Their difficulties are bold and honest, but they are taxidermists, not poets, and their poems are likely to be stuffed birds. A better strategy would seem to be the now fashionable translations into free or irregular verse. Yet this method commonly turns out a sprawl of language, neither faithful nor distinguished, now on stilts, now low, as Dryden would say. It seems self-evident that no professor or amateur poet, or even good poet writing hastily, can by miracle transform himself into a fine metricist. I believe that poetic translation—I would call it an imitation—must be expert and inspired, and needs at least as much technique, luck and rightness of hand as an original poem.

My licenses have been many. My first two Sappho poems are really new poems based on hers. Villon has been somewhat stripped; Hebel is taken out of dialect; Hugo's 'Gautier' is cut in half. Mallarmé has been unclotted, not because I disapprove of his dense medium but because I saw no way of giving it much power in English. The same has been done with Ungaretti and some of the more obscure Rimbaud. About a third of 'The Drunken Boat' has been left out. Two stanzas have been added to Rilke's 'Roman Sarcophagus,' and one to his 'Pigeons.' 'Pigeons' and Valéry's 'Helen' are more idiomatic and informal in my English. Some lines from Villon's 'Little Testament' have been shifted to introduce his 'Great Testament.' And so forth! I have dropped lines, moved lines, moved stanzas, changed images and altered meter and intent.

Pasternak has given me special problems. From reading his prose and many translations of his poetry, I have come to feel that he is a very great poet. But I know no Russian. I have rashly tried to improve on other translations, and have been helped by exact prose versions given me by Russian readers. This is an old practice; Pasternak himself, I think, worked this way with his Georgian poets. I hope I have caught something worthy of his all-important tone.

This book was written from time to time when I was unable to do anything of my own. It began some ten years ago when I read a parallel French translation of Rilke's 'Orpheus,' and felt that a much better job might be done in English. I had long been amazed by Montale, but had no idea how he might be worked until I saw that unlike most good poets—Horace and Petrarch are extremes—he was strong in simple prose and could be made still stronger in free verse. My Baudelaires were begun as exercises in couplets and quatrains and to get away from the longer, less concentrated problems of translating Racine's *Phèdre*.

All my originals are important poems. Nothing like them exists in English, for the excellence of a poet depends on the unique opportunities of his native language. I have been almost as free as the authors themselves in finding ways to make them ring right for me.

'La Lune offensée'

See Sect. 4.4, above, for Walter Benjamin's German version, the source text, and a literal translation.

The Injured Moon

Oh Moon, discreetly worshipped by our sires,
Still riding through your high blue countries, still
Trailed by the shining harem of your stars,
Old Cynthia, the lamp of our retreats . . .

The lovers sleep open-mouthed! When they breathe,
They show the white enamel of their teeth.
The writer breaks his teeth on his work-sheets,
The vipers couple under the hot hill.

Dressed in your yellow hood, do you pursue
Your boy from night to dawn, till the sun climbs
Skyward, where dim Endymion disappears?

'I see your mother, Child of these poor times,
Crushed to her mirror by the heavy years.
She cunningly powders the breast that nourished you.'

Racine's *Phaedra*

Excerpts from Robert Lowell's Preface, 'On Translating Phèdre', from Phaedra: Racine's Phèdre, *trans. Robert Lowell (1961; London: Faber and Faber 1963)*

[In their somewhat despairing way, these prefatory remarks again argue for 'free' translations. *Phèdre* has proved a challenge to a number of contemporary English language poets (see Sect. 5.16 and 5.23, below, for the same passage, translated by Ted Hughes into English and by Edwin Morgan into Scots respectively.]

Racine's plays are generally and correctly thought to be untranslatable. His syllabic alexandrines do not and cannot exist in English. We cannot reproduce his language, which is refined by the literary artifice of his contemporaries, and given a subtle realism and grandeur by the spoke idiom of Louis the Fourteenth's court. [. . .] Matisse says somewhere that a reproduction requires as much talent for colour as the original painting. I have been tormented by the fraudulence of my own heavy touch.

My meter, with important differences, is based on Dryden and Pope. In his heroic plays, Dryden uses an end-stopped couplet, loaded with inversions, heavily alliterated, and varied by short un-rhymed lines. My couplet is run on, avoids inversions and alliteration, and loosens its rhythm with shifted accents and occasional extra syllables.

I gain in naturalness and lose in compactness and epigrammic resonance. I have tried for an idiomatic and ageless style, but I inevitably echo the English Restoration, both in ways that are proper and in my sometimes unRacinian humor and bombast. [. . .]

Racine's verse has a diamond-edge. He is perhaps the greatest poet in the French language, but he uses a smaller vocabulary than any English poet—beside him Pope and Bridges have a Shakespearian luxurance. He has few verbally inspired lines, and in this is unlike Baudelaire and even La Fontaine. His poetry is great because of the justness of its rhythm and logic, and the glory of its hard, electric rage. I have translated as a poet, and tried to give my lines a certain dignity, speed, and flare.

Act 2, Scene 5, From Lowell, Phaedra: Racine's Phèdre, *pp. 43–4*

[John Cairncross's allegation (see his blank-verse version in *Jean Racine: Iphigenia, Phaedra, Athalia,* trans. and introd. John Cairncross (London: Penguin Books, 1963)) that Lowell 'over-energizes the less important details and adds a lot more of his own, while under-energizing the great moments . . .' is hard to gainsay, when one is faced by a passage such as the last lines of Phaedra's guilty declaration [of her love for her stepson Hippolytus, son of her husband, King Theseus: see below.]

> PHAEDRA
>
> > [. . .]
> > I love you! Fool, I love you, I adore you!
> > Do not imagine that my mind approved
> > my first defection, Prince, or that I loved
> > your youth light-heartedly, and fed my treason
> > with cowardly compliance, till I lost my reason.
> > I wished to hate you, but the gods corrupt
> > us; though I never suffered their abrupt
> > seductions, shattering advances, I
> > too bear their sensual lightnings in my thigh.
> > I too am dying. I have felt the heat
> > that drove my mother through the fields of Crete [. . .]
> > [. . .] Prince, I only spoke
> > about myself! Avenge yourself, invoke
> > your father; a worse monster threatens you
> > than any Theseus ever fought and slew.
> > The wife of Theseus loves Hippolytus!
> > See. Prince! Look, this monster, ravenous
> > for her execution, will not flinch.
> > I want your sword's spasmodic final inch

Source text and literal translation by Daniel Weissbort of last section of above, in Phèdre
(Paris: Petits Classiques Larousse, 1998), 82

Hélas! Je ne t'ai pu parler que de toi-même!
Venge-toi, punis-moi d'un odieux amour:
Digne fils du héros qui t'a donné le jour,
Délivre l'univers d'un monster qui t'irrite.
La veuve de Thésée ose aimer Hippolyte!
Crois-moi, ce monstre affreux ne doit point t'échapper;
Voilà mon coeur: c'est là que ta main doit frapper.
Impatient déjà d'expier son offense,
Au-devant de ton bras je le sens qui s'avance.
Frappe: ou si tu le crois indigne de tes coups,
Si ta haine m'envie un supplice si doux,
Ou si d'un sang trop vil ta main serait trempée,
Au défaut de ton bras prête-moi ton épée;
Donne.

Alas! I have been able to speak to you only of yourself!
Take your revenge, punish me for this odious love:
Worthy son of the hero who gave you life,
Rid the universe of a monster who offends you.
Theseus's widow dares to love Hippolytus!
Believe me, this dreadful monster must not escape you;
Here is my heart, that is where your hand must strike.
Impatient already to expiate its offence,
I feel it go before to meet your arm.
Strike: or if you think it unworthy of your blows,
If your hatred grudges me so easy a punishment,
Or if my blood is too vile to stain your hand,
Instead of your hand, lend me your sword.
Give [it to me].

Aeschylus, *The Oresteia*

From Robert Lowell, The Oresteia of Aeschylus *(1978; London, Faber and Faber, 1979)*

[The translation is accompanied by a note by Lowell himself.]

I do not want to cry down my translation of Aeschylus, but to say what I've tried to do and not tried. I have written from other translations, and not from the Greek. One in particular, Richmond Lattimore's, has had my admiration for years, it is so elaborately exact. I have aimed at something else: to trim, cut, and be direct enough to satisfy my own mind and at a first hearing the simple ears of a theatre audience.

No version of the *Oresteia*, even a great one, such as Marlowe or Milton might have written, can be anything like what was performed first in Athens with music, dance, masks, and an audience of thirty thousand or more—an event we cannot recover and something no doubt grander than any play we can see.

From Agamemnon, *in Lowell,* The Oresteia of Aeschylus, *p. 6*

See below, Sect. 5.16, for Ted Hughes's version. Lowell's is much abbreviated.

> I know the omen of the angry birds
> Hurled Agamemnon and Menelaus
> like a spear at Troy—two thrones, one mind!
> Two eagles came to our kings,
> one white-tailed, the other black.
> They lit on the spear-hand side of the palace.
> Everyone saw them. They killed a hare.
> Her unborn young were bursting from her side.

From the Agamemnon *of Aeschylus, trans. Richmond Lattimore, in* Greek Tragedies, *vol. i, ed. Richard Grene and Richmond Lattimore (2nd edn., Chicago, University of Chicago Press, 1991), 8*

> I have mastery yet to chant the wonder at the wayside
> given to kings. Still by god's grace there surges within me
> singing magic
> grown to my life and power,
> how the wild bird portent
> hurled forth the Achaeans'
> twin-stemmed power single hearted,
> lords of the youth of Hellas,
> with spear and hand of strength
> to the land of Teucrus.
> Kings of birds to the kings of the ships,
> one black, one blazed with silver,
> clear seen by the royal house
> on the right, the spear hand,
> they lighted, watched by all
> tore a hare, ripe, bursting with young unborn yet,
> stayed from her last fleet running.
> Sing sorry, sorrow: but good wins out in the end.

'The Vanity of Human Wishes'

From Robert Lowell's version of Juvenal's Tenth Satire, 'The Vanity of Human Wishes', in Near the Ocean *(1967; New York: Farrar Straus and Giroux, First Noonday printing 1971), 54–5*

See Sect. 2.16, above for literal version and Samuel Johnson's translation of this passage.

> Why do we hunger so for vicious things?
> Our wishes bend the statues of the gods.
>
> How many men are killed by Power, by Power
> and Power's companion, Envy! Your long list
> of honor breaks your neck. Statues follow
> the rope and crash, the axe cuts down the two-
> wheeled chariot's wheels and snaps the horse's legs.
> Fierce hiss the fires, the bellows roar, the head
> all-popular and adored by all once, burns—
> Sejanus crackles, and his crude bronze face,
> the second in the world, melts down to jars,
> frying pans, basins, platters, chamber pots.

4.11 STANLEY BURNSHAW

Stanley Burnshaw (1906–2005) was a poet, critic, novelist, playwright, publisher, editor, and translator. He is probably best known as the author of *The Seamless Web* (1970), a study of the ontology of poetry and an analysis of its role in human life. In the Depression era, his work reflected Marxist ideas, even though it was never particularly doctrinaire. In 1927 Burnshaw began a long association with the French poet André Spire. *André Spire and His Poetry* appeared in 1933, revealing Burnshaw's knowledge of European literature and languages. Burnshaw was co-editor of the New York weekly *The New Masses* (1934–6). He is best known, in the field of translation, for his innovative 1960 anthology *The Poem Itself*, which presented poems in the source language, accompanied by a succinct commentary and literal prose version. *The Modern Hebrew Poem Itself* (1965) applies the same principles to Hebrew poetry. Burnshaw's internationalist outlook is reflected also in *Varieties of Literary Experience* (1962). His collection of poetry, *In the Terrified Radiance* (1972), includes a sequence of poems on the life of Mallarmé. Stanley Burnshaw's *The Collected Poems and Selected Prose* was published in 2002.

From the Introduction to *The Poem Itself*, ed. Stanley Burnshaw (1960; New York, Simon & Schuster, 1989), pp. xi–xv

Thirty years ago in *This Quarter*, I published 'A Note on Translation' which suggested that the only way one could experience the poetry of a language one did not command was by learning to hear and pronounce (if only approximately) the sounds of the originals and 'simultaneously' reading literal renditions. Since the poetry inheres in the tonal language (the sounds of the poem in its original tongue), how could one possibly experience a Spanish poem in any language but Spanish, a French poem in any language but French? The 'Note' appeared at a time when translators felt free to do anything: they were 're-creating originals'! Bilingual editions had not yet become familiar—nor had Frost's definition of poetry as 'that which gets lost from verse and prose in translation.' Before long a publisher expressed interest in my notion, and I embarked on a small anthology. But then he insisted that verse translations also be included, despite the danger of confusing and distracting the reader. And so for the time being I abandoned the project certain as ever that mine was the only means by which a reader could begin to experience the poetry of other languages.

But my method had not gone far enough, as I discovered many years later when I found myself working on some poems by Mallarmé. My literal renditions were scrupulous, yet in certain key places a single French word could not be rendered by a single English word— pieces of two or even of three might be required. Other words, with double denotations in the French, had to be halved in English or equated by impossible compounds. And certain phrases that looked easy in the dictionaries carried quite untranslatable connotations essential as meaning. As for syntax, the reader would have to untangle it for himself. And the allusions—though at times they might hold the key to the poem, they could not even be considered, since they stand outside the purview of all translation.

What sort of experience, then, did my confident method offer? Obviously a most inadequate one: a great deal more would have to be added before an English-speaking reader could begin to experience Mallarmé. And if this were true of so familiar a poet, then it must be true of other 'difficult' moderns, such as Rilke, Vallejo, Montale; it must be true to some degree of every participant in the poetic revolution of the last hundred years. The method had to be expanded, the line-by-line rendition enriched, at least with alternate equivalents where necessary and with leads where ellipsis and syntax might frustrate a reader. Other clues had also to be given: to telescoped images, private allusions, specialized symbols, systems of belief, and similar problems. And what of the poem as a work of sonal art? For a reader who wishes to hear and pronounce the original, however approximately, any number of interesting points might be signalled; not only of rime, assonance, meter, and strophe, but of graces, stops, turns, and the sonal felicities of the whole. To be faithful to its intent, the method had to be enlarged into a literal rendering plus commentary—into a discussion aimed at enabling the reader both to *understand* the poem and to begin to *experience it as a poem.*

The result of these thoughts [. . .] fell short of its maker's ideal, yet it served to show others how a somewhat 'difficult' poem in a foreign language could be made accessible to English-speaking readers through a new type of presentation. [. . .] One poet-critic thought that the discussion should be made twice as searching, but he soon saw the unwisdom of trying to analyze too much. For once the reader begins, he can plunge as deep as he wishes. The aim is to help him *into* the poem itself.

There are, of course, various ways of approaching foreign poetry; when a writer uses one, he does not thereby surrender his right to use others. Those of us who are drawn to particular poems in other languages will always be free to revivify them with English verses—and as one of this group, I applaud the practice and hail the occasional achievements. But these are personal preoccupations, and translation is of public concern. English versions of foreign writings abound, but the reader who wants to experience the poetry of other literatures must look elsewhere; the vast stock of verse translations provides no answer.

It provides no answer for several reasons. First, and overwhelming, a verse translation offers an experience in *English* poetry. It takes the reader away from the foreign literature and into his own, away from the original and into something different. The instant he departs from the words of the original, he departs from *its* poetry. For the words are the poem. Ideas can often be carried across, but poems are not made of ideas (as Degas was informed): they are made of words. Regardless of its brilliance, an English translation is always a different thing: it is always an *English* poem.

In this fact about words lies the source of all the slanderous remarks that have been made about translators, from Frost's sentence quoted above to the notorious Italian pun *traduttore-traditore* ('translator-traitor'). Says Poggioli: 'Both original and translation deal with a single substance, differentiated into two unique, and incommensurable, accidents'; and Nida: 'There can never be a word-for-word type of correspondence which is fully meaningful or accurate.'[1] When Coleridge proposed as 'the infallible test of a blameless style' 'its *untranslateableness* in words of the same language without injury to the meaning,' he took care to 'include in the *meaning* of a word not only its correspondent object, but likewise all the associations which it recalls.' For every 'meaningful' word is a unique totality—unique in sound, denotation, connotation, and doubtless much more.

But the order that words make is no less crucial to the translator than the words themselves. For when they appear in a sequence (as in a poem) they begin to mean in a special way—their uniquenesses act, as it were, selectively. The position that each word holds in relation to the others causes parts of its content to be magnified and other parts diminished. Yet even though some meanings recede as others come to the fore, all of them are to some degree also active—whence the multiform richness of feeling and thought conveyed (the 'suggestions, ambiguities, paradoxes, levels of meaning' of current terminology). These facts may be read into Coleridge's definition of poetry as 'the best words in the best order,' especially into his famous remark about 'a more than usual state of emotion, with more than usual order.' Today we talk of the 'affective' phrase or sentence, whose word arrangement differs from that of prose; we say each poem is an organization of such phrases. But some critics go further: each affective phrase is a rhythmic metaphor—a poem is a series of rhythmic metaphors which evokes a physical response in the reader's body, in his internal and external muscles. Not only the mind, but the total organism moves with and 'mirrors' the pattern of the words. For a translator to evoke this response by different words and word order would of course be impossible. But, all corporeal concurrences aside, could a translator even think of trying to carry across into a different language the 'more than usual order' of the original words?

And yet, with all its limitations, verse translation has given us almost all we know of the poets of the rest of the world.[2] And from what we have been given we have formed our judgments. Can they be trusted? The only works we could read have been those that happened to appeal to translators who happened to succeed in turning them into English poems that happened to get published. This fortuitousness should be enough to make us suspect that the picture has been skewed; but there is more. We naturally judge the quality of a foreign poem by the quality of the English poem it inspired, even though we know such correspondence is rare. As a result, verse translation being the poorest subdivision of English verse, we must continually assure ourselves that the originals are much better—which is safe enough, but only a wishful assumption. And what of all the poetry that has never been carried across because it seemed too long or too compact or too difficult or too delicate to fashion into an English poem?

The method of *The Poem Itself* should overcome all three obstacles we have noted in verse translation. Because each word of a foreign poem is unique in itself and in its order, we ask the reader to read the original along with our English approximations (usually set in italics, with alternate meanings in parentheses and explanations in brackets). Our comments on allusion, symbol, meaning, sound, and the like will enable him to see what the poem is saying and *how*, though the poem itself is an unparaphrasable totality. As to how much the reader will hear of the sound of the poem, this depends on what knowledge he already has and on what effort he is willing to invest in learning to hear. This book, then, offers poems and the means toward experiencing them.

[...]

Before inviting the reader to begin, we make five qualifications. (1) Each poem (and each unit of a long poem) is presented on a two-page spread, to enable the reader to see everything without turning pages: a few of our discussions could have used additional space. (2) Ideally each poem should be available in a recording. (3) The book makes no claim to being representative of the last hundred years—how could it be, in so few pages and with so much to choose from? Yet many of the finest poets and poems have been included. (4) The notes on 'The Prosodies' and 'The Pronunciations' will be most useful to the reader who recognizes the intentional brevity of the first and the avowed inadequacy of the second. Every likening of a foreign sound to an English sound is at best an approximation, often only remote. [...]

NOTES

1. *On Translation*, edited by Reuben A. Brower, Harvard University Press, 1959. Renato Poggioli: 'The Added Artificer', p. 138; [Eugene A.] Nida: 'Principles of Translation as Exemplified by Bible Translating', p. 13.

2. Even when we are not aware—as, for example, when a revision of an original passage appears without acknowledgment [...].

Rainer Maria Rilke, 'Archäisher Torso Apollos'

From The Poem Itself, *p. 146, commentary by Gregor Sebba*

> Wir kannten nicht sein unerhörtes Haupt,
> darin die Augenäpfel reiften. Aber
> sein Torso glüht noch wie ein Kandelaber,
> in dem sein Schauen, nur zurückgeschraubt,
>
> sich hält und glänzt. Sonst könnte nicht der Bug
> der Brust dich blenden, und im leisen Drehen

4

der Lenden könnte nicht ein Lächeln gehen
zu jener Mitte, die die Zeugung trug.   8

Sonst stünde dieser Stein entstellt und kurz
unter der Schultern durchsichtigem Sturz
und flimmerte nicht so wie Raubtierfelle;

und bräche nicht aus allen seinen Rändern   12
aus wie ein Stern: denn da ist keine Stelle,
die dich nicht sieht. Du mußt dein Leben ändern.

(Der Neuen Gedichte anderer Teil, 1908)

We did not know his unheard-of (unbelievable) head (2) wherein the eye-apples ripened. But (3) his torso still glows like a candelabrum (4) in which his gaze, merely turned down low [like the flames of a candelabrum, no longer visible but still sending out an afterglow] (5) holds on and gleams. Else the curve (6) of the chest could not blind you, and in the slight twist (7) of the loins there could not go a smile [there would not be a smile, going] (8) towards that center that bore procreation [the genitals]. (9) Else this stone would be standing disfigured and short (10) under the shoulders' transparent fall (plunge) (11) and [it] would not glint like the fell (skin) of beasts of prey; (12) and would not break out from all its [sharp] edges (13) like a star: For here [on this torso] is no place (14) that does not see you. You must change your life.

The sonnet does not describe the 'Archaic Torso of Apollo.' It states its impact upon the beholder: an immediate confrontation, almost a collision, with a work of art that defies even mutilation. The interplay of internal and end rimes (6–7) beautifully reflects the characteristic turn of the body: *blenden—Drehen—Lenden—gehen* ('blind—twist—loins—go') as the line gracefully breaks between substantive and attribute (*Drehen / der Lenden*).

Head and limbs have been broken off, but the stone's vitality, controlled and firmly contained where the sculptor's hand shaped it, 'erupts' at the rough broken surfaces 'like a star.' The lost eyes' gaze is all-present in the marble: every spot you look at looks at you. Confronted with such overwhelming beauty, such power over time and destruction, only one attitude is possible, and the last line proclaims it: You must become essential like this stone; nothing less will do.

Version by Stephen Mitchell, from *The Selected Poetry of Rainer Maria Rilke*, ed. and trans. Mitchell (New York: Random House, 1984), 61

Archaic Torso of Apollo

We cannot know his legendary head
with eyes like ripening fruit. And yet his torso
is still suffused with brilliance from inside,
like a lamp, in which his gaze, now turned to low,

gleams in all its power. Otherwise
the curved breast could not dazzle you so, nor could
a smile run through the placid hips and thighs
to that dark center where procreation flared.

Otherwise this stone would seem defaced
beneath the translucent cascade of the shoulders
and would not glisten like a wild beast's fur:

would not, from all the borders of itself,
burst like a star: for here there is no place
that does not see you. You must change your life.

4.12 LAURA BOHANNAN

Laura Bohannan is an American anthropologist, who received a doctorate at Oxford in 1951. She lectured in anthropology at the University of Chicago and at Northwestern University, and later became professor at the University of Illinois. She has contributed to anthropological journals and books on Africa. Her Shakespeare article, included below, was originally written for the BBC's Third Programme in 1954 under the title 'Miching Mallecho, That Means Witchcraft'. With her husband Paul, she co-authored *The Tiv of Central Nigeria* (1953) and in 1954, she published, under the pseudonym Elenore Smith Bowen, an anthropological novel, *Return to Laughter*, about her work among an (unnamed) African tribe.

Anthropology, originating in the study of 'primitive' cultures, has relied heavily on, and involved, translation (see also below, Sect. 5.7 on Ethnopoetics and Sect. 5.12 on Talal Asad). Cultural translation is clearly an ambivalent concept, on the one hand representing a radically foreign experience in a modern, usually 'Western' context, on the other risking appropriation, a kind of neo-colonialization, since it brings a modern Western rationality to bear on cultural material that does not possess an equal symbolic and political status. Bohannan's article indicates an awareness of this dilemma and of the risks of substituting the familiar for the unfamiliar, although in this case it is, ironically, a canonical Western source that is being appropriated by a 'primitive' tribe.

Laura Bohannan, 'Shakespeare in the Bush' *Natural History* **(the Journal of the American Museum of Natural History), 75 (Aug.–Sept. 1966), 28–33**

Just before I left Oxford for the Tiv in West Africa, conversation turned to the season at Stratford. 'You Americans,' said a friend, 'often have difficulty with Shakespeare. He was, after all, a very English poet, and one can easily misinterpret the universal by misunderstanding the particular.'

I protested that human nature is pretty much the same the whole world over; at least the general plot and motivation of the greater tragedies would always be clear—everywhere—although some details of custom might have to be explained and difficulties of translation might produce other slight changes. To end an argument we could not conclude, my friend gave me a copy of *Hamlet* to study in the African bush: it would, he hoped, lift my mind above its primitive surroundings, and possibly I might, by prolonged meditation, achieve the grace of correct interpretation.

It was my second field trip to that African tribe, and I thought myself ready to live in one of its remote sections—an area difficult to cross even on foot. I eventually settled on the hillock of a very knowledgeable old man, the head of a homestead of some hundred and forty people, all of whom were either his close relatives or their wives and children. Like the other elders of the vicinity, the old man spent most of his time performing ceremonies seldom seen these days in the more accessible parts of the tribe. I was delighted. Soon there would be three months of enforced isolation and leisure, between the harvest that takes place just before the rising of the swamps and the clearing of new farms when the water goes down. Then, I thought, they would have even more time to perform ceremonies and explain them to me.

I was quite mistaken. Most of the ceremonies demanded the presence of elders from several homesteads. As the swamps rose, the old men found it too difficult to walk from one homestead to the next, and the ceremonies gradually ceased. As the swamps rose even higher, all activities but one came to an end. The women brewed beer from maize and millet. Men, women, and children sat on their hillocks and drank it.

People began to drink at dawn. By midmorning the whole homestead was singing, dancing, and drumming. When it rained, people had to sit inside their huts: there they drank and sang or they drank and told stories. In any case, by noon or before, I either had to join the party or retire to my own hut and my books. 'One does not discuss serious matters when there is beer. Come, drink with us.' Since I lacked their capacity for the thick native beer, I spent more and more time with *Hamlet*. Before the end of the second month, grace descended on me. I was quite sure that *Hamlet* had only one possible interpretation, and that one universally obvious.

Early every morning, in the hope of having some serious talk before the beer party, I used to call on the old man at his reception hut—a circle of posts supporting a thatched roof above a low mud wall to keep out wind and rain. One day I crawled through the low doorway and found most of the men of the homestead sitting huddled in their ragged cloths on stools, low plank beds, and reclining chairs, warming themselves against the chill of the rain around a smoky fire. In the center were three pots of beer. The party had started.

The old man greeted me cordially. 'Sit down and drink.' I accepted a large calabash full of beer, poured some into a small drinking gourd, and tossed it down. Then I poured some more into the same gourd for the man second in seniority to my host before I handed my calabash over to a young man for further distribution. Important people shouldn't ladle beer themselves.

'It is better like this,' the old man said, looking at me approvingly and plucking at the thatch that had caught in my hair. 'You should sit and drink with us more often. Your servants tell me that when you are not with us, you sit inside your hut looking at a paper.'

The old man was acquainted with four kinds of 'papers': tax receipts, bride price receipts, court fee receipts, and letters. The messenger who brought him letters from the chief used them mainly as a badge of office, for he always knew what was in them and told the old man. Personal letters for the few who had relatives in the government or mission stations were kept until someone went to a large market where there was a letter writer and reader. Since my arrival, letters were brought to me to be read. A few men also brought me bride price receipts, privately, with requests to change the figures to a higher sum. I found moral arguments were of no avail, since in-laws are fair game, and the technical hazards of forgery difficult to explain to an illiterate people. I did not wish them to think me silly enough to look at any such papers for days on end, and I hastily explained that my 'paper' was one of the 'things of long ago' of my country.

'Ah,' said the old man. 'Tell us.'

I protested that I was not a storyteller. Story-telling is a skilled art among them; their standards are high, and the audiences critical—and vocal in their criticism. I protested in vain. This morning they wanted to hear a story while they drank. They threatened to tell me no more stories until I told them one of mine. Finally, the old man promised that no one would criticize my style 'for we know you are struggling with our language.' 'But,' put in one of the elders, 'you must explain what we do not understand, as we do when we tell you our stories.' Realizing that here was my chance to prove *Hamlet* universally intelligible, I agreed.

The old man handed me some more beer to help me on with my storytelling. Men filled their long wooden pipes and knocked coals from the fire to place in the pipe bowls; then, puffing contentedly, they sat back to listen. I began in the proper style, 'Not yesterday, not yesterday, but long ago, a thing occurred. One night three men were keeping watch outside the homestead of the great chief, when suddenly they saw the former chief approach them.'

'Why was he no longer their chief?'

'He was dead,' I explained. 'That is why they were troubled and afraid when they saw him.'

'Impossible,' began one of the elders, handing his pipe on to his neighbor, who interrupted, 'Of course it wasn't the dead chief. It was an omen sent by a witch. Go on.'

Slightly shaken, I continued. 'One of these three was a man who knew things'—the closest translation for scholar, but unfortunately it also meant witch. The second elder looked triumphantly at the first. 'So he spoke to the dead chief saying, "Tell us what we must do so you may rest in your grave," but the dead chief did not answer. He vanished, and they could see him no more. Then the man who knew things—his name was Horatio—said this event was the affair of the dead chief's son, Hamlet.'

There was a general shaking of heads round the circle. 'Had the dead chief no living brothers? Or was this son the chief?'

'No,' I replied. 'That is, he had one living brother who became the chief when the elder brother died.'

The old men muttered: such omens were matters for chiefs and elders, not for youngsters; no good could come of going behind a chief's back; clearly Horatio was not a man who knew things.

'Yes, he was,' I insisted, shooing a chicken away from my beer. 'In our country the son is next to the father. The dead chief's younger brother had become the great chief. He had also married his elder brother's widow only about a month after the funeral.'

'He did well,' the old man beamed and announced to the others, 'I told you that if we knew more about Europeans, we would find they really were very like us. In our country also,' he added to me, 'the younger brother marries the elder brother's widow and becomes the father of his children. Now, if your uncle, who married your widowed mother, is your father's full brother, then he will be a real father to you. Did Hamlet's father and uncle have one mother?'

His question barely penetrated my mind; I was too upset and thrown too far off balance by having one of the most important elements of *Hamlet* knocked straight out of the picture. Rather uncertainly I said that I thought they had the same mother, but I wasn't sure—the story didn't say. The old man told me severely that these genealogical details made all the difference and that when I got home I must ask the elders about it. He shouted out the door to one of his younger wives to bring his goatskin bag.

Determined to save what I could of the mother motif, I took a deep breath and began again. 'The son Hamlet was very sad because his mother had married again so quickly. There was no need for her to do so, and it is our custom for a widow not to go to her next husband until she has mourned for two years.'

'Two years is too long,' objected the wife, who had appeared with the old man's battered goatskin bag. 'Who will hoe your farms for you while you have no husband?'

'Hamlet,' I retorted without thinking, 'was old enough to hoe his mother's farms himself. There was no need for her to remarry.' No one looked convinced. I gave up. 'His mother and the great chief told Hamlet not to be sad, for the great chief himself would be a father to Hamlet. Furthermore, Hamlet would be the next chief: therefore he must stay to learn the things of a chief. Hamlet agreed to remain, and all the rest went off to drink beer.'

While I paused, perplexed at how to render Hamlet's disgusted soliloquy to an audience convinced that Claudius and Gertrude had behaved in the best possible manner, one of the younger men asked me who had married the other wives of the dead chief.

'He had no other wives,' I told him.

'But a chief must have many wives! How else can he brew beer and prepare food for all his guests?'

I said firmly that in our country even chiefs had only one wife, that they had servants to do their work, and that they paid them from tax money.

It was better, they returned, for a chief to have many wives and sons who would help him hoe his farms and feed his people; then everyone loved the chief who gave much and took nothing—taxes were a bad thing.

I agreed with the last comment, but for the rest fell back on their favorite way of fobbing off my questions: 'That is the way it is done, so that is how we do it.'

I decided to skip the soliloquy. Even if Claudius was here thought quite right to marry his brother's widow, there remained the poison motif, and I knew they would disapprove of fratricide. More hopefully I resumed, 'That night Hamlet kept watch with the three who had seen his dead father. The dead chief again appeared, and although the others were afraid, Hamlet followed his dead father off to one side. When they were alone. Hamlet's dead father spoke.'

'Omens can't talk!' The old man was emphatic.

'Hamlet's dead father wasn't an omen. Seeing him might have been an omen, but he was not.' My audience looked as confused as I sounded. 'It *was* Hamlet's dead father. It was a thing we call a "ghost." ' I had to use the English word, for unlike many of the neighboring tribes, these people didn't believe in the survival after death of any individuating part of the personality.

'What is a "ghost?" An omen?'

'No, a "ghost" is someone who is dead but who walks around and can talk, and people can hear him and see him but not touch him.'

They objected. 'One can touch zombis.'

'No, no! It was not a dead body the witches had animated to sacrifice and eat. No one else made Hamlet's dead father walk. He did it himself.'

'Dead men can't walk,' protested my audience as one man.

I was quite willing to compromise. 'A "ghost" is the dead man's shadow.'

But again they objected. 'Dead men cast no shadows.'

'They do in my country,' I snapped.

The old man quelled the babble of disbelief that arose immediately and told me with that insincere, but courteous, agreement one extends to the fancies of the young, ignorant, and superstitious, 'No doubt in your country the dead can also walk without being zombis.' From the depths of his bag he produced a withered fragment of kola nut, bit off one end to show it wasn't poisoned, and handed me the rest as a peace offering.

'Anyhow,' I resumed, 'Hamlet's dead father said that his own brother, the one who became chief, had poisoned him. He wanted Hamlet to avenge him. Hamlet believed this in his heart, for he did not like his father's brother.' I took another swallow of beer. 'In the country of the great chief, living in the same homestead, for it was a very large one, was an important elder who was often with the chief to advise and help him. His name was Polonius. Hamlet was courting his daughter, but her father and her brother

... [I cast hastily about for some tribal analogy] warned her not to let Hamlet visit her when she was alone on her farm, for he would be a great chief and so could not marry her.'

'Why not?' asked the wife, who had settled down on the edge of the old man's chair. He frowned at her for asking stupid questions and growled, 'They lived in the same homestead.'

'That was not the reason,' I informed them. 'Polonius was a stranger who lived in the homestead because he helped the chief, not because he was a relative.'

'Then why couldn't Hamlet marry her?'

'He could have,' I explained, 'but Polonius didn't think he would. After all, Hamlet was a man of great importance who ought to marry a chief's daughter, for in his country a man could have only one wife. Polonius was afraid that if Hamlet made love to his daughter, then no one else would give a high price for her.'

'That might be true,' remarked one of the shrewder elders, 'but a chief's son would give his mistress's father enough presents and patronage to more than make up the difference. Polonius sounds like a fool to me.'

'Many people think he was,' I agreed. 'Meanwhile Polonius sent his son Laertes off to Paris to learn the things of that country, for it was the homestead of a very great chief indeed. Because he was afraid that Laertes might waste a lot of money on beer and women and gambling, or get into trouble by fighting, he sent one of his servants to Paris secretly, to spy out what Laertes was doing. One day Hamlet came upon Polonius's daughter Ophelia. He behaved so oddly he frightened her. Indeed'—I was fumbling for words to express the dubious quality of Hamlet's madness—'the chief and many others had also noticed that when Hamlet talked one could understand the words but not what they meant. Many people thought that he had become mad.' My audience suddenly became much more attentive. 'The great chief wanted to know what was wrong with Hamlet, so he sent for two of Hamlet's age mates [school friends would have taken long explanation] to talk to Hamlet and find out what troubled his heart. Hamlet, seeing that they had been bribed by the chief to betray him, told them nothing. Polonius, however, insisted that Hamlet was mad because he had been forbidden to see Ophelia, whom he loved.'

'Why,' inquired a bewildered voice, 'should anyone bewitch Hamlet on that account?'

'Bewitch him?'

'Yes, only witchcraft can make anyone mad, unless, of course, one sees the beings that lurk in the forest.'

I stopped being a storyteller, took out my notebook and demanded to be told more about these two causes of madness. Even while they spoke and I jotted notes, I tried to calculate the effect of this new factor on the plot. Hamlet had not been exposed to the beings that lurk in the forests. Only his relatives in the male line could bewitch him. Barring relatives not mentioned by Shakespeare, it had to be Claudius who was attempting to harm him. And, of course, it was.

For the moment I staved off questions by saying that the great chief also refused to believe that Hamlet was mad for the love of Ophelia and nothing else. 'He was sure that something much more important was troubling Hamlet's heart.'

'Now Hamlet's age mates,' I continued, 'had brought with them a famous storyteller. Hamlet decided to have this man tell the chief and all his homestead a story about a man who had poisoned his brother because he desired his brother's wife and wished to be chief himself. Hamlet was sure the great chief could not hear the story without making a sign if he was indeed guilty, and then he would discover whether his dead father had told him the truth.'

The old man interrupted, with deep cunning, 'Why should a father lie to his son?' he asked.

I hedged: 'Hamlet wasn't sure that it really was his dead father.' It was impossible to say anything, in that language, about devil-inspired visions.

'You mean,' he said, 'it actually was an omen, and he knew witches sometimes send false ones. Hamlet was a fool not to go to one skilled in reading omens and divining the truth in the first place. A man-who-sees-the-truth could have told him how his father died, if he really had been poisoned, and if there was witchcraft in it; then Hamlet could have called the elders to settle the matter.'

The shrewd elder ventured to disagree. 'Because his father's brother was a great chief, one-who-sees-the-truth might therefore have been afraid to tell it. I think it was for that reason that a friend of Hamlet's father—a witch and an elder—sent an omen so his friend's son would know. Was the omen true?'

'Yes,' I said, abandoning ghosts and the devil; a witch-sent omen it would have to be. 'It was true, for when the storyteller was telling his tale before all the homestead, the great chief rose in fear. Afraid that Hamlet knew his secret he planned to have him killed.'

The stage set of the next bit presented some difficulties of translation. I began cautiously. 'The great chief told Hamlet's mother to find out from her son what he knew. But because a woman's children are always first in her heart, he had the important elder Polonius hide behind a cloth that hung against the wall of Hamlet's mother's sleeping hut. Hamlet started to scold his mother for what she had done.'

There was a shocked murmur from everyone. A man should never scold his mother.

'She called out in fear, and Polonius moved behind the cloth. Shouting, "A rat!" Hamlet took his machete and slashed through the cloth.' I paused for dramatic effect. 'He had killed Polonius!'

The old men looked at each other in supreme disgust. 'That Polonius truly was a fool and a man who knew nothing! What child would not know enough to shout, "It's me!" ' With a pang, I remembered that these people are ardent hunters, always armed with bow, arrow, and machete; at the first rustle in the grass an arrow is aimed and ready, and the hunter shouts 'Game!' If no human voice answers immediately, the arrow speeds on its way. Like a good hunter Hamlet had shouted, 'A rat!'

I rushed in to save Polonius's reputation. 'Polonius did speak. Hamlet heard him. But he thought it was the chief and wished to kill him to avenge his father. He had meant to kill him earlier that evening. . . . ' I broke down, unable to describe to these pagans, who had no belief in individual afterlife, the difference between dying at one's prayers and dying 'unhousell'd, disappointed, unaneled.'

This time I had shocked my audience seriously. 'For a man to raise his hand against his father's brother and the one who has become his father—that is a terrible thing. The elders ought to let such a man be bewitched.'

I nibbled at my kola nut in some perplexity, then pointed out that after all the man had killed Hamlet's father.

'No,' pronounced the old man, speaking less to me than to the young men sitting behind the elders. 'If your father's brother has killed your father, you must appeal to your father's age mates; *they* may avenge him. No man may use violence against his senior relatives.' Another thought struck him. 'But if his father's brother had indeed been wicked enough to bewitch Hamlet and make him mad that would be a good story indeed, for it would be his fault that Hamlet, being mad, no longer had any sense and thus was ready to kill his father's brother.'

There was a murmur of applause. *Hamlet* was again a good story to them, but it no longer seemed quite the same story to me. As I thought over the coming complications of plot and motive, I lost courage and decided to skim over dangerous ground quickly.

'The great chief,' I went on, 'was not sorry that Hamlet had killed Polonius. It gave him a reason to send Hamlet away, with his two treacherous age mates, with letters to a chief of a far country, saying that Hamlet should be killed. But Hamlet changed the writing on their papers, so that the chief killed his age mates instead.' I encountered a reproachful glare from one of the men whom I had told undetectable forgery was not merely immoral but beyond human skill. I looked the other way.

'Before Hamlet could return, Laertes came back for his father's funeral. The great chief told him Hamlet had killed Polonius. Laertes swore to kill Hamlet because of this, and because his sister Ophelia, hearing her father had been killed by the man she loved, went mad and drowned in the river.'

'Have you already forgotten what we told you?' The old man was reproachful. 'One cannot take vengeance on a madman; Hamlet killed Polonius in his madness. As for the girl, she not only went mad, she was drowned. Only witches can make people drown. Water itself can't hurt anything. It is merely something one drinks and bathes in.'

I began to get cross. 'If you don't like the story I'll stop.'

The old man made soothing noises and himself poured me some more beer. 'You tell the story well, and we are listening. But it is clear that the elders of your country have never told you what the story really means. No, don't interrupt! We believe you when you say your marriage customs are different, or your clothes and weapons. But people are the same everywhere; therefore, there are always witches and it is we, the elders, who know how witches work. We told you it was the great chief who wished to kill Hamlet, and now your own words have proved us right. Who were Ophelia's male relatives?'

'There were only her father and her brother.' Hamlet was clearly out of my hands.

'There must have been many more; this also you must ask of your elders when you get back to your country. From what you tell us, since Polonius was dead, it must have been Laertes who killed Ophelia, although I do not see the reason for it.'

We had emptied one pot of beer, and the old men argued the point with slightly tipsy interest. Finally one of them demanded of me, 'What did the servant of Polonius say on his return?'

With difficulty I recollected Reynaldo and his mission. 'I don't think he did return before Polonius was killed.'

'Listen,' said the elder, 'and I will tell you how it was and how your story will go, then you may tell me if I am right. Polonius knew his son would get into trouble, and so he did. He had many fines to pay for fighting, and debts from gambling. But he had only two ways of getting money quickly. One was to marry off his sister at once, but it is difficult to find a man who will marry a woman desired by the son of a chief. For if the chief's heir commits adultery with your wife, what can you do? Only a fool calls a case against a man who will someday be his judge. Therefore Laertes had to take the second way: he killed his sister by witchcraft, drowning her so he could secretly sell her body to the witches.'

I raised an objection. 'They found her body and buried it. Indeed Laertes jumped into the grave to see his sister once more—so, you see, the body was truly there. Hamlet, who had just come back, jumped in after him.'

'What did I tell you?' The elder appealed to the others. 'Laertes was up to no good with his sister's body. Hamlet prevented him, because the chief's heir, like a chief, does not wish any other man to grow rich and powerful. Laertes would be angry, because he would have killed his sister without benefit to himself. In our country he would try to kill Hamlet for that reason. Is this not what happened?'

'More or less,' I admitted. 'When the great chief found Hamlet was still alive, he encouraged Laertes to try to kill Hamlet and arranged a fight with machetes between them. In the fight both the young men were wounded to death. Hamlet's mother drank the poisoned beer that the chief meant for Hamlet in case he won the fight. When he saw his mother die of poison, Hamlet, dying, managed to kill his father's brother with his machete.'

'You see, I was right!' exclaimed the elder.

'That was a very good story,' added the old man, 'and you told it with very few mistakes. There was just one more error, at the very end. The poison Hamlet's mother drank was obviously meant for the survivor of the fight, whichever it was. If Laertes had won, the great chief would have poisoned him, for no one would know that he arranged Hamlet's death. Then, too, he need not fear Laertes' witchcraft; it takes a strong heart to kill one's only sister by witchcraft.

'Sometime,' concluded the old man, gathering his ragged toga about him, 'you must tell us some more stories of your country. We, who are elders, will instruct you in their true meaning, so that when you return to your own land your elders will see that you have not been sitting in the bush, but among those who know things and who have taught you wisdom.'

4.13 VLADIMIR NABOKOV

Jenefer Coates

Vladimir Nabokov (1899–1977) is best known as a bilingual novelist of dark themes and brilliant style, and as a controversial translator, chiefly of Pushkin's *Eugene Onegin*. Nabokov was, in fact, constantly engaged in turning his own and others' texts between Russian, English, and French in the course of a long working life. His mixed approach, however, led to accusations of double standards: translating his own work with great artistry, he came to adopt a literalist approach for others. Nabokov the translator was closely related to Nabokov the writer: the two evolved in tandem, with the mid-career switch from Russian to English sharpening sensitivity to ineluctable cultural and linguistic difference. His thoughts were shaped into poems, stories, and novels as well as polemical essays, lectures, commentaries, and reviews, in which scorn for commonplace practices gave way to an impassioned justification of literalism (a term he dismissed, however, as 'more or less nonsense'). His novels meanwhile increasingly embodied themes of transformation and translation in a broad and narrow sense.

Born in St Petersburg, Nabokov described his upbringing as that of 'a normal tri-lingual child in a family with a large library', declaring in 1964: 'I am an American writer, born in Russia and educated in England where I studied French literature, before spending fifteen years in Germany' (*Strong Opinions* (New York: McGraw-Hill, 1973), 26). The leading Russian writer in émigré Berlin, Nabokov began to experiment with English in the 1930s. Fleeing Nazism for America in 1940, he embarked on a new career as university teacher, lepidopterist, and writer in English. After moderate success, he finally attracted worldwide note and notoriety with *Lolita* (Paris: Olympia Press 1955; New York: Putnam's 1958) which enabled him to devote himself entirely to literature for the first time. Moving to Switzerland, he completed his Pushkin translation (*Eugene Onegin: A Novel in Verse*, trans. Vladimir Nabokov (Bollingen Series, 72, New York: Pantheon 1964; rev. Princeton: Princeton University Press, 1975)) and composed, *inter alia*, two major works in English, *Pale Fire* (New York: Putnam's, 1962) and *Ada* (New York: McGraw-Hill, 1969), whilst continuing to translate his earlier novels in both directions, to meet the new demand.

Switching Languages

Nabokov published (under the pseudonym 'Vladimir Sirin') two Russian translations before his own first novel: Romain Rolland's pseudo-medieval *Colas Breugnon* (1914) from

French (*Nikolka Persik*, Berlin: Slovo 1922) and Lewis Carroll's *Alice in Wonderland* from English (*Anya v strane chudes*, Berlin: Gamayun, 1923). Both playfully hark back, the one to courtly England, the other to Rabelaisian France. Nabokov cheerfully russianized both, trawling dictionaries for suitable archaic equivalents. He also made fine appropriative translations of French and English poets, amongst them Verlaine, Rimbaud, Supervielle, Rupert Brooke, and Yeats.

The switch to primary use of English brought changes of approach. His translations into Russian, for all the interlingual play and neologizing that characterize Nabokov's style, remained essentially domesticating: innovation is, after all, relative to normative form. The 'russianizing' of *Lolita*, for instance, which he took into his own 'safe hands' (1967), sparkles with all the energy of the original, featuring hundreds of new usages, and Russian in place of Anglophone allusions. Creative adjustments were defended on grounds of authorial licence.

Into English, however, the pattern is more complex: 'fair imitation' was abandoned for more or less word-for-word solutions when translating others, but for his own work, Nabokov always produced approximate replicas. Working methods varied, however: whereas Russian was always handled alone, Nabokov came to prefer collaboration into English, revising and polishing drafts prepared by skilled translators (mostly, and most happily, with his son Dmitri as 'docile assistant'). Translation, he complained, drained him of precious energies needed for new writing and required 'another section of the brain than the text of my book, and switching from the one to another by means of spasmodic jumps causes a kind of mental asthma' (Letter to James Laughlin, 16 July 1942, in *Selected Letters 1940–1977*, ed. Dmitri Nabokov and Matthew J. Bruccoli (New York: Harcourt Brace Jovanovich, 1989), 40).

The temptation to improve on the 'greener fruits' of an earlier self was irresistible to such a prolific, inventive writer. In two cases, translation turned into serial rewriting: *Otchaianie* (1932), first composed in Russian, was self-translated into English as *Despair* (1935), but further revised for republication, still as *Despair*, in 1966 (New York: Putnam's, 1966). Nabokov's memoirs began as *Conclusive Evidence* (1951), were reworked into Russian as *Drugie berega* (1954), and then underwent further transformation before final publication as *Speak, Memory: An Autobiography Revisited* (New York: Putnam's, 1966), a process he described thus: 'This re-Englishing of a Russian re-version of what had been an English re-telling of Russian memories in the first place, proved to be a diabolical task, but some consolation was given me by the thought that such multiple metamorphosis, familiar to butterflies, had not been tried by any human before' (*Speak, Memory* (1966), 12–13).

On his painful switch of language, Nabokov would later write:

None of my American friends have read my Russian books and thus every appraisal on the strength of my English ones is bound to be out of focus. My private tragedy, which cannot, indeed should not, be anybody's concern, is that I had to abandon my natural language, my natural idiom, my rich, infinitely rich and docile Russian tongue, for a second-rate brand of English. ('On a Book Entitled Lolita', 1956, postscript to *Lolita* (1958), 316)

The achievement of *Lolita* is all the greater for this sense of loss, yet its success is, paradoxically, partly due to the relative weakness of Nabokov's early English. Discovering he was 'tri-literary' rather than tri-lingual—never having lived in an English-speaking household, he lacked what he called 'domestic diction'—Nabokov turned what he perceived as an impediment to advantage by giving his style a baroque, hyper-literary tone ('You talk like a book,' Lolita complains to Humbert). It would also engender some memorable, tragicomic outsiders (Pnin, Humbert, and Kinbote). The mature Nabokovian voice would be self-conscious, richly intertextual, and always a little foreign. It would resist easy access through involute structures and intricate language, its complexity increasing in inverse proportion to the rugged plainness of translation, although in fact both called for close attention ('the re-reader' being addressed in *Ada*).

Teaching Russian and European literature in translation gave further impetus to literalism. A literal translation did not seek to entertain or delight, but to educate and inform. Appalled at the shortcomings of versions praised by publishers and critics, Nabokov complained:

I am teaching a course in European Fiction at Cornell University and have selected as a permanent item Flaubert's 'Madame Bovary'. In September I ordered, for a class of 133 students [...] your edition of that novel [...] I devoted seven class meetings to the discussion of the novel, and at least 10 minutes of every such period had to be spent in correcting the incredible mistranslations (more exactly, only the worst of them). In point of fact every page of the book contains at least three or four blunders—either obvious mistakes, or slovenly translations giving the wrong slant to Flaubert's intention. His lovely descriptions of visual things, clothes, landscapes, Emma's hairdo etc. are completely botched by the translator. I had to revise all this, going through each word of the book with a copy of the French first edition before me and have found, in addition to the various blunders due to the translator's insufficient French, a number of misprints due, in most cases, to faulty proofreading ('beads' for 'meads', 'came' for 'cane'—that sort of thing) [...]

My intention was to use the book next year and in later years. As my classroom analysis of Flaubert's style is a close one, and as my students are not expected to have enough French to turn to the French original, the situation is an alarming one [...] My suggestion is that before you make a new printing of your new edition (the one 'based on the Eleanor Marx Aveling translation with corrections and modernization by the editor', 1946), you accept from me a list of more than 1000 corrections [. . .] I have also come to the conclusion that a number of notes elucidating local, literary and historical allusions, which are absolutely incomprehensible to the American student, ought to be added to the English translation of the book [. . .] and this I would also be willing to do [. . .] (To John Selby, Editor at Rinehart, 17 January 1951 (*Selected Letters* (1989), 111–12))

Here are all the signs of Nabokov's growing functionalism. The good reader, he believed, should be ready to work at the text, to take a Schleiermachian journey into an estranged world and meet the author (or translator) at least halfway:

> The good reader is one who has imagination, memory, a dictionary and some artistic sense [. . . and who will] notice and fondle details ... Up a trackless slope climbs the master artist, and at the top, on a windy ridge, whom do you think he meets? The panting and happy reader, and there they spontaneously embrace and are linked for ever, if the book lasts forever [. . .] ('Good Readers and Good Writers', *c.*1940s, in Vladimir Nabokov, *Lectures on Russian Literature*, ed. Fredson Bowers (New York: Harcourt Brace Jovanovich, 1981 / London: Weidenfeld and Nicolson, 1982), 1–6)

The Art of Translation

Nabokov had begun to air his views soon after arrival in America, publishing the 'The Art of Translation' in 1941. Despite a taxonomist's tendency to draw up rules and categories, he eschewed the abstractions of theory proper: sarcastically descriptive and stridently prescriptive, he appealed to an aesthetics that informed his own work. Couched in measured scholarly discourse, his views might have won more friends, but the colourful disparagements of a little-known foreign writer only raised hackles.

From 'The Art of Translation', *The New Republic*, New York, 4 Aug. 1941; repr. in *Vladimir Nabokov: Lectures on Russian Literature*, ed. Fredson Bowers (New York: Harcourt Brace Jovanovich, 1981 / London: Weidenfeld and Nicolson, 1982), 315

> Three grades of evil can be discerned in the queer world of verbal transmigration. The first, and lesser one, comprises obvious errors due to ignorance or misguided knowledge. This is mere human frailty and thus excusable. The next step to Hell is taken by the translator who intentionally skips words or passages that he does not bother to understand or that might seem obscure or obscene to vaguely imagined readers; he accepts the

blank look that his dictionary gives him without any qualms; or subjects scholarship to primness: he is as ready to know less than the author as he is to think he knows better. The third, and worst, degree of turpitude is reached when a masterpiece is planished and patted into such a shape, vilely beautified in such a fashion as to conform to the notions and prejudices of a given public.

[...]

Barring downright deceivers, mild imbeciles and impotent poets, there exist, roughly speaking, three types of translators—and this has nothing to do with my three categories of evil; or, rather, any of the three types may err in a similar way. These three are: the scholar who is eager to make the world appreciate the works of an obscure genius as much as he does himself; the well meaning hack; and the professional writer relaxing in the company of a foreign confrère. The scholar will be, I hope, exact and pedantic: footnotes—on the same page as the text and not tucked away at the end of the volume— can never be too copious and detailed. The laborious lady translating at the eleventh hour the eleventh volume of somebody's collected works will be, I am afraid, less exact and less pedantic; but the point is not that the scholar commits fewer blunders than a drudge; the point is that as a rule both he and she are hopelessly devoid of any semblance of creative genius. Neither learning nor diligence can replace imagination and style.

Now comes the authentic poet who has the two last assets and who finds relaxation in translating a bit of Lermontov or Verlaine between writing poems of his own. Either he does not know the original language and calmly relies upon the so-called 'literal' translation made for him by a far less brilliant but a little more learned person, or else, knowing the language, he lacks the scholar's precision and the professional translator's experience. The main drawback, however, in this case is the fact that the greater his individual talent, the more apt he will be to drown the foreign masterpiece under the sparkling ripples of his own personal style. Instead of dressing up like the real author, he dresses up the author as himself.

We can deduce now the requirements that a translator must possess in order to be able to give an ideal version of a foreign masterpiece. First of all he must have as much talent, or at least the same kind of talent, as the author he chooses [...] Second, he must know thoroughly the two nations and the two languages involved and be perfectly acquainted with all details relating to his author's manner and methods; also, with the social background of words, their fashions, history and period associations. This leads to the third point: while having genius and knowledge he must possess the gift of mimicry and be able to act, as it were, the real author's part by impersonating his tricks of demeanor and speech, his ways and his mind, with the utmost degree of verisimilitude [...]

During the 1950s, Nabokov translated chiefly for academic purposes. His version of the anonymous *Slovo o polku Igoreve*, for example, was originally prepared for teaching at Harvard in 1949, but when published, with commentary and notes, in 1960 under the title *The Song of Igor's Campaign. An Epic of the Twelfth Century* (Vintage 1960; repr. Ann Arbor: Ardis 1988), Nabokov deliberately rendered it still 'less readable', warning: 'I have ruthlessly sacrificed manner to matter and have attempted to give a literal rendering of the text as I understand it.' Despite the rough-hewn texture, it retains some poetry: the Old Russian text, originally composed in the twelfth century, or perhaps forged in the eighteenth, is rendered in broadly modern English, with archaisms employed in token rather than in toto, matching perceived anachronisms for the sake of 'historical exactitude'. In this, he differed significantly from Pound, for example, whose transposition of an entire text to a past, dead form Nabokov considered fake, no matter how (or, especially, whether) 'inspired'. The abstruse lexis that occurs everywhere in Nabokov is used always for precision of meaning rather than effect.

The Song of Igor's Campaign, p. 36, lines 130–50

Igor leads Donwards his warriors.
His misfortunes already
are forefelt by the birds in the oakscrub.
The wolves, in the ravines,
conjure the storm.
The erns with their squalling
summon the beasts to the bones.
The foxes yelp
at the vermilion shields.
O Russian land,
you are already behind the culmen!

Long does the night keep darkling.
Dawn sheds its light.
Mist has covered the fields.
Stilled is the trilling of nightingales;
the jargon of jackdaws has woken.
With their vermilion shields
the sons of Rus have barred the great prairie,
seeking for themselves honor,
and for their prince glory.

From foreword to the translation, in collaboration with Dmitri Nabokov of Lermontov's
A Hero of our Time (New York: Doubleday, 1958)

This is the first English translation of Lermontov's novel. The book has been paraphrased into English several times, but never translated before. The experienced hack may find it quite easy to turn Lermontov's Russian into slick English clichés by means of judicious omission, amplification, and levigation; and he will tone down everything that might seem unfamiliar to the meek and imbecile reader visualized by his publisher. But the honest translator is faced with a different task.

In the first place we must dismiss, once and for all the conventional notion that a translation 'should read smoothly' and 'should not sound like a translation' (to quote the would-be compliments, addressed to vague versions, by genteel reviewers who have and never will read the original texts). In point of fact, any translation that does *not* sound like a translation is bound to be inexact upon inspection; while, on the other hand, the only virtue of a good translation is faithfulness and completeness. Whether it reads smoothly or not, depends on the model, not on the mimic.

Pushkin

In a lecture given in Paris in 1937 (attended by James Joyce) entitled 'Pouchkine: ou le vrai et le vraisemblable' ('Pushkin, or the Real and the Plausible', trans. Dmitri Nabokov, *New York Review of Books*, 31 March 1988), Nabokov had declared:

Those of us who really know him revere him with unparalleled fervor and purity, and experience a radiant feeling when the richness of his life over-flows into the present to flood our spirit [...] To read his works [. . .] and to reread them endlessly is one of the glories of earthly life.

Nabokov's early efforts at translating Pushkin were considered 'the best translations of poetry of any kind' by the American critic Edmund Wilson (*The Nabokov-Wilson Letters : Correspondence between Vladimir Nabokov and Edmund Wilson, 1941–1971*, ed. Simon Karlinsky (New York: Harper and Row, 1979), 42), who encouraged the publication of a small collection (*Three Russian Poets: Pushkin, Lermontov and Tyutchev*, Vladimir Nabokov, Norfolk: New Directions, 1945). Nabokov later dismissed these translations as 'graceful imitations', however, and in 1955 expressed his deep misgivings about 'traducing' Pushkin in a poem published in *The New Yorker*. Ostensibly a model of the fourteen-line Onegin stanza, Nabokov's poetic apology was reprinted in his translator's introduction to *Eugene Onegin* (1964 and 1975, vol. i. 9). It begins:

What is translation? On a platter
A poet's pale and glaring head,
A parrot's screech, a monkey's chatter,
And profanation of the dead.
[. . .].

Nabokov felt ambivalent about translating Pushkin. He longed to reveal to the Anglophone world a poet that meant more to himself (and all Russian speakers) than any other, yet found the impersonation involved in conventional translation increasingly abhorrent, especially while he still feared sounding second-rate in his own creative voice. He knew that Pushkin's special magic, like that of all great poets, lay in the specific 'combinational delights' of sound and sense that would always elude recapture in another language. In the Nabokovian universe, the specific is constantly opposed to the general, while mimicry, masquerade, and imitation are always equated with falsity, fakery, and phoneyness. After years of experimentation, Nabokov finally hit on the 'right approach' but only disclosed it a decade later. He meanwhile outlined the difficulties in 'Problems of Translation: "Onegin" in English'.

From 'Problems of Translation: "Onegin" in English', *Partisan Review*, 22 (1955), Repr. in R. Schulte and J. Biguenet (eds.), *Theories of Translation* (Chicago: Chicago University Press 1992); and in L. Venuti (ed.), *The Translation Studies Reader* (New York & London: Routledge 2000)

I

I constantly find in reviews of verse translations the following kind of thing that sends me into spasms of helpless fury: 'Mr (or Miss) So-and-so's translation reads smoothly.' In other words, the reviewer of the 'translation,' who neither has, nor would be able to have, without special study, any knowledge whatsoever of the original, praises as 'readable' an imitation only because the drudge or the rhymster has substituted easy platitudes for the breathtaking intricacies of the text. 'Readable,' indeed! A schoolboy's boner is less of a mockery in regard to the ancient masterpiece than its commercial interpretation or poetization. 'Rhyme' rhymes with 'crime,' when Homer or Hamlet are rhymed. The term 'free translation' smacks of knavery and tyranny. It is when the translator sets out to render the 'spirit'—not the textual sense—that he begins to traduce his author. The clumsiest literal translation is a thousand times more useful than the prettiest paraphrase.

[. . .]

IV

The person who desires to turn a literary masterpiece into another language, has only one duty to perform, and this is to reproduce with absolute exactitude the whole text, and nothing but the text. The term 'literal translation' is tautological since anything but that is not truly a translation but an imitation, an adaptation or a parody.

The problem, then, is a choice between rhyme and reason: can a translation while rendering with absolute fidelity the whole text, and nothing but the text, keep the form of the original, its rhythm and its rhyme? To the artist whom practice within the limits of one language, his own, has convinced that matter and manner are one, it comes as a shock to discover that a work of art can present itself to the would-be translator as split into form and content, and that the question of rendering one but not the other may arise at all. Actually what happens is still a monist's delight: shorn of its primary verbal existence, the original text will not be able to soar and to sing; but it can be very nicely dissected and mounted, and scientifically studied in all its organic details [...]

VII

[...] Here are three conclusions I have arrived at: 1. It is impossible to translate Onegin in rhyme. 2. It is possible to describe in a series of footnotes the modulations and rhymes of the text as well as all its associations and other special features. 3. It is possible to translate Onegin with reasonable accuracy by substituting for the fourteen rhymed tetrameter lines of each stanza fourteen unrhymed lines of varying length, from iambic diameter to iambic pentameter.

These conclusions can be generalized. I want translations with copious footnotes, footnotes reaching up like skyscrapers to the top of this or that page so as to leave only the gleam of one textual line between commentary and eternity. I want such footnotes and the absolutely literal sense, with no emasculation and no padding—I want such sense and such notes for all the poetry in other tongues that still languishes in 'poetical' versions, begrimed and beslimed by rhyme. And when my Onegin is ready, it will either conform exactly to my vision or not appear at all.

[Nabokov's *Onegin* finally reached publication in 1964. The method was didactic and scholarly. Rather than recreating Pushkin's 'limpid harmonies [...] multiple melodies [...] and precise and luminous images' in the usual Byronic pastiche, Nabokov attempted to match not only meaning word-for-word but the syllabic rhythm of the Russian as well. The stanzaic form was retained but all other rhetorical features suppressed, although lyric moments still glint like shards among rubble. The English translation was interlinear, designed to keep pace exactly with Pushkin's cyrillic on a second line and its roman transliteration on a third. Notes would ideally be accommodated close to the relevant text, even though some of them ran to many sides. In the event, the published edition comprised four separate volumes, one each for the English and Russian texts, and two for the 1200 pages of compendious notes and commentaries. These analyse details of style, variants, and sources and place both poem and poet in full historical, intellectual, and artistic contexts. Nabokov's provocative Foreword sets the tone.]

From *Eugene Onegin: A Novel in Verse* by Aleksandr Pushkin, trans. from the Russian, with commentary, by Vladimir Nabokov, (Bollingen Series 72, 1964); Princeton: Princeton University Press, rev. 1975), vol. i, Foreword, pp. vii–x

[. . .] Can Pushkin's poem, or any other poem with a definite rhyme scheme, be really translated? To answer this we should first define the term 'translation.' Attempts to render a poem in another language fall into three categories:

(1) Paraphrastic: offering a free version of the original, with omissions and additions prompted by the exigencies of form, the conventions attributed to the consumer, and the translator's ignorance. Some paraphrases may possess the charm of stylish diction and idiomatic conciseness, but no scholar should succumb to stylishness and no reader be fooled by it.

(2) Lexical (or constructional): rendering the basic meaning of words (and their order). This a machine can do under the direction of an intelligent bilinguist.

(3) Literal: rendering, as closely as the associative and syntactical capacities of another language allow, the exact contextual meaning of the original. Only this is true translation.

Let me give an example of each method. The opening quatrain of *Eugene Onegin*, transliterated and prosodically accented, reads:

> *Moy dyádya sámih chéstnih právil,*
> *Kogdá ne v shútku zanemóg,*
> *On uvazhát sebyá zastávil,*
> *I lúchshe vídumat' ne móg . . .*

This can be paraphrased in an infinite number of ways. For example:

> My uncle, in the best tradition,
> By falling dangerously sick
> Won universal recognition
> And could devise no better trick . . .

The lexical or constructional translation is:

> My uncle [is] of most honest rules [:]
> when not in jest [he] has been taken ill,
> he to respect him has forced [one],
> and better invent could not . . .

Now comes the literalist. He may toy with 'honorable' instead of 'honest' and waver between 'seriously' and 'not in jest'; he will replace 'rules' by the more evocative 'principles' and rearrange the order of words to achieve some semblance of English construction and retain some vestige of Russian rhythm, arriving at:

> My uncle has most honest principles:
> when he was taken ill in earnest,
> he has made one respect him
> and nothing better could invent ...

And if he is still not satisfied with his version, the translator can at least hope to amplify it in a detailed note.

[...]

We are now in a position to word our question more accurately: can a rhymed poem like *Eugene Onegin* be truly translated with the retention of its rhymes? The answer, of course, is no. To reproduce the rhymes or yet translate the entire poem literally is mathematically impossible. But in losing its rhyme the poem loses its bloom, which neither marginal description nor the alchemy of a scholium can replace. Should one then content oneself with an exact rendering of the subject matter and forget all about form? Or should one still excuse an imitation of the poem's structure to which only twisted bits of sense stick here and there, by convincing oneself and one's public that in mutilating its meaning for the sake of a pleasure-measure rhyme one has the opportunity of prettifying or skipping the dry and difficult passages?

[...]

In transposing *Eugene Onegin* from Pushkin's Russian into my English I have sacrificed to completeness of meaning every formal element including the iambic rhythm, whenever its retention hindered fidelity. To my ideal of literalism I sacrificed everything (elegance, euphony, clarity, good taste, modern usage, and even grammar) that the dainty mimic prizes higher than truth. Pushkin has likened translation to horses changed at the posthouses of civilization. The greatest reward I can think of is that students may use my work as a pony. [...]

The Shift to Literalism

Nabokov attempted to translate Pushkin at three different stages of his career: as an emerging English writer in 1945; as an acclaimed author in 1964, and as a bilingual master in 1976. The shift towards 'bony literalism' can be traced in his handling of a single stanza.

Three translations by Nabokov of *Eugene Onegin* by Alexander Pushkin, chapter 1, stanza, XXXII,

Russian Review, 4/2 (1945), 38–9

Diana's bosom, Flora's dimple
are very charming, I agree—
but there's a greater charm, less simple,
—the instep of Terpsichore.
By prophesying to the eye
a prize with which no prize can vie
'tis a fair token and a snare
for swarms of daydreams. Everywhere
its grace, sweet reader, I admire:
at long-hemmed tables, half-concealed,
in spring, upon a velvet field,
in winter, at a grated fire,
in ballrooms, on a glossy floor,
on the bleak boulders of a shore.

Eugene Onegin: A Novel in Verse *(Bollingen Series 72, New York: Pantheon Press 1964; London: Routledge & Kegan Paul, 1964), i. 111*

Diana's bosom, Flora's cheeks, are charming,
dear friend! Nevertheless, for me
something about it makes more charming
the small foot of Terpsichore.
By prophesying to the gaze
an unpriced recompense,
with token beauty it attracts the willful
swarm of desires.
I like it, dear Elvina,
beneath the long napery of tables,
in springtime on the turf of meads,
in winter on the hearth's cast iron,
on mirrory parquet of halls,
by the sea on granite of rocks.

Eugene Onegin *(Bollingen Series, Princeton: Princeton University Press, (1964; rev. 1975), i. 109*

Diana's bosom, Flora's cheeks,
are charming, dear friends!

However, the little foot of Terpsichore
is for me in some way more charming.
By prophesying to the gaze
an unpriced recompense,
with token beauty it attracts
the willful swarm of longings.
I'm fond of it, my friend Elvina,
beneath the long napery of tables,
in springtime on the turf of meads,
in winter on the hearth's cast iron,
on mirrory parquet of halls,
by the sea on granite of rocks.

NOTES TO CHAPTER ONE: XXXII. COMMENTARY, VOL . 2 : 118–120 (EXCERPTS). [1964 AND 1975]

3–4/Cf. *Le joli-pied* of Nicolas Edme Restif de la Bretonne, a mediocre but entertaining writer of the eighteenth century (1974–1806) [. . .]

7/with token beauty /*uslóvnoyu krasóy* . Although *uslovniy* means 'conditional' or 'conventional,' the only possible sense here must turn on the idea of *un signe convenu*, with the emphasis on the sign, the emblem, the cipher, the code of beauty, the secret language of those narrow little feet [. . .]
Cf. Shakespeare, *Troilus and Cressida*, IV, v. 55:

> There's language in her eye, her cheek, her lip
> Nay, her foot speaks . . .

8/ willful swarm /*svoevól'niy róy* : a common Gallicism, *essaim*, with *svoevól'niy*, 'self-willed' echoing alliteratively such cliché epithets as *volage, frivole, folâtre* [. . .]

9/Elvina: I suspect this is a natural child of Macpherson's Malvina. It occurs in French imitations of the Ossian poems [. . .]

Reception of Onegin

By the time *Eugene Onegin* finally appeared in 1964, Nabokov was internationally acclaimed as a virtuoso stylist. His translation was thus perceived not as the product of a thorough but idiosyncratic scholar, but of a writer who talked of aesthetic bliss while giving short shrift to the creator of the 'greatest poem in the Russian language'; and a writer, moreover, who had flouted his own strictures when translating his own work. Despite the frankness of Nabokov's aims, hostility has persisted. Yet no student or translator can ignore his study: Nabokov gained Pushkin due recognition as a universal poet, and enhanced scholarship in the field. His detailed historical analysis establishes crucial intertextual links between the Russian masterpiece and European writing, and shows how Pushkin often relied on sources read in translation. This point is commonly seen as spiteful condescension on the part of the superior multilingualist, but like Pushkin, Nabokov saw translation as cultural synthesis, a vital stage or staging post in literary evolution; unlike him, however, he saw 'misrepresentations' as obstructions to that process.

Nabokov's *Onegin* ignited one of the most celebrated literary rows of the twentieth century. The loudest detractor was his erstwhile friend and supporter Edmund Wilson, who chose to ignore its advertised purpose, and derided the lack of poetic form, the stilted, archaic diction, awkward syntax, and elephantine prose that so betrayed the glories of the Russian. Nabokov rose in defence and a bitter debate over prosody and style dragged on for many months. Nabokov wearily stated his cause for the last time in 'Reply To My Critics':

From: 'Reply To My Critics', *Encounter* **(Feb. 1966), repr. in** *Strong Opinions* **(New York: McGraw Hill, 1973), 241–67**

[. . . If] adverse criticism happens to be directed not at those acts of fancy [my novels], but at such a matter-of-fact work of reference as my annotated translation of *Eugene Onegin*, other considerations take over. Unlike my novels, EO possesses an ethical side, moral and human elements. It reflects the compiler's honesty or dishonesty, skill or sloppiness. If told I am a bad poet, I smile; but if told I am a poor scholar, I reach for my heaviest dictionary.

[. . . O]ne might conclude that literal translation represents an approach entirely devised by me; that it had never been heard of before; and that there was something offensive and even sinister about such a method and undertaking. Promoters and producers of what Anthony Burgess calls 'arty translations'—carefully rhymed, pleasantly modulated versions containing, say, eighteen percent of sense plus thirty-two of nonsense and fifty of neutral padding—are I think more prudent than they realize. While ostensibly tempted by impossible dreams, they are subliminally impelled by a kind of self-preservation. The 'arty translation' protects them by concealing and camouflaging ignorance or incomplete information or the fuzzy edge of limited knowledge. Stark literalism, on the other hand, would expose their fragile frame to unknown and incalculable perils.

[. . .]

As a result the canned music of rhymed versions is enthusiastically advertised, and accepted, and the sacrifice of textual precision applauded as something rather heroic, whereas only suspicion and blood-hounds await the gaunt, graceless literalist groping around in despair for the obscure word that would satisfy impassioned fidelity and accumulating in the process a wealth of information which only makes the advocates of pretty camouflage tremble or sneer.

[. . .]

My EO falls short of the ideal crib. It is still not close enough and not ugly enough. In future editions I plan to defowlerize it still more drastically. I think I shall turn it entirely into utilitarian prose, with a still bumpier brand of English, rebarbative barricades of square brackets and tattered banners of reprobate words, in order to eliminate the last vestiges of bourgeois poesy and concession to rhyme. [...]

[As threatened, the 1975 edition was revised to be even more 'bumpy'.]

Nabokov's Oeuvre

The order of publication suggests that Nabokov wrote *Lolita* before translating Pushkin. In fact the translation was completed well before *Lolita* catapulted him to prominence, but a further decade was devoted to the commentary. Yet work on the two did overlap by several years and noticeable similarities have given rise to critical speculation. *Lolita* has been posited as a 'free' translation of *Onegin* that complements the 'faithful' literal. Intertextual sleuths have suspected a plundering or, more puzzlingly, a parody of Pushkin. Both novels are luminous examples of the romantic genre, and both are what Nabokov called a "phenomenon of style" (*Eugene Onegin*, Translator's Introduction, i. 7) for both recall their own precursors through homage, parody and multiple allusions: *Onegin* looks back from the 1820s while *Lolita* looks back from the 1950s—by which time, *Onegin* was just one more romance resonating among the many.

Both employ the usual romantic devices, including the epistolary declaration descended from the French: thus Charlotte's letter to Humbert resembles Tatiana's confession to Onegin in its sentimental phrasing and gallic flavour. Pushkin conveys this in a Russian that touchingly calques the French. This is lost in the deliberate clichés of Nabokov's translation (excerpted below), but is richly amplified in his notes. However, his grotesque reincarnation of the moment in *Lolita*, with Charlotte's transatlantic gush punctuated by genteel franglais, speaks to us far more directly.

Tatiana's Letter to Onegin, chapter three, stanza XXXI,
Nabokov's 1964 translation

> I write to you—what would one more?
> What else is there that I could say?
> 'Tis now, I know, within your will
> to punish me with scorn.
> [...]

Why did you visit us?
In the backwoods of a forgotten village,
I would have never known you
nor have known this bitter torment.
[...]
Another! ... No, to nobody on earth
would I have given my heart away!
That has been destined in a higher council,
that is the will of heaven: I am thine;
my entire life has been the gage
of a sure tryst with you;
I know that you are sent to me by God,
you are my guardian to the tomb ...
You had appeared to me in dreams,
unseen, you were already dear to me,
your wondrous glance would trouble me,
your voice resounded in my soul
long since ... No, it was not a dream!
Scarce had you entered, instantly I knew you,
I felt all faint, I felt aflame,
and in my thoughts I uttered: It is he!
Is it not true that it was you I heard:
you in the stillness spoke to me
when I would help the poor
or assuage with a prayer
the anguish of my agitated soul? [...]

Charlotte's Letter to Humbert, From *Lolita*, part I, chapter 16, p. 67

This is a confession: I love you (so the letter began; and for a distorted moment I mistook its hysterical scrawl for a schoolgirl's scribble). Last Sunday in church—bad you, who refused to come to see our beautiful new windows!—only last Sunday, my dear one, when I asked the Lord what to do about it, I was told to act as I am acting now. You see, there is no alternative. I have loved you from the minute I saw you. I am a passionate and lonely woman and you are the love of my life.

Now, my dearest, dearest, *mon cher, cher monsieur*, you have read this; now you know. So, will you please, at once, pack and leave. This is a landlady's order. I am dismissing a lodger. I am kicking you out. Go! Scram! *Departez*! I shall be back by dinnertime, if I do eighty both ways and don't have an accident (but what would it matter?), and I do not wish to find you in the house. Please, please, leave at once, now, do not even read this absurd note to the end. Go. *Adieu.* [. . .]

Themes, images, and calques of translation are woven with increasing complexity into Nabokov's mature novels, his late works subtly interrogating the very fundamentals of word, world and meaning. The entire process of 'text production' is represented from pencils and sharpeners to proofs and misprints, with a cast of writers, translators, editors, critics, and readers, whose every blunder serves as counterpoint to a coded, overarching truth. The text-and-commentary structure of *Pale Fire* (1962), for example, is a model of critical reading that draws the reader into interpreting the interpretations, whilst passages in *Ada* (1969) playfully blur linguistic borders by bending and blending at least three languages at once.

No writer has engaged with the intricacies of cross-cultural exchange in such vivid detail, nor made such an eloquent contribution to not one, but two, major literary traditions.

From *Ada* (New York: McGraw-Hill, 1969), 76

'*Et pourtant,*' said the sound-sensitive governess, wincing, 'I read to her twice Ségur's adaptation in fable form of Shakespeare's play about the wicked usurer.'
'She also knows my revised monologue of his mad king,' said Ada:

> *Ce beau jardin fleurit en mai,*
> *Mais en hiver*
> *Jamais, jamais, jamais, jamais, jamais*
> *N'est vert, n'est vert, n'est vert, n'est vert,*
> *n'est vert.*

'That's good,' said Greg with a veritable sob of admiration.
'Not so *energichno*, children!' cried Marina [. . .]

Further Reading

The Garland Companion to Vladimir Nabokov ed. V. Alexandrov (New York and London: Garland, 1995), articles on translation, self-translation, and bilingualism plus treatments of specific texts, with useful bibliographies.

Beaujour, Elizabeth Klosty *Alien Tongues: Bi-lingual Russian Writers of the 'First' Emigration* (Ithaca, NY: Cornell University Press, 1989).

Boyd, Brian, *Vladimir Nabokov: The Russian Years* and *Vladimir Nabokov: The American Years* (Princeton: Princeton University Press, 1990 and 1991), 2-volume biography with textual analysis.

Grayson, Jane, *Nabokov Translated* (Oxford: Oxford University Press, 1977), detailed study of Nabokov as self-translator.

Leighton, Lauren G, *Two Worlds, One Art* (Dekalb, JU.: Northern Illinois Univerity Press, 1991).

CHAPTER 5

RECENT AND CONTEMPORARY WRITINGS

5.1 INTRODUCTION

It has often been said that it is not until the 1960s that translation studies becomes a discipline in its own right. While it may be hard to draw any firm lines in this regard, and while many of the key statements in the field pre-date the 1960s, even by centuries, it is true that certain book-length studies appeared in the sixties that helped define the scope of a separate field of scholarly study—books such as G. Mounin's *Les Problèmes théoriques de la traduction* (1963), Jiři Levý's *Umění překladu* (1963; see Sect. 4.8, above), Eugene A. Nida's *Toward a Science of Translating* (1964; see Sect. 4.9, above), and J. C. Catford's *A Linguistic Theory of Translation: An Essay in Applied Linguistics* (1965). In the 1970s this field starts developing apace, and in retrospect—as regards literary translation studies in English—George Steiner's *After Babel* (1975) and a couple of books of critical essays co-edited by James S Holmes, *The Nature of Translation: Essays on the Theory and Practice of Literary Translation* (1970) and *Literature and Translation: New Perspectives in Literary Studies* (1978), appear to be the landmark publications from that period. It seems appropriate, therefore, that these two scholars should open the last and longest chapter of the volume, devoted to recent and contemporary writings.

Steiner and Holmes are very different in their approaches to translation. *After Babel* is a monumental and magisterial book, immensely ambitious in its compehensiveness. The book has been discussed and criticized, but figuring out in what ways it has shaped translation studies is no easy task. In his 'Preface to the Second Edition' (1992), Steiner notes: 'Since it first appeared, *After Babel* has been drawn upon and pilfered, often without acknowledgement. A considerable secondary literature has grown up around many of the themes first stated in the book.'[1] It is, indeed, true that the legacy of *After Babel* remains an

---

[1] George Steiner, 'Preface to the Second Edition', *After Babel: Aspects of Language and Translation* (2nd edn., Oxford: Oxford University Press, 1992), p. xi.

open topic. James Holmes was a much less prolific scholar, but he wrote some key essays which helped define translation studies as we know it (including the very name of the field). His legacy also rests in his active collaboration with scholars from several countries, people such as José Lambert, Anton Popovič, and Itamar Even-Zohar, these collaborative efforts clearly influencing the careers of several other scholars in the field, such as André Lefevere, Gideon Toury, Susan Bassnett, and Theo Hermans.

Some of these scholars are represented in the following chapter, as well as some other prominent contemporary translation scholars, such as Mary Snell-Hornby, Douglas Robinson, and Lawrence Venuti (see introductory comments in each section). However, we are not able to include as many theorists in what has become a vibrant academic discipline, as we would have liked, the reason being that this volume is not limited to translation studies in the strictly theoretical sense of that term. Emphasizing the vital connection between theory and practice, we have included texts by several writers who have translated important texts into English, as well as making significant comments on their work and on the act of translation in general—i.e. the following writers: A. K. Ramanujan, Gayatri Spivak, Gregory Rabassa, Suzanne Jill Levine, Ted Hughes, Everett Fox, John Felstiner, W. S. Merwin, Joseph Brodsky, Edwin Morgan, and Seamus Heaney. Some of these individuals are both translators and academic critics, some are poets and translators, some work in all these capacities; similarly, several of the theorists mentioned above are also active translators.

Broad as the concept of 'translation studies' is in both this and previous chapters of the volume, it is nevertheless focused in one way or another on literary translation. Even when we include an autobiographical account of moving between languages and cultures (see Sect. 5.13 below, on Eva Hoffman), or an excerpt from an anthropological discussion of cultural translation (cf. Sect. 5.12, below, on Talal Asad), these have been chosen because they have significant implications for translation as a creative act. Of course, critical explorations of literary translation can often be brought to bear on other kinds of translation (and vice versa), but we would have immeasurably expanded an already compendious volume if we had attempted to account for the various philosophical and linguistic theories of translation which have flourished in recent years, or for computerized translation, or other kinds of 'practical' translation, including simultaneous oral translation (interpreting), not to mention the many kinds of what Roman Jakobson calls 'intersemiotic translation' (see Sect. 4.7, above). There are many interesting areas of investigation here, including film translation (both via dubbing and subtitling), or indeed film adaptation of literary texts—or various kinds of dramatizations or stage versions of literary and dramatic texts: we are of course aware that theatre translation is not very prominently represented in this volume (although see e.g. Sect. 5.16, 5.19, and 5.23, below, on Ted Hughes, Susan Bassnett, and Edwin Morgan respectively). In its broadest ramifications, intersemiotic translation has a long and colourful history of interartistic interpretation (poetry to music, music to dance, painting to prose, novel to film, and so on). Given the cultural and semiotic complexities of moving from one language to another, the study of literary translation should always have a good deal to contribute to translation studies in this broader sense.

Some of the following entries bear witness to the fact that English as a language of literary translation is increasingly facing non-Western, often post-colonial, challenges. It is still too early to say, with Goethe, that 'the epoch of world literature is at hand', as least as far as English is concerned, for the increasing global dissemination of the English language does not go hand in hand with a proportional growth of translation into English. In fact, in the United States and Britain, the inverse proportion seems closer to the truth. Still, certain works make their way into English, for instance from Latin America and India. In India, English is an official language but it must coexist with several indigenous languages and this results in a 'translation culture' which is quite different from that of most other English-speaking countries.

While these non-Western sources may gradually make an increasing impact on English as a literary language, it is interesting to note that some of the most imporant English-language modernist poets of the twentieth century continue to cultivate key texts from the Western tradition. Pound's urge to 'make it new' appears to have been heard by Robert Lowell, Ted Hughes, W. S. Merwin, Edwin Morgan, and Seamus Heaney, all of whom have attended to the European tradition, both the Classical Greek and Roman, but also the Anglo-Saxon and the Celtic. These translators thus help anchor the continuities that may be traced through the whole history reflected by this volume, while also reminding us that 'the experience of the foreign', in Antoine Berman's words,[2] is often close to home; it is often in what seemed most familiar in history.

---

[2] Antoine Berman: *The Experience of the Foreign: Culture and Translation in Romantic Germany*, trans. S. Heyvaert (Albany, NY: State University of New York Press, 1992). So actually the words are those of Berman's translator. Originally published as *L'Épreuve de l'étranger: Culture et traduction dans l'Allemagne romantique* (Paris: Gallimard, 1984).

5.2   GEORGE STEINER

George Steiner (b. 1929), scholar, critic, fiction writer, was educated at the universities of Paris, Chicago, Harvard, Oxford, and Cambridge. He has been Extraordinary Fellow of Churchill College, Cambridge since 1969 and was Professor of English and Comparative Literature, University of Geneva (1974–94). Steiner is a Fellow of the British Academy and has held visiting professorships at Yale, New York University, the University of Geneva, and Oxford University. His non-fiction includes a number of major studies, including *Tolstoy or Dostoevsky* (1958), *The Death of Tragedy* (1961), *In Bluebeard's Castle: Some Notes towards the Redefinition of Culture* (1971). *After Babel* (1975) was preceded by his ground-breaking anthology of *Modern Verse Translation* (1966), which focuses on the translators rather than translated. In addition Steiner has edited *Homer in English* (1996), an anthology of translations/translators of Homer, from Lydgate and Chaucer to the present day. He is also the author of a number of works of fiction including *Portage to San Cristobal of AH* (1981), which was adapted for the stage by Christopher Hampton. A volume of autobiography, *Errata: An Examined Life,* was published in 1997. Steiner regularly contributes reviews and articles to journals and newspapers, including the *New Yorker,* the *Times Literary Supplement*, and the *Guardian.*

After Babel: Aspects of Language and Translation was published by Oxford University Press in 1975. A second, revised, edition was brought out in 1992, and a third edition, from which the following quotations and excerpts are taken, appeared in 1998.

Steiner's view and theories of translation in *After Babel* are embedded in a wide-ranging exploration of language and hermeneutics. While the book contains valuable analyses of translations of texts from one language to another, it also dwells extensively on the translatory nature of understanding, interpretation, communication, and various aspects of language. Steiner's philosophical, literary, and linguistic sources are legion, but prominent among them are hermeneutic traditions stemming from both Jewish Gnosticism and Kabbalism, in part as inflected by Walter Benjamin, and the modern hermeneutic-existential philosophy of Heidegger and Gadamer.

Having argued how, within the parameters of language, understanding establishes itself as translation—the opening chapter is entitled 'Understanding as Translation'—one of the issues Steiner actually fleshes out in the book is the resistance of language to understanding and translation. 'It may be—I will argue so—that communication outward is only a secondary, socially stimulated phase in the acquisition of language. Speaking to oneself would be the primary function [. . .]' (p. 125). This provocative stance does not imply that 'internalized' language (p. 181) is a tidy and smooth affair, for it seems to be the

very force that most strongly encounters the deadening elements of language in the so
sphere. Indeed, 'it is its great untidiness that makes human speech innovative ¿
expressive of personal intent. It is the anomaly, as it feeds back into the general histo
of usage, the ambiguity, as it enriches and complicates the general standard of definition,
which gives coherence to the system. A coherence, if such a description is allowed, "in
constant motion" ' (p. 213).

This conception of language also shapes Steiner's view of translation. Good translators
resist the temptation to smooth out the resistant elements in the original, for the result of
such a procedure can be a 'deceptive ease of transfer. We do not feel the resistant
particularity of the "other". But great translation must carry with it the most precise
sense possible of the resistant, of the barriers intact at the heart of understanding' (p. 397).
'We must not trust the translation whose words are entirely "unbroken". As with a sea-
shell, the translator can listen strenuously but mistake the rumour of his own pulse for the
beat of the alien sea' (p. 398).

As Steiner's discussion of a number of actual translations makes clear, these hermeneutic
statements do not constitute a formula for any single method of translating. It seems that
there are different ways—none of which are easy—of capturing or reinventing the beat of
the alien sea.

From *After Babel: Aspects of Language and Translation* (3rd edn., Oxford and New York: Oxford University Press, 1998)

'Interpretation' as that which gives language life beyond the moment and place of immediate utterance or transcription, is what I am concerned with. The French word *interprète*
concentrates all the relevant values. An actor is *interprète* of Racine; a pianist gives *une
interprétation* of a Beethoven sonata. Through engagement of his own identity, a critic
becomes *un interprète*—a life-giving performer—of Montaigne or Mallarmé. As it does not
include the world of the actor, and includes that of the musician only by analogy, the English
term *interpreter* is less strong. But it is congruent with French when reaching out in another
crucial direction. *Interprète/interpreter* are commonly used to mean *translator.*
   This, I believe, is the vital starting point. (p. 28)

Polysemy, the capacity of the same word to mean different things, such difference ranging
from nuance to antithesis, characterizes the language of ideology. Machiavelli noted that
meaning could be dislocated in common speech so as to produce political confusion.
Competing ideologies rarely create new terminologies. As Kenneth Burke and George
Orwell have shown in regard to the vocabulary of Nazism and Stalinism, they pilfer and
decompose the vulgate. In the idiom of fascism and communism, 'peace', 'freedom',
'progress', 'popular will' are as prominent as in the language of representative democracy.

But they have their fiercely disparate meanings. The words of the adversary are appropriated and hurled against him. When antithetical meanings are forced upon the same word (Orwell's Newspeak), when the conceptual reach and valuation of a word can be altered by political decree, language loses credibility. Translation in the ordinary sense becomes impossible. To translate a Stalinist text on peace or on freedom under proletarian dictatorship into a non-Stalinist idiom, using the same time-honoured words, is to produce a polemic gloss, a counter-statement of values. At the moment, the speech of politics, of social dissent, of journalism is full of loud ghost-words being shouted back and forth, signifying contraries or nothing. It is only in the underground of political humour that these shibboleths regain significance. When the entry of foreign tanks into a free city is glossed as 'a spontaneous, ardently welcomed defence of popular freedom' (*Izvestia*, 27 August 1968), the word 'freedom' will preserve its common meaning only in the clandestine dictionary of laughter.

That dictionary, one supposes, plays a large role in the language of children. Here diachronic and synchronic structures overlap. At any given time in a community and in the history of the language, speech modulates across generations. Or as psycholinguists put it, there are 'phenomena of age grading' in all known languages. The matter of child-speech is a deep and fascinating one. Again, there are numerous languages in which such speech is formally set apart. Japanese children employ a separate vocabulary for everything they have and use up to a certain age. More common, indeed universal, is the case in which children carve their own language-world out of the total lexical and syntactic resources of adult society. So far as children are an exploited and mutinous class, they will, like the proletariat or ethnic minorities, pilfer and make risible the rhetoric, the taboo words, the normative idioms of their oppressors. The scatological doggerels of the nursery and the alley-way may have a sociological rather than a psychoanalytic motive. The sexual slang of childhood, so often based on mythical readings of actual sexual reality rather than on any physiological grasp, represents a night-raid on adult territory. The fracture of words, the maltreatment of grammatical norms which, as the Opies have shown, constitute a vital part of the lore, mnemonics, and secret parlance of childhood, have a rebellious aim: by refusing, for a time, to accept the rules of grown-up speech, the child seeks to keep the world open to his own, seemingly unprecedented needs. In the event of autism, the speech-battle between child and master can reach a grim finality. Surrounded by incomprehensible or hostile reality, the autistic child breaks off verbal contact. He seems to choose silence to shield his identity but even more, perhaps, to destroy his imagined enemy. Like murderous Cordelia, children know that silence can destroy another human being. Or like Kafka they remember that several have survived the song of the Sirens, but none their silence.

[. . .]

The speech of children and adolescents fascinated Dostoevsky. Its ferocious innocence, the tactical equivocations of the maturing child, are reproduced in *The Brothers Karamazov*. St Francis's ability to parley with birds is closely echoed in Alyosha's understanding of Kolya and the boys. But for all their lively truth, children in the novels of James and Dostoevsky remain, in large measure, miniature adults. They exhibit the uncanny percipience of the 'aged' infant Christ in Flemish art. Mark Twain's transcriptions of the secret and public idiom of childhood penetrate much further. A genius for receptive insight animates the rendition of Huck Finn and Tom Sawyer. The artfulness of their language, its ceremonies of insult and kinship, its tricks of understatement are as complex as any in adult rhetoric. But they are unfailingly re-creative of a child's way. The discrimination is made even more exact by the neighbouring but again very different 'childishness' of Negro speech. For the first time in Western literature the linguistic terrain of childhood was mapped without being laid waste. After Mark Twain, child psychology and Piaget could proceed.

When speaking to a young boy or girl we use simple words and a simplified grammar; often we reply by using the child's own vocabulary; we bend forward. For their part, children will use different phrasings, intonations, and gestures when addressing a grown-up from those used when speaking to themselves (the iceberg mass of child language) or to other children. All these are devices for translation. J. D. Salinger catches us in the act:

> Sybil released her foot. 'Did you read "Little Black Sambo"?' she said.
>
> 'It's very funny you ask me that,' he said. 'It so happens I just finished reading it last night.' He reached down and took back Sybil's hand. 'What did you think of it?' he asked her.
>
> 'Did the tigers run all around that tree?'
>
> 'I thought they'd never stop. I never saw so many tigers.'
>
> 'There were only six,' Sybil said.
>
> '*Only* six!' said the young man. 'Do you call that *only?*'
>
> 'Do you like wax?' Sybil asked.
>
> 'Do I like what?' asked the young man.
>
> 'Wax.'
>
> 'Very much. Don't you?'
>
> Sybil nodded. 'Do you like olives?' she asked.
>
> 'Olives—yes. Olives and wax. I never go anyplace without 'em.'
>
> . . .
>
> Sybil was silent.
>
> 'I like to chew candles,' she said finally.
>
> 'Who doesn't?' said the young man, getting his feet wet.

This is the '*perfect* day for bananafish', the swift passage from Pentecost to silence. Being so near death, Seymour, the hero of the story, translates flawlessly. Usually, the task is more difficult. There is so much we do not know. Even more than the illiterate and the oppressed, children have been kept in the margin of history. Their multitudinous existence has left comparatively few archives. How, for instance, do class-lines cut across age gradients? Is it true that the current revolution in the language of sex is entirely a middle-class phenomenon, that sex-talk of the most anatomical and disenchanted kind has always been in use among children of the working-class? One thing is clear. The entry of the child into complete adult notice, a heightened awareness of its uniquely vulnerable and creative condition, are among the principal gains of the recent past. The stifled voices of children that haunt Blake's poetry are no longer a general fact. No previous society has taken as much trouble as ours to hear the actual language of the child, to receive and interpret its signals without distorting them.

In most societies and throughout history, the status of women has been akin to that of children. Both groups are maintained in a condition of privileged inferiority. Both suffer obvious modes of exploitation—sexual, legal, economic—while benefiting from a mythology of special regard. Thus Victorian sentimentalization of the moral eminence of women and young children was concurrent with brutal forms of erotic and economic subjection. Under sociological and psychological pressure, both minorities have developed internal codes of communication and defence (women and children constitute a symbolic, self-defining minority even when, owing to war or special circumstance, they outnumber the adult males in the community). There is a language-world of women as there is of children. (pp. 35–9)

Any model of communication is at the same time a model of translation, of a vertical or horizontal transfer of significance. No two historical epochs, no two social classes, no two localities use words and syntax to signify exactly the same things, to send identical signals of valuation and inference. Neither do two human beings. Each living person draws, deliberately or in immediate habit, on two sources of linguistic supply: the current vulgate corresponding to his level of literacy, and a private thesaurus. The latter is inextricably a part of his subconscious, of his memories so far as they may be verbalized, and of the singular, irreducibly specific ensemble of his somatic and psychological identity. Part of the answer to the notorious logical conundrum as to whether or not there can be 'private language' is that aspects of every language-act are unique and individual. They form what linguists call an 'idiolect'. Each communicatory gesture has a private residue.
[. . .]

I have been trying to state a rudimentary but decisive point: interlingual translation is the main concern of this book, but it is also a way in, an access to an inquiry into language itself. 'Translation', properly understood, is a special case of the arc of communication which every successful speech-act closes within a given language. On the inter-lingual level, translation will pose concentrated, visibly intractable problems; but these same problems abound, at a more covert or conventionally neglected level, intra-lingually. The model 'sender to receiver' which represents any semiological and semantic process is ontologically equivalent to the model 'source-language to receptor-language' used in the theory of translation. In both schemes there is 'in the middle' an operation of interpretative decipherment, an encoding-decoding function or synapse. Where two or more languages are in articulate interconnection, the barriers in the middle will obviously be more salient, and the enterprise of intelligibility more conscious. But the 'motions of spirit', to use Dante's phrase, are rigorously analogous. So, as we shall see, are the most frequent causes of misunderstanding or, what is the same, of failure to translate correctly. In short: *inside or between languages, human communication equals translation*. A study of translation is a study of language. (pp. 47–9)

My conviction is that we shall not get much further in understanding the evolution of language and the relations between speech and human performance so long as we see 'falsity' as primarily negative, so long as we consider counter-factuality, contradiction, and the many nuances of conditionality as specialized, often logically bastard modes. *Language is the main instrument of man's refusal to accept the world as it is.* Without that refusal, without the unceasing generation by the mind of 'counter-worlds'—a generation which cannot be divorced from the grammar of counter-factual and optative forms—we would turn forever on the treadmill of the present. Reality would be (to use Wittgenstein's phrase in an illicit sense) 'all that is the case' and nothing more. Ours is the ability, the need, to gainsay or 'un-say' the world, to image and speak it otherwise. In that capacity in its biological and social evolution, may lie some of the clues to the question of the origins of human speech and the multiplicity of tongues. It is not, perhaps, 'a theory of information' that will serve us best in trying to clarify the nature of language, but a 'theory of misinformation'. (p. 228)

We need a word which will designate the power, the compulsion of language to posit 'otherness'. That power, as Oscar Wilde was one of the few to recognize, is inherent in every act of form, in art, in music, in the contrarieties which our body sets against gravity and repose. But it is pre-eminent in language. French allows *altérité*, a term derived from the Scholastic discrimination between essence and alien, between the tautological integrity of God and the shivered fragments of perceived reality. Perhaps 'alternity' will do: to define the 'other than the case', the counter-factual propositions, images, shapes of will and evasion with which we charge our mental being and by means of which we build the changing, largely fictive milieu of our somatic and our social existence. 'We invent for ourselves the major part of experience,' says Nietzsche in *Beyond Good and Evil* ('wir erdichten …' signifying 'to create fictionally', 'to render dense and coherent through *poiesis*'). Or as he puts it in *Morgenröte*, man's genius is one of lies. (pp. 232–3)

The hermeneutic motion, the act of elicitation and appropriative transfer of meaning, is fourfold. There is initiative trust, an investment of belief, underwritten by previous experience but epistemologically exposed and psychologically hazardous, in the meaningfulness, in the 'seriousness' of the facing or, strictly speaking, adverse text. We venture a leap: we grant *ab initio* that there is 'something there' to be understood, that the transfer will not be void. All understanding, and the demonstrative statement of understanding which is translation, starts with an act of trust. This confiding will, ordinarily, be instantaneous and unexamined, but it has a complex base. It is an operative convention which derives from a sequence of phenomenological assumptions about the coherence of the world, about the presence of meaning in very different, perhaps formally antithetical semantic systems, about the validity of analogy and parallel. The radical generosity of the translator ('I grant beforehand that there must be something there'), his trust in the 'other', as yet untried, unmapped alternity of statement, concentrates to a philosophically dramatic degree the human bias towards seeing the world as symbolic, as constituted of relations in which 'this' can stand for 'that', and must in fact be able to do so if there are to be meanings and structures.

[. . .]

As he sets out, the translator must gamble on the coherence, on the symbolic plenitude of the world. Concomitantly he leaves himself vulnerable, though only in extremity and at the theoretical edge, to two dialectically related, mutually determined metaphysical risks. He may find that 'anything' or 'almost anything' can mean 'everything'. This is the vertigo of self-sustaining metaphoric or analogic enchainment experienced by medieval exegetists. Or he may find that there is 'nothing there' which can be divorced from its formal autonomy, that every meaning worth expressing is monadic and will not enter into any alternative mould. There is Kabbalistic speculation, to which I will return, about a day on which words will shake off 'the burden of having to mean' and will be only themselves, blank and replete as stone.

After trust comes aggression. The second move of the translator is incursive and extractive. The relevant analysis is that of Heidegger when he focuses our attention on understanding as an act, on the access, inherently appropriative and therefore violent, of *Erkenntnis* to *Dasein*. *Da-sein*, the 'thing there', 'the thing that is because it is there', only comes into authentic being when it is comprehended, i.e. translated.[1] The postulate that all cognition is aggressive, that every proposition is an inroad on the world, is, of course, Hegelian. It is Heidegger's contribution to have shown that understanding, recognition, interpretation are a compacted, unavoidable mode of attack. We can modulate Heidegger's insistence that understanding is not a matter of method but of primary being, that 'being consists in the understanding of other being' into the more naïve, limited axiom that each act of comprehension must appropriate another entity (we translate *into*). Comprehension, as its etymology shows, 'comprehends' not only cognitively but by encirclement and ingestion. In the event of interlingual translation this manoeuvre of comprehension is explicitly invasive and exhaustive. Saint Jerome uses his famous image of meaning brought home captive by the translator. We 'break' a code: decipherment is dissective, leaving the shell smashed and the vital layers stripped. Every schoolchild, but also the eminent translator, will note the shift in substantive presence which follows on a protracted or difficult exercise in translation: the text in the other language has become almost materially thinner, the light seems to pass unhindered through its loosened fibres. For a spell the density of 'hostile or seductive 'otherness' is dissipated. Ortega y Gasset speaks of the sadness of the translator after failure. There is also a sadness after success, the Augustinian *tristitia* which follows on the cognate acts of erotic and of intellectual possession.

[. . .]

The third movement is incorporative, in the strong sense of the word. The import, of meaning and of form, the embodiment, is not made in or into a vacuum. The native semantic field is already extant and crowded. There are innumerable shadings of assimilation and placement of the newly-acquired, ranging from a complete domestication, an at-homeness at the core of the kind which cultural history ascribes to, say, Luther's Bible or North's Plutarch, all the way to the permanent strangeness and marginality of an artifact such as Nabokov's 'English-language' *Onegin*. But whatever the degree of 'naturalization', the act of importation can potentially dislocate or relocate the whole of the native structure. The Heideggerian 'we are what we understand to be' entails that our own being is modified by each occurrence of comprehensive appropriation. No language, no traditional symbolic set or cultural ensemble imports without risk of being transformed. Here two families of metaphor, probably related, offer themselves, that of sacramental intake or incarnation and that of infection. The incremental values of communion pivot on the moral, spiritual state of the recipient. Though all decipherment is aggressive and, at one level, destructive, there are differences in the motive of appropriation and in the context of 'the bringing back'. Where the native matrix is disoriented or immature, the importation will not enrich, it will not find a proper locale. It will generate not an integral response but a wash of mimicry (French neo-classicism in its north-European, German, and Russian versions).

[. . .]

Societies with ancient but eroded epistemologies of ritual and symbol can be knocked off balance and made to lose belief in their own identity under the voracious impact of premature or indigestible assimilation. The cargo-cults of New Guinea, in which the natives worship what airplanes bring in, provide an uncannily exact, ramified image of the risks of translation.

This is only another way of saying that the hermeneutic motion is dangerously incomplete, that it is dangerous because it is incomplete, if it lacks its fourth stage, the piston-stroke, as it were, which completes the cycle. The a-prioristic movement of trust puts us off balance. We 'lean towards' the confronting text (every translator has experienced this palpable bending towards and launching at his target). We encircle and invade cognitively. We come home laden, thus again off-balance, having caused disequilibrium throughout the system by taking away from 'the other' and by adding, though possibly with ambiguous consequence, to our own. The system is now off-tilt. The hermeneutic act must compensate. If it is to be authentic, it must mediate into exchange and restored parity.

The enactment of reciprocity in order to restore balance is the crux of the *métier* and morals of translation. But it is very difficult to put abstractly. The appropriative 'rapture' of the translator—the word has in it, of course, the root and meaning of violent transport—leaves the original with a dialectically enigmatic residue. Unquestionably there is a dimension of loss, of breakage—hence, as we have seen, the fear of translation, the taboos on revelatory export which hedge sacred texts, ritual nominations, and formulas in many cultures. But the residue is also, and decisively, positive. The work translated is enhanced. This is so at a number of fairly obvious levels. Being methodical, penetrative, analytic, enumerative, the process of translation, like all modes of focused understanding, will detail, illumine, and generally body forth its object. The over-determination of the interpretative act is inherently inflationary: it proclaims that 'there is more here than meets the eye', that 'the accord between content and executive form is closer, more delicate than had been observed hitherto'. To class a source-text as worth translating is to dignify it immediately and to involve it in a dynamic of magnification (subject, naturally, to later review and even, perhaps, dismissal). The motion of transfer and paraphrase enlarges the stature of the original. Historically, in terms of cultural context, of the public it can reach, the latter is left more prestigious. But this increase has a more important, existential perspective. The relations of a text to its translations, imitations, thematic variants, even parodies, are too diverse to allow of any single theoretic, definitional scheme. They categorize the entire question of the meaning of meaning in time, of the existence and effects of the linguistic fact outside its specific, initial form. But there can be no doubt that echo enriches, that it is more than shadow and inert simulacrum. We are back at the problem of the mirror which not only reflects but also generates light. The original text gains from the orders of diverse relationship and distance established between itself and the translations. The reciprocity is dialectic: new 'formats' of significance are initiated by distance and by contiguity. Some translations edge us away from the canvas, others bring us up close. (pp. 312–17)

Thus the translator at close quarters is at every point under contradictory stress. He is aware that he will always know too little about his source-text because there is a sense in which he 'knows what he does not know'. This is to say that his experience of the 'other' language and 'other' culture is so abundant, so collusive, as to suggest to him a strong sense of the total context. He recognizes the 'infinite regression', the formally undecidable compass of historical information, linguistic sensibility, local ambience which could bear on the meaning of the work which he is translating. On the other hand, he 'knows too much'. He brings to the performance of translation a deceptive bias to transparency. The apparatus of critical comparison, cultural familiarity, immersive identification with which he works proliferates and can do so unconsciously. He knows more or better than his author. Pound can make *Cathay* spare and translucent because he, and his Western readers, know next to nothing of the original. The English translator of Flaubert, the German translator of Shakespeare are drawn into a complex space of recognition. The organization of his own sensibility is in part a product of that which he is about to translate. Hence the paradox of restoration and homecoming which Celan elicits from Sonnet 79. Where translation takes place at close cultural-linguistic proximity, therefore, we can distinguish two main currents of intention and semantic focus. The delineation of 'resistant difficulty', the endeavour to situate precisely and convey intact the 'otherness' of the original, plays against 'elective affinity', against immediate grasp and domestication. In perfunctory translation these two currents diverge. There is no shaping tension between them, and paraphrase attempts to mask the gap. Good translation, on the contrary, can be defined as that in which the dialectic of impenetrability and ingress, of intractable alienness and felt 'at-homeness' remains unresolved, but expressive. Out of the tension of resistance and affinity, a tension directly proportional to the proximity of the two languages and historical communities, grows the elucidative strangeness of the great translation. The strangeness is elucidative because we come to recognize it, to 'know it again', as our own. (pp. 412–13)

NOTE

1. Cf. Paul Ricoeur, 'Existence et herméneutique' in *Le Conflit des interprétations* (Paris, 1969).

5.3 JAMES S HOLMES

James S Holmes (1924–86), poet, poetry translator, and translation theorist, was born in rural Iowa and emigrated to the Netherlands in the 1940s, becoming not only the most prominent translator of Dutch poetry into English, but also a pioneering translation theorist and among the leading translation activists of the post-war era. From 1960, Holmes taught in the Department of General Literary Studies of the University of Amsterdam, where he pioneered translation studies as a discipline and helped establish a Department of Translation Studies (1982). As a practising translator himself and commentator on the pragmatics of translation, Holmes also attempted to define the role of translation in literary culture. He was concerned to minimize the evident and (as the discipline developed) growing gap between theory and practice, maintaining that practical translation training could benefit from theoretical insights, such as those offered by feminism or by queer studies. He also facilitated contact and promoted dialogue between the different centres of translation studies, such as those in the Low Countries (e.g. the universities of Amsterdam, Antwerp, Leuven/Louvain) and, for instance, the Porter Institute of Semiotics, Tel Aviv University. Another focus of Holmes's activities was in persuading literature departments to recognize the cultural significance of translation. Although he published comparatively little, Holmes's role and influence was pivotal in this field, as emerges clearly from his posthumously published gathering of essays and papers, *Translated!* (1988). He engaged in or initiated a number of essential projects, leading for instance to the compilation of comprehensive bibliographies and identification of key historical texts for the teaching of translation. He also edited a number of landmark collections of essays, among them *The Nature of Translation* (1970) and *Literature and Translation* (1978; see also *Translation Studies: The State of the Art*, Proceedings of the First James S. Holmes symposium on Translation Studies (1991), ed. Kitty M. van Leuven-Zwart and Ton Naaijkens). His groundbreaking work in the field of translation studies is symbolically reflected in the fact that he is the one who gave this name to the field—in the 1972 paper 'The Name and Nature of Translation Studies' (reprinted in *Translated!*).

Holmes, the Theorist

In his article 'Poem and Metapoem: Poetry from Dutch to English', Holmes first discusses the 'limits between poetry and prose', arguing that the translator of prose is usually able to bypass the 'root problem of all translation', namely the 'the fact that the semantic field of a word, the entire complex network of meaning it signifies, never matches exactly the semantic field of any one word in any other language'. While it is true that in prose literature the context often provides space for the translator to manoeuvre the 'fit between the original and the translation', one can certainly find plenty of examples in both prose and drama texts, along with poetry, that very much problematize the issue of 'equivalence', *if* that term is taken to imply any kind of sameness of meaning. In other words, what Holmes sees as a burning issue in the field of poetry translation, is to an extent a concern of all literary translation. Holmes goes on to discuss how one can identify the relation between the two 'structures' of original and translation, suggesting that translation is a kind of 'meta-literature', i.e. 'writing which makes use of language to communicate something about literature itself'. The translated poem, a 'metapoem', is 'from this point of view a fundamentally different kind of object from the poem from which it derives. This difference is perhaps best defined in the following proposition: MP:P:: P:R—the relation of the metapoem to the original poem is as that of the original poem to "reality"'. Criticism is another kind of meta-literature, in which the critic interprets by analysis. 'The metapoem, on the other hand, interprets, as William Frost has pointed out, not by analysis, but by enactment.' In what follows, Holmes valuably points out the specificity of the translator's act, and then discusses the constraints of his or her enactment when translating between closely related languages, and when translating from 'little-translated languages' into, for instance, English, where the translator may feel heavily restricted by the 'wants' of the literary system at the receiving end. He then discusses two of his own translations of Dutch poems into English. (Holmes placed the originals of these poems in footnotes. These have been included here in the body of the text.)

From 'Poem and Metapoem: Poetry from Dutch to English', (1969), repr. in *Translated! Papers on Literary Translation and Translation Studies* (Amsterdam: Rodopi, 1988), 9–22

It is frequently said that to translate poetry one must be a poet. This is not entirely true, nor is it the entire truth. In order to create a verbal object of the metapoetic kind, one must perform some (but not all) of the functions of a critic, some (but not all) of the functions of a poet, and some functions not normally required of either critic or poet. Like the critic, the metapoet will strive to comprehend as thoroughly as possible the many features of the original poem, against the setting of the poet's other writings, the literary traditions of the source culture, and the expressive means of the source language. Like the poet, he will strive to exploit his own creative powers, the literary traditions of the target culture, and the expressive means of the target language in order to produce a verbal object that to all appearances is nothing more nor less than a poem. He differs, in other words, from the critic in what he does with the results of his critical analysis, and from the poet in where he derives the materials for his verse.

Linking together these two activities, the critical and the poetic, is an activity which is uniquely the metapoet's: the activity of organizing and resolving a confrontation between the norms and conventions of one linguistic system, literary tradition, and poetic sensibility, as embodied in the original poem as he has analysed it, and the norms and conventions of another linguistic system, literary tradition, and poetic sensibility to be drawn on for the metapoem he hopes to create. This activity of confrontation and resolution is, as the late Jiří Levý pointed out,[1] an elaborate process of decision-making, in which every decision taken governs to some extent the nature of all decisions still to be taken, and the appropriateness of each decision must be tested in terms of its appositeness within the emerging structure of the metapoem as a whole.

It is these three factors—acumen as a critic, craftsmanship as a poet, and skill in the analysing and resolving of a confrontation of norms and conventions across linguistic and cultural barriers: in the making of appropriate decisions—that determine the degree to which the metapoet is capable of creating a new verbal object which, for all its differences from the original poem at every specific point, is nevertheless basically similar to it as an overall structure.[2]

The problems involved in resolving a confrontation of the kind I have just mentioned may vary greatly in emphasis according to the languages and the cultures concerned. In what follows I shall attempt to identify some of the impediments to appropriate decision-making in the process of creating a metapoem in one specific language, English, on the basis of a poem in another specific language, Dutch. A first major impediment is one that is common to all translation between closely related languages. Let me illustrate it by an example not from Dutch, but from German. In the opening line to a familiar poem, Goethe asks, 'Kennst du das Land, wo die Zitronen blühn . . .?' Much of the effect of this line lies in the characteristically Goethean combination of the exotic image of lemon trees in blossom with the straightforward syntax of everyday interrogative speech: 'Kennst du das Stück, das jetzt im Theater spielt?' 'Kennst du das Haus, das gestern verbrannt ist?'

Semantically the line presents few problems for the English translator, and a dynamic rendering into prose of an equivalent register might be: 'Do you know the country where the lemon trees blossom?' or 'Do you know the country of the blossoming lemon trees?' In poetry, however, 'the temptation', as Jackson Mathews has pointed out, 'is much greater . . . than in prose to fall under the spell of the model, to try to imitate its obvious features, even its syntax . . .'.[3] And even, he might have added, when formally similar syntax has a quite different function, or a dysfunction, in the target language. Those who have attempted to render Goethe's 'Mignon' into English verse have repeatedly fallen into the trap which this line opens for them, and 'Kennst du das Land . . .' time and again becomes 'Knowst thou the land . . .'[4] Syntactically and morphologically the two passages are close parallels, yet the shift in the total message conveyed is tremendous. The interrogatory inversion instead of an auxiliary construction with 'do', the use of the old second-person singular forms for the verb and the pronoun, the translation of German Land as 'land' in place of 'country': all these elements combine to lend the English passage the wan, archaic quality of a dead poetic tradition, far removed from the colloquial vigour of the German.

There is a frequent tendency of this kind when the source and target languages are closely related. A type of linguistic interference, it may manifest itself in such features as the matching of form to form regardless of meaning, the intrusion of source-language vocabulary and syntax in the target language, and the contamination of semantic areas,[5] and the result is often a mechanistic translation at the lowest ranks, without the preliminary operations of poem analysis and interlinguistic confrontation. In memory of those translators of Goethe, I have sometimes referred to the phenomenon as the 'citric syndrome.' But whatever we may choose to call it, it is a phenomenon that repeatedly stands in the way of satisfactory translation from Dutch to English.[6]

A second impediment to appropriate decision-making in Dutch–English verse translation is one that is particular to translation from little-translated languages. Professor Rabin has called attention to the fact that the more and the longer translations are made from language A to language B, the easier it becomes to translate from A to B (though not, it should be noted, in the reverse direction). This fact Rabin attributes to the accumulation of what he calls a 'translation stock,' a collection of proven solutions to specific problems that frequently arise in A-to-B translation. This translation stock, once developed, may be passed on for centuries, or it may die out rapidly as A-to-B translation dwindles.[7]

Such a translation stock is clearly available for the translator from English to Dutch, since a long and continuous tradition of translation in this direction, for a wide variety of purposes, has led to the development of a large number of practical solutions to translation problems and the creation of a certain degree of consensus regarding 'right' and 'wrong' renderings. This is much less the case for translation from Dutch to English. True, there is a fairly long tradition of Dutch-to-English translation within the Low Countries, and a stock of solutions of a certain kind has accumulated. But these solutions, the work of generations of philologists and schoolmasters with one specific aim in view, are largely unsuited to the needs of translation in any genuine sense, as distinguished from translation as a didactic method presumed to impart and test linguistic skills. On the level of literary translation, the translator from Dutch to English has almost invariably had to start from scratch, working outside a tradition and finding his own solutions as he went along. This has been particularly true in the case of poetry, where there has never been anything even approaching a tradition of translation in the

Dutch-English direction, solely the work of scattered individuals, isolated in time, place, and readership. Only in the past few years has this situation begun to change, as more Dutch poetry than hitherto has been published more widely than heretofore, in translations by more English and American metapoets.[8]

A similar impediment to appropriate decision-making derives from the position of little-known literatures. Concomitant with an absence of a translation tradition is a lack of knowledge of the literary background against which a poem translated from the Dutch should be read when it appears. A rendering into English of a poem by Georg Trakl or Apollinaire falls into (or perhaps contradicts) a general pattern of German or French poetry already available to the English poetry reader. A rendering of a poem by, say, Paul van Ostaijen must stand by itself, isolated both from the remainder of Van Ostaijen's work and from the entire body of Dutch poetry. This means that the translator of a poem by Van Ostaijen has to approach his task in quite a different way from the translator of Trakl or Apollinaire.

[...]

A few of the problems that come to the fore during the attempt to transform a Dutch poem into an English metapoem may be illustrated by two examples. The first is an English rendering of a poem by the contemporary Flemish poet Paul Snoek.

> 'Rustic Landscape'
>
> The ducks are like our cousins:
> they waggle and walk
> and slavering at the mouth
> in the mud grow old.
>
> But all at once a terrific
> bang almost breaks
> their pleasant peasant membranes.
>
> That was the farmer himself of course:
> he's trying the shotgun out,
> the lout. He cut an apple
> in the snout and cried, stark red
> with relief: 'I'm dressing,
> yes, a golden pear.'
>
> And did those quacking cousins have a laugh.
> (1) They prune their roses
> with a crooked knife;
> (2) How old are the ducks?[9]

'Rustiek landschapje'

De ganzen zijn net onze tantes:
zij waggelen en wandelen
en worden watertandend
in de modder oud.

Maar plots doet een geweldig
knalletje hun landelijke,
liefelijke vliezen bijna scheuren.

Dat was een hereboer natuurlijk:
hij schiet met loden spek,
de gek. Hij sneed een appel
in de bek en riep spierrood
van ontspanning: 'Ik mest,
jawel, ik mest een gulden peer'.

Of die kwakende tantes moesten lachen.
1. Zij snoeien hun rozen
met een kromgekweekt mes;
2. Hoe oud zijn de ganzen?

This is not the place for a detailed comparison of the English text against the Dutch original, Snoek's 'Rustiek landschapje',[10] but even a cursory reading of the two texts in conjunction is enough to uncover the major decision-requiring problem. A fundamental theme of the Dutch poem is the juxtaposition of *ganzen* (geese) and *onze tantes* (our aunts), with such descriptive terms as *waggelen, wandelen, worden...oud*, and *kwakende* applying to both. These juxtaposed and coalescing images (suddenly separated again in the two 'clues' which close the poem, turning it into a picture puzzle) are reinforced acoustically by a complex system of alliteration and internal rhyme.

A low-rank translation of the opening line would yield 'The geese are like our aunts' or a similar rendering. But that lacks the acoustic complexity of the Dutch. Moreover it leads the translator to the further problem that in English geese do not quack (see line fourteen) but honk or possibly hiss. Retention of the geese leads to honking relatives, and that to a suggestion, disturbingly inappropriate in this context, of honking car-horns. Retention of the quacking, on the other hand, leads from geese to ducks. A choice for ducks and quacking instead of honking and geese opens up the possibility of turning the aunts into cousins and so to beginning the metapoem with the initial elements for an acoustic system parallel to that of the Dutch ('De ganzen zijn net onze tantes...'; 'The ducks are like our cousins...'). This choice, however, leaves the human image less concrete at the end of the first line than in the Dutch, since cousins, unlike aunts, are of unspecified sex and relative age; the translator who has given preference to this series of choices must rely on the rest of the first stanza, reinforced by the last, to make it clear that the cousins, too, are female and growing old. In other words the major cluster of choices facing the translator of this poem is that of either reconstructing the acoustic qualities of the Dutch at the cost of shifting the nature of two of the poem's major images (though preserving the nature of their juxtaposition) or retaining the images at the cost of introducing alien implications with the 'honking'[11] and failing to parallel the acoustic qualities of the poem.

The second translation reflects a similar problem of choice between emphasis on the aspect of sound and the aspect of image. But in the case of this poem, Hubert van Herreweghen's 'Avond aan zee',[12] the factors governing the choice are quite different. Where in 'Rustiek landschapje' the nature of the relationship between the two juxtaposed images was central, not the precise nature of the images themselves, in 'Avond aan zee' the emphasis is squarely on an image as such: that of a sow as metaphor for the evening sky as the sun sets in the sea. In a poem of this kind any shift even in subordinate imagic details can be quite precarious. On the formal level, Snoek's poem is highly individual, contained in an organic form developed for this poem and it alone; Van Herreweghen's poem, on the other hand, is formally quite traditional: five four-line stanzas rhyming *abba* (stanzas one, two, four, and five) or *abab* (stanza three), each line with six (masculine-rhyme lines) or seven (feminine-rhyme) syllables and three accents. The sole unorthodox elements in the form are the rhyming of *zinkt* with *zingt* in stanza three[13] and the somewhat uneven rhythm throughout.

Such close adherence to traditional form is more common among contemporary Dutch poets (at least in Flanders) than among their English and American counterparts, and there is little reason for the translator to concentrate on reproducing a familiar poetic form at the cost of introducing major shifts in the imagic material of the poem. On the other hand, by expanding the incidental use of consonance in the Dutch poem into a basic formal principle of consonance and assonance in the English metapoem, while at the same time admitting two-accent lines alongside the three-accent of the original, the translator can create a form for the English metapoem which has two important advantages. Situationally, it is actually more closely equivalent to the Dutch than a correspondent form would be. And it has the flexibility to provide a close fit for the semantic and imagic material of the Dutch poem. The result is an English metapoem which is formally quite different from the Dutch poem but in every other way follows the original with a minimum of skewing.

> 'Evening by the Sea'
>
> An evening of olives;
> a lemon sky
> surfaces its belly
> on a green sea.

A sow lying on its side
grumbling and dangerous,
a belly of thwacking light,
teeth gleeful with rage.

From here to where the earth
slopes away and sinks,
the gigantic red-haired beast
flames and flashes and sings.

Vicious mother with lips
of froth across yellow teeth,
eyes of a lightning white,
asquint with ruttish tricks;

belly, your teats hang there
maternally light and full,
plenty of milk for all.
Evening licks our desire.[14]

'Avond aan zee'

Een avond van olijven,
een hemel van citroen,
komt op een zee van groen
met zijn buik boven drijven.

Een zeug die op de zijde
grommend gevaarlijk ligt,
een buik vol kletsend licht,
tanden van woede blijde.

Ver tot de hellende aarde
onder de einder zinkt,
het vlammend rood behaarde
groot beeest dat blinkt en zingt.

Wrede moeder met schuimen
lip over geel gebit,
ogen bliksemend wit,
loens van bronstige luimen,

buik, moederlijk daar hangen,
uw tepels licht en melk,
zatheit van dronk voor elk.
Avond likt ons verlangen.

NOTES

1. Jiří Levý, 'Translation as a Decision Process', in *To Honor Roman Jakobson. Essays on the Occasion of His Seventieth Birthday* (three vols.; The Hague: Mouton, 1967), II, pp. 1171–1182. Cf. Levý, *Umění překladu* (Prague: Československý spisovatel, 1963), p. 148; Anton Popovič, 'Translation Analysis and Literary History: A Slovak Approach to the Problem', *Babel* (Avignon), 14 (1968), pp. 68–76, esp. p. 73.

2. The views expressed in the first part of this essay were developed further in a paper presented at the conference on literary translation theory held in Bratislava late in May, 1968 and printed in the proceedings of the conference, James S Holmes with Frans de Haan and Anton Popovič (eds.), *The Nature of Translation: Essays on the Theory and Practice of Literary Translation* (Bratislava: Publishing House of the Slovak Academy of Sciences and The Hague: Mouton, 1970), under the title 'Forms of Verse Translation and the Translation of Verse Form'.

3. Jackson Mathews, 'Third Thoughts on Translating Poetry', in Reuben A. Brower (ed.), *On Translation* (Harvard Studies in Comparative Literature, Vol. 23; Cambridge, Mass.: Harvard University Press, 1959), pp. 67–77, quotation p. 67.

4. See the translations listed in Lucretia Van Tuyl Simmons, *Goethe's Lyric Poems in English Translation prior to 1860* (University of Wisconsin Studies in Language and Literature, vol. 6; Madison: [University of Wisconsin], 1919), and in Stella M. Hinz, *Goethe's Lyric Poems in English Translation after 1860* (same series. vol. 26; 1928).

5. Cf. Irène C. Spilka, 'On Translating the Mental Status Schedule', *Meta* (Montreal), 13 (1968), pp. 4–20; esp. p. 13.

6. One striking example may emphasize my point. A few years ago the following text was published in the authoritative American review *Poetry*:

'The Old Man'

> An old man in the street
> his small story to the old woman
> it is nothing it sounds like a thin tragedy
> his voice is white
> like a knife that so long was whetted
> till the steel was thin
> Like an object outside him hangs the voice
> over the long black coat
> The old meager man in his black coat
> seems a black plant
> You see this stasps the fear through your mouth
> the first taste of an anaesthetic

(translation Hidde Van Ameyden van Duym; *Poetry* [Chicago], 104 [1964]. p. 175). There is some remarkable English here. A reading of the Dutch poem by Paul van Ostaijen on the facing page of *Poetry* shows why.

'De oude man'

> Een oud man in de straat
> zijn klein verhaal aan de oude vrouw
> het is niets het klinkt als een ijl treurspel
> zijn stem is wit
> zij gelijkt een mes dat zo lang werd aangewet
> tot het staal dun werd
> Gelijk een voorwerp buiten hem hangt deze stem
> boven de lange zwarte jas
> De oude magere in zijn zwarte jas
> gelijkt een zwarte plant
> Ziet gij dit snokt de angst door uw mond
> het eerste smaken van een narkose

(Paul van Ostaijen, *Verzameld werk: Poëzie* [two vols.; Antwerp: De Sikkel, The Hague: Daamen, and Amsterdam: Van Oorschot. (1952)], II. p. 244).

One can see the lexis and syntax of the original Dutch constantly breaking through the surface of the English, across the barrier of language. At the rank of lexis, a *klein verhaal* is equated to a 'small story', an *ijl treurspel* to a 'thin tragedy, *mager* to 'meager', and *de angst* to 'the fear'. At a higher rank 'Gelijk een voorwerp buiten hem hangt deze stem' is rendered as 'Like an object outside him hangs the voice', and 'zij gelijkt een mes dat zo lang werd aangewet/tot het staal dun werd' as the contamination 'like a knife that so long was whetted / till the steel was thin'. The last line of the poem but one is particularly unclear in the English, partly perhaps because of what may be a misprint, but primarily because the translator has depended on lexical translation to solve his dilemma for him, instead of making a choice between two readings ('Ziet gij dit/snokt de angst door uw mond' or 'If/When you see this fear quivers through your mouth', and 'Ziet gij/dit snokt de angst door uw mond' or 'You see, this sucks the fear through your mouth'). The result is that, by retaining the syntax of the Dutch, he has created a line which must be read either as approximating the less probable of the two Dutch meanings ('You see/this stasps the fear through your mouth') or as meaningless ('You see this/stasps the fear through your mouth').

A translation of this kind, though presented formally as a poem, becomes rather a comment on the general nature of Dutch syntax than a comment on a specific Dutch poem. Indeed, the deviations from the syntactic norms of English stand in the way of an appreciation of the English text as poetry. (This is not true of all kinds of syntactic deviation of course. But there is apparently a fundamental difference in effect between the deviations from the norm of 'translationese' and those of 'poetic licence'.)

7. C. Rabin, 'The Linguistics of Translation', in *Aspects of Translation* (The Communication Research Centre, University College, London: Studies in Communication, Vol. 5; London: Secker and Warburg, 1958), pp. 123–145. esp. pp. 144–145.

8. More Dutch poetry was published in English translation during the single decade 1955–1965 than in all the preceding years of this century taken together.

9. My translation. First printed in *Delta: A Review of Arts, Life, and Thought in the Netherlands* (Amsterdam), 8, No. 2 (Summer 1965), p. 49.

10. Paul Snoek, *De heilige gedichten, 1956–1958* [Antwerp: Ontwikkeling and Rotterdam: Donker, 1959], 39.

11. There is of course also the literalist's alternative of retaining both the quacking and the geese, at the cost of confusing the image and tearing the fabric of the poem.

12. Hubert van Herreweghen, *Vleugels* [Hasselt: Heideland, (1962)], p. 52.

13. Since Van Herreweghen is Belgian, perhaps also the rhyme *ligt*—*licht* should be considered consonance rather than *rime riche*.

14. My translation. First printed in *The Literary Review: An International Journal of Contemporary Writing* (Teaneck, New Jersey), 7, No. 3 (Spring 1964: special Flanders Number), p. 466.

The article 'Describing Literary Translations: Models and Methods' is an ambitious attempt to formulate a model not just of the process of translation itself, but of the way in which the translation scholar may come to an understanding of, in fact to some extent retrace, this process. The article, in a word taken from within it, is a kind of 'map' of the sphere and activity of the translation scholar and critic who analyses both the original and the translation in order to discover how the latter came into being and what 'rules' governed this genesis.

In the opening words of his article, Holmes notes the scarcity of studies that attempt to describe the relations between a literary text and its translation(s), and claims that such studies also tend to be 'so haphazard, so piecemeal, so normative. And so naïve in their methodology' (p. 81). He then tackles the issue of the translation process.

From 'Describing Literary Translations: Models and Methods' (1978), repr. in *Translated!,* **81–91**

The earliest explicit, more or less formalized models of the translation process were designed in the late forties and early fifties as bases for programs of research into the feasibility of so-called automatic translation. These models started from the notion that texts were strings of words (or 'lexical items') which could, in the main, be translated item by item, if only a few allowances were made for the unfortunate tendency of languages to exhibit language-pair differences in syntax and to create divergent exocentric (that is, 'idiomatic') phrases.[1] Later this basically lexical-rank model was replaced by a sentence-rank model, in which (to cite the terminology used by one of its foremost advocates, Nida) a source-language passage was converted into a receptor-language passage via a tripartite process of analysis, kernel-level transfer, and restructuring.[2]

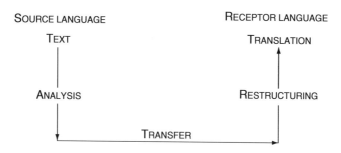

Figure 1. Nida's model of the translation process (Nida 1969: 484).

The shift from lexical rank to sentence rank was a significant step towards sophistication, but the basic premise remained that a text is a string of units, essentially serial in nature.

A fundamental fact about texts, however, is that they are both serial *and* structural—that after one has read a text in time, one retains an array of data about it in an instantaneous form. On these grounds, it has more recently been suggested (though nowhere, as far as I know, clearly set out in model form) that the translation of texts (or at least of extensive texts, or at least of complex texts) takes place on two planes: a serial plane, where one translates sentence by sentence, and a structural plane, on which one abstracts a 'mental conception' of the original text, then uses that mental conception as a kind of general criterion against which to test each sentence during the formulation of the new, translated text. This model might be sketched as follows:

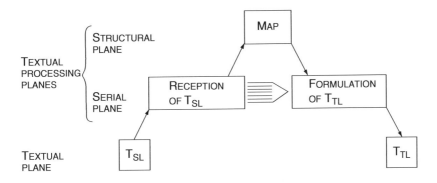

Figure 2. Two-plane text-rank translation model (T_{SL} = source-language text; T_{TL} = target-language text).

Such a two-plane model would seem to come much closer than the earlier serial models to describing the translation process as it takes place in the translator's study. The introduction of an abstract text-rank[3] 'mental conception'—or, as I propose to call it henceforward, 'map'—would seem to be a further step forward.

I would question, however, whether one such map or mental conception is sufficient to model the actual translation process adequately. Consider for a moment. Mr X, who sometimes translates poetry into English, has just reread a poem in French, say Baude-laire's 'La géante'. Among the details in the map which he abstracts from the original poem will be (to restrict myself to a few of the more elementary features) that it is in sonnet form, rhyming *abba abba cde cde*, in syllabic verse, twelve (or thirteen) syllables to the line. X, if he is like most English-language translators, will not automatically decide to 'retain' the rhyme scheme, the syllabic verse, or the twelve- (or thirteen-) syllable lines. Rather, he has a number of options to select from. On the basis of these selections (and a great many others) he in fact develops a second map, in various ways like the first, but in others quite different. It is this second map, not the first, which he uses as his criterion to guide him in carrying out his translation on the serial plane. If this really approximates the way in which the translator works, then we arrive at the following two-plane, two-map model.[4]

In my sketch of this model I have taken the further step of introducing three sets of rules by which specific phases of the translation process would seem to be carried out. (It goes without saying that in actual practice the different phases are not always separated from each other in time; like other human beings, the translator can be doing various things at once.[5]) Of the three rule sets, the first, that of derivation rules (DR), determines the way in which the translator abstracts his map of the source text from the text itself, and the third, that of projection rules (PR), determines the way in which he makes use of his map of the prospective target text in order to formulate the text, while the second, that of correspondence rules (CR) or matching rules (MR)—or, if one prefers, equivalence rules (ER)—determines the way in which he develops his target-text

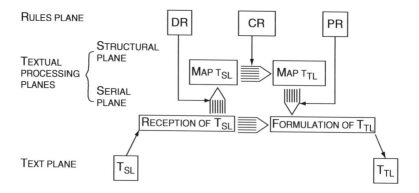

Figure 3. Two-map two-plane text-rank translation model (T_{SL} = source-language text; T_{TL} = target-language text; DR = derivation rules; CR = correspondence rules; PR = projection rules).

map from his source-text map. It should be noted that the first of the three phases described here the translator shares with every reader of literary texts, the third with every writer; the second, however, that of developing a target-text map from his source-text map by means of correspondence rules, is uniquely a translational (or at least a specific kind of metatextual) operation, and as such deserves our special attention.

It should be realized in this connection that the map of the source text, if the translator-to-be who abstracts it is a skilled and experienced reader, will be a conglomerate of highly disparate bits of information. In the first place, as a map of a linguistic artefact, it will contain information, at a variety of ranks, regarding features of the text in its relation to the linguistic continuum within which (or violating the rules of which) it is formulated, that is, contextual information. Secondly, as a map of a literary artefact, it will contain information, at a variety of ranks, regarding features of the text in its relation to the literary continuum within which (or rebelling against which) it is formulated, that is, intertextual information. And third, as a map of a socio-cultural artefact, it will contain information, at a variety of ranks, regarding features of the text in its relation to the socio-cultural continuum within which (or transcending which) it is formulated, that is, situational information.[6]

[Holmes goes on to discuss what Jiří Levý called the translator's 'decision process': how the translator seeks correspondences between the different features, forms, and functions in the two different languages (see also Sect. 4.8, above, on Levý). The translator may be compelled to abandon certain qualities of the source text, while highlighting others. Thus, 'the translator, whether or not he is conscious of it, establishes a hierarchy of correspondences' (p. 86).]

If this is a fair description of the literary translation process, in other words of the way in which the literary translator goes about his business, then the task for the scholar who wishes to describe the relationship between the translated text and its original would seem to be obvious. He must attempt to determine the features of the translator's two maps and to discover his three systems of rules, those of derivation, projection, and, above all, correspondence—in other words, the translator's poetics.

[...]

In most cases, however, the analyst is left with little or no material beyond the two (or more) texts, the original and its translation(s), and it is from these alone that he must attempt to derive his description. How can he set about his task? At the risk of simplifying the problem, I should like to restrict myself here to considering what I have suggested is the major aspect of this task, that of attempting to retrace the translator's two maps and the correspondence rules determining their relationship.

Clearly, the analyst will have to approach this problem in a different way from that of the translator. The translator, I have argued, derives a map of the source text from the text itself, next applies a set of correspondence rules, some of them more or less predetermined and some more or less *ad hoc*, to develop a target-text map from the source-text map, and finally uses this second map as a guide while formulating his target text. The analyst, on the other hand, starting from the two texts, will as a first step apply a set of derivation rules to each text in turn, in order to obtain maps of the two texts. His next step will be, with the aid of a set of comparison rules, to compare the two maps in order to determine the network of correspondences between their various features. This will then be followed by a third step in which, with the aid of a set of abstraction rules, he derives a set of correspondence rules and a correspondence hierarchy from the network of correspondences.

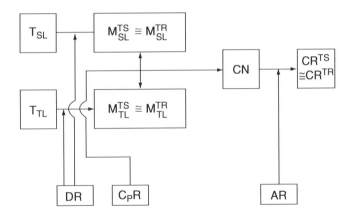

Figure 4. Model of the translation-descriptive process (T = text; SL = source language; TL = target language; M = map; TR = translator; TS = translation scholar; CN = network of correspondences. CR = correspondence rules; DR = derivation rules; CpR = comparison rules; AR = abstraction rules).

Only in one phase of one of these steps does the work of the analyst parallel that of the translator: in the operation of deriving the source-text map from the text. The operation of deriving the target-text map, on the other hand, is for the analyst the reverse of the operation performed by the translator (though at the same time parallel to the analyst's operation of deriving the source-text map, and requiring comparable discovery procedures). Similarly, the abstraction of a network of correspondences from the maps, and of correspondence rules and a correspondence hierarchy underlying that network, is an operation of quite a different kind from those performed by the translator.

A further complication is one that applies to all studies of mental processes. Since in most cases there is little or no tangible evidence of what has taken place in the translator's 'mind' except the text he has produced as compared to the original text, the scholar attempting to trace the relationship of the two texts likewise in most cases has no material except those two texts from which to derive his conclusions. And since the descriptive process he pursues is, though in a different way from the translator's process, extremely complex, there is great danger that the results of his analysis will be highly subjective and so of little value to other scholars. Assuming that objectivity in any true sense is in such a matter a goal even more unattainable than in research dealing with tangible objects and/ or events observable outside the 'mind', one can nevertheless posit that a high degree of intersubjectivity is an aim worth striving after in a research situation of this kind.

There would seem to be a choice for the analyst between two basic working methods. In the first, the descriptive scholar, upon studying the two texts, will derive from them a list of distinctive features which strike him as significant and deserving of comparative analysis; frequently he will also determine a hierarchical ordering of the features. The well-trained analyst will, it must be assumed, bring with him a detailed knowledge of linguistic, literary, and socio-cultural theory such that he can identify contextual, inter-textual, and situational elements in the texts in a manner acceptable to other scholars, and this, it must likewise be assumed, will provide at least a modicum of intersubjectivity to his application of linguistic, literary, and socio-cultural research methods. But the fact remains that none of the disciplines concerned with the nature of texts has given us a generally accepted intersubjective method for determining distinctive features in a concrete text, so that their selection remains to a large extent an *ad hoc* operation. The result will consequently be that the maps of the two texts derived by the analyst, like the translator's two maps, will be incomplete: the analyst, for instance, may very likely discover blank spaces (indications of *terrae incognitae*) in the translator's maps, but overlook the blank spaces in his own—and precisely in such *terrae incognitae*, as in parts of Africa in the old maps, may be lions.

A second working method, at least in theory, would be to circumvent the problem of *ad hoc* selection of distinctive features by determining beforehand a required repertory of features always to be analysed, regardless of what specific text is involved. This method, too, has at least one major drawback: if its results are to lead to a map that is generally acceptable as within reach of completeness, the repertory would have to be quite extensive, and the task of providing full details on the texts would be one that is arduous and tedious to the researcher and largely uninteresting to the reader.

The repertory method would, however, assure a higher degree of intersubjectivity to the results of the analysis based on it—provided, of course, that scholars in the field could reach agreement as to what elements should be included in such a repertory. Lambert has made an explorative attempt at a listing;[7] it would seem to me that a further filling out and structuring of this listing should be one of the major foci of research and discussion in the near future for scholars interested in translation description. It is clear that the repertory must not only be quite complete, but also complex enough in structure to accommodate a number of parametric axes. Among these a major one, of course, is the axis microstructure-mesostructure-macrostructure (from grapheme/morpheme via lexeme, sentence, and suprasentential units to text; in verse moreover via line, stanza, and suprastanzaic units). But other axes intersect this one, notably that of form-meaning-function (morphologue-semasiologue-analogue) and that of (linguistic) contextuality—(literary) intertextuality—(socio-cultural) situationality, and these axes too would have to be incorporated.

The task of working out such a repertory would be enormous. But if scholars were to arrive at a consensus regarding it, in the way, for instance, that botanists since Linnaeus have arrived at a consensus regarding systematic methods for the description of plants, it would then become possible, for the first time, to provide descriptions of original and translated texts, of their respective maps, and of correspondence networks, rules, and hierarchies that would be mutually comparable. And only on the basis of mutually comparable descriptions can we go on to produce well-founded studies of a larger scope: comparative studies of the translations of one author or one translator, or—a greater leap—period, genre, one-language (or one-culture), or general translation histories.

Such goals, of course, the scholars of our generation have tended to reject: they seem to us unattainable, and so outside the range of our less-than-vaulting ambition. It is in any case certain that they exceed the grasp of the subjective, largely intuitive and impressionist methods still so often being applied today. And only a more explicit, a more precise, a stricter and more intersubjective approach holds any promise of greater things to come.

NOTES

1. See e.g. the discussions in various early computer-oriented studies.
2. In the various models developed at this level, the main difference of opinion is in just what is being transferred: syntactic elements (Nida's kernel or near-kernel sentences) or semantic kernels. (Eugene A. Nida, 'Science of Translation', *Language*, 45 [1969], pp. 483–498). The fullest discussion of these and other serial models of the translation process is to be found in V. N. Komissarov, *Slovo o perevode* (Moscow: IMO, 1973), a book which I am unfortunately unable to read, though manuscript translations of several portions of it made by various students at the University of Amsterdam have given me confidence that it is a work of high significance which needs to be translated into a Western language *in toto*.

3. Obviously, in the case of longer texts there will also be mesostructural ranks, ranging from those of paragraphs and/or stanzas to those of chapters of novels, cantos of long poems, scenes or acts of plays.

4. Of course the charge can be made that this model, too, is an oversimplification of the translation process, ignoring as it does the mesostructural ranks. Eventually it may therefore prove necessary to abandon it in favour of a more complex model introducing a hierarchical series of maps, ranging from sentence-rank maps via a number of mesostructural maps to the text maps.

5. It also goes withoug saying that there is a great deal of feedback not indicated in the model; details of the target-text map, and in some cases even of the source-text map, may change drastically in the course of sentence-by-sentence (or transeme-by-transeme) translation.

6. On this terminology see André Lefevere, 'The Translation of Literature: An Approach', *Babel*, 16 (1970), pp. 75–79, and James S Homes, 'Rebuilding the Bridge at Bommel: Notes on othe Limits of Translatability', *Translated!*, pp. 45–52.

7. José Lambert, 'Echanges littéraires et traduction: Discussion d'un projet', James S. Holmes, José Lambert, & Raymond van den Broeck (eds.). *Literature and Translation: New Perspectives in Literary Studies* (Leuven, Acco, 1978), pp. 142–160, esp. pp. 154–155.

Holmes, the Translator

James S. Holmes received major awards for his translations of Dutch poetry (including *Dutch Interior, Postwar Poetry of the Netherlands and Flanders*, co-edited with William Jay Smith, 1984). He also published a series of modestly produced chapbooks with translations of Paul van Ostaijen, Piet Paaltjens, Gerrit Komrij, and others. Some of these translations, *Poems for Men after Martial* (1983) being among them, were published under the pseudonym Jacob Lowland. As noted in the Colophon to the Martial chapbook: 'These versions, close adaptations of poems from Books Eight to Twelve of Martial's Epigrams were made by Jacob Lowland in August & September 1983 [...] [T]he rendition of IX:59 was influenced by a late seventeenth-century version often tho probably erroneously, attributed to Henry Killigrew. *Martial Music* was issued in a limited edition of ninety copies on the occasion of the colloquium on homo-erotic literature held in Amsterdam in November 1983.'

In 'Translating Martial and Vergil: Jacob Lowland among the Classics', from a talk given by James S. Holmes (*Translating Poetry: The Double Labyrinth*, ed. Daniel Weissbort, 1989), Holmes remarks about the translation of Catullus, an ongoing project of his, that 'one of the major problems [...] has been not his homosexual feelings, but his obscenity, the street language. Only since about 1965 has it been possible for people to use such languaqe in poetry and get it published. It's not a question of what poets dare to do often, but of what publishers dare to publish, because of the censorship laws'. As for Martial, he notes: 'I hadn't done anything more with Latin until this past summer. I picked up a book called *From Daphne to Laurel* [1982], which is a very interesting anthology of how English-language translators [. . .] have dealt with the classics, from the Middle Ages up to today [. . .] It's arranged not by poets but by translators [like George Steiner's landmark anthology of translators, *The Penguin Book of Modern Verse Translation*, 1966] [. . .] Well, I came across a poem that I didn't know, in an anonymous late seventeenth-century version, by someone who brought out a book of Martial translations. [. . .]' He continues in this casual manner, while drawing attention to the inhibitions standing in the way of adequate translations of this important Latin poet. His account of translating homoerotic Latin poetry challenges a number of theoretical assumptions.

As regards the inevitably limited life of a 'modernizing' translation, Holmes comments: 'That doesn't worry me at all. I'm quite willing for translation to age very fast. In fact, I'm quite willing for my own poetry to age very fast. I'm very much concerned with communication *now*. [. . .] I believe firmly in new translations for every generation . . . '. The versions of Martial, printed below, though doubtless dated, are probably still accessible to the present generation. As regards 'Window Shopping', Holmes comments: 'Mamurra is a name that goes back to the time of Catullus, and I suspect that Martial knew that. Julius Caesar's friend, his lover until he died, was named Mamurra, and Catullus absolutely hated him. [. . .] Peter Wigham, in the Penguin translation of Catullus, translated Mamurra with a pun, as O'Toole [*The Poems of Catullus*, trans. and introd. Peter Wigham, 1966] [. . .] When I started 'I decided that I wanted to translate this so that it communicated in the present day, to gay people in the present day; that was the first decision I made. [. . .]'

Martial IX 57

Latin original

Nil est tritius Hedyli lacernis:
non ansae veterum Corinthiorum,
nec crus compede lubricum decenni,
nec ruptae recutita colla mulae,
nec quae Flaminiam secant salebrae,
nec qui litoribus nitent lapilli,
nec Tusca ligo vinea politus,
nec pallens toga mortui tribulis,
nec pigri rota quassa mulionis,
nec rasum cavea latus visontis,
nec dens iam senior ferocis apri.
res una est tamen (ipse non negabit)
culus tritior Hedyli lacernis.

Literal translation

Nothing is worn smoother than Hedylus' mantles:
not the handles of antique Corinthian vases,
nor a shank polished by a ten-years-worn fetter,
nor the scarred neck of a broken-winded mule,
nor the ruts that intersect the Flaminian Way,
nor the pebbles that shine on the sea beach,
nor a hoe polished by a Tuscan vineyard,
nor the shiny toga of a defunct pauper,
nor the ramshackle wheel of a lazy carrier,
nor a bison's flank scraped by its cage,
nor the tusk, now aged, of a fierce boar.
Yet there is one thing—he himself will not deny it:
Hedylus' rump is worn smoother than his mantle.

James S. Holmes's version, Martial Music, *p. x*

Nothing's worn smoother than Harry's coat:
not the handle on a long-used stein,
a slave's wrist polished by years of rope,
a city-dog's neck, rubbed by the line,

the ruts that cut country rods in spring,
the gleaming pebbles on ocean beaches,
a hoe for suburban gardening,
the shiny seat of a beggar's britches,

rickety wheels on a market cart,
the bare-scraped flanks of a zoo-caged lion,
the horns on a butt-prone billy goat.
Wait! There's one thing I wouldn't deny him:
His bum's worn smoother than Harry's coat.

Martial IX 59

Latin original

In Saeptis Mamurra diu multumque vagtus,
  hic ubi Roma suas aurea vexat opes,
inspexit molles pueros oculisque comedit,
  non hos quos primae prostituere casae,

sed quos arcanae servant tabulata catastae
    et quos non populus nec mea turba videt.
inde satur mensas et opertos exuit orbes
    expositumque alte pingue poposcit ebur,
et testudineum mensus quater hexaelinon
    ingemuit citro non satis esse suo.
consuluit nares an olerent aera Corinthon,
    culpavit statuas et, Polyclite, tuas,
et, turbata brevi questus crystallina vitro,
    murrina signavit seposuitque decem.
expendit veteres calathos et si qua fuerunt
    pocula Mentorea nobilitata manu,
et viridis picot gemmas numeravit in auro,
    quidquid et a nivea grandius aure sonat.
sardonychas veros mensa quaesivit in omni
    et pretium magnis fecit iaspidibus.
undecima lassus cum iam discederet hora,
    asse duos calices emit et ipse tulit.

Literal translation

Mamurra, long and often wandering in the Saepta,
here where Golden Rome flings about her wealth,
inspected and devoured with his eyes dainty boys,
not those the outer stalls made public,
but those who are guarded by the platform of a secret stand,
and whom the people do not see, nor the crowd of such as I. Then, sated with the view,
he had tables and round covered table-tops laid bare,
and must needs have their high-hung glistening ivory supports brought down;
and after four measurements of a tortoise-shell couch for six,
he said with a sigh that it was too small for his citrus wood table.
He took counsel of his nose whether the bronzes smelt of Corinth,
and condemned even your statuary, Polyclitus;
and, complaining that the crystal vases were disfigured by a small piece of glass,
he put his seal on ten murrine articles, and set them aside.
He weighed antique tankards, and any cups
made precious by Mentor's handiwork,
and counted the emeralds set in chased gold,
and every large pearl that tinkles from a snow-white ear. Genuine sardonyxes he
looked for on every table,

and offered a price for some big jaspers.
When at the eleventh hour, fagged out, he was at last departing,
for a penny he bought two cups—and bore them off himself.

'Window-shopping', trans. anon

[This is attributed by the British Library catalogue to Henry Killigrew (1613–1700), although this seems unlikely.]

> Mamurra many hours does vagrant tell
> I' th' shops, where Rome her richest ware does sell.
> Beholds fair boys, devours them with his eyes,
> Not those of common note, one first espies;
> But which in inner rooms they closely mew,
> Remov'd from mine, and from the people's view.
> Glutted with these, choice tables he uncases,
> Others of ivory, set high, displaces.
> Rich tortoise beds he measures four times o'er.
> Sighs, they fit not, and leaves them on that score.
> Consults the statues of Corinthian brass
> By the scent; and not without blame lets pass
> Thy pieces, Polyclet. He next complains
> Of crystals mix'd with glass, and then disdains.
> Marks porcelain cups, sets ten of them apart:
> Weighs antique plate (of Mentor's noble art
> If any be); counts, i' the' enamell'd gold,
> The gems that stand. Rich pendants does behold:
> For the sardonyx makes a search most nice,
> And of the biggest jaspers beats the price.
> Tir'd now, at last, after eleven hours' stay,
> Two farthing pots he bought, and himself bore away.

James S Holmes's version, 'Window Shopping', Martial Music, p. xl

[See introduction to 'Holmes, the Translator', above, for Holmes's general translation strategy here. Notes, supplied by Holmes and obviously no longer current, explain the allusions, e.g. ' "Rob Himself", Rob of Amsterdam, runs an art gallery in Amsterdam [. . .]'.]

> O'Toole in ennui
>   (life is *such* a bore)
> goes shopping
>   in the Gay Department Store.

First to the Slave Department
   With his eyes
he eats 'em up:
   not those on show for guys

like you & me,
   but prime-type types locked tight
in special rooms
   tucked out of common sight.

None's *hot* enough,
   Now Stocks & Pillories.
He checks out this one, that.
   None of them *please*.

He measures all the slings,
   twice, three times, four.
None of them *fit*.
   When *will* you have some *more*?

Now on to Art.
   There's this new set of drawings
just in from Finland.
   Look! A *flaw*!

O *Tom*, how *could* you!
   Time to contemplate
the silver cockrings.
   Silver! Silver *plate*!

He *loves* the harnesses,
   has three of them
laid by, *adores* a belt
   (each studded gem

selected & set in
   by Rob Himself
counts every stone,
   then moves on to the shelf

with rings & earrings,
   Oooh, the *diamond's* nice.
The *big* one.
   Oh? *That* much? At *half* the price . . .

Exhausted after four hours' stay,
   he'll buy
two jars of Lube &
   really have to *fly.*

5.4 ITAMAR EVEN-ZOHAR

Itamar Even-Zohar (b. 1939), Professor of Culture Research and Porter Chair Professor of Semiotics and Literary Theory, Tel Aviv University, former editor of *Poetics Today* (1987–93), is a leading Israeli translation scholar, probably best known for his Polysystem Theory, in which is outlined the structure and evolution of literary systems. Even-Zohar and some of his Israeli colleagues, notably Gideon Toury, worked closely with James S Holmes and other colleagues in the Netherlands, Belgium, and the UK, this collaboration being important in the development of Translation Studies in the 1970s and after. In recent years, he has been researching the development of cultural systems, already an implied feature of his work in the 1970s, as instanced in his essay 'The Position of Translated Literature within the Literary Polysystem' (1978; rev. 1990), reprinted below.

'The Position of Translated Literature within the Literary Polysystem' (1978), repr. in *Polysystem Studies*, special issue of *Poetics Today*, 11/1 (1990), 45–51.

Dedicated to the memory of James S Holmes—a great student of translation and a dear friend

I

In spite of the broad recognition among historians of culture of the major role translation has played in the crystallization of national cultures, relatively little research has been carried out so far in this area. As a rule, histories of literatures mention translations when there is no way to avoid them, when dealing with the Middle Ages or the Renaissance, for instance. One might of course find sporadic references to individual literary translations in various other periods, but they are seldom incorporated into the historical account in any coherent way. As a consequence, one hardly gets any idea whatsoever of the function of translated literature for a literature as a whole or of its position within that literature. Moreover, there is no awareness of the possible existence of translated literature as a particular literary system. The prevailing concept is rather that of 'translation' or just 'translated works' treated on an individual basis. Is there any basis for a different assumption, that is for considering translated literature as a system? Is there the same sort of cultural and verbal network of relations within what seems to be an arbitrary group of translated texts as the one we willingly hypothesize for original literature? What kind of relations might there be among translated works, which are presented as completed facts, imported from other literatures, detached from their home contexts and consequently neutralized from the point of view of center-and-periphery struggles?

My argument is that translated works do correlate in at least two ways: (a) in the way their source texts are selected by the target literature, the principles of selection never being uncorrelatable with the home co-systems of the target literature (to put it in the most cautious way); and (b) in the way they adopt specific norms, behaviors, and policies—in short, in their use of the literary repertoire—which results from their relations with the other home co-systems. These are not confined to the linguistic level only, but are manifest on any selection level as well. Thus, translated literature may possess a repertoire of its own, which to a certain extent could even be exclusive to it. (See Toury 1985 and 1985a.)

It seems that these points make it not only justifiable to talk about translated literature, but rather imperative to do so. I cannot see how any scholarly effort to describe and explain the behavior of the literary polysystem in synchrony and diachrony can advance in an adequate way if that is not recognized. In other words, I conceive of translated literature not only as an integral system within any literary polysystem, but as a most active system within it. But what is its position within the polysystem, and how is this position connected with the nature of its overall repertoire? One would be tempted to deduce from the peripheral position of translated literature in the study of literature that it also permanently occupies a peripheral position in the literary polysystem, but this is by no means the case. Whether translated literature becomes central or peripheral, and whether this position is connected with innovatory ('primary') or conservatory ('secondary') repertoires, depends on the specific constellation of the polysystem under study.

II

To say that translated literature maintains a central position in the literary polysystem means that it participates actively in shaping the center of the polysystem. In such a situation it is by and large an integral part of innovatory forces, and as such likely to be identified with major events in literary history while these are taking place. This implies that in this situation no clear-cut distinction is maintained between 'original' and 'translated' writings, and that often it is the leading writers (or members of the avant-garde who are about to become leading writers) who produce the most conspicuous or appreciated translations. Moreover, in such a state when new literary models are emerging, translation is likely to become one of the means of elaborating the new repertoire. Through the foreign works, features (both principles and elements) are introduced into the home literature which did not exist there before. These include possibly not only new models of reality to replace the old and established ones that are no longer effective, but a whole range of other features as well, such as a new (poetic) language, or compositional patterns and techniques. It is clear that the very principles of selecting the works to be translated are determined by the situation governing the (home) polysystem: the texts are chosen according to their compatibility with the new approaches and the supposedly innovatory role they may assume within the target literature.

What then are the conditions which give rise to a situation of this kind? It seems to me that three major cases can be discerned, which are basically various manifestations of the same law: (a) when a polysystem has not yet been crystallized, that is to say, when a literature is 'young,' in the process of being established; (b) when a literature is either 'peripheral' (within a large group of correlated literatures) or 'weak,'' or both; and (c) when there are turning points, crises, or literary vacuums in a literature.

In the first case translated literature simply fulfills the need of a younger literature to put into use its newly founded (or renovated) tongue for as many literary types as possible in order to make it serviceable as a literary language and useful for its emerging public. Since a young literature cannot immediately create texts in all types known to its producers, it benefits from the experience of other literatures, and translated literature becomes in this way one of its most important systems. The same holds true for the second instance, that of relatively established literatures whose resources are limited and whose position within a larger literary hierarchy is generally peripheral. As a consequence of this situation, such literatures often do not develop the same full range of literary activities (organized in a variety of systems) observable in adjacent larger literatures (which in consequence may create a feeling that they are indispensable). They may also 'lack' a repertoire which is felt to be badly needed vis-à-vis, and in terms of the presence of, that adjacent literature. This lack may then be filled, wholly or partly, by translated literature. For instance, all sorts of peripheral literature may in such cases consist of translated literature. But far more important is the consequence that the ability of such 'weak' literatures to initiate innovations is often less than that of the larger and central literatures, with the result that a relation of dependency may be established not only in peripheral systems, but in the very center of these 'weak' literatures. (To avoid misunderstanding, I would like to point out that these literatures may rise to a central position in a way analogous to the way this is carried out by peripheral systems within a certain polysystem, but this cannot be discussed here.)

Since peripheral literatures in the Western Hemisphere tend more often than not to be identical with the literatures of smaller nations, as unpalatable as this idea may seem to us, we have no choice but to admit that within a group of relatable national literatures, such as the literatures of Europe, hierarchical relations have been established since the very beginnings of these literatures. Within this (macro-) polysystem some literatures have taken peripheral positions, which is only to say that they were often modelled to a large extent upon an exterior literature. For such literatures, translated literature is not only a major channel through which fashionable repertoire is brought home, but also a source of reshuffling and supplying alternatives. Thus, whereas richer or stronger literatures may have the option to adopt novelties from some periphery within their indigenous borders, 'weak' literatures in such situations often depend on import alone.

The dynamics within the polysystem creates turning points, that is to say, historical moments where established models are no longer tenable for a younger generation. At such moments, even in central literatures, translated literature may assume a central position. This is all the more true when at a turning point no item in the indigenous stock is taken to be acceptable, as a result of which a literary 'vacuum' occurs. In such a vacuum, it is easy for foreign models to infiltrate, and translated literature may consequently assume a central position. Of course, in the case of 'weak' literatures or literatures which are in a constant state of impoverishment (lack of literary items existing in a neighbor or accessible foreign literature), this situation is even more overwhelming.

III

Contending that translated literature may maintain a peripheral position means that it constitutes a peripheral system within the polysystem, generally employing secondary models. In such a situation it has no influence on major processes and is modelled according to norms already conventionally established by an already dominant type in the target literature. Translated literature in this case becomes a major factor of conservatism. While the contemporary original literature might go on developing new norms and models, translated literature adheres to norms which have been rejected either recently or long before by the (newly) established center. It no longer maintains positive correlations with original writing.

A highly interesting paradox manifests itself here: translation, by which new ideas, items, characteristics can be introduced into a literature, becomes a means to preserve traditional taste. This discrepancy between the original central literature and the translated literature may have evolved in a variety of ways, for instance, when translated literature, after having assumed a central position and inserted new items, soon lost contact with the original home literature which went on changing, and thereby became a factor of preservation of unchanged repertoire. Thus, a literature that might have emerged as a revolutionary type may go on existing as an ossified *système d'antan*, often fanatically guarded by the agents of secondary models against even minor changes.

The conditions which enable this second state are of course diametrically opposite to those which give rise to translated literature as a central system: either there are no major changes in the polysystem or these changes are not effected through the intervention of interliterary relations materialized in the form of translations.

IV

The hypothesis that translated literature may be either a central or peripheral system does not imply that it is always wholly one or the other. As a system, translated literature is itself stratified, and from the point of view of polysystemic analysis it is often from the vantage point of the central stratum that all relations within the system are observed.

This means that while one section of translated literature may assume a central position, another may remain quite peripheral. In the foregoing analysis I pointed out the close relationship between literary contacts and the status of translated literature. This seems to me the major clue to this issue. When there is intense interference, it is the portion of translated literature deriving from a major source literature which is likely to assume a central position. For instance, in the Hebrew literary polysystem between the two world wars literature translated from the Russian assumed an unmistakably central position, while works translated from English, German, Polish, and other languages assumed an obviously peripheral one. Moreover, since the major and most innovatory translational norms were produced by translations from the Russian, other translated literature adhered to the models and norms elaborated by those translations.

The historical material analyzed so far in terms of polysystemic operations is too limited to provide any far-reaching conclusions about the chances of translated literature to assume a particular position. But work carried out in this field by various other scholars, as well as my own research, indicates that the 'normal' position assumed by translated literature tends to be the peripheral one. This should in principle be compatible with theoretical speculation. It may be assumed that in the long run no system can remain in a constant state of weakness, 'turning point,' or crisis, although the possibility should not be excluded that some polysystems may maintain such states for quite a long time. Moreover, not all polysystems are structured in the same way, and cultures do differ significantly. For instance, it is clear that the French cultural system, French literature naturally included, is much more rigid than most other systems. This, combined with the long traditional central position of French literature within the European context (or within the European macro-polysystem), has caused French translated literature to assume an extremely peripheral position. The state of Anglo-American literature is comparable, while Russian, German, or Scandinavian would seem to show different patterns of behavior in this respect.

V

What consequences may the position taken by translated literature have on translational norms, behaviors, and policies? As I stated above, the distinction between a translated work and an original work in terms of literary behavior is a function of the position assumed by the translated literature at a given time. When it takes a central position, the borderlines are *diffuse, so* that the very category of 'translated works' must be extended to semi- and quasi-translations as well. From the point of view of translation theory I think this is a more adequate way of dealing with such phenomena than to reject them on the basis of a static and a-historical conception of translation. Since translational activity participates, when it assumes a central position, in the process of creating new, primary models, the translator's main concern here is not just to look for ready-made models in his home repertoire into which the source texts would be transferable. Instead, he is prepared in such cases to violate the home conventions. Under such conditions the chances that the translation will be close to the original in terms of adequacy (in other words, a reproduction of the dominant textual relations of the original) are greater than otherwise. Of course, from the point of view of the target literature the adopted translational norms might for a while be too foreign and revolutionary, and if the new trend is defeated in the literary struggle, the translation made according to its conceptions and tastes will never really gain ground.But if the new trend is victorious, the repertoire (code) of translated literature may be enriched and become more flexible. Periods of great change in the home system are in fact the only ones when a translator is prepared to go far beyond the options offered to him by his established home repertoire and is willing to attempt a different treatment of text making. Let us remember that under stable conditions items lacking in a target literature may remain untransferable if the state of the polysystem does not allow innovations. But the process of opening the system gradually brings certain literatures closer and in the longer run enables a situation where the postulates of (translational) adequacy and the realities of equivalence may overlap to a relatively high degree. This is the case of the European literatures, though in some of them the mechanism of rejection has been so strong that the changes I am talking about have occurred on a rather limited scale.

Naturally, when translated literature occupies a peripheral position, it behaves totally differently. Here, the translator's main effort is to concentrate upon finding the best ready-made secondary models for the foreign text, and the result often turns out to be a non-adequate translation or (as I would prefer to put it) a greater discrepancy between the equivalence achieved and the adequacy postulated.

In other words, not only is the socio-literary status of translation dependent upon its position within the polysystem, but the very practice of translation is also strongly subordinated to that position. And even the question of what is a translated work cannot be answered *a priori* in terms of an a-historical out-of-context idealized state: it must be determined on the grounds of the operations governing the polysystem. Seen from this point of view, translation is no longer a phenomenon whose nature and borders are given once and for all, but an activity dependent on the relations within a certain cultural system.

NOTE

1. On the concept of 'weak' see 'Interference in Dependent Literary Polysystems' [Itamar Even-Zohar, *Polysystem Studies*, *Poetics Today*, 11/1 (1990), 79–84].

BIBLIOGRAPHY

Toury, G. (1985) 'Translational Solutions on the Lexical Level and the Dictionary', in J. Tomaszczyk and B. Lewandowska-Tomaszczyk (eds), *International Conference on Meaning and Lexicography: Abstracts*, Lodz, Poland: University of Lodz.

Toury, G. (1985a) 'A Rationale for Descriptive Translation Studies', in T. Hermans (ed.) *The Manipulation of Literature: Studies in Literary Translation*, London: Croom Helm, pp. 16–41.

5.5 André Lefevere

André Lefevere (1945–96), translation theorist and historian, translator, was born in Belgium and was educated there (Ghent) and in England (Essex), teaching in Hong Kong and Antwerp as well as the USA. He came to the University of Texas in Austin in 1984 to take over the Netherlandic Studies Program, and was also very active in the Comparative Literature Program, where he contributed a vision of how the study of translations illuminates our understanding of cultures. Lefevere was a leading theoretician in the field of literary translation, associated with the descriptive and target-oriented approach of such as Gideon Toury. He was also a prolific author of polemical works and editor of textbooks, such as *Translation/History/Culture: A Sourcebook* (1992), with contributions to books, as well as translations of poetry from French, Dutch, Latin, German, English, into Dutch and English. He co-authored books with Susan Bassnett, such as *Constructing Cultures: Essays on Literary Translation* (1990) and was joint general editor with Bassnett of the Routledge Translation Studies series. Not unlike James Holmes, he insisted on the need for theory to be based in experience or practice. Lefevere developed the notion of refraction or rewriting to characterize the process of successful translation as a refocusing and redirecting of a source text into a target culture (see also his *Translation, Rewriting, and the Manipulation of Literary Fame*, 1992).

From 'Why Waste Our Time on Rewrites: The Trouble with Interpretation and the Role of Rewriting in an Alternative Paradigm', included in Theo Hermans (ed.), *The Manipulation of Literature: Studies in Literary Translation* (London: Croom Helm, and New York: St. Martin's Press, 1985), 215–43

Criticism, which has often given the impression that it is trying to describe and interpret works of literature or whole historical epochs from the outside, should be seen for what it is: an attempt to influence the development of a given literature in a certain direction, the direction which happens to coincide with the poetics and ideology of the dominant critical school of the moment. To do so, criticism, in its historical avatar, will not hestitate to rewrite history until it fits the said ideology and poetics, nor will it give up trying to influence the way in which a reader reads a certain work of literature.

Deconstructionist criticism is, at last, beginning openly to acknowledge this state of affairs. Criticism is put squarely where it belongs: with literature, not with any kind of analysis of literature as a social phenomenon and not, as has been the case for too long, somewhere in between, occupying a fundamentally ambiguous position, and forced to occupy that position by the interplay of systemic constraints (how else could it ever hope to become and/or remain dominant?), yet obscuring the workings of those constraints by the very position it occupies. The realization that criticism is part of the rough and tumble of the development of a literary system, not a description of that system, may prove productive in opening the way for an analysis of literary systems as such. 'Since', in Paul de Man's words, 'they are not scientific, critical texts have to be read with the same awareness of ambivalence that is brought to the study of non-critical literary texts' (1979: 110). They should no longer be taken for what they are not.

To recognize the fact that criticism, being part of a literary system, can never be autonomous, will not spell the end of literary studies, as those who produce interpretations and swear by them would have us believe, but it may spell the end of a study of literature in which interpretation functions as the central concept. It may also spell the breakthrough of another kind of study of literature which would not only take into account the literature that is written, but also the ways in which what is written gets rewritten, in the service of which ideology, which poetics, and with what results.

The study of literature would then no longer consist of the rewriting of literature in various ways, and the theory of literature would not be 'the attempt to govern interpretations of particular texts by appealing to an account of interpretation in general' [Knapp & Michaels 1982: 723]. Rather, literary theory would try to explain how both the writing and the rewriting of literature are subject to certain constraints, and how the interaction of writing and rewriting is ultimately responsible, not just for the canonization of specific authors or specific works and the rejection of others, but also for the evolution of a given literature, since rewritings are often designed precisely to push a given literature in a certain direction. Think, for example, of the often quoted rewritings of T'ang poetry in Pound's *Cathay*, which have helped to push the evolution of modern English-language poetry in a certain direction. And if we were able to find out about the evolution of a given literature, if we could discover certain regular, recurring patterns, we might even try to formulate a theory of what makes literature tick, a theory that would not focus primarily on 'literary practice as an intimate mental process of writing' (Dubois: 1978: 34), since a few decades of focusing primarily on that aspect seem to have made us sadder rather than wiser, but on 'the concept (and the reality) of a socialized apparatus that takes literature in charge and organizes it' (ibid.). This does most emphatically not mean that the writer is now relegated to the periphery, banished from the limelight for ever, but merely that he or she will have to share the limelight with re-writers, since they share the responsibility for the evolution of a literature, and to no small extent. (pp. 218–20)

Literature is one of the systems which constitute the (super)system known as society, which also encompasses other systems, such as physics, law, and many more. A further word of warning may be in order here: I use the term system with a fair degree of flexibility, ranging far and wide in history (the Medieval System in Western Europe, say) and geography (the Euramerican system, or the Islamic system). I trust that the reader will read the term with a corresponding flexibility of mind, the result of a willing suspension of attitude, so to speak.

Alternatively, a society, a culture is the environment of a literary system. The literary system and the system of society are open to each other, they influence each other. There is, in fact, a control factor in the literary system which sees to it that that system does not fall too far out of step with other systems the society consists of. Or rather, it would be more accurate to say that this control function is shared by two elements, one of which belongs squarely in the literary system, whereas the other is to be found outside of that system. The first element tries to control the literary system from the inside, within the parameters set by the second element. The first element is represented by interpreters, critics, reviewers, teachers of literature, translators. They will occasionally repress certain works of literature because these works go all too blatantly against the dominant concept of what literature should (be allowed to) be—the poetics—and of what society should (be allowed to) be—the ideology, the world view—of a certain society at a certain moment. But these rewriters will much more frequently adapt works of literature until they can be claimed to correspond to the poetics and the ideology of their age. French neo-classical translations of Homer, for example, in which all that was felt to be 'uncouth', such as the entrails of both men and animals, was resolutely left out, are an obvious example of the process, as long as we realize that these features of the original were not left out because the translators knew no Greek, or because the Greek-French dictionaries of the period were strangely deficient in certain areas, but because the 'uncouth' simply ran counter to the dominant poetics/ideology of that period—to such an extent even that when Leconte de Lisle translated Homer about a hundred and fifty years later, and with all entrails in place, he was seriously accused, in certain quarters, of having mutilated the original, whereas he was, in fact, restoring it.

The second control factor, the one which operates mostly outside the literary system proper, will be called 'patronage' here, and it will be understood to mean something like 'the powers (persons, institutions) which help or hinder the writing, reading and rewriting of literature.' Patronage is usually more interested in the ideology of literature than in its poetics, or it could be said that the patron 'delegates' authority to the interpreter where poetics is concerned. A paradigmatic example of this, which will serve to make matters clearer, may be found in the relationship between the critic Sainte-Beuve and his patron, the later Napoleon III. As Chris Baldick puts it, 'the political "strong man" for whom Sainte-Beuve was to be the literary equivalent was Louis Bonaparte and it was in the (far from "disinterested") Bonapartist journal *Le Constitu-tionnel* and the official government paper *Le Moniteur* that he published his *Causeries*' (Baldick 1983: 13).

Patronage consists of three elements, which can be seen to interact in various combinations. There is an ideological component, which acts as a constraint on the choice and development of both form and subject-matter. There is also an economic component: the patron sees to it that writers and re-writers are able to make a living, by giving them a pension, appointing them to some office (Chaucer, as is not too widely known outside the circles frequented by medievalists, acted as 'the King's envoy, the controller of customs on wool, hides and sheepskins or the subforester of North Petherton,' cf. Bennett 1952: 5), paying royalties on the sale of books, or employing writers and rewriters as teachers and reviewers. There is, finally, also an element of status involved: 'acceptance of patronage signaled integration into an elite and acceptance of the style of life associated with that elite' (Clark & Clark 1977: 201). Goethe's Tasso provides us with perhaps the most succinct description of this element when he exclaims: 'here is my fatherland, here is the circle/in which my soul is pleased to dwell/I listen here, I pay attention to every hint/ here speak the voices of experience, science and taste' (lines 449–452). 'Here' is, of course, the court of Ferrara, and Goethe himself had, as is well known, found a patron in another court. In more recent times, on the other hand, acceptance of patronage may simply mean integration into the lifestyle of a support group, or subculture, which certainly need not always be described in terms of an élite. (pp. 226–8)

All writing of literature takes place under the two constraints mentioned above, patronage and poetics, to which two more constraints must be added. One is what linguists often call 'universe of discourse' these days, i.e. the knowledge, the learning, but also the objects and the customs of a certain time, to which writers are free to allude in their work. The other is the natural language in which the work is composed. For rewriters a fifth constraint must be added, namely that of the original work itself. The original is the locus where ideology, poetics, universe of discourse and language come together, mingle and clash.

All rewriting of literature, be it interpretation, criticism, historiography, the putting together of anthologies, or translation, takes place under at least one of the constraints mentioned, and implies the others. (pp. 232–3)

Translation is probably the most obvious instance of rewriting, since it operates under all four constraints. Yet all different forms of rewriting tend to work together in a literary system. No translation, published as a book, is likely to give you just the translation. It is nearly always accompanied by an introduction, which is a form of criticism cum interpretation. If the translation is successful, acclaimed, taken up into the mainstream, it is sure to be anthologized sooner or later, and historians of literature writing on literatures other than those of which they know the languages, will rely on translations to get their impressions of what a work is like. No one form of rewriting alone can establish or disestablish, make or break the reputation of a writer and/or a work inside the receiving culture, just as functional and inventory innovations in the poetics of the receiving literature may be initiated by translation, but they are then reinforced by other forms of rewriting.

Translation operates first of all under the constraint of the original, itself the product of constraints belonging to a certain time. Second, the language changes, quite dramatically. Third, the universe of discourse very often poses insuperable problems for any kind of so-called 'faithful' translation. Universe of discourse features are those features particular to a given culture, and they are, almost by definition, untranslatable or at least very hard to translate. They can be things, like 'bistro' in French, or concepts, like 'völkisch' in German. They belong to a certain time, like 'völkisch' in German or 'tunica' in Latin, and they go under with their time as far as their language of origin is concerned. In translation, however, they need to be resuscitated, though nobody is quite sure in what form: loan translation, calque, footnote, a combination of the three?

Voltaire's translations of Shakespeare provide us with a good example of the poetological adaptation works of literature are forced to undergo: the alexandrine takes the place of the iambic pentameter and the alexandrine does, of course, rhyme. Shakespeare, in other words, has to sound a lot more like Racine in order to be acceptable as Shakespeare for the French audience of Voltaire's time. In Victor Hugo's time, on the other hand, Shakespeare does not have to sound like Racine any more—proof of the fact that no poetics remains dominant in a given system for ever. The same fact also highlights the relationship between patronage and poetics: the poetics of Victor Hugo's time is so different from that of Voltaire's time because the patronage has shifted dramatically: the people who extended patronage to Hugo were the people who, among other things, survived the French Revolution and even profited from it. Many of the people who were Voltaire's patrons, and went to applaud his tragedies which are now almost completely forgotten, did not.

Writers are rewritten when their work passes from one literature into another, just as they are rewritten inside a given literature. But why, it may be asked, do writers have to submit to these indignities? First of all, they don't really submit. In many cases they have long been dead, in most they have precious little say in the matter. Writers are powerless to control the rewriting of their work, which may be a bad thing; but so, in the long run, is anybody else, which may not be such a bad thing after all. Second, if the writer does not 'submit', he or she will simply not exist in the receiving literature at all. Third, these indignities usually stop after a while. True, the foreign writer may have to adopt the native guise, but once he or she is established in the receiving literature, new translations tend to be made with the aim of revealing him or her on his or her own terms to the receiving literature, and no longer on terms dictated by the receiving literature itself. The example of Brecht's *Mother Courage* in English/American, which I have analysed in more detail elsewhere (Lefevere 1982), is instructive in this context.

It is and remains a fact of literary life that patrons and critics are, in the final analysis, influential in deciding what will 'make it' in a given literature and what will not. They do the screening and they pronounce the verdict. The fight to influence that verdict one way or the other is fought with weapons taken not primarily from the writings of the author in question, but by means of rewritings of all kinds, which are used against each other until a certain consensus is reached in systems with differentiated patronage. In systems with undifferentiated patronage the matter is usually settled with more efficiency and dispatch: what does not fit in with the dominant poetics or ideology is simply labelled 'denatured', or 'vile', or 'trivial', or even 'popular and entertaining'.

Whether or not a literature dictates its terms to potential imports will often depend on the self-image that literature has developed. If, like French literature in the eighteenth century, it was convinced that it represented the very epitome of wit and elegance, it would have every reason to screen out whatever did not fulfil its requirements, or else change it in such a way as to make it acceptable. It did that to foreign works by means of translations, it also did that to French works written in a French that was not quite the French of Paris (and therefore dismissed as 'popular', even though, on occasion, 'charmingly naive'), and it also did that to French works not written to its specifications, ideological or otherwise, such as those of the Marquis de Sade.

If, on the other hand, the potential receiving literature does not have all that much of a self-image, like German literature in that same eighteenth century, it will not (and did not) dictate any terms at all. On the contrary, it will accept at least the poetics of the source literature as a potentially liberating influence and one that will, through patient imitation, allow it finally to emerge from the depths of obscurity and to play an important part on the stage of world literature as a whole.

Translation, then, is the visible sign of the openness of the literary system, of a specific literary system. It opens the way to what can be called both subversion and transformation, depending on where the guardians of the dominant poetics, the dominant ideology stand. No wonder, therefore, that there have been all kinds of attempts to regulate translation, to make sure that it does not exert any subversive influence on the native system, to use it to integrate what is foreign by naturalizing it first. Various historical periods, dominated by completely different poetics, have formulated rules for the translator to follow, different rules, of course, contradictory rules even, but rules nonetheless. In fact it could be said that long after the normative (handbooks of) poetics disappeared from Western literature—and those always contained at least one chapter on translation—translation remained the only literary activity still supposed to be bound by rules also, and with a vengeance, in the Romantic period which claimed to have abolished all rules of any kind in poetic composition.

It should be clear, by now, that translation does not manage to subvert or transform a literature all on its own. Translation does so in conjunction with other forms of rewriting, which explains why translation should also be studied in conjunction with other forms of rewriting, and not on its own. If the study of translation is to be made productive for the study of literary theory and, especially, literary history, it is quite clear that translation can no longer be analysed in isolation, but that it should be studied as part of a whole system of texts and the people who produce, support, propagate, oppose, censor them. Or, to put it differently, translation can be studied in isolation only if it is reduced to one half of one of the constraints under which it is produced: that of the locutionary level of language.

The translation of literature, then, must be heavily regulated because it is potentially—and often actually—subversive, precisely because it offers a cover for the translator to go against the dominant constraints of his or her time, not in his or her own name which, in most cases, would not happen to be all that well known anyway, but rather in the name of, and relying on the authority of a writer who is considered great enough in another literature so as not to be ignored in one's own, at least not if one wants to safeguard that literature against provincialism and other forms of atrophy. It goes without saying that all this holds equally true for other forms of rewriting; translation only makes it all so much more obvious, though still not as obvious as the production of drama. But then translations are more difficult to ferret out and destroy than drama. It is not too difficult to close down theatres, or to censor plays, or to forbid specific performances of specific plays. It is much more difficult to destroy all potentially subversive translations.

Not all translations produced do, of course, fit the mould described here. A fair number of them tend to be produced by 'technicians' rather than 'prophets'. By technicians I mean scholars of literature who are able to make works of literature belonging to other systems available in their own systems through translations. This is a sorely needed contribution to literary studies, since in the present state of literary affairs the natural language in which a work of literature is written does not infrequently militate against that work being given wider exposure. As a result, certain systems of literature (particularly the Islamic one, in my opinion) are rather less well known than others, and generalizations in surveys and histories of literature are made on the basis of what is best known. Most generalizations about literature have, in fact, been made on the basis of a more or less unashamedly Eurocentric poetics, and, more precisely, of a certain historical phase in the evolution of that poetics.

It is clear, however, that 'literature' cannot be adequately studied if it is, in practice, restricted to the literature of Europe and the Americas, and that non-Western literary systems, so often relegated to the mysterious and therefore largely ignorable status of the 'exotic', are as vital for any understanding of literature as is the Western system on its own. Generalizations are, therefore, very often made in good faith, though just as often on the basis of the kind of ignorance that could be relatively easily remedied by translation.

It should also be clear that the translations I have in mind at this point should be seen as a heuristic tool to profit the study of literature—which does, of course, not mean that they should be forbidden to delight and please the reader as well—and not as an 'interpretive' weapon in the struggle between rival poetics inside the receiving system. The aim of this kind of translation would be to make literature produced in other systems available for description and analysis, which is why it should, ideally, be a 'descriptive' rather than an interpretive translation. In practice, of course, translations will tend to be more or less descriptive or more or less interpretive, simply because nobody is ever able to escape from the ideology and/or the poetics prevalent in the literary system of his or her own time, to which his or her translation will be seen to belong. (pp. 234–9)

REFERENCES

Baldick, Chris. (1983). *The Social Mission of English Criticism, 1848–1932*, Oxford, Clarendon.

Bennett, H. S. (1952). *English Books and Readers,* Cambridge, Cambridge UP.

Clark, P. P. Clark, T. N. 1977. 'Patrons, Publishers and Prizes: The Writer's Estate in France', in J. Ben-David & T. N. Clark (eds.), *Culture and its Creators*, Chicago, Chicago UP: 197–225.

Dubois, Jean. 1978. *L'institution de la littérature*, Brussels, Editions Labor.

Knapp, S. & Michaels, W. B. 1982. 'Against Theory', *Critical Inquiry,* viii, 4: 723–42.

Lefevere, André. 1982. 'Mother Courage's Cucumbers: Text, System and Refraction in a Theory of Literature', *Modern Language Studies*, xii, 4: 3–20.

Man, Paul de. 1979. *Allegories of Reading*, New Haven, Yale UP.

5.6 MARY SNELL-HORNBY

Mary Snell-Hornby, translation theorist, is professor of translation studies at the University of Vienna. She is the author of *Translation und Text* (1996); she collaborated with Franz Pochhacker and Klaus Kaindl on *Translation Studies: An Interdiscipline* (1994), and with a number of scholars in asssembling *Handbuch Translation* (1999). Snell-Hornby writes alternately in English and German and her work often mediates valuably between the German and English-language dimensions of the field. Her approach to translation studies is broad-based and interdisciplinary. Snell-Hornby is among those who wish to develop the discipline holistically, avoiding the kind of specialization which would compartmentalize different genres of translation; hence she treats literary translation as inherently and culturally linked to 'practical' translation. This is reflected in the excerpt below, from her book *Translation Studies*, which, significantly, is subtitled 'An integrated approach'.

From *Translation Studies: An Integrated Approach* (1988; rev. ed., Amsterdam/ Philadelphia: John Benjamins, 1995), 26–35

1.3 Categorization and text-type

The tendency to categorize is innate in man and essential to all scientific development, and to be able to categorize we need concepts. Our discussion so far has centred round concepts (such as the unstable concept of equivalence) and the categories that ensue from them. Looking back at the definitions and descriptions quoted so far in this study, we see that these too fall into distinct categories, the most striking being the *dichotomy*, or rigid polarization. In 20th century linguistics the dichotomy as a mode of categorization is associated especially with Saussure, whose distinction between form and substance in linguistic items is directly reflected in Nida's dichotomy of formal vs. dynamic equivalence and Catford's dichotomy of formal correspondence vs. textual equivalence. Another kind of categorization is the *typology*, or system of box-like compartments, as in Kade's system of equivalence types, each of these being clear-cut and sharply delimited from the others.

Both the dichotomy and the typology are fundamental to the classical theory of categorization that is part of our Western culture. In recent years however, the validity of this theory has been challenged within a number of cognitive sciences: relevant for our present purpose is the work done in psychology by Eleanor Rosch and its development within linguistics by George Lakoff.[1]

1.3.1 Prototype and gestalt

In his study *Categories and Cognitive Models* (1982), Lakoff presents a brief survey of the classical theory of categorization: this entails *clear boundaries* between categories without borderline cases or fuzziness of any kind, *shared properties* as conditions for category membership (the so-called 'checklist theory'), *uniformity* among all members of the category, *inflexibility* of category boundaries, *internal definition*, strictly *objective conditions* for category membership, and the reductionist principle of ultimate *primitives* (Lakoff 1982: 15).

[. . .]

On the basis of experiments, Eleanor Rosch set out to test the classical theory of categorization as expounded in objectivist psychology, where *experiential aspects* (perception, mental imagery, bodily experiences, desires and expectations, social experiences, understanding one thing in terms of another) were ruled out completely. Rosch's experiments disproved the classical theory on all counts and led to her own theory of natural categorization (1973), according to which human beings categorize in the form of *prototypes*—in other words, the natural category has a focus or 'hard core' and fades off at the edges. [. . .]

The notion of the 'blurred edge' as applied to concepts is of course by no means new: this phrase was used by Wittgenstein in his *Philosophical Investigations* of 1953. Another of Wittgenstein's celebrated notions, that of 'family resemblances,' is also confirmed by Rosch's experiments, where it is used in the sense of 'perceived similarities between representative and nonrepresentative members' of the category concerned (Lakoff 1982: 16). Thus category membership is not dependent on necessary and fixed conditions, as in the classical theory, but rather on 'clusters of attributes that characterize the most representative members' (Lakoff 1982: 16).

A second important conclusion Rosch made in her experiments is derived from what she calls *basic level results*, her basic categories being situated between superordinate and subordinate. Thus *chair* represents the basic level between the superordinate *furniture* and the subordinate *rocking-chair*. The use of such taxonomies is of course nothing new in linguistic theory (and was essential to structural semantics—cf. Snell-Hornby 1983), but of interest for the present study are Rosch's conclusions and the research they led to. Rosch contends that the basic categories (such as *chair*) do not depend on the objects themselves, but on the way people interact with them, perceive and use them. Hence while a chair is imagined as something to sit on, there is no such interactional image connected with the more abstract superordinate category *furniture*. Rosch's notion of the basic level category stimulated research in ethnobiology by Brent Berlin (Berlin et al. 1974), who concludes that this 'folk-generic level' (in his terminology) is in several respects psychologically basic: at that level languages have simple names, categories have greater cultural significance and things are more easily remembered, but above all—and for our purposes this is the essential point:

> At that level, things are perceived *holistically, as a single gestalt*, while for identification at a lower level, specific details have to be picked out. (Lakoff 1982: 20, emphasis added)

It is the holistic principle of the *gestalt* that will be essential in our integrated approach to translation, which for far too long was thought to be merely a matter of isolatable words. Like the notion of 'blurred edges,' the gestalt-concept links up with the European tradition: the main principle of the school of Gestalt psychology, itself based on experimental studies carried out by Max Wertheimer, Wolfgang Köhler and Kurt Kofka (Wertheimer 1912), is that the whole is more than the mere sum of its parts, and an analysis of the parts cannot provide an understanding of the whole. This principle—a foregone conclusion in literary studies—was until very recently totally ignored by philologists and linguists: the study of language, and with it the 'scientific,' linguistically oriented translation theory, remained atomistic, fragmented and out of touch with language in its concrete realization. The change took place in the 1970s, mainly—as in the case of the prototype and gestalt—via other disciplines such as sociology (sociolinguistics), moral philosophy (the speech act theory of Austin and Searle), ethnology and psychology, and with the development of text-linguistics a more holistic approach to language was made possible.[2] In America, Berlin's ethnobiological notion of the gestalt was taken up and developed as a linguistic concept by Lakoff in his study 'Linguistic Gestalts' (1977). At the same time the Finnish linguist Raimo Anttila published an essay drawing on the same principles of Gestalt psychology with the title 'Dynamic fields and linguistic structure: A proposal for a Gestalt linguistics' (1977), and in Germany a book was published by Stephan Langhoff with the title *Gestaltlinguistik* (1980). Even if the term *Gestalt linguistics* is used in only a few individual studies, the holistic principle itself has become increasingly dominant in the study of language over the last few years, and in recent translation theory it is of primary importance.

1.3.2 Text-typologies and the prototypology

The conclusion drawn by Lakoff in *Categories and Cognitive Models* is that the theory of natural categorization 'requires not only a very different theory of categories, but a different world-view to go with it' (1982: 22). Central to this new theory are *experiential* aspects: mental imagery, memory, social functions, human intentions, gestalt perception—'all matters that have to do with human interaction with and functioning in the world, rather than with objective properties of the world' (Lakoff 1982: 22).

Language as part of the world: this notion is central to the integrated approach adopted in the present study, and at the same time it represents the point of departure from the 'world-view' that dominated the linguistically oriented translation theory.

As we have already seen, the main categorization-types governing translation theory have been the dichotomy and the typology, the latter being a system of box-like compartments as in Kade's equivalence-types. The use of the typology in translation theory extends beyond the concept of equivalence however: it was of basic importance as a tool for categorizing texts.

In her pioneering study *Möglichkeiten und Grenzen der Übersetzungskritik* (1971) Katharina Reiss aims at deriving strictly objective criteria for assessing the quality of translations. Her approach is based on a translation-related text-typology (1971: 31 ff.), whereby the text-type is presented as a "literary category of translation critique" (1971: 52 f.). Reiss' typology is founded on Karl Bühler's organon-model (Bühler 1965: 28), where the three functions of language are shown to be *Darstellung* (representation), *Ausdruck* (expression) and *Appell* (appeal). From this three-fold division Reiss derives corresponding 'dimensions of language' and corresponding text-types.[3] This she represents in the following diagram:

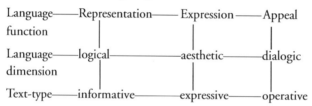

Reiss then offers criteria for translation according to the respective texttype: a metaphor in an 'expressive' text, for example, must be rendered as a metaphor in the translation, but this is not necessary for a metaphor in an 'informative' text (1971: 62). The same principle applies for idioms: the Spanish idiom 'miente más que el gobierno,' for example, would—according to Reiss—be rendered into German as 'er lügt allzuviel (he often lies)' in an 'informative' text, whereas in an 'expressive' text a better translation would be the German idiom 'er lügt wie gedruckt (he lies like mad)' (1971: 81 f.). Such prescriptive generalizations can be extremely misleading, and indeed Reiss has been severely criticized (cf. Koller 1979) for being too rigid. As Reiss herself actually indicates (1971: 32), most texts are in fact hybrid forms, multi-dimensional structures with a blend of sometimes seemingly conflicting features: Shakespeare's sonnets contain technical terminology of his day, while modern economic texts abound in lexicalized metaphor, and advertisements (which would be categorized by Reiss as strictly 'operative' (cf. Reiss 1976)) are characterized by the varying methods they use to present information. As a starting-point Bühler's model undoubtedly has great possibilities for translation theory; as a frame of reference for objective criteria Reiss' typology, as presented here, though modified in Reiss (1976), is too clear-cut for real-life translation in all its complexity. What is wrong is the use of box-like categories as a kind of prescriptive grid, creating an illusion of the scientific objectivity that was required of academic thinking at the time.

Reiss's text-typology demonstrates the shortcomings of the classical theory of categorization. In its concrete realization language cannot be reduced to a system of static and clear-cut categories. In the present study the rigid typology of the objectivist and reductionist tradition will therefore be replaced by the *prototypology*,[4] a dynamic, gestalt-like system of relationships, whereby the various headings represent an idealized, prototypical focus and the grid-system gives way to blurred edges and overlappings. Blend-forms are part of the conceptual system and not the exception. Whereas the typology aims at separation and sharp delimitation, the prototypology aims at focussing and at subtle differentiation.

1.4 An integrated approach

The ideas discussed so far will now be presented in concrete form as a basis for an integrated concept of translation studies. In the diagram [below] a system of relationships is established between basic text-types—as prototypes—and the crucial aspects of translation. On the horizontal plane the diagram represents a spectrum or cline,[5] where sharp divisions have been replaced by the notion of gradual transition, hence no demarcation lines have been drawn in. At the same time, on the vertical plane, the diagram represents a *stratificational model* which, in accordance with the gestalt-principle, proceeds from the most general level (A) at the top, downwards to the most particular level (F) at the bottom—or, in other words, from the macro- to the micro-level.

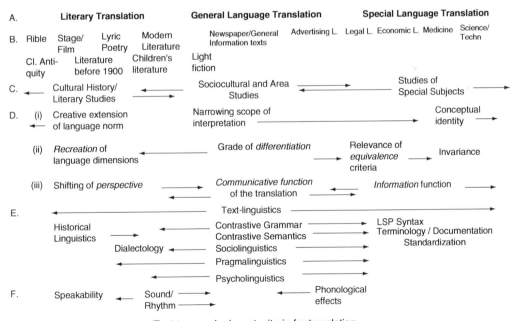

Text-type and relevant criteria for translation

Level A presents the conventional areas of translation which up to now have been kept all too separate: on the left literary translation, traditionally the province of poets and scholars and once the only area thought worthy of the theorist, and on the right special language translation, traditionally inferior and the main concern of the translation schools. 'General language translation' is still a vague concept which up to now has only been negatively defined as 'not literary' and 'not technical,'[6] but which is nonetheless implicitly the concern of the linguistically oriented *Übersetzungswissenschaft*. In this concept the historical dichotomy has been replaced by a fluid spectrum, whereby, for example, prototypically literary devices such as word-play and alliteration can be accommodated both in 'general' newspaper texts and in the language of advertising, and conversely prototypically technical terms from the language of science or culture-bound items from the 'general' area of politics or everyday living can be explained and interpreted as literary devices.

Level B presents a prototypology of the basic text-types, from the Bible to the language of modern technology, which are the main concern of the translator. While traditional theory concentrated on the items situated at the extreme left of the spectrum, the Bible, the monuments of Classical Antiquity and the great works of the European tradition, particularly Shakespeare's plays, only a few of these areas have been given detailed attention in modern theory, and even then the focus has been limited to specific aspects (for Bible translation see Nida and Taber 1969, for lyric poetry Levý 1969 and Beaugrande 1978). The special problems of children's literature and stage-translation until recently only received scant attention (cf. Verch 1976, Reiss 1982 on children's literature and Snell-Hornby 1984, Bassnett-McGuire 1985 and Schultze 1986 on the translation of drama). At the other end of the scale are the special language text-types, the main fare of the modern professional translator; in the training institutes the major areas are law, economics, medicine, science and technology, and these are now being dealt with intensively in academic studies (cf. Schmitt 1986; Stellbrink 1984a and 1985; Gerzymisch-Arbogast 1986 and 1987). On the diagram limited space permitted only a narrow selection of basic text-types; there are of course many others, along with numerous blend forms.

Level C shows the non-linguistic disciplines—or areas of so-called 'extralinguistic reality'—which are inseparably bound up with translation. The terms are placed at the point of the cline where they are thought to apply most, but again, we are concerned here with the dynamic concept of focus and not with grid-like compartments involving rigid classification; the arrows indicate the range of application or, where they overlap, interaction. Essential for special language translation, for example, is specialized factual knowledge of the subject concerned, while literary translation presupposes a background in literary studies and cultural history. A necessary precondition for all translation is knowledge of the sociocultural background, both of the source culture and the target culture concerned.

Level D names important aspects and criteria governing the translation process itself, an extremely complex area which at this point is dealt with only briefly, as most of them form the main topic of chapters to follow. D(i) focusses on the source text: crucial here is the *understanding* of the text, which does not simply involve familiarity with words and structures, but presupposes the ability to penetrate the sense of the text, both as a complex multidimensional whole and at the same time in its relationship to the cultural background. With certain special language texts involving standardized concepts (particularly in science and technology) the scope of interpretation is narrowed down considerably. D(ii) names focal criteria for the envisaged translation: the notion of invariance can only apply in cases of conceptual identity (standardized terminology), while the concept of equivalence is here still considered to be of some relevance for certain types of special language translation where the focus is on isolatable lexical items. Basically however, our conception of translation supports the more dynamic approach pioneered by Hönig and Kußmaul (1982), whose dominant criterion is the *communicative function* of the target text (the stage indicated in D(iii)), which governs what they call the 'notwendigen Grad der Differenzierung' (the necessary degree of precision) (see Hönig and Kußmaul 1982: 58 ff.). With texts involving the *creative extension* of the language norm—this applies mainly but not exclusively to literary texts—translation involves *recreating* language *dimensions* and results in a shift of *perspective* in the target text.

Level E names those areas of linguistics which are relevant for translation. Of basic importance is text-linguistics in all its aspects, from the analysis of the macrostructure, thematic progression and sentence perspective (cf. Gerzymisch-Arbogast 1986) to coherence and cohesion. Older literature requires knowledge of Historical Linguistics, while special language translation presupposes familiarity with work in terminology and access to data-banks. Contrastive Linguistics, both in syntax and lexicology, has great potential for translation theory, although up to now its results in this respect have been meagre. Other disciplines of relevance for translation as an act of communication within a specific situational context would be sociolinguistics (as the study of language varieties), pragmalinguistics (in particular the speech act theory), and psycholinguistics (as regards the interdependence of language, experience and thought). And finally, the lowest level F names phonological aspects of specific relevance for certain areas of translation, as for example, speakability in stage translation, alliteration and rhythm in advertising language.

With this prototypological framework the foundations have been laid for our conception of translation studies as an integrated and independent discipline that covers all kind of translation, from literary to technical. In this view, translation draws on many disciplines, but is not equal to the sum total of their overlapping areas and is not dependent on any one of them. As a discipline in its own right, translation studies needs to develop its own methods based, not on outside models and conventions from other disciplines, but on the complexities of translation. The present study is intended as a step in that direction.

At this stage I should like to summarize, in four briefly worded hypotheses, the results of what has been established so far:

(1) Translation studies should not be considered a mere offshoot of another discipline or sub-discipline (whether Applied Linguistics or Comparative Literature): both the translator and the translation theorist are rather concerned with a world *between* disciplines, languages and cultures.

(2) Whereas linguistics has gradually widened its field of interest from the micro- to the macro-level, translation studies, which is concerned essentially with texts against their situational and cultural background, should adopt the reverse perspective: as maintained by the gestalt psychologists, an analysis of parts cannot provide an understanding of the whole, which must be analyzed from 'the top down'.

(3) Translation studies has been hampered by classical modes of categorization, which operate with rigid dividing-lines, binary opposites, antitheses and dichotomies. Frequently these are mere academic constructs which paralyze the finer differentiation required in all aspects of translation studies. In our approach the typology is replaced by the prototypology, admitting blends and blurred edges, and the dichotomy gives way to the concept of a spectrum or cline against which phenomena are situated and focussed.

(4) While the classic approach to the study of language and translation has been to isolate phenomena (mainly words) and study them in depth, translation studies is essentially concerned with a web of relationships, the importance of individual items being decided by their relevance in the larger context of text, situation and culture.

NOTES

1. See especially Lakoff 1977 and 1982; also Lakoff and Johnson 1980.
2. In practice, only those branches of text-linguistics are relevant for translation which concentrate on concrete texts as against abstract models (cf. Beaugrande and Dressler 1981 and Stolze 1982: 55 ff.). In this study the term *text-linguistics* is used in the concrete sense in its relevance for translation.
3. In this study the term *dimension* is extended beyond the threefold division proposed by Reiss. The English term *text-type* as used here includes German *Texttyp* (as used by Reiss) and *Textsorte* (as in diagram on p. 447).
4. The term *Prototypologie* goes back to Neubert (Brussels 1984, personal communication), who applies the concept of the prototype to lexicography in Neubert 1986a.
5. This conception of the *cline* as well as that of the *stratificational model* go back to the British linguist M. A. K. Halliday (see Halliday 1976).
6. The German term *Gemeinsprache* is matched in English by both *general language* (as against technical language) and *ordinary language* (as against literary language).

REFERENCES

Anttila, Raimo. 1977. 'Dynamic fields and linguistic structure: A proposal for a Gestalt linguistics,' in: *Sprache* 23, 1–10.

Bassnett-McGuire, Susan. 1985. 'Ways Through the Labyrinth: Strategies and Methods for Translating Theatre Texts,' in: T. Hermans (ed.), *The Manipulation of Literature*. London: Crooms Helm, 87–102.

Beaugrande, Robert de. 1978. *Factors in a Theory of Poetic Translating*, Assen: Van Gorcum.

Berlin, Brent, Dennis E. Breedlove and Peter H. Raaven. 1974. *Principles of Tzeltal Plant Classification*, New York: Academic Press.

Bühler, Karl. 1965. *Sprachtheorie*, Stuttgart: Fischer.

Gerzymisch-Arbogast, Heidrun. 1986. 'Zur Relevanz der Thema-Rhema-Gliederung für den Übersetzungsprozeß,' in: M. Snell-Hornby (ed.), *Übersetzungswissenschaft—Eine Neuorientierung*, Tübingen: Francke, 160–183.

Gerzymisch-Arbogast, Heidrun. 1987. *Zur Thema-Rhema-Gliederung in amerikanischen Wirtschaftstexten. Eine exemplarische Analyse*, Tübingen: Narr.

Halliday, M. A. K. 1976. *System and Function in Language. Selected Papers*, ed. G. R. Kress, Cambridge: Cambridge University Press.

Hönig, Hans G. and Paul Kußmaul. 1982. *Strategie der Übersetzung. Ein Lehr- und Arbeitsbuch*, Tübingen: Narr.

Koller, Werner. 1979. *Einführung in die Übersetzungswissenschaft*, Heidelberg: Quelle & Meyer.

Lakoff, George. 1977. 'Linguistic Gestalts,' in: *Proceedings of the Thirteenth Regional Meeting of the Chicago Linguistic Society*, Chicago, 236–287.

Lakoff, George. 1982. *Categories and Cognitive Models*. Trier: LAUT.

Lakoff, George and Mark Johnson. 1980. *Metaphors We Live By*, Chicago: University of Chicago Press.

Langhoff, Stephan. 1980. *Gestaltlinguistik. Eine ganzheitliche Beschreibung syntaktisch-semantischer Sprachfunktionen am Beispiel modaler Infinitivkonstruktionen des Deutschen und Englischen*, Frankfurt: Lang.

Levý, Jiří. 1969. *Die literarische Übersetzung. Theorie einer Kunstgattung*, transl. Walter Schamschula, Frankfurt: Athenäum.

Neubert 1986a. 'Dichtung und Wahrheit des zweisprachigen Wörterbuchs,' in: *Sitzungsberichte der Sächsischen Akademie der Wissenschaften zu Leipzig*, Vol. 126, 4, 1–23.

Nida, Eugene A. and Charles R. Taber. 1969. *The Theory and Practice of Translation*, Leiden: Brill.

Reiss, Katharina. 1971. *Möglichkeiten und Grenzen der Übersetzungskritik. Kategorien und Kriterien für eine sachgerechte Beurteilung von Übersetzungen*, München: Hueber.

Reiss, Katharina. 1976. *Texttyp und Übersetzungsmethode. Der operative Text*, Kronberg: Scriptor.

Reiss, Katharina. 1982. 'Zur Übersetzung von Kinder- und Jugendbüchern. Theorie und Praxis,' in: *Lebende Sprachen*, 1, 7–13.

Rosch, Eleanor. 1973. 'Natural categories,' in: *Cognitive Psychology* 4, 328–350.

Schmitt, Peter A. 1986. 'Die 'Eindeutigkeit' von Fachtexten: Bemerkungen zu einer Fiktion,' in: M. Snell-Hornby (ed.), *Übersetzungswissenschaft—Eine Neuorientierung*, Tübingen: Francke, 252–282.

Schultze, Brigitte. 1986. 'Theorie der Dramenübersetzung—1960 bis heute. Ein Bericht zur Forschungslage,' unpubl. ms.

Snell-Hornby, Mary. 1983. *Verb-descriptivity in German and English. A contrastive study in semantic fields*, Heidelberg: Winter.

Snell-Hornby, Mary. 1984. 'Sprechbare Sprache—Spielbarer Text. Zur Problematik der Bühnenübersetzung,' in: R. Watts and U. Weidmann (eds.), *Modes of Interpretation. Essays Presented to Ernst Leisi*, Tübingen: Narr, 101–116.

Stellbrink, Hans-Jürgen. 1984a. 'Die Aufgaben eines Fremdsprachendienstes beim Abschluß von fremsprachigen Verträgen,' Guest Lecture Hildesheim 12.11. 1984, unpubl. ms.

Stellbrink, Hans-Jürgen. 1985. 'Die Tätigkeit des Dolmetschers und Übersetzers in der Industrie: Meistens nicht wie im Lehrbuch,' Guest Lecture Heidelberg 1.2. 1985, unpubl. ms.

Verch, Maria. 1976. 'Zum Problem englisch-deutscher Übersetzungen von Jugendliteratur,' in: *Revue d'Allemagne* VIII, 3, 466–473.

Wertheimer, Max. 1912/1959. *Productive Thinking*, Chicago: Chicago University Press.

5.7 ETHNOPOETICS: TRANSLATION OF THE ORAL AND OF ORAL PERFORMANCE—DENNIS TEDLOCK AND JEROME ROTHENBERG

Ethnopoetics, a movement originating in the 1950s and 1960s, which now has a substantial academic presence in the USA, combines anthropology/ethnography/linguistics and poetry in an attempt to confront the problem not just of representing or preserving the vanishing oral literary legacies of the world, but also of connecting them with living literature. It seems part of a broader impulse, harking back to nineteenth-century Romanticism, with its interest in the folk ethos, as well as to avant-garde experiments and Modernist, especially Dadaist, interest in 'primitivism' and performance. Ethnopoetics, however, is not to be dismissed as mere exhibitionism. It challenges the traditional emphasis on semantics, taking its lead from the fieldwork of anthropologists. For the poets who were directly involved in this movement, and others indirectly affected, ethnopoetics represented a way out of, or at least through, the absorption in self, and in the written as against the oral. Post-colonial aspirations are evident in Jerome Rothenberg's remark that 'a poetics without a concurrent ethnopoetics is stunted, partial, therefore faulty in a time like ours that can only save itself by learning to confront its multiple identities and definitions—its contradictions, therefore, & its problematics'[1]. The connections between ethnopoetics and ecology are here clearly relevant.

The origin and theoretical basis of the ethnopoetics movement is addressed below by the anthropologist Dennis Tedlock and the poet Jerome Rothenberg, who were its principal originators. This is followed by accounts of ethnopoetics in action.

Dennis Tedlock is Professor of Anthropology at the State University of New York/Buffalo; his fields of research include oral performances of Mongol shamans, Zuñi verbal arts, Yoruba spoken and written verbal arts. Among his books are: *The Human Design: 2000 Years of Mayan Literature; Breath on the Mirror: Mythic Voices and Visions of the Living Maya*, (1997); *The Dialogic Emergence of Culture* (1995); and *Teachings from the American Earth: Indian Religion and Philosophy* (1992). Tedlock has also edited a number of periodicals, including the *American Anthropologist* and *Alcheringa/Ethnopoetics*, 'A First Magazine of the World's Tribal Poetries', co-founded in 1970 and co-edited with Jerome Rothenberg (1970–6), editor-in-chief (1977–80).

---

[1] In conversation with Gavin Selerie, *The Riverside Interviews*, iv, ed. G. Selerie (London: Binnacle Press, 1984), 58.

From a State University of New York/Buffalo course description by Dennis Tedlock

Ethnopoetics is a decentred poetics, an attempt to hear and read the poetries of distant others, outside the Western tradition as we know it now. [. . .]

Ethnopoetics does not merely contrast the poetics of 'ethnics' with just plain poetics, but implies that any poetics is always an ethnopoetics. [. . .]

Practitioners of ethnopoetics treat the relationship between performances and texts as a field for experimentation. [. . .] An ethnopoetic score not only takes account of the words but silences, changes in loudness and tone of voice, the production of sound effects, and the use of gestures and props. [. . .]

Jerome Rothenberg (b. 1931) is an American poet, editor, and translator. His concern for the relationship between 'primitive' and modern poetry led in 1968 to the publication of *Technicians of the Sacred*. He ventured further into this field, collaborating with Seneca songmen in the translation of a series of Navajo horse-blessing songs. Rothenberg called his approach 'total translation', attempting to account for every element in the original language, including the so-called 'meaningless' vocables, word distortions, and redundancies. This project led to another anthology, *Shaking the Pumpkin: Traditional Poetry of the Indian North Americas* (1972). With Dennis Tedlock (see above), Rothenberg co-edited *Alcheringa*; with Diane Rothenberg he also edited *Symposium of the Whole: A Range of Discourse Toward An Ethnopoetics* (1983). Another and related aspect of his work is the exploration of his own ancestral themes, specifically the world of Jewish Poland.

From 'Ethnopoetics at the Millennium', a talk for the Modern Language Association of America (29 December 1994) by Jerome Rothenberg, available at <http://epc.buffalo.edu/authors/rothenberg/ethnopoetics.html> (accessed 7 May 2004)

[. . .] For me such an ethnopoetics—which looks away from the modern & experimental, to focus on ancient & autochthonous cultures (often under threat of mass extinction or long since blown away)—is the product (as study & praxis) of our most dedicated & outrageous modernism, even surviving (under fire) into that *post*modernism taken as the older movement's *early* & forever problematic offspring. *Early*, I say, remembering that it was Tristan Tzara [. . .], who in his Weimar manifesto-lecture of 1922 declared: 'You are mistaken if you take Dada for a modern school, or as a reaction against the schools of today. . . . Dada is not at all modern. It is more in the nature of an almost Buddhist religion of indifference.' [. . .]

The decade that followed [after the First World War] also saw a revival of the concern that we later came to call ecological, with an environment—local & global—under increasing developmental pressure, & the view—emerging from that concern—that just those cultures that were repositories of the old poetries were the models thereby for a more sane relation to the natural world & its other-than-human as well as its human inhabitants. Gradually this would open up to a concern & need for what sacred language in traditional bioregional cultures [. . .]

It was while preparing my second ethnopoetic gathering, *Shaking the Pumpkin*, that I received a packet from Dennis Tedlock including his translation—I would later call it his *total* translation—of a Zuñi Indian [oral] narrative called *The Boy & the Deer*. What it had to say about the nature of talking & story-telling as those related to poetry (I mean *our* poetry as well as *theirs*) was one of the most electrifying experiences in my life as a poet. It also led quickly to our founding of *Alcheringa* as an ongoing venue (we hoped) for a new ethnopoetics: a convergence of poets & scholars toward a re-imagining of poetry based on its actual development and presence in the life of many different peoples & cultures.

From 'On the Translation of Style in Oral Narrative', by Dennis Tedlock, *Journal of American Folklore*, 84 331–4 (1971), 114–33

[. . .] A discriminating reader, hoping to find collections of American Indian narratives which are at one and the same time thoroughly authentic and respectable as literature, is likely to be disappointed. When he [sic] explores the narratives published before the field methods of Franz Boas' were widely employed, he may decide that their style seems more Victorian than Indian. [. . .]

Wishing for greater authenticity, our reader may turn at last to the vast scholarly collections produced by Boasian anthropologists. But he will soon wonder whether the original style of these narratives was as choppy and clumsy as that of most English translations. If he takes these translations to represent, as Boas claimed, 'faithful rendering of the native tales', and if he remains disappointed with popularizations, he may end by agreeing with La Farge[2] who said, 'the literary value of a great deal of primitive literature, whether myths or tales, is nil. That of much of the rest is apparent, in the raw form, only to connoisseurs, while those who undertake to retell some of it often achieve only emasculation.'

Unless it is true that many of the oral narratives of non-Western peoples have little or no literary value, and that what value they do have is untranslatable, then something has gone wrong along the way from the oral performance to the printed page. [. . .]

The Zuñi narratives collected by Frank Hamilton Cushing[3] in the 1880s have always attracted more attention than others. [. . .]

The most distressing of all Cushing's inventions are his moralistic passages. [. . .] The didactic content of Zuñi tales is usually either implicit or addressed by one tale character to another, and it is never addressed by the narrator directly to his audience. But Cushing begins one tale this way: 'Listen, ye young ones and youths, and from what I say draw inference. For behold! The youth of our nation in these recent generations have become less sturdy than of old; else what I relate had not happened.' [. . .]

In some cases the neglect of translation is doubtless related to a belief that style, or at least the better part of it, is simply untranslatable. [. . .] If [this] view is combined with the view that content survives even bad translation then there is no room at all for an art of translation. It may be that no one scholar has ever held both these views simultaneously in their pure form, but many scholars of the past four generations might as well have done so. [. . .]

While it may be that past translations of Zuñi narratives have suffered somewhat from neglect of the "linguistic" features of style discussed above, they have suffered much more from neglect of 'oral' or 'paralinguistic' features such as voice quality (tone of voice), loudness, and pausing. Boas wrote long ago that 'the form of modern prose is largely determined by the fact that it is read, not spoken, while primitive prose is based on the art of oral delivery and is therefore, more closely related to modern oratory than to the printed literary style.' [. . .]

Loudness and voice quality are obviously worth noting, but it seems to me that pausing is foremost among the paralinguistic devices that give shape to Zuñi narrative and distinguish it from written prose, and the same could probably be said of many other oral narrative traditions. [. . .]

The treatment of oral narrative as dramatic poetry has a number of analytical advantages. Some of the features or oral narrative which have been branded 'primitive,' on the basis of comparisons with written prose fiction, can now be understood as 'poetic' instead. It has been said for example, that while most of our own prose narrative is highly 'realistic', primitive narrative is full of fantasy: a stone moves about like an animal, an animal speaks like a man, a man jumps through a hoop and becomes a coyote. Yet when we encounter gross and unexplained distortions of reality in Yeats, for example, we are apt to call them not 'primitive' but 'dream-like' or 'mystical' and to regard them as highly poetic. [. . .]

Another distinguishing feature of 'primitive' narrative, according to Boas and many others, is repetition, ranging from the level of words or phrases to that of whole episodes. [. . .] But the same device is common in epic poetry [. . .]. Unless we want to call epic poetry 'primitive', this particular kind of repetition must be properly understood as 'oral' and not 'primitive,' and the same thing goes for the repeated use of stock formulas in both epic poetry (epithets, for example) and Zuñi narrative [. . .]

The treatment of oral narrative as dramatic poetry, then, clearly promises many analytical rewards. It should also be obvious that there are immediate esthetic rewards. The apparent lack of literary value in many past translations is not a reflection but a distortion of the originals, caused by the dictation process, an emphasis on content, a pervasive deafness to oral qualities, and a fixed notion of the boundary between poetry and prose.

NOTES

1. Franz Boas (1858–1942), German born and educated anthropologist, later Professor at Columbia University, established a new concept of culture and race, in which everything was important to the study of culture, so that collecting all manner of date was essential. He believed in historical particularism, insisting that the differences between peoples were the result of historical, social and geographic conditions and all populations had complete and equally developed cultures. His views thus ran counter to earlier evolutionist ones.
2. Oliver La Farge (1901–63), American writer and anthropologist, who conducted archaeological expeditions to Arizona and ethnological ones to Guatemala and Mexico. He also wrote a novel of Navajo life for which he was awarded the 1930 Pulitzer Prize.
3. Cushing's translation may be found in Frank Hamilton Cushing, 'Zuñi Fetiches,' *Annual Report of the Bureau of American Ethnology*, 2 (1883). Frank Hamilton Cushing (1857–1900), pioneer ethnologist whose work at Zuñi Pueblo made him one of the most important white observers of Native American culture. In his methods and thinking, he was a forerunner of anthropologists today. Cushing lived among the Zuñi, being one of the first professional anthropologists to live with the people he was studying, not adopting the typical stance of detached and superior observer. His analysis of Zuñi life took him several steps along the path of cultural relativism which was later to become critical to the development of anthropology as a discipline.

From 'Total Translation: An Experiment in the Translation of American Indian Poetry', from Jerome Rothenberg, *Pre-Faces & Other Writing* (1981); repr. in *Writing through Translations and Variations* (Middletown, Conn.: Wesleyan University Press, 2004).

A final recorded version appeared nearly ten years after the essay as *6 Horse Songs for 4 Voices* (New Wilderness Audiographics, 1978), available at <http://www.ubu.com/sound/> along with a number of other performance works.]

The big question, which I was immediately aware of with both poetries [Seneca and Navago], was if & how to handle those elements in the original works that weren't translatable literally. As with most Indian poetry, the voice carried many sounds that weren't, strictly speaking, 'words.' These tended to disappear or be attenuated in translation, as if they weren't really there. [. . .]

Here's an immediate example of what I mean. In the first of Frank Mitchell's seventeen [Navago] Horse Songs, the opening line comes out as follows in McAllester's transcription:

dzo—wowode sileye shi, dza—na desileye shiyi dzanadi sileye shiya'e

but the same segment given 'as spoken' reads:

dz____di silá shi dz____di silá shi dz____di silá shi

which translates as 'over-here it-is-there-(&) mine' repeated three times. So does the line as sung if all you're accounting for is the meaning. In other words, translate only for meaning & you get the three-fold repetition of an unchanging single statement; but in the Navajo each time it's delivered there's a sharp departure from the spoken form: thus three distinct sound-events, not one-in-triplicate!

Another thing I try not to overlook is that the singers & I, while separated in Seneca, are joined in English. That they have to translate for me is a problem at first, but the problem suggests its own solution. Since they're bilingual, sometimes beautifully so, why not work from that instead of trying to get around it? [...]

(nana na) Sun—(Yeye ye) Standing-within (neye ye) Boy

(Heye ye) truly his horses

('Eye ye) abalone horses

('Eye ye) made of sunrays

(Neye ye) their bridles

(Gowo wo) coming on my right side

(Jeye yeye) coming into my hand (yeye neyowo 'ei).

Now this, which even so doesn't show the additional word distortions that turn up in the singing, might be brought closer to English word order & translated for meaning alone as something like

Boy who stands inside the Sun

with your horses that are

abalone horses

bridles

made of sunrays

rising on my right side

coming to my hand

etc.

Translation is carry-over. It is a means of delivery & of bringing to life. It begins with a forced change of language, but a change too that opens up the possibility of greater understanding. Everything in these song-poems is finally translatable: words, sounds, voice, melody, gesture, event, etc., in the reconstitution of a unity that would be shattered by approaching each element in isolation. A full & total experience begins it, which only a total translation can fully bring across.

5.8 LOUIS AND CELIA ZUKOFSKY

The son of Russian orthodox Jewish immigrants, his native language Yiddish, Louis Zukofsky (1904–78) was the founder of the Objectivist movement in poetry in 1931, along with with George and Mary Oppen of the Objectivist Press. Working as a teacher, mostly at the Polytechnic Institute of Brooklyn, Zukofsky drew on many sources, including the avant-garde modernist work of Ezra Pound, W. C. Williams, and Wallace Stevens; his own major work, the epic poem '*A* is perhaps 'the most hermetic poem in English' (Hugh Kenner). With his wife, the composer Celia Thaew, Zukofsky translated the Latin poetry of Catullus musically, trying, as he put it, 'to breathe with' the source text (see below). The translators retain the rhythm and the actual number of syllables of the original, a 'never-never land of phonetic aping', according to Burton Raffel (*Arion*, 1969). Even Guy Davenport, an admirer of Zukofsky's work, including his translations, regarded the translation, in this case from *The Book of Job*, as 'a feat so astounding as to seem mad' (*Contemporary Authors*, 1994).

André Lefevere (*Translating Poetry: Seven Strategies and a Blueprint* (Assen: Van Gorcum, 1975) describes the Zukofskys' approach as 'phonemic', quoting Zukofsky's preface: 'This translation of Catullus follows the sound, rhythm and syntax of his Latin—tries, as is said, to breathe the "literal" meaning with him.' In other words, the translators here confront directly what may be regarded as the impossibility of achieving identity of sound and at the same time some degree of semantic fidelity. They attempt to reproduce the sound or some semblance of it, to the exclusion of all except a (marginally) defendable modicum of sense. Lefevere analyses one of the results of this procedure and shows how far the translator is driven from the source text, even if each transgression or straying can, as suggested above, be glossed. Nevertheless, as he also points out, 'the phonemic translator can, occasionally, achieve satisfactory results without having to exploit the more obvious outward similarities of words [...]'. And, even if, in general, the cost may be said to be catastrophic, this ultra-radical procedure, putting the target language under extreme pressure, does at the very least oblige the translator to dig deep into the target language, as well as to listen with the greatest attention to the sound-structure of the original, abstractly considered. Not surprisingly, the translated text is bound to mix registers, however ingeniously, and will often resort to archaisms and other anachronistic usages, although one might do well to remember that, for instance, a poet like Thomas Hardy also resuscitates archaic or dialect words, and this is quite characteristic of the work of modernist writers, notably of James Joyce. This exercise or experiment, while conclusively, most would think, demonstrating the impossibility or even absurdity of the enterprise, and while being productive only of a sort of hybrid, 'testifying', as Lefevere remarks, 'at best to the translator's linguistic virtuosity and inventiveness', may also sensitize the translator, if not his/her reader, to the source text's musical structure, which is so often neglected or even ignored.

By way of illustration, what follows is a very short poem by Caius Valerius Catullus, followed by Celia Zukofsky's literal version, a 'literate' version from the Loeb Library edition, and finally Zukofsky's 'phonemic' version.

Catullus 112

Latin original

Multos home es, Naso neque tecum multus homost qui
descendit: Naso, multus es et pathicus

literal translation (by Celia Zukofsky)

Much a man you are, Naso, and that you much a man it is who
comes down: Naso, much you are and pathetic/lascivious.

Loeb Classical Library (used by Zukofsky)

You are many men's man, Naso, but many men
go down town with you: Naso, you are many
men's man and minion.

Louis Zukofsky's version in Catullus (Cape Golliard, 1969)

Mool 'tis homos' Naso, 'n' queer take 'im mool 'tis ho most he
descended: Naso, mool 'tis is it pathic, cuss.

5.9 TRANSLATION OF VERSE FORM

Translation of verse form is a much and sometimes hotly disputed topic. Inevitably, the question is touched upon in a number of entries in this volume. Many translators believed that, with the advent of so-called free verse, attempts to preserve verse form in translation were rendered obsolete. It was pointed out, quite correctly, that, for instance, the Classical hexameter had no proper equivalent in English, being based on a syllable count, whereas English poetry was accentual, or at least, accentual-syllabic. If syllables were counted, the iambic measure tended, in any case, to assert itself. Since iambic pentameters (rhymed couplets or unrhymed blank-verse) were so much more flexible, a clear advance on the monotonous fourteener, it was taken as a functional equivalent of the hexameter (or, for that matter, the alexandrine) permitting greater semantic accuracy.

Since the earlier part of the twentieth century, the debate has started up again, with a vengeance. The excerpts below, centre around the late Nobel laureate, poet, and essayist (in Russian and English) Joseph Brodsky (1940–96). Brodsky is heir to a Russian tradition of mimetic verse translation, which dismisses any translation not imitative of the original's form, even when mimesis is achieved—inevitably one might think—at the cost of semantic accuracy. As against this, of course, there were those (see Sect. 4.13, above, on Vladimir Nabokov and Sect. 5.10, below, on A. K. Ramanujan), who insisted on almost literal transmission of the source text. Introducing his own translation of Pushkin's *Eugene Onegin* (1955), Nabokov is unequivocal: 'The person who desires to turn a literary masterpiece into another language has only one duty to perform, and this is to reproduce with absolute exactitude the whole text, and nothing but the text.' Form should be sacrificed without any qualms. Nabokov could not have been more opposed to the notion advanced by those who believed (like Denham; see Sect. 2.10, above) that only 'poesie could open poesie', or, more recently Robert Lowell (see Sect. 4.10, above) who in his introduction to *Imitations* (1962) likens strict metrical translators to 'taxidermists'.

The late James S Holmes (see Sect. 5.3, above), characteristically tried to take some of the heat out of the debate by describing the options non-prescriptively. As a verse translator himself, Holmes particularly in his 'Jacob Lowland' alias, is identified with free translation, imitation, even with what might be termed parody. In 'Forms of Verse Translation and the Translation of Verse Form' (in *Translated! Papers on literary Translation and Translation Studies* (Amsterdam: Rodopi, 1988, 23–33), he begins by defining the translation of a poem as belonging to a spectrum or fan of 'meta-literature' around the poem, as do critical commentary, criticism in the source language, critical essays in another language, and various types of translation which accumulate around primary work. However, verse translation is also fundamentally different 'in the very basic fact that it makes use of verse as its medium, and hence manifestly aspires to be a poem in its own right, about which a new fan of meta-literature can take shape'. A major problem is that of 'choosing the most appropriate form of verse in which to cast the metapoem'.

There appear to be four basic approaches, two 'form-derivative', two 'content-derivative'. (1) 'The first traditional approach is that usually described as retaining the form of the original. [...] The translator making use of [what might be called] mimetic form looks squarely at the original poem when making his choice of verse form, to the exclusion of all other considerations.' (2) 'A second school of translators has traditionally looked [...] to the function of its form within its poetic tradition, then sought a form that filled a parallel function with the poetic tradition of the target language [...] The principal underlying this approach is that of "analogical form" [...]' (3) '[M]any translators have turned away from form-derivative form [...], resorting to a verse form which is basically 'content-derivative', and might be called 'organic form'. The translator [...] starts from the semantic material, allowing it to take on its own unique poetic shape as the translation develops.' (4) 'This form does not derive from the original poem at all, and might therefore be classified as "deviant form" or "extraneous form" [...] in no way implicit in either the form or the content of the original.' [...]

'The effect of the analogical form is to bring the original poem within the native tradition, to "naturalize" it [...] [I]t follows that the analogical form is the choice to be expected in a period that is inturned and exclusive, believing that its own norms provide a valid touchstone by which to test the literature of other places and other times.' The mimetic form, on the other hand, 'tends to have the effect of re-emphasizing, by its strangeness, the strangeness which for the target-language reader is inherent in the semantic message of the original poem. Rather than interpreting the original in terms of the native tradition; the mimetic metapoem requires the reader to stretch the limits of his literary sensibility [...] It follows that the mimetic form tends to come to the fore among translators in a period when genre concepts are weak, literary norms are being called into question, and the target culture as a whole stands open to outside impulses.' The organic form of the metapoem 'is a corollary of an organic and monistic approach to poetry as a whole: since form and content are inseparable [...], it is impossible to find any prede-termined extrinsic form into which a poem can be poured in translation, and the only solution is to allow a new intrinsic form to develop from the inward workings of the text itself. As fundamentally pessimistic regarding the possibilities of cross-cultural transference as the mimetic approach is fundamentally optimistic, the organic approach has naturally come to the fore in the twentieth century.' 'There remains the extraneous form, which on closer examination is perhaps in some cases not so extraneous after all, but an older collateral of the organic form [...].'

Holmes concludes by stressing that these different approaches cannot be regarded 'solely as period forms' and also that they do not necessarily exist only in their pure form.

From 'Beyond Consolation' by Joseph Brodsky (trans. Barry Rubin), *New York Review of Books* (7 February 1974), 13–16

[This is a review of *Hope Abandoned* by Nadezhda Mandelstam, trans. Max Hayward; *Osip Mandelstam: Selected Poems*, trans. Clarence Brown and W. S. Merwin; *Complete Poetry of Osip Emilevich Mandelstam*, trans. Burton Raffel and Alla Burago; *Osip Mandel'stam, Selected Poems*, trans. David McDuff]

> Translation is a search for an equivalent, not for a substitute. Mandelstam is a formal poet in the highest sense of the word. For him, a poem began with a sound, with a 'sonorous molded shape of form,' as he himself called it. Logically, a translator should begin his work with a search for at least a metrical equivalent to the original form. Some translated poems indicate that the translators are aware of this. But the tension involved is too high, it excessively shackles individuality [...] This happens primarily because these translators are themselves poets and their own individuality is dearest of all to them. Their conception of individuality precludes the possibility of sacrifice [...] This is especially sad in the case of Merwin, from whom more should have been expected than a translation of Mandelstam into Merwin.

[Here Brodsky offers an example, first in Russian transliteration, then in Merwin's translation, finally in a "stiff literal version", presumably by himself. He continues:]

> Mandelstam's poem is in regular iambic pentameter with regular feminine rhymes [...] Meters in verse are kinds of spiritual magnitudes for which nothing can be substituted. They cannot even be replaced by each other, and especially not by free verse. I don't mean that by rejecting meter in translation the translator commits sacrilege, but he is certainly deceiving the reader. In general, it seems to me that a specific system of coordinates must be created for poems written in free verse. This is a special genre of verbal art, like graphics in relation to painting. It is a genre with its own aesthetics. To apply to poems written in free verse the critical terminology that is applied to metrical poetry is to mislead both oneself and others.
>
> [...]
>
> A poem is the result of a certain necessity: it is inevitable, and so is its form. 'Necessity,' as Nadezhda Mandelstam says in 'Mozart and Salieri,' 'is not a compulsion and is not the curse of determinism, but is a link between times, if the torch inherited from forebears

has not been trampled.' Form too is noble for it is hallowed and illumined by time. It is the vessel in which meaning is cast; they need each other and sanctify each other reciprocally—it is an association of soul and body. Break the vessel, and the liquid will leak out. [. . .]

Russian poetry has set an example of moral purity and firmness, which to no small degree has been reflected in the preservation of so-called classical form without any damage to content. Herein lies her distinction from her Western sisters, though in no way do I presume to judge whom this distinction favors most. However, it is a distinction, and if only for purely ethnographic considerations that quality ought to be preserved in translation and not forced into a common mold.

[Brodsky's remarks on translation, entirely unlike Holmes's, are unashamedly normative. He will not accept that a translation is inevitably a substitution, since it cannot be identical with the source text. When he talks about free verse, 'a special genre of verbal art', it is clear that he is quite out of sympathy with it. When he claims that he does not mean that the translator who rejects meter in translating is committing sacrilege, it is hard to take him at his word. Similarly, when he claims that 'Russian poetry has set an example of moral purity and firmness', preserving the 'so-called classical form without any damage to content', he *does*, indeed, 'presume to judge between it and its Western sisters'.]

From Clarence Brown's Introduction to *Selected Poems of Osip Mandelstam*, trans. Clarence Brown and W. S. Merwin (London: OUP, 1973), pp. v–xviii

[This, of course, preceded Brodsky's review (see above), which emphatically rejects its arguments.]

For more years than I find it comfortable to admit I have been preparing a study of Mandelstam's life and poetry [. . .], and in the course of that I developed a habit of preparing worksheets on each poem. These included, along with notes on every aspect of the poem that struck me, notations of variant readings, semantic nuances of the diction, peculiarities of the prosody, and so on, a plain English translation, often with numerous alternative translations. [. . .] [T]he first stage in our work was my simply turning over to Merwin my worksheets. From these, with a truly heroic effort of decipherment, he produced first versions. In the intervening couple of years, we have [. . .] debated the early results [. . .] Bargains were struck, but no compromises were undertaken, I hope, with the English poem that was trying to be born out of Mandelstam's Russian.

The poems that resulted are of course no longer *calques* of the original [. . .], but we have not consciously invented thoughts or images that the original could in no sense warrant. It need scarcely be said, I suppose, that we never considered the folly of trying to convey to the ear of our English readers the sounds of the Russian.

[Brown then gives as an example poem No. 394, the same poem Brodsky considers in his review-essay. He proceeds:]

Would Mandelstam approve? I cannot quite bring myself up to the presumption of answering in his name, so I shall rather let him answer for himself by an account of his own practice.

Mandelstam also translated. Like most of the Russian poets who brought about the great reflowering of their art around the turn of the century, he was at home in the languages of culture, and translation was a part of his response to the world. [...] He had to translate [translation being his only means of making a living] under sweatshop conditions, the texts assigned him being the trash in vogue at the time with the authorities [...]

But even under these conditions he sometimes managed to translate in response to the old genuine urgency—out of love. In 1933 he turned four sonnets of Petrarch into Russian. [...] I had received the texts alone, with no indication of where the originals might be among Petrarch's hundreds of sonnets, so my first concern was naturally to seek these out. If was an awful headache. No sooner would I have identified this or that image in an opening line or two than some wild divergence would convince me that Mandelstam must have been working from another original. The 'other original' stubbornly refusing to turn up, I was driven back to my starting point, and had to conclude what is the point of this little narrative: that Mandelstam had translated Petrarch not into Russian, but into Mandelstam.

Lest any reader think that by lending myself to this undertaking I have switched sides in the Lowell-Nabokov debate let me say, first, that he should inspect my several tributes to Nabokov, and secondly, that that controversy, now that time had dissipated the fog of animus, can be seen for what it was, a pseudo-controversy. Lowell does not translate into English, but into Lowell; Nabokov can be said to translate into literal English only by those who will accept his definition of literal English: in reality, it is Nabokov. Merwin has translated Mandelstam into Merwin. When one is speaking of writers of the stature of Lowell, Nabokov, and Merwin this strikes me as being the happiest of situations.

I can imagine, if only just, an English poem that might reproduce what one critic has called the 'cello sound' of this or that poem by Mandelstam [...] [W]hat is more, I can imagine the only audience that might, or should, appreciate this English poem: a roomful of native Russians who, with the original itself unfolding in their mind's ear, have just enough English to collate the two, and approve the result. They would approve it, happily unaware of the exorbitant price that had been paid, and consequently as happily unable to assess its merit as an English poem of our own time.

We [...] have accepted the responsibility entailed in the fact that to translate is to change. Those of my colleagues in the academy who are sent up the wall by 'mistakes' in the translation of poetry, those who are happy to maintain that poetry is untranslatable here on earth, and the arbiters of their own brand of literalism everywhere, have probably by now read far enough in this book.

[Brown takes it as axiomatic (a) that no attempt can be made to reproduce the sound of the Russian and (b) that a translator of poetic distinction will translate not so much into the target language, as into his 'own' language. Brodsky, though he does not refer directly to Brown's remarks, clearly disagrees. What else can a poet do, asks Brown, but translate into his own voice; a poetry translator, insists Brodsky, must resist precisely this temptation.]

From W. S. Merwin's Foreword to his *Selected Translations 1968–1978* (New York: Atheneum, 1980), pp. vii–xiv

[Among leading contemporary American poets, Merwin is perhaps the most active as a translator (*The Song of Roland, The Cid, The Satires of Persius,* and of work by individual poets, besides Mandelstam, such as Roberto Juarroz, Jean Follain, Pablo Neruda, and Nicanor Parra).]

When Pope set out to translate Homer almost everything (as it appears to us) was known beforehand. He knew who most of his immediate readers would be: they had subscribed for the translations. They, in turn knew—or thought they knew—who Homer was, and they knew the text, in the original. Both the subscribers and the translator took it for granted that the proper form for heroic verse, in English, must of course be the heroic couplet. Pope's work was expected to display the wit, elegance, and brilliance with which he could render a generally accepted notion of the Homeric poems into a familiar English verse form [...]

[...] In our time, an individual or social literary culture without it [translation] is unthinkable. What is it that we think we need? We begin with the idea that it is the original—which means our relative conception of the original, as scholars, potential translators, or readers. At the outset, the notion is probably not consciously involved with any thought of the available means of translation. The 'original' may even figure as something that might exist in more forms than one, just as it can be understood by more than one reader. But if we take a single word of any language and try to find an exact equivalent in another, even if the second language is closely akin to the first, we have to admit that it cannot be done. A single primary denotation may be shared; but the constellation of secondary meanings, the moving rings of associations, the etymological echoes, the sound and its own levels of association, do not have an equivalent because they cannot [...] The surprising thing is that at this point the hope of translation does not fade altogether, but begins to emerge. Not that these rudiments of form in the original language can be matched [...] But the imaginative force which they embody [...] may suggest convocations of words in another language that will have a comparable thrust and sense.

By 'rudiments of form' I mean recognizable elements of verbal order, not verse forms. I began with what I suppose was, and perhaps still is, a usual preconception about the latter: that fidelity in translating a poem should include an ambition to reproduce the original verse form. Besides, I started translating partly as a discipline, hoping that the process might help me learn to write. [Merwin describes his early visit to Ezra Pound and the latter urging him to 'get as close to the original as possible' and to keep the rhyme scheme if he could.] When I did come, gradually, to abandon more and more often the verse forms of poems that I was translating, I did not try to formulate any precise principle for doing so. Translation is a fairly empirical practice, usually, and the 'reason' for making particular choices, however well grounded in scholarship, is seldom wholly explicable. I would have recognised, probably, quite early, a simple reluctance to sacrifice imagined felicities of the potential English version, to keep a verse pattern that was, in a sense, abstract. [. . .] Verse conventions are to a large degree matters of effects, that depend partly on a familiarity which cannot, of course, be translated at all. [. . .]

From an interview with W. S. Merwin, conducted by Christopher Merrill, on 12 October 2001, at 'Lost & Found: The Art of Translation', the 2nd annual International Writing Program Festival, University of Iowa, transcription provided by C. Merrill, Director of the IWP

I've come to believe that in general, the musical elements, by which I mean formal elements, of poetry are embedded in the original language [. . .] You can suggest, you can torment your own language into repeating them, but even if you do, you're not going to get the form doing in your language what it did in the original.

The startling thing for me, apart from the excitement of the material itself [here he alludes to Budge's edition of 'The Egyptian Book of the Dead', with its hieroglyphs, and the literal rendering under each] was when you turned to the back, where he's got it in good English—flat as can be... And I thought of something that I've heard two very different poets say in different ways, and each time it was very revealing [. . .] Berryman and Allen Ginsberg both said to me that in real poems [. . .] the focus is twisted somehow, there's something a little bit out of perspective. Berryman's example was Blake's never spoken language [. . .]. The comparison I would make would be something like Cézanne's 'Bathers', where everything is just a little bit out of proportion. [. . .] Look at the difference between 'Should I say you're like a day in summer?' which is the obvious way to say 'Shall I compare thee to a summer's day?' [. . .]

I'm in the middle of trying to work on Mandelstam—by the way [. . .] [Brodsky] said, you know, you have to keep the meter and the rhyme of the original. And I said, well, the meter and the rhyme of the original—Mandelstam generally wrote in rhymed quatrains [. . .] There's a history of rhymed quatrains in English, and if I were really lucky, it might sound like not very good Auden, and if I weren't lucky, it might sound like not very good Longfellow. [. . .] And finally he said, well, I would maybe agree with you if it were not Russian poetry. I said, Well, what is different about Russian poetry? And he said, Russian poetry is, how shall I say, sacred. And I said, Oh sure, just like all other poetry.

[. . .] I have a sense, and through Clarence's [Brown] conversation I have to feel that I have a sense of what makes that poem exciting in the original. I don't want to mislead about the real meaning of the poem. But I want it to be a poem that has that same kind of—I don't know—drama, that same kind of [. . .] urgency. It won't be exactly the urgency. But if it doesn't have any urgency, if it's flat, it doesn't matter whether it rhymes or has meter or anything. You've lost the poem.

And of course Mandelstam [. . .] said that poets really shouldn't translate unless they were getting as close as they could to writing their own poems. [. . .]

From 'On the Translation of Form in Poetry' by Yves Bonnefoy, *World Literature Today*, 52–3 (1979), 374–9

[Yves Bonnefoy, major French poet, is also an important translator into French, especially of Shakespeare and Yeats. He categorically refutes Brodsky's insistence on formal mimetic translation and especially his condemnation of the use of free verse.]

[Brodsky] emphasizes the value and meaning of poetic form; he shows its relatedness with the most inner quality of the poem [. . .]—and I cannot but agree with these ideas [. . .] But there is this other point about the inferior [. . .] quality of free verse in general, and even more surprising, this moral judgment which Brodsky makes in unequivocal terms indeed. [. . .] Brodsky makes it very clear that he [. . .] rejects every use of it [free verse], every poem written with its help. Actually, he finds in free verse the main distinction between Russian poetry and what he calls 'her Western sisters' and makes us suspicious that he believes his own poetic tradition the only one inflexible if not heroic [. . .] while the decadent literatures of the West, with their free verse as a proof of their laziness, would indulge in all the easy delights of their corrupted civilization. [. . .]

Yes, it cannot be doubted that poetry is form as well as meaning, so that I surely do not believe that the Russian poets, for instance, must be deprived, by our way of translating them, of their rights to be understood as formal artists [. . .] and yet, when I began to translate Shakespeare and later some poems of John Donne [as did Brodsky] and Yeats, I did not hesitate to adopt free verse, and I still believe I was right. [. . .] I also knew that the laws of reading, understanding, translating a poem are not simple and that perhaps we must lose in the beginning in order to be able later to recover more fully. [. . .]

[. . .] Nothing can be rightly analyzed in itself, independently of the whole to which it belongs; we must think in terms of structure. In the case of poetry this means that *no part of a poem, not even its form*, has a detached or constant meaning [. . .] None of us can use instinctively, unambiguously, the old regular forms, deprived as we are of the old spirit, which had been for such a long time their principal cause. And even in the case of translation we cannot but experience this impediment [. . .].

Against Brodsky I therefore affirm that, even when we have to translate some of these poems of the past, whose regularity was so important an aspect, almost the soul, we can no longer sincerely and seriously use regular, 'classical' meters. Indeed, the more regularity was intense or significant in the original poetry, the more our faked or dispirited regularity of now must be, at the very first, dismissed.

[But] there is another reason why regular meter must be proscribed from all serious translation. Whatever the resources of regular verse can be today, we must not forget that we cannot think only in terms of what is desirable, without checking what can actually be made. And this examination will rule out, at the level of the translator's word-by-word work, any possibility of satisfying regularity. Why? Because exactly as we discovered a while ago that a poem is a whole whose formal elements have no meaning as such independently of the others, so now we must understand that writing, the act of writing, is in itself an unbreakable unity whose formal operations are conceived and executed in constant interaction with, for example, the invention of the images and the elaboration of meaning. If the meaning of the future poem were totally given in advance, let us say, there could conceivably be a way for the author to make it known, and this even clearly; but that would be a prosaic expression, and every attempt to adorn this precooked meaning with the feathers of a beautiful prosody would be artificial and lifeless. [. . .]

But this necessary freedom is not, unfortunately, within reach of the translator. In his case, meaning, the whole meaning of the poem, is already determined; he cannot invent anything about it without betraying the intent of the author. Consequently, were he to decide to adopt the alexandrine or the pentameter, this regular pattern would be for him nothing but a frame to which the meaning would have to adjust itself, obliging him to pure virtuosity. [. . .] [P]assiveness instead of responsibility and freedom would be his joyless destiny, with discouragement at the end. [. . .]

Far from considering free verse as a minor way of approaching the musicality of language I will therefore say that it is the full exercise of it [. . .] In brief, free verse is only one aspect among others of modernity as such, and if it is not recognized in this quality in Russia today, the reason is probably not so much a better understanding of classical forms by Russian poets as it is a consequence of the distance which keeps all the arts in Leningrad or Moscow so isolated from the evolution of their counterparts in the western world.

[Bonnefoy concludes with some reflections and observations on his own free verse translations of Shakespeare, in which the repetitive pattern of the original poetry 'is enough [. . .] to pervade what is said in my modern words with some colour of the old relationship between the poet and the world'.]

Translations of Mandelstam

Comparison of Translations of poem 94, stanza 2 (using numbering in *Selected Poems of Osip Mandelstam*, trans. Clarence Brown and W. S. Merwin, p. 99)

[This poem is cited by Brodsky in his review. Brodsky gives a transliteration of the Russian, the poem as translated by Brown/Merwin, and an *ad verbum* version, presumably by himself. The Merwin translation is characterized as a travesty, since it reproduces neither metre nor rhyme. For purpose of comparison, a number of other translations are given below. Remarks by other translators are appended to these versions.]

Clarence Brown and W. S. Merwin's translation

There are women with the dampness of the earth in their veins.
Every step they take there's a sobbing in a vault.
They were born to escort the dead, and be at the grave
First to greet those who rise again.
It would be terrible to want a caress from them
but to part with them is more than a man could do.
One day angel, next day the worm in the grave,
The day after that, a sketch.
What used to be within reach—out of reach.
Flowers never die. Heaven is whole.
But ahead of us we've only somebody's word.

Joseph Brodsky, ad verbum *version*

There are women who are akin to the damp earth,
And their every step is reverberating sobbing;
To escort the dead and be first
To greet the resurrected is their calling.
And demanding caresses from them is criminal.
And parting with them is beyond one's strength.
To-day—an angel, tomorrow—a worm in the grave,
And the day after tomorrow—only an outline.
What was—the walk—becomes unreachable.

Flowers are immortal. Heaven is whole.
And that which will be is only a promise.

Bernard Meares's translation, from Osip Mandelstam: 50 Poems,
(New York: Persea, 1977), 98

There are some women who are kin to the raw earth,
Whose every pace is resonant with weeping;
To accompany the dead and be the first
To greet the resurrected is their vocation.
To plead caresses from them would be a crime
And to part with them is more than one can bear.
Today an angel, tomorrow a worm in the tomb,
The next day just an outline, nothing more.
What's been—a step—will be one step beyond our reach.
Flowers are immortal, heaven a single whole,
And what shall be is nothing but a promise.

[In his 'Translator's Introduction' Meares says nothing about his approach to translation. Since Brodsky contributes an introduction to the collection, it is to be supposed that he approves of it. Meares uses rhyme and keeps roughly to a five-stress line.]

James Greene's translation, from Osip Mandelstam Poems,
(London: Paul Elek, 1977), 85

There are women who are natives of the sodden earth:
Their every step a hollow sobbing,
Their calling to accompany the dead,
To be first to meet the risen.
And we would trespass to demand caresses of them,
And to part from them is beyond our strength.
Today—angel, tomorrow—the cryptic worm,
The day after—a stark outline,—
What was a step, now beyond us ...

But what shall be is, for us,
A promise.

From James Greene, 'Translator's Preface' Osip Mandelstan Poems
[Greene quotes Akhmatova on Mandelstam's poetry: 'We know the sources of Pushkin and Blok, but who will tell us where that new, divine harmony, Mandelstam's poetry came

from?' He defends his decision to translate freely, sometimes going so far as to suppress lines and whole stanzas or even to compress two poems.]

Mandelstam's poems are rhymed and strictly metrical ... I have mostly had to eschew rhyme (but not half-rhyme, internal rhymes or assonance), and have tried to feel my way towards what might be the right rhythm for English. Some may say that my 'from' versions are not translations at all but 'adaptations' or 'imitations'. [...] However, in planting Mandelstam's trees over again in foreign soil, I hope I have not deviated too much from his sense or spirit.

To the non-Russian-speaking reader who wants to know about the relation between Mandelstam's metres (which I have not consciously set out to re-enact), length of line, etc., and mine, I can only say: 'decisions' of this kind are made intuitively, or in heaven; don't eat my—or any other translator's—menus or pontifical recipes; total 'faithfulness', were it possible—the 'same' metre, rhyme-scheme, pattern of sounds, number of syllables, line-length, etc, etc.—would be an absurdity.

[Greene, like others, emphasizes the subjective nature of the operation; Brodsky flatly insists on the sanctity of the original form.]

Richard and Elizabeth McKane's translation, from The Voronezh Notebooks, Osip Mandelstam, Poems 1935–1937 *(Newcastle upon Tyne: Bloodaxe, 1996), 95*

> There are women, who are so close to the moist earth;
> their every step is loud mourning,
> their calling is to accompany the resurrected,
> and be first to greet the dead.
> It is a crime to demand kisses from them,
> and it is impossible to part from them.
> Today angels, tomorrow worms in the graveyard,
> and the day after, just an outline.
> The steps you once took, you won't be able to take.
> Flowers are immortal. Heaven is integral.
> What will be is only a promise.

From Richard McKane's Preface, The Voronezh Notebooks, *pp. 11–14*

Late Mandelstam is very difficult even in the original Russian. His technique of composing by mouthing words with his lips as opposed to sitting at a table with pen and paper, gives the poems a distinctive sound quality, and a unique voice, ranging from the colloquial to the elegiac. Not only do Mandelstam's poems rhyme, but also sounds and roots evoke other sounds and roots. Form and content unite in an unsplittable whole in the Russian. So our interpretative capacities were tested to the full in trying to render meaningful poems in English.

W. S. Merwin

Interestingly, Merwin, in a recent translation, seems to be approaching a more literal or foreignizing form of translation. Paradoxically perhaps, in view of his dispute with Brodsky, he seems less concerned about the strain imposed on English, just as Brodsky—granted from a non-native perspective—was able to bend English in attempting to convey the sound-feel of the Russian source texts.

A Sonnet by Dante

[This sonnet from *La Vita Nuova* ('Deh peregrini che pensosi andate . . .') was composed by Dante on seeing pilgrims pass before the house of Beatrice after her death. Merwin's version was published in a hand-set edition, on the occasion of the translator's reading in Iowa City at the translation conference where he was interviewed (see above for excerpts from this interview; other excerpts, relating to this translation, have been appended here). By way of stark contrast, we end with Dante Gabriel Rossetti's version from his translation of *la Vita Nuova* (1861) (see also Sect. 3.5, above, on Rossetti).]

W. S. Merwin's translation (Iowa City, 2001)

Oh pilgrims who walk thinking it may be
of something that is not there now before you
do you come from people as far away
as it seems from the appearance of you
for you do not weep as you travel through
the center of the sorrowing city
as though you might be of those people who
seem not to understand her gravity

If you will pause wishing to hear of that
my heart sighing tells me certainly that
you will be weeping when you go away
She has lost her Beatrice and what
one can say of her in words is able to
make tears fall from all of those who hear it

From the interview with W. S. Merwin, Iowa City, 12 October 2001

I tried to get a sonnet in English out of it. I've tried to get it as close [. . .] It's metrically not the same, but the kind of measure of lines is the same. But the sonnet does not do in

English what the sonnet does in Italian. And the associations of a sonnet in English are not the associations in Italian. It seemed worth doing because I love the poem. [. . .] But I don't feel that I've contributed an enormous amount to it just by making it a sonnet. And of course the run-on quality of the line is quite different from Dante.

I wanted something that was closer to the literal meaning of the original than the prose translation. Because as I looked through the translations, I thought they all take liberties. [. . .] [R]hyme is more important in the Italian than it can ever be in the English. Pace is immensely important [. . .] the pace of the 'Inferno' and the 'Purgatory' are totally different. You lose that and you've lost something very, very important. But rhyme—you know, we don't hear the way the Italians did. [. . .] Dante said he wanted it to be in the plain language of his time. [. . .] On the other hand, of course—I wanted the translation to be a poem. I think that when you're translating poetry, or when you're writing poetry, any conditions that you set yourself becomes a form. If you say literal meaning is one of the conditions, I don't want to take liberties, not for the sake of the form or anything else, I don't want to mislead anyone—that's a condition, a form of the writing. just as the sonnet is a form [. . .].

Dante Gabriel Rossetti's version

Ye pilgrim-folk, advancing pensively
As if in thought of distant things, I pray,
Is your own land indeed so far away
As by your aspect it would seem to be—
That nothing of our grief comes over ye
Though passing through the mournful town midway;
Like unto men that understand to-day
Nothing at all of her great misery?
Yet if ye will but stay, whom I accost,
And listen to my words a little space,
At going ye shall mourn with a loud voice.
It is her Beatrice that she hath lost;
Of whom the least word spoken holds such grace
That men weep hearing it, and have no choice.

Joseph Brodsky

An indication of what Brodsky wanted in translations is suggested by his own versions of his own poems, of which an example, 'May 24, 1980', is given below. This is a mock-heroic birthday poem to himself. A near literal translation of it by the present writer is also given.

For a comprehensive discussion of this poem, see V. Polukhina, 'I, Instead of a Wild Beast' (in Lev Loseff and Valentina Polukhina, *Joseph Brodsky, The Art of a Poem* (London: Macmillan [1999]), 68–91; also Daniel Weissbort, *From Russian with Love* (London: Anvil, 2004). Brodsky takes considerable liberties, for the sake of what seemed to him a truer literalism, or truth to the source as a sound/sense artefact.

'May 24, 1980'

Literal version by Daniel Weissbort

It was I, no wild beast, that entered the cage,
with a nail scorched my prison term and nickname in the barrack hut,
lived by the sea, played roulette,
dined in coat-tails with the devil-knows-who.
From the top of a glacier, I surveyed half the world,
thrice drowned, twice was unpicked/unstitched.
You could people a town with those who have forgotten me.
I mooched about in the steppes, recalling the howl of the Hun,
clothed myself in what again has become fashionable,
sowed rye, tarred barn roofs,
and dry water wasn't my only beverage.
I admitted into my dreams the sentry's burnished pupil,
guzzled the bread of exile, not leaving even a crust.
I've permitted my vocal cords to utter all manner of
    sounds, except for a howl.
I passed over to a whisper. Now I am forty.
What should I say about life? That it turned out to be long.
It is only with sorrow/grief that I can identify.
But until my mouth is crammed with clay,
only gratitude will resound/ring out from it.

Translation of Brodsky by Brodsky

I have braved, for want of wild beasts, steel cages,
carved my term and nickname on bunks and rafters,
lived by the sea, flashed aces in an oasis,
dined with the-devil-knows-whom, in tails, on truffles.
From the height of a glacier I beheld half a world, the earthy
width. Twice have drowned, thrice, let knives rake my nitty-gritty.
Quit the country that bore and nursed me.

Those who forgot me would make a city.
I have waded the steppes that saw yelling Huns in saddles,
worn the clothes nowadays back in fashion in every quarter,
planted rye, tarred the roofs of pigsties and stables,
guzzled everything save dry water.
I've admitted the sentries' third eye into my wet and foul
dreams. Munched the bread of exile: it's stale and warty.
Granted my lungs all sounds except the howl;
switched to a whisper. Now I am forty.
What should I say about life? That it's long and abhors
transparence.
Broken eggs make me grieve; the omelette, though, makes me vomit.
Yet until brown clay has been crammed down my larynx,
only gratitude will be gushing from it.

[If this version by Brodsky does not 'speak for itself' with total conviction, it is perhaps because it marks an interim stage in his mastery of English. It can hardly be denied, even by those committed to the advancement of the art of translation, that Brodsky had better things to do than translate his own poetry into English. Nevertheless, it is perhaps not wholly wishful thinking either to see some sort of a convergence between, for instance, a Merwin and a Brodsky.]

5.10 A. K. RAMANUJAN

Vinay Dharwadker
(University of Wisconsin, Madison)

A. K. Ramanujan (1929–93) was a multilingual poet, fiction writer, translator, and scholar. As a translator, he brought together an unparalleled variety of languages, texts, genres, literatures, historical periods, and past and present cultures. He translated literary works mainly from various forms of Kannada and Tamil into English, and also from English into Kannada; with the help of collaborators, he rendered texts from Malayalam, Telugu, Marathi, and Sanskrit into English. He focused his attention on verse as well as prose, rendering epic and classical poetry from the ancient period (chiefly works composed between about 500 BC and AD 500), early and late poetic texts from the middle period (from the eighth to the eighteenth centuries), and poems, short stories, novelistic fiction, and numerous folktales from the modern period (the nineteenth and twentieth centuries).

During his lifetime, Ramanujan's reputation as a translator grew around seven finely crafted books. Among these, *The Interior Landscape* (1967) and *Poems of Love and War* (1985) contained selections of his English versions of Classical Tamil poetry, both including scholarly commentary on the language and culture of the original texts, but the latter offering a larger and more representative body of work and a more comprehensive critical account of the tradition. *Speaking of Shiva* (1973) brought together Ramanujan's translations of more than two hundred *vachanas* ('sayings') by four major *bhaktas* ('devotees,' in this case of the god Shiva) in the 'counter-cultural' Vira-shaiva religious tradition in Kannada, from the early centuries of the past millennium. *Hymns for the Drowning: Poems for Vishnu by Nammalvar* (1981) consisted of Ramanujan's renderings of nearly ninety poems by a tenth-century Tamil saint-poet in the very different Shri Vaishnava *bhakti* tradition, complementing in language, religious orientation, and poetic quality his versions of the Kannada *vachanas* in *Speaking of Shiva*. In *Samskara: A Rite for a Dead Man* (1976, 1978), Ramanujan produced a version of U. R. Anantha Murthy's existentialist Kannada novel which had been 'Popular with critic and common reader alike since its [original] publication in 1965,' and 'was made into an award-winning, controversial film in 1970' (*Samskara*, p. viii). Moving away from high culture and touching on a new boundary of translation in the last years of his life, Ramanujan presented in *Folktales from India* (1991) his retellings and edited versions in English prose of nineteenth- and twentieth-century oral narratives from twenty-two Indian languages.

At the time of his death, Ramanujan left behind several other translated works in various stages of completion, which have appeared posthumously. *When God Is a Customer* (1994), a small book co-translated and co-authored with V. Narayana Rao and David Shulman, offers a selection of Telugu *bhakti* poems by a single poet from the mystic-erotic temple tradition of the late middle period of southern Indian literary history. *The Oxford India Anthology of Contemporary Poetry*, which he co-edited with Vinay Dharwadker between about 1984 and 1992, brings together poems by 125 twentieth-century poets writing in fifteen Indian languages and in English, most of them translated by over sixty contemporary translators, and includes Ramanujan's versions of more than thirty recent Kannada, Tamil, Telugu, and Malayalam poems. During the last few years of his life Ramanujan also worked energetically on one of his longest-term projects, *A Flowering Tree and Other Kannada Folktales* (1998), a large collection of orally narrated stories that he had recorded, transcribed, and translated over three decades of fieldwork in Karnataka, and which Stuart Blackburn edited for posthumous publication. By the end, Ramanujan had translated, in various senses of this term, ranging from playful prose retelling to precise poetic metaphrase, produced independently and in collaboration with others, some three thousand individual texts from the full spectrum of Dravidian and Indo-Aryan languages into English.

Statements on Translation

From Speaking of Shiva (Harmondsworth: Penguin, 1973), 12–13

A translation has to be true to the translator no less than to the originals. He cannot jump off his own shadow. Translation is choice, interpretation, an assertion of taste, a betrayal of what answers to one's needs, one's envies. I can only hope that my needs are not entirely eccentric or irrelevant to the needs of others in the two traditions, the one I translate from and the one I translate into [. . .]

In the act of translating, 'the Spirit killeth and the Letter giveth Life'. Any direct attack on the 'spirit of the work' is foredoomed to fuzziness. Only the literal text, the word made flesh, can take us to the word behind the words. I have tried therefore to attend closely to the language of the Originals, their design, detail by detail; not to match the Kannada with the English, but to *map* the medieval Kannada onto the soundlook of modern English; in rhythm and punctuation, in phrase-breaks, paragraphs and lineation to suggest the inner form of the originals as I see them. Medieval Kannada manuscripts use no punctuation, no paragraph-, word-, or phrase-divisions, though modern editions print the [*vachanas*] with all the modern conventions. The few liberties I have taken are towards a close structural mimicry, a re-enactment in English, the transposition of a structure in one texture onto another. Valéry said of a translation of St John of the Cross: 'This is really to *translate*, which is to reconstitute as nearly as possible the *effect* of a certain cause'.

From 'On Translating a Tamil Poem', in *The Collected Essays of A. K. Ramanujan* (New Delhi: Oxford University Press, 1999), 229–31

At least four things, maybe even four articles of faith, help the translator.

1. *Universals.* If there were no universals in which languages participate and of which all particular languages were selections and combinations, no language learning, translation, comparative studies or cross-cultural understanding of even the most meager kind would be possible. If such universals did not exist, as Voltaire said of God, we would have to invent them. [. . .] Universals of structure, in both signifiers (e.g., sound systems, grammar, semantics, rhetoric, and poetics) and the signifieds (e.g., what poems are about [. . .] and what they mean within and across cultures), are necessary fictions, the indispensable 'as ifs' of our fallible enterprise.

2. *Interiorised contexts.* However culture-specific the details of a poem are, poems . . . interiorise the entire culture. Indeed, we know about the culture of the ancient Tamils only through a careful study of [their] poems. [. . .]

3. *Systematicity.* The systematicity of such bodies of poetry, the way figures, genres, personae, etc., intermesh in a master-code, is a great help in entering this intricate world of words. One translates not single poems but bodies of poetry that create and contain their original world. Even if one chooses not to translate all the poems, one chooses poems that cluster together, that illuminate one another, so that allusions, contrasts, and collective designs are suggested. One's selection then becomes a metonymy of their world, re-presenting it. Here intertextuality is not the problem, but the solution. [. . .]

4. *Structural mimicry.*[. . .] [The] work of translating single poems in their particularity is the chief work of the translator. In this task, [. . .] the structures of individual poems, the unique figures they make out of all the given codes of their language, rhetoric, and poetics, become the points of entry. The poetry and the significance reside in these figures and structures as much as in the untranslatable verbal textures. So one attempts a structural mimicry, to translate relations, not items—not single words but phrases, sequences, sentences; not metrical units but rhythms; not morphology but syntactic patterns.

To translate is to 'metaphor', to 'carry across'. Translations are transpositions, re-enactments, interpretations. Some elements of the original cannot be transposed at all. One can often convey a sense of the original rhythm, but not the language-bound metre; one can mimic levels of diction, but not the actual sound of the original words. Textures are harder (maybe impossible) to translate than structures, linear order more difficult than syntax, lines more difficult than larger patterns. Poetry is made at all these levels—and so is translation. That is why nothing less than a poem can translate another.

Yet 'anything goes' will not do. The translation must not only represent, but *re*-present, the original. One walks a tightrope between the To-language and the From-language, in a double loyalty. A translator is an 'artist on oath'. Sometimes one may succeed only in *re*-presenting a poem, not in closely representing it. At such times one draws consolation from parables like the following. A Chinese emperor ordered a tunnel to be bored through a great mountain. The engineers decided that the best and quickest way to do it would be to begin work on both sides of the mountain, after precise measurements. If the measurements were precise enough, the two tunnels would meet in the middle, making a single one. 'But what happens if they don't meet?' asked the emperor. The counselors, in their wisdom, answered, 'If they don't meet, we will have two tunnels instead of one.' So too, if the representation in another language is not close enough, but still succeeds in 'carrying' the poem in some sense, we will have two poems instead of one.

Selection of Translations

Kapilar (before third century), translated from Classical Tamil

'What She Said,' 1, from Poems of Love and War *(New York: Columbia University Press, 1985), 7–8*

In his country,
summer west wind blows
flute music
through bright beetle-holes in the waving bamboos.
The sweet sound of waterfalls is continuous,
dense as drums.
The urgent lowing voices of a herd of stags
are oboes,
the bees on the flowering slopes
become lutes.

Excited by such teeming voices,
an audience of female monkeys
watches in wonder
the peacock on the bamboo hill
sway and strut
like a dancer
making an entrance
on a festival stage.

He had a garland on his chest,
a strong bow in his grip,
arrow already chosen,
and he asked which way
the elephant went
with an arrow buried in its side.

He stood at the edge
of a ripe-eared millet field.

But, among all the people
who saw him standing there,
why is it
that I alone
lie in bed
in this harsh night,
eyes streaming,
arms growing lean?

'What She Said,' 2, from Poems of Love and War, p. 13

You ask me to forget him,
how can I?

His mountain,
wearing its dark raincloud
white-crested

as a bean flower
the east wind opens,

his mountain,
that blue sapphire,
is never out of sight.

'What She Said,' 3, from Poems of Love and War, p. 17

Only the thief was there, no one else.
And if he should lie, what can I do?

There was only
a thin-legged heron standing
on legs yellow as millet stems

and looking
            for lampreys
in the running water
when he took me.

'What She Said', 4, from Poems of Love and War, *p.25*

He is from those mountains

where the little back-faced monkey,
playing in the sun,
rolls the wild peacock's eggs
on the rocks.

Yes, his love is always good
as you say, my friend,

but only for those strong enough
to bear it,

who will not cry their eyes out
or think anything of it

when he leaves.

Ponmutiyar (before third century), translated from Classical Tamil

'A Young Warrior', from Poems of Love and War, *p. 165*

O heart
sorrowing
for this lad

once scared of a stick
lifted in mock anger
when he refused
a drink of milk,

                  now
not content with killing
war elephants
with spotted trunks,

this son
of the strong man who fell yesterday

seems unaware of the arrow
in his wound,

his head of hair is plumed
like a horse's,

he has fallen
on his shield,

his beard still soft.

'A Mother's List of Duties', from Poems of Love and War, p. 185

To bring forth and rear a son is my duty.
To make him noble is the father's.
To make spears for him is the blacksmith's.
To show him good ways is the king's.

And to bear
a bright sword and do battle,
to butcher enemy elephants,
and come back:

that is the young man's duty.

Erumai Veliyanar (before third century), translated from Classical Tamil

'The Horse Did Not Come Back', from Poems of Love and War, p. 179

The horse did not come back,
his horse did not come back.
All the other horses have come back.

The horse
of our good man,

who was father in our house
to a little son
with a tuft of hair
like a plume on a steed,

it did not come back.

Has it fallen now,
his horse
that bore him through battle,

has it fallen
like the great tree
standing at the meeting place
of two rivers?

Devara Dasimayya (tenth–eleventh centuries?), translated from Old Kannada

Poem 133, from Speaking of Shiva, *p. 110*

If they see
breasts and long hair coming
they call it woman,

if beard and whiskers
they call it man:

but, look, the self that hovers
in between
is neither man
nor woman,

O Ramanatha

Basavanna (c. 1106–67), translated from Old Kannada

Poem 820, from Speaking of Shiva, *p. 88*

The rich
will make temples for Shiva.
What shall I,
a poor man,
do?

My legs are pillars,
the body the shrine,
the head a cupola
of gold.

Listen, O lord of the meeting rivers,
things standing shall fall,
but the moving ever shall stay.

Mahadevi (mid-twelfth century), translated from Old Kannada

Poem 17, from Speaking of Shiva, *p. 116*

Like a silkworm weaving
her house with love

from her marrow,
                    and dying
in her body's threads
winding tight, round
and round,
                    I burn,
desiring what the heart desires.

cut through, O lord,
my heart's greed,
and show me
your way out,

O lord white as jasmine.

Allama Prabhu (twelfth century), translated from Old Kannada

Poem 972, from Speaking of Shiva, *p. 168*

Looking for your light
I went out:

  it was like the sudden dawn
  of a million million suns,

  a ganglion of lightnings
  for my wonder.

  O Lord of Caves,
  if you are light,
  there can be no metaphor.

N. Revathi Devi (1951–81), translated from Modern Telugu, with V. Narayana Rao

'This Night', from The Oxford India Anthology of Contemporary Poetry,
ed. V. Dharwadker and A. K. Ramanujan
(Delhi: Oxford University Press, 1994, 1996)

If this night passes
which does not surrender even to sleeping pills
if this night passes

the night that spreads under my back
like a bed of arrows
for not compromising with man

the night that flows in my veins
like blood from the thorns of the toddy palm
for not compromising with God
if this night passes

covering the face of honesty
with a blanket of light
another day
another day another night another day

at some time another night another day
if honesty stands naked, smooth
not finding light
if that night stands without passing
it will pass, it will move away, honestly

5.11 GAYATRI CHAKRAVORTY SPIVAK

Gayatri Chakravorty Spivak (b. 1942), literary theorist, feminist critic, translator, studied in Calcutta and at Cornell University and has taught at a number of universities in the United States, Europe, and Asia. Spivak's influential translation of and introduction to Jacques Derrida's *De la grammatologie* (1967), *Of Grammatology*, was published in 1976. She is on the editorial board of several journals and is active in rural literacy teacher training in India and Bangladesh. Among her many publications are translations of the fiction of Mahasweta Devi: *Imaginary Maps, Breast Stories, Old Women* (1993) and *Chotti Munda and His Arrow* (2003), as well as the following books: *In Other Worlds: Essays in Cultural Politics* (1987); *Outside in the Teaching Machine* (1993); *A Critique of Postcolonial Reason: Towards a History of the Vanishing Present* (1999); and *Death of a Discipline* (2003). Spivak is the recipient of the Sahitya Akademi (National Academy of Literature) 1999 Translation Prize in India. She is Avalon Professor of the Humanities at Columbia University, New York.

Translation of scholarly and critical material is rarely discussed in the same breath as the rendering of literary texts from one language to another. The former is supposed to require conceptual and linguistic accuracy, and while it may certainly call for a considerable creative grasp of language, it is not expected to involve the more subtle nuances of aesthetic recreation seen as the crux of literary translation. There are of course borderline genres that make any such division fuzzy, especially the essay, which has played a vital role in literary criticism as it has in other areas of writing.

However, in the case of some literary theorists and philosophers, the very act of linguistic delivery forms such an important part of the 'content' expressed in their scholarly works, that translators have to cope with polysemy, ambiguities, or creative wordplay in the terms, conceptual formulations, and critical arguments encountered in the text. The writing of the French philosopher Jacques Derrida, who has greatly influenced literary scholarship in the past few decades, is characterized by a use of words, terms, and expressions that engage his topics at a linguistic level, while admitting, if not reinforcing, the openness, the slipperiness, sometimes indeed the uncanniness, of language.

In the introduction to her translation of Derrida's *Of Grammatology*, Spivak discusses the very 'untranslatability' of Derrida's text, but then joins Derrida in regarding this 'negative' quality not as a flaw, but rather as a fate of language, which can can never be repeated in total sameness, although it is caught in an infinite web of intertextuality, i.e. the connections of text with other texts that contribute to its making and understanding. From this point of view, translation is in some sense 'primary', since it draws out the very difference between the signifier (the sound or the physical signal) and the signified (the concept or abstract 'meaning') which together make up the signs used for any kind of reference to things, relations, emotions, etc. A translator may substitute one signifier for another, yet cannot be certain that an analogous change of signifieds has taken place, nor that the former signified has stayed in 'place'.

This may give an idea of how translation becomes for Derrida one of the clues to a philosophy of language, and this holds true for some other thinkers too (see Walter Benjamin's 'The Task of the Translator', in Sect. 4.4, above; and Sect. 5.2 on George Steiner).[1] In Spivak's article, 'The Politics of Translation', based in part on her experience of translating eighteenth-century poetry and the contemporary fiction of Mahasweta Devi from Bengali into English, translation is also seen as a crucial gateway to the language of others, as well as a testing ground for the way in which the individual (the 'agent') seeks and forms the faultlines between logic, rhetoricity, and silence in language. For Spivak, translation is a matter of risk and intimacy; it challenges the identity of the translator as it brings her face to face with political, post-colonial, and feminist issues. The 'exchange of language' which takes place in translation must not be made subservient to the safety of the logical aspects of the third-world source language or the 'majority' target language (English). 'Without a sense of the rhetoricity of language,' which also works 'in the silence between and around words', 'a species of neocolonialist construction of the non-Western scene is afoot.'

English texts are being translated into countless languages around the globe, but Spivak's discussion takes us to what is probably the most active site of translation *into* English today. India and Pakistan have a huge bilingual population, and there is a great deal of literary traffic into English from the several other languages of the Subcontinent. As yet, this activity may not have made a large impression upon the English-language culture of the Western world, less indeed than works originally written in English by writers from this part of the world, for instance Salman Rushdie, works which often involve a great deal of cultural translation and border-crossings. But as Spivak points out, actual works of translation from one language to another may reveal more about the politics of exchange between languages, cultures, countries, and continents, not to forget race and gender.[2]

---

[1] For Derrida's views of translation, see also his 'Des Tours de Babel' (in French and in Joseph F. Graham's translation), in Joseph F. Graham (ed.), *Difference in Translation* (Ithaca, NY and London: Cornell University Press, 1985), and *The Ear of the Other: Otobiography, Transference, Translation*, trans. Peggy Kamuf and Avital Ronell (New York: Schocken Books, 1985).

[2] See Sect. 5.12, below on Talal Asad, for another interesting discussion about the inequality of languages, and Sect. 4.12, above, on Bohannan for an insightful reverse situation. See also, for a historical perspective on the Indian-English translation scene, Tejaswini Niranjana: *Siting Translation: History, Post-Structuralism, and the Colonial Context* (Berkeley and Los Angeles: University of California Press, 1992).

From Gayatri Chakravorty Spivak's 'Translator's Preface' to Jacques Derrida, *Of Grammatology* **(Baltimore and London: The Johns Hopkins University Press 1976), pp. ix–lxxxvii**

It is customary at this point to say a few words about the problem of translation. Derrida's text certainly offers its share of 'untranslatable' words. I have had my battles with 'exergue' and 'propre.'¹ My special worry is 'entamer.' As we have seen, it is an important word in Derrida's vocabulary. It means both to break into and to begin. I have made do with 'broach' or 'breach,' with the somewhat fanciful confidence that the shadow-word 'breach' or 'broach' will declare itself through it. With 'entamer' as well as with other words and expressions, I have included the original in parenthesis whenever the wording and syntax of the French seemed to carry a special charge. To an extent, this particular problem informs the entire text. Denying the uniqueness of words, their substantiality, their transferability, their repeatability, *Of Grammatology* denies the possibility of translation. Not so paradoxically perhaps, each twist of phrase becomes at the same time 'significant' and playful when language is manipulated for the purpose of putting signification into question, for deconstructing the binary opposition 'signifier-signified.' That playfulness I fear I have not been able remotely to capture. Even so simple a word as 'de' carries a touch of play—hinting at both 'of' and 'from.' (I have once resorted to 'from/of,' where the playfulness seemed to ask for special recognition.) But that sort of heavy-handedness cannot punctuate an entire text where 'penser' (to think) carries within itself and points at 'panser' (to dress a wound); for does not thinking seek forever to clamp a dressing over the gaping and violent wound of the impossibility of thought? The translation of the title, suggesting 'a piece of' as well as 'about,' I have retained against expert counsel.

I began this preface by informing my readers that Derrida's theory admitted—as it denied—a preface by questioning the absolute repeatability of the text. It is now time to acknowledge that his theory would likewise admit—as it denies—translation, by questioning the absolute privilege of the original. Any act of reading is besieged and delivered by the precariousness of intertextuality. And translation is, after all, one version of intertextuality.² If there are no unique words, if, as soon as a privileged concept-word emerges, it must be given over to the chain of substitutions and to the 'common language,' why should that act of substitution that is translation be suspect? If the proper name or sovereign status of the author is as much a barrier as a right of way, why should the translator's position be secondary? It must now be evident that, desiring to conserve the 'original' (*De la grammatologie*) and seduced by the freedom of the absence of a sovereign text (not only is there no *Of Grammatology* before mine, but there have been as many translations of the text as readings, the text is infinitely translatable), translation itself is in a double bind.

And, from quite another point of view, most practically and rigorously speaking, both Derrida and I being very roughly bilingual—his English a cut above my French—where does French end and English begin?

I shall not launch my philosophy of translation here. Instead I give you a glimpse of Derrida's:

> Within the limits of its possibility, or its *apparent* possibility, translation practices the difference between signified and signifier. But, if this difference is never pure, translation is even less so, and a notion of *transformation* must be substituted for the notion of translation: a regulated transformation of one language by another, of one text by another. We shall not have and never have had to deal with some 'transfer' of pure signifieds that the signifying instrument—or 'vehicle'—would leave virgin and intact, from one language to another, or within one and the same language. (*Pos* 31)

'From one language to another, *or* within one and the same language.' Translation is a version of the intertexuality that comes to bear also within the 'same' language. Ergo...

Heidegger's deconstructive (or 'destructive') method is often based on consideration of how the so-called content of philosophy is affected by the exigencies of translation. Derrida writes of this in 'La différance' and 'Ousia et grammè.' (*MP* 3–29, *SP* 129–60; *MP* 31–78) In the latter example there is a double play: Heidegger laments the loss for philosophy when the lone Latin 'presence' was pressed into service to translate the many nuanced Greek words signifying philosophical shadings of the idea of presence. Derrida engages in the parallel lament—how translate the many nuanced Heideggerian German words signifying philosophical shadings of the idea of presence through the lone Romance 'présence?' Derrida goes on to use the business of 'mistranslations' as an effective deconstructive lever of his own. The most sustained example is 'La pharmacie de Platon,' where he appropriately asks: why have translators obliterated the word '*pharmakon*' by providing a collection of different words as its translated substitute?

And all said and done, that is the sort of reader I would hope for. A reader who would fasten upon my mistranslations, and with that leverage deconstruct Derrida's text beyond what Derrida as controlling subject has directed in it. (pp. lxxxv–lxxxvii)

NOTES

1. For a cogent discussion of the problems relating to these two words as used by Derrida, see 'White Mythology', trans. by F. C. T. Moore, *New Literary History* VI.i. Autumn 1974, p. 5.
2. For a cogent discussion of translation and intertextuality, see Jeffrey Mehlman, 'Portnoy in Paris,' *Diacritics* 2, iv (Winter 1972), p. 21.

BIBLIOGRAPHY

Pos: Jacques Derrida: *Positions*, Paris 1972.
MP: Jacques Derrida: *Marges de la philosophie*, Paris 1972.
SP: Jacques Derrida: *Speech and Phenomena*, trans. by David B. Allison, Evanston 1973.

From Spivak's 'The Politics of Translation', in her *Outside in the Teaching Machine* (New York and London: Routledge 1993), 179–200

The idea for this title comes from the British sociologist Michèle Barrett's feeling that the politics of translation takes on a massive life of its own if you see language as the process of meaning-construction.[1]

In my view, language may be one of many elements that allow us to make sense of things, of ourselves. I am thinking, of course, of gestures, pauses, but also of chance, of the subindividual force-fields of being which click into place in different situations, swerve from the straight or true line language-in-thought. Making sense of ourselves is what produces identity. If one feels that the production of identity as self-meaning, not just meaning, is as pluralized as a drop of water under a microscope, one is not always satisfied, outside of the ethicopolitical arena as such, with 'generating' thoughts on one's own. [. . .] I have argued in Chapter Six that one of the ways of resisting capitalist multiculturalism's invitation to self-identity and compete is to give the name of 'woman' to the unimaginable other. The same sort of impulse is at work here in a rather more tractable form. For one of the ways to get around the confines of one's identity as one produces expository prose is to work at someone else's title, as one works with a language that belongs to many others. This, after all, is one of the seductions of translating. It is a simple miming of the responsibility to the trace of the other in the self.

[. . .]

How does the translator attend to the specificity of the language she translates? There is a way in which the rhetorical nature of every language disrupts its logical systematicity. If we emphasize the logical at the expense of these rhetorical inferences, we remain safe. 'Safety' is the appropriate term here, because we are talking of risks, of violence to the translating medium.

I felt that I was taking those risks when I recently translated some eighteenth-century Bengali poetry. I quote a bit from my 'Translator's Preface':

> I must overcome what I was taught in school: the highest mark for the most accurate collection of synonyms, strung together in the most proximate syntax. I must resist both the solemnity of chaste Victorian poetic prose and the forced simplicity of 'plain English,' that have imposed themselves as the norm ... Translation is the most intimate act of reading. I surrender to the text when I translate. These songs, sung day after day in family chorus before clear memory began, have a peculiar intimacy for me. Reading and surrendering take on new meanings in such a case. The translator earns permission to transgress from the trace of the other—before memory—in the closest places of the self.[2]

Yet language is not everything. It is only a vital clue to where the self loses its boundaries. The ways in which rhetoric or figuration disrupts logic themselves point at the possibility of random contingency, beside language, around language. Such a *dis*semination cannot be under our control. Yet in translation, where meaning hops into the spacy emptiness between the two named historical languages, we get perilously close to it. By juggling the disruptive rhetoricity that breaks the surface in not necessarily connected ways, we feel the selvedges of the language-textile give way, fray into *frayages* or facilitations.[3] Although every act of reading is a bit of this risky fraying which scrambles together somehow, our stake in agency keeps the fraying down to a minimum except in the communication and reading of and in love. [...] The task of the translator is to facilitate this love between the original and its shadow, a love that permits fraying, holds the agency of the translator and the demands of her imagined or actual audience at bay. The politics of translation from a non-European woman's text too often suppresses this possibility, because the translator cannot engage with, or cares insufficiently for, the rhetoricity of the original.

[...]

Let us now think that, in that other language, rhetoric may be disrupting logic in the matter of the production of an agent, and indicating the founding violence of the silence at work within rhetoric. Logic allows us to jump from word to word by means of clearly indicated connections. Rhetoric must work in the silence between and around words in order to see what works and how much. The jagged relationship between rhetoric and logic, condition and effect of knowing, is a relationship by which a world is made for the agent, so that the agent can act in an ethical way, a political way, a day-to-day way; so that the agent can be alive, in a human way, in the world. Unless one can at least construct a model of this for the other language, there is no real translation.

Unfortunately it is only too easy to produce translations if this task is completely ignored. [...]

Without a sense of the rhetoricity of language, a species of neocolonialist construction of the non-Western is afoot. [...] Poststructuralism has shown some of us a staging of the agent with a three-tiered notion of language (as rhetoric, logic, silence). We must attempt to enter or direct that staging, as one directs a play, as an actor interprets a script. That takes a different kind of effort from taking translation to be a matter of synonym, syntax, and local color.

[Spivak then discusses the need to bring texts into English, 'the language of the majority'.] On the other hand, there is nothing essentially noble about the law of the majority either. It is merely the easiest way of being 'democratic' with minorities. In the act of wholesale translation into English there can be a betrayal of the democratic ideal into the law of the strongest. This happens when all the literature of the Third

World gets translated into a sort of with-it translatese, so that the literature by a woman in Palestine begins to resemble, in the feel of its prose, something by a man from Taiwan. [...]

Let us consider an example where attending to the author's stylistic experiments can produce a different text. Mahasweta Devi's 'Stanadāyini' is available in two versions.[4] Devi has expressed approval for the attention to her signature style in the version entitled 'Breast-Giver.' The alternative translation gives the title as 'The Wet-Nurse,' and thus neutralizes the author's irony in constructing an uncanny word; enough like 'wet-nurse' to make that sense, and enough unlike to shock. It is as if the translator should decide to translate Dylan Thomas's famous title and opening line as 'Do not go gently into that good night.' The theme of treating the breast as organ of labor-power-as-commodity and the breast as metonymic part-object standing in for other-as-object—the way in which the story plays with Marx and Freud on the occasion of the woman's body—is lost even before you enter the story. In the text Mahasweta uses proverbs that are startling even in the Bengali. The translator of 'The Wet-Nurse' leaves them out. She decides not to try to translate these hard bits of earthy wisdom, contrasting with class-specific access to modernity, also represented in the story. In fact, if the two translations are read side by side, the loss of the rhetorical silences of the original can be felt from one to the other.

First, then, the translator must surrender to the text. She must solicit the text to show the limits of its language, because that rhetorical aspect will point at the silence of the absolute fraying of language that the text wards off, in its special manner. Some think this is just an ethereal way of talking about literature or philosophy. But no amount of tough talk can get around the fact that translation is the most intimate act of reading. Unless the translator has earned the right to become the intimate reader, she cannot surrender to the text, cannot respond to the special call of the text.

The presupposition that women have a natural or narrative-historical solidarity, that there is something in a woman or an undifferentiated women's story that speaks to another woman without benefit of language-learning, might stand against the translator's task of surrender. Paradoxically, it is not possible for us as ethical agents to imagine otherness or alterity maximally. We have to turn the other into something like the self in order to be ethical. To surrender in translation is more erotic than ethical. In that situation the good-willing attitude 'she is just like me' is not very helpful. In so far as Michèle Barrett is not like Gayatri Spivak, their friendship is more effective as a translation. In order to earn that right of friendship or surrender of identity, of knowing that the rhetoric of the text indicates the limits of language for you as long as you are with the text, you have to be in a different relationship with the language, not even only with the specific text.

Learning about translation on the job, I came to think that it would be a practical help if one's relationship with the language being translated was such that sometimes one preferred to speak in it about intimate things. This is no more than a practical suggestion, not a theoretical requirement, useful especially because a woman writer who is wittingly or unwittingly a 'feminist'—and of course all woman writers are not 'feminist' even in this broad sense—will relate to the three-part staging of (agency in) language in ways defined out as 'private,' since they might question the more public linguistic maneuvers. (pp. 179–83)

NOTES

1. The first part of this essay is based on a conversation with Michèle Barrett in the summer of 1990.

2. Forthcoming from Seagull Press, Calcutta. [*Song for Kali: A Cycle of Drawings and Songs* (Nirode Mazumdar Interprets Ramprasad), trans. Gayatri Chakravorty Spivak (Seagull Private Books Limited, 2000)]

3. 'Facilitation' is the English translation of the Freudian term *Bahnung* (pathing) which is translated *frayage* in French. The dictionary meaning is:

   Term used by Freud at a time when he was putting forward a neurological model of the functioning of the psychical apparatus (1895): the excitation, in passing from one neurone to another, runs into a certain resistance; where its passage results in a permanent reduction in this resistance, there is said to be facilitation; excitation will opt for a facilitated pathway in preference to one where no facilitation has occurred. (J. B. Pontalis, *The Language of Psychoanalysis* [London: Hogarth Press, 1973], 157.).

4. 'The Wet-Nurse,' in Kali for Women, eds., *Truth Tales: Stories by Indian Women* (London: The Women's Press, 1987), pp. 1–50 (first published by Kali for Women, Dehli, 1986), and 'Breast-Giver,' in Spivak, *In Other Worlds*, pp. 222–240.

5.12 TALAL ASAD

Talal Asad is Distinguished Professor of Anthropology at the City University of New York (CUNY) Graduate Center. He has done extensive research on the complex relations between modernity, secularism, and religion (including modern religious revivals). His publications include the books *Genealogies of Religion: Discipline and Reasons of Power in Christianity and Islam* (1993) and *Formations of the Secular: Christianity, Islam, Modernity* (2003).

Asad begins his article 'The Concept of Cultural Translation in British Social Anthropology', part of which is reprinted below, by briefly mentioning anthropological interest in language and translation, reminding his readers 'that the phrase "the translation of cultures," which increasingly since the 1950s has become an almost banal description of the distinctive task of social anthropology, was not always so much in evidence' (p. 141). He then refers to Godfrey Lienhardt's 1954 paper 'Modes of Thought' as an early example of the use of this notion of translation (p. 142), quoting Lienhardt's statement: 'The problem of describing to others how members of a remote tribe think then begins to appear largely as one of translation, of making the coherence primitive thought has in the languages it really lives in, as clear as possible in our own.' Asad goes on to cite (p. 142) the noted British anthropologist Edmund Leach's comments on how the 'essential problem' of coming to terms with 'the others' is 'one of translation'.

As part of his pursuit of the role of 'cultural translation' in British anthropology, Asad then critically examines the article 'Concepts and Society' by another noted scholar in the field, Ernest Gellner. Gellner's basic argument, says Asad, 'is that (a) contemporary anthropologists insist on interpreting exotic concepts and beliefs within a social context, but that (b) in doing so they ensure that apparently absurd or incoherent assertions are always given an acceptable meaning, and that (c) while the contextual method of interpretation is in principle valid, the "excessive charity" that usually goes with it is not'. Asad cites (p. 146) Gellner's comments on how the anthropologist has 'no third language which could mediate between the native language and his own, in which equivalences could be stated and which would avoid the pitfalls arising from the fact that his own language has its own way of handling the world'; and as a result the anthropologist proceeds to locate equivalent sentences in his own language, but these tend to be loaded with the value connotations of his own culture. In doing so, the anthropologist, eager to make sense, is often guilty of excessive charity instead of maintaining critical distance.

Asad claims that 'Gellner's parable of the anthropologist-translator requires the assumption that it is sentences that the latter matches' (p. 147), whereas he (Asad) sees this translation as a matter 'of *learning to live another form of life* and to speak another kind of language. Which contexts are relevant in different discursive events is something one learns in the course of living, and even though it is often very difficult to verbalize that knowledge, it is still knowledge about something "in the nature of society," about some aspect of living, that indicates (although it does not "dictate") just how much context is relevant to any given utterance' (p. 149). Asad concludes his detailed analysis of Gellner's article by explaining why he has insisted 'that anyone concerned with translating from other cultures must look for coherence in discourses' and yet he has devoted several pages 'to showing that Gellner's text is largely incoherent'. 'Gellner and I speak the same language, belong to the same academic profession, live in the same society. In taking up a critical stance toward his text I am *contesting* what he says, not *translating* it, and the radical difference between these two activities is precisely what I insist on. [...] In order for criticism to be responsible, it must always be addressed to someone who can contest it' (pp. 155–6).

All of the above has important implications for the issues of translation covered by other authors represented in this volume, but this is even more true of Asad's subsequent discussion, contained below.

From: 'The Concept of Cultural Translation in British Social Anthropology', in James Clifford and George E. Marcus (eds.), *Writing Culture: The Poetics and Politics of Ethnography* (Berkeley and Los Angeles: University of California Press 1986), 141–64

The Inequality of Languages

A careful reading of Gellner's paper shows that although he raises a number of important questions, he not only fails to answer them but misses some of the most crucial aspects of the problem with which the ethnographer is engaged. The most interesting of these, it seems to me, is the problem of what one might call 'unequal languages'—and it is this I want now to discuss in some detail.

All good translation seeks to reproduce the structure of an alien discourse within the translator's own language. How that structure (or 'coherence') is reproduced will, of course, depend on the genre concerned ('poetry,' 'scientific analysis,' 'narrative,' etc.), on the resources of the translator's language, as well as on the interests of the translator and/ or his readership. All successful translation is premised on the fact that it is addressed within a specific language, and therefore also to a specific set of practices, a specific form of life. The further that form of life is from the original, the less mechanical is the reproduction. As Walter Benjamin wrote: 'The language of a translation can—in fact must—let itself go, so that it gives voice to the *intentio* of the original not as reproduction but as harmony, as a supplement to the language in which it expresses itself, as its own kind of *intentio*' (1969: 79). It is, incidentally, for the reader to evaluate that *intentio*, not for the translator to preempt the evaluation. A good translation should always precede a critique. And we can turn this around by saying that a good critique is always an 'internal' critique—that is, one based on some shared understanding, on a joint life, which it aims to enlarge and make more coherent. Such a critique—no less than the object of criticism—is a point of view, a (contra) *version*, having only provisional and limited authority.

What happens when the languages concerned are so remote that it is very difficult to rewrite a harmonious *intentio*? Rudolf Pannwitz, quoted in the Benjamin essay on which I have just drawn, makes the following observation:

> Our translations, even the best ones, proceed from a wrong premise. They want to turn Hindi, Greek, English into German instead of turning German into Hindi, Greek, English. Our translators have a far greater reverence for the usage of their own language than for the spirit of the foreign works.... The basic error of the translator is that he preserves the state in which his own language happens to be instead of allowing his language to be powerfully affected by the foreign tongue. Particularly when translating from a language very remote from his own he must go back to the primal elements of language itself and penetrate to the point where work, image, and tone converge. He must expand and deepen his language by means of the foreign language. (1969: 80–1)

This call to transform a language in order to translate the coherence of the original, poses an interesting challenge to the person satisfied with an absurd-sounding translation on the assumption that the original must have been equally absurd: the good translator does not immediately assume that unusual difficulty in conveying the sense of an alien discourse denotes a fault in the latter, but instead critically examines the normal state of his or her *own* language. The relevant question therefore is not how tolerant an *attitude* the translator ought to display toward the original author (an abstract ethical dilemma), but how she can test the tolerance of her own language for assuming unaccustomed forms.

But this pushing beyond the limits of one's habitual usages, this breaking down and reshaping of one's own language through the process of translation, is never an easy business, in part because (if I may be allowed a hypostatization) it depends on the willingness of the translator's *language* to subject itself to this transforming power. I attribute, somewhat fictitiously, volition to the language because I want to emphasize that the matter is largely something the translator cannot determine by individual activity (any more than the individual speaker can affect the evolution of his or her language)—that it is governed by institutionally defined power relations between the languages/modes of life concerned. To put it crudely: because the languages of Third World societies—including, of course, the societies that social anthropologists have traditionally studied—are 'weaker' in relation to Western languages (and today, especially to English), they are more likely to submit to forcible transformation in the translation process than the other way around. The reason for this is, first, that in their political-economic relations with Third World countries, Western nations have the greater ability to manipulate the latter. And, second, Western languages produce and deploy *desired* knowledge more readily than Third World languages do. (The knowledge that Third World languages deploy more easily is not sought by Western societies in quite the same way, or for the same reason.)

Take modern Arabic as an example. Since the early nineteenth century there has been a growing volume of material translated from European languages—especially French and English—into Arabic. This includes scientific texts as well as 'social science,' 'history,' 'philosophy,' and 'literature.' And from the nineteenth century, Arabic as a language has begun as a result to undergo a transformation (lexical, grammatical, semantic) that is far more radical than anything to be identified in European languages—a transformation that has pushed it to approximate to the latter more closely than in the past. Such transformations signal inequalities in the power (i.e., in the *capacities*) of the respective languages in relation to the *dominant* forms of discourse that have been and are still being translated. There are varieties of knowledge to be learnt, but also a host of models to be imitated and reproduced. In some cases knowledge of these models is a precondition for the production of more knowledge; in other cases it is an end in itself, a mimetic gesture of power, an expression of desire for transformation. A recognition of this well-known fact reminds us that industrial capitalism transforms not only modes of production but also kinds of knowledge and styles of life in the Third World. And with them, forms of language. The result of half-transformed styles of life will make for ambiguities, which an unskillful Western translator may simplify in the direction of his own 'strong' language.

What does this argument imply for the anthropological concept of cultural translation? That perhaps there is a greater stiffness in ethnographic linguistic conventions, a greater intrinsic resistance than can be overcome by individual experiments in modes of ethnographic representation.

In his perceptive essay 'Modes of Thought,' which Gellner criticizes for making overcharitable assumptions about the coherence of 'primitive thought,' Lienhardt has this to say:

> When we live with savages and speak their languages, learning to represent their experience to ourselves in their way, we come as near to thinking like them as we can without ceasing to be ourselves. Eventually, we try to represent their conceptions systematically in the logical constructs we have been brought up to use; and we hope, at best, thus to reconcile what can be expressed in their languages, with what can be expressed in ours. We mediate between their habits of thought, which we

have acquired with them, and those of our own society; in doing so, it is not finally some mysterious 'primitive philosophy' that we are exploring, but the further potentialities of our thought and language. (1954: 96–97)

In the field, as Lienhardt rightly suggests, the process of translation takes place at the very moment the ethnographer engages with a specific mode of life—just as a child does in learning to grow up within a specific culture. He learns to find his way in a new environment, and a new language. And like a child he needs to verbalize *explicitly* what the proper way of doing things is, because that is how learning proceeds. (Cf. A. R. Luria on 'synpraxic speech' in Luria and Yudovich 1971: 50.) When the child/anthropologist becomes adept at adult ways, what he has learnt becomes *implicit*—as assumptions informing a shared mode of life, with all its resonances and areas of unclarity.

But learning to live a new mode of life is not the same as learning about another mode of life. When anthropologists return to their countries, they must write up 'their people,' and they must do so in the conventions of representation already circumscribed (already 'written around,' 'bounded') by their discipline, institutional life, and wider society. 'Cultural translation' must accommodate itself to a different language not only in the sense of English as opposed to Dinka, or English as opposed to Kabbashi Arabic, but also in the sense of a British, middle class, academic game as opposed to the modes of life of the 'tribal' Sudan. The stiffness of a powerful established structure of life, with its own discursive games, its own 'strong' languages, is what among other things finally determines the effectiveness of the translation. The translation is addressed to a very specific audience, which is waiting to read *about* another mode of life and to manipulate the text it reads according to established rules, not to learn *to live* a new mode of life.

If Benjamin was right in proposing that translation may require not a mechanical reproduction of the original but a harmonization with its *intentio*, it follows that there is no reason why this should be done only in the same mode. Indeed, it could be argued that 'translating' an alien form of life, another culture, is not always done best through the representational discourse of ethnography, that under certain conditions a dramatic performance, the execution of a dance, or the playing of a piece of music might be more apt. These would all be *productions* of the original and not mere interpretations: transformed instances of the original, not authoritative textual representations of it (cf. Hollander 1959). But would they be thought of by most social anthropologists as valid exercises in the 'translation of culture'? I think not, because they all raise an entirely different dimension of the relationship between the anthropological 'work' and its audience, the question of different *uses* (practices), as opposed merely to different *writings and readings* (meanings) of that work. And as social anthropologists we are trained to translate other cultural languages as texts, not to introduce or enlarge cultural capacities, learnt from other ways of living, into our own. It seems to me very likely that the notion of culture as *text* has reinforced this view of our task, because it facilitates the assumption that translation is *essentially* a matter of verbal representation.

Reading Other Cultures

This inequality in the power of languages, together with the fact that the anthropologist typically writes about an illiterate (or at any rate non-English-speaking) population for a largely academic, English-speaking audience, encourages a tendency I would now like to discuss: the tendency to read the *implicit* in alien cultures.

According to many social anthropologists, the object of ethnographic translation is not the historically situated speech (that is the task of the folklorist or the linguist), but 'culture,' and to translate culture the anthropologist must first read and then reinscribe the implicit meanings that lie beneath/within/beyond situated speech. Mary Douglas puts this nicely:

> The anthropologist who draws out the whole scheme of the cosmos which is implied in [the observed] practices does the primitive culture great violence if he seems to present the cosmology as a systematic philosophy subscribed to consciously by individuals. ... So the primitive world view which I have defined above is rarely itself an object of contemplation and speculation in the primitive culture. It has evolved as the appanage of other social institutions. To this extent it is produced indirectly, and to this extent the primitive culture must be taken to be unaware of itself, unconscious of its own conditions. (1966: 91)

One difference between the anthropologist and the linguist in the matter of translation is perhaps this: that whereas the latter is immediately faced with a specific piece of discourse produced within the society studied, a discourse that is *then* textualized, the former must construct the discourse *as* a cultural text in terms of meanings *implicit* in a range of practices. The construction of cultural discourse and its translation thus seem to be facets of a single act. [...]

The business of identifying unconscious meanings in the task of 'cultural translation' is therefore perhaps better compared to the activity of the psychoanalyst than to that of the linguist. Indeed British anthropologists have sometimes presented their work in precisely these terms. Thus David Pocock, a pupil of Evans-Pritchard's, writes:

> In short, the work of the social anthropologist may be regarded as a highly complex act of translation in which author and translator collaborate. A more precise analogy is that of the relation between the psychoanalyst and his subject. The analyst enters the private world of his subject in order to learn the grammar of his private language. If the analysis goes no further it is no different in kind from the understanding which may exist between any two people who know each other well.[!] It becomes scientific to the extent that the private language of intimate understanding is translated into a public language, however specialized from the layman's point of view, which in this case is the language of psychologists. But the

particular act of translation does not distort the private experience of the subject and ideally it is, at least potentially, acceptable to him as a scientific representation of it. Similarly, the model of Nuer political life which emerges in Professor Evans-Pritchard's work is a scientific model meaningful to his fellow-sociologists as sociologists, and it is effective because it is *potentially acceptable to the Nuer in some ideal situation in which they could be supposed to be interested in themselves as men living in society.* The collaboration of natural scientists may from this point of view be seen as developing language enabling certain people to communicate with increasing subtlety about a distinct area of natural phenomena which is defined by the name of the particular science. Their science is, in the literal meaning of the term, their commonsense, their common meaning. To move from this common sense to the 'common sense' of the wider public involves again an act of translation. The situation of social anthropology, or sociology in general, is not at this level so very different. The difference lies in the fact that sociological phenomena are objectively studied only to the extent that their subjective meaning is taken into account and that the people studied are potentially capable of sharing the sociological consciousness that the sociologist has of them. (1961: 88–89; emphasis added)

I have quoted this remarkable passage in full because it states very lucidly a position that is, I think, broadly acceptable to many anthropologists who would otherwise consider themselves to be engaged in very different kinds of enterprise. I have quoted it also because the nature of the collaboration between 'author and translator' is neatly brought out in the subsequent reference to the psychoanalyst as scientist: if the anthropological translator, like the analyst, has final authority in determining the subject's meanings—it is then the former who becomes *the real author* of the latter. In this view, 'cultural translation' is a matter of determining implicit meanings—not the meanings the native speaker actually acknowledges in his speech, not even the meanings the native listener necessarily accepts, but those he is 'potentially capable of sharing' with scientific authority 'in some ideal situation': it is when he can say, for example, with Gellner, that *vox Dei* is in reality *vox populi*, that he utters the true meaning of his traditional discourse, an essential meaning of his culture. The fact that in that 'ideal situation' he would no longer be a Muslim Berber tribesman, but something coming to resemble Professor Gellner, does not appear to worry such cultural translators.

This power to create meanings for a subject through the notion of the 'implicit' or the 'unconscious,' *to authorize them*, has of course been discussed for the analyst-analysand relationship (e.g., recently in Malcolm 1982). It has not, to my knowledge, been considered with regard to what the cultural translator does. There are, of course, important differences in the case of the anthropologist. It may be pointed out that the latter does not *impose* his translation on the members of the society whose cultural discourse he unravels, that his ethnography is therefore not authoritative in the way the analyst's case study is. The analysand comes to the analyst, or is referred to the latter by those with authority over him, as a patient in need of help. The anthropologist, by contrast, comes to the society he wants to read, he sees himself as a learner, not as a guide, and he withdraws from the society when he has adequate information to inscribe its culture. He does not consider the society, and neither do its members consider themselves to be, sick: the society is never subject to the anthropologist's authority.

But this argument is not quite as conclusive as it may seem at first sight. It remains the case that the ethnographer's translation/representation of a particular culture is inevitably a textual construct, that as representation it cannot normally be contested by the people to whom it is attributed, and that as a 'scientific text' it eventually becomes a privileged element in the potential store of historical memory for the nonliterate society concerned. In modern and modernizing societies, inscribed records have a greater power to shape, to reform, selves and institutions than folk memories do. They even construct folk memories. The anthropologist's monograph may return, retranslated, into a 'weaker' Third World language. In the long run, therefore, it is not the personal authority of the ethnographer, but the social authority of his ethnography that matters. And that authority is inscribed in the institutionalized forces of industrial capitalist society (see page 158 [p. 497 in this volume] above), which are constantly *tending* to push the meanings of various Third World societies in a single direction. This is not to say that there are no resistances to this tendency. But 'resistance' in itself indicates the presence of a dominant force. (pp. 156–63)

REFERENCES

Asad, Talal. 1983a. 'Anthropological conceptions of Religion: Reflections on Geeretz', in *Man* 18, pp. 237–259.

Benjamin, Walter. 1969. 'The Task of the Translator', translated by Harry Zohn, in *Illuminations: Essays and Reflections*, edited and with an introduction by Hannah Arendt, pp. 69–82.

Douglas, Mary. 1966. *Purity and Danger*, London, Routledge & Kegan Paul.

Dummett M. 1981. 'Objections to Chomsky', in *London Review of Books*, September 3–16, pp. 5–6.

Gellner, Ernest. 1970. 'Concepts and Society', in *Rationality*, ed. by B.R. Wilson, Oxford, Basil Blackwell, pp. 18–49.

Hollander, J. 1959. 'Versions, Interpretations, and Performances', in *On Translation*, ed. R. A. Brower, Cambridge Mass., Harvard University Press, pp. 205–231.

Lienhardt, Godfrey. 1954. 'Modes of Thought', in *The Institutions of Primitive Society* by E. E. Evans-Pritchard et al., Oxford, Basil Blackwell, pp. 95–107.

Luria, A. R., and F. I. Yudovich. 1971. *Speech and the Development of Mental Processes in the Child*, London, Penguin Books.

Malcolm, J. 1982. *Psychoanalaysis: The Impossible Profession*, London, Pan Books.

Pocock, David. 1961. *Social Anthropology*, London and New York, Sheed and Ward.

5.13   EVA HOFFMAN

Eva Hoffman (b. 1945) was born in Cracow, Poland into a Jewish family, emigrating to Canada when she was 13. She served as an editor of the *New York Times Book Review* from 1979 to 1990, but now lives in London. In her first book, *Lost in Translation: A Life in a New Language* (1989), she explores the emotional and linguistic dislocation suffered by an exile. She has also published *Exit Into History: A Journey through the New Eastern Europe* (1993); *Shtetl: The Life and Death of a Small Town in the World of Polish Jewry* (2000); and *After Such Knowledge: Where Memory of the Holocaust Ends and History Begins* (2004). Hoffman is the author of numerous essays and articles on cultural and political topics for, among others, *The New York Times*, *The Atlantic Monthly*, and *The Yale Review*.

Lost in Translation is a autobiographical work describing the journey of a 13-year-old Jewish girl who leaves her native Poland with her family to settle in North America (first Canada and later the US). With ties to both the *Bildungsroman* and postmodern metanarratives, Hofman's story describes the struggles and challanges facing a person whose border between childhood and maturity becomes also a divide between countries, cultures, and languages. Not only her title—the familiar phrase about how meaning risks getting lost when moving between languages—but a substantial part of Hoffman's work revolves around the cultural, existential, and metaphorical implications of the term 'translation'. As a young immigrant she attempts in various ways to translate her identity, to make the world of her childhood somehow 'fit' her new linguistic and socio-cultural environment, even as she realizes that one 'can't transport human meanings whole from one culture to another'.[1]

In this respect, Hoffman's experience is not unlike that of many translators, who when seeking to transport culturally complex works from one language to another, often get the strong sense that it cannot be done—yet they, like she, go ahead and do it. The keyword in the sentence quoted is 'whole'; one has to let go of a whole, hoping to create another that represents and extends it honourably. And while one may celebrate both the glories of translation and the multiculturalism that results from a migrant mobility such as the one Hoffman describes, she also manifests that this is a process fraught with anxiety. This is also borne out, in the context of postcolonial studies, by Homi Bhabha, who emphasizes the 'anxiety of enjoining the global and the local; the dilemma of projecting an international space on the trace of a decentered, fragmented subject. Cultural globality is figured in the *in-between* spaces of double-frames: its historical originality marked by

---

[1] Eva Hoffman, *Lost in Translation: Life in a New Language* (London: Minerva 1991), 175.

a cognitive obscurity; its decentred "subject" signified in the nervous temporality of the transitional, or the emergent provisionality of the "present".'[2]

This is indeed the 'translational' experience Ewa, later Eva, Hoffman goes through; she has to negotiate this in-between (non)territory, this 'interstitial' space, which unsettles any rigid mapping of cultural locations, and only allows them to exist in hybrid forms. A part of every translation is a text in exile; yet that very text cannot be separated from what Walter Benjamin has termed the labour pains of the language of the translation.[3]

From *Lost in Translation: Life in a New Language* (1989; London: Minerva, 1991)

When the brass band on the shore strikes up the jaunty mazurka rhythms of the Polish anthem, I am pierced by a youthful sorrow so powerful that I suddenly stop crying and try to hold still against the pain. I desperately want time to stop, to hold the ship still with the force of my will. I am suffering my first, severe attack of nostalgia, or *tęsknota*—a word that adds to nostalgia the tonalities of sadness and longing. It is a feeling whose shades and degrees I'm destined to know intimately, but at this hovering moment, it comes upon me like a visitation from a whole new geography of emotions, an annunciation of how much an absence can hurt. (p. 4)

'Shut up, shuddup,' the children around us are shouting, and it's the first word in English that I understand from its dramatic context. My sister and I stand in the schoolyard clutching each other, while kids all around us are running about, pummeling each other, and screaming like whirling dervishes. Both the boys and the girls look sharp and aggressive to me—the girls all have bright lipstick on, their hair sticks up and out like witches' fury, and their skirts are held up and out by stiff, wiry, crinolines. I can't imagine wanting to talk their harsh-sounding language. (pp. 104–5)

Every day I learn new words, new expressions. I pick them up from school exercises, from conversations, from the books I take out of Vancouver's well-lit, cheerful public library. There are some turns of phrase to which I develop strange allergies. 'You're welcome,' for example, strikes me as a gaucherie, and I can hardly bring myself to say it—I suppose because it implies that there's something to be thanked for, which in Polish would be impolite. The very places where language is at its most conventional, where it should be most taken for granted, are the places where I feel the prick of artifice.

Then there are words to which I take an equally irrational liking, for their sound, or just because I'm pleased to have deduced their meaning. Mainly they're words I learn

---

[2] Homi K. Bhabha, 'How Newness Enters the World', *The Location of Culture* (London and New York: Routledge 1994), 216.

[3] Cf. Walter Benjamin's article 'The Task of the Translator', in Sect. 4.4, above.

from books, like 'enigmatic' or 'insolent'—words that have only a literary value, that exist only as signs on the page.

But mostly, the problem is that the signifier has become severed from the signified. The words I learn now don't stand for things in the same unquestioned way they did in my native tongue. 'River' in Polish was a vital sound, energized with the essence of riverhood, of my rivers, of my being immersed in rivers. 'River' in English is cold—a word without an aura. It has no accumulated associations for me, and it does not give off the radiating haze of connotation. It does not evoke.

The process, alas, works in reverse as well. When I see a river now, it is not shaped, assimilated by the word that accommodates it to the psyche—a word that makes a body of water a river rather than an uncontained element. The river before me remains a thing, absolutely other, absolutely unbending to the grasp of my mind.

When my friend Penny tells me she is envious, or happy, or disappointed, I try laboriously to translate not from English to Polish but from the word back to its source, to the feeling from which it springs. Already, in that moment of strain, spontaneity of response is lost. And anyway, the translation doesn't work. I don't know how Penny feels when she talks about envy. The word hangs in a Platonic stratosphere, a vague prototype of all envy, so large, so all-emcompassing that it might crush me—as might disappointment or happiness. (pp. 106–7)

For my birthday, Penny gives me a diary, complete with a little lock and key to keep what I write from the eyes of all intruders. It is that little lock—the visible symbol of the privacy in which the diary is meant to exist—that creates my dilemma. If I am indeed to write something entirely for myself, in what language do I write? Several times, I open the diary and close it again. I can't decide. Writing in Polish at this point would be a little like resorting to Latin or ancient Greek—an ancient thing to do in a diary, in which you're supposed to set down your most immediate experiences and unpremeditated thoughts in the most unmediated languages. Polish is becoming a dead language, the language of the untranslatable past. But writing for nobody's eyes in English? That's like doing a school exercise, or performing in front of yourself, a slightly perverse act of self-voyeurism.

Because I have to choose something, I finally choose English. If I'm to write about the present, I have to write in the language of the present, even if it's not the language of the self. As a result, the diary becomes surely one of the more impersonal exercises of that sort produced by an adolescent girl. These are no sentimental effusions of rejected love, eruptions of familial anger, or consoling broodings about death. English is not the language of such emotions. Instead, I set down my reflections on the ugliness of wrestling; on the elegance of Mozart, and on how Dostoyevsky puts me in mind of El Greco. I write down Thoughts. I Write.

There is a certain pathos to this naïve snobbery, for the diary is an earnest attempt to create a part of my persona that I imagine I would have grown into in Polish. In the solitude of this most private act, I write, in my public language, in order to update what might have been my other self. The diary is about me and not about me at all. But on one level, it allows me to make the first jump. I learn English through writing, and, in turn, writing gives me a written self. Refracted through the double distance of English and writing, this self—my English self—becomes oddly objective; more than anything, it perceives. It exists more easily in the abstract sphere of thoughts and observations than in the world. For a while, this impersonal self, this cultural negative capability, becomes the truest thing about me. When I write, I have a real existence that is proper to the activity of writing—an existence that takes place midway between me and the sphere of artifice, art, pure language. This language is beginning to invent another me. However, I discover something odd. It seems that when I write (or, for that matter, think) in English, I am unable to use the word 'I.' I do not go as far as the schizophrenic 'she'—but I am driven, as by a compulsion, to the double, the Siamese-twin 'you.' (pp. 120–1)

In the politics of daily perception, I'm at a distinct disadvantage. My American Friends are so many, and they share so many assumptions that are quite invisible to them, precisely because they're shared. These are assumptions about the most fundamental human transactions, subcutaneous beliefs, which lie just below the stratum of political opinion or overt ideology: about how much 'space,' physical or psychological, we need to give each other, about how much 'control' is desirable, about what is private and what public, about how much interest in another person's affairs is sympathy and how much interference, about what's a pretty face or a handsome body, about what we're allowed to poke fun at and what we have to revere, about how much we need to hide in order to reveal ourselves. To remain outside such common agreements is to remain outside reality itself—and if I'm not to risk a mild cultural schizophrenia, I have to make a shift in the innermost ways. I have to translate myself. But if I'm to achive this without becoming assimilated—that is, absorbed—by my new world, the translation has to be careful, the turns of the psyche unforced. To mouth foreign terms without incorporating their meanings is to risk becoming bowdlerized. A true translation proceeds by the motions of understanding and sympathy; it happens by slow increments, sentence by sentence, phrase by phrase. (pp. 210–11)

I'm a vigilant Culture watcher, like everyone else. And undoubtedly, like everyone else, I've ingested parts of the Culture even while I've prudishly pulled my skirts around me. I see this paradox in my friends clearly enough, culture turning into counterculture and counterculture into culture despite everyone's best intentions, the organization man giving way to the dropout and the dropout to a new technocrat, loneliness to love-ins and then loneliness again, as if any set of cultural terms necessarily determines the terms of the subsequent rebellion, and the rejections carry in them the seeds of what is rejected. It is always difficult to know how a culture flows through our veins, and by now I've lost track of how much America flows through mine. Fragments of Janis Joplin songs and the Rolling Stones surface in my mind as I walk down the street; the landscape of Amagansett, where I've spent several summers, is just under my retina, to be retrieved whenever I think vacation, time off; films about New York are films about my hometown; 'Gimme a break,' I say, when a street vendor gets pushy, and the issues I debate—how to conduct one's career without losing one's sanity, what to eat without becoming contaminated, how to deal with passive-aggressive lovers—are American conversations, dictated by 'the Culture' as much as this season's fashions. And I never, never say 'It's only psychological' anymore. Maybe, behind my back and while I wasn't looking, I've acquired a second unconscious, an American one, made up of diverse cultural matter. Like any unconscious, this one is hard to pin down. I only know that the hybrid creature I've become is made up of two parts Americana, that the pastiche has lots of local color. Despite my resistance, or perhaps through its very act, I've become a partial American, a sort of resident alien. (p. 221)

For me, therapy is partly translation therapy, the talking cure a second-language cure. My going to a shrink is, among other things, a rite of initiation: initiation into the language of the subculture within which I happen to live, into a way of explaining myself to myself. But gradually, it becomes a project of translating backward. The way to jump over my Great Divide is to crawl backward over it in English. It's only when I retell my whole story, back to the beginning, and from the beginning onward, in one language, that I can reconcile the voices within me with each other; it is only then that the person who judges the voices and tells the stories begins to emerge.

The tiny gap that opened when my sister and I were given new names can never be fully closed up; I can't have one name again. My sister has returned to her Polish name— Alina. It takes a while for me to switch back to it; Alina, in English, is a different word than it is in Polish: it has the stamp of the unusual, its syllables don't fall as easily on an English speaker's tongue. In order to transport a single word without distortion, one would have to transport the entire language around it. My sister no longer has one, authentic name, the name that is inseparable from her single essence.

When I talk to myself now, I talk in English. English is the language in which I've become an adult, in which I've seen my favorite movies and read my favorite novels, and sung along with Janis Joplin records. In Polish, whole provinces of adult experience are missing. I don't know Polish words for 'microchips,' or 'pathetic fallacy,' or *The Importance of Being Earnest*. If I tried talking to myself in my native tongue, it would be a stumbling conversation indeed, interlaced with English expressions. (pp. 271–72)

5.14 GREGORY RABASSA

Gregory Rabassa (b. 1922), American translator, whose father was Cuban, has produced more than three dozen translations from the Spanish and the Portuguese, the best known being the novel *One Hundred Years of Solitude* (1970), a translation of Nobel Prize laureate Gabriel García Márquez's *Cien años de soledad* (1967). This translation is widely acclaimed, and so is that of Márquez's novel *The Autumn of the Patriarch*; Márquez himself has called Rabassa the 'best Latin American writer in the English language.' Rabassa's translations include works by several other writers, mainly Latin American: Octavio Paz, Miguel Angel Asturias, Julio Cortázar, Mario Vargas Llosa, Jorge Amado, José Lezama Lima, Clarice Lispector, and Luisa Valenzuela. He has received numerous awards, including the National Book Award for translation in 1967 for *Hopscotch* by Cortázar.

Rabassa received a doctorate from Columbia University. He is still teaching, as a professor of Romance languages and Comparative Literature at Queens College, City University of New York. During the Second World War, he served in North Africa and Italy, his first assignment including breaking secret military codes ('That's where my translating career started . . .'). After graduate school, he worked as an editor at *Odyssey Review*, a literary magazine that published new literature from Europe and Latin America. Some of his translations were published in the magazine, and this led to an opportunity to produce *Hopscotch*, his award-winning translation of *Rayuela* by Cortázar. It can truly be said that Rabassa never looked back from that. Together with Helen R. Lane, Suzanne Jill Levine (see Sect. 5.15, below), and a number of other translators he has been instrumental in bringing to the English-language world the 'boom' writing of Latin America, including key works associated with 'magic realism'.

From Rabassa's article 'If This Be Treason: Translation and Its Possibilities', in William Frawley (ed.), *Translation: Literary, Linguistic, and Philosophical Perspectives* (Newark, Del. University of Delawere Press/London and Toronto: Associated University Presses 1984), 21–9

> *Traduttore, traditore*
> —Italian cliché

In this age of the bad mouth, where a kind word is as rare as a Buick in college town, translation has had more than its share of opprobrium. This is probably due to its being a kind of bastard art, an intermediate form, and as such always vulnerable to attack.

Translation is almost as old as language, certainly as old as the contact of a language with alien speakers. In spite of the fact that it is an ancient craft, its ways are still rather mysterious, and most analyses have fallen short of the mark in defining what translation is or, at least, what it should be. The inconsequence of the last fact would seem to make translation an art, something defined by its very existence or by its uses, as Ortega might have put it. (p. 21)

The basic problem of the writer as he moves along is that he must name things: objects, actions, ideas. He must often choose among possibilities and synonyms for the *mot juste*; but since it is his creation, at some point he can sit back and cease pondering. It is his work, take it or leave it. The translator, however, is at one remove. He must find the *mot juste* for a *mot juste* out of his own bag of possibilities in a different language. The original agonizing is still there with his own added to it. Borges once advised his translator, Norman Thomas Di Giovanni, to write what he was trying to say, not what he was saying. In that case it was easier because the writer was on hand and knew English. The advice is good, but how can we be sure what Tasso was 'trying to say'? [...] (p. 22)

[...] We come to the part of the tree that grows out of the main trunk, called *rama* in Spanish. What shall we call it in English? It is a branch, a bough, a limb, or what? We can simply call it *branch*, for *rama* also possesses the figurative meaning *branch* has in English, but that might be too easy, something might be lost—we might be missing the poetry. This is the time to follow the Borgesian dictum. Who is speaking? Would his Anglo-phonic equivalent be a branch-man, a bough-man, or a limb-man? And we seek help from our bilingual dictionary. This drab old friend, sneered at by the 'fluent,' is a great font of synonyms and is quite useful in jogging the memory. The ultimate solution is, more often than not, instinctive. This means that the translator must be close in one way or another to the writer. At least, he must have some understanding of him and his ways.

The translator, therefore, like the critic and scholar, must be a reader. The ideal translator must be the ideal reader, a rare breed, for a translation ought to be the closest possible reading of a work. [...] (p. 23)

If translations have difficulty enduring in time, they have an even harder struggle, in many cases, making spatial adjustments. Some books are very mulish about being 'led across'. Regional and local literature has a flavour that is immediately sensed in the original language. Only when that flavour is limited to the *mise-en-scène* and does not affect the language to any large degree can the translator score a subtle success in preserving it. Just as words do not have real equivalents in other languages, neither do dialects or local patterns of speech. Rustics are rustics the world over, but it is absurd and outlandish to have a Brazilian *sertanejo* talking like an Appalachian mountain man. Even black English is poorly served by translation into black Spanish. The African roots are too remote, and the diverging histories of forced migration under two distinct European cultures have produced two quite different modes of expression. The transfer of local or regional idiom into another language, therefore, must be listed as another of the impossibilities of translation.

A similar problem, but one that can be solved, is the problem that arises when an environment that is commonplace in one culture becomes exotic in the other. I recall that the Peruvian novelist Mario Vargas Llosa was concerned that the English translation of his novel *The Green House*, which I was working on, would give an exotic tone to what in Peru was commonplace. He was worried about the names of the flora and fauna that have no translation, since they do not exist in English-speaking countries and no Anglo-Saxon Adam had passed through to give them lexical identity. I did not think it serious enough to warrant a certain dilution I had come across while working on the Guatemalan novelist Miguel Angel Asturias. In that case, I had been faced with a tree under which someone had sat and which bore an ever-so-exotic Mayan name. The French translation preceded mine, and when I got my hands on it, I figured that the solution lay there, and in a good bilingual dictionary. Alas, I found that the man had sat down under an *arbre*. [. . .] The Peruvian trees remained with their aboriginal names, for, as I explained to the author, many commonplace aspects of Peru are, per se, exotic to the outsider. If a novel is universal, the universality should not be hindered by the strange. [. . .] (p. 24–5)

We have seen that the translator is not the free-flying artist that the writer can be, that it is, indeed, the writer who causes the translator to hew to a narrow path if he is to do his job well and correctly. Even when the translator is compared to the performing musician who interprets an extant composition written by someone else, the comparison is not exact because the musician is, above all, interpretive and has the freedom to enhance the piece being played, as Billie Holiday would by her rendition convert the most banal pop tune into a masterpiece. I have said that the translator qua translator must never engage in the silk-purse business, regardless of the temptation to do so. To continue the musical analogy, there is no place for riffs in translation.

Having looked into a few of the many possibilities and impossibilities in the making of a translation, now we must look to the other side, how a translation should be judged, what a critic should look for, and who, ideally, he should be. A translator's ego is most wounded, of course, when the review fails to mention him, even to the point of omitting his name from the heading and risking a letter of admonishment from the novelist B. J. Chute, who, with her watchful eye, has done a splendid job seeing that translators receive their due. Some reviewers will also go on about the magnificent language of a novel without mentioning the fact that is the language of translation, as if the book had been written in English to begin with. Even when the translator is mentioned and praised, he should be wary and not let it go to his head. Quite often this sort of encomium really only covers half of his accomplishment, for it may be that the reviewer, perceptive as he may be, has no knowledge of the work in the original and more than likely is not familiar with the language it was first written in. In this case, the translator has been told that he writes well, not that he translated well. Many reviewers of this type, however, will then go on to discuss and analyze the book with great intelligence and insight, which, by indirection, tells the translator that he has translated well. Gabriel García Márquez has said that American reviewers, on the whole, have understood *One Hundred Years of Solitude* much better than critics in his own language. And, of course, many of these American reviewers have had to rely completely on the English version. This would imply that it is almost possible for an astute reader to judge the merits of a translation without recourse to the original language.

The bane of the translator more often than not is the critic who does know the other language; he is usually an academician who has done his homework and checked out the English against the original. If there is a mistake or a slip, he will surely find it, and he is not above suggesting alternate possibilities, some of which are as cogent as that exasperating last entry on multiple-choice exams, 'None of these.' Sara Blackburn has dubbed this fellow Professor Horrendo, and he is too much with us as he brings the nastiness of the academic *ninguneo* (Mexican for put-down) into literary criticism. But it is his mood that offends, for in truth he is often right: there have been mistakes, they should be corrected, which is why it is impossible for a translation ever to be final. The translator is irked, of course, and is left wondering why the full-dress court-martial when company punishment would suffice. (pp. 26–7)

It is time for at least one definitive statement about translation: it is impossible to make a handsome living from it. Like so many other artistic endeavors, it is an adjunct or a labor of love. A person frugal in his wants can possibly live off it. The successful translator, catalyst that he is, is not rewarded to the degree that the successful writer is. (p. 28)

Heaven-sent or hell-bent, according to the critic, translation is really something apart from the other arts. But it is, indisputably, an art. Too often people have defined it in terms that only partially apply, for it has never received the massive attention given to other aspects of literature. It follows, it serves, it is the squire of the arts, but it was Sancho Panza who made Don Quixote possible. (p. 29)

Gabriel García Márquez, *One Hundred Years of Solitude* (1967), trans. Gregory Rabassa (1970; New York: Avon Books 1971)

Many years later, as he faced the firing squad, Colonel Aureliano Buendía was to remember that distant afternoon when his father took him to discover ice. At that time Macondo was a village of twenty adobe houses, built on the bank of a river of clear water that ran along a bed of polished stones, which were white and enormous, like prehistoric eggs. The world was so recent that many things lacked names, and in order to indicate them it was necessary to point. Every year during the month of March a family of ragged gypsies would set up their tents near the village, and with a great uproar of pipes and kettledrums they would display new inventions. First they brought the magnet. A heavy gypsy with an untamed beard and sparrow hands, who introduced himself as Melquíades, put on a bold public demonstration of what he himself called the eighth wonder of the learned alchemists of Macedonia. He went from house to house dragging two metal ingots and everybody was amazed to see pots, pans, tongs, and braziers tumble down from their places and beams creak from the desperation of nails and screws trying to emerge, and even objects that had been lost for a long time appeared from where they had been searched for most and went dragging along in turbulent confusion behind Melquíades' magical irons. 'Things have a life of their own,' the gypsy proclaimed with a harsh accent. 'It's simply a matter of waking up their souls.' José Arcadio Buendía, whose unbridled imagination always went beyond the genius of nature and even beyond miracles and magic, thought that it would be possible to make use of that useless invention to extract gold from the bowels of the earth. Melquíades, who was an honest man, warned him: 'It won't work for that.' But José Arcadio Buendía at that time did not believe in the honesty of gypsies, so he traded his mule and a pair of goats for the two magnetized ingots. Úrsula Iguarán, his wife, who relied on those animals to increase their poor domestic holdings, was unable to dissuade him. 'Very soon we'll have gold enough and more to pave the floors of the house,' her husband replied. For several months he worked hard to demonstrate the truth of his idea. He explored every inch of the region, even the riverbed, dragging the two iron ingots along and reciting Melquíades' incantation aloud. The only thing he succeeded in doing was to unearth a suit of fifteenth-century armor which had all of its pieces soldered together with rust and inside of which there was the hollow resonance of an enormous stone-filled gourd. When José Arcadio Buendía and the four men of his expedition managed to take the armor apart, they found inside a calcified skeleton with a copper locket containing a woman's hair around its neck. (Opening paragraph, pp. 11–12)

5.15 SUZANNE JILL LEVINE

Suzanne Jill Levine, professor of Spanish, University of California, Santa Barbara, is a leading translator of Latin American fiction, including works by Adolfo Bioy Casares, Jorge Luis Borges, Carlos Fuentes, Severo Sarduy, and Manuel Puig. She is the author of numerous studies in Latin American literature, including the book *Manuel Puig and the Spider Woman: His Life and Fictions* (2000). She is also the author of a book on the art and theory of translation, *The Subversive Scribe: Translating Latin American Fiction* (1991). A chapter from that book, reprinted below, includes examples from her translation of the Cuban writer Guillermo Cabrera Infante.

From *The Subversive Scribe: Translating Latin American Fiction* (St Paul, Minn.: **Graywolf Press, 1991**).

From the 'Preface'

> *To write about translation is to write about one of writing's most conscious operations, the one that lays open the function of writing as a manipulation of words and not of realities.*
>
> E. Rodríguez Monegal,
> *Borges: A Literary Biography*

Why has the art of translating poetry eclipsed that of prose in the history of translation studies? The answer seems simple: We have commonly believed that the poetry translator must be a poet, and therefore that his technique or philosophy deserves our inquiry, but any somewhat bilingual individual with dictionary in hand can translate a prose text. Again, the common belief is that novels are easier to translate than poetry. The traditional virtue of translators, particularly prose translators, has been their invisibility as humble scribes, scribbling transparent texts in the cellar of the castle of Literature.

The formal and linguistic complexities of twentieth-century fiction obviously belie these feudal notions. Exposing the poetics of prose translation and the prose translator's role as creative writer and literary critic can provide invaluable insights, for translation is the most concrete form of the interpretive act performed by all readers, scholars, and teachers of foreign literatures. Translations and the practice of translating, says Gideon Toury, are *observational facts*; the description of these facts is not only essential but prior to any possible theory. Self-referential inquisitions by prose translators should provide useful models for translation studies as well as models of self-questioning for all interpreters.

Umberto Eco speaks of telling the process of writing as an activity apart from the writing itself:

> Telling how you wrote something does not mean proving it is 'well' written. Poe said that the effect of the work is one thing and the knowledge of the process is another.... Sometimes the most illuminating pages on the artistic process have been written by minor artists, who achieved modest effects but knew how to ponder their own processes. (11–12)

With this *excusatio propter infirmitatem* in mind, I would like to explain briefly what motivated me to write a book about translation.

The project began as a collection of the various notes, articles, and essays I had written from 1971 to 1984. My first attempt to record the challenging process of my first two translations, *Three Trapped Tigers* and *Betrayed by Rita Hayworth*, was guilelessly called 'Notes on Translation.' What struck me almost immediately about these early translation experiences was how much richer the process was than the final product. Writing about translation made me even more keenly aware that the reader could gain a more intimate knowledge of the literary work, and of the languages and cultures involved in the dialogue between original and translation, if only he or she knew how translation decisions were made, and how possible choices were finally set aside for what were considered better solutions.

These early translations were also close collaborations, or 'closelaborations,' a neologism coined by Guillermo Cabrera Infante. As I worked with him, and later with Manuel Puig, I observed that the dilemma of one word versus another was not a problem unique to translation. The original writer constantly chooses words and phrases, compelled by intuitions and reasons that often have more to do with language than with his own intentions; as the composer Maurice Ravel once responded to a eulogizing critic, creativity is not a matter of inspiration but of choices, of decision-making. The original is one of many possible versions. When jotting down these first notes, I realized that not only did the reader 'lose' the constant dilemmas and fugitive process of the translation but also my ongoing dialogue with the authors. Since their letters reveal tantalizing views of the relationship between original and translation—both as product and process—I have translated excerpts that will serve as primary material in my presentations of translation strategies.

Other reasons for writing such a study took shape as I made the transition from freelance translator to university professor. The academic community is still under the sway of the positivist prejudice against translation as an unimaginative and unscholarly activity, and as Carol Maier observes, it still sees translation as 'a task that does not occur in the realms of thought but between the pages of a dictionary' (25). Especially the translation of contemporary fiction situates me in a sphere that is too 'literary' in the eyes of more traditional colleagues. The translation of poetry, both classical and modern, and of classical drama, have been marginal scholarly concerns, but does contemporary fiction merit the same respect? So far only James Joyce, the genius of modernism: *Finnegans Wake*, paradigm of the modern, provides in fiction what Pound forged in poetry, a theoretical though controversial place for translation as interpretation and creation.

But what can we learn from the translation of contemporary fiction—most of it not yet canonized—and particularly of works from 'marginal' countries such as Cuba and Argentina? Much of contemporary Latin Amerian literature, beginning perhaps with the master fabulist Jorge Luis Borges, falls under the rubric of 'postmodernism,' a tendency that reflects (for some) exhaustion; John Barth describes Borges's originality and obsessive, implicit theme as the 'difficulty, perhaps unnecessity of writing original works' (22). Postmodern writers such as those I've translated and am writing about—Cabrera Infante, Puig, Severo Sarduy—have attempted to revitalize Literature by turning to popular forms. Is such writing worthy of translation, and do the problems involved in translating it deserve our attention?

I attempt here to address and to redress these questions. In a world preoccupied more with present than past, English speakers today need to know the concerns expressed in other languages; North American readers need to hear the voices of that 'other' America alienated from the United States by a torturous political history. But these readers also need to understand *how* Latin American writing is transmitted to them, and *how* differences and similarities between cultures and languages affect *what* is finally transmitted. Knowing the other and how we receive or hear the other is a fundamental step toward knowing ourselves. (pp. xii–xv)

'The Ides of March': Post-TTT Exercises, *The Subversive Scribe*, pp. 74–81

> *Literature is all that is read as such...*
>
> G. Cabrera Infante,
> *Exorcismos de esti(l)o*

TTT [Cabrera Infante's *Three Trapped Tigers*] was written to be read aloud, and the American English translation followed suit, but doesn't the written page in translation inevitably make the textual texture of the spoken more *pronounced*? To remake a text that amuses or moves the reader by the sheer fact of being written in a very local, hence very 'real' version of spoken language is surely a task worthy of Pierre Menard. After *TTT* I briefly experienced (to avoid 'experiment,' that scientific word Cabrera Infante detests) with Menardian fervor Cabrera Infante's *Exorcismos de esti(l)o* (1976), a collection of comic miscellany in evident homage to Queneau's *Exercices de style*. These set pieces really are exorcisms, excessive games with language and literary forms high and low, Cabrera

Infante blowing off steam accumulated in *TTT*, especially in 'Brainteasers,' by continuing to abuse texts and to amuse himself. He explains in an interview in the *Paris Review*:

> *Exorcismos de esti(l)o* . . . means many things: the exorcising of style, exercises in summertime, even the lure of the pen—all in a send-up of *Exercices de style*. This is one of my favorites among my own books, and it closes the cycle begun in my collected movie reviews, *Un oficio del siglo XX* (1962). In *Exorcismos*, I expanded my experience (not experiment, a word I loathe when I see it applied to art instead of science) with Havanese, the idiom of *habaneros*, who might perhaps be called hablaneros or total talkers. (166)

I chose to do for *Review* (Fall 1974) an 'exorcism' titled '"*Los Idus de Marzo*", *según Plutarco . . . y según Shakespeare, y según Mankiewicz, y según el limpiabotas Chicho Charol*' (16). In this monologue, a shoeshine boy narrates to a silent client his innocent or at least biased version of the plot of Joseph L. Mankiewicz's movie version of Shakespeare's tragedy *Julius Caesar*. '"The Ides of March," According to Plutarch . . . According to Shakespeare, According to Mankiewicz, According to the Shoeshine Boy, Ol' Leatherlip,' a delirious piece in vulgate, exposes a very literary subject: how culture is handed down through the metamorphoses of interpretation, that is, translation. Writers (Shakespeare) interpret history and/or writers (Plutarch); one genre translates another (in this case, theater reconstructs history and film pirates theater); and readers or spectators of another age, language, and class interpret history-as-popular-legend converted into high art to return inevitably to the *vox populi*.

The translation of this piece confirms once again that literary parodies of the spoken become, need to become, more *written*, more literary when transposed into another language. Unlike the original parody, the translation mimics a written text.

'*Los Idus . . .*' already challenges the reader, becomes a veritable obstacle course in interpreting, indeed in translating spoken Cuban. Chicho's speech is 'recorded' phonetically and forces the reader to translate it into a more communicative code. *C* becomes *s* (*socio = sosio*), *s* disappears, making two words into one (*quete = que este*), and *r* becomes *l*, as in Hollywood's popular and racist representations of Chinese pronunciation. The problem of reading Chicho is multiplied by all sorts of wordplays and alliterations. These can be read as Chicho's 'natural' invention, but we know the author is using Chicho as a mouthpiece for his own double entendres: The noble Brutus becomes *Bruto* in Spanish, which also means stupid.

'The Ides of March' is a grotesquerie, low humor straight from the gutter, the satirical representation of a racial cliché. This text descends from a popular tradition that harks back to the *Menippea* and certainly to the Renaissance farce and Spanish Golden Age *entremeses*, in which social satire often plays upon the innocence or ignorance of the underdog. The black man as the butt of humor is a theme of low farce in both Cuban and Anglo-American vaudeville, particularly his misperceptions of the rules of the game in white society and his mispronunciations.[1]

'Boy' in English figuratively, demeaningly denotes a black man of unspecified age who can be unmistakably identified in the Spanish by the Cuban reader. His language, his unabashed illiteracy, his low station in society, and even his name (*Chico* suggests 'burnt,' thus by metonymy darkened; *Charol* means 'patent leather') belie his racial and, in this milieu, social identity. Ol' Leatherlip attempts to duplicate the parodic effect of the original name by identifying the character with his trade, but also multiplies or makes more explicit the parodic thrust of the text by the addition of 'lip': The text we read is indeed a product of Chicho's 'lip service.'

Chicho is linguistically, even psychologically plausible in Cabrera Infante's rendition. The humor here derives from the contrast between Chicho's low or comically incorrect language and the complex literary plot he tries to unravel, as well as the written play with spoken language that turns the piece into a graphic puzzle that the reader must unravel.

The translation attempts to reproduce both the tension between low language and high art and written and spoken, but the problem that remains is how to maintain Chicho's plausibility. For the sake of humor—the piece's *raison d'être*—verisimilitude is inevitably undermined when the text loses its raw material and passes into English. The humor derived from writing words the way they are slurred in Spanish, again, cannot be repeated to the same effect in English. 'This guy' approximates the tone but is not as comically confusing as *quete* (*que este*). The spoken can only be rendered into yet another version of the spoken, but also the original already demands, implicitly speaks of translating into 'proper' writing when it is read in Spanish. Here's the first sentence of this ludic interlude in spoken 'Cuban':

> *bueno sosio la cosa e quete tipo Sesal no quie sel rey pero si quiere o no quie pero si quiere la corona que no e pa tanto poque no ejuna corona deoro ni de plata ni con joya ni na ni na sino quee de yelba asi como de gajo emata y no se polque tanta boba—que si' se la pone que si se la quita quetan neneso como un siglo.* (p. 35)

For the non-Cuban readers' sake, here is the above *translated* to proper phonetics, if not grammar:

> *bueno socio la cosa es que este tipo Cesar no quiere ser rey pero si quiere o no quiere pero si quiere la corona que no es para tanto porque no es una corona de oro ni de plata ni con joyas ni nada ni nada sino que es de yerba así como de gajo de mata yo no se porque tanta bohada—que si la pone que se la quita que están en eso como un siglo.*

Now, in Slanglish:

> Well man the thing is that this guy Ceezer dont wanna be king but he really duz or duznt but he really wants the crown which dont mount to much cos it aint made of

gold or silver or tin or nuttin but sum weeds or branches and I dont know what's the big deal about him puttin it on or takin it off which they fuss about for ages.

Cabrera Infante's comment on this translation (May 25, 1974):

> I really like it, especially since I know how damned difficult it was, so much so that I wonder how you could understand the whole thing, since I myself got confused at certain points of this exercise. I think you've transposed it very well into American.

In the original, the authenticity of the transcription of spoken Cuban is what brings home vividly the distortions but also hidden truths of interpretation, that is, translation.[2] I write 'hidden truths' because behind Chicho's innocence and misunderstandings (of, for example, the symbolic importance of the crown, which he perceives literally as being a thing made of 'weeds or branches') there is implicit criticism. The movie is a melodrama, and its referent, the high-minded, 'high art' drama (and in turn its point of departure, ancient history) seem on the surface irrelevant to Chicho's daily existence, except in and/or through Chicho's interpretation.

Chicho can certainly identify hypocrisy, deceit, and betrayal in the followers surrounding Caesar, except that Chicho uses a word that translates as 'asslickers' rather than the word 'hypocrites.' And he finds a political issue that strikes home: When the populace crowds around Caesar begging for favors, Chicho interprets their pleas for 'amnisty' for some relative. Maybe Chicho can understand this detail because, like the Everymen of Rome, he lives under the double shadow of a dictator's tyranny: Chicho speaks as a citizen of Batista's Cuba, but Cabrera Infante writes the text in the Seventies of Fidel Castro. Chicho doesn't consciously admit historical parallels, but they are implied in his unconsciously devious though direct discourse, as transcribed by his invisible scribe.

The translation can't possibly reproduce Cuban Black speech but vaguely simulates spoken Black American, the closest equivalent. What makes this speech humorous to the reader in Spanish, however, is that it already is written. Chicho's speech becomes literature, that is, Cabrera Infante subtly undermines Chicho's mentality by making jokes that *could* sprout from Chicho's streetwise know-how but which *are* the author's. Something needed to be added in the English, beyond the simulated Black American: What made Chicho's speech humorous is the way Cesar becomes Sesal, so I made Caesar into Ceezer, writing it as it could be heard. Again, I could invent graphic distortions in English precisely because, unlike Spanish, it often doesn't (duznt) sound as it is written, but failure always lurks: An invented distortion is certainly not as funny as a 'natural' one.

I had to go further, and, following the author's lead as in the Brutus/Bruto play, play with words. When Chicho says Caesar's smart but perhaps too smart for his own good, repeating the word *vivo* (wise guy), which takes on an ironic twist since this *vivo* (live wire) ends up *muerto* (dead), I say 'and Ceezer who's no geezer' with tongue in cheek since he will never reach old age. And I responded to Brutus and Bruto with 'his pal Brutish comes along who aint so brutish.' 'The crown which dont mount to much' plays with the spoken, which slurringly leaves out syllables, and with a sexual suggestion, 'mount': Chicho compares Caesar later on to a cuckolded husband who's the last to know—in this case, that he's in danger of being assassinated—so that a sexual innuendo fits well in Chicho's vulgarized version. These additional jokes compensate somehow for the loss of the local, and correspond to the text's underlying 'thrusts.'

The translation recognizes its status as translation by 'spickin' instead of 'speaking,' self-consciously saluting the language of the original and participating in the two-tongued play between English and Spanish already in Cabrera Infante's original. Translation means substitution here, as in *TTT*: In both cases, the reader is led to respond to a humor based on language's distortions and language distorted.

Here is the rest of the translation. Some added or changed puns and alliteration are in italics:

> The thing is that this guy Cashius who's givin Ceezer the *hairy* eyeball wants the little ol' crown too altho it's only made of newspaper and he's eyein it from above on a balconey with one colum after anotha and he smiles kind of off the side of his mouth and that's when this other guy his pal Brutish comes along who aint so brutish but who's damn brutish at the end cos Ceezer is like he was his father in a manner of *spickin* and who really loves him and is goin to hand him down the kingdom someday with the crown and the branch and the whole *shebang*. But this here Brutish what he duz is start whispering in corners with Cashius and conspiring and all that and Ceezer who's no *geezer* makes like he dont know what's happening but he must know unless kings are like husbands who are always the last to know. Well, the thing is that Brutish knows it and Ceezer's friends suspect it and Ceezer's wife dreams it and the Sen'dors know it and everybody and his *aunt* knows it except Ceezer who keeps making speeches and walkin up and *down aroun Rome* wrapped in a white sheet the whole damn day until morning. Then comes this guy with a beard and a roll *of toilet paper* in his hand who the friend of some fortuneteller who already tol Ceezer what was goin to happin to him on the *Idas or Ideas of* March which seems to be a bad month, for crazy people and *hares and so on*, and Ceezer who jus dont want to unnerstand and when the bad guys come over to im it aint that way cos before he saw a fat man happily bouncing down the stairs and Ceezer has this thing with fat guys that he sez you shunt mistrust em but the skinny guys you should, poor Ceezer who dont know that fat dogs bite harder than skinny dogs cos theyre fat and grab you wid their strong jores and the party's over. But this Ceezer guy goes ahead as if nuttin happened and on and on til he gets to the Senit which is a cave of Ali babas and the fifty theeves and is chock full o' asslickers who are lying on the floor and crawlin over and kneelin before Ceezer askin to get on the

gravy train and to get amnisty for some relative and with all that bunch of beggars Ceezer dont see the reel bad guys comin and with what intensions besides the knives which arent *sceesors* but *bonafido* knives theyre hidin under their sheets. Well the thing is they cover him with knife *wombs* cos in dose days they didn't have guns or revolvers and they sew his sheet with knives but before this guy Ceezer who's as tough as *snails and tougher than the marbles, even the loose ones, in that statchue of his right next to im* turns halfway aroun like this and sort of from his profile he seez his son who aint his son but is Brutish come over but he sez his son and then Ceezer *spicks* to him in *sumfin* that sounds like Italian and his son who aint his son dont seem to know Italian cos he dont breathe a word but clams up and keeps a tight upper and lower lip and makes a tremendous slash in the bread basket and finishes him off and Ceezer dies like this wrapped up in his sheet which can also be used as a funeral shroud. And then comes Marlo Brando who dont have to be no *Marlowe* to finger out who killed Ceezer, and that they'll kill him too if he dont watch out and he picks up Ceezer who's lookin more and more like a salad and carries him out to the stairs and makes a tremendous fuss saying that he didn't come to berry Ceezer but to put him up *dere and down below* lissening to the speech there's a load of people who now that Ceezer died there's a bigger crowd than before and a tremendous meeting and sayin that thing about not comin to *berry confucion* and a mess cos it seems there's a war but there isn't a war and you dont see one fight and afterwoods, what happins afterwoods? Well, Brutish does and Brando comes to say he was brutish but also nobull and Cashius who's no clay pigeon like Brutish and even more brutish *besides being British* cos he kills himself when nobody not even enemies are around on his birfday cos it seems that's the way ancient peoples killed themselves to die on the same day they was born and that's the story, Joe. Hey, you want plain or black?

War and confusion are the outcome of Brando's speech, confusion reigning over the literal-minded spectator Chicho, who never sees war acted out in this movie pretending to be a play (or vice versa): hence, berry confucion. Brutish led to British in reaction to Chicho's reaction to this travesty of high-style British acting. *Alice in Wonderland's* March hare enters on cue as our Marlowe Chicho gropes to interpret the words of the Shakespearean soothsayer who whispers or probably shouts into 'Sesal's' ear about March being a bad month for *gente ida* (crazy people), *ida*, the past participle of the verb *ir*, literally, 'gone.' Associative thinking drives the groping interpreters Chicho and his translator from the mysterious Ides to the more accessible *ida* and *Ida* (the feminine name) and to *Ideas*, to berry the reader in confucion.

Yes, I'll admit I've taken liberties for humor's sake, making Ol' Leatherlip a mite more sophisticated and self-conscious than the relatively raw Chicho, but the seed of these liberties lies in the original itself. Cabrera Infante uses Chicho's speech as a vehicle of parody, imposing his subtle and critical differences upon 'another's' discourse, a discourse (re)created by him out of the piquant potpourri of spoken Cuban.

NOTES

1. See chapter VI, 'You Always Can Tell,' of *Infante's Inferno*, prefaced by a reference to the figures of 'Blackie and the Spaniard—traditional comic characters, from as far back as the gay nineties.' (193)
2. 'Natural' inconsistencies in the 'transcription' include *porque*, pronounced once without the *r*, *poque*, and the next time, with the *r* slurred into *l*, *polque*—two possible pronunciations in lower-class Cuban.

BIBLIOGRAPHY

Barth, John. 'The Literature of Exhaustion', *Atlantic*, August 1967.

Carbrera Infante, G. *Infante's Inferno*, trans. S. J. Levine with the author. New York: Harper & Row, 1984.

Carbrera Infante, G. *Three Trapped Tigers*, trans. Donald Gardner and Suzanne Jill Levine in collaboration with the author, New York: Harper & Row, 1971.

Carbrera Infante, G. *Tres tristes tigres*. Barcelona: Seix Barral, 1967.

Eco, Umberto. *Postscript to the Name of the Rose*, trans. William Wewaver, San Diego: Harcourt Brace Jovanovich, 1984.

Maier, Carol. 'Some Thoughts on Translations, Imagination and (Un)academic Activity', *Translation Review*, 6, Winter 1986.

Toury, Gideon. *In Search of a Theory of Translation*, Jerusalem: Porter Institute, 1980.

5.16 TED HUGHES

Ted Hughes (1930–98), British Poet Laureate (1984–98) must also be regarded as among the major poetry translators in the English tradition. His interest in translation pre-dates his 1965 co-founding with Daniel Weissbort of the journal *Modern Poetry in Translation* (*MPT*). But *MPT* helped to bring a number of poets to his attention: notably the Israeli Yehuda Amichai, the Hungarian János Pilinszky, and the Yugoslav Vasko Popa. The first two of these he translated and the last he did much to promote.

One impulse for the journal had been Hughes's encounter with poets from Eastern Europe at various international festivals, and he remained particularly interested in the post-war East European poets of the generation immediately preceding his own, writers the circumstances of whose lives 'had brought their poetry down to such precisions, discriminations and humilities that it is a new thing'.[1] Hence also the allurement for him of the English versions produced by the Israeli poet Yehuda Amichai of his own poems, or of the scrupulously literal renderings from the Hungarian of János Pilinszky by another Hungarian poet, János Csokits. Hughes was struck by the way these versions powerfully conveyed material of great urgency, which was apparently dissipated in more polished or, as we might now say, 'domesticated' versions.

Ted Hughes's severe approach to the translation of poetry suggests a belief in the ability of poetry to cross language frontiers, provided the translator does not interpose himself overmuch. That his interest in translation was no passing phase is evidenced by his continuing work in this area throughout his life. Although he did not take part in the polemics, he can be said to have represented a foreignizing tendency, relatable to changes in the literary atmosphere and a new openness of the English language. More immediately, though, it can be related to his own needs as a writer and it provides important clues to his development which have been largely ignored. It has been observed that paradoxically Hughes, while remaining close to the *ad verbum* text, has created works of translation which are unmistakably Hughesian. But then, his translations *were* an integral part of his oeuvre, just as the promotion of translation was an intrinsic part of his professional activity as a writer.

Hughes himself wrote only one short (uncollected) essay describing the translation boom of the previous decade, while at the same time re-formulating his bias towards literal translation: 'Modern Poetry in Translation' (*Modern Poetry in Translation: 1983, An Annual*

---

[1] Ted Hughes's 'Introduction' to Vasko Popa, *Collected Poems,* trans. Anne Pennington (Manchester: Carcanet, 1978), 1

Survey (Manchester: Carcanet, 1983)). He refers to a work that for him represented a kind of model, *Specimens of Bushmen Folklore*, collected in the 1870s by the German-trained ethnographer and philologist William Bleek: 'Ideally we would have liked to see at least some poems translated [...] as meticulously as Bleek's translation of Bushman lore—though we understood the limited appeal of anything so raw and strange' (p. 12). (See Sect. 5.7 on Ethnopoetics, for W. S. Merwin's interest in the near contemporary of Bleek, E. A. Wallace Budge, who translated *The Egyptian Book of the Dead*). As in the early *MPT* editorials, Hughes inveighed against translations that aimed to produce a 'parallel equivalent' of some original's unique verbal texture. He commented that, in fact, 'we found the closest thing to it in translations made by poets whose first language was not English, or by scholars who did not regard themselves as poets' (pp. 12–13).

Yehuda Amichai

From Yehuda Amichai, *Amen*, translated from the Hebrew by the author and Ted Hughes, with an introduction by Ted Hughes (New York: Harper & Row, 1977)

From 'Letter of Recommendation' (p. 66)

[...]
I remember my father waking me up
for early prayers. He did it caressing
my forehead, not tearing the blanket away.

Since then I love him even more.
And because of this
let him be woken up
gently and with love
on the Day of Resurrection.

[Hughes made minimal changes in the draft given him by the author. In the last stanza, Amichai offers an alternative for 'And because of this' (In merit of this) which Hughes does not take up. And in the following line, Amichai has 'may he be woken up'. Of course, in other poems, the changes are more considerable. But in general, Hughes's versions of Amichai do not shrink from a certain foreignness. Hughes was as good as his word: 'The translations were made by the poet himself. All I did was correct the more intrusive oddities and errors of grammar and usage, and in some places shift about the phrasing and line endings. What I wanted to preserve above all was the tone and cadence of Amichai's own voice speaking in English which seems to me marvellously true to the poetry, in these renderings.']

János Pilinszky

From János Pilinszky, *Selected Poems*, trans. Ted Hughes and János Csokits (Manchester: Carcanet, 1977)

From 'The French Prisoner' (the last two stanzas, p. 30)

Why go on. Guards came for him.
He had escaped from the nearby prison camp.
And just as I did then, in that garden,
I am strolling here, among garden shadows, at home.
I look into my notes and quote:
If only I could forget that Frenchman . . .
And from my ears, my eyes, my mouth
The scalding memory shouts at me:

'I am hungry!' And suddenly I feel
the eternal hunger
which that poor creature has long ago forgotten
and which no earthly nourishment can lessen.
He lives on me. And more and more hungrily!
And I am less and less sufficient for him.
And now he, who would have eaten anything,
Is clamouring for my heart.

[In addition to the literal translations János Csokits provided Hughes with contextual notes. Here is Csokits's literal [unpublished]:]

Go on with this—what for? Guards came for him;
he had escaped from the near-by prisoners' camp.
And I am wandering about, as I did in that garden then,
among the shadows of this garden at home.
I look into my notes and quote:
'If only I could forget him, that Frenchman . . .'
And from my ears, my eyes, my mouth
the fierce memory fervently shouts at me:

'I am hungry!' And all at once I feel
that immortal hunger which
the poor wretch does not feel since long,
and which no earthly food can still.
He lives on me! And ever more hungrily!

And I am less and less enough for him!
He who would have subsisted on any aliment:
is demanding now my heart.

From Ted Hughes's 'Introduction' to János Pilinszky, Selected Poems

Very many lines of his [Csokits's] rough draft have been impossible to improve, as far as I could judge, and besides that odd inevitability and 'style' which a poet's translation into language other than his own often seems to have, he retained naturally an unspoiled sense of the flavour and the tone of the originals—that very intriguing quality which is the translator's will-o'-the-wisp, the foreignness and strangeness. (pp. 13–14)

Seneca

Ted Hughes's adaptation of Seneca's play *Oedipus* was first performed by the National Theatre Company in March 1968, produced and designed by Peter Brook, with John Gielgud in the title role and Irene Worth as Jocasta. A version had been commissioned from David Turner, but, as Hughes put it in his introduction: 'Peter Brook had clear ideas about the type of production he wanted, and when he found the translation [by Turner] did not quite suit them he invited me in to go over it and adapt it [. . .] and after some tentative false starts, we found the only way forward was for me to go back to the original Seneca, eking out my Latin with a Victorian crib and so make a completely new translation' (*Seneca's Oedipus*, adapted by Ted Hughes (London: Faber & Faber, 1969), 7). Brook, in fact, got the actors to study the play in the Miller version, which Hughes described as 'being extremely weighty and extremely literal' (from Ted Hughes's unpublished account).

As Hughes notes: 'I was in complete sympathy with Peter Brook's guiding idea, which was to make a text that would release whatever inner power this story, in its plainest, bluntest form, still has, and to unearth, if we could, the ritual possibilities within it' (pp. 7–8). The Seneca adaptation inaugurated Ted Hughes's collaboration with Peter Brook, culminating in a play, 'Orghast', written by Ted Hughes in a language which he invented and called Orghast (see A. C. H. Smith, *Orghast in Persepolis*, 1972).

In the excerpt below, King Oedipus, in dialogue with Creon, Jocasta's brother, calls for expiation for the murder of his predecessor Laius, so as to bring about deliverance from the scourge that is afflicting Thebes. He himself, of course, was responsible for this, having unwittingly killed Laius, his father, and afterwards married his own mother Jocasta, Laius's wife. The lineation, supervised by Hughes, has been retained. Note the absence of punctuation and the spacing of the words. (See also, Sect. 2.6, above, for Alexander Neville's translation, 1563, of the same passage).

Seneca, *Oedipus*, Act II

From Seneca's Oedipus, *adapted by Ted Hughes (London: Faber & Faber, 1969), 24*

OEDIPUS:

the movers the guides the lawgivers   are above
they are demanding expiation for this murder
vengeance for Laius   the King of Thebes
where is the man

you great gods   you who choose Kings from among
men and set them up and keep them in power
come down and hear these words   you who made
this whole Universe and the laws we have to live and
die in   hear me   and you   great burning
watcher   who look after the seasons of this earth
who give sap and blood its strength   who pace out
the centuries   and you who govern darkness   and
you   muscle of the earth   who move and speak
in the winds and in water   and you who manage the
dead   be with me now   hear these words I
speak now [. . .]

Literal version from Seneca VlII, Tragedies 1, *trans. Frank Justus Miller (1917; Cambridge, Mass. and London: Loeb Classical Library, 1979), 449.*

Now at Heaven's command let the crime be expiated.

Whoever of the gods dost look with favour upon kingdoms—though, thou, whose are the laws of the swift-revolving heavens; and thou, greatest glory of the unclouded sky, who presidest over the twelve signs in thy changing course, who dost unroll the slow centuries with swift wheel; and thou, his sister, ever faring opposite to thy brother, Phoebe, night-wanderer; thou whom the winds obey, who over the level deep dost speed thy azure car; and thou who dost allot homes devoid of light—do ye all attend: [. . .]

Version by David Anthony Turner, from Classical Tragedy: Greek and Roman: Eight Plays, *ed. Robert W. Corrigan (New York: Applause Theatre Book Publishers, 1990), 454–5*

Well, the Gods demand it. Now someone will pay for that atrocity. All you gods who look kindly on the work of kings, be near me. May no house be a haven, no home secure, may no country welcome in his banishment the man whose hand struck down King Laius. May shame torment his bed, may his seed mock heaven. With that same hand may he kill even his own father, and may he—can any curse be more deadly?—may he do all the things I have escaped. There shall be no forgiveness anywhere. Apollo who moves the lips of the priestess to speak the future, come yourself as witness to my words. By the kingdom here of which I am guest, and master, by the gods of that home I left behind—I make this oath. My father, and a quiet old age for him, peaceful possession of a high majesty till death, for Merope my mother—marriage to Polybus only, never to—someone else ... On all this may mercy for the guilty man depend. May I not spare him ...

But the scene of that foul murder—where did it take place? Tell me again. Was it a fair fight or an ambush?

Racine

Ted Hughes's version of *Phèdre* was first performed, in London, by the Almeida Theatre Company, August 1998, directed by Jonathan Kent, with Diana Rigg as Phèdre and Toby Stephens as Hippolytus. That there was an earlier version by Robert Lowell, who also produced a version of *The Oresteia* is perhaps not without significance (see Sect. 4.10, above, on Lowell, for excerpts of the same passages of *Phèdre* and *Oresteia*).

For Ted Hughes, blank verse was not a viable option. Implicitly he recognizes the limits of translation by aiming to convey an aspect of Racine's masterpiece rather than the play in its literary-historical context, or by means of an updated or personalized transcription. That he felt able to do so is surely because the mythical substratum for him was a permanent feature of human existence.

From Jean Racine, *Phèdre*, new translation version by Ted Hughes (1998; New York: Farrar, Straus and Giroux, 1999), 37

[Act 2: Queen Phèdre confesses her fatal love for her stepson Hippolytus, son of her husband, King Theseus. See Sect. 4.10, above, for Robert Lowell's version and his remarks on the translation of *Phèdre*; also Edwin Morgan's version into Scots, in Sect. 5.23, below.]

> [...]
> I am in love.
> But do not suppose for a second
> I think myself guiltless
> For loving you as I love you.
> I have not
> Indulged myself out of empty boredom.
> I have not drunk this strychnine day after day
> As an idle refreshment.

Wretched victim of a divine vengeance!
I detest myself
More than you can ever detest me.
You are right, the gods are watching me.
Yes, the same gods
Who have filled me with these horrible flames
That are killing me—as they have killed
All the women in my family.
[. . .]
O prince, I cannot speak to you
Of anything but you. Avenge yourself.
I am depraved. Act. Punish me.
Prove yourself the son of your father—
Rid the world of a monster!
The widow of King Theseus has dared
To fall in love with his son, Hippolytus.
This disgusting pest should be killed.
Look—my heart. Here.
Bury your sword here.
This heart is utterly corrupt.
It cannot wait to expiate its evil.

Ovid

Ted Hughes was one of the contributors to *After Ovid, New Metamorphoses*, ed. Michael Hofmann and James Lasdun (1994), and continued thereafter to translate the *Metamorphoses*, which was so important to Shakespeare, a primary focus for Hughes (cf. his *A Choice of Shakespeare's Verse* and *Shakespeare and the Goddess of Complete Being*). Hughes completed a substantial part of the *Metamorphoses*, and his *Tales from Ovid* was among his most acclaimed works.

Ovid, *Metamorphoses*, 'Salmacis and Hermaphroditus'

From Tales from Ovid: Twenty Passages from the Metamorphoses *(London: Faber and Faber, 1997), 226–7*

[see Arthur Golding for his translation of the same passage, p. 88. Hughes referred to Golding's translation, as well as to the Latin source text. Hughes's elaborations or additions (e.g. 'slippery as the roots of big lilies'; 'helpless to her burrowing kisses . . .'; 'A tangle of

constrictors, nippled with suckers'), seem designed (as in Golding's version) to make the
scene more graphically vivid.]

'I've won!' shrieked Salmacis. 'He's mine!'
She could not help herself.
'He's mine!' she laughed, and with a couple of bounds
Hit the pool stark naked
In a rocking crash and thump of water
The slips of her raiment settling wherever
They happened to fall. Then out of the upheaval
Her arms reach and wind round him,
And slippery as the roots of big lilies
But far stronger, her legs below wind round him.
He flounders and goes under. All his strength
Fighting to get back up through a cloud of bubbles
Leaving him helpless to her burrowing kisses.
Burning for air, he can do nothing
As her hands hunt over him, and as her body
Knots itself every way around him
Like a sinewy otter
Hunting some kind of fish
That flees hither and thither inside him,
And as she flings and locks her coils
Around him like a snake
Around the neck and legs and wings of an eagle
That is trying to fly off with it,
And like ivy which first binds the branches
In its meshes, then pulls the whole tree down,
And as the octopus
A tangle of constrictors, nippled with suckers,
That drag towards a maw
Embraces its prey.

Line-by-line modern version by D. E. Hill, Ovid, Metamorphoses I–IV *(Warminster: Aris &*
Phillips, 1985), 375

'I have won, and he is mine,' cried out the Naiad, and she threw
all her clothing well away from her and rushed into the middle of the waters
and held him as he fought against her, violently snatching kisses
and bringing her hands up under him and touching his unwilling breast;

and now she draped herself around the youth this way and that.
At last, though he struggled against her in his desire to get away,
she entwined herself around him like a snake picked up by the king of birds
and snatched aloft (as she hangs from him she binds his head
and feet and entwines her tail around his spreading wings),
or like ivy which likes to weave its way up tall tree trunks,
or like an octopus catching and holding its enemy
beneath the sea by spreading its tentacles in all directions.

Aeschylus

In his translation of Aeschylus' *The Oresteia*, (New York: Farrar, Straus and Giroux, 1999), as with Seneca and Racine, Hughes does not attempt to reproduce the metre, but sparely and vividly confronts the myth. In general he exercises much self-restraint, remaining true to his own 'literalistic' aims, and if he takes liberties, these are in deleting rather than adding. While clearly aiming at immediacy, he is mindful of formal considerations (more than a shadow of the alexandrine lies over his translation of *Phèdre*).

The Oresteia

From Ted Hughe's translation of Aeschylus' The Oresteia *(New York: Farrar Strauss and Giroux, 1999), 10–11*

[The lines below from *Agamemnon* (the first play in the Oresteian trilogy) are spoken by the Chorus and describe the embarcation for Troy of the Argive fleet under the twin monarchs, Agamemnon and Menelaus, after Helen, wife to Menelaus, has been abducted to Troy by Paris. It recounts the ominous killing of a pregnant hare by two birds of prey, representing the two royal brothers. See Sects. 4.10 and 3.5 above, for versions by Lowell and Browning respectively of the same passage.]

I am the man to tell this tale.
Old age
Takes away everything
Except a few words the gods have tested,
For the eye
That opens towards the grave
Sees the core of things and is prophetic.
As our two Kings set out,

As their floating forest of spears
Lifted anchor,
Two birds,
Hook-beaked, big-winged birds,
Sailed over
On the right—on the right!
Good fortune!
The whole army cheered the good omen—
Victory!
Then those two birds,
The black bird and the white bird,
Flushed and drove and killed
A hare heavy with her twins.
The whole army
Saw them kill the pregnant hare. They saw
The black bird and the white bird
That had brought them promise of victory
Rip the mother's womb and drag from it
The living unborn tenants—
The whole army watched from start to finish
That murder of the unborn.
If evil is in this wind, let it blow over.

Calchas the seer
Recognised the birds,
The white bird and the black,
Menelaus and Agamemnon.
Calchas
Cried to the whole army and the two Kings:
'What does this kill mean? I will tell you.
It means
Victory with a twist.
Fate will destroy
All Troy's cattle,
All Troy's crops,
And at last
Will open to you the city's holy of holies.
But when you have empted Troy of her blood and her babies,
Then you can expect the anger of heaven.
Artemis, the moon-faced, the goddess,

The mother of the hares,
Beautiful Artemis,
Deity of the womb and its mystery,
Protectress of mothers and their darlings,
She has heard the death-cry of the hare,
She has seen what her father's birds have done,
She has looked through the bloody spy-hole
Where the hare's womb was plucked out.
She has seen the bigger murder behind it
Still to be committed
By the hooked heads,
The white bird and the black bird—
What will she do now?
[. . .]

Recent scholarly version by Hugh Lloyd-Jones of the first part of this passage
(Aeschylus, Oresteia *(1982; London, Duckworth, 2001), 21–2*

I have power to tell of the auspicious command of the expedition, the command of men
in authority; for still from the gods am I inspired
With persuasive power, my strengh in song, by the life that has grown up with me:
To tell how the two-throned command of the Achaeans, of the youth of Hellas
the concordant leadership,
was sped with avenging spear and arm
by the warlike bird of omen to the Teucrian land,
the king of birds appearing to the kings of the ships,
the black eagle and behind it the white one,
appearing near the palace on the hand in which the spear is brandished,
in seats conspicuous,
feeding upon the hare, her womb teeming with young,
checked from running her final course.
[. . .]

Sir Gawain and the Green Knight

Ted Hughes managed almost to complete a draft of the whole poem, although only a
section was revised for publication in *The School Bag*, ed. Seamus Heaney and Ted Hughes

(London: Faber and Faber, 1997). *Wodwo*, the title of Hughes's 1967 collection, alludes to a kind of forest troll, a wodwo, which makes an appearance in *Sir Gawain*.

The passage below describes the encounter between the Green Knight and Sir Gawain, who has sought him out in the Green Chapel, so as to receive a blow, in return for the decapitating one dealt the Green Knight when the latter had presented himself at King Arthur's court a year before and issued his challenge. Gawain flinches the first time. Here he prepares to withstand the second blow. See Sect. 5.22, below, for a literal version of this passage and a translation by W. S. Merwin, whose career as poet and translator Hughes followed with much attention.

From *The School Bag*, ed. Seamus Heaney and Ted Hughes (London Faber and Faber, 1997), 489–90

'But hurry up, warrior, for God's sake come to the point.
Deal me my destiny, and do it quickly.
I shall stand to your stroke with not one stir
Till your axe-head hits me. I give you my word.'
'Then here it comes,' cried the other, and heaved it upwards
With a gargoyle grimace as if he were mad.
And with all his strength hauled down, yet never touched him.
He stopped the blade mid-stroke, before it could harm.
Gawain patiently waited, not a nerve twitched.
He stood there still as a rock or some stiff stump
That grips the stony ground with a hundred roots.
Then the Man in Green spoke pleasantly:
'Now that your heart is whole again, may I ask you,
Let your high rank, that Arthur gave you, preserve you
And recover your neck from my stroke, if it is able.
Then Gawain ground his teeth and shouted in anger:
'Why, hack away, you savage, you threaten too long.
I think you have frightened yourself with your bragging.'
'What's this?' cried the other. 'Rough words from Sir Gawain?
I will no longer withhold from such an appeal
                    Justice.'
        And he braced himself for the stroke—
        Clenching both lip and brow.
        No wonder he did not like it
        Who saw no rescue now.

Pushkin

Ted Hughes's last known poem is, in fact, a translation, a version of Alexander Pushkin's 'The Prophet' (*Prorok*). This was for a collection of Pushkin translations, by various hands *After Pushkin*, (London, The Folio Society, 1999), edited by Elaine Feinstein, on the occasion of the bicentenary of the poet's birth.

Hughes was provided by Daniel Weissbort and Valentina Polukhina with a literal version of the Russian and a guide to the sound and prosody. Evidently he sensed something 'primitive' in Pushkin's highly sophisticated poem or in the language, insofar as this could be gleaned from the English versions he had read and the crib he used. What is thus signalled presumably is that he had found a starting point, as with Pilinszky and Amichai.

Conclusion of 'The Prophet'

ad verbum *version, with alternative words suggested (published in* Modern Poetry in Translation, *15 (1999), 146)*

> I lay like a corpse in the desert/wilderness,
> And the voice of God called out to me/summoned me:
> 'Arise, prophet, and see, and hear,
> Carry out my will,
> And passing by sea and land,
> Burn the hearts of people with the word.

Translation by Ted Hughes in After Pushkin, *26*

> I lay on stones like a corpse.
> There God's voice came to me:
> 'Stand, Prophet, you are my will.
> Be my witness. Go
> Through all seas and lands. With the Word
> Burn the hearts of the people.'

5.17 DOUGLAS ROBINSON

Douglas Robinson (b. 1954), professor of English at the University of Mississippi, studied at the universities of Washington and of Jyväskylä, Finland. He lived and taught in Finland for fourteen years; co-edited, with Ilkka Rekiaro, a Finnish-English-Finnish Dictionary (1989); and has translated Finnish poetry into English; he has also translated from Russian, Spanish, and German. Robinson is a prolific and versatile translation scholar. He is the author of *Translation and Taboo* (1996), *Translation and Empire: Postcolonial Approaches Explained* (1997), *What Is Translation?: Centrifugal Theories, Critical Interventions* (1997), and *Who Translates?: Translator Subjectivities Beyond Reason* (2001). He also edited the textbook *Western Translation Theory from Herodotus to Nietzsche* (1997). The title of his book *The Translator's Turn* (1991) illustrates his emphasis on how the act of translation, even when under considerable institutional and normative strain, is a matter of creative, personal and physical reaction and expression.

From *The Translator's Turn* (Baltimore and London: The Johns Hopkins University Press, 1991)

Conclusion

The argument of this book could be reduced to a few fairly simple and truistic propositions:

1. Translators choose the TL [target language] words and phrases that *feel* right.
2. Translators feel their way to the 'right' TL words and phrases in a complex two-way dialogue with the writer of the SL [source language] text and the reader of the TL text.
3. Translators turn from the SL text toward a TL rephrasing in a wide variety of ways.
4. Translators act upon their TL readers and can direct their influence over the TL reader in a wide variety of ways.

Put like this, these claims seem so commonsensical and obvious, so inevitable, even, that it would be difficult to quarrel with them—difficult, indeed, to imagine what possible position I could be arguing against. And certainly, if my case were that these propositions should simply be added to the current prepositional content of mainstream translation theory—that mainstream theory be supplemented with them, expanded to contain them—I doubt that many readers would protest.

In fact, of course, my theoretical revisionism is much more radical. The negative burden of my argument would include at least the following as well:

5. Equivalence between texts is not the final goal of all translation. Equivalence is an interpretive fiction that helps the translator work toward the true goal of translation, a working TL text—and is only one of many such fictions.

6. The striving for sense-for-sense equivalence is based on a reductive and ideologically contingent interpretation of the SL text and is really only fruitful with certain relatively uninteresting texts: unprepossessing technical and scholarly texts, for example. Most SL texts are more demanding and will require more innovative turnings.

7. Normative rules intended to govern the translator's choice of TL words and phrases are not only irrelevant to the practice of translation, they are, insofar as they alienate translators from their best intuitions about texts, actively pernicious.

8. Translators are never, and should never be forced to be (or to think of themselves as), neutral, impersonal transferring devices. Translators' personal experiences— emotions, motivations, attitudes, associations—are not only allowable in the formation of a working TL text, they are indispensable.

This second group of propositions underlines the oppositional thrust of my argument. I want to incorporate from mainstream theories certain practical approaches to the act of translation—attempting to render in the TL the sense of individual words, sentences, or whole texts (metonymy), for example, and attempting to persuade the TL reader to the SL writer's position (conversion)—but only as specific methods of limited scope in a broad and complex field; and I want to displace the *entire* rhetoric and ideology of mainstream translation theory, which, as I claim, is medieval and ecclesiastical in origin, authoritarian in intent, and denaturing and mystificatory in effect.

The specific taxonomic formulations that I offer are expendable. The six tropes (metonymy, synecdoche, metaphor, irony, hyperbole, and metalepsis) and the seven versions (conversion, reversion, subversion, perversion, aversion, diversion, and conversation), my specific conceptions of those tropes and versions, and even my conception of translation in tropological and ethical terms—these are more illustrations of the paradigm shift that I want to effect than its substance, which is, I suppose, best summed up in the eight propositions listed above. I certainly do not expect my tropes and versions to be adopted wholesale, and I would be horrified if they were adopted wholesale in an authoritarian, normative manner, imposed on translators as 'correct' or 'acceptable' approaches to translation. They are, I repeat, entirely expendable, and it is my sincere hope that they *will* be expended in translatological debate: literally used up, subsumed into future (and finer) formulations of the translator's hermeneutical tools and stances. (pp. 259–60)

From 'The Ascetic Foundations of Western Translatology: Jerome and Augustine' in *Translation and Literature*, 1 (Edinburgh: Edinburgh University Press, 1992), 3–25

[...] The ascetic imperialism of the medieval Church was first channelled through superstitious fear of an angry deity monopolized by the clergy; and in some sense, despite an escalating series of bourgeois demystifications throughout the modern era, that imperialism of the spirit is with us still today. Gradually, however, the monasteries extended their worldly sway into overtly socio-political spheres, through the amassing of vast ecclesiastical land holdings, for example—a kind of parallel or mirror-image feudalism informed not by territorialism but by an ascetic ideology that structured even decadent opulence in totalitarian ways. Toward the end of the Middle Ages, in the fourteenth and fifteenth centuries, the monastic opposition to the territorial ideology of might makes-right began to assume political form in the rise of the absolute state, which can be seen as the socio-ideological extension of monastic rule.[1] And finally—and most importantly, though also most indirectly—ecclesiastical asceticism 'seized power' in Western society through the rise of a secular but insistently ascetic bourgeoisie, dedicated to monetary profit through a new ascetic regimen: temperance, silence, order, resolution, frugality, industry, sincerity, justice, moderation, cleanliness, tranquillity, chastity, and humility, in Benjamin Franklin's late-eighteenth-century list.[2] This transformed ascetic ideology has been so successful in the past few centuries that Franklin's (or we could say Augustine's) ascetic 'virtues' have become naturalized in Western society, inscribed in what we unthinkingly take to be human 'nature,' in a discipline that (we believe) it is only 'natural' for all humans to undertake.

[...]

Certainly the importance of asceticism for the history of Western translatology cannot be over-emphasized. 'Normal' translation as it has been imagined in the West for sixteen centuries, and continues to be imagined today, is hegemonically ascetic (although humanistic strains from Cicero and the other classical theorists survive even within Christian asceticism, encouraging the translator to develop, to grow, through translation). Indeed it is difficult to recall (or even to imagine) a Western definition of translation, simple or complex, old or new, that does not immediately betray its ascetic aims. Consider only the 'renunciations' that are now and have long been expected of the translator: the renunciation of source-language syntax and 'colour' or 'feel' or 'mood', in the reduction of the source-language text to an abstract 'sense'; the renunciation of personal biases, predilections, preferences, and opinions in the education of the translator into a neutral transfer-machine. Consider the diatribes launched at 'word-for-word' and 'free' translations, and the temptation good translators feel and resist to indulge those pleasures: to cling 'too' closely to the source-language text, to trace its contours lovingly in the target language, by translating word for word; or to strike off 'too' boldly in a new direction, to sever ideologically-controlled ties with source language meaning, by translating freely. Consider the discipline required of the translator to renounce all this, to resist such temptations, and the institutional support (translator training, translator organizations and conferences, legal and financial sanctions) provided to back up that discipline. The history of Western translatology is many things, but above all it is a history of ascetic discipline. After Jerome and Augustine, even the worldly rebels against ascetic translatology typically only modify the prescribed ascesis.

Christian asceticism begins in a double tradition, eremitic and cenobitic, and the history of Western translatology reflects that split from the beginning. The eremite was the hermit who took drastic and dramatic steps to still the lure of the world in himself: starvation, motionlessness, sleep deprivation, the refusal to lie or sit down, sitting on poles. The cenobite was the monk or nun who submitted to monastic discipline, surrendered all decision-making to the father or mother superior and to the founder of the order, in the form of a monastic 'rule'. [...]

The worldly success of cenobitism has rendered the ascetic tradition in Western translatology more hegemonically cenobitic than eremitic; the ideal Western translator has always been more a disciplined monk or nun than a self-dramatizing hermit. As [Geoffrey Galt] Harpham says, the cenobite, like the ideal translator, is 'faultless rather than excellent, a subtracted rather than an achieved self.'[3] It is tempting, therefore, to set the eremitic tradition to one side and focus on the development of translatology out of cenobitism. The exclusion of the eremite—the maverick, the bull-headed loner, the individualist, the Hölderlin, the Pound, the Nabokov—is in fact one of the great temptations of mainstream Western translatology, and one that I am going to have to resist if I am to explore the complexities of ascetic translation. Although it is true, for example, that most Western translators have received overwhelming instruction of one kind or another in cenobitic invisibility (the 'subtracted self'), and have more or less successfully resisted the temptation to enter into eremitic self-dramatizations, the two most famous Western translatologists were eremites: Jerome, the hermit who ended his life in a monastery in Bethlehem, and Martin Luther, the Augustinian monk who broke free of the monastery and became one of the first modern eremites, a famous ascetic who ate and drank and married and clamoured for attention. Jerome's 'Letter to Pammachius' (395) and Luther's 'Circular Letter on Translation' (1530) are powerfully eremitic documents that have shaped translatology from the ideological periphery: wild, shaggy letters aflame with the passionate tempers and animal fears of their writers, documents that have been more quoted than read precisely because they are so embarrassingly unkempt and uncouth.

Calm, rational, presentable (cenobitic) translatology begins in the West in Book II of Augustine's *On Christian Doctrine*, his discussion of signs. [...] Where Jerome's eremitic translatology is personal, pragmatic, and riddled with internal contradictions,

Augustine's cenobitic translatology is impersonal, perfectionist, and systematic; where Jerome's is rhetorically hot, Augustine's is cool.

[...]

Jerome writes to Pammachius because he has been charged with 'ignorance and falsehood ... by an inexperienced, bumptious tongue', (probably Rufinus). He goes on:

> This tongue, it seems, claims that I have made mistakes through misinterpretation or carelessness when I translated into Latin a letter written by another in Greek ... My enemies tell the uneducated Christian crowd that Jerome falsified the original letter, that Jerome has not translated word for word, that Jerome has written 'beloved friend' in place of 'honorable Sir', and that—more disgraceful still— Jerome has maliciously condensed by omitting the epithet 'most reverend'.[4]

Jerome is at some pains to defend himself against these charges—to show that they are based on ignorance and inexperience of translation—and lashes back at his enemies with his own 'bumptious tongue'. Compared with his slightly younger and infinitely more authoritative contemporary Augustine,[5] Jerome is a quirky, crotchety hothead whose blood boils throughout the letter:

> At the very beginning, before I defend my translation, I wish to interrogate those men who call cunning and malice prudence. Where did you obtain your copy of my translation? Who gave it to you? How dare you display something obtained by your fraud? What place will be safe when a man cannot keep his secrets even behind his own walls and in his private desk? (p. 134)

[...]

In the defence that follows of his sense-for-sense Latin translation of a Greek letter from Epiphanius, Bishop of Constantia, to John, Bishop of Jerusalem, Jerome vacillates tellingly between eremitic self-dramatizations as an experienced translator who knows the right way to translate and cenobitic submission to the authority of a whole string of classical and Christian authors (Cicero, Horace, Terence, Plautus, Caecilius, and Bishop Evagrius of Antioch, who translated Athanasius's *Life of Anthony* into Latin). Here, for example, is an eremitic passage, which Jerome quotes from his own preface to an earlier translation:

> 'In the following sentence composed by another man, it is difficult not to diverge somewhere; and in translating it is hard to preserve the beauty of idiom which in the original is most distinguished. Each particular word has a significance of its own. Possibly I have no equivalent, by which to express some word, and if I then must go out of my way to reach the goal, miles are spent to cover what in reality is a short city block. To this difficulty must be added the windings of word transpositions, the dissimilarities in the use of cases, the varieties in figures of speech, and, most

difficult of all, the peculiar vernacular marrow of the language itself. If one translates each and every word literally, the passage will sound absurd; and if by necessity I change anything in the order and wording, it will seem that I have abused the function of translator.' Then, after a lengthy discussion, which would be a bit boring to follow here, I added the following: 'If anyone does not see how translation adulterates the charm of the original, let him squeeze Homer word for word into Latin—I will go even further and ask him to render Homer into Latin prose: the result will be that the order of the words will seem ridiculous, and that the most eloquent of poets will be hardly articulate.' (pp. 138–9)

[. . .]

Jerome does not stick to this rhetorical stance throughout, however; he sandwiches these particular eremitic claims, for example, between quotations from Cicero and Bishop Evagrius that establish his cenobitic credentials as submissive follower of a 'Rule' ('for this practice I have behind me the authority of Cicero himself'; 'now if my own opinion seems to lack authority ... read and consider this short preface from a biography of St Anthony of Egypt', pp. 137, 139). Indeed the remainder of the letter is devoted to a close reading of the Seventy's translations from the Hebrew and the evangelists' free interpretations or misreadings of the Old Testament, in order to show that the greatest authorities of all, the Greek translators of the Old Testament (whom Jerome at this writing, following Philo, still believed to have been divinely inspired) and the writers of the four gospels, tacitly approved of his translation practice, and thus lent him their considerable exegetical weight.

Tellingly, however, the cumulative effect of Jerome's citations from the Septuagint and the gospels is subversive of cenobitic discipline—undermines his implicit self-presentation as the submissive follower of a Rule. The impetus of his citations, ostensibly submissive and honorific, is almost invariably accusatory:

> Though the sense is identical with that in the Septuagint, the words are dissimilar, and are quite differently arranged. (p. 141)
>
> Even greater discrepancies may be discovered in another passage from Matthew. (p. 144)
>
> Similar trifling mistakes occur in the Apostle Paul. (p. 146)
>
> One of the most striking misquotations is made by Stephen, Christ's first martyr. (p. 147)

He is supposedly defending the writers and translators in question; but rhetorically his enumeration of their failings is carefully balanced between praise for sense-for-sense equivalence and blame for word-for-word deviation:

Should one accuse the Apostle Matthew of adulterating his translation? It agrees neither with the Hebrew original, nor with the Greek Septuagint, and, worse than that, one could claim that Matthew has mistaken even the author's name, attributing the passage to Jeremiah instead of Zechariah.

Far be it from Jerome, however, to speak like this about a follower of the Christ. The truth is that Matthew made it his business to formulate dogmas rather than scurry after words and syllables. (pp. 141–2)

It is a canny move: at the simplest level, he is providing a model for both praise and blame, hoping to force his accusers into an extension of their attack on him to the Seventy and the authors of the New Testament, and thus, since that position is politically untenable (i.e., heretical), to force them back into praise for his own position.

But there is another, and more devious (more eremitic), side to Jerome's claims—or rather, not a 'side', but an ascetic tension between opposed resistances. Jerome does blame the Seventy and the evangelists, it seems to me, for their inaccuracies; and he also praises them for their creative deviances, their eremitic wanderings beyond the faceless cenobitic discipline of the scholars. He takes a fierce pleasure in enumerating the 'defects' in these texts, the slippages from the Old Testament Hebrew to the Greek of the Septuagint and the New Testament, and the pleasure seems to me to be steeped in an eremitic imitation of Christ. This mimetic pleasure in effect conflates Jerome's implicit praise and blame for the Seventy and the evangelists, for it suggests simultaneously that the writers of the Greek Bible are nothing compared with Christ (and hence are as subject to blame as anyone else) and that their greatness, like Jerome's own, lies in their imitation of Christ (hence they are to be admired and emulated).

This reading of Jerome's duplicitous letter would corroborate Harpham's claim that, 'conceiving of himself as a direct or primary imitation of Christ, the eremite actually stands in the position of the transcription of the spoken Word. The highly mediated nature of even this posture undercuts any pretension to true originality on the part of the eremite, but this is not the real point. The eremite had predecessors but not intermediaries; he placed himself in direct relation, if it can be called that, to the Mediator' (p. 43). The eremitic Jerome has predecessors—Cicero, Horace, Bishop Evagrius, the Seventy, the evangelists—but they are not intermediaries in the sense of mastering or mediating his understanding of the source-language text (especially in the most radical Christian sense, of Jesus as the divine source-language Text or Word). They are only humans like himself, predecessors in the sense of having gone before, having attempted (like himself) to place themselves in an unmediated relation to truth. Faced as translator and Bible scholar with the textual traces of their imitations, he sees the inadequacies of those traces (as he sees the inadequacies of his own), and is not impressed—certainly is not silenced by them. But because he is attempting to achieve the same unmediated relation through his translations, he also recognizes the visionary power of their failures, the courage and determination that led them to deviate from mediated models of understanding and strike off on their own, hoping to transcribe the transformative Word on and through their own bodies by wandering like Jesus in the desert.

[. . .]

This crisscrossing of temptations and resistances is in fact inscribed within Jerome's own eremitic translatological regimen, in what may be the oddest note in the letter: 'Now I not only admit but freely announce that in translating from the Greek—except of course in the case of Holy Scripture, where even the syntax contains a mystery—I render, not word for word, but sense for sense' (pp. 136–7). Given the absence of support for (or later recurrence to) this 'exception', Jerome's insistence that he renders the Bible word for word sounds superficially like kneejerk piety—perhaps an attempt to protect himself against charges of heresy. Read this way, his word-for-word exceptionalism becomes a claim to resist the eremitic temptation to 'deviate' from the sense of the original.

But it is more complicated than that. Word-for-word translation is 'normal' for ecclesiastical authorities ignorant of translation, who believe that piety toward the source-language text requires piety toward every word in it. This renders word-for-word translation an ideological haven for those afraid of heresy charges—like Jerome, who writes this letter precisely in order to defend himself against such charges. At the same time, however, it is 'deviant' for ecclesiastical authorities with experience of translation, who believe that the translator should show piety not toward the source-language text but rather toward its transcendental *meaning*. This renders word-for-word translation a temptation to be resisted, a delight in the felicity of the source-language text that the ascetic translator must renounce. As Jerome's claim that 'even the syntax contains a mystery' suggests, word-for-word translation is at least implicitly kabbalistic: it reveals too great an attachment to the 'world', to 'fleshly' utterances, to the 'mystery' of specific articulations. The ascetic translator is expected to resist this temptation through idealization, abstraction, the transcendentalization of meaning especially through sense-for-sense translation, where the 'sense' to be translated is regarded as dwelling not in individual words or even utterances, but beyond all natural language in the mind of God (as circumscribed by the Church), and perceived by the pious translator only *through* the source-language text as through a veil.

Inscribed in the temptations and resistances of Jerome's letter, therefore, is a whole mutually defining system of translatological oppositions that will inform translation theory until our own [twentieth] century. On the one hand, there is 'humble' or 'self-effacing' or cenobitic translation, predicated on the translator's pious submission to the source-language author's intention as defined by the ecclesiastical (or other social) institution; on the other, there is 'arrogant' or 'self-dramatizing' or eremitic translation, predicated on the translator's assumption that he or she knows best and will translate any way he or she sees fit. Each of these positions is then divided into a sense-for-sense/word-for-word opposition: the ignorant cenobite translates, or requires that others translate, word for word' while the learned cenobite translates, or requires that others translate, sense for sense; and the orthodox eremite translates (etc.) sense for sense, while the kabbalistic eremite translates (etc.) word for word.

[. . .]

Jerome instituted translatology almost by accident, individualistically, eremitically, in situational self-defence and self-creation; the cenobitic Augustine took a larger, more dogmatic view. Augustine instituted translatology as a systematic undoing of the scattering of tongues at the Tower of Babel—specifically by identifying the *translatum* or transferred message with the unitary Word of God and then policing the transfer. [. . .]

In order to envisage perfect translation, then, and thus the Church, Augustine charts out a dual ascesis, a cenobitic purification at once of the *translatum* and of the translator. Everything in language that is not pure, simple, stable, permanent, must be excised; living language use, especially speech, must be derogated and dismissed as mere dross, a distortion of stable *logoi* (which are themselves distortions of the divine *Logos*) that is in turn subject to further distortion by listeners. And everything in human response that proliferates individuated meanings, all interpretive idiosyncrasies, inclinations, impulses, must be silenced, from within and without: both renounced by the interpreter and denounced by the monastic institution. Nomadic translation, marketplace translation, translation as a free-flowing series of encounters with other speakers in a fluid social sphere all this must be thematized as a temptation to be resisted, a sickness to be purged, an evil to be exorcised. The ideal translator for Augustine was a monk in a cell, purified of personality, perfectly conformed to cenobitic rule, wholly spoken from within by the voice of God.

[. . .]

When selfishness at Babel bred dissension, then, that dissension led to vocal dissonance, which led to the need for translation; but in the 'scattering' of Bible translations across the world Augustine sees a potential reversal of the Babelian scattering of tongues:

> Thus it happened that even the Sacred Scripture, by which so many maladies of the human will are cured, was set forth in one language, but so that it could be spread conveniently through all the world it was scattered far and wide in the various languages of translators that it might be known for the salvation of people who desired to find in it nothing more than the thoughts and desires of those who wrote it and through these the will of God, according to which we believe those writers spoke.[6]

The aporias that drive Augustine's idealization run deep: the scattering of translations allows all humans to hear 'nothing more' than the single and unified voice of God. More is less: more languages, more translations, more voices mean less dissension, less plurality, less selfish individuation.

Augustine can only envisage this transformation of more into less through the ascetic regimen that he outlines in *On Christian Doctrine* (II. vii), the seven-step path to wisdom that enables the Bible reader (and thus also the translator) to renounce the 'selfish' impulses that proliferate interpretations and preclude hegemonic understanding. [The seven steps are *fear, piety, knowledge, fortitude, mercy, cleansing,* and *wisdom.*] What makes this ascetic regimen so successful (witness how well it still works for us today, sixteen centuries after Augustine invented it) is partly that each step in some sense erases or subsumes the one previous, so that the pious translator no longer needs to be afraid, the knowledgeable translator no longer needs to conceive his or her quest for knowledge in terms of piety, and so on, until the arrival at 'wisdom' or perfect submission to cenobitic discipline erases everything that has gone before, leaving only (at least ideally) the perfectly neutral translator, the translator as robot, the 'machine' translator that continues to practice all seven ascetic disciplines but has forgotten that it does so (has *forgotten* that it has been programmed and believes that it is 'free'). This is the sense in which machine translation, the great cenobitic project of twentieth-century translatology, would be the ultimate fulfilment of Augustine's ascetic program.

But this forgetful internalization is only part of the reason for the program's success. Another part is institutional enforcement, the maintenance of *communal* discipline that provides for sanctions when ideological programming fails. And it always does: this is the problem. We are 'only human', we say—not (quite) machines. We try to maintain our fear of the critics and our respect for the source-language author, but they are too pathetic, too absurd in their ignorance, too backward in their attempts to write comprehensible source-language (the author) or target-language (the critics) prose, and we 'fix things up'. We try to purge ourselves of distracting personality, but it sneaks back in when we least expect it. We try to banish despair with determined fortitude, but fail (and despair at our failure). We try to be merciful to the target-language reader, but the source-language words delight us too much, we can't turn away from them, and so we pepper our translation with source-languagisms, literal renditions.

[. . .]

This institutional enforcement of built-to-fail ascetic programs is central to Augustine's cenobitic translatology. It is not enough to internalize and then forget fear, piety, knowledge, fortitude, mercy, purification, and wisdom; one must be repeatedly guided by institutional authorities to the proper fulfilment of those steps. [. . .]

[Robinson further discusses Augustine's emphasis on Church authority, but points out how institutional authority is traditionally vested in an 'alien word', a 'foreign word that is just domesticated enough to be almost understandable but still alien enough to be elevated, solemn, sacred, powerful'. Greek was for Augustine the main source of this word, not least the Greek word for word: *logos*, and the Greek Septuagint translation was the prime example of how divine authority is confirmed in human inspiration; we should, Augustine says, 'cede to the divine dispensation' by which the seventy translators worked.]

This insistence on the centrality of the alien Greek word to Augustine's cenobitic semiotic may seem to be undermined by the close attention Augustine pays to Latin translations; but in fact there is no conflict. The key for Augustine is not the use of an alien language, but the *alienation* of whatever language one uses. Nor is this alienation entirely at odds with familiarity, for in some sense he requires that both the alien and the familiar be resisted: the utterly alien is not understood and therefore has no impact, while the utterly familiar has no impact because it is unremarkable. By domesticating the foreign and alienating the familiar, the user of language creates a kind of ascetic Esperanto, an 'alien word' that is at once familiar and strange, understandable and shot through with awe.

We should recognize this 'alien word' as the interlanguage into which translators are systematically encouraged to render their source-language texts, even by translatologists like Eugene A. Nida, a vocal advocate of not making the translation sound like a translation. Nida disapproves of alien Bible translations, like the radically literal renditions of Buber and Rosenzweig or Chouraqui, or like the outdated English of the King James Version, and calls for easily understandable colloquial translations; but he also disapproves of overly assimilated translations, slangy translations, modernized translations, and so on. The translation should be familiar but not too familiar—and alien, but not too alien.

In fact, of course, this dialectical resistance to both the alien and the familiar means in practice that, depending on the readership for whom the translator is translating, the ascetic alien word may take any number of forms: from the qualified colloquialism of a Nida translation to the literalism of David Rosenberg in *The Book of J* to the modernization of Clarence Jordan's Cotton Patch Version; from the radical plainness of a Pound translation to the radical ugliness of Nabokov's *Eugene Onegin*. [. . .]

[. . .] Translation remains normatively a cenobitic discipline; but in the repressive dualism of Western thought, norms are predicated upon deviations, and therefore depend on them for their impact. Cenobitic translation, bound as it is by the subtracted self's dialectics of success and failure and of the familiar and the alien, is built upon the repression of eremitism. Eremitic translation, bound as it is by the isolated self's dialectics of brilliance and heresy, mystical oneness with the source-language author and audience response, is built upon the repression of cenobitism. Ascetic translation itself, eremitic and cenobitic, is built upon the repression of classical humanism, which was bound by the created self's dialectics of passive reception and anxious appropriation, outer- and inner-direction.

And the key to the complexity of Western translation theory is this: what is repressed in each successive theory does not thereby vanish, but survives in the resistance that maintains the repression, survives in a vital enough form to anticipate and in some sense engineer its own return. Cicero and Luther sound in Jerome. Quintilian and Goethe sound in Augustine. Repressed echoes striate each theory, every voice. It is only by listening to those echoes and tracing those striations that we can begin to move beyond the hegemonic repetition—Cicero and Jerome and Luther and Dryden and everybody between and since calling for sense-for-sense rather than word-for-word translation—to which the history of Western translation theory has conventionally been, and continues today to be, reduced.

NOTES

1. I'm drawing here on Norbert Elias, *Power and Civility*, Volume II of *The Civilizing Process*, translated by Edmund Jephcott (New York, 1982).

2. For the classic discussion of the bourgeois transformation of ascetic ideology, see Max Weber, *The Protestant Ethic and the Spirit of Capitalism*, translated by Talcott Parsons (New York, 1976). For a discussion of the transformation of 'profit' from spiritual in the fourth century to monetary in the seventeenth and eighteenth, see Geoffrey Galt Harpham, *The Ascetic Imperative in Culture and Criticism* (Chicago, 1987), pp. 62–4.

3. Harpham, *The Ascetic Imperative in Culture and Criticism*, p. 28.

4. Jerome, 'Letter to Pammachius (On the Best Kind of Translator)', in *The Satirical Letters of Jerome*, translated by Paul Carroll (Chicago, 1958), pp. 132–4.

5. Jerome was born c. 347, Augustine nine years later in 356, Jerome dies around the age of 73 in c. 420, Augustine at the age of 74 in 430.

6. Augustine, *On Christian Doctrine*, translated by D. W. Robertson, Jr (Indianapolis, 1958), II. v. 6; pp. 36–7.

5.18 LAWRENCE VENUTI

Lawrence Venuti (b. 1953) is a professional translator (mostly from Italian), translation theorist, and educator, editor of *Rethinking Translation: Discourse, Subjectivity, Ideology* (1992) and *The Translation Studies Reader* (a selection of twentieth-century texts, from Benjamin to Venuti himself; 2000). He is the author of the *The Scandals of Translation: Towards an Ethics of Difference* (1998) as well as of the influentially polemical *The Translator's Invisibility: A History of Translation* (1995), in which he strenuously argues against the notion of neutrality in translation, basing his argument on a historical account of developments from the seventeenth century to the present. He makes the post-colonial, post-imperial case for translation which attempts to preserve the foreignness of the foreign text, countering the domesticating, familiarizing, appropriative effect of what might be seen as the mainstream approach to translation in the English tradition, drawing on a hegemonic Classical legacy. Venuti has himself translated much Italian prose and recently (2002) he published a selection of the work of the Italian author Antonia Pozzi: *Breath: Poems and Letters*. The same year, he also published an anthology, *Italy: A Traveler's Literary Companion*. Lawrence Venuti is Professor of English at Temple University, Philadelphia.

In the essay printed below, Venuti again assembles the historical evidence, in support of a proposition in support of a translator's activism, which might counter the effect of domestication, translatory or whatever, which he characterizes as violence perpetrated on source cultures.

From 'Translation as Cultural Politics: Regimes of Domestication in English', *Textual Practice*, 7/2 (Summer 1993), 208–23

> A metalanguage is always terrorist.
> Roland Barthes (trans. Richard Howard)

> All violence is the illustration of a pathetic stereotype.
> Barbara Kruger

I propose these two epigraphs as an extravagant but pointed metaphor for translation. The statement from Roland Barthes concludes his incisive 1961 review of Michel Foucault's *Histoire de la folie*.[1] For Barthes, Foucault's history shows that madness is the discourse of reason about unreason, and this discourse, apart from the physical exclusions of exile, imprisonment, and hospitalization which it makes possible, also excludes the discourse of unreason about unreason, hence reducing the object of which it professes knowledge. In Barthes's conclusion, a metalanguage, a second-order discourse that takes a prior signifying system as its object, is found to be reductive and exclusionary and thus likened to terrorism, violent action that is both intense and damaging, that intimidates and coerces, usually in the service of social interests and political agendas, often under the aegis of reason or truth. The epigram from the artist Barbara Kruger was part of a 1991 installation, in which the accusatory aphoristic statements that distinguish her photo-montages were painted across the walls and floors of the Mary Boone Gallery in New York.[2] Here violence is likened to a metalanguage: it is action with the function of representation, a second-order discourse illustrating a prior stereotype, which can be seen as pathetic in its destructiveness, its reductive and exclusionary relation to a person or social group. Violence is the enactment of a cultural discourse that already constitutes a conceptual or representational violence. Reflection on translation in the context of Barthes's and Kruger's statements undoubtedly cheapens violent action, trivializing its serious physical and psychological costs, its brutal materiality. But such reflection will also illuminate the discursive conditions of violence by attending to the material effects of another metalanguage, the power of translation to (re)constitute and cheapen foreign texts, to trivialize and exclude foreign cultures, and thus potentially to figure in racial discrimination and ethnic violence, international political confrontations, terrorism, war.

The violence of translation resides in its very purpose and activity: the reconstitution of the foreign text in accordance with values, beliefs and representations that pre-exist it in the target language, always configured in hierarchies of dominance and marginality, always determining the production, circulation, and reception of texts. Translation is the forcible replacement of the linguistic and cultural difference of the foreign text with a text that will be intelligible to the target-language reader. This difference can never be entirely removed, of course, but it necessarily suffers a reduction and exclusion of possibilities— and an exorbitant gain of other possibilities specific to the translating language. Whatever difference the translation conveys is now imprinted by the target-language culture, assimilated to its positions of intelligibility, its canons and taboos, its codes and ideologies. The aim of translation is to bring back a cultural other as the same, the recognizable, even the familiar; and this aim always risks a wholesale domestication of the foreign text, often in highly self-conscious projects, where translation serves an imperialist appropriation of foreign cultures for domestic agendas, cultural, economic, political.

Thus, the violent effects of translation are felt at home as well as abroad. On the one hand, translation wields enormous power in the construction of national identities for foreign cultures and hence can play a role in racial and ethnic conflicts and geopolitical confrontations. On the other hand, translation enlists the foreign text in the maintenance or revision of literary canons in the target-language culture, inscribing poetry and fiction, for example, with the various poetic and narrative discourses that compete for cultural dominance in the target language. Translation also enlists the foreign text in the maintenance or revision of dominant conceptual paradigms, research methodologies, and clinical practices in target-language disciplines and professions, whether physics or architecture, philosophy or psychiatry, sociology or law. It is these social affiliations and effects—written into the materiality of the translated text, into its discursive strategy and its range of allusiveness for the target-language reader, but also into the very choice to translate it and the ways it is published, reviewed, and taught—all these conditions permit translation to be called a cultural political practice, constructing or critiquing ideology-stamped identities for foreign cultures, affirming or transgressing discursive values and institutional limits in the target-language culture. The violence wreaked by translation is partly inevitable, inherent in the translation process, partly potential, emerging at any point in the production and reception of the translated text, varying with specific cultural and social formations at different historical moments.

The most urgent question facing the translator who possesses this knowledge is: What to do? Why and how do I translate? Although I have construed translation as the site of multiple determinations and effects—linguistic, cultural, ideological, political—I also want to indicate that the translator always exercises a choice concerning the degree and direction of the violence at work in his practice. This choice was given its most decisive formulation at the beginning of the nineteenth century by the theologian and philosopher Friedrich Schleiermacher. In an 1813 lecture on the different methods of translation, Schleiermacher argued that 'there are only two. Either the translator leaves the author in peace, as much as possible, and moves the reader towards him; or he leaves the reader in peace, as much as possible, and moves the author towards him.'[3] Admitting (with qualifications like 'as much as possible') that translation can never be completely adequate to the foreign text, Schleiermacher allowed the translator to choose between a domesticating method, an ethnocentric reduction of the foreign text to target-language cultural values, bringing the author back home, and a foreignizing method, an ethno-deviant pressure on those values to register the linguistic and cultural difference of the foreign text, sending the reader abroad.

Schleiermacher made clear that his choice was foreignizing translation, and this has led the French translator and translation theorist Antoine Berman to treat Schleiermacher's argument as an ethics of translation, concerned with making the translated text a place where a cultural other is manifested—although, of course, an otherness that can never be manifested in its own terms, only in those of the target language, and hence always already encoded.[4] The 'foreign' in foreignizing translation is not a transparent representation of an essence that resides in the foreign text and is valuable in itself, but a strategic construction whose value is contingent on the current target-language situation. Foreignizing translation signifies the difference of the foreign text, yet only by disrupting the cultural codes that prevail in the target language. In its efforts to do right abroad, this translation method must do wrong at home, deviating from native norms to stage an alien reading experience.

I want to suggest that in so far as foreignizing translation seeks to restrain the ethnocentric violence of translation, it is highly desirable today, a strategic intervention in the current state of world affairs, pitched against the hegemonic English-language nations and the unequal cultural exchanges in which they engage their global others. For the fact is that only 2–3 per cent of the books published in the US and UK each year are translations, whereas foreign titles, many from English, count for as much as 25 per cent (or more) of the books published annually in other countries.[5] And yet foreignizing translation has always been marginalized in Anglo-American culture. This method is specific to certain European countries at particular historical moments: formulated first in German culture during the classical and romantic periods, it has recently been revived in a French cultural scene characterized by postmodern developments in philosophy, literary criticism, psychoanalysis, and social theory that have come to be known as 'poststructuralism'.[6] English-language translation, in contrast, has been dominated by domesticating theories and practices at least since the seventeenth century.

In 1656, Sir John Denham prefaced *The Destruction of Troy*, his version of the second book of the *Aeneid*, with the remark that 'if *Virgil* must needs speak English, it were fit he should speak not only as a man of this Nation, but as a man of this age.'[7] Denham saw himself as presenting a naturalized English Virgil. He felt that poetic discourse in particular called for domesticating translation because 'Poesie is of so subtle a spirit, that in pouring out of one Language into another, it will all evaporate; and if a new spirit be not added in the transfusion, there will remain nothing but a *Caput mortuum*' (p. 65). The 'new spirit' Denham 'added' to Virgil belonged to Denham ('my Art', 'my self'), and he was acutely aware that it was specifically English, so that domestication was a translation method laden with nationalism, even if expressed with courtly self-effacement:

> if this disguise I have put upon him (I wish I could give it a better name) fit not naturally and easily on so grave a person, yet it may become him better than that Fools-Coat wherein the French and Italian have of late presented him. (p. 65)

Domestication became the preferred method for English-language poetry translation by the end of the seventeenth century, when it received its authoritative formulation in John Dryden's *Dedication of the Aeneis* (1697). 'I have endeavoured to make Virgil speak such English,' wrote Dryden, 'as he would himself have spoken, if he had been born in England, and in this present age.'[8] In Dryden's wake, from Alexander Pope's multi-volumed Homer (1715–26) to Alexander Tytler's systematic *Essay on the Principles of Translation* (1791), domestication dominated the theory and practice of English-language translation in every genre, prose as well as poetry. William Guthrie, for example, in the preface to his version of *The Orations of Marcus Tullius Cicero* (1741), argued that 'it is *living Manners* alone that can communicate the Spirit of an Original' and so urged the translator to make 'it his Business to be as conversant as he cou'd in that Study and Manner which comes the nearest to what we may suppose his Author, were he now to live, wou'd pursue, and in which he wou'd shine.'[9] Hence, Guthrie cast his Cicero as a member of Parliament, 'where,' he says, 'by a constant Attendance, in which I was indulg'd for several Years, I endeavour'd to possess myself of the Language most proper for this translation.'

It is important not to view such instances of domestication as simply inaccurate translations. Canons of accuracy and fidelity are always locally defined, specific to different cultural formations at different historical moments. Both Denham and Dryden recognized that a ratio of loss and gain inevitably occurs in the translation process and situates the translation in an equivocal relationship to the foreign text, never quite faithful, always somewhat free, never establishing an identity, always a lack and a supplement. Yet they also viewed their domesticating method as the most effective way to control this equivocal relationship and produce versions adequate to the Latin text. As a result, they castigated methods that either rigorously adhered to source-language textual features or played fast and loose with them, that either did not sufficiently domesticate the foreign text or did so by omitting parts of it. Following Horace's dictum in *Ars Poetica*, Denham 'conceive[d] it a vulgar error in translating Poets, to affect being *Fides Interpres*', because poetic discourse required more latitude to capture its 'spirit' in the target language than a close adherence to each foreign word would allow. But he also professed to 'having made it my principal care to follow [Virgil]', noting that 'neither have I any where offered such violence to his sense, as to make it seem mine, and not his'. Dryden similarly 'thought it fit to steer betwixt the two extremes of paraphrase and literal translation', i.e. between the aim of reproducing primarily the meanings of the Latin text, usually at the cost of its phonological and syntactical features, and the aim of rendering it word for word, respecting syntax and line break. And he distinguished his method from Abraham Cowley's 'imitations' of Pindar, partial translations that revised and, in effect, abandoned the foreign text. The ethnocentric violence performed by domesticating translation rested on a double fidelity, to the source-language text as well as to the target-language culture, but this was clearly impossible and knowingly duplicitous, accompanied by the rationale that a gain in domestic intelligibility and cultural force outweighed the loss suffered by the foreign text and culture.

By the turn of the nineteenth century, a translation method of eliding the linguistic and cultural difference of the foreign text was firmly entrenched as a canon in English-language translation, usually linked to a valorization of transparent discourse. In 1820, a translator of Aristophanes, John Hookham Frere, unfavourably reviewed Thomas Mitchell's versions of *The Acharnians* and *The Knights*, their principal 'defect' being 'the adoption of a particular style; the style of our ancient comedy in the beginning of the 16th century'.[10] Frere faulted Mitchell's use of an archaic literary and dramatic discourse, English Renaissance comedy, because the language of translation ought, we think, as far as possible, to be a pure, impalpable and invisible element, the medium of thought and feeling, and nothing more; it ought never to attract attention to itself; hence all phrases that are remarkable in themselves, either as old or new; all importations from foreign languages and quotations, are as far as possible to be avoided … such phrases as [Mitchell] has sometimes admitted, 'solus cum solo', for instance, 'petits pates', &c. have the immediate effect of reminding the reader, that he is reading a translation, and … the illusion of originality, which the spirited or natural turn of a sentence immediately preceding might have excited, is instantly dissipated by it. (p. 481)

Frere advocated a fluent strategy, in which the language of the translation is made to read with a 'spirited or natural turn', so that the absence of any syntactical or lexical peculiarities produces the illusionistic effect of transparency, the appearance that the translation reflects the foreign writer's intention ('It is the office, we presume, of the Translator to represent the forms of language according to the intention with which they are employed') (p. 482) and therefore the appearance that the translation is not in fact a translation, but the original, still within the foreign writer's control, not worked over by the translator. Fluency produces an individualistic illusion, in which the text is assumed to originate fundamentally with the author, to be authorial self-expression, free of cultural and social determinations. Since fluency is here a translation strategy, it can be considered a discursive sleight of hand by which the translator domesticates the foreign text, causing its difference to vanish by making it intelligible in an English-language culture that values easy readability, transparent discourse, and the illusion of authorial presence.

And, once again, the domestication enacted by a fluent strategy does not necessarily result in an inaccurate translation. In 1823, the anonymous reviewer of William Stewart Rose's *Orlando Furioso* recommended this strategy in the pronouncement that

> the two characteristics of a good translation are, that it should be *faithful*, and that it should be *unconstrained*. Faithful, as well in rendering correctly the meaning of the original, as in exhibiting the general spirit which pervades it: unconstraincd, so as not to betray by its phraseology, by the collocation of its words, or construction of its sentences that it is only a copy.[11]

Fluency can be associated with fidelity because it means foregrounding the conceptual signified in the translation, checking the drift of language away from communication, minimizing any play of the signifier which calls attention to its materiality, to words as words, their opacity, their resistance to immediate intelligibility, empathic response, interpretive mastery. What the fluent strategy conceals with the effect of transparency, what it makes seem faithful, is in fact the translator's interpretation of the foreign text, the signified he has demarcated in the translation in accordance with target-language cultural values. The fluent translation is seen as 'rendering correctly the meaning of the original' because it constitutes an interpretation that conforms or can be easily assimilated to those values, not only the valorization of 'unconstrained' language, but also the understanding of the foreign text or literature that concurrently prevails in the target culture.

In Frere's case fluency entailed a linguistic homogenization that avoided 'associations exclusively belonging to modern manners' as well as archaism, that removed as many of the historically specific markers of the foreign text as possible by generalizing or simply omitting them. The translator will,

> if he is capable of executing his task upon a philosophic principle, endeavour to resolve the personal and local allusions into the genera, of which the local or personal variety employed by the original author is merely the accidental type; and to reproduce them in one of those permanent forms which are connected with the universal and immutable habits of mankind. (p. 482)

Frere rationalized these admitted 'liberties' by appealing to a 'philosophic principle':

> The proper domain of the Translator is, we conceive, to be found in that vast mass of feeling, passion, interest, action and habit which is common to mankind in all countries and in all ages; and which, in all languages, is invested with its appropriate forms of expression, capable of representing it in all its infinite varieties, in all the permanent distinctions of age, profession and temperament. (p. 481)

In Frere's view, a fluent strategy enables the translation to be a transparent representation of the eternal human verities expressed by the foreign author.

The principle on which Frere's translation theory rests is liberal humanism, in which subjectivity is seen as at once self-determining and determined by human nature, individualistic yet generic, transcending cultural difference, social conflict, and historical change to represent 'every shade of the human character'; Frere's theory may appear to be democratic in its appeal to what is 'common to mankind', to a timeless and universal human essence, but it actually involved an insidious domestication that allowed him to imprint the foreign text with his conservative sexual morality and cultural élitism. He made plain his squeamishness about the physical coarseness of Aristophanic humour, its grotesque realism, and felt the need to explain it away as inconsistent with the author's intention: the 'lines of extreme grossness' were 'forced compromises', 'which have evidently been inserted, for the purpose of pacifying the vulgar part of the audience, during passages in which their anger, or impatience, or disappointment, was likely to break out' (p. 491). Hence, 'in discarding such passages,' Frere asserted, 'the translator is merely doing that for his author, which he would willingly have done for himself'—were he not 'often under the necessity of addressing himself exclusively to the lower class'

(p. 491). Frere's advocacy of a fluent strategy was premissed on a bourgeois snobbery, in which the moral and political conservatism emerging in early nineteenth-century English culture resulted in a call for a bowdlerized Aristophanes that represented the 'permanent' class divisions of humanity, what Frere described as 'that true comic humour which he was directing to the more refined and intelligent part of his audience' (p. 491).[12] For Frere, 'the persons of taste and judgment to whom the author occasionally appeals, form, in modern times, the tribunal to which his translator must address himself' (p. 491).

Fluency is thus a discursive strategy ideally suited to domesticating translation, capable not only of executing the ethnocentric violence of domestication, but also of concealing this violence by producing the illusionistic effect of transparency. And it is this strategy that, with very few exceptions (the Victorian archaism of Francis Newman and William Morris, for example, or the modernist experiments of Ezra Pound and Louis and Celia Zukofsky), has continued to dominate the theory and practice of English-language translation to this day. Perhaps the clearest indication of this dominance is Eugene Nida's influential concept of 'dynamic' or 'functional equivalence' in translation, formulated first in 1964, but restated and developed in numerous books and articles over the past twenty-five years. 'A translation of dynamic equivalence aims at complete naturalness of expression,' states Nida, 'and tries to relate the receptor to modes of behavior relevant within the context of his own culture.'[13] The phrase 'naturalness of expression' signals the importance of a fluent strategy to this theory of translation, and in Nida's work it is evident that fluency involves domestication. As he has recently put it, 'the translator must be a person who can draw aside the curtains of linguistic and cultural differences so that people may see clearly the relevance of the original message.'[14] This is of course a relevance to the target-language culture, something with which foreign writers are usually not concerned when they write their texts, so that relevance can be established in the translation process only by replacing source-language features that are not recognizable with target-language ones that are. Thus, when Nida asserts that 'an easy and natural style in translating, despite the extreme difficulty of producing it ... is nevertheless essential to producing in the ultimate receptors a response similar to that of the original receptors' (*Science*, p. 163), he is in fact imposing the English-language valorization of transparent discourse on every foreign culture, masking a basic disjunction between the source- and target-language texts which puts into question the possibility of eliciting a 'similar' response.

Like earlier theorists in the Anglo-American tradition, however, Nida has argued that dynamic equivalence is consistent with a notion of accuracy. The dynamically equivalent translation does not indiscriminately use 'anything which might have special impact and appeal for receptors'; it rather 'means thoroughly understanding not only the meaning of the source text but also the manner in which the intended receptors of a text are likely to understand it in the receptor language' (*One Language*, pp. vii–viii, 9). For Nida, accuracy in translation depends on generating an equivalent effect in the target-language culture: 'the receptors of a translation should comprehend the translated text to such an extent that they can understand how the original receptors must have understood the original text' (ibid., p. 36). The dynamically equivalent translation is 'interlingual communication' which overcomes the linguistic and cultural differences that impede it (ibid., p. 11). Yet the understanding of the foreign text and culture which this kind of translation makes possible answers fundamentally to target-language cultural values while veiling this domestication in the transparency evoked by a fluent strategy. Communication here is initiated and controlled by the target-language culture, and therefore it seems less an exchange of information than an imperialist appropriation of a foreign text. Nida's theory of translation as communication does not adequately take into account the ethnocentric violence that is inherent in every translation process—but especially in one governed by dynamic equivalence.

As with John Hookham Frere, Nida's advocacy of domesticating translation is explicitly grounded on a transcendental concept of humanity as an essence that remains unchanged over time and space. 'As linguists and anthropologists have discovered,' Nida states, 'that which unites mankind is much greater than that which divides, and hence there is, even in cases of very disparate languages and cultures, a basis for communication' (*Science*, p. 2). Yet the democratic potential of Nida's humanism, as with Frere's, is contradicted by the more exclusionary values that inform his theory of translation, specifically Christian evangelism and cultural elitism. From the very beginning of his career, Nida's work has been motivated by the exigencies of Bible translation: not only have problems in the history of the Bible translation served as examples for his theoretical statements, but he has written studies in anthropology and linguistics designed primarily for Bible translators and missionaries. [. . .]

To advocate foreignizing translation in opposition to the Anglo-American tradition of domestication is not to do away with cultural political agendas. Clearly, such an advocacy is itself an agenda. The point is rather to develop a theory and practice of translation that resists dominant target-language cultural values so as to signify the linguistic and cultural difference of the foreign text. Philip Lewis's concept of abusive fidelity can be taken as a first step in such a theorization: it acknowledges the equivocal relationship between the foreign text and the translation and eschews a fluent strategy in order to reproduce in the translation whatever features of the foreign text abuse or resist dominant cultural values in the source language.[15] Abusive fidelity directs the translator's attention away from the conceptual signified to the play of signifiers on which it depends, to phonological, syntactical, and discursive structures, resulting in a 'translation that values experimentation, tampers with usage, seeks to match the polyvalencies or plurivocities or expressive stresses of the original by producing its own' (p. 41). Such a translation strategy can best be called resistancy, not merely because it avoids fluency, but because it challenges the target-language culture even as it enacts its own ethnocentric violence on the foreign text.

The notion of foreignization can alter the ways translations are read as well as produced because it assumes a concept of human subjectivity that is very different from the humanist assumptions underlying domestication. Neither the foreign author nor the translator is conceived as the transcendental origin of the text, freely expressing an idea about human nature or communicating it in transparent language to a reader from a different culture. Rather, subjectivity is constituted by cultural and social determinations that are diverse and even conflicting, that mediate any language use, and that vary with every cultural formation and every historical moment. Human action is intentional, but determinate, self-reflexively measured against social rules and resources, the heterogeneity of which allows for the possibility of change with every self-reflexive action.[16] Textual production may be initiated and guided by the producer, but it puts to work various linguistic and cultural materials which make the text discontinuous, despite its appearance of unity, and which result in meanings and effects that may exceed the producer's intention, creating an unconscious that is at once personal and social, psychological and ideological. Thus, the translator consults many different target-language cultural materials, ranging from dictionaries and grammars to texts, discursive strategies, and translations to values, paradigms, and ideologies, both canonical and marginal. Although intended to reproduce the source-language text, the translator's consultation of these materials inevitably reduces and supplements it, even when source-language cultural materials are also consulted, and their sheer heterogeneity leads to discontinuities in the translation that are symptomatic of its ethnocentric violence. Discontinuities at the level of syntax, diction, or discourse allow the translation to be read as a translation, revealing the strategy at work in it, foreignizing a domesticating translation by showing where it departs from target-language cultural values, domesticating a foreignizing translation by showing where it depends on them. [...]

In many translations [...] the discontinuities are readily apparent, unintentionally disturbing the fluency of the language or deliberately establishing the linguistic heterogeneity that distinguishes a resistant strategy. Literary translations, in particular, often bear prefaces which announce the translator's strategy and alert the reader to the presence of noticeable stylistic peculiarities. But perhaps translations in other disciplines should also contain prefaces that not merely describe the problems posed by the foreign text and the translator's solutions, but rationalize the global strategy developed and implemented by the translator, including the specific kind of discourse chosen for the translation and the specific interpretations assigned to key concepts. Such prefaces will ultimately force translators and their readers to reflect on the ethnocentric violence of translation and possibly to write and read translated texts in ways that seek to recognize the linguistic and cultural difference of foreign texts. What I am advocating is not an indiscriminate valorization of every foreign culture or a metaphysical concept of foreignness as an essential value; indeed, the foreign text is privileged in a foreignizing translation only in so far as it enables a disruption of target-language cultural values, so that its value is always strategic, depending on the cultural formation into which it is translated. My goal is not an essentializing of the foreign, but resistance against ethnocentrism and racism, cultural narcissism and imperialism, in the interests of democratic geopolitical relations.'' Hence, my project is the elaboration of the theoretical, critical, and textual means by which translation can be studied and practised as a focus of difference, instead of the homogeneity that widely characterizes it today. Once the violence of translation is recognized, the choices facing the writers and readers of translated texts become clear—however difficult they are to make.

[handwritten annotation: shouldn't this depend more on the work?]

[handwritten annotation: implies that translation intends to disrupt cultural values]

NOTES

1. Roland Barthes, 'Taking sides', in *Critical Essays*, trans. Richard Howard (Evanston, Ill.: Northwestern University Press, 1972), pp. 163–70.
2. Barbara Kruger, Mary Boone Gallery, 5–26 January 1991.
3. Friedrich Schleiermacher, 'On the different methods of translating', in *Translating Literature: The German Tradition from Luther to Rosenzweig*, ed. and trans. André Lefevere (Assen: Van Gorcum, 1977), pp. 67–89.
4. Antoine Berman, *L'épreuve de l'étranger: Culture et traduction dans l'Allemagne romantique* (Paris: Gallimard, 1984). See also Berman's 'La traduction et la lettre, ou l'auberge du lointain', in *Les Tours de Babel: Essais sur la traduction* (Mauvezin: Trans-Europ-Repress, 1985), pp. 31–150, especially pp. 87–91. Schleiermacher's theory, despite its stress on foreignizing translation, is complicated by the nationalist cultural programme he wants German translation to serve: see my article 'Genealogies of translation theory: Schleiermacher', in *TTR: Traduction, Terminologie, Rédaction: Etudes sur le texte et ses transformations*, vol. 4, no. 2 (1991), pp. 125–50.
5. See the annual statistics for the American publishing industry presented by Chandler B. Grannis in *Publishers Weekly*, 19 September 1989, pp. 24–5, 9 March 1990, pp. 32–5, and 8 March 1991, pp. 36–9. For the British statistics, see *Whittaker's Almanack* for the years 1986 to 1991. The volume of translations published annually in a European country like Italy can be gauged from Herbert R. Lottman, 'Milan: A world of change', *Publishers Weekly*, 21 June 1991, pp. s5–s11.
6. I discuss the impact of French poststructuralism on translation theory and practice in the introduction of my anthology, *Rethinking Translation: Discourse, Subjectivity, Ideology* (London and New York: Routledge, 1992) pp. 1–17. The present article develops theoretical issues set forth in that introduction. Although I am theorizing translation from within Anglo-American culture, the foreign theoretical discourses I put to work considerably complicate my 'home' position, creating possibilities for cultural critique and resistance. In a previous article—'The translator's invisibility', *Criticism*, 28, (1986), pp. 179–212—I offer an assessment of current English-language translation that is indebted as much to Althusserian Marxism as to poststructuralism.
7. Sir John Denham, 'Preface' to The Destruction of Troy, in *English Translation Theory, 1650–1800*, ed. T. R. Steiner (Assen: Van Gorcum, 1975), pp. 64–5.
8. John Dryden, 'Dedication of the *Aeneis*,' in *English Translation Theory*, pp. 72–4.
9. William Guthrie, 'Preface' to *The Orations of Marcus Tullius Cicero*, in *English Translation Theory*, pp. 96–9.
10. John Hookman Frere, Review of Thomas Mitchell's translation of *The Comedies of Aristophanes*, *Quarterly Review*, 23 (July 1820), pp. 474–505.
11. Review of William Stewart Rose's translation of *Orlando Furioso*, *Quarterly Review*, 30 (October 1823), pp. 40–61.
12. For the emergence of moral and political conservatism in early nineteenth-century England, see Maurice J. Quinlan, *Victorian Prelude: A History of English Manners, 1780–1830* (New York: Columbia University Press, 1941) and Lawrence Stone, *The Family, Sex and Marriage in England, 1500–1800* (New York: Harper & Row, 1977).

13. Eugene A. Nida, *Toward a Science of Translating, with Special Reference to Principles and Procedures Involved in Bible Translating* (Leiden: Brill, 1964), p. 159. Further references to this work will be indicated by *Science*.

14. Jan de Waard and Eugene A. Nida, *From One Language to Another: Functional Equivalence in Bible Translating* (Nashville: Thomas Nelson, 1986), p. 14. Further references to this work will be indicated by *One Language*.

15. Philip E. Lewis, 'The measure of translation effects', in *Difference in Translation*, ed. Joseph Graham (Ithaca, N.Y.: Cornell University Press, 1985), pp. 31–62.

16. These remarks assume Anthony Giddens' concept of agency in *Central Problems in Social Theory: Action, Structure, and Contradiction in Social Analysis* (Berkeley and Los Angeles: University of California Press, 1979), especially ch. 2.

5.19 SUSAN BASSNETT

Susan Bassnett (b. 1945), literary scholar, translation theorist, translator, poet, has served as Pro-Vice-Chancellor of the University of Warwick, and is Professor in the Centre for Translation and Comparative Cultural Studies which she founded in the 1980s. She was educated in several European countries and has lectured widely. Bassnett is author of over twenty books, and her *Translation Studies* (1980; 3rd edn. 2002) has remained in print and has become one of the most important textbooks around the world in the expanding field of Translation Studies. Her *Comparative Literature: A Critical Introduction* (1993), polemically seeking to situate translation studies in the centre rather than on the fringe of comparative literature, has itself been translated into several languages. Recent books include *Constructing Cultures* (1998) co-authored with André Lefevere, with whom she collaborated (see introduction to Sect. 5.5 on Lefevere) on many projects, and *Post-Colonial Translation* (1999) co-edited with Harish Trivedi. With Piotr Kuhiwczak, who also teaches at Warwick, she has translated and edited an anthology: *Ariadne's Thread: Polish Women Poets* (1988). Her own latest collection of poetry is *Exchanging Lives* (2002). Susan Bassnett also writes for several national newspapers. One of her specialities is the semiotics of theatre and theatre translation.

From 'Theatre and Opera', in Peter France (ed.), *The Oxford Guide to Literature in English Translation* (Oxford: Oxford University Press, 2000), 96–103

The Problem of the Play-Text

[U]nlike other types of text, the play is written to be spoken and is therefore a kind of blueprint that actors use as the basis of their performance. It has been argued that the play text is incomplete without that physical dimension, that in its written version it awaits realization in performance. Pavis warns that any discussion of the translation of a play text needs to take the performance dimension into account, since the play is not simply a literary text, written to be read, but a text that 'reaches the audience by way of the actors' bodies' [P. Pavis, *Theatre and the Crossroads of Culture* (London and New York: 1992)]. [...]

André Helbo makes a distinction between four types of stage direction, suggesting that some are meant for the actors, some for the staging, some for the implied spectator and some for the reader [A. Helbo, *Theory of the Performing Arts* (Amsterdam, 1987)]. What is clear is that there are very different kinds of stage direction, and very different kinds of play, and in consequence some plays are more easily accessible to readers even without the performance dimension.[...]

Any theory of translation of theatre and opera texts needs to take into account both the problem of determining exactly what the relationship between written text and performance is, and the problem of huge variations in reading and writing practices. Is the dramatic text literature [. . .], or is it another kind of text altogether, a hybrid that cannot be considered as a complete entity? Depending on the response to this question, translation practice varies considerably.

Theatre and opera are multi-dimensional arts. Tadeusz Kowzan proposes five semiotic systems that underpin all performance, and may be present together or separately, according to the type of performance being staged. The first of these is the spoken text, for which there may or may not be a written script, the second is bodily expression, the third the actor's physical appearance (height, gestures, features, etc), the fourth the playing space (size, shape, lighting, props, etc), and the fifth non-spoken sound, including music [T. Kowzan, *Littérature et spectacle* (Paris and The Hague, 1975)]. From these five categories, he determines 13 distinct subsections: words, intonation, mime, gesture, movement, make-up, hairstyle, costume, props, decor, lighting, music, and sound effect, which he classifies as either auditive or visual signs. This structuralist breakdown of performance serves as a basic map, and remains a useful tool for understanding the complex interrelationship between sign systems in theatre. For theatre is above all a collaborative process, and the final performance is the result of interaction between different sign systems and different individuals. The spoken text (or written text, if there is one at all) exists as only one element of that collaboration.

The task of the translator, therefore, is to render the single element of written text into another language. This might not seem, on the surface, any different from any other kind of translation practice, but the difficulties arise when we return to the vexed question of determining exactly what a play-text is. For if there is some kind of coded gestural text inside the play, which actors, directors, designers and other practitioners can decode and render actual in corporeal terms, then it follows that the translator needs to take this factor into account, for practitioners in the target culture will also want to actualize the play in their own language and physicality.

Speakability

[. . .] In his introduction to six plays by Chekhov in English, Robert Corrigan declares:

> The first law in translating for the theatre is that everything must be speakable. It is necessary at all times for the translator to hear the actor speaking in his mind's ear. He must be conscious of the gestures of the voice that speak—the rhythm, the cadence, the interval. He must also be conscious of the look, the feel, and the movement of the actor while he is speaking. He must, in short, render what might be called the whole gesture of the scene.
>
> (A. Chekhov, *Six Plays*, tr. R. Corrigan, New York, 1962) [. . .]

Malcolm Griffiths claims that:

> Translators for the theatre are enmeshed in a protean activity which requires as
> much familiarity with theatre practice, cultural contexts and social history as it does
> with spoken and written languages.

(M. Griffiths, 'Presence and Presentation: Dilemmas in Translating for the Theatre',
in T. Hermans, ed. *Second Hand: Papers on the Theory and Historical Study of
Literary Translation*, ALW-Cahier. 3, 1985).

This is a large statement, but serves to illustrate the futility of relying upon an ill-defined
notion of 'speakability' as a criterion for translation. What is being suggested here is that
theatre practice in different cultures has its own genealogy and its own traditions;
audiences in different cultures have different horizons of expectation. [...]

The point is that audience expectations are by no means universal, and performance
styles are geared to accommodate those different expectations. Actors adjust their
rhythms in accordance with the conventions and expectations of their own culture and
tradition. [...] This means that any modern French performance of a Racine tragedy is a
form of translation, and any version in any other language is doubly a translation, both
interlingual and intersemiotic.

Dialogue and Deixis

[...] In the 1980s, theatre analysts turned their attention to the fact that at the heart of
dramatic dialogue there lies the notion of the *deixis*, the '*I* addressing *a you here* and *now*'
[K. Elam, *The Semiotics of Theatre and Drama* (London 1980)]. This means that a
dramatic text can be broken down into a series of deictic units, which give indications
of where speech is to be directed. [...]

Version, Adaptation, and Translation

The terms 'version' or 'adaptation' are frequently used with reference to translation of
texts for theatre, and this terminology can have different meanings. One use of the terms
implies a degree of variation from the source text, so that a 'translation' might be
perceived as closer to the original than something described as a 'version' or as an
'adaptation'. But 'adaptation' can also be used to describe the process for dramatizing a
novel, for example, and in this sense it is often used as a synonym for 'screenplay' when
the source text is not set out in the form of a play. [...]

Some critics argue about the use of this terminology, suggesting that a translation is
somehow more 'faithful' to the original than a version or an adaptation. This argument is
based on the flawed premiss that there *is* such a thing as a 'faithful' translation in the first
place, an assumption called into question by Translation Studies. For all translations
reflect the translator's interpretation of the source text, so that a translation is basically the

product firstly of a single individual's reading and then of his or her second-language rewriting. Translation inevitably involves rewriting and manipulation of the source, as translators and theorists, from Dryden to Derrida have pointed out, and the act of translating always leads to changes.

There is also another, more recent use of the terms 'version' and 'adaptation'. In some countries, particularly in the English-speaking world, it is common to market translations as being made by well-known playwrights, even if these have no access to the source language. [. . .] [P]roblems arise when the term 'translation', which implies knowledge of more than one language, is used to describe the work of English writers, and a way round this ethical and legal difficulty can be found by use of the term 'translation' to describe the text produced by interlingual transfer and 'adaptation' or 'version' to describe the text rewritten in English. [. . .]

Acculturation in Translation

[. . .] Translation of a play involves deliberate choices on the part of theatre managements, funding bodies, actors and directors, and foreign texts are often chosen because of the specific needs of the target system. Many play translations are undertaken in order to expand a repertoire [. . .] A period of intense playwriting activity is generally not one of great theatre translation, but conversely, a period where there is relatively little native theatre being produced tends to be a time of increased translation. [. . .]

A recent development in the theatre is the transcultural performance, which draws upon a range of different theatrical systems. It is possible to argue that this kind of theatre, famously developed by such figures as Peter Brook or Pina Bausch, does not have a source text at all, since the foreign text and culture are not taken as points of departure. [. . .] In this kind of theatre, the communication of the foreign is not posited as a feature of the performance; rather, the performance seeks to combine different elements in a new whole. Discussing Eugenio Barba's intercultural work with *Faust*, Pavis defines it as a western vision conveyed by eastern traditions that is reworked by a western director, using performers from both east and west, which results in the 'neutralization' of one theatrical and cultural tradition by another [P. Pavis, *Theatre at the Crossroads of Culture*, (London and New York, 1992)].

Although intercultural theatre may be a new development, opera has long had an intercultural dimension, made possible by a more restricted concept of translation. When operas are performed in the source language, singers learn their roles in that language, combining music and sound patterns without necessarily having any conversational or writing ability in the language. It is therefore commonplace to have singers from China, Bulgaria, the United States or Italy all performing in the same opera, provided there is a common language in which all will sing. The increased internationalization of opera means that this pattern is likely to continue.

5.20 EVERETT FOX

Everett Fox, educated at Brandeis University, is the Allen M. Glick Professor of Judaic and Biblical Studies at Clark University in Worcester, Massachusetts. He has investigated the rhetoric and internal coherence of the Hebrew Bible, with the object of conveying these qualities, as far as possible, in his translations. These have appeared in *The Five Books of Moses* (1995), and in *Give Us a King!: Samuel, Saul, and David* (1999). Fox has relied substantially on the theory and practice of Martin Buber and Franz Rosenzweig. Together with Lawrence Rosenwald, he has also translated Buber and Rosenzweig's *Scripture and Translation* (1994; see Sect. 4.5, above, on Buber and Rosenzweig).

From Everett Fox's 'Translator's Preface' to *The Five Books of Moses: Genesis, Exodus, Leviticus, Numbers, Deuteronomy* **(New York: Schocken Books, 1995)**

> ... read the Bible as though it were something entirely unfamiliar, as though it had not been set before you ready-made.... Face the book with a new attitude as something new.... Let whatever may happen occur between yourself and it. You do not know which of its sayings and images will overwhelm and mold you.... But hold yourself open. Do not believe anything a priori; do not disbelieve anything a priori. Read aloud the words written in the book in front of you; hear the word you utter and let it reach you.
>
> —*adapted from a lecture of Martin Buber, 1926*

The purpose of this work is to draw the reader into the world of the Hebrew Bible through the power of its language. While this sounds simple enough, it is not usually possible in translation. Indeed, the premise of almost all Bible translations, past and present, is that the 'meaning' of the text should be conveyed in as clear and comfortable a manner as possible in one's own language. Yet the truth is that the Bible was not written in English in the twentieth or even the seventeenth century; it is ancient, sometimes obscure, and speaks in a way quite different from ours. Accordingly, I have sought here primarily to echo the style of the original, believing that the Bible is best approached, at least at the beginning, on its own terms. So I have presented the text in English dress but with a Hebraic voice.

The result looks and sounds very different from what we are accustomed to encountering as the Bible, whether in the much-loved grandeur of the King James Version or the clarity and easy fluency of the many recent attempts. There are no old friends here; Eve will not, as in old paintings, give Adam an apple (nor will she be called 'Eve'), nor will

Moses speak of himself as 'a stranger in a strange land,' as beautiful as that sounds. Instead, the reader will encounter a text which challenges him or her to rethink what these ancient books are and what they mean, and will hopefully be encouraged to become an active listener rather than a passive receiver.

This translation is guided by the principle that the Hebrew Bible, like much of the literature of antiquity, was meant to be read aloud, and that consequently it must be translated with careful attention to rhythm and sound. The translation therefore tries to mimic the particular rhetoric of the Hebrew whenever possible, preserving such devices as repetition, allusion, alliteration, and wordplay. It is intended to echo the Hebrew, and to lead the reader back to the sound structure and form of the original.

Such an approach was first espoused by Martin Buber and Franz Rosenzweig in their monumental German translation of the Bible (1925–1962) and in subsequent interpretive essays. *The Five Books of Moses* is in many respects an offshoot of the Buber-Rosenzweig translation (hereafter abbreviated as B-R). I began with their principles: that translations of individual words should reflect 'primal' root meanings, that translations of phrases, lines, and whole verses should mimic the syntax of the Hebrew, and that the vast web of allusions and wordplays present in the text should be somehow perceivable in the target language (for a full exposition in English, see now Buber and Rosenzweig 1994). In all these areas I have taken a more moderate view than my German mentors, partly because I think there are limitations to these principles and partly because recent scholarship points in broader directions. As a result, my translation is on the whole less radical and less strange in English than B-R was in German. This, however, does not mean that it is less different from conventional translations, or that I have abandoned the good fight for a fresh look at the Bible's verbal power.

Buber and Rosenzweig based their approach on the Romantic nineteenth-century notion that the Bible was essentially oral literature written down. In the present century there have been Bible scholars who have found this view attractive; on the other hand, there has been little agreement on how oral roots manifest themselves in the text. One cannot suggest that the Bible is a classic work of oral literature in the same sense as the *Iliad* or *Beowulf*. It does not employ regular meter or rhyme, even in sections that are clearly formal poetry. The text of the Bible that we possess is most likely a mixture of oral and written materials from a variety of periods and sources, and recovering anything resembling original oral forms would seem to be impossible. This is particularly true given the considerable chronological and cultural distance at which we stand from the text, which does not permit us to know how it was performed in ancient times.

A more fruitful approach, less dependent upon theories whose historical accuracy is unprovable, might be to focus on the way in which the biblical text, *once completed*, was copied and read. Recent research reveals that virtually all literature in Greek and Roman times—the period when the Hebrew Bible was put into more or less the form in which it has come down to us (but not the period of its composition)—was read aloud. This holds for the process of copying or writing, and also, surprisingly, for solitary reading. As late as the last decade of the fourth century, Saint Augustine expressed surprise at finding a sage who read silently. Such practices and attitudes seem strange to us, for whom the very definition of a library, for instance, is a place where people have to keep quiet. But it was a routine in the world of antiquity, as many sources attest.

So the Bible, if not an oral document, is certainly an aural one; it would have been read aloud as a matter of course. But the implications of this for understanding the text are considerable. The rhetoric of the text is such that many passages and sections are understandable in depth only when they are analyzed *as they are heard*. Using echoes, allusions, and powerful inner structures of sound, the text is often able to convey ideas in a manner that vocabulary alone cannot do. A few illustrations may suffice to introduce this phenomenon to the reader; it will be encountered constantly throughout this volume.

Sound plays a crucial role in one of the climactic sequences in Genesis, Chapters 32–33. Jacob, the protagonist, has not seen his brother Esau for twenty years. Now a rich and successful adult, he is on his way back to Canaan after a long exile. He sends messengers to forestall Esau's vengeance—for twenty years earlier, Jacob had stolen the birthright and the blessing which Esau felt were rightly his own. When Jacob finds out that his brother 'is already coming … and four hundred men are with him' (32: 7), he goes even further, preparing an elaborate gift for Esau in the hopes of appeasing his anger. The text in vv.21–22 presents Jacob's thoughts and actions (the translation is taken from the New English Bible):

> for he thought, 'I will appease him with the present that I have sent on ahead, and afterwards, when I come into his presence, he will perhaps receive me kindly.' So Jacob's present went on ahead of him.…

This is an accurate and highly idiomatic translation of the Hebrew, and the reader will notice nothing unusual about the passage as it reads in English. The sound of the Hebrew text, on the other hand, gives one pause. It is built on variations of the word *panim*, whose basic meaning is 'face,' although the Hebrew uses it idiomatically to encompass various ideas. (Note: in Hebrew, the sound *p* is pronounced as *ph* under certain circumstances.) If the text is translated with attention to sound, its quite striking oral character emerges (italics mine):

> For he said to himself:
> I will wipe (the anger from) his *face* (*phanav*)
> with the gift that goes ahead of my *face*; (*le-phanai*)

afterward, when I see his *face*, (*phanav*)

perhaps he will lift up my *face!* (*phanai*)

The gift crossed over ahead of his *face.* . . . (*al panav*)

Comparison of these two English versions is instructive. In the New English Bible, as in most other contemporary versions, the translators are apparently concerned with presenting the text in clear, modern, idiomatic English. For example, they render the Hebrew *yissa phanai* as 'receive me kindly.' The N.E.B. translates the *idea* of the text; at the same time it translates *out* the sound by not picking up on the repetition of *panim* words.

What does the reader gain by hearing the literalness of the Hebrew? And what is lost by the use of its idiomatic meaning? As mirrored in the second translation, it is clear that our text is signaling something of significance. The motif of 'face' (which might be interpreted as 'facing' or 'confrontation') occurs at crucial points in the story. The night before his fateful meeting with Esau, as he is left to ponder the next day's events, Jacob wrestles with a mysterious stranger—a divine being. After Jacob's victory, the text reports (32: 31):

Yaakov called the name of the place: Peniel/*Face of God*,

for: I have seen God,

face to face,

and my life has been saved.

The repetition suggests a thematic link with what has gone before. One could interpret that once the hero has met and actually bested this divine being, his coming human confrontation is assured of success. Thus upon meeting Esau at last, Jacob says to him (33: 10):

For I have, after all, seen your *face*, as one sees the *face* of God,

and you have been gracious to me.

It could be said that in a psychological sense the meetings with divine and human adversaries are a unity, the representation of one human process in two narrative episodes. This is accomplished by the repetition of the word *panim* in the text.

The above interpretation depends entirely on sound. Once that focus is dropped, either through the silent reading of the text or a standard translation, the inner connections are simply lost and the reader is robbed of the opportunity to make these connections for himself. Clearly there is a difference between translating what the text means and translating what it says.

While the Jacob passages use the sound of a specific word to indicate an important motif in the narrative, there are other cases where sound brings out structure, and the structure itself conveys the principal idea of the passage. A striking example of this is found at the beginning of Genesis. God's first acts of creation in 1: 3–5 are portrayed in a highly ordered fashion, suggesting that creation itself is orderly, and this idea is the thematic backbone of the whole chapter. We are meant to experience the orderliness of God's activity through the sensuality of the language and through the particular way in which the text speaks. A translation keyed to the sound of the Hebrew reads:

> God said: Let there be light! And there was light.
> God saw the light: that it was good.
> God separated the light from the darkness.
> God called the light: Day! and the darkness he called: Night!

The four occurrences of 'God' plus verb accomplish the narrator's goal, and give a tone to the creation account that makes it akin to poetry. In contrast, virtually all modern translations treat the passage as prose, rendering it into clear written English but simultaneously removing its inner structure. What remains is a statement of what is taking place in the narrative, but without its underlying thrust. Again the New English Bible:

> God said, 'Let there be light,' and there was light; and God saw that the light was good, and he separated light from darkness. He called the light day, and the darkness night.

This translation is cast in good English style. For just that reason two occurrences of 'God' have been omitted, and the passage consequently reads smoothly—so smoothly that one glides past it as if creation were the same as any other narrated action. But what has been lost is the characteristic oral ring of the text, and simultaneously its intent to say something beyond the content of words alone.

Another example of translating with an ear to the sound and structure of the original, this time from the book of Exodus, comes from the dramatic story of the Sea of Reeds (14: 11–12). The newly freed Israelites find themselves pursued by their former masters, the Pharaoh and his army; with their backs to the Sea, they panic, and bitterly harangue their would-be deliverer, Moses. The present translation, attempting to reflect the repetition and structure of the original, yields the following:

> they said to Moshe:
> Is it because there are no graves in Egypt
> that you have taken us out to die in the wilderness?
> What is this that you have done to us, bringing us out of Egypt?
> Is this not the very word that we spoke to you in Egypt,
> saying: Let us alone, that we may serve Egypt!

Indeed, better for us serving Egypt
than our dying in the wilderness!

This passage demonstrates several aspects of a rhetorical translation method, if we may so
term it: the laying out of the text in 'cola' or lines meant to facilitate reading aloud (more
on this below); the repetition of words—'Egypt' five times and 'wilderness' twice—to
stress the irony of the Israelites' predicament (as they see it, Egypt means life, and the
wilderness, certain death); and the double use of 'serve,' the very word that Moses
constantly drummed into Pharaoh's ears in the early part of the book to denote the
Israelites' desire to go and worship their God ('Send free my people, that they may serve
me'). If we juxtapose the above translation with that found in, say, the New International
Version, the importance of this approach to the text becomes clear:

> They said to Moses, 'Was it because there were no graves in Egypt that you brought
> us to the desert to die? What have you done to us by bringing us out of Egypt?
> Didn't we say to you in Egypt, "Leave us alone; let us serve the Egyptians"? It would
> have been better for us to serve the Egyptians than to die in the desert!'

Here the rhetorical force of the Hebrew has been ignored. The Hebrew text does not
transpose 'desert to die' to 'die in the desert' at the end of the passage (the word order
repeats in the original, for emphasis); it does not distinguish in sound between 'Egypt'
and 'Egyptians'; and it certainly does not read like standard colloquial prose. Indeed, all
of Chapter 14 of Exodus demonstrates the Bible's use of an intermediate form between
poetry and prose, a form designed to instruct as well as to inspire.

But it is not only in narrative that the rhetoric of biblical language makes itself felt.
Fully half of the book of Exodus is law or instruction, and one can find there further
examples of the importance of sound structure in the Bible. Take, for instance, the law
concerning the protection of widows and orphans (22: 23–24). This time I shall present
the text first through the eyes of the Jerusalem Bible:

> You must not be harsh with the widow, or with the orphan; if you are harsh with
> them, they will surely cry out to me, and be sure that I shall hear their cry; my anger
> will flare and I shall kill you with the sword, your own wives will be widows, your
> own children orphans.

This is powerful language, especially in a law code. But the Hebrew text goes much
farther, utilizing as it does a double form of the verb rarely found in multiple sequence:

> Any widow or orphan you are not to afflict.
> Oh, if you afflict, afflict them ...!
> For (then) they will cry, cry out to me,
> and I will hearken, hearken to their cry,

> my anger will flare up
>
> and I will kill you with the sword,
>
> so that your wives become widows, and your children,
>
>   orphans!

Here the text is in effect slowed down by the division into lines, and the verb forms are isolated to underscore their unique rhetoric. The effect of the whole is to focus attention on this particular law among a host of others. (pp. ix–xv)

Genesis 11: 1–9, as translated in Fox, *Five Books of Moses*, pp. 48–9.

[Cf. other versions of the same passage, pp. 9–10, 13–14, 43–6, 66–7, 72, 113–14, 119–20, 321–2, 351, and 568.]

1. Now all the earth was of one language and one set-of-words.
2. And it was when they migrated to the east that they found a valley in the land of Shinar and settled there.
3. They said, each man to his neighbour:
   Come-now! Let us bake bricks and let us burn them well-burnt!
   So for them brick-stone was like building-stone, and raw-bitumen was for them like red-mortar.
4. Now they said:
   Come-now! Let us build ourselves a city and a tower, its top in the heavens,
   and let us make ourselves a name,
   lest we be scattered over the face of all the earth!
5. But YHWH came down to look over the city and the tower that the humans were building.
6. YHWH said:
   Here (they are) one people with one language for them all,
   and this is merely the first of their doings—
   now there will be no barrier for them in all that they scheme to do!
7. Come-now! Let us go down and there let us baffle their language,
   so that no man will understand the language of his neighbour.
8. So YHWH scattered them from there over the face of all the earth,
   and they had to stop building the city.
9. Therefore its name was called Bavel/Babble,
   for there YHWH baffled the language of all the earth-folk,
   and from there, YHWH scattered them over the face of all the earth.

5.21 JOHN FELSTINER

John Felstiner (b. 1936) graduated from Harvard. Since 1965 he has been teaching literature at Stanford, where he is Professor of English, with stints at the University of Chile, the Hebrew University in Jerusalem, and Yale. He has held Rockefeller, Guggenheim, NEH, and NEA fellowships. He is the author of *The Lies of Art: Max Beerbohm's Parody and Caricature* (1972), *Translating Neruda: The Way to Macchu Picchu* (1980), and *Paul Celan: Poet, Survivor, Jew* (1995). Felstiner has received a number of awards for his work on and translations of Neruda and Celan. His *Selected Poems and Prose of Paul Celan* appeared in 2001. Like some other scholars and practitioners of translation, Felstiner has noted how translation constitutes an exceptionally attentive and energized form of reading. His article, 'Kafka and the Golem', reprinted in its entirety below, exemplifies the many connections between reading, interpretation and translation.

John Felstiner, 'Kafka and the Golem: Translating Paul Celan', in Daniel Weissbort (ed.), *Translating Poetry: The Double Labyrinth* (Iowa City: University of Iowa Press, 1985), 35–50

Einem, der vor der Tür stand
    eines
Abends:
ihm
tat ich mein Wort auf –: zum
Kielkropf sah ich ihn trotten,
    zum
halb-
schürigen, dem
im kotigen Stiefel des
    Kriegsknechts
geborenen Bruder, dem
mit dem blutigen
Gottes-
gemächt, dem
schilpenden Menschlein.

Rabbi, knirschte ich, Rabbi
Löw:

To one who stood before the
    door, one
evening:
to him   toward
I opened my word –: ~~to~~ the
clod I saw him trot~~ting, to the~~
    toward
the half-
baked   begot
brother ~~born~~ in ~~the~~ a
    dough boy's ~~hireling's~~
dung-caked, boot, ~~him~~
~~with his blood~~   him with his
    god-
~~on God's~~   like loins
~~handiwork, the~~   all bloody,
    the
chittering manikin.

Rabbi, I gnashed, Rabbi
Loew:

Diesem

beschneide das Wort,

diesem

schreib das lebendige

Nichts ins Gemüt,

diesem

spreize die zwei

Krüppelfinger zum heil-

bringenden Spruch.

Diesem.

. . . .

Wirf auch die Abendtür zu,
    Rabbi.

. . . .

Reiß die Morgentür auf
    Ra- –

For this one –

circumcise *his* word,

for this one –

write the living

Nothing~~ness~~ on his heart,

for this one

spread your two

cripple ~~bent~~ fingers in a

~~sav-~~   safe-

~~ing saying.~~   keeping prayer.

For this one

. . . .

And slam (shut) the evening
    door, Rabbi.

. . . .

Throw the morningdoor open,
    Ra- –

Because attentiveness or *Aufmerksamkeit*—as in a saying that Walter Benjamin took to identify Kafka's genius and that Paul Celan then took up in thinking of his own poetic practice: 'Attentiveness is the natural prayer of the soul'—because attentiveness mattered so critically to Celan, I try in translating him to make translating into the fullest possible and the closest act of reading and of writing.[1] A translator, I think, needs to become the reader *par excellence*—or perhaps I should say *par exigence*. Here I would borrow from Kafka's *Trial*, where Joseph K., trying to interpret the parable 'Before the Law', is told by a priest: 'The Scripture is unalterable and its interpretations often merely betray bewilderment at this.'[2]

At the enigmatic text before me now, '*Einem, der vor der Tür stand*', 'To one who stood before the door',[3] I feel a kindred bewilderment. I can at least perceive in this poem a dynamic linking divine creative speech to failing mortal clay. And I think I hear Paul Celan crying out for admission into a spiritual realm that we may (unknowingly) suppose he entered when in mid-career, a quarter-century after the catastrophe that took away his parents, culture and homeland, he took his own life by drowning. To begin tracing him through this poem, I think of what Franz Rosenzweig once said about his work on Judah Halevi: 'I myself understand a poem only when I have translated it.'[4]

Einem, in the dative, an indefinite pronoun initiating a subordinate clause followed by a colon; then a second dative, *ihm*, with a line to itself, leading to a dash and another colon: punctuation, line breaks, syntax and grammar already seem to compose the law of this poem, as if language and speech themselves formed a prior, primary reality governing anything the poem may refer to. Yet a translator's exactness with these technical elements does not dispel the reader's questions. Who is speaking, and to whom? Before what door, and when—Shabbat, or some other pivot in time? Maybe the fact of a door barring entrance to something matters more at first than the something behind it.

> To one who stood before the door, one
> evening:
> to him
> I opened my word

'*ihm/tat ich mein Wort auf*'. Usually with *auftun* in the German Bible—in Job and Psalms, for instance—a divine or human speaker opens his mouth or lips, or doors and gates open up. In Celan's poem, a word is opened, but what word—or does the very act of opening, of speaking, matter most here?

Now if line by line I seem to be deferring and frustrating the interpretive impulse, I think Celan's poem requires just that of its reader-translator. We have not even come to the close of a sentence yet; and we have not yet come upon Rabbi Loew.

Having opened his word to someone standing before the door, the speaker saw him approach someone else. A broken, staggered syntax and an impasto of crude, animal-like images convey this scene. I sense here a derisiveness pulsing through all five adjectives with the same dropping cadence: *schürigen, kotigen, geborenen, blutigen, schilpenden*— a derisiveness I have tried to catch in fairly rough sound and rhythmic patterns:

> ... toward the
> clod I saw him trot, toward
> the half-
> baked
> brother begot in a
> doughboy's dung-caked boot,
> him with his god-
> like loins all
> bloody, the
> chittering manikin.

What is the 'clod', the *Kielkropf*, that spawns these phrases? A dialect term meaning changeling, abortion, monster or, colloquially, dolt; my word 'clod' indicates an earthy, soulless creature like the golem, but it loses the idea of something misbegotten and also weakens the bite of *Kielkropf*, with those two sharp k's that cut through again in *Kriegsknecht*. To regain a little in translation, instead of 'born' I have said 'begot' in a boot, for the verb's raw rhyme with 'trot' and its half-biblical, half-bestial overtones.

If Celan has the golem in mind here, he has certainly laded on more than its usual legendary traits. The word *half-schürig*—'of the second shearing', i.e. imperfect—does tally closely with the biblical term *golem*, 'unformed', and also with the colloquial sense of 'golem', a dumbhead; both senses are perhaps audible in the English 'half-baked'. But Celan's next phrase gives a strange lineage to this creature the doorkeeper trotted toward, this 'brother begot in a/doughboy's dung-caked boots'.[5] Possibly some folk tale lies behind the image, with muck on a trooper's boot making do for the clay that formed humankind. Yet the *Kriegsknecht*, a 'mercenary', still baffles me. In sixteenth-century and later versions the golem as bodyguard or spy does defend Jews against their enemies, yet no source I have been able to find says that Joseph Golem actually served as a hired soldier, much less that he was born in the boot of one.[6] Provisionally, 'doughboy' will do for a common trooper, and the word jostles interestingly with 'dungcaked'. It also suggests the shaping of Adam, the miracle of creating human life that so powerfully underlies the golem tradition. In a kind of sacred parody written not long before this poem, and called 'Psalm', Celan begins by countering Creation: 'No one kneads us again out of earth and clay,/no one conjures our dust.'[7] This 'psalm', a quintessential expression of despair after the Jewish catastrophe, makes a bleak backdrop to the poem *Einem, der vor der Tür stand'*, with its wretched creaturely hero.

Now why *Bruder*? Is this creature a brother to the 'one who stood before the door', the one who trots toward him? Is he something less worthy, an Esau perhaps, deprived of blessing, or even a Cain, the baneful side of humankind? Celan sees him with a bloody 'form', and here the word *Gemächt*, an unusual term, gives me pause. In Psalm 103: 14 Luther uses it to translate the Hebrew *yetser*, 'frame': 'For He knoweth our frame; He remembereth that we are dust.' That Hebrew root occurs in Genesis 2: 7, 'God *formed* man of the dust of the ground', and in *Sefer Yetsirah*, the third-century Book of Creation from which derived the earliest idea of magically fashioning a person such as the golem. So *Gemächt* signifies something made, and *Gottesgemächt*, 'God's handiwork'. But Celan's creature, created in the image of God, has blood on his frame. What is more, *Gemächt* can also mean something else: the male genitals; indeed for *dem blutigen Gottesgemächt* a French version of this poem has *le membre sanglant de Dieu*, 'God's bloody member'.[8] Although I cannot quite see Celan entertaining such an image, his poem (like the golem legend) certainly involves the question of (pro)creativeness as well as createdness. I try to resolve both senses of *Gemächt*, 'frame' and 'generative power', in the word 'loins'. I call them 'godlike' to reflect the Genesis story, and I break the word to replicate Celan's linebreak, which (if only momentarily and prosodically) sunders God from his handiwork.

But why then 'bloody'? If this brother has something of Cain in him, then his 'brother's blood cries out from the ground' (Gen. 4: 10). Or we remember that the Golem defended Prague's Jews against the Passover blood libel. Or perhaps bloody loins really signal the idea of circumcision that will decisively enter this poem in a moment; after all, the painful violence of 'his godlike loins all bloody' might possibly express Paul Celan's sense of having been inscribed in the Mosaic covenant. Fortunately a translation does not entail specifying one sense or another. I think the clodbrother-manikin in some way incarnates the animal and unredeemed side of human nature, and thus may reflect all those possibilities lodged in 'blood'. As in Psalm 139: 16, the only biblical occurrence of the word *golem*, this creature is imperfect, Adam not yet touched by the breath of God. Then remembering that Rabbi Loew's homunculus cannot speak helps explain why this *schilpenden Menschlein* is called a chirping, or cheeping, or twittering, or chittering manikin.

Here the speaker stops, and moves from report—'I opened my word', 'I saw him trot'—into direct speech. This brief transition—

> Rabbi, I gnashed, Rabbi
> Loew:

—becomes the poem's fulcrum, identifying as the Maharal of Prague the person who stood before the door and trotted toward the manikin. And in one unexpected verb, *knirschte*, 'gnash' or 'grate' or 'grind', the speaker takes on a desperateness that imbues everything he says from here on. Simply to utter the word 'Rabbi', which appears nowhere else in Celan's ten books of poetry, and to utter it twice, bespeaks for him a rare because openly Jewish urgency. In early 1961, when I believe he wrote this poem, Celan was acutely afflicted by a public charge of plagiarism against him and by its connection to recent German anti-semitism.[9] He might well have turned then to the wonder-working Prague Rabbi, the man whose golem fought against libel. And the name *Löw* itself, poised alone as an entire verse, may be calling up Celan's father Leo, in Russian Lev. Around the time of this poem Celan jokingly signed a letter 'Pavel Lvovitsch', Paul son of Lev.[10] As a boy he had not felt close to his father, a man whose Orthodox, Zionist persuasions represented a Judaism which, but for the Nazi war, he might have sloughed off.[11] So to single out the name *Löw* in this poem grounds a religious and historical urgency in a difficult private invocation.

After this invocation, again pointed by a colon, we hear twelve lines of direct speech for the duration of the poem. A much firmer syntax and grammar move these lines than in the poem's first half. And now a demonstrative pronoun, again a dative, opens the sentence:

> Diesem
> beschneide das Wort.

Celan builds so much into the dative with its verb that I have (reluctantly) added punctuation and emphasis to make this fulcral point decisive in English:

> For this one –
> circumcise *his* word.

Here again an enigmatic figure generates a cluster of possibilities. Given Celan's inexhaustible linguistic curiosity, a pun on *brit mila*—Covenant of the 'Word' as well as of circumcision—may inhabit the phrase *beschneide das Wort* (a pun audible only in the phrase's Hebrew overtones and thus not for German ears). 'For this one—circumcise *his* word', the speaker pleads, meaning not only the wordless golem but someone like Moses of 'uncircumcised lips' (Exod. 6: 12), perhaps the poet himself in exile and wanting prophetic speech. The only English translation I know of renders this phrase as 'remove the word', since *beschneiden* does literally mean 'to cut off'.[12] Yes, Rabbi Loew removes the name of God from the golem's mouth every Shabbat, and ultimately tears away the aleph from *emeth*, 'truth', on the creature's forehead, leaving him *meth*, 'dead'. But an image of cutting off would deter the prayer rising in this sentence: 'For this one ... for this one ... for this one.' If only because Nazism construed circumcision as a fatal sign, I think Celan would have wanted to 'circumcise the word', to bring his own German language itself, however murderously abused, somehow within the covenant. Jacques Derrida has called circumcision *une blessure lisible*.[13] Virtually every poem Celan wrote bears a 'legible wound'.

And no other figure of speech exposes that wound as acutely as paradox:

> for this one
> write the living
> Nothing on his heart

Again I regret having to use three words for Celan's inflected pronoun, especially now that the charged word *diesem*, flush left and filling a line of its own, begins to give a vertebral structure to this plea or prayer. As for the paradox of 'living Nothing', it may well be *emeth* written on the golem's forehead and then removed. But it also belongs to a larger dimension, as does the paradox of circumcision, the wound that sanctifies an organ of regeneration. 'The Nothing is the Nothing of God ... from which all true Creation springs,' writes Gershom Scholem, whom Celan was reading at the time.[14] Yet a poet who had felt the pain of annihilations as if inscribed on his own back could not wholly regard *das Nichts* as sheer creative potential. For a survivor the paradox retains historical, experiential force, palpable even in the turn of Celan's verse, the sudden break after *lebendige*: 'write the living/Nothing on his heart'.[15]

And why 'write' it? Celan came to prize the kabbalistic theory of language and creation: 'Every word'—he marked this sentence once in Scholem's little book *The Secrets of Creation*—'Every word is a name of God.'[16] Yet long before that Celan had felt his mother tongue become one and the same with life, with survival. 'In the midst of the losses,' he said after the war, 'this one thing remained: language.'[17] It was literally all he had left. He wrote—not as if, but because his life depended on it. So a poem that says *'schreib' das lebendige Nichts*, 'write' the paradox of life and death, only makes explicit an imperative implied in every poem.

Now a third *diesem*, holding to the spine of the poem, comes to enforce the dative case with its power of 'giving' to or going towards someone:

> diesem
> spreize die zwei
> Krüppelfinger zum heil-
> bringenden Spruch.

With no more syllables, an English version can attempt equivalence:

> for this one
> spread your two
> cripple-fingers in a safe-
> keeping prayer.

What English as always cannot do, however, is mimic the intimacy built up in *beschneide, schreib* and now *spreize*, three imperatives spoken in the second person singular. This form of address to Rabbi Loew seems slightly surprising, just as when Joseph K. uses it to a priest in *The Trial's* cathedral scene.

Why then *two* fingers? For a while I tried various explanations: Do those bent fingers form the name of the Almighty, *Shaddai*, as in an ancient benediction?—but that would take three fingers![18] Do they symbolize the two-letter combinations recited by medieval golem-makers?[19] Finally on last Rosh Hashanah morning, much later than it should have, the correct image dawned on me: spread the third and fourth fingers of each upraised hand in the Priestly Blessing (Num. 6: 24–7). 'The Lord bless thee, and keep thee': with these words in mind, I changed my 'sav-ing saying'—so as to cleave to Celan's *heil-/bringenden Spruch*—into 'safe-keeping saying', and then, for a better rhythm and sound, into 'safe-keeping prayer'. Yet the word 'prayer' may lose more than my prosody gains: namely the fact of 'saying', as in *Segensspruch*, German for 'benediction'. This whole poem has proceeded by virtue of language and speech: 'I opened my word', 'the chittering manikin', 'circumcise his word', 'write the living Nothing', and now a benedictive 'saying'. Well, perhaps in some other world the translation will come right!

We should still ask why these two fingers are not straight but bent, maimed, stunted, stumped, crooked. I tried all those adjectives, to stress the paradox in this blessing, and then realized that the cognate does it best: 'cripple-fingers' for *Krüppelfinger*. Images of a bruised, broken or contradicted faith abound in Celan's poetry, above all in the 1963 volume that includes this poem, *Die Niemandsrose* ('The No-One's-Rose').[20] The year before he had given an East German magazine *'Einem, der vor der Tür stand'* plus two other poems of a similar temper.[21] One of them begins:

> You prayer-, you blasphemy-, you
> prayersharp knives
> of my
> silence.
>
> You my words with me go-
> ing crippled, you
> my straight ones.

Such writing resists the need Celan's readers often feel to rationalize his harshest paradoxes. Likewise the appeal to Rabbi Loew comes to full stop in an opposition, a healing yet crippled word, the only kind of truth Celan could credit. Then a final verse, *Diesem*, gathers into one word the plea that blessing and safekeeping, light and graciousness, favour and peace be granted 'For this one', for a half-baked, misbegotten, bloody, cheeping handiwork of God.

After this highly liturgical period, *Diesem . . . , diesem . . . , diesem . . . Diesem*, a pause ensues, longer than any line- or stanza-break—and alas, the only thing a translation can perfectly convey. Clearly this silence marks off a time of waiting, of expectation. Then the speaker goes on, still in the intimate imperative of prayer:

> Wirf auch die Abendtür zu, Rabbi.
> . . . .
> Reiß die Morgentür auf, Ra- —

Not much defies translation here, except perhaps the German verbs' separable prepositions *zu* and *auf,* reserving their impact until the end of the phrase. English can try this with adjectives:

> And slam the eveningdoor shut, Rabbi.
> . . . .
> Throw the morningdoor open, Ra- —

Maybe my adjectives even take Celan's prepositions up a few decibels—not unjustifiably, I hope.

The poem climaxes here, if beseeching alone can make a climax. And wherever they may ultimately lead, these doors first lead us back to the beginning—not only to the poem's beginning, where 'To one who stood before the door, one evening . . . I opened my word', but to Genesis itself: 'And there was evening and there was morning: one day.' This poem of Celan's has at heart to do with the mystery of creation, or more truly, with mortal access to the mystery of creation and renewal. Is this evening encounter a Sabbath encounter? Does evening give way to morning? We can hope so. On another level Celan's plea to shut the *Abendtür* and open the *Morgentür* carries overtones of *Abendland* and *Morgenland,* Occident and Orient; in his letters of the time he turns away from 'this so golden West' toward Eastern Europe and his homeland.[22] But whatever they ask, the poem's last two imperatives, like the three before them, do not necessarily guarantee a response.

An earlier poem also speaks of two doors in a way that can darken our sense of Rabbi Loew's *Abendtür* and *Morgentür*.[23] Celan wrote 'Epitaph for François' in 1953, when a son born to his wife Gisèle died within hours of birth:

> The world's two doors
> stand open:
> opened by you
> at twinight.
> We hear them banging, banging . . .

The doors of life and of death stand dreadfully close to each other, as Celan already knew well enough. So when his later poem asks Rabbi Loew to 'slam the eveningdoor shut . . . Throw the morningdoor open', the hope, the force of this prayer must reside in the asking.

At this point another kind of source for the evening and morning doors comes to mind. It occurred to me, again much later than it should have but in fact on Yom Kippur, that Celan's final appeal in this poem echoes the Neilah prayer at sunset on the Day of Atonement: 'Open the gates to us when the gates are being closed, for the day is about to set. The day shall set, the sun shall go down and set—let us enter Your gates!' Whether Celan actually had this paradox of salvation in mind, or had it dimly in mind, matters only up to a point. If he did, it would firmly orient his poem, and would certainly make me grip my pen more firmly as I translate. But even the fact that earlier on Yom Kippur Psalm 103 is sung, in which God 'knoweth our frame', our *Gemächt* that is formed from dust—even this coincidence does not make Celan's poem a Yom Kippur cipher so much as it manifests the deeper coherence of his poetic imagination. He never made an explicit religious profession or wholehearted commitment, like Franz Rosenzweig, who converted *to* Judaism, as it were, after a Yom Kippur service. So I see the Neilah prayer as confirmation rather than source for the poem's closing lines.

Something unexpected and unliturgical happens at the very close of this poem. In the magazine version Celan had written *Reiß die Morgentür auf, Ra . . .* , with three dots after *Ra . . .* , a sort of trailing off or giving up. Later he changed that to *Ra* with a hyphen and a dash—not merely to prevent the interference of an Egyptian sun god supplanting a Prague rabbi, but to break off his own voice more abruptly. The hyphen ruptures a word, the dash ruptures speech. To translate effectively, need one only reproduce punctuation and not decide the vital question: whether this muting signifies an end or an onset, darkness or radiance, exile or entrance? I think again of Rosenzweig, his voice paralyzed for years, dictating as he died what 'the Lord has truly granted to me', 'the point of all points for which there . . .'[24] I think also of Kafka, speechless at the end from tuberculosis of the larynx. Of course the golem story itself, in which Rabbi Loew tears the holy name from his creature's mouth, furnishes close enough reference for the sudden end to Celan's poem. And by now the poet has grown into the golem-figure; in pleading 'For this one . . . for this one', he ends up pleading for himself.

Paul Celan's final silence remains open to the largest possibilities. Nightfall or morning: he had to tolerate that irreconcilable ambiguity at the heart of his Judaism, living as he did in exile while holding somehow to a spiritual expectation. So he put the hyphen after *Ra-*, breaking off a Jew's appeal in mid-voice. Yet the dash can point to something still to come.

Here the poem stops, and by rights this essay in translation ought to stop at the same moment. But throughout it all a presence has been hovering that I want to bring, forward. Franz Kafka's parable *'Vor dem Gesetz'*, 'Before' or 'In Front of' the Law, first came into Celan's hands when he was sixteen or seventeen.[25] Then just after the war, in Bucharest, he translated it into Rumanian, and in 1959 he underscored some thoughts about it in Walter Benjamin's Kafka essay.[26] The parable begins quite simply: 'Before the Law stands a doorkeeper. To this doorkeeper comes a man from the country and asks for entrance into the Law. But the doorkeeper says he cannot grant him entrance now. The man thinks it over and then asks if he'll be permitted to enter later. "It's possible," says the doorkeeper, "but not now." '

Celan's lifelong, adherent kinship with Kafka starts with childhood, where they both felt the burden of an unsympathetic father caught between petit bourgeois and normative Jewish behavior; Celan once told a friend that Kafka's *Letter to His Father* had to be written over and over again in Jewish homes.[27] And Celan sometimes associated his mother, cherished throughout his poetry while the father appears only once, with Bohemia and Prague: he calls Bohemia his mother's 'three-year land' because she fled there during the first world war.[28] In Czernowitz, the Austrian Empire's eastern outpost ceded to Rumania after 1918, a German-speaking Jew could feel alien both nationally and linguistically, as likewise in Prague. Early in 1962, at the high pitch of his anxiety about post-war anti-semitism, Celan adopted a refrain from Kafka's story 'A Country Doctor'—*'s ist nur ein Arzt*, 'it's only a doctor'—and signed a letter with it: *'s ist nur ein Jud*, 'it's only a Jew'.[29] Both writers tried at times to counter their displacement as assimilated western Jews by gravitating toward eastern or hasidic Judaism, and Kafka even sketched in his diary a version of the golem theme.[30]

First and last, Celan identified with the writer in Kafka. Fleeing Bucharest in 1947, Celan carried a letter of introduction from his mentor, calling his poetry 'the only lyric pendant to Kafka's work'.[31] Later he would buy first editions of Kafka and give his French students Kafka to read and translate. Writing in April 1970 to an Israeli friend, Celan said his Kafka seminar was going well, and he quoted Kafka's remark about the difficulty of getting happiness from writing—'happiness only if I can raise the world into the pure, the true, the immutable'.[32] Ten days later Celan took his own life.

At bottom, I think Celan saw in Kafka a radical, essentially human estrangement. He marked vigorously the diary passage where Kafka asks: 'What have I in common with Jews? I have hardly anything in common with myself.'[33] Yet he also knew that the seemingly nameless, causeless *Angst* of Kafka's protagonists, grounded though it was in Austrian bureaucratic Prague, had still to find its ultimate name and cause in Nazism. Celan's guilt at having survived when his parents did not, his loneliness in France, his corrosive suspicion that neo-Nazism and anti-semitism were preying upon him—these anxieties have a more drastic and specific basis than Kafka's.

Despite—or I should say because of—this historical rift between the two writers, Celan's poem 'To one who stood before the door' compellingly recalls the voice of Kafka's parable *'Vor dem Gesetz'*. 'You're very friendly to me,' Joseph K. tells the priest in *The Trial*, 'With you I can speak openly.' Then K. hears the parable in which a man waits many years, beseeching a doorkeeper for entrance into the Law. The man grows old and finally almost blind and deaf. 'But now in the dark he perceives a radiance that streams inextinguishably from the door of the Law.' Gathering all his years of trial into one question, the man asks why, since everyone strives after the Law, no one but himself has come demanding admission. 'No one else could obtain admission here,' the doorkeeper shouts at the dying man, 'because this entrance was meant only for you. I will now go and shut it.'

In rehearsing Celan's poem with Kafka in the wings, I see the poet stationing himself within the frame of the parable and hear him opening his word to a guardian of the Law. Maybe this guardian trots over towards the only sort of person eligible for entrance into the Law, one of those animal-like creatures ridden with guilt in Kafka's stories. And now the crude name 'Kafka' itself seems to crop up in Celan's text. Possibly the double k's in this poem's *Kielkropf* and *Kriegsknecht* are hidden signatures—I should have translated: 'toward the *klutz* I saw him trot, toward the half-baked brother begot in a *kossack's* dung-caked boot'.[34]

'For this one' Celan's poem intercedes, commingling the golem legend with Kafka's parable: for him some radiance or *Glanz*, as the parable says, may finally break from the door. Kafka's word *Glanz* sends me momentarily back to another poem Celan wrote just after his first son's death.[35] Entitled 'Assisi', it has 'animals trotting' toward Saint Francis, and the poem ends: *Glanz, der nicht trösten will, Glanz./Die Toten—sie betteln noch, Franz.* 'Radiance that will not comfort, radiance./The dead—they still go begging, Franz.' Speaking at once to the saint and to his lost son François, Celan also addresses the Franz whose parable promises radiance at the moment of death. The later poem, 'To one who stood before the door', also begs some of that radiance for a golem, a speechless creature revertible to clay and dust.

Finally the dative *Diesem* drops away and the poet speaks for himself. Just as we do not actually know whether Kafka's doorkeeper shuts the door or leaves it open, Celan can only ask for the eveningdoor shut, the morningdoor open. And as in Kafka we are never to hear the last word. In fact it literally breaks off.[36] 'Throw the morningdoor open, Ra- —', our poem ends, with that much prayer and no more. Let me close now with a motto from Kafka's notebook that holds equally for Celan and also, if I may say so, for his translator: *Schreiben als Form des Gebetes*, 'Writing as a form of prayer'.[37]

NOTES

This essay originated as a paper for the Association for Jewish Studies, Boston, 16 December 1985. I wish to thank Gisèle Celan-Lestrange for her generous assistance in my work; Mary Lowenthal Felstiner for her critique of this essay; and Sigrid Mayer, Jerry Glenn, Al Hoelzel, James K. Lyon for their helpful counsel.

1. Walter Benjamin, 'Franz Kafka', in *Schriften*, ed. Th. W. Adorno and Gretel Adorno (Frankfurt, 1955) 2: 222. For a translation of this and other essays see Benjamin, *Illuminations*, ed. Hannah Arendt, trans. Harry Zohn (New York, 1969) p. 134. Celan cited the sentence in his speech 'Der Meridian' (1960): Celan, *Gesammelte Werke* (Frankfurt: Suhrkamp, 1983) 3: 198. (This collected edition, in five volumes, is hereafter referred to as *GW*.)

2. *Der Prozeß* (1925; Frankfurt, 1979) ch. 9, p. 185. All translations in this essay are mine.

3. *GW*, 1: 242–3.

4. Letter to Margarete Susman, 22 Aug. 1924, in Franz Rosenzweig, *Briefe und Tagebücher*, 2 (1918–29) ed. Rachel Rosenzweig and Edith Rosenzweig Scheinmann (The Hague, 1979) p. 982.

5. Kafka's 'man from the country', who approaches the doorkeeper in 'Before the Law', evidently derives from the Hebrew *'am ha' arets*, 'the common people; an ignoramus', or literally a person of the land, and more literally of the earth: see Heinz Politzer, *Franz Kafka: Parable and Paradox* (Ithaca, NY, 1966) p. 174.

6. See Gershom Scholem, 'The Idea of the Golem', in *On the Kabbalah and Its Symbolism*, trans. Ralph Manheim (New York, 1969) pp. 158–204. Celan owned the German edition, *Zur Kabbala und ihrer Symbolik* (Zurich, 1960). On the golem legend see also Micha Josef bin Gorion, *Der Born Judas* (Wiesbaden, 1959); Sigrid Mayer, *Golem: Die literarische Rezeption eines Stoffes* (Bern, 1975).

7. *GW*, 1: 225.

8. Celan, *La Rose de Personne*, trans. Martine Broda (Paris, 1979) p. 71.

9. For biographical material see John Felstiner, 'Paul Celan: The Strain of Jewishness', *Commentary* (April 1985) 44–55.

10. Letter to Reinhard Federmann, 23 Feb. 1962, in 'In Memoriam Paul Celan', *Die Pestsäule* 1 (Sept. 1972) 18.

11. For material on Celan's early years see Israel Chalfen, *Paul Celan: Eine Biographie seiner Jugend* (Frankfurt, 1979).

12. 'To One Who Stood at the Door', trans. Cid Corman, *Origin*, 3rd Series 15 (Oct. 1969): 34.

13. Derrida, 'Shibboleth', in Geoffrey Hartman and Sanford Budick (eds) *Midrash and Literature* (New Haven: Yale University Press, 1986). This paper was originally given in French at the International Paul Celan Symposium, University of Washington, Seattle, 14 Oct. 1984. Derrida also makes a connection between the opening of a door in this poem and Elijah, since the person holding the infant during circumcision sits on 'Elijah's Chair'.

14. *Von der mystischen Gestalt der Gottheit* (Zurich, 1962) p. 128. In his 1958 poem 'El Golem', Jorge Luis Borges twice makes his subject rhyme with 'Scholem': Mayer, p. 77.

15. For the word *Gemüt*, 'mind', 'soul' or 'spirit' would perhaps do better than 'heart'. Something of a poeticism, the word occurs only this once in Celan's poetry. I settle on 'heart', maybe by contagion with Judah *Lev* ben Bezalel, *Lev* being Hebrew for 'heart', or with the 'circumcision of the heart' (Deut. 10: 16, 30: 6).

16. *Die Geheimnisse der Schöpfung: Ein Kapitel aus dem Sohar* (Berlin, 1935) p. 29.

17. 'Ansprache anläßlich der Entgegennahme des Literaturpreises der freien Hansestadt Bremen' (1958) in *GW*, 3: 185.

18. Joshua Trachtenberg, *Jewish Magic and Superstition* (New York, 1979) p. 80.

19. Scholem, *On the Kabbalah*, pp. 185–6.

20. *Die Niemandsrose* (Frankfurt, 1963).

21. *Sinn und Form* 14, 5–6 (1962) 701–3. The third poem was *Es war Erde in ihnen*, which begins:

> There was earth inside them, and
> they dug.
>
> they dug and dug, so their day
> went by, their night. And they did not praise God …

22. Letter to Alfred Margul-Sperber, 8 Feb. 1962, in 'Briefe an Alfred Margul-Sperber', *Neue Literatur*, 7 (1975): 57.

23. 'Grabschrift für François', *GW*, 1: 105.

24. Rosenzweig, p. 1237.

25. Chalfen, p. 67. A recent article on the presence of Kafka in Celan's work does not mention 'Einem, der vor der Tür stand': Dietmar Goltschnigg, 'Zur lyrischen Kafka-Rezeption nach 1945 am Beispiel Paul Celans', *Literatur und Kritik*, 197–8 (1985) 316–26.

26. *Zeitschrift für Kulturaustausch*, 3 (1982) 286.

27. Otto Pöggeler, 'Kontroverses zur Ästhetik Paul Celans (1920–1970)', *Zeitschrift für Ästhetik und allgemeine Kunstwissenschaft*, 25: 2 (1980) 226.

28. Celan, 'Es is alles anders', *GW*, 1: 285.

29. Kafka's story 'A Country Doctor' appeared in the same collection—*Ein Landarzt* (1919)—as the parable 'Before the Law'. The parable later formed part of *The Trial*, ch. 9. Celan's letter to Reinhard Federmann, 23 Feb. 1962, in 'In Memoriam', p. 18.

30. Kafka, *Tagebücher 1910–1923*, ed. Max Brod (Frankfurt, 1973) p. 310 (20 April 1916). Kafka reportedly liked the atmosphere of Prague's old Jewish quarter evoked in Gustav Meyrink's novel *Der Golem* (1915): Gustav Janouch, *Conversations with Kafka* (New York, 1953) p. 47. Johannes Urzidil says that one Friedrich Thieberger was a Hebrew teacher of Kafka's: 'Two Recollections', *The World of Franz Kafka*, ed. J. P. Stern (New York, 1980) p. 60; Thieberger later published *The Great Rabbi Loew of Prague* (London, 1955). Marthe Robert, *As Lonely as Franz Kafka*, trans. Ralph Manheim (New York, 1982), deals beautifully with Kafka's vexed Jewishness.

31. Letter from Alfred Margul-Sperber to Otto Basil, printed in part in *Plan* (Vienna) 6 (1948) 423; reprinted in Milo Dor, 'Paul Celan', in *Über Paul Celan*, ed. Dietlind Meinecke (Frankfurt, 1973) p. 282.

32. Kafka, *Tagebücher*, p. 333 (25 Sept. 1917).

33. Kafka, *Tagebücher*, p. 219 (8 Jan. 1914).

34. In a diary entry of 27 May 1914 (*Tagebücher*, p. 234) Kafka remarks: 'I find the letter K ugly, it almost sickens me yet I write it down, it must be characteristic of me.' Celan's poem 'In Prag' (ca. 1966) bears mention in relation to 'Einem, der vor der Tür stand'. Against a somewhat ghastly background, 'In Prag' speaks of the Hradcany Castle Hill, where alchemy was practised, and then of 'bone-Hebrew/ground to sperm'.

35. 'Assisi' (1954), *GW*, 1:108.

36. In a 1966 poem ('Frankfurt, September', *GW*, 2:114) that quotes Kafka and plays on 'jackdaw', his name in Czech, Celan also recalls Kafka's tuberculosis of the larynx—the *Kehlkopf*—and his final story, 'Josephine the Singer'. The poem ends:

> Der Kehlkopfverschlußlaut   The glottal stop
> singt.   sings.

37. Kafka, 'Fragmente', in *Hochzeitsvorbereitungen auf dem Lande*, ed. Max Brod (Frankfurt, 1966) p. 348.

5.22 W. S. MERWIN

W. S. Merwin (b. 1927) is a leading American poet, awarded the Pulitzer, Bollingen, Tanning, and PEN Translation Prizes, as well as the Lila Wallace-Reader's Digest Writers' Award and the Ruth Lilly Poetry Prize. He is a Fellow of the Academy of American Poets. Author of numerous collections of poetry, of plays, and of prose, he has also been a prolific translator from Spanish, French, Italian, Middle English, as well as Russian, Vietnamese and Chinese, and other languages. His translation of *Sir Gawain and the Green Knight* was published in 2002. Merwin's example as a scrupulous translator was one Ted Hughes (to whom and Sylvia Plath, Merwin dedicated an early volume of translations, *Some Spanish Ballads*, 1961) had constantly before him. It was perhaps Merwin's quite straightforward, semantically faithful approach, dispensing with or avoiding direct imitation of the source text's formal qualities that particularly commended itself to Hughes, that and the discoveries Merwin shared with his readers. Merwin himself, as noted in an interview excerpted in Sect. 5.9, above, was encouraged by Ezra Pound, whom he visited in St Elizabeth's Hospital and who recommended translation, since at age 18, although the young poet might think he did, he in fact had little to write about! It was Pound, too, who directed his attention to Provence and the highly sophisticated but little known poetry of the *jongleurs* and troubadors.

For more on Merwin's views on verse translation, readers are referred to Sect. 5.9, above. Merwin has written comparatively little about translation. As he noted in a letter, 'I continue in the belief that I don't know how to translate, and that nobody does. It is an impossible but necessary process, there is no perfect way to do it, and much of it must be found for each particular poem, as we go.'[1] Nevertheless, his Foreword to *Selected Translations 1968–1978* (1979) is an important statement. He has maintained that he really has nothing further to say on the subject.

For a translation from the Russian of Osip Mandelstam, which W. S. Merwin made with Clarence Brown, as also for Merwin's translation of a Sonnet of Dante, see Sect. 5.9, above. The selection below is, therefore, limited to a passage from his most recent translation, *Sir Gawain and the Green Knight*. The same passage, translated by Ted Hughes, can be found in Sect. 5.16, above.

Merwin's translations include, among others: *Poem of The Cid* (1959); *Some Spanish Ballads* (1961); *Selected Translations, 1968–1978* (1979), with a foreword; *East Window* (1968), translations from Asian languages, including Urdu, Chinese, Sanskrit, Japanese,

---

[1] (See Daniel Weissbort (ed.), *Translating Poetry: The Double Labyrinth* (Iowa City: University of Iowa Press, 1989), 139.

Persian, and Vietnamese, selected from previously published volumes, with a preface; *Sir Gawain & The Green Knight* (2002), with a foreword.

From *Sir Gawain and The Green Knight: A New Verse Translation* (New York: Alfred A. Knopf, 2002)

[The New Year's feast at King's Arthur's Court is interrupted by the entry of a huge green knight, on a green horse. In response to a challenge, Sir Gawain decapitates the knight. The knight exits carrying his severed head. The condition, however, is that Sir Gawain must present himself at the Green Chapel, a year later, and receive a blow in return from the Green Knight. At this point, late in the poem, the Green Knight is set to strike for the second time, Gawain having flinched the first time.

In his Iowa interview (see Sect. 5.9, above.), Merwin comments on his translation. His Foreword reiterates that the translator's own interest in the troubadour and chivalric tradition dates from his student years. He continues: 'As I translated, I wanted to keep what I could of the movement of the lines, what I felt as their vitality and rush, their pitch and momentum, and to keep an alliterative recurrence of sounds that would echo in modern English the stressed alliterative patterns of the original. I did not want, though, to cram and twist the lines in an effort to make an exact replica of a verse form in what has become, in six hundred years, another language. And for every reason I wanted to keep as close as I could to the meaning of the original words, so as not to mislead my first reader— myself.' He felt that he had picked up a familiar accent, the Welsh intonations overheard in the mining city of Scranton, Pennsylvania, where he was raised. It is interesting to note that Ted Hughes, also drawn to this poem, remarked that the diction reminded him of West Yorkshire dialect, which of course is quite likely, since the poem is held to have originated in that general area of England.]

> But have at it, knight, by your faith, and bring me to the point.
> Deal me my destiny, and do it out of hand,
> For I shall stand for your stroke and not flinch again
> Until your ax strikes me, here is my word upon it.'
> 'Have at you, then,' the other said, and heaves it up high,
> His face as fierce as that of a madman.
> He aims a heavy blow at him but never touches him,
> Withheld his hand suddenly before the harm was done.
> Gawain stood waiting for the blow, no part of him moving,
> Still as a stone or as the stump of a tree
> Which a hundred roots have anchored in rocky ground.

Then merrily the man in green says to him,
'So now that you have your courage up I must make my stroke.
Uphold the high knighthood that Arthur bestowed on you
And see whether your neck can survive this blow.'
Then Gawain was angry and in a rage he said,
'Well, strike then, you fierce fellow. Your threats take too long.
I begin to believe you are afraid of yourself.'
'Indeed,' that other knight said, 'you speak so boldly,
I will not leave your mission unfulfilled
    Any longer.'
  Then he plants his feet to strike
  With set mouth and frowning brow.
  What was there for him to like
  With no hope of rescue?

5.23 EDWIN MORGAN

Edwin Morgan (b. 1920) was born in Glasgow. He studied at Glasgow University in the late 1930s, during which time he encountered French Symbolism and Russian Futurism. He returned to the university, as a lecturer, in 1946. That year he also took part in a discussion regarding the use of Scots in verse, which brought him into disagreement with Hugh MacDiarmid. Morgan retired from Glasgow University as Professor of English in 1980, by which time he had produced a vast corpus of poetry and critical writings. In 1999, Edwin Morgan was appointed Glasgow's first Poet Laureate. He was awarded the Queen's Gold Medal for Poetry in 2000 and in 2001 received the Weidenfeld Prize for Translation. In 2004, Edwin Morgan was nominated as Scots Makar, the first Poet Laureate or National Poet of Scotland. He has received numerous other honours and awards.

His voluminous output includes many translations. His 1952 translation of *Beowulf* was widely used in the USA and Australia. Other translations include: *Selected Poems* of Sandor Weöres (from Hungarian, 1970); *Wi the haill Voice: 25 Poems by Vladimir Mayakovsky* (from Russian into Scots, 1972); Edmond Rostand's *Cyrano de Bergerac* (1992); Jean Racine's *Phaedra* (into Scots, 2000); *Attila József Sixty Poems* (From Hungarian, 2001). Morgan, thus, has translated poetry from a number of languages, including Italian, Russian, German, Spanish, French, Portuguese, Anglo-Saxon, ancient Greek, Dutch, Khmer, Armenian, and Hungarian. Carcanet, which has published his *Collected Poems* (1990), has also published his *Collected Translations* (1996).

His translations extended an already formidable vocal range. This also formed part of an attempt to turn Modernism away from the right-wing orientation of Eliot and Pound and towards the overt political radicalism of such writers as Vladimir Mayakovsky (1894–1930) and Attila József (1905–37). As regards Mayakovsky, Morgan commented that he was drawn by the combination of committed political content and adventurous style. During the 1950s, when use of Scots vernacular in verse was a highly political issue, Morgan devised a form of proletarian Scots speech, which is exemplified, for instance, in his 1972 translations of Mayakovsky.

Edwin Morgan, 'Language at Play, in Conversation with Joseph Farrell', in *Stages of Translation*, ed. David Johnston (Bath: Absolute Classics, 1996), 219–27

> JF: You are known principally as a poet, so I presume that your first work of translation was of poetry. How did you become involved in theatre translation?

EM: Yes, my first translations were poetry translations. As far as theatre is concerned, it began in two ways. The most important was my contact with the Medieval Players, now unfortunately disbanded, but dedicated to the idea that pre-Shakespearean drama was something a modern audience could enjoy. Although they did quite a number of plays which had originally been written in medieval English, they also staged various anonymous plays from other countries. They asked me to take a hand in translating these and preparing them for performance, which I did. I did two plays with them, and they seemed to work all right on the stage. That was probably what got me interested in the stage.

JF: Where did these plays come from?

EM: The titles were *The Apple Tree* and *Master Peter Pathelin*. The first of these was Dutch, and I worked with a Dutch translator. The other was a French farce, written in medieval French. *The Apple Tree* is a morality play, with a decidedly grim morality, but the other was quite a famous work of farce, with lots of scope for linguistic play, which is why I got so much enjoyment from doing it.

JF: What kind of work did you actually do with the plays? I start from the premise that the distinction between translation and adaptation is fundamental. Were these translations in a conventional sense, or were you doing an adaptation for the tastes of a modern audience?

EM: No, these were fairly faithful translations. That was how the company wanted to present these plays, so both translations are close to the original. With *Master Peter Pathelin* there are no substantial changes in the text or action, and I kept as closely as possible to the form. The translation has metre and rhyme, as had the original. It was much the same with the Dutch play. Both the plays were translated into standard English, although there were occasional bits of Scots, and other languages too:

PATHELIN

Paid? You don't pay such grasping men.
The devil gets *mafeesh faloos*.
He's coming here to eat a goose
And this is what we have to do.
Long before he starts to chew
He's going to cry to be paid pronto.
The bed is what I must get onto.
You understand? I'm a sick man.
He knocks, you open, lift your hand
To your lips, say 'Shush!' You sigh
You're sad, you say, 'Don't even try
To see him, poor man, ill in bed
For two months, oh, with what a head!'

EM: There is quite a lot of linguistic play in them, but the basic language is English. It was much the same with *The Apple Tree*. Being a morality play, I gave them names which reflected this, names like Frank Goodheart, Faith Trustwell, Willie Wildoats, or Jenny Joycat.

JF: I'm assuming you don't speak Dutch, so how did you work when you were translating that play?

EM: You are correct in your assumption. I had a translation given to me, a direct word-for-word translation into English.

JF: I would be curious to know how you actually worked in these circumstances. Was it a joint enterprise, did you work together, did you have him there at your elbow, or did he simply send you the translation?

EM: He sent me the translation, and I got to work on it, and thereafter we kept in correspondence. There are problems in interpretation or intelligibility, as there always are with any translation, but perhaps they were more severe in this case because of the age of the text. It is obviously frustrating not to have a knowledge of the original language, and it can never be the best way. I did it in this case because I was invited, it was a pleasing challenge, and I thought I would enjoy doing it. I seemed to get into the spirit of the piece, and it worked well on stage. Plainly I much prefer to work as I did with the French play, seeing it as I would see it and knowing exactly what the words meant. With *The Apple Tree*, it was not unduly difficult, because it was a short play and fits into a known genre—you know what medieval morality plays are like. It is similar to various early English morality plays. You are not entirely at sea. You are not hopelessly distant from the text.

JF: Your part, when you are basing yourself on a literal translation, is to devise speakable dialogue.

EM: It is no use—ever—having a translation which might be pedantically accurate or scholarly if it cannot be spoken on stage. Any translator has to bear that in mind, always. As it happens, I relish thinking in those terms and working in that kind of way. I find myself speaking the individual lines to myself. I knew that with the Medieval Players, actors and actresses would be working on those lines very soon after I had finished putting them on paper:

FROM THE PREFACE TO THE APPLE TREE *(1982)*

Clearly, it would not do to turn the Dutch text into an imaginary English version contemporary with it (i.e. about 1500); any such historical pastiche would seem forced and fraudulent. At the same time, the whole nature of the play resisted absolute modernisation. The solution adopted was to make the language itself modern, but set within the structure of a four-stress alliterative line which would hold associations with the earlier English drama and poetry. The Dutch original is written in a rough four-stress line, in rhyming couplets, and the use of alliteration in English may be taken as some kind of equivalent for the use of rhyme in the Dutch text. It can give a certain shape, a certain formal interest, to the colloquial language, without destroying the raciness required. Not all the speeches have this quality of raciness. Some lines and couplets have more 'set', chorus-like, proverbial character, which has to be indicated. Also there are on three occasions examples of a more marked formality, a sort of interlacing 'round' of repeated phrases suggesting something ritualistic, perhaps musical, perhaps gestural. ... It was important that these features should be reproduced as far as possible, since they are part of the linguistic variety and verve of the play.

EM: I said at the beginning that there were two factors which had induced me to take up translation for the stage. The second was that I had been writing opera libretti just around that time. I worked with Thomas Wilson, and did a script based on the life of St Columba. It was very lively, because Columba may have been a saint, but he was a very forceful character who made his presence felt.

JF: Your poetry too has a quality which lends itself to theatre.

EM: I think that lies at the back of it all. The kind of poetry I write is often incipient theatre. I like dramatic situations, and characters, and the poem is often like a scene from a play, so I found it natural to take the extra step. I have always liked the presence of the voice in poetry. Long before there were books, poetry was spoken or chanted.

JF: Do you use a different technique for translating poetry, compared to what you would use when translating for theatre?

EM: The difference lies entirely in the realisation that dialogue has to be spoken. I have never translated plays for publication, or not primarily for publication; there was always some company waiting for the script. With a poem, there might be a complex concatenation of ideas, or the images might be unusual, so you would have to think of the best way of rendering them, but without the urgency of producing words to be spoken aloud. I probably enjoy best poets from other languages like Mayakovsky who, like myself, believe in the primacy of voice.

JF: Your best known translation, or perhaps it is just the most recent, was the *Cyrano de Bergerac* you did for the Communicado Theatre Company. Had you always had a special fondness for this play, or was it just a telephone call?

EM: I was asked to do it. Communicado wanted a new version for the Edinburgh Festival in 1992, and they asked me to think about it. I have to confess that I had never read the play before. I knew the story, but I had never read the play. I read an American version, and decided it was something I would like to attempt. Gerry Mulgrew, the director, wanted a Scottish version, although he did not specify it absolutely. There was no time for theorising about the type of Scots to be employed, because it had to be done very quickly. Rehearsal schedules meant that I only had three months to do what was a full five act play.

I concluded that it should be in Scots, but not the kind of 'historical' Scots used by the playwrights of the thirties and forties like MacLellan and Kemp, which was a deliberate attempt to reproduce an older Scots language. These plays have mostly fallen by the wayside now. I felt that it would have to be a Scots which could be spoken today by actors, and since it was me who was writing it, it would need to be a Scots with a strong Glasgow basis—a Glaswegian Scots if you like. It uses words from other parts of the country, but I was not too worried about purity of the language. I wanted something which would meet the demands of the play, while always being speakable. The main part is very long and demanding, so it was vital that the actor playing that part had a language he was at ease with. Tom Mannion is from Glasgow, and that did work for him. We experimented with the first act, and it was felt to be successful. I was there during rehearsals, and if they felt I had used a word which was too obscure, I met their objections. There is no point in being too precious about this.

I wanted to keep it racy, but formal. I kept the original metre. The original has metre and rhyme, and it seemed to me that there was no point in abandoning that, because part of the joy of the play is in the rhyme. The play itself is linguistically sparkling, and I felt that to do it in some kind of free verse or blank verse would not meet the case. The actors were initially surprised to be confronted by metre and verse, because so few plays today are written in that style, but they rose to the challenge:

FROM THE INTRODUCTION TO CYRANO DE BERGERAC (1992)

In the age of Ibsen, the play came as a delightful release. The hero was a poet, and the brilliant verse of the play, full of pyrotechnics and wit, but racily colloquial also, and capable of a moving lyricism when the need arose, was a reminder of what poetry can do in theatre. The play was robust and boisterous, yet sad also, and it at once inhabited a territory of its own, escaping gritty naturalism and *fin-de-siècle* decadence. That robust quality. theatrical yet human, is what keeps the play alive today.

Various English translations of the play have been made, but it is one of those plays which need to be translated again and again, in different circumstances and for different purposes, readerly and actorly. The time seemed ripe for a Scottish version, but one that would be thoroughly stageworthy and not incomprehensible to an international audience at the Edinburgh International Festival. I decided that urban Glaswegian Scots would offer the best basis, since it is widely spoken, can accommodate contemporary reference, is by no means incapable of the lyrical and the poetic, and comes unburdened by the baggage of the older Scots which used to be thought suitable for historical plays. I kept English for the Count de Guiche, and for some of the minor characters (the fops, the nuns, Roxane's duenna).

JF: Did you change the play, not in its structure or plot, but in its tone? The Communicado production was uproariously funny in parts, but I once saw the play done by the Comédie Française. It was an infinitely more stately production, especially the famous speech about Cyrano's nose, which was delivered by an actor in the grandest of classical styles, and stilled the entire audience. Were you trying to write as you thought Rostand intended, bringing out a comedy others might have missed, or were you consciously altering the style?

EM: Well, I have never seen a French production, so I cannot judge that. I thought I was getting into the spirit of the play, which seemed to me both comic and serious, in different ways and at different moments. Obviously you can be serious by being funny, but in that long speech about noses, it seemed to me that the joy with which the character spoke about all the ways in which someone could have spoken about his nose, if they had the language to do it, must communicate itself. It is a very funny speech, and this must be brought out. Cyrano is not only a swordsman, but he is a poet, and the translator must address himself to the problem of getting the poetic verve across. That was my aim in that speech—to forge a kind of poetry which would show how his mind worked, how it leapt from one subject to another very rapidly and very convincingly, while at the same time bringing out the comedy.

> Yer *canto*'s no *bel*, young man.
> Ye could have said—oh lotsa things, a plan
> For each, tae suit yer tone o'voice, like so:
> *Thuggish*: 'If Ah'd a nose like yours, Ah'd go
> Straight to the surgery fur amputation'.
> *Freen-like*: 'Dinnae dunk it in a cup, fashin
> yersel a Munich tankard for tae slurp fae'.
> *Descriptive*: 'A rock? A peak? A cape? the survey
> Shaws the cape's a haill peninsula!'
> *Pawky*: 'If it's in a boax, and no a fistula,
> Whit's in it, pens or pins or penny needles?'
> *Gracious*: 'Ye're a right Saint Francis, ye weedle
> The buds o the air tae wrap their gentle tootsies
> Roon yer pirch and rest their weary Guccis'.
> *Truculent*: 'Puff yir pipe until the smoke
> Comes whummlin oot yer nose, and the big toke
> Has awe yer neebors cryin—Lum's on fire!'

Saft-hertit: 'Whit if it fadit at high noon?
Make a wee parasol tae keep the sun aff!'
Bummin: 'Nae wind, o hypermacho nose,
Could give ye snuffles but blasts fae Muckle Flugga!'
Dramatic: 'Bleeds a haill Rid Sea, the bugger!'

EM: In other parts of the play I aimed to bring out the lyrical note, which clashes with the more boisterous parts of the play, for ultimately we are dealing with a tragic love story. It would be easy to overlook the moving, touching mood which emerges most strongly in the latter part of the play. I suppose I was after a flexible kind of language which could be funny when needed, yet straight and serious at other times.

JF: Are you tempted to improve on the original, to write in jokes when you think that Rostand, or any other author, could have, or should have been funnier than he actually managed to be?

EM: I think to some extent, because theatre is a living process, some changes are necessary. Some characters have to be dropped or amalgamated, or little bits have to be added. For *Cyrano* I was asked to write a nuns' song at the beginning of the last act, and this too I did. In addition, when the director, or some actor, found some part appealing, he asked me to write a few extra lines, which I did. So there were some changes.

JF: As an instance, the *distributrice* of Rostand's original Act 1, sells nothing more remarkable than 'oranges, milk, strawberry water, lime juice', while the 'usherette' of your version offers:

Ices, ginger, tea,
Raspberry yoghurt, Greek yoghurt, aw the yoghurts,
Lovely Turkish delight, licorice awsorts,
Popcoarn, hote chestnits, marshmallows,
Chewin gum, candy-floss . . . . .

EM: However, I decided not to change the main setting of the play. It was tempting to switch the action to Scotland, and make it a Scottish historical play, but the work needed its French environment. Cyrano, after all, was a character from history, his life is documented so it seemed to me important to respect that element. The play remained set in seventeenth-century France, even if the language used was Scots.

JF: Do you have any feelings about that in general? There are many Scottish versions of Molière or Goldoni which have been transported holus bolus to Glasgow or to Edinburgh's New Town. There are two points of view on this—one that it makes the work more immediate for an audience, or alternatively that it is a refusal of the challenge of foreign, unfamiliar ideas and an invitation to couthy provincialism.

EM: I think it varies. At times it can be illuminating to have the play in a very different setting, but on the whole I prefer to respect the original. In my *Cyrano* I have some anachronistic references to Gucci shoes, for instance, or to the Body Shop, but paradoxically these references may have a very limited lifespan. But a play is a very fluid thing.

JF: The voice that people are getting is yours and not that of Rostand, or of the anonymous authors of medieval morality plays.

EM: Is it?

JF: I put that as a general point. I don't know if it is any more strongly true in your case, although I suspect it is.

EM: I don't know about this. I suppose in general that must be true. I suppose that you as the writer are responsible for the words and the arrangement of the words, so it is inevitable that something of yourself must get into it. On the other hand, I don't try to do this. Some translators make a deliberate effort to make the translations an integral part of their own output. I am thinking of Ezra Pound or Robert Lowell. Their translations are just Pound poetry or Lowell poetry. But I do try to be fair to the other writer, to reproduce the effects of his or her style as far as I can. Where I have published translations of different authors from different periods, I would hope that this would appear as an anthology of writings by different people.

JF: So you regard that as a value of your translation, or an aim of translation in general—the retention of the flavour, the voice of the original author, as against the contrary view which would be, more or less, that all that counts is producing something which reads well or works on stage here and now.

EM: Yes, I think I am with the first view. It is hard to be exactly sure of what was in the original author's mind. Rostand belonged to another century, but I think I got into his way of thinking fairly well. I did a lot of research, I read others of his plays . . . But theatre is still something else. If you read the play in a book, you still have not seen the play as it was presented on the French stage in 1897. I would love to have seen that!

JF: Do you find you have greater liberty when you are writing in Scots, as against writing in English?

EM: I think the answer has to be 'yes'. It is a strange thing that it should be so, but it is. It may just be because you are doing something uncommon. Quite a lot of my poetry is in Scots, or other languages—invented languages—but it is true that you do have more liberty precisely because of the freshness of the enterprise. *Cyrano* does not use many words which would not be known to people in Scotland, but there is another curious thing: people seem to get a disproportionate delight from hearing Scots words which they use frequently enough, but which acquire an extra dimension for them when they hear them in the theatre. Also, there is a stimulus for the writer to be writing in Scots. If I translate into straight English, as I did with French and Dutch plays, it works all right, but they lack that spice which you get from something slightly different.

JF: Another topic. Both in poetry and theatre, what are you ultimately translating? Is it some inner core of meaning you believe you have identified, and how do you work out the balance between the desire to deal with the emotion or thought contained in a poem or speech and the need to keep some sense of the linguistic richness present in the original?

EM: That is the hardest thing of all. You are working as you go, and it is very difficult to start from a theory. It is very much a question of practice. I like to do it thoroughly. I like to get to know the original poem or play as deeply as possible, and this means you have a double task. You have to understand, if you can, the semantic part of the meaning, but you also have to do a different kind of reading. You have to soak yourself in it, to let it float into your mind at different times until you get a feeling for what the work is like at levels other than that of the literal meaning. Not all poems are amenable to this kind of treatment, but if a poem is at all complex, it will have both an intellectual and an emotional dimension, and you must aim to transmit both of these aspects, which is not easy, but I think it can be done. It is a slow process, unless you are lucky.

JF: Since you have translated both from languages you know, and from languages where you had to rely on the 'literal' translation, can you draw up some kind of balance sheet of the advantages and disadvantages of these processes? What do you lose by not being able to read the words of the original writer?

EM: Obviously you do lose a lot. *The Apple Tree* seemed to work, and everyone was pleased with it, but from my point of view, I really want to be able to read the text—play or poem—and get to know it as deeply as I can. But there is an important qualification to be made. As well as the Dutch translation, I have worked on quite a lot of Hungarian poetry. Modern Hungarian poetry is of a very high class but because their language is so isolated, the Hungarians find it hard to persuade people of this. They are very keen to have their literature translated, especially into English. I have visited Hungary, I know a bit of the language, so I am not totally ignorant of what the language is like, but I need assistance. Even if I have a literal translation, I go through the text for myself, I know the sounds and know something of the background. With all these qualifications, I still am reliant on others for access to the text, but I think that in certain circumstances that is unavoidable, and it is preferable to not having valuable work made available in other countries.

From the 'Preface' to *Beowulf* (1952; new edn., Manchester: Carcanet, 2002), p. ix

The translation, which was begun shortly after I came out of the army at the end of the Second World War, was in a sense my unwritten war poem and I would not want to alter the expression I gave to its themes of conflict and danger, voyaging and displacement, loyalty and loss.

From *Beowulf* (Old English), pp. 21–2

[Beowulf's fight with Grendel (lines 791–819). See Sect. 3.5 above, for William Morris's version, and, Sect. 5.24, below, for Seamus Heaney's.]

> Nothing would make the protector of warriors
> Let slaughter's emissary escape alive,
> Nor would he reckon many days left to him
> Of profit to any man. Then Beowulf's soldiers
> Brandished here and there their ancient swords,
> Anxious to defend the body of their lord,
> Of the illustrious prince, as they might be able—
> Ignorant of this, when they moved to fight,
> Iron-minded men of arms,
> Thinking to strike on every side,
> To pierce to his spirit; that the lawless ravager
> Was not to be reached by any war-blade,
> Not by the choicest metal on earth,
> For every sword-edge and weapon of victory
> He had blunted by wizardry.—Wretched his future
> Now at that hour of this earthly life
> Cut off from breath; far had the uncanny
> Soul to wander into fiends' dominions.
> For then he discovered, who often before
> Had in his transgressions tormented the mind
> Of human kind, he God's antagonist,
> That his own body would not obey him,
> But the kinsman of Hygelac in undaunted encounter
> Had him in his grasp; each was to the other
> Abhorrent if alive. The appalling demon
> Bore flesh-agony; on his shoulder became manifest
> A monstrous wound, sinews quivering,
> Tendons ripped open. To Beowulf was granted
> Triumph in the fight [. . .]

The opening of 'The Seafarer' (Anglo-Saxon), from *Rites of Passage, Selected Translations* (1976); also in *Collected Translations* (Manchester: Carcanet, 1996), 246–8

[See Sect. 4.2, above for Ezra Pound's version.]

> This verse is my voice, it is no fable,
> I tell of my travelling, how in hardship

I have often suffered laborious days,
endured in my breast the bitterest cares,
explored on shipboard sorrow's abodes,
the welter and terror of the waves. There
the grim night-vigil has often found me
at the prow of the boat when gripped by the cold
it cuts and noses along the cliffs.
There my feet were fettered by frost,
with chains of zero, and the cares were whistling
keen about my heart, and hunger within me
had torn my sea-dazed mind apart.
The theme is strange to the happy man
whose life on earth exults and flourishes,
how I lived out a winter of wretchedness
wandering exiled on the ice-cold sea,
bereft of my friends, harnessed in frost,
when the hail flew in showers down.
There I heard only the ocean roar,
the cold foam, or the song of the swan.
The gannet's call was all my pleasure,
curlew's music for laughter of men,
cries of a seagull for relish of mead.
There tempests struck the cliffs of rock,
and the frozen-feathered tern called back,
and often the eagle with glistening wings
screamed through the spindrift: [...]

From Jean Racine, *Phaedra*, translated into Scots by Edwin Morgan (Manchester: Carcanet, 2000), 36

[From Act 2, Scene 5, Phèdre has declared her love for her stepson Hippolytus and now begs him to avenge his father, her husband Theseus, and kill her for this heinous sin. See above, Sects. 4.10 and 5.16 for Robert Lowell's and Ted Hughes's versions respectively.]

Gode, Ah kid only speak t'ye aboot yirsel!
Avenge it, pey hame this laithlie love:
Gret son o a gret faither, syne oot
The universe, gie yir gyre-carlin hur quietus.
If Theseus' weeda daurs tae love Hippolytus,
Make shair the coorse gyre-carlin gets hur paiks;

Here's ma hert: luft yir haun tae it noo.
Ah feel it, though yir erm is at yir side,
Ma hert gaes oot tae feel it, earn it, thole it.
Hut me: or if ye hink this hert's no wurth it,
If yir hatred hus te hae a merr fell dunch,
Or if ma bluid's ower mankit fur ye tae skail,
Gie's a len a—no yir erm—yir blade—
See's it!

Russian agitprop poem from 1917, the year of the Bolshevik Revolution

'To the Bourgeoisie', from Wi the Haill Voice: 25 Poems
by Vladimir Mayakovsky (1972), included in Edwin Morgan,
Collected Translations *(Manchester: Carcanet, 1996), 119*

Stick in, douce folk.—Pineaipple, feesant's breist:
stuff till ye boke, for thon is your last feast.

Literal translation of Russian source text

Eat pineapples, chew grouse,
your last day is coming, bourgeois.

5.24 SEAMUS HEANEY

Seamus Heaney (b. 1939) was born into a farm family in County Derry, Northern Ireland. He attended St Columb's College, a Catholic boarding school, where he was taught Latin and Irish. In Belfast, he studied Anglo-Saxon at Queen's University, and lectured there (1966–72). He was involved with the Field Day theatre company, founded in 1980, contributing a version of Sophocles' *Philoctetes*, *The Cure at Troy*. Having moved to Dublin, Heaney lectured in English until 1982. He taught at Harvard University, becoming Boylston Professor of Rhetoric and Oratory, a position that he occupied for some years. In 1989, he was elected for a five-year period as Professor of Poetry at Oxford University. Heaney served for five years on The Arts Council in the Irish Republic (1973–8) and has acted as judge and lecturer. He has received several honorary degrees and other honours, culminating, in 1995, in the award of the Nobel Prize for Literature.

With Stanislaw Baranczak, he is co-translator of the Renaissance Polish poet Jan Kochanowski's *Laments* (1995), and in 1999 published his award-winning version of *Beowulf*. Other translations include *A Song Cycle by Leoš Janáček*, commissioned by the English National Opera for a series of international performances, opening in Dublin in October 1999 (1999). In 2004, returning to an earlier engagement with the plays of Sophocles, he completed *The Burial at Thebes*, a version of *Antigone*, to mark the centenary of Dublin's Abbey.

In 1986, Seamus Heaney delivered a paper, 'The Impact of Translation', (*The Government of the Tongue*, 1988). It appears that, like Ted Hughes, an equally rooted poet, Heaney was attuned to the poetry of Eastern Europe and Russia that was being made available through translation, to such an extent, indeed, that his own engagement, as a translator, comes as no surprise. Like Hughes he seems, however, to have moved from a focus on the poetry of near contemporaries to that of the distant past—the Classical past, with which he had some direct connection through his Catholic heritage and the Celtic and Anglo-Saxon past. Thus Heaney's command of contemporary English is deepened and contextualized by an awareness of other cultural and linguistic legacies and of the extreme conditions shaping the work of near coevals. In this connection as well, his close friendship with the late Joseph Brodsky, the exiled Russian poet, also a Nobel laureate, is surely to be noted.

From 'The Impact of Translation', included in *The Government of the Tongue* (London: Faber, 1988), 36–44

> What translation has done over the last couple of decades is not only to introduce us to new literary traditions but also to link the new literary experience to a modern

martyrology, a record of courage and sacrifice which elicits our unstinted admiration. [...] We have been made conscious, for example, of the passionate spirits of Russian poetry in the teens, twenties and thirties of this century. [...] It seems self-evident that what the reader who does not speak Russian experiences as the poem in translation is radically and logically different from what the native speaker experiences, phonetics and feelings being so intimately related in the human makeup. What I am suggesting, rather, is that our sense of the fate and scope of modern Russian poetry has implicitly established a bench at which subsequent work will have to justify itself. [...] For these poets, the mood of writing is the indicative mood and for that reason they constitute a shadow-challenge to poets who dwell in the conditional, the indeterminate mood [...] (pp. 38–9)

I am reminded of Stephen Dedalus's enigmatic declaration that the shortest way to Tara was via Holyhead, implying that departure from Ireland and inspection of the country from the outside was the surest way of getting to the core of Irish experience. Might we not nowadays affirm, analogously, that the shortest way to Whitby, the monastery where Caedmon sang the first Anglo-Saxon verses, is via Warsaw and Prague? To put it more directly, contemporary English poetry has become aware of the insular and eccentric nature of English experience in all the literal and extended meanings of those adjectives. England's island status, its off-centre European positioning, its history of non-defeat and non-invasion since 1066, these enviable and (as far as the English are concerned) normative conditions have ensured a protracted life within the English psyche for the assumption that a possible and desirable congruence exists between domestic and imagined reality. [...] (pp. 40–41)

I should propose, then, that there was a road not taken in poetry in English in this century [...] Further, because we have not lived the tragic scenario which such imaginations presented to us as the life appropriate to our times, our capacity to make a complete act of faith in our vernacular poetic possessions has been undermined. Consequently, we are all the more susceptible to translations which arrive like messages from those holding their own much, much further down the road not taken by us—because, happily, it was a road not open to us [...] (p. 44)

From an interview with Grigory Kruzhkov, Heaney's Russian translator, 2003 (*Ars Interpres*, 2004) in Seamus Heaney's cottage, his 'dacha', in Co. Wicklow.

[In this revealing conversation with a fellow translator, Heaney shows how his Sweeney translation is intimately linked to his ongoing work as a poet.]

North [1975] was all written here. And the translation *Sweeney Astray* [1983], because when I resigned my job and came here, at first it was all very unusual. Nine years teaching in the schools and so on. I was not sure how I would fill my days. So *Sweeney Astray* appeared, which I got from the Early Irish Texts Society volume [J. G. O'Keeffe's bilingual edition, 1913], Irish on one side and English on the other. I knew it was a long job, so it kept me busy for a year. I returned to it six years later. [. . .]

It's a translation mediated by the scholars' translation. [. . .] I followed associations of the Irish, treated it freely. [. . .]

It was the added question, the added problem of stanza form and rhyme. The early Irish text is strict. And somehow there was a softness and a tentativeness about the movement of this first version. That wasn't quite right. I wanted to finish one version. But then I knew I had to redo it, but I was too scared to start it. After six years I did begin it again.

First of all I saw bits of *Sweeney Astray* in Flann O'Brien's book *At-Swim-Two-Birds* where Sweeney is a comic figure in the novel. And Flann O'Brien has translations. Some of them are overdone and comic, but there is a sense of Irish nature, early Irish nature poetry in them. The second place where I came across it was an anthology *Celtic Miscellany*, edited by Kenneth H. D. Jackson. There I found those little extracts, real jewels reminding of Chinese or Japanese nature poems. So that wakened me to it. Then when I looked at it I have to confess that there was a large inflation, a self-inflation involved, because the story of Sweeney involves a king, springing out of battle and roaming Ireland. He's a king from the North, from a place, which is quite close to where I grew up. And I had an analogy—here I was in Wicklow, displaced from the North, because of violence in a way. [. . .] And the other truth is, if you look out of the window here, you can see leaves on the trees, you can see ivy [. . .] it was like entering the first world again. And the Sweeney poetry, giving opportunity for this straightforward, enraptured nature poetry. So it was something about living in these fields that wakened in me. [. . .] The sense of being withdrawn here was strong, you know. It's also there in some poems that I wrote afterwards in *Station Island*, a sequence called *Sweeney Redivivus* [. . .]

From 'Earning a Rhyme: Notes on Translating Buile Suibhne', included in Rosanna Warren (ed.), *The Art of Translation: Voices from the Field* (Boston: Northeastern University Press, 1989), 13–20

The Irish Literary Revival is by now a historical phenomenon. And the Norman invasion of England, the Tudor conquest of Ireland, and English colonization of North America, all these are even more suspended and remote. Yet in Northern Ireland in the late sixties and early seventies, when the international excitement of the civil rights movement got grafted on to the political appetites of the Nationalist minority, when questions about identity and cultural difference, which were being newly plied by blacks and Native Americans in the United States, came up again urgently and violently in Northern

Ireland; when the poets there—who had ignored their different religio-political origins in the name of that greater humility and flexibility which the imaginative endeavor entails—began to find themselves tugged by undercurrents of historical memory and pleas for identification with the political aims of their groups; when the whole unfinished business of the England/Ireland entanglement presented itself at a local level as a conflict of loyalties and impulses—when all this happened, historical parallels and literary precedent began to assume fresh relevance, and to offer distances and analogies which could ease the strain of the present. The poets were needy for ways in which they could honestly express the exacerbations of the local quarrel without turning that expression into just another manifestation of the aggressions and resentments which had been responsible for the quarrel in the first place.

It was under these circumstances that I began work on *Buile Suibhne* [. . .]

From *Sweeney Astray*, (1st pub. Derry, Ireland: Field Day Theatre Company, 1983, rev. text London: Faber & Faber, 2001)

Conclusion of Sweeney's lament on his fate, p. 40

[Sweeney had been transformed into a wandering bird-creature by St Ronan, whom he had offended.]

> Mendicant forever,
> frayed, scant and raggedy,
> high in the mountains
> like a crazed, frost-bitten sentry.
>
> I find no bed, no quarter,
> no place in the sun—
> not even in this reddening
> covert of tall fern.
>
> My only rest: eternal
> sleep in holy ground
> when Moling's earth lets fall
> dark balm on my wound.
>
> But now that sudden bleating
> and belling in the glen!
> I am a timorous stag
> feathered by Ronan Finn.

Sweeney is pursued by headless torsos and disembodied heads, pp. 60–1

They rose in a flock, coming for him, but he soared away in front, skimming from thicket to thicket; and no matter how wide the glen that opened before him, he bounded from edge to edge, from the top of one hill to the top of the next.

> The heads were pursuing him,
> lolling and baying,
> snapping and yelping,
> whining and squealing.
>
> They nosed at his calves and his thighs,
> they breathed on his shoulder,
> they nuzzled the back of his neck,
> they went bumping off tree-trunks and rock-face,
> they spouted and plunged like a waterfall,
> until he gave them the slip and escaped
> in a swirling tongue of low cloud.

From 'Fretwork: On Translating Beowulf', a version of the 1999 St Jerome Lecture, *TLS*, 12 November 1999, 13/14; included in *In Other Words*, (Autumn/Winter 1999/2000), 23–33

The translation that Norton commissioned was intended to replace a scholarly prose version by E. Talbot Donaldson, an authority on the poem and one of the editors of the *Norton Anthology*, where his translation has heretofore appeared. The publishers therefore wanted to be sure that my work would not depart too far from the line-by-line meaning established by generations of editors and commentators, so in order to keep their minds at rest and me on my toes, they appointed a reader who was a kind of minder. Once I had completed five or six hundred lines, I sent them to the New York office and the office sent them on to this man whom I did not then know except as a name at the bottom of a letter. His brief was to keep me from my own mistakes and to point out what might be considered my oversteppings, and I was lucky that he combined a deep knowledge of Beowulf's language and meanings with a real feel for what might be permitted if not altogether required in a new translation.

Here's an example of what went on. In the Anglo-Saxon, there is a famous description of the mountain tarn where Grendel and his mother dwell. It contains the following lines about how it is so deep and so forbidding that a hunted deer will allow itself to be torn apart by the hounds rather than enter it:

> Ðǣr mæg nihta gehwǣm   nīðwundor sēon,
> fȳr on flōde.   Nō þæs frōd leofað

> gumena bearna   þaet þone grund wite.
> Ðēah þe hǣðstapa   hundum geswenced,
> heorot hornum trum   holtwudu sēce,
> feorran geflȳmed,   ǣr hē feorh seleð,
> aldor on ōfre,   āer hē in wille
> hafelan hȳdan.
>
> (ll. 1365–72)

My first version went as follows:

> At night there, something uncanny happens:
> the water burns. And the water is bottomless.
> Nobody alive has ever fathomed it.
> There too the heather-stepper halts:
> the hart in flight from pursuing hounds
> will face up to them with firm-set horns
> and die in the wood rather than dive
> beneath its surface.

My reader was prepared to let me off for letting myself off the job of alliteration in a line like 'Nobody alive has ever fathomed it', but alliteration could not quite compensate for what I had written in the previous line: 'the water burns. And the water is bottomless'. His note read: ' "bottomless." Well, the water is so deep that no one has ever fathomed the bottom: "it" in the next line must refer to some bottom.' And then came his reminder about the kenning for the hart:

> Heather-stepper. [Is the literal sense not] heath-stepper? Again, a short line—especially if heather becomes heath. Possibly re-arrange? 'There the hart halts, the heath-stepper/hard-pressed in flight by pursuing hounds...' I like how the 'firm-set horns' become functional in the translation. In the original they are simply an attribute of the hart.

My letter back on this occasion seems to me to be worth quoting at length since it reveals all the contradictory commands which the literary translator will feel called upon to obey. It so happens I had not answered directly until this moment because my instinct was to defer consideration of the comments until I was so deeply engaged with the work that I could not be put off my stride—not that stride was exactly the word for the pace I was going at. 'I am writing now,' I said,

> on impulse, having got to that moment in the text where I call the heath-stepper the heather-stepper and where I want to persist with my perverse rendering... In general, however, I have made the revisions on the lines you suggest... glad to be

convinced in so many places that what is called for is a more literal rendering, more of a word-for-word match with the original. Hence, this morning I've tried to rewrite the bit where Hrothgar describes the prowlers on the moor; and have got to the 'bottomless' water of the mere, which you rightly point out goes beyond what the original warrants.

At this point, I might have pleaded out that 'bottomless' occurs as the last word in an early poem of my own, but even if I did not adduce the chapter and verse, I went on to say that for me 'bottomless' was a word

> with *mere-y* suggestions, since as a child I was always being warned awav from bog pools in our district—because they had 'no bottom to them'. So I was prepared to transgress, and paused for a while before coming round to a different rendering. In general, after my pauses, I *have* come round. I dropped 'thole', early on; dropped 'wallstead' but then retained it; foresee a reluctance to drop 'gap of danger'; must warn you about the appearance of *seanachaí* (an Irish/Hiberno-English word for a professional storyteller); and so on... And to come to this morning's heatherings and thitherings, so to speak—heather is a word deeply within my own first speech whereas heath is [to my first ear] very much a literary word—Danelaw-y, English and admittedly very thrilling in its deep [King] Lear-y wildness. I have nothing against literary words, of course, and in fact I thrill to the depth-charges in 'heath', back through Hopkins's 'wiry heath-packs' and Brontë's Heathcliff, and so on—but somehow, 'heather-stepper' has more spring in its step for me and since the heath is contained in the heather, I want to hold on to it.

I said earlier that I wanted my anchor to be lodged on the Anglo-Saxon seafloor, down in the consonantal rock, but I had a second mooring down in the old soft vowel-bog of the local speech. I was honour-bound to the feel and sense of the original, but at the same time could not desert whatever it is in my ear that makes me sound convincing to myself.

At a seminar on translation last year [Nobel Symposium on Translation of Poetry and Prose, 1998], Efim Etkind quoted Samuel Marshak, a great translator of poetry from English into Russian. 'Poetry is impossible to translate,' Marshak declared. 'Each time it is an exception to the rule.' So I would not claim that there is anything exceptional about the work I have done, just that it constantly manifests the impossibility factor. Consider, for example, the problem of translating a line that occurs earlier in the heath-stepper passage. The original tells us that the country people have seen two 'micle mearcstapan mōras healdan/ellorgǣstas' (lines 1348–9)—two big border-steppers keeping to the moors, spirits from elsewhere. In the final version, I rendered this as 'two such creatures/prowling the moors, huge marauders/from some other world'. I liked the menace and stealth in the word 'prowling'. It seemed to catch what was shadowy and ghostly about these 'ellorgǣstas', as well as what was wild-beastish and brute-dangerous.

An earlier version, however, had rendered them as two such creatures, '*ranging* the moors, huge marauders/from some other world', because 'ranging' alliterated with the stressed syllable in 'marauding', and I was wanting to keep as much as possible to the four-stress pattern and the alliterative requirements of the Anglo-Saxon line. Neverthe-less, in spite of the falconish sweep of the verb 'range' and the glamour it still retains four and a half centuries after Sir Thomas Wyatt used it in his poem 'They flee from me' (where his former lovers 'range/Busily seeking with a continual change') – in spite of all this, I went for the unalliterating 'prowl' because it contained more darkness and danger. On the other hand, when it came to telling where the monsters dwelt, on 'windswept crags/and treacherous keshes, where cold streams/pour down the mountain', the word 'kesh', meaning a causeway or log bridge, presented itself uncontradictably, combining as it did the local and the alliterative, the drag of the golden chain and the fret-free exhilaration of having slipped the leash.

[. . .]

In the end, the point is this: 'words of the fragrant portals' come glimmering up out of the merest puddles, from the very capillary roots of consciousness in forgotten or half-remembered sensation. 'Literary' does not mean 'lofty' The proper translation—'proper' in the Latin sense of belonging, belonging recognisably to the original and to the oeuvre of the translator—exists half-way between a crib and an appropriation. [. . .]

Given such an audience[readers of the *Norton Anthology*], some light editing is certainly called for. My favourite instance refers to a word used to render the poet's laconic description of what was going on in Heorot Hall when Grendel and Beowulf were in the throes of their combat. 'Dryht-sele dynede,' says the Anglo-Saxon; 'Denum eallum wearð,/ceaster-būendum, cenra gehwylcum,/eorlum ealuscerwen' (lines 767–9). 'The lord's hall resounded; to all the Danes, the dwellers in the castle, to each brave one, it was a warriors' ale-sharing.' My version went like this:

> And now the timbers trembled and sang,
> a hall-session that harrowed every Dane
> inside the stockade: stumbling in a fury,
> the two contenders crashed through the
> building. (767–70)

And the footnote in the anthology is to read: 'In Hiberno-Ellglisli the word 'session' ('*seisián*' in Irish) can mean a gathering where musicians and singers perform for their own enjoyment. (Translator's note).' Enough. The examples could be multiplied. What they all go to prove is that one of the most acute dilemmas faced by a contemporary poet is one that is also shared by the contemporary literary translator. Moreover, since this dilemma is explicated so vividly in Ted Hughes's extraordinary essay on 'Myths, Metres, Rhythms', I want to turn to that in order to conclude. The essay is essentially a meditation on the middle state of the writer, poised between his own idiolect and the vast sound-wave and sewage-wash of the language's total availability, but, being the poet he was, Ted Hughes eschewed the use of a technical term like idiolect. His critical prose, in spite of recent insinuations to the contrary, was never at odds with the flourishing of his creative impulse, so in this instance he typically invented one of his animal parables.

> One gazelle flicks its tail—and the tail flick goes from gazelle to gazelle right through the herd, while they keep their heads down, nonchalantly feeding. To the individual gazelle it must feel like a communal brief prayer, meaning: while we all exist as one gazelle, I exist as full strength gazelle, immortal gazelle.

In fact, this parable could equally well be a parable for the indissolubility of individual consciousness, shared language and cosmic at-homeness that we suppose existed in the world before Babel. Hughes employs it, however, to illustrate the way the non-standard language of any sub-group functions as a means of communicating and conserving 'the voltage of the whole group's awareness and energy'. This shared inner language is also, however, a badge of the group's eccentricity when they come to speak it as part of society's lingua franca. 'From the point of view of the lingua franca,' Hughes writes, 'the solidarity system and mythology of any sub-group tends to appear parochial, old-fashioned, limited and limiting—to be indulged, if at all, only as local colour.' On the other hand, from the point of view of the sub-group, 'the lingua franca appears shallow, arbitrary, empty, degraded and degrading, even destructive, if not altogether meaningless'.

As ever with Ted Hughes, there is great cogency in this writing, and it does not lessen when he goes on to outline its implications for the writer.

> Setting aside just how any writer resolves or fails to resolve this dilemma, the fact remains that each modern literary work has to take its place on a continuum between some sub-group's (author's) system of shared understandings... and the most inclusive, ideally global wave-length of a multi-cultural lingua franca.
>
> Whether the writer intends it or not, is even conscious of it or not, by the very act of bringing the work to linguistic focus they fix it at some point on that continuum. Just where that point is only becomes clear after publication.

So, in a sense, there is nothing more to say. The translator, like the writer in Hughes's parable, 'can only grope along, transmitting what are intended to be meaningful signals, the most meaningful possible'. If the work is successful, the flash of the right word-choice should create a tremor that makes readers feel they exist as 'full strength' members of the language-group. A voltage should travel up the line, from the hoard into the herd, a sensation of being tied into an extensive and self-fortifying network, a far-reaching system of pulse and beat and heft and hold. The individual translator of *Beowulf* shoulders the burden of the past and tries to launch it into the swim of the present.

My own metaphor for this process comes from a poem called 'The Settle Bed', about a big unwieldy piece of rural furniture, as solid and clinker-built as a Viking longship. The settle in question came into my possession after a cousin of my father's left it to me in her will, mine to keep, to have and hold and bequeath in turn—so the following lines seemed an appropriate epigraph for the translation:

> and now this is 'an inheritance'—
> Upright, rudimentary, unshiftably planked
> In the long ago, yet willable forward
>
> Again and again and again.

To the literary translator, this attempt to will a thing forward is the raison d'être of the whole business and belongs, as such, with the larger effort of poetry itself, especially if poetry is conceived of as Czeslaw Milosz has conceived of it, 'a dividend from what you know and what you are'. Put in a different way, this means that our language pays tribute to itself when tribute is exacted from it; it suggests that our value to ourselves as individuals or as a group or even as a species can be re-estimated and increased by dwelling upon the sum total of the experience stored in our word-hoard. Our fret as investors in ourselves can, if you like, be allayed when poetry recirculates the language's hidden wealth, a recirculation that is not only etymologically renovating, but psychologically and phenomenologically so as well.

From an interview with Grigory Kruzhkov (see above), regarding the success of his translation of *Beowulf*

That was an accident, mere accident. *Beowulf* is based on my reading of Anglo-Saxon poetry when I was a student. Not that I knew very much about it; I liked the noise of it, the meter, the alliteration. And it's like Hopkins. Hopkins is a neo-Anglo-Saxon writer [...]. I actually loved doing it, that it was so magnificently resistant. [...]

I read it aloud on the BBC [reads a few lines] and so on, and so on... just telling, telling, telling, telling... That's what people like about it, the sense of a straightforward and clear story being told. But nobody could predict what happened to *Beowulf*. Let's face it, it's a part of the phenomenon of a consumer society. [...] It has to do with some extra glamour, or whatever.

From *Beowulf* (London: Faber, 1999), 26–7

[Beowulf fights Grendel. See Sects. 3.5 and 5.23, above, for William Morris's and Edwin Morgan's versions of this passage.]

But the earl-troop's leader was not inclined
to allow his caller to depart alive:
he did not consider that life of much account
to anyone anywhere. Time and again,
Beowulf s warriors worked to defend
their lord's life, laying about them
as best they could with their ancestral blades.
Stalwart in action, they kept striking out
on every side, seeking to cut
straight to the soul. When they joined the struggle
there was something they could not have known at the time,
that no blade on earth, no blacksmith's art
could ever damage their demon opponent.
He had conjured the harm from the cutting edge
of every weapon. But his going away
out of this world and the days of his life
would be agony to him, and his alien spirit
would travel far into fiends' keeping.

Then he who had harrowed the hearts of men
with pain and affliction in former times
and had given offence also to God
found that his bodily powers failed him.
Hygelac's kinsman kept him helplessly
locked in a handgrip. As long as either lived,
he was hateful to the other. The monster's whole
body was in pain, a tremendous wound
appeared on his shoulder. Sinews split
and the bone-lappings burst. Beowulf was granted
the glory of winning [...]

POSTFACE

Daniel Weissbort

Since this collection provides, as needed, a historical background to translation in the English tradition, it seems appropriate to provide an account of its own genealogy. We have drawn on a very large number of related works, as the apparatus indicates. Nevertheless, it was the lack specifically of a textbook (a selection of primary texts) which might function as an introduction to the field that prompted us to undertake this task. That the book has been so long in the making has much to do with the fact that the discipline itself was evolving, even as we tried to get it into perspective.

For the present writer it all began with the magazine *Modern Poetry in Translation* (*MPT*), co-founded with Ted Hughes in 1965. From the start the journal had the support of the British Arts Council, and of a number of poets interested in translation (e.g. Michael Hamburger, Nathaniel Tarn, Anselm Hollo, Peter Redgrove). Like the Penguin Modern European Poets series (General Editor A. Alvarez), *MPT* was initially a response to a growing awareness of the writings, particularly the poetry, emanating from 'the other Europe', Eastern Europe, in the period after Stalin's death in 1953. The aim was to publish work by contemporary poets, in translations that tended towards the literal, as we understood the term. Early issues of the journal contained a minimum of comment, although this changed somewhat as we became more aware of current debates on translation and of the work of such individuals as James S Holmes (see Sect. 5.3, above) and others. But *MPT* ('at least a novelty', as a *Times Literary Supplement* editorial called it) was not alone in the field. The idea for such a publication had occurred to Ted Hughes when he and Sylvia Plath were living in the USA (late 1950s) and there was, even at that time, at least one other similar project, edited by the American poet, translator, and critic Willis Barnstone, this eventuating, however, in a landmark anthology, rather than in several issues of a journal: *Modern European Poetry*, ed. Willis Barnstone (New York: Bantam Books, 1966).

In 1972/3 I was invited by Paul Engle, one of the earliest subscribers to *MPT*, to the University of Iowa, as a member of the International Writing Program, which, with his wife Hualing Nieh, he had founded in 1967. Paul Engle is renowned, among other things, for having developed the Iowa Creative Writing Program, of which he became director in

1942, and for including among its offerings an 'invention' of his, the Translation Workshop, this being the first such course in the English-speaking world.

Like most of my English contemporaries, I was uneasy about the notion of Creative Writing Workshops, and I didn't really know what to make of a *Translation* Workshop. It seems that in 1963, when he was director of the Iowa Writers Workshop, Paul Engle had invited Edmund (Mike) Keeley, fiction writer and translator of Greek poetry (Cavafis, Seferis, among others) to try out a Translation Workshop.[1] This project was a natural enough outcome of Engle's interest in the larger world. He had for some years accepted foreign student-writers in the Iowa Creative Writing Program. Translation became a preoccupation, although his personal interest in it pre-dated the Workshop, since he had translated modern German poetry, including Rilke.

As Keeley explained, there was at that time no public forum for translators, no publication devoted primarily to translation, no association of translators: 'Evidence of an imminent turning point was the second revelation of my year in Iowa, namely that there were students of writing eager to learn about the craft of translation.'[2] Keeley was given a free hand, the guiding principle being that English was the language into which translation was to be made.

When I arrived in Iowa (1973/4), Gayatri Spivak, chairperson of Comparative Literature, was herself working on a translation of Jacques Derrida's *De la grammatologie* (1967), *On Grammatology* (1976; see Sect. 5.11, above). She was interested in introducing a translation programme, taking advantage of the favourable situation in Iowa. This initiative led swiftly enough to the establishment of an MFA Program in Translation, in Comparative Literature, and it was agreed that this new programme would also have a theoretical/historical component, which called for a course in the history and theory of translation. It was Paul Engle, in fact, who had been particularly adamant about the need for such a course, having in mind a historically focused rather than theory-based one. The teaching of this course inevitably fell to me, the course concerning itself, above all, with the history of theory in the English tradition, from its roots in Classical writings (Cicero, Horace, Quintillian, etc.) up to, say, Ezra Pound. I attempted to carry on beyond EP, but found contemporary translation theory, especially that which drew on French critical theory (Derrida, for instance) rather daunting. Our primary interest was in the production

---

[1] For a detailed account of the American translation Workshop and its place in the development of the academic discipline of Translation Studies, readers should consult Edwin Gentzler's 'The North American Translation Workshop' in his *Contemporary Translation Theories* (1993; rev. 2nd edn., Clevedon, Multilingual Matters 2001) This is based on first-hand experience, since Gentzler, as program assistant to Paul Engle's International Writing Program in the early 1970s, participated in the early Translation Workshops.

[2] See Keeley's Closing Address to the 1980 Symposium of the American Literary Translators Association, 'The State of Translation' (*MPT*, 41–2, Mar. 1981).

of translated texts, rather than in the consideration of the theoretical dimension of translation. Somewhat prior to these developments at Iowa, James S Holmes (1924–86), like Paul Engle a native Iowan, was at work, at the University of Amsterdam, identifying texts and assembling bibliographies which might render feasible the teaching of a course on historical translation theory. It was Holmes, incidentally, who first used the term 'Translation Studies'[3] and certainly it was he who did most to define the scope of the emerging discipline (see Sect. 5.3, above). I met Holmes in Bratislava at an FIT (International Federation of Translators, a UNESCO-affiliated body) conference, in 1968, and he contributed translations of Dutch poetry and articles on historical translation theory to *MPT*, also regularly visiting Iowa where he kept an avuncular eye on the Translation Workshop. Holmes made the bibliographies he was compiling 'for the use of students doing graduate work in translation studies at the University of Amsterdam' available to me and these lists enabled me to begin assembling a course pack for the course in the history of translation theory.

The lack of a suitable textbook had been apparent as early as 1973. Indeed, in a report 'On the Place of Translation in Comparative Literature', submitted to the American Comparative Literature Association by Rainer Schulte, himself the originator of the American Literary Translators Association (ALTA) in the late 1970s, it was stated that: 'The Course in History of Translation [...] is one of the most tradition-bound areas of comparative literature, yet [...] almost impossible to teach, since suitable materials for study are shamefully lacking.' It continues: '[T]he class is faced with a paucity of available materials, from the translations of bygone ages and a plethora of materials from contemporary (or at least twentieth-century) translations.'

There was, to be sure, an array of relevant materials, by far the most significant and inspiring being George Steiner's compendious work, *After Babel: Aspects of Language and Translation* (1975; see Sect. 5.2, above). Some pre-indication of its scope was given by the same author's *Penguin Book of Modern Verse Translation* (1966), which for the first time allowed translators comparable status with source language poets. Steiner's introduction to this anthology is one of the most important contemporary texts on the translation of poetry and on literary translation in general. Scrupulously, he draws attention to the work of a number of other scholars and poets, some associated with the short-lived National Translation Center in Texas (founded in 1968), including, for instance, D. S. Carne-Ross and William Arrowsmith.

---

[3] See 'The Name and Nature of Translation Studies' (1972), included in James S Holmes, *Translated!: Papers on Literary Translation and Translation Studies* (Amsterdam: Rodopi, 1988).

In an essay written for *Modern Poetry in Translation: 1983*, Ted Hughes speculates on the reason for the apparent boom in poetry translation in the 1960s and early 1970s. When *MPT* began, the people consulted included the poet and translator Nathaniel Tarn who, between 1967 and 1969, was general editor of Cape Editions, published by Jonathan Cape, which made available in English translations, especially from the French, a number of important short texts of literary criticism, linguistics, and anthropology (by Claude Lévi-Strauss, Roland Barthes, Michel Leiris among others). A noted translator from Spanish (Neruda, in particular), Tarn was an advisory editor of *MPT* and was also involved with the first Poetry International readings in London, in 1967, directed by Ted Hughes and Patrick Garland.

Meanwhile, or shortly before these developments in England, Paul and Hualing Engle, at the University of Iowa, had embarked on a similar if even more ambitious project, namely the publication, through funds raised by them and made available to the University of Iowa Press, of a series of international anthologies. In their General Foreword, the Engles wrote that it was intended to bring together 'people with creative talent (who, in some instances, may not even know the language being translated) with a poet native to the language. Together they attempt a version in English which tries to be partly as imaginative as the original.'[4] Paul Engle had pioneered, through the Translation Workshop, this 'tandem method' of translating poetry. It is worth recording that later, in the spirit of what the IWP had begun, an attempt was made to formalize the relationship between visiting writers and student-writers in Creative Writing and Translation by setting up a workshop the participants of which consisted of visiting foreign writers and student writers in the Creative Writing Program wanting to collaborate with them on the translation of their work.

The project to assemble a collection of primary texts, with historical notes and commentaries moved forward, but was overtaken by some others, including the late André Lefevere's *Translation/History Culture: A Sourcebook*, eventually published in 1992 in the Routledge Translation Studies series, the general editors of which were Lefevere himself, a Belgian scholar from the University of Antwerp, and Susan Bassnett of the University of Warwick. (The Routledge series was actually the second of its kind, the first, less widely available, being 'Approaches to Translation Studies', published by Van Gorcum, Amsterdam, under the editorship of James S Holmes.) Lefevere's useful short volume, with its thematic rather than chronological arrangement and its emphasis on translation as manipulation, was probably the offshoot of a larger project, under the aegis of the

---

[4] See e.g. General Editors' Introduction to *Russian Poetry: The Modern Period*, ed. John Glad and Daniel Weissbort (Iowa City: University of Iowa Press, 1978).

ICLA (International Comparative Literature Association), for a world historical reader in translation studies. I had participated in discussions about this with Holmes and Lefevere.

The University of Iowa supported our efforts to bring to fruition work on a Historical Reader in Translation Studies. My principal collaborator for a while was a doctoral candidate, Stephen Welchselblatt. In 1997, Astradur Eysteinsson, who had earned his doctorate in Comparative Literature at Iowa, returned to teach translation courses, and it was around this time that he and I decided to collaborate on the project. In the course of our co-editorship, the project was substantially reshaped. Addi Eysteinsson supplied the enthusiasm and discipline, the practical experience and theoretical knowledge, that made it possible to complete a far more ambitious project than had originally been envisaged. However, in the spirit of the earlier work, this volume has tried to keep the scope as open as may be, emphasizing the link between theory and practice, as this emerges from a historical survey of historical developments. The primary writers on translation have been the translators themselves, as noted in the General Introduction to the present volume. These statements, frequently in the unobtrusive form of prefaces, often reflect differences of opinion regarding for instance the use of blank verse rather than heroic (rhyming) couplets in the translation of the Homeric epic (William Cowper as against Alexander Pope). We have represented some of these specific controversies, although our focus has remained the work of individual translators and their contributions to a more general ongoing debate. We have also attempted, with the twentieth century, to represent work of writers who might be described primarily as theorists or critics. Even in these cases, though, the theoretical comments were often drawn from or accompanied by actual translation.

It is true that some translation theory has detached itself from the practice of translation, so as to gain a perspective on this rapidly developing discipline. If there is any bias in this volume, then, it is probably towards theory as it affects or is reflected in and reflects practice, this, in its turn, being determined by circumstances. In providing examples where possible of translations by the likes of Dryden, Pope, Pound, as well as by such as Benjamin and others who are not primarily creative writers (to use that problematical but convenient term), we have tried to flesh out the theory. As a rough guide to the translations, we have provided literal or ad verbum versions of the source texts. Of course, the very notion of literalism is problematical; nevertheless, these texts do give some additional purchase on otherwise inaccessible source material. Naturally, if the literal version provided was also one used by the translator—assuming he or she needed or made use of such an intermediate version by someone else—this was an additional bonus. As we have seen, Ted Hughes—and he was not alone (see, in particular, Sect. 5.22, above, on W. S. Merwin)—wanted versions that aspired to verbal accuracy rather than to any kind of literariness. His aim when translating was, as far as possible, to preserve the 'foreignness', bringing into English that which could not possibly have been there before. If this seems to accord with post-colonial developments in critical theory, in particular with the advocacy of 'foreignizing' translation by such as Lawrence Venuti, it suggests a current of thought flowing both ways between theory and practice.

At the same time, we became increasingly aware that anything to do with human communication can be related to translation: all transactions between human beings, whether from different languages and cultures, within the same language, between social groups, between the sexes, between adults and children and so forth involve translation; the act of writing may itself be regarded as one of translation. And then, there is the business of adaptation, for instance the screen treatment of a work of fiction. There is also the translation of oral poetry into written, when the whole social situation or context is obviously pertinent, a question with which those involved in ethnopoetics are very much concerned (see Sect. 5.7, above, on Ethnopoetics and *passim*). Translation has been globalized, in so far as its universal implications have been recognized, and the broadening of the field has become conceivable and indeed practical, greatly extending the scope or relevance of literature.

These developments may have somewhat obscured the distinction between original writing and translation. Nevertheless, that there is a distinction is not, we believe, an assumption based wholly on convenience. While, as stated, we have tried to keep the field open, we have also tried not to broaden it to such an extent that it becomes virtually indefinable. As regards the place of translation studies in academia, Professor Susan Bassnett of Warwick University has gone so far as to state that 'there are now so many people working in the field of Translation Studies that some of the old assumptions about the marginality of this work have been radically challenged, principal among which is the notion that the study of translation can be relegated to a sub-category of Comparative Literature. The current perspective reverses that assessment and proposes instead that comparative literature be considered a branch of the much wider discipline that is Translation Studies.'[5]

As editors of this volume, we have felt it incumbent on us to press for inclusiveness, keeping Translation Studies as a whole open, rather than exclusive, fortified by more or less impenetrable jargon. The discipline does, after all, propose a new way of looking at least at

---

[5] See Preface to the Revised Edition of *Translation Studies* by Susan Bassnett-McGuire (1980; London and New York, Routledge, 1991), p. xi; see also Susan Bassnett's *Comparative Literature: A Critical Introduction* (Oxford and Cambridge, Mass.: Blackwell).

one area of scholarship: the study of literature. With the emphasis here on the actual business of writing, of translating, we hope to have been able to preserve the connection at least with literary life in its historical dimension. One thing translation apparently is not— even if it may have seemed so and may still seem so to some of its practitioners—is a purely scribal business, engendering numerous local problems requiring action. At the same time, of course, that is also precisely what it is! These contradictions and dilemmas account for the perennial fascination of translation, as an art, as a practical activity or polemic, and so forth. This fascination, the wide appeal of translation and of any discussion of it, makes it a most effective introduction, as well, to the study of literature (arguably, no reading of a text is closer or more critical than that of its translator). Translation can provide the link, often missing between theory and practice, between writing about writing and writing itself.

The normativeness or ideological nature of much writing about translation has, of course, much to do with the fact that it is, by and large, tied to a consideration of certain practical problems. We hope that the present volume will help readers put the often passionate views of writers on translation into historical perspective, at the same time as relating them to supposedly more enduring aesthetic considerations. In any case, translation has, for most of its history, been concerned with broadening readerships, making more widely available what has been accessible only to a privileged few. To that extent, while recognizing the conservative or even reactionary tendencies of society, as it tries to preserve or even roll back the status quo, translation activists do well also to acknowledge the legitimacy of resistance—for instance, among many publishers—to some of the more radical approaches, such as radical foreignization.

There has been in the post-Second World War period and, particularly from the mid-1960s, a concerted effort to interrogate the process of translation, as well as to promote the actual business of translation. Consciousness-raising in the academy and generally in the media has inevitably been a slow process. We feel privileged to have been part of this historical movement and fortunate, too, to be in a position to pay tribute to fellow prospectors. This volume is also dedicated to the many individuals who directly or indirectly had a hand in its making, under the peculiarly favourable circumstances that prevailed in certain places in the last quarter of the twentieth century.

ACKNOWLEDGEMENTS

We are grateful to all the publishers and translators of texts quoted in this book and in particular to the following for the translations or articles indicated:

Extracts from The Authorized Version of the Bible (The King James Bible), the rights in which are vested in the Crown, are reproduced by permission of the Crown's Patentee, Cambridge University Press.

Extracts from The Good News Bible (The Bible Societies, Collins/Fontana, 1976), copyright © The Bible Societies, reprinted by permission of HarperCollins Publishers Ltd.

Yehuda Amichai: from 'Letter of Recommendation', in *Amen*, translated from the Hebrew by the author and Ted Hughes (Harper & Row, 1977), copyright © 1977 by Yehuda Amichai, reprinted by permission of HarperCollins Publishers, USA.

Talal Asad: from 'The Concept of Cultural Translation in British Social Anthropology', in James Clifford and George E. Marcus (eds.), *Writing Culture: The Poetic and Politics of Ethnography* (University of California Press, 1986), copyright © The Regents of The University of California, reprinted by permission of the author and the University of California Press.

Susan Bassnett: from 'Theatre and Opera', in Peter France (ed.), *The Oxford Guide to Literature in English Translation* (OUP, 2000), reprinted by permission of Oxford University Press.

Walter Benjamin: 'Die Kränkung der Luna', German translation of 'La Lune offensée' by Charles Baudelaire, in *Illuminationen: Ausgewählte Schriften* (Suhrkamp, 1955), reprinted by permission of Suhrkamp Verlag.

J. W. Binns: from *Intellectual Culture in Elizabethan and Jacobean England: The Latin Writings of the Age* (ARCA Classical and Medieval Texts, Papers and Monographs 24, Leeds, 1990), reprinted by permission of Francis Cairns (Publications) Ltd.

Laura Bohannan: 'Shakespeare in the Bush', from *Natural History*, 75 (August–September 1966); copyright holder not traced.

Yves Bonnefoy: from 'On the Translation of Form in Poetry', *World Literature Today*, 52–3 (1979); copyright holder not traced.

Anthony Bonner: 'Pierre Menard, author of Don Quixote', in Jorge Luis Borges, *Ficciones*, ed. and introd. Anthony Kerrigan (Weidenfeld and Nicolson/Grove Press, Inc. 1962), reprinted by permission of Grove/Atlantic, Inc.

Clarence Brown: from Introduction to *Osip Mandelstam: Selected Poems*, ed. Clarence Brown and W. S. Merwin (OUP, 1973), reprinted by permission of Oxford University Press.

Joseph Brodsky: 'May 24, 1980', from *Joseph Brodsky: Collected Poems in English* (Carcanet), first published in *To Urania* (Farrar, Straus & Giroux), reprinted by permission of Carcanet Press Ltd and Farrar Straus & Giroux, LLC.

Martin Buber with **Franz Rosenzweig:** Translation of Genesis 11: 1–9 into German in *Die Schrift (Die fünf Bücher der Weisung)* (WBG Darmstadt, 1997), reprinted by permission of the Estates of Martin Buber and of Franz Rosenzweig.

Stanley Burnshaw: from the introduction to *The Poem Itself* (Simon & Schuster 1989, first published in 1960): copyright holder not traced.

F. H. Colson: from Philo Judaeus, *The Life of Moses*, vol. vi, Loeb Classical Library 289, (Cambridge, Mass: Harvard University Press, 1935), reprinted by permission of the Trustees of the Loeb Classical Library, Harvard University Press. The Loeb Classical Library 1 is a registered trademark of the President and Fellows of Harvard College.

Edward Crankshaw: from Memoir of Constance Garnett published in *The Listener*, 30 January 1947, copyright © Edward Crankshaw 1947, reprinted by permission of PFD on behalf of the Estate of Edward Crankshaw.

David Daniell: from *Tyndale's Old Testament, Being the Pentateuch of 1530, Joshua to 2 Chronicles of 1537, and Jonah, in a modern-spelling edition* (Yale University Press, 1992), reprinted by permission of the publisher.

Stavros Deligiorgis: 'The Septuagint' including translation of Genesis 11: 1–9 from the Greek, printed by permission of Stavros Deligiorgis.

Itamar Even-Zohar: 'The Position of Translated Literature within the Literary Polysystem' (1978; rev. 1990) as published in *Polysystem Studies*, a special issue of *Poetics Today*, 11/1 (1990), reprinted by permission of the author.

John Felstiner: from 'Kafka and the Golem: Translating Paul Celan', in Daniel Weissbort (ed.), *Translating Poetry: The Double Labyrinth* (University of Iowa Press, 1985), reprinted by permission of the author.

Susanne Flatauer: from the German by Walter Schamshula of Jiří Levý, 'Translation as an Art Form', previously unpublished; copyright holder not traced.

Everett Fox: from the 'Translator's Preface' to *The Five Books of Moses: Genesis, Exodus, Leviticus, Numbers, Deuteronomy* (Schocken Books, 1995), copyright © 1983, 1986, 1990, 1995 by Schocken Books, reprinted by permission of Schocken Books, a division of Random House, Inc. [see also at **Lawrence Rosenwald** with **Everett Fox**]

Constance Garnett: from 'The Art of Translation' (in her own words from notes made by Richard Garnett published in *The Listener*, 30 January 1947), and from Fyodor Dostoevsky: *Crime and Punishment* (Heinemann, 1914), reprinted by permission of A P Watt Ltd on behalf of the Executors of the Estate of Constance Garnett.

James Greene: extract from preface and 'There are women who are natives' from *Osip Mandelstam Poems* (Paul Elek, 1977), copyright © James Greene 1977, reprinted by permission of HarperCollins Publishers Ltd.

Seamus Heaney: extracts from 'The Impact of Translation', in *The Government of the Tongue, The 1986 T. S. Eliot Memorial Lectures and Other Critical Writings* (Faber, 1988), from *Sweeney Astray* (Faber, 1984, 2001), and from *Beowulf* (Faber, 1999), all reprinted by permission of the publishers, Faber & Faber Ltd and Farrar Straus & Giroux, LLC; from 'Earning a Rhyme: Notes on Translating Buile Suibhne', in *The Art of Translation: Voices from the Field,* ed. Rosanna Warren (Northeastern University Press, 1989), reprinted by permission of Faber & Faber Ltd; from 'Fretwork on Translating Beowulf', first given as a BCLT St Jerome Lecture and published in *In Other Words* (Journal of the Translators Association) (Autumn/Winter 1999/2000), No 13/14, reprinted by permission of the British Centre for Literary Translation and Faber & Faber Ltd.

D. E. Hill: Ovid's 'Salamacis and Hermaphroditus', in *Metamorphoses I–IV* (Aris & Philips, 1985), reprinted by permission of Oxbow Books Ltd.

Eva Hoffman: from *Lost in Translation: Life in a New Language* (Minerva, 1991), copyright © Eva Hoffman 1991, reprinted by permission of The Random House Group Ltd and Rogers, Coleridge & White Ltd, 20 Powis Mews, London W11 1JN.

James S Holmes: 'Poem and Metapoem: Poetry from Dutch to English', in *Translated! Papers on Literary Translation and Translation Studies* (Rodopi, 1988), reprinted by permission of Editions Rodopi BV; from introduction to and from Estienne Dolet: *La manière de bien traduire d'une langue en lautre* [The way to translate well from one language to another], in *Modern Poetry in Translation*, 41–2 (March 1981), reprinted by permission of the Editors of *Modern Poetry in Translation*.

Ted Hughes: from *Seneca: Oedipus* (Faber, 1969), from *Jean Racine: Phèdre* (Faber, 1999), from *Tales from Ovid, Twenty Passages from the Metamorphoses* (Faber, 1997), from *Aeschylus: The Oresteia* (Faber, 1999), and from 'Sir Gawain and the Green Knight' in *The School Bag* edited by Seamus Heaney and Ted Hughes (Faber, 1997), all reprinted by permission of the publishers, Faber & Faber Ltd; from 'Letter of Recommendation' by Yehuda Amichai in *Amen* translated from the Hebrew by the author and Ted Hughes (Harper & Row, 1977), copyright © 1977 by Yehuda Amichai, reprinted by permission of HarperCollins Publishers, USA; and from 'The French Prisoner' translated with János Csokits and from the introduction to János Pilinszky, *The Desert of Love* (Anvil, 1989), reprinted by permission of Anvil Press Poetry.

Roman Jakobson: 'On Linguistic Aspects of Translation', first published in Reuben Brower, *On Translation* (Harvard, 1959), reprinted here from Krystyna Pomorska and Stephen Rudy (eds.), *Language in Literature* (The Belknap Press of Harvard University Press, 1987), copyright © 1987 by The Jakobson Trust, reprinted by permission of The Roman Jakobson Trust and Harvard University Press.

André Lefevere: translations of Johann Wolfgang von Goethe and Friedrich Schleiermacher from *Translating Literature: The German Tradition from Luther to Rosenzweig* (Van Gorcum, 1977), reprinted by permission of Dr Ria Vanderauwera; from 'Why Waste Our Time in Rewrites: The Trouble with Interpretation and the Role of Rewriting in an Alternative Paradigm', in Theo Hermans (ed.), *The Manipulation of Literature: Studies in Literary Translation* (Croom Helm, 1985), reprinted by permission of Palgrave Macmillan.

Suzanne Jill Levine: from *The Subversive Scribe: Translating Latin American Fiction* (Graywolf, 1991), copyright © 1991 by Suzanne Jill Levine, reprinted by permission of Graywolf Press, Saint Paul, Minnesota.

Hugh Lloyd-Jones: from *Aeschylus: The Oresteia* (Duckworth, 2001), reprinted by permission of Gerald Duckworth & Co Ltd.

Robert Lowell: from the Preface and from *Phaedra: Racine's Phèdre* (Faber, 1963, first published 1961), from *The Oresteia of Aeschylus* (Faber, 1979), from introduction and translation of Charles Baudelaire's 'The Injured Moon' ['La lune offensée'] in *Imitations* (Farrar, Straus & Giroux, 1961), copyright © 1959 by Robert Lowell, copyright renewed 1987 by Harrier Sheridan and Caroline Lowell, all reprinted by permission of the publishers, Faber & Faber Ltd and Farrar, Straus & Giroux, LLC.

Richard and Elizabeth McKane: from *Osip Mandelstam: The Moscow & Voronezh Notebooks* (Bloodaxe, 2003), reprinted by permission of Bloodaxe Books Ltd.

Bernard Meares: lines from poem 394, in *Osip Mandelstam: 50 Poems* (Persea, 1977), translation copyright © 1977 by Bernard Meares, reprinted by permission of Persea Books, Inc. (New York).

W. S. Merwin: from *Sir Gawain and The Green Knight: A New Verse Translation*, (Knopf, 2002) copyright © W. S. Merwin 2002, reprinted by permission of The Wylie Agency, Inc. and Alfred A Knopf, a division of Random House, Inc; from the foreword to *Selected Translations 1968–1978* (Atheneum, 1980), copyright © W. S. Merwin 1980; lines from poem 394 (with Clarence Brown) from *Selected Poems of Osip Mandelstam* (OUP, 1973), copyright © W. S. Merwin 1973; 'La Vita Nuova' by Dante (International Writing Program Festival, University of Iowa, 2001), copyright © W. S. Merwin 2001; and from an interview conducted by Christopher Merrill October 2001 at 'Lost and Found: The Art of Translation', International Writing Program Festival, University of Iowa, all reprinted by permission of the Wylie Agency, Inc.

Frank Justus Miller: from Ovid, vol. iv, Loeb Classical Library 43 (1916) in *Ovid: Metamorphoses Books I–VIII,* rev. G. P. Goold (Cambridge, Mass.: Harvard University Press, 1999) and from Seneca: *Oedipus*, vol. viii, Loeb Classical Library 62 (1917) in *Seneca Tragedies I* (Cambridge, Mass: Harvard University Press, 1979), reprinted by permission of the Trustees of the Loeb Classical Library, Harvard University Press. The Loeb Classical Library 1 is a registered trademark of the President and Fellows of Harvard College.

Stephen Mitchell: 'Archaic Torso of Apollo', copyright © 1982 by Stephen Mitchell from *The Selected Poetry of Rainer Maria Rilke,* trans. Stephen Mitchell, reprinted by permission of Random House, Inc.

Edwin Morgan: 'Language at Play, in Conversation with Joseph Farrell', in *Stages of Translation,* ed. David Johnston (Absolute Classics, 1996), reprinted by permission of Edwin Morgan and Joseph Farrell; from *Beowulf* and from his introduction (Carcanet, 2002); from 'The Seafarer' and from 'To the Bourgeoisie' by Vladimir Mayakovsky in *Collected Translations* (Carcanet, 1996); and from Jean Racine: *Phaedra* (Carcanet, 2000), all reprinted by permission of the publishers, Carcanet Press Ltd.

Vladimir Nabokov: from *Vladimir Nabokov: Selected Letters 1940–1977*, ed. Dmitri Nabokov and Matthew J Bruccoli (Harcourt, 1989), copyright © 1989 by the Article 3b Trust under the Will of Vladimir Nabokov; from *Lolita* (Putnam, 1955/Weidenfeld & Nicolson, 1959), reprinted by permission of Weidenfeld and Nicolson, an imprint of the Orion Publishing Group; from 'The Art of Translation' in *Vladimir Nabokov: Lectures on Russian Literature,* ed. Fredson Bowers (Harcourt, 1981), copyright © 1981 by the Estate of Vladimir Nabokov, reprinted by permission of Harcourt, Inc; from *Onegin: A Novel in Verse* by Alexandr Pushkin, translated from the Russian with commentary by Vladimir Nabokov, Bollingen Series 72, vol. 1 (Princeton, 1964), copyright © 1964 by Bollingen, 1975 rev. edn., copyright © 1975, renewed 1992, 2003 by Princeton University Press. reprinted by permission of Princeton University Press; from 'Problems of Translation: "Onegin" in English', in L. Venuti (ed.), *The Translation Studies Reader* (Routledge 2000); from *The Song of Igor's Campaign, An Epic of the Twelfth Century* (Ardis, 1988); from 'Reply to my Critics' in *Strong Opinions* (McGraw Hill, 1973); from *Ada* (McGraw Hill, 1969); and from foreword to Lermontov: *A Hero of our Time* (Doubleday, 1958) translated in collaboration with Dimitri Nabokov, all reprinted by permission of the Estate of Vladimir Nabokov via Smith Skolnik Literary Management. All rights reserved.

Eugene A. Nida: from *Toward a Science of Translating: With Special Reference to Principles and Procedures Involved in Bible Translating* (E. J. Brill, 1964), reprinted by permission of Brill Academic Publishers.

Ezra Pound: from *Selected Letters of Ezra Pound* (1950), copyright © 1950 by Ezra Pound; from *The Cantos of Ezra Pound* (1993), copyright © 1934, 1937, 1940, 1948, 1956, 1959, 1962, 1966, 1968 by Ezra Pound; from *Personae: The Collected Shorter Poems of Ezra Pound* (1971), copyright © 1926 by Ezra Pound; from *Literary Essays of Ezra Pound*, introd. T. S. Eliot (1968), copyright © 1935 by Ezra Pound; and from *The Translations of Ezra Pound* (1970), copyright © 1953 by Ezra Pound, all reprinted by permission of the publishers, Faber & Faber Ltd and New Directions Publishing Corp.

Gregory Rabassa: from 'If This Be Treason: Translation and Its Possibilities', in William Frawley (ed.), *Translation: Literary, Linguistic and Philosophical Perspectives* (University of Delaware Press, 1984), reprinted by permission of the Associated University Presses; from Gabriel García Márquez, *One Hundred Years of Solitude* (Cape, 1970), reprinted by permission of The Random House Group Ltd.

A. K. Ramanujan: from *Speaking of Shiva* (Penguin Classics, 1973), copyright © A. K. Ramanujan 1973, reprinted by permission of Penguin Books Ltd; poems from *Poems of Love and War: From the Eight Anthologies and the Ten Long Poems of Classical Tamil* (Columbia University Press, 1985), copyright © 1985 Columbia University Press, reprinted by permission of the publishers, Columbia University Press and Molly A. Daniels Ramanujan; from 'On Translating a Tamil Poem', in *The Collected Essays of A. K. Ramanujan* (OUP India, 1999) and 'This Night' by N. Revathi Devi, trans. A. K. Ramanujan with V. Narayana Rao in *Oxford India Anthology of Contemporary Poetry* edited by Vinay Dharwadker and A. K. Ramanujan (OUP India, 1996), reprinted by permission of Oxford University Press India, New Delhi.

Rainer Maria Rilke: 'Archaischer Torso Apollo' from *Neue Gedichte* (Insel-Verlag, 2000), reprinted by permission of the publisher.

Norma Rinsler: literal translations of 'La Lune offensée' by Charles Baudelaire and of the German translation by Walter Benjamin, reprinted by permission of Norma Rinsler.

Douglas Robinson: from *The Translator's Turn* (The Johns Hopkins University Press, 1991), copyright © Douglas Robinson 1991, reprinted by permission of the publisher; and from 'The Ascetic Foundations of Western Translatology: Jerome and Augustine', in *Translation and Literature*, vol. i (Edinburgh University Press, 1992), reprinted by permission of the publishers, www.eup.ed.ac.uk

Lawrence Rosenwald with **Everett Fox**: from Martin Buber: 'Leitwort Style in Pentateuch Narrative', 'On Word Choice in Translating the Bible: In Memoriam Franz Rozenzweig', and 'A Translation of the Bible'; from Franz Rozenzweig: 'Scripture and Word: On the New Bible Translation' and 'Scripture and Luther', all in *Scripture and Translation* [*Die Scrift und Ihre Verdeutschung*] (Indiana University Press, 1994), reprinted by permission of the publisher, Indiana University Press.

Franz Rosenzweig [see **Martin Buber**]

Barry Rubin: 'Beyond Consolation' by Joseph Brodsky, *New York Review of Books*, 7 February 1974; copyright holder not traced.

Niall Rudd: from *Johnson's Juvenal, London and the Vanity of Human Wishes* (Bristol Classical Press, 1981), reprinted by permission of Gerald Duckworth & Co. Ltd.

James Harry Smith and **Edd Winfield**: from Joachin du Bellay, *The Defence and Illustration of the French Language [La Defense et illustration de la langue francayse]* in *The Great Critics: An Anthology of Literary Criticism*, ed. J. H. Smith and E. Winfield (3rd edn., Norton, 1951), copyright 1932, 1939, 1951 by W. W. Norton & Co., Inc., renewed © 1967 by James Harry Smith and Edd Winfield Parks, reprinted by permission of W. W. Norton & Company, Inc.

Mary Snell-Hornby: from *Translation Studies: An Integrated Approach* (John Benjamins Publ. Co. 1994; rev. edn. 1995), reprinted by permission of John Benjamins Publishing Company, Amsterdam,/Philadelphia. www.benjamins.com and the Foundation of Language.

Gayatri Chakravorty Spivak: from 'Translator's Preface' to Jacques Derrida, *Of Grammatology* (The Johns Hopkins University Press, 1976), copyright © Gayatri Chakravorty Spivak 1976, reprinted by permission of the publisher; from 'The Politics of Translation', in *Outside in the Teaching Machine* (Routledge, 1993), copyright © Gayatri Chakravorty Spivak 1993, reprinted by permission of Routledge/Taylor & Francis Books, Inc.

George Steiner: from *After Babel: Aspects of Language and Translation* (3rd edn., OUP, 1998), reprinted by permission of Oxford University Press.

Dennis Tedlock: from 'On the Translation of Style in Oral Narrative', in *Journal of American Folklore*, 84; and from a State University of Buffalo course description on 'Ethnopoetics'; copyright holder not traced.

David Anthony Turner: from *Oedipus* in *Classical Tragedy: Greek and Roman: Eight Plays,* ed. Robert W. Corrigan (Applause, 1990), reprinted by permission of Hal Leonard Corporation on behalf of Applause Theatre & Cinema Books.

Lawrence Venuti: from 'Translation as Cultural Politics: Regimes of Domestication in English', in *Textual Practice* 7/2 (1993), reprinted by permission of Taylor & Francis (UK).

Edd Winfield [see at **James Harry Smith**]

Celia and Louis Zukofsky: from *Catullus* (Cape Golliard, 1969); copyright holder not traced.

Despite every effort to trace and contact copyright holders before publication, this has not been possible in those cases indicated. If contacted, the publisher will be pleased to rectify any errors or omissions at the earliest opportunity.

SELECT BIBLIOGRAPHY

INTRODUCTORY NOTE

Selecting material to include in a reader such as this is always a daunting task. When it came to deciding what to include in a bibliography, which would 'round off' the volume, the editors felt they were facing one of the most difficult decisions in this whole process of selection.

The concept of our anthology rests on a wide-ranging and flexible understanding of the field, drawing not only on a scholarly framework of translation studies in the 'stricter' meaning of the term, but also on various discussions and commentaries on the idea and practice of translation; on introductions, interviews, notes of practising translators, etc., and not least of course on the very practice of translation itself (albeit chiefly literary translation).

It is clearly impractical to include an extensive bibliography along those lines, and a short, selected one would inevitably constitute an awkward case of arbitrariness, more so than our selection of materials which is contextualized by the volume itself. This is especially true of translated literary works. The volume contains samples of the work of only some of the important translators who have enriched the English language through the ages. Trying to make up for shortcomings by including a list or 'canon' of great translators and translations is not something we were eager to attempt.

It would have been easier to select a number of scholarly books and articles which have appeared in the past several decades and which have helped to define the academic field of translation studies. The volume contains, either in part or in whole, several seminal texts in this category, i.e. works that could be classified as translation theory, a discipline we have participated in as university teachers and researchers. But we have also consulted other writings pertaining to translation, be they of a critical, introductory, speculative, experimental, or experiential bent, and we have both worked as practising translators. Hence, while we are very much aware of the key role played by translation theory in translation studies as a discipline, we could not help but wonder whether we wouldn't be undermining our own approach—the concept of translation studies constituted in and by the reader—if we chose to 'close' it with a bibliography constituted according to a disciplinary framework which the volume itself displaces, to some extent replacing it with a different model.

Did we want to tell students using this anthology, as they are discovering the whole field of translation and translation studies, that they should now move on to the 'central' academic authorities on translation? Wouldn't we prefer them to continue 'thinking the field' in the broad, open sense, in which we felt we had tried to approach and outline it?

That said, it should of course be acknowledged that the seminal works of translation theory comprise a critical sprectrum which is applicable in various ways to both the many methods and examples of translation and the many different accounts of, and comments on, translation. The useful theoretical works are not pieces of dogma; they contain models and ideas which students of translation can work with creatively as they discover their own paths in the field. This includes putting together many 'bibliographies' that still need to be worked out, for there are many documents 'out there' that touch on translation in a multiplicity of ways—and there are of course thousands of translations which remain to be discussed and analysed.

Some of the important publications in the history of translation studies have contained extensive general bibliographies that reflect a discipline which is both versatile and in fact very much in-progress, as this field has been and perhaps still is. This is true for instance of Bayard Quincy Morgan's 'Bibliography, 46BC–1958', included in Reuben Brower's *On Translation* (1959), the bibliography Eugene A. Nida includes in his *Toward a Science of Translating* (1964), and more recently the chronological bibliography in George Steiner's *After Babel* (3rd edn., 1998).

One of the options we considered for the present volume was simply to collect all the bibliographies and bibliographical references contained within the reader itself and replicate them as a whole. Ultimately we decided against this. These references are already available in the book and we felt that a more 'simple' list of works would be of greater service, one that would not attempt to reflect specialized areas of research, but would relate to a more general framework. As a result, the lists below are restricted to books in English that either collect material and information in the field or present broad accounts of translation and translation studies. There is also a short list of journals that specialize in translation (not, therefore, including journals that have intermittently focused on translation or have even, occasionally, put out special issues on translation).

A. JOURNALS

Babel, international journal of the Federation of Translators, (1955–).

The Bible Translator (London, 1949–).

Delos, National Translation Center, University of Texas at Austin (1968–71).

Exchanges, (http://www.uiowa.edu/~xchanges/index.htm), University of Iowa (1989–).

IJT (*International Journal of Translation*) (New Delhi, 1994–).

In Other Words, the journal of the Translators Association, produced in collaboration with the British Centre for Literary Translation at the University of East Anglia, (1993–).

Meta, University of Montreal (1966–).

Modern Poetry in Translation (London, 1965–).

New Voices in Translation Studies (http://www.iatis.org/newvoices/) (2005–).

Target (Amsterdam/Philadelphia, 1989–).

Translation, Columbia University (New York, 1973–94).

Translation and Literature, Edinburgh University Press (1992–).

Translation Journal (*http://accurapid.com/journal/*) (1997–).

Translation Review University of Texas (Dallas, 1978–).

The Translator (Manchester, 1995–).

TRANSST: International Newsletter for Translation Studies, Tel Aviv University (1987–).

TTR (Montreal, 1988–).

Two Lines: A Journal of Translation (San Francisco, 1994–).

B. Encyclopedias, Anthologies, Essay Collections

Arrowsmith, William and Shattuck Roger, (eds.), *The Craft and Context of Translation* (Austin: University of Texas Press, 1961).

Baker, Mona (ed.), *Routledge Encyclopedia of Translation* (London: Routledge, 2001).

Bassnett, Susan and Lefevere, André (eds.), *Translation, History and Culture* (London and New York: Pinter Publishers 1990).

—— and Trivedi, Harish (eds.), *Post-Colonial Translation: Theory & Practice* (London: Routledge 1998).

Biguenet, John and Schulte, Rainer (eds.), *The Craft of Translation* (Chicago and London: University of Chicago Press, 1989).

—— —— *Theories of Translation: An Anthology of Essays from Dryden to Derrida* (Chicago and London: University of Chicago Press, 1992).

Bowker, Lynne et al. (eds.), *Unity in Diversity: Current Trends in Translations Studies* (Manchester: St Jerome, 1998).

Brower, Reuben A. (eds.), *On Translation* (Cambridge, Mass.: Harvard University Press, 1959).

Budick, Sanford, and Iser, Wolfgang (eds.), *The Translatability of Cultures: Figurations of the Space Between* (Stanford: Stanford University Press, 1996).

Chan, Leo Tak-hung (ed.), *One into Many: Translation and the Dissemination of Classical Chinese Literature* (Amsterdam and New York: Editions Rodopi, 2003).

Classe, Olive (ed.), *Encyclopedia of Literary Translation into English* (Chicago and London: Fitzroy Dearborn Publishers, 2000).

France, Peter (ed.), *The Oxford Guide to Literature in English Translation* (Oxford: OUP, 2001).

Frank, Armin Paul et al. (eds.), *Übersetzung—Translation—Traduction: Ein Internationales Handbuch Zur Übersetzungsforschung/An International Encyclopedia of Translation Studies/ Encyclopedie Internationale Des Sciences De Traduction*, i (Berlin and New York: Walter de Gruyter, 2004).

Frawley, William (ed.), *Translation: Literary, Linguistic, and Philosophical Perspectives* (Newark: University of Delaware Press and London/Toronto: Associated University Presses, 1984).

Graham, Joseph F. (ed.), *Difference in Translation* (Ithaca, NY and London: Cornell University Press, 1985).

Grähs, L., Korlén, G., and Malmbert, B. (eds.), *Theory and Practice of Translation* (Nobel Symposium 39) (Stockholm, 1978).

Guenthner, F, and Guenthner-Reutter, M. (eds.), *Meaning and Translation: Philosophical and Linguistic Approaches* (London: Duckworth, 1978).

Hermans, Theo (ed.), *The Manipulation of Literature: Studies in Literary Translation* (New York: St Martin's Press 1985).

—— *Second Hand: Papers on the Theory and Historical Study of Literary Translation* (Vlaamse Vereniging voor Algemene en Vergelijkende Literatuurwetenschap (ALW-CAHIER nr. 3), 1985).

Holmes, James S (ed.), *The Nature of Translation: Essays on the Theory and Practice of Literary Translation* (The Hague and Paris: Mouton, 1970).

—— Lambert, J. and van den Broeck, R. (eds.), *Literacy and Translation* (Leuven: Acco, 1978).

Honig, Edwin, *The Poet's Other Voice: Conversations on Literary Translation* (Amherst: University of Massachusetts Press, 1985).

Hung, Eva (ed.), *Translation and Cultural Change: Studies in History, Norms and Image-Projection* (Amsterdam: John Benjamins, 2005).

Johnston, David (ed.), *Stages of Translation: Essays and Interviews on Translating for the Stage* (Bath: Absolute Classics, 1996).

Kittel, Harald, and Frank, Armin Paul (eds.), *Interculturality and the Historical Study of Literary Translation* (Berlin: Erich Schmidt Verlag, 1991).

Lefevere, André (ed.), *Translating Literature: The German Tradition* (Amsterdam and Assen: Van Gorcum, 1977).

—— *Translation/History/Culture: A Sourcebook* (London and New York: Routledge, 1992).

Orero, Pilar, and Sager, Juan C. (eds.), *The Translator's Dialogue* (Philadelphia and Amsterdam: John Benjamins, 1997).

Pálsson, Gísli (ed.), *Beyond Boundaries: Understanding, Translation and Anthropological Discourse* (Oxford and Providence: Berg, 1993).

Petrilli, Susan (ed.), *Translation Translation* (Amsterdam and New York: Editions Rodopi, 1993).

Radice, William, and Reynolds, Barbara (eds.), *The Translator's Art: Essays in Honour of Betty Radice* (Harmondsworth: Penguin Books, 1987).

Riccardi, Alessandra (ed.), *Translation Studies: Perspectives on an Emerging Discipline* (Cambridge: Cambridge University Press, 2002).

Robinson, Douglas (ed.), *Western Translation Theory: From Herodotus to Nietzsche* (Manchester: St Jerome, 1997).

Snell-Hornby, Mary (ed.), *Translation and Lexicography* (Euralex Colloquium 1987. A Special *Paintbrush* Monograph) (Philadelpia and Amsterdam: John Benjamins, 1989).

——, Jettmarova, Zuzana, and Kaindl, Klaus (eds.), *Translation as Intercultural Communication: Selected Papers from the EST Congress—Prague, September 1995* (Philadelphia and Amsterdam: John Benjamins, 1997).

Steiner, T. R. (ed.), *English Translation Theory 1650–1800* (Assen and Amsterdam: Van Gorcum, 1975).

Tymoczko, Maria, and Gentzler, Edwin (eds.), *Translation and Power* (Amherst: University of Massachusetts Press, 2002).

Van Leuven-Zwart, Kitty M., and Naaijkens, Ton (eds.), *Translation Studies: The State of the Art. Proceedings of the First James S Holmes Symposium on Translation Studies* (Amsterdam and New York: Editions Rodopi, 1991).

Venuti, Lawrence (ed.), *Rethinking Translation: Discourse, Subjectivity, Ideology* (London and New York: Routledge, 1992).

—— (ed.), *The Translation Studies Reader* (London and New York: Routledge, 2000).

Warren, Rosanna (ed.), *The Art of Translation: Voices from the Field* (Boston: Northeast University Press, 1989).

Weissbort, Daniel (ed.), *Translating Poetry: The Double Labyrinth* (Iowa City: University of Iowa Press, 1989).

C. General or Introductory Books on the Practice of Translation and/or the Field of Translation Studies

Aaltonen, Sirkku, *Time-Sharing on Stage: Drama Translation in Theatre and Society* (Clevedon, UK: Multilingual Matters, 1999).

Amos, Flora Ross, *Early Theories of Translation* (1920; New York: Octagon Books, 1973).

Apter, Ronnie, *Digging for the Treasure: Translation after Pound* (New York: Peter Lang Publishing, 1984).

Austermühl, Frank, *Electronic Tools for Translators* (Manchester: St Jerome, 2001).

Baker, Mona, *In Other Words: A Coursebook on Translation* (London and New York: Routledge, 1992).

Barnstone, Willis, *The Poetics of Translation: History, Theory, Practice* (New Haven and London: Yale University Press, 1993).

Bassnett, Susan, *Translation Studies* (1980; 3rd edn. London: Routledge, 2002).

Bell, Roger T., *Translation and Translating: Theory and Practice* (London and New York: Longman, 1991).

Benjamin, Andrew, *Translation and the Nature of Philosophy: A New Theory of Words* (London and New York: Routledge, 1989).

Berman, Antoine, *The Experience of the Foreign*, trans. S. Heyvaert (Albany, NY: State University of New York Press, 1992).

Buber, Martin, and Rosenzweig, Franz, *Scripture and Translation*, trans. Lawrence Rosenwald and Everett Fox (Bloomington and Indianapolis: Indiana University Press, 1994).

Catford, J. C., *A Linguistic Theory of Translation* (London: Oxford University Press, 1965).

Cohen, J. M., *English Translators and Translations* (London: Longmans, Green, 1962).

Conley, C. H., *The First English Translators of the Classics* (1927; Port Washington, NY: Kennikat Press, 1967).

Cronin, Michael. *Translating Ireland* (Cork: Cork UP, 1996).

Delisle, Jean, and Woodsworth, Judith, *Translators through History* (Amsterdam: John Benjamins, 1995).

Even-Zohar, Itamar, *Polysystem Studies*, special issue of *Poetics Today*, 11/1 (Spring 1990).

Friedberg, Maurice, *Literary Translation in Russia: A Cultural History* (University Park: Pennsylvania State University Press, 1997).

Gentzler, Edwin, *Contemporary Translation Theories* (1993; 2nd rev. edn. Clevedon, UK: Multilingual Matters, 2001).

Hatim, Basil, and Mason, Ian, *Discourse and the Translator* (London: Longman, 1990).

Hermans, Theo, *Translation in Systems: Descriptive and System-oriented Approaches Explained* (Manchester: St Jerome Publishing, 1999).

Hofstadter, Douglas R., *Le Ton beau de marou: In Praise of the Music of Language* (New York: Basic Books, 1997).

Holmes, James S, *Translated! Papers on Literary Translation and Translation Studies* (Amsterdam: Rodopi, 1988).

Jacobsen, Eric, *Translation: A Traditional Craft* (Copenhagen: Nordisk Forlag, 1958).

Kelly, Louis G., *The True Interpreter: A History of Translation Theory and Practice in the West* (New York: St Martin's Press, 1979).

Kussmaul, Paul, *Training the Translator* (Amsterdam: John Benjamins, 1995).

Landers, Clifford E., *Literary Translation: A Practical Guide* (Clevedon, UK: Multilingual Matters, 2001).

Lefevere, André, *Translating Poetry : Seven Strategies and a Blueprint* (Assen : Van Gorcum, 1975).

—— *Translating Literature: The German Tradition from Luther to Rosenzweig* (Amsterdam and Assen: Van Gorcum, 1977).

—— *Translating Literature: Practice and Theory in a Comparative Literature Context* (New York: The Modern Language Association of America, 1992).

—— *Translation, Rewriting, and the Manipulation of Literary Fame* (London and New York: Routledge, 1992).

Matthiessen, F. O., *Translation: An Elizabethan Art* (1931; New York: Octagon Books, 1965).

Munday, Jeremy, *Introducing Translation Studies: Theories and Applications* (London: Routledge, 2001).

Nida, Eugene A., *Toward a Science of Translating: With Special Reference to Principles and Procedures Involved in Bible Translating* (Leiden: E. J. Brill, 1964).

—— and Taber, Charles R., *The Theory and Practice of Translation* (Leiden: Brill Academic Publishers, 2003).

Niranjana, Tejaswini, *Siting Translation: History, Post-Structuralism and the Colonial Context* (Berkeley and Los Angeles: University of California Press, 1992).

Neubert, Albrecht, and Shreve, Gregory M., *Translation as Text* (Kent, Ohio, and London: Kent State University Press, 1992).

Newmark, Peter, *Approaches to Translation* (Oxford: Pergamon Press, 1981).

Nord, Christiane, *Translating as a Purposeful Activity* (Manchester: St Jerome, 1997).

Oittinen, Riitta, *Translating for Children* (New York: Garland Publishing, 2000).

Postgate, J. P., *Translation and Translations: Theory and Practice* (London: G. Bell and Sons, 1922).

Pym, Anthony, *Method in Translation History* (Manchester: St Jerome, 1998).

Rener, Frederick M., *Interpretatio: Language and Translation from Cicero to Tytler* (Amsterdam and New York: Editions Rodopi, 1989).

Reiss, Katharina, *Translation Criticism—The Potentials and Limitations: Categories and Criteria for Translation Quality Assessment* (Manchester: St Jerome and New York: American Bible Society, 2000).

Robinson, Douglas, *The Translator's Turn* (Baltimore: Johns Hopkins University Press, 1991).

—— *What Is Translation? Centrifugal Theories, Critical Interventions* (Kent, Ohio, and London: Kent State University Press, 1997).

Savory, Theodore, *The Art of Translation* (London: Cape, 1957).

Schwartz, W., *Principles and Problems of Biblical Translation: Some Reformation Controversies and their Background* (Cambridge: Cambridge University Press, 1955).

Simon, Sherry, *Gender in Translation: Cultural Identity and the Politics of Transmission* (London: Routledge, 1996).

Snell-Hornby, Mary, *Translation Studies: An Integrated Approach* (1988; 2nd, rev. edn., Amsterdam and Philadelphia: John Benjamins, 1995).

Sofer, Morry, *The Translator's Handbook* (1996; 4th, rev. edn. Rockville, Md: Schreiber Publishing, 2002).

Steiner, George, *After Babel: Aspects of Language and Translation* (1975; 3rd rev. edn. Oxford: OUP, 1998).

Tabakowska, Elzbieta, *Cognitive Linguistics and Poetics of Translation* (Tübingen: Narr, 1993).

Toury, Gideon, *Descriptive Translation Studies and Beyond* (Amsterdam and Philadelphia: John Benjamins, 1995).

—— *In Search of a Theory of Translation* (Tel Aviv: Porter Institute for Poetics and Semiotics, 1980).

Tytler, Alexander Fraser, *Essay on the Principles of Translation* (1791; 3rd rev. edn. London, 1813).

Venuti, Lawrence, *The Translator's Invisibility: A History of Translation* (London and New York: Routledge, 1995).

——— *The Scandals of Translation: Towards an Ethics of Difference* (London: Routledge, 1998).

Wilss, Wolfram, *The Science of Translation: Problems and Methods*, trans. from German by the author (Tübingen: Gunter Narr Verlag, 1982).

INDEX OF TRANSLATED TEXTS

Works in translation, included in part or whole, in the various entries of the volume (this index does not include texts *on translation* of which there are a fair number in the book).

Aeschylus: *Agamemnon* 222–3, 250–1, 357–8, 529–31
Amichai, Yehuda: Amen 522
Arabian Nights 252

Ballata (anon., from Italian) 254–5
Baudelaire: La lune offensée 307–9, 355
Beowulf 256–7, 594, 606–7
Bible:
    Babel (Genesis 2:1–9) 9–10, 13–14, 43–6, 66–7, 72, 113–14, 119–20, 321–2, 351, 568
    Psalm 23:1–6 120
    St. John 1:1–5 120
Boccaccio: Sigismonda and Guiscardo 157–8
Brodsky, Joseph: May 24, 1980 474–5

Calahorra, Diego Ortúnez de: *The Mirrour of Princely Deedes and Knyghthood* 132
Cavacanti, Guido: sonnet 279
Catullus 112 459
Celan, Paul: To One Who Stood Before the Door 569–70
Chaucer: *Troilus and Criseyde* 107
Corneille: *La Mort de Pompée* 134–5

Dante: *Divine Comedy* 242–4
Dante: sonnet 472–3
Dostoevsky: *Crime and Punishment* 296

Epictetus 143

The Flower and the Leaf 158–9

Goethe: Wanderers Nachtlied II 244
Grettis Saga 257

Herreweghen, Hubert van: Evening by the Sea 412–13
Homer: *Iliad* 158, 172–3, 226, 232
Homer: *Odyssey*, Book XI 97–8, 173, 187, 239–40, 255–6, 286–7
Horace: *Ars poetica* 22–3
Horace: Ode 29, Book 3 152–3

Indian Subcontinental Poetry:
    Kalipar (poems, from Classical Tamil) 479–81
    Ponmutiyar (poems, from Cl. Tamil) 481–2
    Erumai Veliyanar (poem, from Cl. Tamil) 482–3
    Devara Dasimayya (poem, from Old Kannada) 483
    Basavanna (poem, from Old Kannada) 483
    Mahadevi (poem, from Old Kannada) 483–4
    Allama Prabhu (poem, from Old Kannada) 484
    N. Revathi Devi: This Night (from Modern Telugu) 484–5
Infante, G. Cabrera: The Ides of March 516–19

Juvenal: The Tenth Satire 153–5, 179–82, 359

Khayyam, Omar: *Rubáiyát* 247–8

Lucretius: *Against the Fear of Death* 137–8, 151–2

Mandelstam, O.: Poem 94, stanza 2 469–71
Márquez, G. G.: *One Hundred Years of Solitude* 510–11
Martial IX 57 and 59 423–8
Mayakovsky, V.: To the Bourgeoisie 596

Orlando, Guido: sonnet 278
Ovid: *The Metamorphoses* 87–8, 527–9

Pilinszky, János: The French Prisoner 523–4
Pindar: The Second Olympique Ode 125–7
Plutarch: *Parallel Lives* 91–3

Po, Li T'ai: South-Folk in Cold Country 280
Pushkin: *Eugene Onegin* 385–91
Pushkin: The Prophet 533

Racine: *Phaedra* 355–7, 526–7, 595–6
Rilke, R. M.: Archäischer Torso Apollos 363–5
Rostand, Edmond: *Cyrano de Bergerac* 589–91

The Seafarer 283–4, 594–5
Seneca: *Oedipus* 85–6, 525–6
Shakespeare: *Hamlet* 366–75
Sir Gawain and the Green Knight 532, 583–4
Snoek, Paul: Rustic Landscape 410–11
The Song of Igor's Campaign 381
Sweeney Astray 600–1

Virgil: *Aeneid* 155–7, 237–8
6 Horse Songs for 4 Voices (Native American) 456–7

INDEX

Ablancourt, Nicolas Perrot de 196 n
Adelard (of Bath) 261
Adlington, W. 265
Aelfric [Ælfric] 19, 34, 38–40, 40–4
    (author & translator)
Aeschines 21, 30
Aeschylus 7, 211–12, 220–1, 222–3
    (author), 233–4, 246, 249, 250
    (author), 260, 282, 286, 352, 357, 358
    (author), 529–31 (author)
Aethelweard [Æthelweard] 38, 40
Akhmatova, Anna 470
Albertus Magnus, St 70, 261
Alexander (the Great) 11
Alfarabi 261
Alfred (the Great, King of Wessex) 2, 18,
    33–6, 36–8 (author), 40, 261–2
Algarotti, Francesco 142
Ali-Shah, Omar 248 (translator)
Allen, William (Cardinal) 110–11
Alured (King) 49
Amado, Jorge 507
Ambrose, St 66
Amichai, Yehuda 521, 522 (author)
Amyot, Jacques 81, 82, 90–1, 92
    (translator) 264–5
Anacreon 160
Andreopulos, Michael 262
Andronicus, Lucius Livius 259
Anthony, St (of Egypt) 27, 538–9
Anttila, Raimo 445
Apollinaire, Guillaume 410
Apter, Ronnie vi, 217, 274–89 (author & editor)
Apuleius, Lucius 265

Aquila 29, 49
Aquinas, Thomas St 130, 261
Arabian Nights 251–2
Aratus (of Soli) 260
Arendt, Hanna 298
Ariosto, Ludovico 106, 198, 201
Aristeas (Epistle or letter of) 11, 12, 23
Aristophanes 160, 550, 553
Aristotle 22, 33, 60, 89, 108, 109, 130,
    260–3, 340
Arnold, Matthew 196, 210, 213, 224, 225,
    227–30 (author), 230–1, 231–2 (author
    & translator), 239, 250 n
Arundel, Thomas (Archbishop) 112
Asad, Talal 366, 394, 487 n, 494–5, 495–501
    (author)
Asser 36, 37
Asturias, Miguel Angel 507, 509
Attar-ut-Tair 246
Athanasius of Alexandria 27, 538
Auden, W. H. 467
Aue, Hartman von 242, 253
Augustus (Emperor) 22
Augustine, St (Aurelius Augustinus) 18, 28, 31,
    32–3 (author), 34–5, 66, 117, 118, 536–8,
    542–5, 564
Aurogallus (Goldhahn) Matthaeus 61
Aveling, Eleanor Marx 379
Averroes (Ibn Rushd) 261
Avicenna 261
Avitus, Tiberius Octavius 260

Bacon, Lord Francis 105–6
Baldick, Chris 437

Baldvinsson, Gardar vii
Baranczak, Stanislaw 597
Barba, Eugenio 561
Barnhouse, Rebecca 39
Barrett, Michèle 490, 492, 493 n
Barthes, Roland 546–7
Barth, John 513
Barton, Bernard 246
Basavanna 483 (author)
Basil, St (the Great) 104, 132
Basselin, Oliver De 247
Bassett, Mary 130–1 (author), 136
Bassnett [also Bassnett-McGuire] Susan 394–5,
    435, 448, 558–61 (author)
Bauchant, André 263
Baudelaire, Charles 6, 297–8, 307–9 (author),
    326, 354–6, 417
Bausch, Pina 561
Beaufort, Lady Margaret 129
Beaugrande, Robert de 448, 450 n
Beaujour, Elizabeth Klosty 392 n
Bede (the Venerable) 35, 112, 262
Beegle, Dewey M. 69
Behn, Aphra 128, 133, 138–41 (author)
Bellay, Joachim du 55, 73, 77–80 (author)
Belloc, Hilaire 349
Ben-David, J. 442 n
Benjamin, Walter 3, 6, 195, 199, 272, 297–8,
    298–307 (author), 308–9 (translator), 337,
    355, 495–6, 498, 503, 546, 570
Benner, Susan vii
Bennett, H. S. 438
Bentley, Richard 166
Beowulf 4, 7, 34, 43, 255–8, 267, 563, 585, 593–4,
    597, 601, 604–7
Berman, Antoine 395, 548, 556 n
Berners, Lord Gerald Tyrwhitt 264
Bergsland, Knut 336 n
Berlin, Brent 444, 445

Berry, George Ricker 9 (translator)
Berryman, John 466
Bersuire, Pierre 263
Beza, Theodore 86
Bhabha, Homi K. 502
Bible v, 1; Authorized (King James) Version 56,
    68, 115–20, 263–4, 310–11, 316–17, 346, 544,
    562; Douay-Reims Bible 8, 68, 110–13;
    Genesis/Tower of Babel 7, 8–10, 13–14, 19,
    34, 38–46, 57, 66–7, 69, 72, 113–14, 119–20,
    310, 317, 321–2, 346, 351, 564, 566, 568, 572;
    Geneva Bible 68; Good News Bible 351;
    Gospels 12, 17–18, 28, 32, 191, 539; Hebrew
    Bible 8–10, 68, 310–11, 562–4; Luther's
    Bible 57–67, 200, 264, 315, 403;
    Septuagint 8, 11–14, 17–18, 20, 23, 29–32,
    118, 218, 346, 539–40, 544; Vulgate 8, 12,
    18, 28, 32–3, 43, 45, 100, 110–11, 113, 164,
    263; see also Buber & Rosenzweig, Fox,
    Tyndale
Biguenet, J. 383
Binns, J. W. 101, 102–9 (author & translator)
Blanke, Heiz 66
Blackburn, Sara 510
Blackburn, Stuart 477
Blackie, John S. 211–13, 216, 220–5 (author &
    translator), 233–5
Bleek, William 522
Blok, Aleksandr 470
Bloomfield, Leonard 346
Boas, Franz 333, 454–5, 456 n
Boccaccio, Giovanni 144, 157–8, 263
Boethius, Anicius Manlius Severinus 18, 33
    (author), 35, 37, 175
Bohannan, Laura 6, 366–75 (author), 487 n
Bohannan, Paul 366
Bohr, Niels 332
Bonnefoy, Yves 467–8 (author), 469
Bonner, Anthony 323–30 (translator)

Borchardt, Rudolph 306

Borges, Jorge Luis 6, 323, 323–9 (author), 508, 512, 514, 580 n

Boswell, James 174–5

Bowers, Fredson 379

Boyd, Brian 392 n

Boyle, Roger (1st Earl of Orrery) 133

Bradley, S. A. J. 34

Brecht, Bertolt 439

Brenton, Sir Lancelot C. L. 8, 10 (translator)

Brett, Richard 104

Bristowe, Richard 110

Brod, Max 581 n

Brodsky, Joseph 271, 394, 460, 462–3 (author), 465–8, 469–70 (translator), 471–3, 474–5 (author & translator), 597

Brooke, Rupert 377

Brook, Peter 524, 561

Broome, William 161, 166

Brower, Reuben A. 330

Brown, Clarence 462, 463–5 (author), 469 (translator), 582

Browning, Robert 7, 222–3 (translator), 241, 249, 249–50 (author & translator), 271, 286, 529

Bruccoli, Matthew J. 377

Buber, Martin 119, 272, 310–11, 313, 316–20 (author), 321 (translator), 544, 562–3

Buckley, Theodore Alois 212, 233–35

Budge, E. A. Wallace 466, 522

Burago, Alla 462 (translator)

Burgess, Anthony 389

Burne-Jones, Edward 255

Burnshaw, Stanley 273, 360–3 (author)

Burt, Mary Anne 217–19

Burke, Kenneth 397

Burton, Richard 251, 252 (translator) 253

Butcher, S. H. 238–40 (author & translator)

Bürger, Gottfried August 217, 266

Bühler, Karl 446

Byrhtferth 38

Byron, Lord George Gordon 211, 266, 384

Caedmon (of Whitby) 49, 598

Caesar, Julius 76, 86

Cairncross, John 356

Caius, John 109

Calahorra, Diego Ortúnez de 132 (author)

Calderón de la Barca, Pedro 201, 204, 246, 266

Callimachus 160, 260

Calvin, John 86, 109

Campbell, George 189–90

Carlyle, Thomas 245, 266

Carne-Ross, D. S. 298, 352

Caro, Annibale 129

Carroll, Lewis 377

Carter, Elizabeth 141, 142–3 (author & translator)

Cary, Edmund 350

Cary, Elizabeth (Lady Falkland) 133

Cary, Herny Francis 235, 242–3

Casares, Adolfo Bioy 512

Cassiodorus (Flavius Magnus Aurelius Cassiodorus Senator) 260

Castiglione, Baldassare 84 (author)

Catford, J. C. 393, 443

Catullus, Gaius Valerius 260, 422–3, 458–9, 459 (author)

Cavalcanti, Guido 274, 276–9, 288

Cavendish, Richard 109

Caxton, William 19, 47, 51–3 (author), 176, 263

Cecil, Mildred (Lady Burghley) 132

Cecil, William (Lord Burghley) 89

Celan, Paul 405, 569–70 (author), 570–81

Cervantes, Miguel de 266, 323, 326–8

Chalcidius 260

Chalfen, Israel 580 n, 581 n

Challoner, Richard 110

Chaloner, Sir Thomas 109

Chapman, George 7, 56, 86, 94–5, 95–7 (author & translator), 166–7, 171, 173, 214, 223–4, 228, 282, 232, 238, 255, 265, 287

Chapone, Hester 129

Charles I (King) 49, 104

Chaucer, Geoffrey 7, 106, 107 (author), 144, 150–1, 166, 175–6, 262–3, 293, 396, 438

Cheke, Sir John 88–9, 109

Chekhov, Anton 290–5, 559

Christopherson, John 102–3

Chouraqui, André 544

Chudleigh, Lady Mary 129

Chute, B. J. 509

Cicero, Marcus Tullius v, 2, 17–18, 20–2, 21 (author), 24–5, 28–31, 74, 76–7, 79, 81–2, 89, 103, 109, 116, 141, 260, 263, 265, 536, 538–40, 545, 549–50

Clark, Mary, *see* Bassett, Mary

Clark, P. P. 438

Clark, T. N. 438

Clement I (Pope) 104

Clemoes, Peter 39

Clifford, James 495

Coates, Jenefer vi, 273, 376–92 (author & editor)

Colson, F. H. 23–4 (translator)

Coleridge, Samuel Taylor 362

Columba, St. 588

Conington, John 220–1, 266

Conley, C. H. 82

Conrad, Joseph 290–1, 294

Constantine, St. 335

Cooke, Anne 130

Cooper, Thomas 109

Corman, Cid 580 n

Corneille, Pierre 133–4, 134–5 (author)

Corrigan, Robert W. 525, 559

Cortázar, Julio 507

Cottrell, Sir Charles 134

Coverdale, Miles 68, 263

Cowell, E. B. 241, 245–6

Cowley, Abraham 121, 124–6 (author & translator), 146, 174–5, 177–8, 550

Cowper, Dame Sarah 128

Cowper, William 167, 173, 183–7 (author & translator), 223–5, 228, 258, 266

Crankshaw, Edward 291–2, 294–6 (author)

Crawford, S. J. 43

Crossley-Holland, Kevin 34

Crousaz, Jean-Pierre 142

Csokits, János 521, 523 (translator)

Cushing, Frank Hamilton 454, 456 n

Cyprian, St 83

Cyril, St (of Alexandria) 12, 103

Dacier, Anne 55, 129, 160–2, 162–5 (author), 166, 170

Damasus (Pope) 27, 28, 115

D'Angoulême, Marguerite 130

Daniell, David 72

Dante Alighieri 4, 196, 211, 235–6, 242–4 (author), 253, 266, 276, 352, 401, 472–3, (author), 582

Dares Phrygius 53

Dasimayya, Devara 483 (author)

Davenport, Guy 458

Dayman, John 235–6

Deligiorgis, Stavros vi, 8, 11–14 (author & translator)

Delille, Jacques 201, 236–7

Denham, Sir John 121–3 (author), 146, 176, 185, 460, 549–50

Demosthenes 21, 30, 31, 76–7, 89–90, 260

Deny 49

Derrida, Jacques 486–9, 561, 574, 580 n

Devi, Mahasweta 486, 487, 492

Devi, N. Revathi 484–5 (author)

Dewey, John 336 n

Dictes 53

Dharwadker, Vinay vi, 476–85 (author &
    editor)

Dillon, Wentworth (4th Earl of
    Roscommon) 138, 177–8

Dionysius (the Areopagite) 262, 335

Diphilus 260

Divus, Andreas (*see* Justinopolitanus)

Doane, A. N. 45

Dodwell, C. R. 39

Dolet, Estienne 55–6, 73–4, 74–6 (author)

Donaldson, E. Talbot 601

Donatus, Aelius 28, 41

Donne, John 476

Doren, Mark Van 280

Dostoevsky, Fyodor 290–5, 296 (author),
    396, 399

Douglas, Gavin 275, 385

Douglas, Mary 499

Dryden, John vi, 2, 7, 56, 101, 121, 124, 137,
    144–5, 145–59 (author & translator), 205,
    212, 214, 226, 236, 237 (translator), 241,
    245, 258–9, 266, 271, 352, 354–5, 545,
    549–50, 561

Dubois, Jean 436

Dudley, John 88

Dummett, M. 501 n

Duym, Hidde van Ameyden van 414 n

Eckerman, Johann Peter 198, 203

Eco, Umberto 513

Eden, Richard 109

Elias, Norbert 545 n

Eliot, George 2, 211, 212 n, 217–20 (author)

Eliot, T. S. 144, 271, 275

Elyot, Sir Thomas 82–3 (author), 109

Elwell-Sutton, L. P. 248

Empson, William 214–15 (author)

Ennius, Quintus 79, 259, 260

Epictetus 128, 142–3, 143 (author)

Epiphanius (Archbishop) 30, 538

Erasmus, Desiderius 68, 70, 109

Erigena [Eriugena], *see* Scotus, John

Eschenburg, Johann Joachim 199

Etkind, Efim 603

Euclid 109, 261

Eusebius Pamphili (of Caesarea) 28–9, 30,
    102, 131

Eusebius (of Cremona) 30

Eustathius (of Thessalonica) 160

Evagrius Scholasticus (Bishop of Antioch) 27
    (author) 102, 538–59

Evans-Pritchard, E. E. 499, 500

Even-Zohar, Itamar 394, 429–34 (author)

Eysteinsson, Astradur vi, 321–2
    (translator), 613

Fairclough, H. Rushton 23 (translator)

Fairfax, Edward 176, 265

Fang, Achilles 350

Fanshaw, Richard 121, 176

Farge, Oliver La 454, 456 n

Farrell, Joseph 585–93 (interview with Edwin
    Morgan)

Feinstein, Elaine 533

Felstiner, John 394, 569–81 (author &
    translator)

Feltham, Owen 176, 178

Fenton, Elijah 166

Firdausi, Tousi 201–2

Fischart, Johann 264

Fitzalan, Lady Jane 130

Fitzalan, Lady Mary 130

FitzGerald, Edward 197, 241–2, 245–7, 247–8
    (author & translator), 253, 266, 275

Fitzmaurice-Kelly, James 197, 258–67 (author)

Flatauer, Susanne 337, 338–45 (translator)

Floranx, Jenix 79

Florio, John (*or* Giovanni) 93–4, 94 (author & translator) 265

Follain, Jean 465

Fontaine, Jean de la 356

Fontenelle, Bernard De 138, 140, 288

Foucault, Michel 546

Fouqué, Friedrich de la Motte 217

Fox, Everett 119 n, 272, 310–13, 320, 346, 394, 562–8 (author & translator)

France, Peter 6, 98 n, 291 n, 311, 558

Franklin, Benjamin 536

Frantzen, Allen 36

Frawley, William 507

Freiligrath, Ferdinand 217, 219

Frere, John Hookham 550–4

Freud, Sigmund 492, 493 n

Froissart, Jean 264

Frost, William 360, 362, 407

Fuentes, Carlos 512

Fulke, William 111

Gadamer, Hans-Georg 396

Galen (Claudius Galenus of Pergamum) 260–2

Gallus (Gaius Cornelius Gallus) 260

Garnett, Constance 272, 290–2, 292–3 (author), 294–6, 296 (translator)

Garnett, Edward 290, 291, 294

Garnett, David 290, 292

Garnett, Richard 290

Garnier, Robert 264

Gasset, Ortega y 403

Sir Gawain and the Green Knight 531–2, 582–4

Gellner, Ernest 494–5, 497, 500

Geoffrey (of Monmouth) 263

Gerard (of Cremona) 261

Gerzymisch-Arbogas, Heidrun 448, 449

Giddens, Anthony 557 n

Giffard, Lady Martha 133

Ginsberg, Allen 466

Giovanni, Norman Thomas Di 508

Goethe, Johann Wolfgang von 195–6, 198–9, 199–204 (author), 211, 214–17, 219, 242, 244 (author), 297, 306, 337, 395, 408–9, 438, 545

Gogol, Nikolay 290–1, 293

Golding, Arthur 86–7, 87–8 (author & translator), 264

Goncharov, Ivan 290

Gorion, Micha Josef bin 580 n

Gottsched, Johann Christoph 195

Gower, John 176

Góngora, Luis de 352

Graham, Joseph E. 487 n

Grannis, Chandler B. 556 n

Graves, Robert 248 (translator)

Grayson, Jane 392 n

Greene, James 470–1 (translator & author)

Gregory, St (the Great) 34, 35, 36, 49, 261–2

Grene, Richard 358

Grettis Saga 255, 257, 266

Grey, Lady Jane 107

Griffiths, Malcolm 560

Guevara, Antonio De 90, 264, 265

Guthrie, William 549, 550

Guyon, Jeanne-Marie Bouvier de la Motte 183

Haan, Frans de 414 n

Hafiz, Mohammad Shams al-Din 198

Halevi, Judah 570

Halliday, M. A. K. 450 n

Hamburger, Michael 271

Hammer-Purgstall, Joseph von 201

Hampton, Christopher 396

Hardy, Thomas 458

Harpham, Geoffrey Galt 537, 540, 545 n

Harpsfield, John 130

Hartman, Geoffrey 580 n

Haute-Seille, Jean de 262

Hayward, Abraham 214 (translator), 215–16, 246

Hayward, Max 462 (translator)

Heaney, Seamus 255, 394–5, 531, 532, 594, 597–607 (author & translator)

Hebel, Johann Peter 354

Heidegger, Martin 348, 396, 402, 489

Helbo, Andre 558

Heliodorus 265

Herberay, Nicolas de 264

Herbert, George 106

Herder, Johann Gottfried 195, 198, 242

Hermann (the German) 261

Hermans, Theo vii, 394, 435, 560

Herodotus 168, 214

Herreweghen, Hubert van 412–13 (author), 415 n

Hesiod 95, 260

Heyvaert, S. 395 n

Heywood, Jasper 84, 264

Herzen, Alexander 290–1

Hieronymus, St 59,

Higden, Ralph 19, 47

Hill, D. E. 528 (translator)

Hippocrates 260–2

Hinz, Stella M. 414 n

Hobbes, Thomas 265

Hoby, Sir Thomas 82, 84 (author)

Hoffman, Eva 6, 502–3, 503–6 (author)

Hofmann, Michael 527

Holland, Philemon 81, 94, 98–9, 176, 265

Hollander, J. 498

Holliday, Billy 509

Holmes, James S. 4, 6, 73–4 (author), 74–6 (translator), 188, 189 (author), 393–4, 406–22 (author & translator), 422–3, 424–8 (translator), 429, 435, 460, 462–3 (see also Lowland, Jacob)

Homeric epics v, 4, 7, 29, 53, 77, 86, 94–5, 97–8, 115, 129, 144, 147, 158, 160–74, 178–9, 183–7, 191, 195–6, 198–9, 201, 210–11, 213–14, 220–1, 223–32, 234, 238–40, 255–6, 260, 265–6, 282–3, 285–7, 348, 352, 383, 396, 437, 465, 539, 549

Hopkins, David vi, 144–59 (author & editor)

Hopkins, Gerald Manley 603, 606

Hora, Josef 335

Horace (Quintus Horatius Flaccus) 17, 22–3 (author), 29, 33, 145, 149, 152–3 (author), 176, 183, 226, 233, 259, 352, 354, 538, 540, 550

Horne, R. H. 213–14 (author)

Howard, Henry (Earl of Surrey) 109, 236–7

Howard, Richard 546 (translator)

Huet, Pierre-Daniel 160

Hughes, Ted 7, 85–6, 222, 250, 310–11, 352–3, 355, 358, 394–5, 521–2, 522–33 (translator & author), 582–3, 595, 597, 604–5

Hugo, Victor 354, 439

Hull, Dame Eleanor 129

Humboldt, Wilhelm von 195, 198, 297

Hume, Anna 133

Humphrey, Laurence 56, 101–4, 107–9

Hunt, William Holman 253

Hurt, James R. 39

Hutchinson, Lucy 131, 136–8 (author & translator)

Hyde, George 291

Hyde, Lawrence (1st Earl of Rochester) 149, 152

Hynd, James 298 (translator)

Hölderlin, Friedrich 297, 303–6, 357

Hölty, Ludwig Heinrich Christoph 217

Hönig, Hans G. 449

Ibsen, Henrik 267, 589

Infante, Guillermo Cabrera 512–20 (in part as author)

Ishak, Honein ibn 260
Isocrates 71, 76, 82, 83, 130

Jackson, Kenneth H. D. 599
Jakobson, Roman 330–6 (author), 394
Jami 246
Janouch, Gustav 581 n
Jarvis, Charles 266
Jebb, Richard Claverhouse 266
Jensson, Gottskalk vi, 98 (translator), 287
    (translator)
Jephcott, Edmund 545 n
Jerome, St (Eusebius Hieronymus) 8, 12, 18, 20,
    27–8, 29–31 (author), 31–3, 49–50, 103,
    110–11, 115–18, 263, 402, 536–45
Jóhannsdóttir, Anna vii
John (Bishop of Jerusalem) 30, 538
John (of Capua) 263
John (of Trevisa) 19, 47–50 (author)
Johnson, Elizabeth 128
Johnson, Samuel 7, 174–5, 175–81 (author &
    translator), 352, 359
Johnston, David 585
Jonson, Ben 22 (translator), 145, 176, 178, 265
Jordan, Clarence 544
Josephus, Flavius 12, 29, 260, 265
Jowett, Benjamin 266
Joyce, James 291, 329, 382, 458, 514
József, Attila 585
Juarroz, Roberto 465
Jurenka, H. 344
Justinopolitanus, Andreas Divus 275, 286, 287
    (translator)
Juvenal, Decimus Iunius 7, 95, 144–5, 153,
    174–5, 178–80, 214, 266, 352, 359

Kade, Max 443, 446
Kafka, Franz 398, 570, 578–81
Kamuf, Peggy 487 n

Kaindl, Klaus 443
Kalidasa 201
Kant, Emanual 211, 217–18
Kapilar 479–81 (author)
Karcevski, S. 334
Karlinsky, Simon 382
Kay, George 353
Keats, John 95, 253, 265
Kelly, Louis G. vi, 20 n, 21 (translator), 25–7
    (translator), 29–31 (translator), 32–3
    (translator)
Kenner, Hugh 280, 283, 288 n, 289 n, 458
Kennedy, B. H. 236, 238
Kerrigan, Anthony 323
Keynes, Simon 36
Khayyam, Omar 241, 245–7, 247–8 (author), 266
Khlebnikov, Velimir 330
Killigrew, Henry 422, 426
Klopstock, Friedrich Gottlieb 217
Knapp, S. 436
Knox, Ronald 111
Kochanowski, Jan 597
Kofka, Kurt 445
Koller, Werner 446
Komissarov, V. N. 421 n
Komrij, Gerrit 422
Kosegarten, Luwig Gotthard 201
Kowzan, Tadeusz 559
Kruger, Barbara 546–7, 556 n
Kruzhkov, Grigory 598, 606
Kuhiwczak, Piotr 558
Kur, Friedrich 66
Kußmaul, Paul 449
Kyd, Thomas 264
Kynaston, Sir Francis 106
Köhler, Wolfgang 445

Labeo, Notker 262
Lakoff, George 443–5, 450 n

Lambert, José 394, 421

Lane, Helen R. 507

Lang, A. 238–40 (author & translator)

Langhoff, Stephan 445

Lapidge, Michael 36

Lasdun, James 527

Latini, Brunetto 263

Lattimore, Richmond 352, 357, 358 (translator)

Lawrence, D. H. 290, 292

Leach, Edmund 494

Lefevere, André 160 n, 195, 199–202
    (translator), 206–9 (translator), 394,
    422 n, 435–42 (author), 458–9, 558

Lermontov, Mikhail Y. 291, 380, 382

L'Estrange, Sir Roger 265

Leuven-Zwart, Kitty M. van 406

Lefèvre, Raoul 51, 52

Leighton, Laura G. 392 n

Lessing, Gotthold Ephraim 195, 266

Levine, Suzanne Jill 394, 507, 512–20 (author &
    translator)

Levý, Jiří 337, 338–45 (author), 393, 408,
    418, 448

Lewis, Phillip 554

Lidgate, Dan John 52

Lienhardt, Godfrey 494, 497–8

Lima, José Lezama 507

Lisle, Leconte de 437

Lispector, Clarice 507

Livy (Titus Livius) 99, 109, 263, 265

Llosa, Mario Vargas 507, 509

Lloyd-Jones, Hugh 250–1 (translator), 531
    (translator)

Lobo, Jeronimo 174

Lockhart 230

Logue, Christopher 7, 167

Longfellow, Henry Wadsworth 230, 241–2,
    243–4 (translator), 253, 266, 467

Loseff, Lev 474

Lottman, Herbert R. 556 n

Lowell, James Russell 246

Lowell, Robert 179, 222, 246, 250, 272, 308,
    352–3, 353–9 (author & translator), 395,
    460, 526, 529, 592, 595

Lowland, Jacob (pseudonym of James S.
    Holmes) 422, 460

Lucian 83

Lucretius (Titus Lucretius Carus) 79, 128, 136,
    137–8 (author), 144–5, 148–52, 259

Luke, David 244 (translator)

Luria, A. R. 498

Luther, Martin 8, 30, 55, 57–67 (author &
    translator), 73, 112, 195, 199, 261, 264, 303,
    305, 311–16, 537, 545, 572

Lönnrot, Elias 241

Mabbe, James 258, 265

Macaulay, Thomas Babington 197

MacCarthy, Denis Florence 266

MacDiarmid, Hugh 585

Machiavelli, Niccolo 397

Magnússon, Eiríkur 255, 257 (translator), 267

Mahadevi 483 (author)

Maier, Carol 513

Malcolm. J. 500

Mallarmé, Stéphane 303, 326, 354, 360–1, 597

Malory, Sir Thomas 51, 90, 263

Mandelstam, Osip 462–7, 469–71 (author), 582

Mandeville, Sir John 263

Mangan, James Clarence 212, 216–17

Manheim, Ralph 581 n

Man, Paul de 436

Manrique, Jorge 242

Mansfield, Katherine 291–2

Mayer, Sigrid 580 n

Marcus, George E. 495

Margaret (Duchess of Burgundy) 52

Marlowe, Christopher 264, 275, 285, 358, 519

Márquez, Gabriel García 507, 510, 510–11 (author)
Marquis de Sade (Donatien Alphonse François) 440
Marshak, Samuel 603
Martial (Marcus Valerius Martialis) 26, 80, 423–8 (author)
Martin, Gregory 110–13 (author)
Martin, H.-J. 129
Mason, H. A. 166 n
Masterson, James R. 336 n
Mathews, Jackson 408
Matthiessen, F. O. 90, 94
Mayakovsky, Vladimir 330, 585, 588, 596 (author)
McAllester, David P. 456
McDuff, David 462 (translator)
McKane, Elizabeth 471 (translator)
McKane, Richard 471 (translator & author)
Meares, Bernard 470 (translator)
Mehlman, Jeffrey 489 n
Meiklejohn, J. M. D. 217–18
Melanchthon, Philip 61
Menander 260
Menard, Pierre (character in J. L. Borges' short story) 323–9, 513
Merrill, Christopher 466
Merwin, W. S. 394–5, 462–4, 465–7 (author), 469 (translator), 472–3 (author & translator), 475, 522, 532, 582, 583–4 (translator)
Methodius 12
Meung, Jean de 262
Meyrink, Gustav 581 n
Michaels, W. B. 436
Millais, John Everett 253
Miller, Frank Justus 85, 88 (translator), 524, 525 (translator)
Miller, John 236, 238
Milosz, Czeslaw 606

Milton, John 161, 167, 171, 183, 185, 276, 282, 358
Mitchell, Frank 456
Mitchell, Stephen 364–5 (translator)
Mitchell, Thomas 550–1
Monegal, E. Rodrígues 512
Montagu, Lady Mary Wortley 142
Montaigne, Michael de 93–4, 259, 264–5, 397
Montchrétien, Antoine de 264
Montale, Eugenio 354, 361
More, Hannah 142
More, Sir Thomas 82, 100, 107, 130
Morgan, Edwin 5, 255, 355, 394–5, 526, 585–96 (author & translator), 606
Mornay, Philippe De 86
Moore, F. C. T. 489 n
Mounin, G. 393
Morris, William 173, 197, 241, 255, 255–7 (translator), 258, 266, 271, 553, 594, 606
Mulgrew, Gerry 588
Munro, David B. 266
Murthy, U. R. Anantha 476
Musa, Mark 243–4 (translator)
Musaeus 95

Naaijkens, Ton 406
Nabokov, Dmitri 377, 382
Nabokov, Vladimir vi, 272–3, 376–7, 378–92 (author & translator), 403, 460, 464, 537, 544
Naevius, Gnaeus 259
Neruda, Jan 344
Neruda, Pablo 465, 569
Neubert, Albrecht 450 n
Neville, Alexander 84, 85–6 (author & translator) 524
Newdigate, Dame Alice 128
Newman, Francis W. 196, 210–11, 213, 225–6 (author & translator), 227–9, 230–1 (author), 232 (translator), 241, 553

Newton, Thomas 84

Nida, Eugene A. 272, 310, 346–51 (author), 393, 416, 421 n, 433, 448, 544, 553–4

Nietzsche, Friedrich 195, 328, 401

Nimms, John Frederick 87

Niranjana, Tejaswini 197 n, 487 n

Norris, John 129

North, Sir Thomas 55, 81–2, 90, 91–3 (author & translator) 94, 98, 265, 403

Norton, Charles Eliot 245

Nuce, Thomas 84

O'Brien, Flann 599

O'Keeffe, J. G. 599

Oldisworth, William 161

Oppen, George and Mary 458

Oresme, Nicolas 263

Origen (Oregenes Adamantius) 28–9, 49–50, 103, 118

Orlando, Guido 278 (author)

Ormsby, John 258

Orosius, Paulus 35, 262

Orwell, George 397–8

O'Shaughnessy, Arthur 267

Ostaijen, Paul van 410, 414 n, 415 n, 422

Ovid (Publius Ovidus Naso) 4, 7, 80, 86–7, 88 (author), 108, 144–5, 148, 151, 214, 264–5, 275, 285, 527, 528–9 (author)

Owen, John 136

Ozell, John 161, 161–2 (author), 162–5 (translator)

Paaltjens, Piet 422

Pacuvius, Marcus 260

Paige, D. D. 280, 288 n

Painter, William 264

Pammachius (letter to) 27–8, 30, 537–8

Pannwitz, Rudolph 306, 496

Parr, Katherine 109

Parra, Niconar 465

Parsons, Talcott W. 235, 545 n

Pasternak, Boris 335, 352, 353–4

Pavis, P. 558, 561

Paz, Octavio 507

Peirce, Charles Sanders 331, 336 n

Peletier du Mans, Jacques 73, 77

Pennington, Mantagu 142

Perionius, Joachim 108

Perrin, Bernadotte 91–2 (translator)

Perron [du Perron], Jacques Davy (Cardinal) 133

Petrarch, Francis 94, 354, 464

Phalereus, Demetrius 11

Phaer, Thomas 236–7, 264

Philadelphus, Ptolemy 11

Phillips, Herbert P. 347

Phillips, J. B. 350

Phillips, Katherine 133, 134–5 (author & translator), 138

Philo Judaeus (of Alexandria) 8, 11, 20, 23–4 (author), 109, 539

Philocrates 23

Pico della Mirandola, Giovanni 82, 83

Pilinszky, János xi, 521, 523–4 (author), 533

Pindar 29, 124–5, 125–7 (author), 146, 177, 214, 306, 550

Pitt, M. Christopher 237

Plato 13, 25, 29, 33, 73, 109, 130, 260

Plautus 160, 260, 358

Playfere, Thomas 105

Pliny the Elder (Gaius Plinius Secundus) 26, 98

Pliny the Younger (Gaius Plinius Caecilius Secundus) 26–7 (author), 81, 98, 265

Plutarch 55, 81–3, 90, 91–3 (author), 99, 128, 129, 264–5, 403, 515

Po, Li T'ai 280 (author)

Pochhacker, Franz 443

Pocock, David 499

Poggioli, Renato 362
Pöggeler, Otto 581 n
Politzer, Heinz 580 n
Pollard, Alfred W. 47, 51
Polukhina, Valentina vii, 474, 533
Pomorska, Krystyna 330
Ponmutiyar 481–2 (author)
Pontalis, J. B. 492 n
Popa, Vasko 521
Pope, Alexander 7, 56, 95, 121, 160, 161 n,
    166–7, 167–74 (author & translator), 179,
    183–4, 191, 212, 214, 220–1, 223–6, 228–9,
    239, 258, 266, 272, 285, 355–6, 465, 549
Popovic, Anton 394, 414 n
Pound, Ezra vi, 5, 7, 86, 115, 167, 173, 249, 253,
    271–3, 274–5, 275–88 (author &
    translator), 381, 395, 405, 436, 458, 466, 513,
    537, 544, 553, 582, 585, 592, 594
Porphyrius (Porphyry) 33, 260
Pozzi, Antonia 546
Prabhu, Allama 484 (author)
Premier Fait, Laureat de 263
Propertius, Sextus 80
Ptolemy, Claudius 218, 261
Puig, Manuel 512, 513, 514
Pushkin, Alexander 272, 376, 383–4, 385–8
    (author), 390–1 (author), 460, 533 (author)

Queen Elizabeth 89–90, 103, 108, 130, 262
Quevedo, Francisco Gómez de 265, 324, 325 n,
    328, 352
Quinlan, Maurice J. 556 n
Quintilian (Marcus Fabius Quintillianus) 17,
    24, 25–6 (author), 89, 545

Rabassa, Gregory 394, 507–11 (author &
    translator)
Rabelais, François 73, 264, 377
Rabin, C. 409

Race, William H. 126–7 (translator)
Racine, Jean 7, 265, 352, 354–5, 356–7 (author),
    397, 439, 526–7 (author), 529, 560, 585,
    595–6 (author)
Raffel, Burton 458, 462
Ramanujan, A. K. vi, 394, 460, 476, 477–85
    (author & translator)
Rao, V. Narayana 477, 484–5 (translator)
Ravel, Maurice 513
Rawley, William 105
Rekiaro, Ilkka 534
Reiss, Katharina 447, 448, 450 n
Retines, Robert de 261
Reynolds, John 110
Ricoeur, Paul 405 n
Rieu, E. V. 348, 350
Rilke, Rainer Maria 354, 361, 363–5 (author)
Rimbaud, Arthur 354, 377
Rinsler, Norma vi, 298, 308–9 (translator)
Robert, Marthe 581 n
Robertson, D. W. Jr. 545 n
Robinson, Douglas 6, 394, 534–45 (author)
Rolland, Romain 376
Ronell, Avital 487 n
Ronsard, Pierre de 77
Roper, Margaret 130
Rosch, Eleanor 443–4
Rose, William Stuart 551
Rosenberg, David 544
Rosenwald, Lawrence 311 (translator), 562
Rosenzweig, Franz 19 n, 195, 272, 310–11, 311–16
    (author), 317, 319–20, 321 (translator), 544,
    562–3, 570, 577
Rossetti, Dante Gabriel 242, 245, 253–5 (author
    & translator), 274–5, 277, 286, 346, 472,
    473 (translator)
Rostand, Edmond 585, 589, 590–1 (author),
    592
Rothenberg, Diane 453

Rothenberg, Jerome 319, 452, 453–4 (author), 456–7 (author & translator)
Rouse, W. H. D. 274, 280, 282
Rowe, Elizabeth 128
Rubin, Barry 462 (translator)
Rudd, Niall 180–2 (translator)
Rudy, Stephen 330
Rufinus 28
Rushdie, Salman 487
Ruskin, John 245–6, 255
Russell, Bertrand 330, 336 n

Sainte-Beuve, Charles-Augustin 437
Salinger, J. D. 399
Sallust (Gaius Sallustius Crispus) 76, 263
Sandys, Edwin 108, 176, 178
San Pedro, Fernández de 264
Sapir, Edward 346
Sappho 160, 354
Sarduy, Severo 512, 514
Saunders, J. W. 128
Saussure, Ferdinand de 443
Savile, Sir Henry 265
Scaliger, Julius Caesar 95
Scheinmann, Edith Rosenzweig 580 n
Schlegel, August Wilhelm & Friedrich von 195, 198, 219, 220, 266, 303
Schleiermacher, Friedrich 189, 195, 198, 205–6, 206–9 (author), 211, 272, 297, 314, 337, 548, 556 n
Schiller, Johann Christoph Friedrich von 211, 217
Schulte, Rainer 383
Scot, Michael 261
Scott, John 49, 211
Scotus, John (Erigena) 262
Sebba, Gregor 363, 364 (author)
Sebillet, Thomas 73, 77
Sedgefield, W. J. 35

Selerie, Gavin 452 n
Sellar, W. Y. 236
Seneca, Lucius Annaeus 7, 82, 84, 85–6 (author), 116, 129, 130, 133, 263–5, 256–7, 524, 525–6 (author), 529
Sergius (of Resaina) 260
Seymour, Edward (Duke of Somerset) 109
Sewell, W. 220
Shakespeare, William 4, 55, 82, 86, 87, 90, 92–3 (author), 101, 128, 174, 195, 199, 201, 211, 212 n, 265, 266, 326, 366–75, 388 n, 392, 405, 439, 446, 448, 467, 469, 515, 519, 527
Schamschula, Walter 337
Schmitt, Peter A. 448
Scholem, Gershom 574
Schultze, Brigitte 448
Shaw, Bernard 291
Sheffield, Edmund 109
Shelley, Percy Byshe 211, 266
Shelton, Thomas 265
Shulman, David 477
Sidney, Mary (Countess of Pembroke) 130
Sidney, Sir Philip 86, 130
Sieburth, Richard 288 n
Simeon Metaphrastes 104
Simmons, Lucretia Van Tuyl 414 n
Smital, J. 344
Smith, A. C. H. 524
Smith, James Harry 77–80 (translator)
Smith, Miles 115
Smith, William Jay 422
Snell-Hornby, Mary 337, 443–51 (author)
Snoek, Paul 410–11 (author), 412
Socrates 102, 131
The Song of Igor's Campaign 381
Sophocles 211, 246, 260, 266, 304, 306, 597
Sotheby, William 221, 225
Southey, R. 183, 222 n, 230
Sozomen 102, 131

Spann, Marcella 271
Spenser, Edmund 77
Spilka, Irène C. 414 n
Spire, André 360
Spivak, Gayatri Chakravorty 307 n, 394,
    486–7, 488–93 (author)
Stackelberg, Jürgen 196 n
Steiner, George 2, 5, 7, 166, 167, 272, 337, 393,
    396–7, 397–405 (author), 423, 487
Steiner, T. R. 122, 174
Stellbrink, Hans-Jürgen 448
Stepniak-Kravchinsky, Sergei 290
Stern, J. P. 581 n
Stevenson, Jane vi, 128–43 (author & editor)
Stevens, Wallace 458
Stone, Lawrence 556 n
Studley, John 84
Störig, Hans Joachim 199 n, 202 n
Suetonius (Gaius Suetonius Tranquillus) 26, 265
Sullivan, J. P. 289 n
Supervielle, Jules 377
Surrey, Earl of (see Howard, Henry)
Syme, David 216
Symmachus 29, 49
Swanton, Michael 34
Sweeney Astray 598–601
Sweet, Henry 35
Swinburne, Charles Algernon 245, 274–5

Taber, Charles R. 346, 448
Tacitus (Publius or Gaius Cornelius
    Tacitus) 26, 123, 265
Tanner, Jennifer vi, 57–67 (translator)
Tasso, Torquato 106, 201, 256, 438, 508
Taylor, Bayard 246
Taylor, William 266
Tedlock, Dennis 319, 452, 453–6 (author)
Tegnér, Esaias 242
Tenison, Thomas 105–6

Tennyson, Alfred 221, 223, 245
Terence (Publius Terentius Afer) 160, 260, 262, 538
Thackeray, William Makepeace 245, 343
Theodoretus 102, 131
Theodore 102
Theodosius 29, 49
Thieberger, Friedrich 581 n
Thomas, Elizabeth 129
Thomas, Dylan 492
Thott, Birgitte 142
Thrale, Hannah 141
Thucydides 265
Tibellus 80
Tieck, Johann Ludwig 217, 220
Tolstoy, Leo 290–2, 294–5, 396
Tomlinson, Charles 5
Toury, Gideon 394, 429–30, 435, 512
Trachtenberg, Joshua 580 n
Trakl, Georg 410
Trivedi, Harish 558
Tudor, Mary 130–1
Turgenev, Ivan 290–6
Turner, David 85, 524
Tyler, Margaret 130, 131–2 (author & translator)
Tyndale, William 55, 68, 69–72
    (author & translator) 115, 263, 311, 346
Tytler, Alexander Fraser 56, 188–9, 189–94
    (author), 549
Twain, Mark 399
Twine, Thomas 236–7
Tzara, Tristan 453

Udall, Nicholas 109
Underdown, Thomas 265
Ungaretti, Giuseppe 354
Urzidil, Johannes 581 n

Vaillant, Andre 335, 336 n
Valenzuela, Luisa 507

Valéry, Paul 325, 327, 328, 354
Valk, E. M. 298 (translator)
Veliyanar, Erumai 482–3 (author)
Venuti, Lawrence 6, 212 n, 394, 546, 546–57 (author)
Verch, Maria 448
Verlaine, Paul 377, 380
Villon, François 253, 275, 288, 354
Virgil 4, 19, 22, 28, 77, 79, 85, 95, 109, 122, 123, 129, 133, 142, 144, 145, 147–50, 155–7 (author), 165, 167–9, 171, 178–9, 196, 211, 214, 223, 230, 236, 237–8 (author), 255, 259–60, 262, 266, 549–50
Volkhovsky, Feliks 290
Voltaire (François-Marie Arouet) 160, 439, 478
Voss, Johann Heinrich 201, 221, 228, 266, 303, 305
Volz, Hanz 66

Waard, Jan de 557 n
Waller, Edmund 145, 185
Walsingham, Sir Francis 108
Warren, Rosanna 599
Watson, J. S. 25 (translator)
Watts, Issac 132
Weber, Max 545 n
Wertheimer, Max 445
Weissbort, Daniel vi, 357 (translator), 422, 474 (translator), 521, 533, 569, 582 n, 609–15 (author)
West, Constance B. 346
Whibley, Charles 81, 93
Whitelock, Dorothy 35, 36, 37
Whitman, Walt 352
Whorf, Benjamin Lee 332, 336 n

Wieland, Christoph Martin 199–201
Wigham, Peter 423
Wilcox, Jonathan vi, 18, 34–54 (author, editor & translator)
Wilde, Oscar 401
William (of Moerbeke) 261
Williams, Raymond 3
Williams, W. C. 352, 458
Wilson, Edmund 382, 389
Wilson, Horace H. 201
Wilson, Thomas 88–9, 89–90 (author), 588
Winfield, Edd 77–80 (translator)
Withers, Benjamin C. 39
Wittgenstein, Ludwig 401, 444
Weores, Sandor 585
Wordsworth, William 211
Worthington, Thomas 110
Wroth, Sir Thomas 107–8
Wulfstan 38
Wyatt, A. J. 255, 256 (translator)
Wyatt, Sir Thomas 109, 604
Wycliffe, John 112, 263
Wærferth [Werferth, Wyrefrith] 36, 49

Xenophon 25, 29, 84, 260, 265

Yeats, William Butler 377, 455, 467
Yip, Wai-lim 289 n
Young, Patrick 104, 106
Young, Richard E. 211
Yudovich, F. I. 498

Zhdanov, Andrei 293
Zohn, Harry 298, 580 n
Zukofsky, Celia and Louis 458–9, 459 (translators) 553

Made in the USA
Las Vegas, NV
09 January 2021